General Motors A-Cars Automotive Repair Manual

by Gradon Mechtel, Larry Warren and John H Haynes
Member of the Guild of Motoring Writers

Models covered:
Buick Century, Chevrolet Celebrity,
Oldsmobile Ciera and Cutlass Cruiser,
Pontiac 6000
1982 through 1996

(4L19 - 38005)

(829)

ABCDE
FGHIJ
KLMNO
PQR

3

Haynes Publishing Group
Sparkford Nr Yeovil
Somerset BA22 7JJ England

Haynes North America, Inc
861 Lawrence Drive
Newbury Park
California 91320 USA

About this manual

Its purpose

The purpose of this manual is to help you get the best value from your vehicle. It can do so in several ways. It can help you decide what work must be done, even if you choose to have it done by a dealer service department or a repair shop; it provides information and procedures for routine maintenance and servicing; and it offers diagnostic and repair procedures to follow when trouble occurs.

We hope you use the manual to tackle the work yourself. For many simpler jobs, doing it yourself may be quicker than arranging an appointment to get the vehicle into a shop and making the trips to leave it and pick it up. More importantly, a lot of money can be saved by avoiding the expense the shop must pass on to you to cover its labor and overhead costs. An added benefit is the sense of satisfaction and accomplishment that you feel after doing the job yourself.

Using the manual

The manual is divided into Chapters. Each Chapter is divided into numbered Sections, which are headed in bold type between horizontal lines. Each Section consists of consecutively numbered paragraphs.

At the beginning of each numbered Section you will be referred to any illustrations which apply to the procedures in that Section. The reference numbers used in illustration captions pinpoint the pertinent Section and the Step within that Section. That is, illustration 3.2 means the illustration refers to Section 3 and Step (or paragraph) 2 within that Section.

Procedures, once described in the text, are not normally repeated. When It's necessary to refer to another Chapter, the reference will be given as Chapter and Section number. Cross references given without use of the word "Chapter" apply to Sections and/or paragraphs in the same Chapter. For example, "see Section 8" means in the same Chapter.

References to the left or right side of the vehicle assume you are sitting in the driver's seat, facing forward.

Even though we have prepared this manual with extreme care, neither the publisher nor the author can accept responsibility for any errors in, or omissions from, the information given.

NOTE

A **Note** provides information necessary to properly complete a procedure or information which will make the procedure easier to understand.

CAUTION

A **Caution** provides a special procedure or special steps which must be taken while completing the procedure where the Caution is found. Not heeding a Caution can result in damage to the assembly being worked on.

WARNING

A **Warning** provides a special procedure or special steps which must be taken while completing the procedure where the Warning is found. Not heeding a Warning can result in personal injury.

Acknowledgements

We are grateful for the help and cooperation of Tomco Industries, 1435 Woodson Road, St. Louis, Missouri 63132, for their assistance with technical information and illustrations. Wiring diagrams produced exclusively for Haynes North America, Inc. by Valley Forge Technical Communications. Technical writers who contributed to this project include Bob Henderson, Jeff Killingsworth and Mike Forsythe.

© **Haynes North America, Inc. 1994, 1995, 1996, 1998**

With permission from J.H. Haynes & Co. Ltd.

A book in the Haynes Automotive Repair Manual Series

Printed in the U.S.A.

ISBN 1 56392 209 6

Library of Congress Catalog Card Number 95-82336

Contents

Haynes mechanic, author and photographer with Pontiac 6000

Introduction to the General Motors A-cars

Since its introduction in 1982, the popular GM A-body design has gone through many changes. Although the basic chassis design has changed little, several engines, fuel systems and ignition systems have been offered.

Most four-cylinder models are equipped with the 2.5 liter overhead valve (OHV) four-cylinder engine, sometimes referred to as the "Iron Duke," because of its all-cast-iron construction. In 1993, this engine was replaced by a 2.2L OHV four-cylinder engine with a cast-iron block and aluminum cylinder head.

Two different OHV V6 engine designs have been used in these models. The narrower 2.8 liter and 3.1 liter V6 engines are from the same general engine family; they have a 60-degree angle between cylinder banks. The second V6 engine family (3.0 liter, 3.3 liter and 3.8 liter engines) are wider because of the 90-degree angle between cylinder banks.

Most models use a Throttle Body Injection (TBI) or multi-port fuel injection system, although some 1985 and earlier V6 models are carbureted.

The engine drives the front wheels through either a manual or automatic trans-

axle via unequal-length driveaxles. The power assisted rack and pinion steering gear assembly is mounted behind the engine.

The front suspension is composed of MacPherson struts, three-point control arms and a stabilizer bar. The rear suspension consists of a solid axle with integral trailing arms, coil springs and shock absorbers.

The brakes are disc at the front and drum at the rear on most models (some models have rear disc brakes), with power assist standard. Some later models are equipped with an Anti-lock Brake System (ABS).

Vehicle identification numbers

Modifications are a continuing and unpublicized process in vehicle manufacturing. Since spare parts manuals and lists are compiled on a numerical basis, the individual vehicle numbers are essential to correctly identify the component required.

Vehicle identification number (VIN)

This very important identification number is located on a plate attached to the top left corner of the dashboard of the vehicle (see illustration). The VIN also appears on the Vehicle Certificate of Title and Registration. It contains valuable information such as where and when the vehicle was manufactured, the model year and the body style.

Body identification plate

This metal plate is normally located on or near the top side of the radiator support. Like the VIN, it contains valuable information concerning the production of the vehicle, as well as information about the way in which the vehicle is equipped. This plate is especially useful for matching the color and type of paint during repair work.

Engine identification numbers

On 2.2 liter four-cylinder engines, the engine number is stamped onto a machined pad, adjacent to the transaxle (see illustration).

The VIN number is visible through the windshield on the driver's side

The engine number on the 2.5 liter four-cylinder engine is either stamped on a pad at the front of the cylinder block, above the timing cover, or at the rear of the block, adjacent to the transaxle (see illustration).

The number on V6 engines is located on a pad at the rear of the cylinder block, just ahead of the transaxle or adjacent to the timing chain cover, just below the water pump (see illustration). Later models also have an ID number attached to the valve cover.

Manual transaxle number

The manual transaxle ID number is located on a pad on the forward side of the transaxle case.

Automatic transaxle numbers

The VIN number is located on a flange pad at either the lower front edge, near the dipstick or the top of the transaxle case. The model code is located at the top of the case.

Alternator numbers

The alternator ID number is located on top of the drive end frame.

Vehicle Emissions Control Information label

The Emissions Control Information label is usually attached to the front of the suspension strut tower (see illustration).

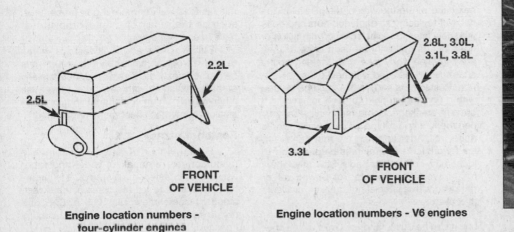

Engine location numbers - four-cylinder engines

Engine location numbers - V6 engines

The Vehicle Emissions Control Information label is located in the engine compartment

Buying parts

Replacement parts are available from many sources, which generally fall into one of two categories - authorized dealer parts departments and independent retail auto parts stores. Our advice concerning these parts is as follows:

Retail auto parts stores: Good auto parts stores will stock frequently needed components which wear out relatively fast, such as clutch components, exhaust systems, brake parts, tune-up parts, etc. These stores often supply new or reconditioned parts on an exchange basis, which can save a considerable amount of money. Discount auto parts stores are often very good places to buy materials and parts needed for general vehicle maintenance such as oil, grease, filters, spark plugs, belts, touch-up paint, bulbs, etc. They also usually sell tools and general accessories, have convenient hours, charge lower prices and can often be found not far from home.

Authorized dealer parts department: This is the best source for parts which are unique to the vehicle and not generally available elsewhere (such as major engine parts, transmission parts, trim pieces, etc.).

Warranty information: If the vehicle is still covered under warranty, be sure that any replacement parts purchased - regardless of the source - do not invalidate the warranty!

To be sure of obtaining the correct parts, have engine and chassis numbers available and, if possible, take the old parts along for positive identification.

Maintenance techniques, tools and working facilities

Maintenance techniques

There are a number of techniques involved in maintenance and repair that will be referred to throughout this manual. Application of these techniques will enable the home mechanic to be more efficient, better organized and capable of performing the various tasks properly, which will ensure that the repair job is thorough and complete.

Fasteners

Fasteners are nuts, bolts, studs and screws used to hold two or more parts together. There are a few things to keep in mind when working with fasteners. Almost all of them use a locking device of some type, either a lockwasher, locknut, locking tab or thread adhesive. All threaded fasteners should be clean and straight, with undamaged threads and undamaged corners on the hex head where the wrench fits. Develop the habit of replacing all damaged nuts and bolts with new ones. Special locknuts with nylon or fiber inserts can only be used once. If they are removed, they lose their locking ability and must be replaced with new ones.

Rusted nuts and bolts should be treated with a penetrating fluid to ease removal and prevent breakage. Some mechanics use turpentine in a spout-type oil can, which works quite well. After applying the rust penetrant, let it work for a few minutes before trying to loosen the nut or bolt. Badly rusted fasteners may have to be chiseled or sawed off or removed with a special nut breaker, available at tool stores.

If a bolt or stud breaks off in an assembly, it can be drilled and removed with a special tool commonly available for this purpose. Most automotive machine shops can perform this task, as well as other repair procedures, such as the repair of threaded holes that have been stripped out.

Flat washers and lockwashers, when removed from an assembly, should always be replaced exactly as removed. Replace any damaged washers with new ones. Never use a lockwasher on any soft metal surface (such as aluminum), thin sheet metal or plastic.

Fastener sizes

For a number of reasons, automobile manufacturers are making wider and wider use of metric fasteners. Therefore, it is important to be able to tell the difference between standard (sometimes called U.S. or SAE) and metric hardware, since they cannot be interchanged.

All bolts, whether standard or metric, are sized according to diameter, thread pitch and length. For example, a standard 1/2 - 13 x 1 bolt is 1/2 inch in diameter, has 13 threads per inch and is 1 inch long. An M12 - 1.75 x 25 metric bolt is 12 mm in diameter, has a thread pitch of 1.75 mm (the distance between threads) and is 25 mm long. The two bolts are nearly identical, and easily confused, but they are not interchangeable.

In addition to the differences in diameter, thread pitch and length, metric and standard bolts can also be distinguished by examining the bolt heads. To begin with, the distance across the flats on a standard bolt head is measured in inches, while the same dimension on a metric bolt is sized in millimeters (the same is true for nuts). As a result, a standard wrench should not be used on a metric bolt and a metric wrench should not be used on a standard bolt. Also, most standard bolts have slashes radiating out from the center of the head to denote the grade or strength of the bolt, which is an indication of the amount of torque that can be applied to it. The greater the number of slashes, the greater the strength of the bolt. Grades 0 through 5 are commonly used on automobiles. Metric bolts have a property class (grade) number, rather than a slash, molded into their heads to indicate bolt strength. In this case, the higher the number, the stronger the bolt. Property class numbers 8.8, 9.8 and 10.9 are commonly used on automobiles.

Strength markings can also be used to distinguish standard hex nuts from metric hex nuts. Many standard nuts have dots stamped into one side, while metric nuts are marked with a number. The greater the number of dots, or the higher the number, the greater the strength of the nut.

Metric studs are also marked on their ends according to property class (grade). Larger studs are numbered (the same as metric bolts), while smaller studs carry a geometric code to denote grade.

It should be noted that many fasteners, especially Grades 0 through 2, have no distinguishing marks on them. When such is the case, the only way to determine whether it is standard or metric is to measure the thread pitch or compare it to a known fastener of the same size.

Standard fasteners are often referred to as SAE, as opposed to metric. However, it should be noted that SAE technically refers to a non-metric fine thread fastener only. Coarse thread non-metric fasteners are referred to as USS sizes.

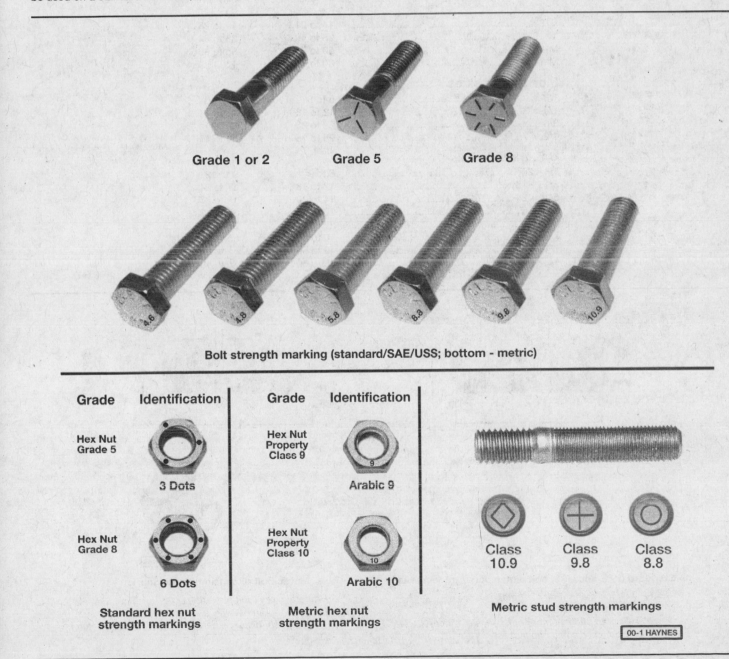

Grade 1 or 2   Grade 5   Grade 8

Bolt strength marking (standard/SAE/USS; bottom - metric)

Grade	Identification
Hex Nut Grade 5	3 Dots
Hex Nut Grade 8	6 Dots

Standard hex nut strength markings

Grade	Identification
Hex Nut Property Class 9	Arabic 9
Hex Nut Property Class 10	Arabic 10

Metric hex nut strength markings

Class 10.9   Class 9.8   Class 8.8

Metric stud strength markings

Since fasteners of the same size (both standard and metric) may have different strength ratings, be sure to reinstall any bolts, studs or nuts removed from your vehicle in their original locations. Also, when replacing a fastener with a new one, make sure that the new one has a strength rating equal to or greater than the original.

Tightening sequences and procedures

Most threaded fasteners should be tightened to a specific torque value (torque is the twisting force applied to a threaded component such as a nut or bolt). Overtightening the fastener can weaken it and cause it to break, while undertightening can cause it to eventually come loose. Bolts, screws and studs, depending on the material they are made of and their thread diameters, have specific torque values, many of which are noted in the Specifications at the beginning of each Chapter. Be sure to follow the torque recommendations closely. For fasteners not assigned a specific torque, a general torque value chart is presented here as a guide. These torque values are for dry (unlubricated) fasteners threaded into steel or cast iron (not aluminum). As was previously mentioned, the size and grade of a fastener determine the amount of torque that can safely be applied to it. The figures listed here are approximate for Grade 2 and Grade 3 fasteners. Higher grades can tolerate higher torque values.

Fasteners laid out in a pattern, such as cylinder head bolts, oil pan bolts, differential cover bolts, etc., must be loosened or tightened in sequence to avoid warping the component. This sequence will normally be shown in the appropriate Chapter. If a specific pattern is not given, the following procedures can be used to prevent warping.

Metric thread sizes	Ft-lbs	Nm
M-6	6 to 9	9 to 12
M-8	14 to 21	19 to 28
M-10	28 to 40	38 to 54
M-12	50 to 71	68 to 96
M-14	80 to 140	109 to 154
Pipe thread sizes		
1/8	5 to 8	7 to 10
1/4	12 to 18	17 to 24
3/8	22 to 33	30 to 44
1/2	25 to 35	34 to 47
U.S. thread sizes		
1/4 - 20	6 to 9	9 to 12
5/16 - 18	12 to 18	17 to 24
5/16 - 24	14 to 20	19 to 27
3/8 - 16	22 to 32	30 to 43
3/8 - 24	27 to 38	37 to 51
7/16 - 14	40 to 55	55 to 74
7/16 - 20	40 to 60	55 to 81
1/2 - 13	55 to 80	75 to 108

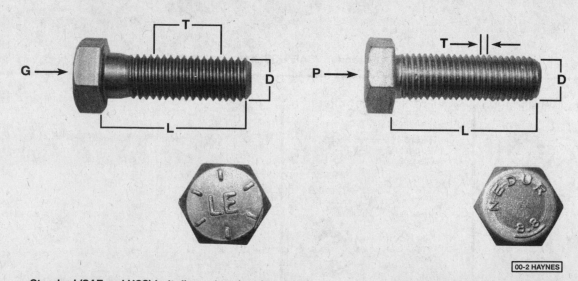

00-2 HAYNES

Standard (SAE and USS) bolt dimensions/grade marks

G   Grade marks (bolt strength)
L   Length (in inches)
T   Thread pitch (number of threads per inch)
D   Nominal diameter (in inches)

Metric bolt dimensions/grade marks

P   Property class (bolt strength)
L   Length (in millimeters)
T   Thread pitch (distance between threads in millimeters)
D   Diameter

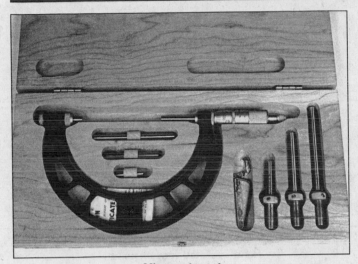

Micrometer set

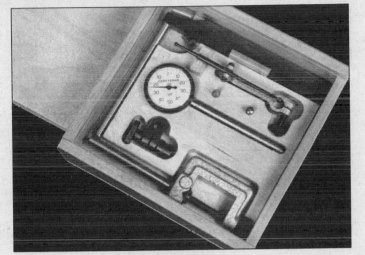

Dial indicator set

Initially, the bolts or nuts should be assembled finger-tight only. Next, they should be tightened one full turn each, in a criss-cross or diagonal pattern. After each one has been tightened one full turn, return to the first one and tighten them all one-half turn, following the same pattern. Finally, tighten each of them one-quarter turn at a time until each fastener has been tightened to the proper torque. To loosen and remove the fasteners, the procedure would be reversed.

Component disassembly

Component disassembly should be done with care and purpose to help ensure that the parts go back together properly. Always keep track of the sequence in which parts are removed. Make note of special characteristics or marks on parts that can be installed more than one way, such as a grooved thrust washer on a shaft. It is a good idea to lay the disassembled parts out on a clean surface in the order that they were removed. It may also be helpful to make sketches or take instant photos of components before removal.

When removing fasteners from a component, keep track of their locations. Sometimes threading a bolt back in a part, or putting the washers and nut back on a stud, can prevent mix-ups later. If nuts and bolts cannot be returned to their original locations, they should be kept in a compartmented box or a series of small boxes. A cupcake or muffin tin is ideal for this purpose, since each cavity can hold the bolts and nuts from a particular area (i.e. oil pan bolts, valve cover bolts, engine mount bolts, etc.). A pan of this type is especially helpful when working on assemblies with very small parts, such as the carburetor, alternator, valve train or interior dash and trim pieces. The cavities can be marked with paint or tape to identify the contents.

Whenever wiring looms, harnesses or connectors are separated, it is a good idea to identify the two halves with numbered pieces of masking tape so they can be easily reconnected.

Gasket sealing surfaces

Throughout any vehicle, gaskets are used to seal the mating surfaces between two parts and keep lubricants, fluids, vacuum or pressure contained in an assembly.

Many times these gaskets are coated with a liquid or paste-type gasket sealing compound before assembly. Age, heat and pressure can sometimes cause the two parts to stick together so tightly that they are very difficult to separate. Often, the assembly can be loosened by striking it with a soft-face hammer near the mating surfaces. A regular hammer can be used if a block of wood is placed between the hammer and the part. Do not hammer on cast parts or parts that could be easily damaged. With any particularly stubborn part, always recheck to make sure that every fastener has been removed.

Avoid using a screwdriver or bar to pry apart an assembly, as they can easily mar the gasket sealing surfaces of the parts, which must remain smooth. If prying is absolutely necessary, use an old broom handle, but keep in mind that extra clean up will be necessary if the wood splinters.

After the parts are separated, the old gasket must be carefully scraped off and the gasket surfaces cleaned. Stubborn gasket material can be soaked with rust penetrant or treated with a special chemical to soften it so it can be easily scraped off. A scraper can be fashioned from a piece of copper tubing by flattening and sharpening one end. Copper is recommended because it is usually softer than the surfaces to be scraped, which reduces the chance of gouging the part. Some gaskets can be removed with a wire brush, but regardless of the method used, the mating surfaces must be left clean and smooth. If for some reason the gasket surface is gouged, then a gasket sealer thick enough to fill scratches will have to be used during reassembly of the components. For most applications, a non-drying (or semi-drying) gasket sealer should be used.

Hose removal tips

Warning: *If the vehicle is equipped with air conditioning, do not disconnect any of the A/C hoses without first having the system depressurized by a dealer service department or a service station.*

Hose removal precautions closely parallel gasket removal precautions. Avoid scratching or gouging the surface that the hose mates against or the connection may leak. This is especially true for radiator hoses. Because of various chemical reactions, the rubber in hoses can bond itself to the metal spigot that the hose fits over. To remove a hose, first loosen the hose clamps that secure it to the spigot. Then, with slip-joint pliers, grab the hose at the clamp and rotate it around the spigot. Work it back and forth until it is completely free, then pull it off. Silicone or other lubricants will ease removal if they can be applied between the hose and the outside of the spigot. Apply the same lubricant to the inside of the hose and the outside of the spigot to simplify installation.

As a last resort (and if the hose is to be replaced with a new one anyway), the rubber can be slit with a knife and the hose peeled from the spigot. If this must be done, be careful that the metal connection is not damaged.

If a hose clamp is broken or damaged, do not reuse it. Wire-type clamps usually weaken with age, so it is a good idea to replace them with screw-type clamps whenever a hose is removed.

Tools

A selection of good tools is a basic requirement for anyone who plans to maintain and repair his or her own vehicle. For the owner who has few tools, the initial investment might seem high, but when compared to the spiraling costs of professional auto maintenance and repair, it is a wise one.

To help the owner decide which tools are needed to perform the tasks detailed in this manual, the following tool lists are offered: *Maintenance and minor repair,*

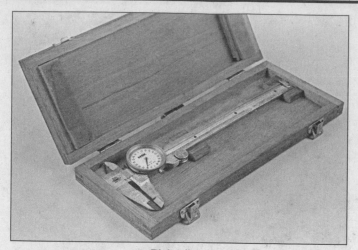

Dial caliper

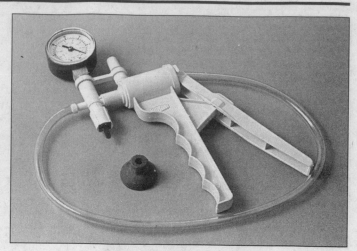

Hand-operated vacuum pump

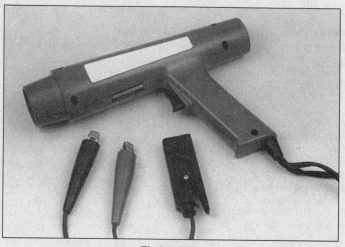

Timing light

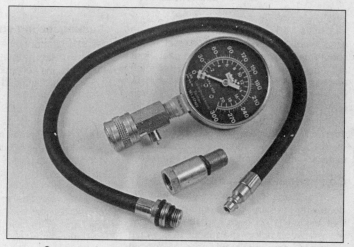

Compression gauge with spark plug   hole adapter

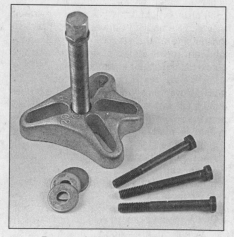

Damper/steering wheel puller

General purpose puller

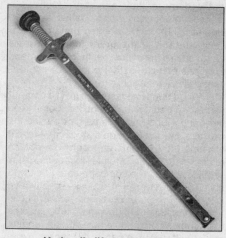

Hydraulic lifter removal tool

Repair/overhaul and *Special.*

The newcomer to practical mechanics should start off with the *maintenance and minor repair* tool kit, which is adequate for the simpler jobs performed on a vehicle. Then, as confidence and experience grow, the owner can tackle more difficult tasks, buying additional tools as they are needed.

Eventually the basic kit will be expanded into the *repair and overhaul* tool set. Over a period of time, the experienced do-it-yourselfer will assemble a tool set complete enough for most repair and overhaul procedures and will add tools from the special category when it is felt that the expense is justified by the frequency of use.

Maintenance and minor repair tool kit

The tools in this list should be considered the minimum required for performance of routine maintenance, servicing and minor repair work. We recommend the purchase of combination wrenches (box-end and open-

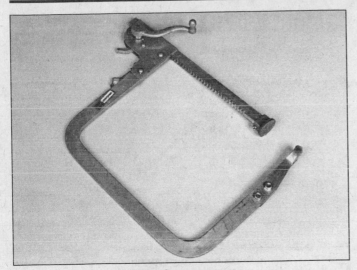

Valve spring compressor

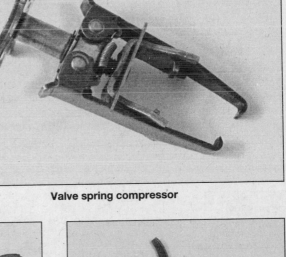

Valve spring compressor

Ridge reamer

Piston ring groove cleaning tool

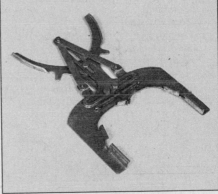

Ring removal/installation tool

end combined in one wrench). While more expensive than open end wrenches, they offer the advantages of both types of wrench.

Combination wrench set (1/4-inch to
    1 inch or 6 mm to 19 mm)
Adjustable wrench, 8 inch
Spark plug wrench with rubber insert
Spark plug gap adjusting tool
Feeler gauge set
Brake bleeder wrench
Standard screwdriver (5/16-inch x
    6 inch)
Phillips screwdriver (No. 2 x 6 inch)
Combination pliers - 6 inch
Hacksaw and assortment of blades
Tire pressure gauge
Grease gun
Oil can
Fine emery cloth
Wire brush
Battery post and cable cleaning tool
Oil filter wrench
Funnel (medium size)
Safety goggles
Jackstands (2)
Drain pan

Note: If basic tune-ups are going to be part of routine maintenance, it will be necessary to purchase a good quality stroboscopic timing

light and combination tachometer/dwell meter. Although they are included in the list of special tools, it is mentioned here because they are absolutely necessary for tuning most vehicles properly.

Repair and overhaul tool set

These tools are essential for anyone who plans to perform major repairs and are in addition to those in the maintenance and minor repair tool kit. Included is a comprehensive set of sockets which, though expensive, are invaluable because of their versatility, especially when various extensions and drives are available. We recommend the 1/2-inch drive over the 3/8-inch drive. Although the larger drive is bulky and more expensive, it has the capacity of accepting a very wide range of large sockets. Ideally, however, the mechanic should have a 3/8-inch drive set and a 1/2 inch drive set.

Socket set(s)
Reversible ratchet
Extension - 10 inch
Universal joint
Torque wrench (same size drive as
    sockets)
Ball peen hammer - 8 ounce
Soft-face hammer (plastic/rubber)

Ring compressor

Standard screwdriver (1/4-inch x 6 inch)
Standard screwdriver (stubby -
    5/16-inch)
Phillips screwdriver (No. 3 x 8 inch)
Phillips screwdriver (stubby - No. 2)
Pliers - vise grip
Pliers - lineman's
Pliers - needle nose
Pliers - snap-ring (internal and external)
Cold chisel - 1/2-inch

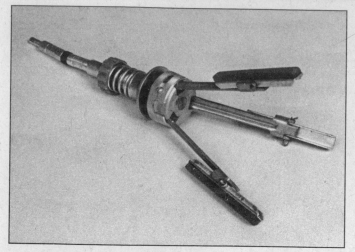

Cylinder hone

Brake hold-down spring tool

Scribe
Scraper (made from flattened copper
   tubing)
Centerpunch
Pin punches (1/16, 1/8, 3/16-inch)
Steel rule/straightedge - 12 inch
Allen wrench set (1/8 to 3/8-inch or
   4 mm to 10 mm)
A selection of files

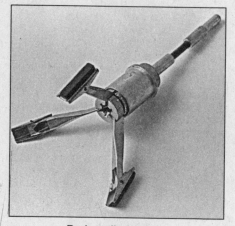

Brake cylinder hone

Wire brush (large)
Jackstands (second set)
Jack (scissor or hydraulic type)

Note: Another tool which is often useful is an electric drill with a chuck capacity of 3/8-inch and a set of good quality drill bits.

Special tools

The tools in this list include those which are not used regularly, are expensive to buy, or which need to be used in accordance with their manufacturer's instructions. Unless these tools will be used frequently, it is not very economical to purchase many of them. A consideration would be to split the cost and use between yourself and a friend or friends. In addition, most of these tools can be obtained from a tool rental shop on a temporary basis.

This list primarily contains only those tools and instruments widely available to the public, and not those special tools produced by the vehicle manufacturer for distribution to dealer service departments. Occasionally, references to the manufacturer's special tools are included in the text of this manual. Generally, an alternative method of doing the job without the special tool is offered. How-

ever, sometimes there is no alternative to their use. Where this is the case, and the tool cannot be purchased or borrowed, the work should be turned over to the dealer service department or an automotive repair shop.

Valve spring compressor
Piston ring groove cleaning tool
Piston ring compressor
Piston ring installation tool
Cylinder compression gauge
Cylinder ridge reamer
Cylinder surfacing hone
Cylinder bore gauge
Micrometers and/or dial calipers
Hydraulic lifter removal tool
Balljoint separator
Universal-type puller
Impact screwdriver
Dial indicator set
Stroboscopic timing light (inductive
   pick-up)
Hand operated vacuum/pressure pump
Tachometer/dwell meter
Universal electrical multimeter
Cable hoist
Brake spring removal and installation
   tools
Floor jack

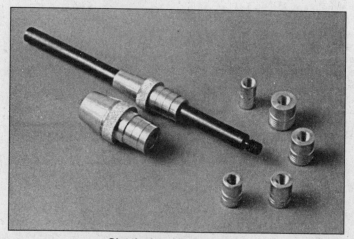

Clutch plate alignment tool

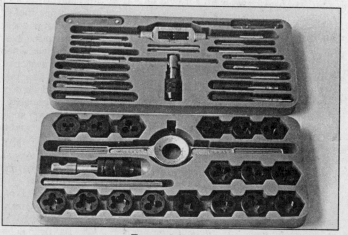

Tap and die set

Buying tools

For the do-it-yourselfer who is just starting to get involved in vehicle maintenance and repair, there are a number of options available when purchasing tools. If maintenance and minor repair is the extent of the work to be done, the purchase of individual tools is satisfactory. If, on the other hand, extensive work is planned, it would be a good idea to purchase a modest tool set from one of the large retail chain stores. A set can usually be bought at a substantial savings over the individual tool prices, and they often come with a tool box. As additional tools are needed, add-on sets, individual tools and a larger tool box can be purchased to expand the tool selection. Building a tool set gradually allows the cost of the tools to be spread over a longer period of time and gives the mechanic the freedom to choose only those tools that will actually be used.

Tool stores will often be the only source of some of the special tools that are needed, but regardless of where tools are bought, try to avoid cheap ones, especially when buying screwdrivers and sockets, because they won't last very long. The expense involved in replacing cheap tools will eventually be greater than the initial cost of quality tools.

Care and maintenance of tools

Good tools are expensive, so it makes sense to treat them with respect. Keep them clean and in usable condition and store them properly when not in use. Always wipe off any dirt, grease or metal chips before putting them away. Never leave tools lying around in the work area. Upon completion of a job, always check closely under the hood for tools that may have been left there so they won't get lost during a test drive.

Some tools, such as screwdrivers, pliers, wrenches and sockets, can be hung on a panel mounted on the garage or workshop wall, while others should be kept in a tool box or tray. Measuring instruments, gauges, meters, etc. must be carefully stored where they cannot be damaged by weather or impact from other tools.

When tools are used with care and stored properly, they will last a very long time. Even with the best of care, though, tools will wear out if used frequently. When a tool is damaged or worn out, replace it. Subsequent jobs will be safer and more enjoyable if you do.

How to repair damaged threads

Sometimes, the internal threads of a nut or bolt hole can become stripped, usually from overtightening. Stripping threads is an all-too-common occurrence, especially when working with aluminum parts, because aluminum is so soft that it easily strips out.

Usually, external or internal threads are only partially stripped. After they've been cleaned up with a tap or die, they'll still work. Sometimes, however, threads are badly damaged. When this happens, you've got three choices:

1) *Drill and tap the hole to the next suitable oversize and install a larger diameter bolt, screw or stud.*

2) *Drill and tap the hole to accept a threaded plug, then drill and tap the plug to the original screw size. You can also buy a plug already threaded to the original size. Then you simply drill a hole to the specified size, then run the threaded plug into the hole with a bolt and jam nut. Once the plug is fully seated, remove the jam nut and bolt.*

3) *The third method uses a patented thread repair kit like Heli-Coil or Slimsert. These easy-to-use kits are designed to repair damaged threads in straight-through holes and blind holes. Both are available as kits which can handle a variety of sizes and thread patterns. Drill the hole, then tap it with the special included tap. Install the Heli-Coil and the hole is back to its original diameter and thread pitch.*

Regardless of which method you use, be sure to proceed calmly and carefully. A little impatience or carelessness during one of these relatively simple procedures can ruin your whole day's work and cost you a bundle if you wreck an expensive part.

Working facilities

Not to be overlooked when discussing tools is the workshop. If anything more than routine maintenance is to be carried out, some sort of suitable work area is essential.

It is understood, and appreciated, that many home mechanics do not have a good workshop or garage available, and end up removing an engine or doing major repairs outside. It is recommended, however, that the overhaul or repair be completed under the cover of a roof.

A clean, flat workbench or table of comfortable working height is an absolute necessity. The workbench should be equipped with a vise that has a jaw opening of at least four inches.

As mentioned previously, some clean, dry storage space is also required for tools, as well as the lubricants, fluids, cleaning solvents, etc. which soon become necessary.

Sometimes waste oil and fluids, drained from the engine or cooling system during normal maintenance or repairs, present a disposal problem. To avoid pouring them on the ground or into a sewage system, pour the used fluids into large containers, seal them with caps and take them to an authorized disposal site or recycling center. Plastic jugs, such as old antifreeze containers, are ideal for this purpose.

Always keep a supply of old newspapers and clean rags available. Old towels are excellent for mopping up spills. Many mechanics use rolls of paper towels for most work because they are readily available and disposable. To help keep the area under the vehicle clean, a large cardboard box can be cut open and flattened to protect the garage or shop floor.

Whenever working over a painted surface, such as when leaning over a fender to service something under the hood, always cover it with an old blanket or bedspread to protect the finish. Vinyl covered pads, made especially for this purpose, are available at auto parts stores.

Jacking and towing

Jacking

The jack supplied with the vehicle should only be used for raising the vehicle when changing a tire or placing jackstands under the frame. **Caution:** *Never work under the vehicle or start the engine while this jack is being used as the only means of support.*

The vehicle should be on level ground with the wheels blocked and the transaxle in Park (automatic) or Reverse (manual). If the wheel is to be changed, pry off the hub cap (if equipped) using the tapered end of the lug wrench - wire wheels require a special tool to remove the lock bolt, which should be stored with the spare tire **(see illustration)**. If the wheel is being changed, loosen the wheel nuts one-half turn and leave them in place until the wheel is raised off the ground.

Place the jack under the side of the vehicle in the indicated position **(see illustration)** and raise it until the jack head groove fits into the rocker flange notch. Operate the jack with a slow, smooth motion until the wheel is raised off the ground.

If a wheel is being changed, remove the nuts and wheel, install the spare wheel and reinstall the lug nuts, bevelled side facing in.

Tighten the nuts snugly, but not completely at this time.

Lower the vehicle, remove the jack and tighten the nuts (if loosened or removed) in a criss-cross sequence by turning the wrench clockwise (see Chapter 1 for the proper torque). Replace the hub cap (if equipped) by placing it in position and using the heel of your hand or a rubber mallet to seat it. On wire-wheel models, reinstall the lock bolt.

Towing

The vehicle can be towed with all four wheels on the ground, provided that speeds do not exceed 35 mph and the distance is not over 50 miles, otherwise transaxle damage can result.

Towing equipment specifically designed for this purpose should be used and should be attached to the main structural members of the vehicle and not the bumper or brackets.

Safety is a major consideration when towing and all applicable state and local laws must be obeyed. A safety chain system must be used for all towing.

While towing, the parking brake should

Use the special wrench stored with the spare tire to remove the center cap and lock bolt

be released and the transaxle should be in Neutral. The steering must be unlocked (ignition switch in the OFF position). Remember that power steering and power brakes will not work with the engine off.

Vehicle jacking points

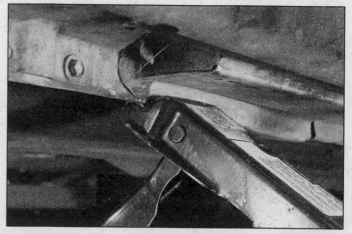

Jacking procedure

Delco-Loc II anti-theft audio system

General information

1   Some 1992 and later models are equipped with the Delco Loc II audio system, which includes an anti-theft feature that will render the stereo inoperative if stolen. If the power source to the stereo is cut with the anti-theft feature activated, the stereo will be inoperative. Even if the power source is immediately re-connected, the stereo will not function. If your vehicle is equipped with this anti-theft system, do not disconnect the battery, remove the stereo or disconnect related components unless you have either turned off the feature or have the individual ID (code) number for the stereo.

2   Refer to your vehicle's owner's manual for more complete information on this audio system and its anti-theft feature.

Disabling the anti-theft feature

3   Press the stereo's 1 and 4 buttons at the same time for five seconds with the ignition on and the radio power off. The display will show SEC, indicating the unit is in the secure mode (anti-theft feature enabled).

4   Press the SET button. The display will show "000."

5   Press the SEEK button to make the first number appear.

6   Rotate the TUNE knob right or left to make the last two numbers agree with your code. The numbers will be displayed as entered.

7   Press the lower BAND knob. "000" will be displayed.

8   Enter the second three digits of the code.

9   Press the lower BAND knob. If the display shows "_ _," you have successfully disabled the anti-theft feature. If SEC is displayed, the code you entered was incorrect and the anti-theft feature is still enabled.

Unlocking the stereo after a power loss

10   When power is restored to the stereo, the stereo won't turn on and LOC will appear on the display. Enter your ID code as follows; pause no more than 15 seconds between Steps.

11   Turn the ignition switch to ON, but leave the stereo off.

12   Press the SET button. "000" should display.

13   Press the SEEK button to make the first number appear.

14   Rotate the TUNE knob right or left to make the last two numbers agree with your code.

15   Repeat Steps 2 through 4 for the last three digits of your code.

16   Press the lower BAND knob. The time should appear, indicating the stereo is unlocked. If SEC appears, the numbers you entered were not correct and the stereo is still inoperative.

Booster battery (jump) starting

Observe these precautions when using a booster battery to start a vehicle:

a) Before connecting the booster battery, make sure the ignition switch is in the Off position.
b) Turn off the lights, heater and other electrical loads.
c) Your eyes should be shielded. Safety goggles are a good idea.
d) Make sure the booster battery is the same voltage as the dead one in the vehicle.
e) The two vehicles MUST NOT TOUCH each other!
f) Make sure the transaxle is in Neutral (manual) or Park (automatic).
g) If the booster battery is not a maintenance-free type, remove the vent caps and lay a cloth over the vent holes.

Connect the red jumper cable to the positive (+) terminals of each battery (see illustration).

Connect one end of the black jumper cable to the negative (-) terminal of the booster battery. The other end of this cable should be connected to a good ground on the vehicle to be started, such as a bolt or bracket on the body.

Start the engine using the booster battery, then, with the engine running at idle speed, disconnect the jumper cables in the reverse order of connection.

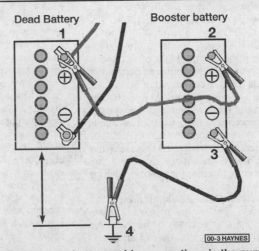

Make the booster battery cable connections in the numerical order shown (note that the negative cable of the booster battery is NOT attached to the negative terminal of the dead battery)

Automotive chemicals and lubricants

A number of automotive chemicals and lubricants are available for use during vehicle maintenance and repair. They include a wide variety of products ranging from cleaning solvents and degreasers to lubricants and protective sprays for rubber, plastic and vinyl.

Cleaners

Carburetor cleaner and choke cleaner is a strong solvent for gum, varnish and carbon. Most carburetor cleaners leave a dry-type lubricant film which will not harden or gum up. Because of this film it is not recommended for use on electrical components.

Brake system cleaner is used to remove grease and brake fluid from the brake system, where clean surfaces are absolutely necessary. It leaves no residue and often eliminates brake squeal caused by contaminants.

Electrical cleaner removes oxidation, corrosion and carbon deposits from electrical contacts, restoring full current flow. It can also be used to clean spark plugs, carburetor jets, voltage regulators and other parts where an oil-free surface is desired.

Demoisturants remove water and moisture from electrical components such as alternators, voltage regulators, electrical connectors and fuse blocks. They are non-conductive, non-corrosive and non-flammable.

Degreasers are heavy-duty solvents used to remove grease from the outside of the engine and from chassis components. They can be sprayed or brushed on and, depending on the type, are rinsed off either with water or solvent.

Lubricants

Motor oil is the lubricant formulated for use in engines. It normally contains a wide variety of additives to prevent corrosion and reduce foaming and wear. Motor oil comes in various weights (viscosity ratings) from 5 to 80. The recommended weight of the oil depends on the season, temperature and the demands on the engine. Light oil is used in cold climates and under light load conditions. Heavy oil is used in hot climates and where high loads are encountered. Multi-viscosity oils are designed to have characteristics of both light and heavy oils and are available in a number of weights from 5W-20 to 20W-50.

Gear oil is designed to be used in differentials, manual transmissions and other areas where high-temperature lubrication is required.

Chassis and wheel bearing grease is a heavy grease used where increased loads and friction are encountered, such as for wheel bearings, balljoints, tie-rod ends and universal joints.

High-temperature wheel bearing grease is designed to withstand the extreme temperatures encountered by wheel bearings in disc brake equipped vehicles. It usually contains molybdenum disulfide (moly), which is a dry-type lubricant.

White grease is a heavy grease for metal-to-metal applications where water is a problem. White grease stays soft under both low and high temperatures (usually from -100 to +190-degrees F), and will not wash off or dilute in the presence of water.

Assembly lube is a special extreme pressure lubricant, usually containing moly, used to lubricate high-load parts (such as main and rod bearings and cam lobes) for initial start-up of a new engine. The assembly lube lubricates the parts without being squeezed out or washed away until the engine oiling system begins to function.

Silicone lubricants are used to protect rubber, plastic, vinyl and nylon parts.

Graphite lubricants are used where oils cannot be used due to contamination problems, such as in locks. The dry graphite will lubricate metal parts while remaining uncontaminated by dirt, water, oil or acids. It is electrically conductive and will not foul electrical contacts in locks such as the ignition switch.

Moly penetrants loosen and lubricate frozen, rusted and corroded fasteners and prevent future rusting or freezing.

Heat-sink grease is a special electrically non-conductive grease that is used for mounting electronic ignition modules where it is essential that heat is transferred away from the module.

Sealants

RTV sealant is one of the most widely used gasket compounds. Made from silicone, RTV is air curing, it seals, bonds, waterproofs, fills surface irregularities, remains flexible, doesn't shrink, is relatively easy to remove, and is used as a supplementary sealer with almost all low and medium temperature gaskets.

Anaerobic sealant is much like RTV in that it can be used either to seal gaskets or to form gaskets by itself. It remains flexible, is solvent resistant and fills surface imperfections. The difference between an anaerobic sealant and an RTV-type sealant is in the curing. RTV cures when exposed to air, while an anaerobic sealant cures only in the absence of air. This means that an anaerobic sealant cures only after the assembly of parts, sealing them together.

Thread and pipe sealant is used for sealing hydraulic and pneumatic fittings and vacuum lines. It is usually made from a Teflon compound, and comes in a spray, a paint-on liquid and as a wrap-around tape.

Chemicals

Anti-seize compound prevents seizing, galling, cold welding, rust and corrosion in fasteners. High-temperature ant-seize, usually made with copper and graphite lubricants, is used for exhaust system and exhaust manifold bolts.

Anaerobic locking compounds are used to keep fasteners from vibrating or working loose and cure only after installation, in the absence of air. Medium strength locking compound is used for small nuts, bolts and screws that may be removed later. High-strength locking compound is for large nuts, bolts and studs which aren't removed on a regular basis.

Oil additives range from viscosity index improvers to chemical treatments that claim to reduce internal engine friction. It should be noted that most oil manufacturers caution against using additives with their oils.

Gas additives perform several functions, depending on their chemical makeup. They usually contain solvents that help dissolve gum and varnish that build up on carburetor, fuel injection and intake parts. They also serve to break down carbon deposits that form on the inside surfaces of the combustion chambers. Some additives contain upper cylinder lubricants for valves and piston rings, and others contain chemicals to remove condensation from the gas tank.

Miscellaneous

Brake fluid is specially formulated hydraulic fluid that can withstand the heat and pressure encountered in brake systems. Care must be taken so this fluid does not come in contact with painted surfaces or plastics. An opened container should always be resealed to prevent contamination by water or dirt.

Weatherstrip adhesive is used to bond weatherstripping around doors, windows and trunk lids. It is sometimes used to attach trim pieces.

Undercoating is a petroleum-based, tar-like substance that is designed to protect metal surfaces on the underside of the vehicle from corrosion. It also acts as a sound-deadening agent by insulating the bottom of the vehicle.

Waxes and polishes are used to help protect painted and plated surfaces from the weather. Different types of paint may require the use of different types of wax and polish. Some polishes utilize a chemical or abrasive cleaner to help remove the top layer of oxidized (dull) paint on older vehicles. In recent years many non-wax polishes that contain a wide variety of chemicals such as polymers and silicones have been introduced. These non-wax polishes are usually easier to apply and last longer than conventional waxes and polishes.

Conversion factors

Length (distance)

Inches (in)	X	25.4	= Millimetres (mm)	X 0.0394	= Inches (in)
Feet (ft)	X	0.305	= Metres (m)	X 3.281	= Feet (ft)
Miles	X	1.609	= Kilometres (km)	X 0.621	= Miles

Volume (capacity)

Cubic inches (cu in; in³)	X	16.387	= Cubic centimetres (cc; cm³)	X 0.061	= Cubic inches (cu in; in³)
Imperial pints (Imp pt)	X	0.568	= Litres (l)	X 1.76	= Imperial pints (Imp pt)
Imperial quarts (Imp qt)	X	1.137	= Litres (l)	X 0.88	= Imperial quarts (Imp qt)
Imperial quarts (Imp qt)	X	1.201	= US quarts (US qt)	X 0.833	= Imperial quarts (Imp qt)
US quarts (US qt)	X	0.946	= Litres (l)	X 1.057	= US quarts (US qt)
Imperial gallons (Imp gal)	X	4.546	= Litres (l)	X 0.22	= Imperial gallons (Imp gal)
Imperial gallons (Imp gal)	X	1.201	= US gallons (US gal)	X 0.833	= Imperial gallons (Imp gal)
US gallons (US gal)	X	3.785	= Litres (l)	X 0.264	= US gallons (US gal)

Mass (weight)

Ounces (oz)	X	28.35	= Grams (g)	X 0.035	= Ounces (oz)
Pounds (lb)	X	0.454	= Kilograms (kg)	X 2.205	= Pounds (lb)

Force

Ounces-force (ozf; oz)	X	0.278	= Newtons (N)	X 3.6	= Ounces-force (ozf; oz)
Pounds-force (lbf; lb)	X	4.448	= Newtons (N)	X 0.225	= Pounds-force (lbf; lb)
Newtons (N)	X	0.1	= Kilograms-force (kgf; kg)	X 9.81	= Newtons (N)

Pressure

Pounds-force per square inch (psi; lbf/in²; lb/in²)	X	0.070	= Kilograms-force per square centimetre (kgf/cm²; kg/cm²)	X 14.223	= Pounds-force per square inch (psi; lbf/in²; lb/in²)
Pounds-force per square inch (psi; lbf/in²; lb/in²)	X	0.068	= Atmospheres (atm)	X 14.696	= Pounds-force per square inch (psi; lbf/in²; lb/in²)
Pounds-force per square inch (psi; lbf/in²; lb/in²)	X	0.069	= Bars	X 14.5	= Pounds-force per square inch (psi; lbf/in²; lb/in²)
Pounds-force per square inch (psi; lbf/in²; lb/in²)	X	6.895	= Kilopascals (kPa)	X 0.145	= Pounds-force per square inch (psi; lbf/in²; lb/in²)
Kilopascals (kPa)	X	0.01	= Kilograms-force per square centimetre (kgf/cm²; kg/cm²)	X 98.1	= Kilopascals (kPa)

Torque (moment of force)

Pounds-force inches (lbf in; lb in)	X	1.152	= Kilograms-force centimetre (kgf cm; kg cm)	X 0.868	= Pounds-force inches (lbf in; lb in)
Pounds-force inches (lbf in; lb in)	X	0.113	= Newton metres (Nm)	X 8.85	= Pounds-force inches (lbf in; lb in)
Pounds-force inches (lbf in; lb in)	X	0.083	= Pounds-force feet (lbf ft; lb ft)	X 12	= Pounds-force inches (lbf in; lb in)
Pounds-force feet (lbf ft; lb ft)	X	0.138	= Kilograms-force metres (kgf m; kg m)	X 7.233	= Pounds-force feet (lbf ft; lb ft)
Pounds-force feet (lbf ft; lb ft)	X	1.356	= Newton metres (Nm)	X 0.738	= Pounds-force feet (lbf ft; lb ft)
Newton metres (Nm)	X	0.102	= Kilograms-force metres (kgf m; kg m)	X 9.804	= Newton metres (Nm)

Vacuum

Inches mercury (in. Hg)	X	3.377	= Kilopascals (kPa)	X 0.2961	= Inches mercury
Inches mercury (in. Hg)	X	25.4	= Millimeters mercury (mm Hg)	X 0.0394	= Inches mercury

Power

Horsepower (hp)	X	745.7	= Watts (W)	X 0.0013	= Horsepower (hp)

Velocity (speed)

Miles per hour (miles/hr; mph)	X	1.609	= Kilometres per hour (km/hr; kph)	X 0.621	= Miles per hour (miles/hr; mph)

Fuel consumption*

Miles per gallon, Imperial (mpg)	X	0.354	= Kilometres per litre (km/l)	X 2.825	= Miles per gallon, Imperial (mpg)
Miles per gallon, US (mpg)	X	0.425	= Kilometres per litre (km/l)	X 2.352	= Miles per gallon, US (mpg)

Temperature

Degrees Fahrenheit = (°C x 1.8) + 32   Degrees Celsius (Degrees Centigrade; °C) = (°F - 32) x 0.56

*It is common practice to convert from miles per gallon (mpg) to litres/100 kilometres (l/100km), where mpg (Imperial) x l/100 km = 282 and mpg (US) x l/100 km = 235

Safety first!

Regardless of how enthusiastic you may be about getting on with the job at hand, take the time to ensure that your safety is not jeopardized. A moment's lack of attention can result in an accident, as can failure to observe certain simple safety precautions. The possibility of an accident will always exist, and the following points should not be considered a comprehensive list of all dangers. Rather, they are intended to make you aware of the risks and to encourage a safety conscious approach to all work you carry out on your vehicle.

Essential DOs and DON'Ts

DON'T rely on a jack when working under the vehicle. Always use approved jackstands to support the weight of the vehicle and place them under the recommended lift or support points.

DON'T attempt to loosen extremely tight fasteners (i.e. wheel lug nuts) while the vehicle is on a jack - it may fall.

DON'T start the engine without first making sure that the transmission is in Neutral (or Park where applicable) and the parking brake is set.

DON'T remove the radiator cap from a hot cooling system - let it cool or cover it with a cloth and release the pressure gradually.

DON'T attempt to drain the engine oil until you are sure it has cooled to the point that it will not burn you.

DON'T touch any part of the engine or exhaust system until it has cooled sufficiently to avoid burns.

DON'T siphon toxic liquids such as gasoline, antifreeze and brake fluid by mouth, or allow them to remain on your skin.

DON'T inhale brake lining dust - it is potentially hazardous (see *Asbestos* below).

DON'T allow spilled oil or grease to remain on the floor - wipe it up before someone slips on it.

DON'T use loose fitting wrenches or other tools which may slip and cause injury.

DON'T push on wrenches when loosening or tightening nuts or bolts. Always try to pull the wrench toward you. If the situation calls for pushing the wrench away, push with an open hand to avoid scraped knuckles if the wrench should slip.

DON'T attempt to lift a heavy component alone - get someone to help you.

DON'T rush or take unsafe shortcuts to finish a job.

DON'T allow children or animals in or around the vehicle while you are working on it.

DO wear eye protection when using power tools such as a drill, sander, bench grinder, etc. and when working under a vehicle.

DO keep loose clothing and long hair well out of the way of moving parts.

DO make sure that any hoist used has a safe working load rating adequate for the job.

DO get someone to check on you periodically when working alone on a vehicle.

DO carry out work in a logical sequence and make sure that everything is correctly assembled and tightened.

DO keep chemicals and fluids tightly capped and out of the reach of children and pets.

DO remember that your vehicle's safety affects that of yourself and others. If in doubt on any point, get professional advice.

Asbestos

Certain friction, insulating, sealing, and other products - such as brake linings, brake bands, clutch linings, torque converters, gaskets, etc. - may contain asbestos. Extreme care must be taken to avoid inhalation of dust from such products, since it is hazardous to health. If in doubt, assume that they do contain asbestos.

Fire

Remember at all times that gasoline is highly flammable. Never smoke or have any kind of open flame around when working on a vehicle. But the risk does not end there. A spark caused by an electrical short circuit, by two metal surfaces contacting each other, or even by static electricity built up in your body under certain conditions, can ignite gasoline vapors, which in a confined space are highly explosive. Do not, under any circumstances, use gasoline for cleaning parts. Use an approved safety solvent.

Always disconnect the battery ground (-) cable at the battery before working on any part of the fuel system or electrical system. Never risk spilling fuel on a hot engine or exhaust component. It is strongly recommended that a fire extinguisher suitable for use on fuel and electrical fires be kept handy in the garage or workshop at all times. Never try to extinguish a fuel or electrical fire with water.

Fumes

Certain fumes are highly toxic and can quickly cause unconsciousness and even death if inhaled to any extent. Gasoline vapor falls into this category, as do the vapors from some cleaning solvents. Any draining or pouring of such volatile fluids should be done in a well ventilated area.

When using cleaning fluids and solvents, read the instructions on the container carefully. Never use materials from unmarked containers.

Never run the engine in an enclosed space, such as a garage. Exhaust fumes contain carbon monoxide, which is extremely poisonous. If you need to run the engine, always do so in the open air, or at least have the rear of the vehicle outside the work area.

If you are fortunate enough to have the use of an inspection pit, never drain or pour gasoline and never run the engine while the vehicle is over the pit. The fumes, being heavier than air, will concentrate in the pit with possibly lethal results.

The battery

Never create a spark or allow a bare light bulb near a battery. They normally give off a certain amount of hydrogen gas, which is highly explosive.

Always disconnect the battery ground (-) cable at the battery before working on the fuel or electrical systems.

If possible, loosen the filler caps or cover when charging the battery from an external source (this does not apply to sealed or maintenance-free batteries). Do not charge at an excessive rate or the battery may burst.

Take care when adding water to a non maintenance-free battery and when carrying a battery. The electrolyte, even when diluted, is very corrosive and should not be allowed to contact clothing or skin.

Always wear eye protection when cleaning the battery to prevent the caustic deposits from entering your eyes.

Household current

When using an electric power tool, inspection light, etc., which operates on household current, always make sure that the tool is correctly connected to its plug and that, where necessary, it is properly grounded. Do not use such items in damp conditions and, again, do not create a spark or apply excessive heat in the vicinity of fuel or fuel vapor.

Secondary ignition system voltage

A severe electric shock can result from touching certain parts of the ignition system (such as the spark plug wires) when the engine is running or being cranked, particularly if components are damp or the insulation is defective. In the case of an electronic ignition system, the secondary system voltage is much higher and could prove fatal.

Troubleshooting

Contents

This Section provides an easy reference guide to the more common problems which may occur during the operation of your vehicle. These problems and possible causes are grouped under various components or systems; i.e. Engine, Cooling system, etc., and also refer to the Chapter and/or Section which deals with the problem.

Remember that successful troubleshooting is not a mysterious "black art" practiced only by professional mechanics; it's simply the result of a bit of knowledge combined with an intelligent, systematic approach to the problem. Always work by a process of elimination, starting with the simplest solution and working through to the most complex - and never overlook the obvious. Anyone can forget to fill the gas tank or leave the lights on overnight, so don't assume that you are above such oversights.

Finally, always get clear in your mind why a problem has occurred and take steps to ensure that it doesn't happen again. If the electrical system fails because of a poor connection, check all other connections in the system to make sure that they don't fail as well; if a particular fuse continues to blow, find out why - don't just go on replacing fuses. Remember, failure of a small component can often be indicative of potential failure or incorrect functioning of a more important component or system.

Engine and engine performance

1 Engine will not rotate when attempting to start

1   Battery terminal connections loose or corroded. Check the cable terminals at the battery; tighten the cable or remove corrosion as necessary .
2   Battery discharged or faulty. If the cable connections are clean and tight on the battery posts, turn the key to the On position and switch on the headlights and/or windshield wipers. If they fail to function, the battery is discharged.
3   Automatic transaxle not completely engaged in Park or clutch not completely depressed.
4   Broken, loose or disconnected wiring in the starting circuit. Inspect all wiring and connectors at the battery, starter solenoid, neutral start switch and ignition switch.
5   Starter motor pinion jammed in flywheel ring gear. If manual transaxle, place transaxle in gear and rock the vehicle to manually turn the engine. Remove starter and inspect pinion and flywheel at earliest convenience.
6   Starter solenoid faulty (Chapter 5).
7   Starter motor faulty (Chapter 5).
8   Ignition switch faulty (Chapter 12).

2 Engine rotates but will not start

1   Fuel tank empty.
2   Battery discharged (engine rotates slowly). Check the operation of electrical components as described in previous Section.
3   Battery terminal connections loose or corroded. See previous Section .
4   Carburetor flooded and/or fuel level in carburetor incorrect. This will usually be accompanied by a strong fuel odor from under the hood. Wait a few minutes, depress the accelerator pedal all the way to the floor and attempt to start the engine.
5   Choke control inoperative - carbureted models (Chapter 1).
6   Fuel not reaching carburetor or fuel-injection system (Chapter 4).
7   Fuel injector or fuel pump faulty (fuel-injected vehicles) (Chapter 4).
8   Excessive moisture on, or damage to, ignition components (Chapter 5).
9   Worn, faulty or incorrectly gapped spark plugs (Chapter 1).
10   Broken, loose or disconnected wiring in the starting circuit (see previous Section).
11   Distributor loose, causing ignition timing to change (HEI ignition systems only). Turn the distributor as necessary to start engine, then set ignition timing as soon as possible (Chapter 1).
12   Broken, loose or disconnected wires at the ignition coil(s) or faulty coil(s) (Chapter 5).
13   Broken or stripped timing chain or gears (Chapter 2)

3 Starter motor operates without rotating engine

1   Starter pinion sticking. Remove the starter (Chapter 5) and inspect.
2   Starter pinion or flywheel teeth worn or broken. Remove the cover at the rear of the engine and inspect.

4 Engine hard to start when cold

1   Battery discharged or low. Check as described in Section 1.
2   Choke control inoperative or out of adjustment - carbureted models (Chapter 4).
3   Carburetor flooded (see Section 2).
4   Insufficient fuel supply reaching the carburetor of fuel-injection system - check fuel pressure (Chapter 4).
5   Leaky fuel injectors, fuel lines or fuel pump outlet check valve, causing fuel pressure to bleed down while the vehicle is sitting (multi-port fuel injection systems) (Chapter 4).
6   Carburetor/fuel injection system malfunctioning (Chapter 4).
7   Distributor rotor carbon tracked (Chapter 1).

5 Engine hard to start when hot

1   Choke sticking in the closed position - carbureted models - (Chapter 1).
2   Carburetor flooded (see Section 2).
3   Air filter clogged (Chapter 1).

4   Malfunction in the carburetor or fuel injection system (Chapter 4).
5   Insufficient fuel supply reaching the carburetor or fuel injection system. Check the fuel pressure (Chapter 4).
6   Leaky fuel injectors, fuel lines or fuel pump outlet check valve, causing fuel pressure to bleed down while the vehicle is sitting (multi-port fuel injection systems) (Chapter 4).

6 Starter motor noisy or excessively rough in engagement

1   Pinion or flywheel gear teeth worn or broken. Remove the cover at the rear of the engine (if so equipped) and inspect.
2   Starter motor mounting bolts loose or missing.

7 Engine starts but stops immediately

1   Loose or faulty electrical connections at distributor, coil or alternator.
2   Insufficient fuel reaching the carburetor/fuel injector(s) - check the fuel pressure (Chapter 4).
3   Vacuum leak at the gasket surfaces of the intake manifold and/or carburetor/throttle body. Make sure that all mounting bolts (nuts) are re-tightened securely and that all vacuum hoses connected to the carburetor/fuel injection unit(s) and manifold are positioned properly and in good condition.

8 Engine "lopes" while idling or idles erratically

1   Vacuum leakage. Check mounting bolts (nuts) at the carburetor/throttle body and intake manifold for tightness. Make sure that all vacuum hoses are connected and in good condition. Use a length of fuel hose held against your ear to listen for vacuum leaks while the engine is running. A hissing sound will be heard. A soapy water solution will also detect leaks. Check the carburetor/throttle body and intake manifold gasket surfaces. Also check the points where the injectors are attached to the intake ports (multi-port fuel injection).
2   Leaking EGR valve or plugged PCV valve (see Chapters 1 and 6).
3   Air filter clogged (Chapter 1).
4   Fuel pump not delivering sufficient fuel to the carburetor/fuel injector(s) - check the fuel pressure (Chapter 4).
5   Carburetor out of adjustment (Chapter 4) or clogged fuel injectors.
6   Leaking head gasket. If this is suspected, take the vehicle to a repair shop or dealer where the engine can be pressure checked.
7   Timing chain and/or gears worn (Chapter 2).
8   Camshaft lobes worn (Chapter 2).

9   Engine misses at idle speed

1   All the causes listed in the previous Section, plus:
2   Spark plugs worn or not gapped properly (Chapter 1).
3   Faulty spark plug wires (Chapter 1).
4   Choke not operating properly - carbureted models (Chapter 1).

10   Engine misses throughout the driving speed range

1   Fuel filter clogged and/or impurities in the fuel system (Chapter 1). Also check the fuel pressure (Chapter 4).
2   Clogged fuel injectors.
3   Faulty or incorrectly gapped spark plugs (Chapter 1).
4   Incorrect ignition timing (Chapter 1).
5   On early models with HEI ignition, check for cracked distributor cap, disconnected distributor wires and damaged distributor components (Chapter 1).
6   Leaking spark plug wires (Chapter 1).
7   Faulty emissions system components (Chapter 6).
8   Low or uneven cylinder compression pressures. Remove spark plugs and test compression with gauge (Chapter 1).
9   Weak or faulty ignition system (Chapter 5).
10   Vacuum leaks at carburetor/throttle body, intake manifold or vacuum hoses (see Section 8).

11   Engine stalls

1   Idle speed incorrect (Chapter 1) or automatic idle speed control circuit malfunctioning.
2   Fuel filter clogged and/or water and impurities in the fuel system (Chapter 1).
3   Choke improperly adjusted or sticking - carbureted models - (Chapter 1).
4   Distributor components damp or damaged - early models with HEI ignition systems (Chapter 5).
5   Faulty emissions system components (Chapter 6).
6   Faulty or incorrectly gapped spark plugs. Also check spark plug wires (Chapter 1).
7   Vacuum leak at the carburetor/throttle body, intake manifold or vacuum hoses. Check as described in Section 8.
8   If the engine stalls after cruising (where the torque converter clutch [TCC] engages), but then re-starts, the problem could be a faulty TCC solenoid. If the solenoid sticks closed, the clutch will remain engaged when the vehicle is coming to a stop, which will stall the engine. Refer to the Haynes Automatic Transmission and Transaxle Overhaul Manual for details on this relatively easy repair.

12   Engine lacks power

1   Incorrect ignition timing - early models with HEI ignition systems - (Chapter 1).
2   Excessive play in distributor shaft (early models with HEI). At the same time, check for worn rotor, faulty distributor cap, wires, etc. (Chapters 1 and 5).
3   Faulty or incorrectly gapped spark plugs (Chapter 1).
4   Carburetor/fuel injection system not adjusted properly or excessively worn (Chapter 4).
5   Faulty ignition coil(s) (Chapter 5).
6   Brakes binding (Chapter 1).
7   Automatic transaxle fluid level incorrect (Chapter 1).
8   Clutch slipping (Chapter 8).
9   Fuel filter clogged and/or impurities in the fuel system (Chapter 1).
10   Emissions control system not functioning properly (Chapter 6).
11   Use of substandard fuel. Fill tank with proper octane fuel.
12   Low or uneven cylinder compression pressures. Test with compression tester, which will detect leaking valves and/or blown head gasket (Chapter 1).

13   Engine backfires

1   Emissions system not functioning properly (Chapter 6).
2   Ignition timing incorrect - early models with HEI ignition systems (Chapter 1).
3   Faulty secondary ignition system (cracked spark plug insulator, faulty plug wires, distributor cap and/or rotor) (Chapters 1 and 5).
4   Carburetor/fuel injection system in need of adjustment or worn excessively (Chapter 4). A clogged fuel injector may also cause this problem.
5   Vacuum leak at carburetor/throttle body, intake manifold or vacuum hoses. Check as described in Section 8.
6   Valve clearances incorrectly set (early 2.8L engines only), and/or valves sticking or burned (Chapter 2).

14   Pinging or knocking engine sounds during acceleration or uphill

1   Incorrect grade of fuel. Fill tank with fuel of the proper octane rating .
2   Ignition timing incorrect (Chapter 1).
3   Carburetor/fuel injection system in need of adjustment (Chapter 4).
4   Improper spark plugs. Check plug type against *Emissions Control Information* label located in engine compartment. Also check plugs and wires for damage (Chapter 1).
5   Worn or damaged distributor components (Chapter 5).

6   Faulty emissions system (Chapter 6).
7   Vacuum leak. Check as described in Section 8.

15   Engine diesels (continues to run) after switching off

1   Vacuum leaks. Check as described in Section 8.
2   Idle speed too high (Chapter 1).
3   Electrical solenoid at side of carburetor not functioning properly (not all models, see Chapter 4).
4   Ignition timing incorrectly adjusted (Chapter 1).
5   Thermo-controlled air cleaner heat valve not operating properly (Chapter 6).
6   Excessive engine operating temperature. Probable causes of this are malfunctioning thermostat, clogged radiator, faulty water pump (Chapter 3).

Engine electrical system

16   Battery will not hold a charge

1   Alternator drivebelt defective or not adjusted properly (Chapter 1).
2   Electrolyte level low or battery discharged (Chapter 1).
3   Battery terminals loose or corroded (Chapter 1).
4   Alternator not charging properly (Chapter 5).
5   Loose, broken or faulty wiring in the charging circuit (Chapter 5).
6   Short in vehicle wiring causing a continual drain on battery
7   Battery defective internally.

17   Alternator light fails to go out

1   Fault in alternator or charging circuit (Chapter 5).
2   Alternator drivebelt defective or not properly adjusted (Chapter 1).

18   Ignition light fails to come on when key is turned on

1   Warning light bulb defective (Chapter 12).
2   Alternator faulty (Chapter 5).
3   Fault in the printed circuit, dash wiring or bulb holder (Chapter 12).

19   "CHECK ENGINE" light comes on

Check for trouble codes stored in the ECM (see Chapter 6).

Fuel system

20 Excessive fuel consumption

1 Dirty or clogged air filter element (Chapter 1).
2 Incorrectly set ignition timing - early models with HEI ignition system (Chapter 1).
3 Choke sticking or improperly adjusted - carbureted models (Chapter 1).
4 Emissions system not functioning properly (Chapter 6).
5 Carburetor/fuel injection internal parts excessively worn or damaged (Chapter 4).
6 Low tire pressure or incorrect tire size (Chapter 1).

21 Fuel leakage and/or fuel odor

1 Leak in a fuel feed or vent line (Chapter 4).
2 Tank overfilled. Fill only to automatic shut-off.
3 Emissions system filter clogged (Chapter 1).
4 Vapor leaks from system lines (Chapter 4).
5 Carburetor/fuel injection internal parts excessively worn or out of adjustment (Chapter 4).

Cooling system

22 Overheating

1 Insufficient coolant in system (Chapter 1).
2 Water pump drivebelt defective or not adjusted properly (Chapter 1).
3 Radiator core blocked or radiator grille dirty and restricted (Chapter 3).
4 Thermostat faulty (Chapter 3).
5 Fan blades broken or cracked.
6 Radiator cap not maintaining proper pressure. Have cap pressure tested by a gas station.
7 Ignition timing incorrect - models with a distributor (Chapter 1).

23 Overcooling

1 Thermostat faulty (Chapter 3).
2 Inaccurate temperature gauge or sending unit (Chapter 12).

24 External coolant leakage

1 Deteriorated or damaged hoses or loose clamps. Replace hoses and/or tighten clamps at hose connections (Chapter 11).
2 Water pump seals defective. If this is the case, water will drip from the ''weep'' hole in the water pump body (Chapter 3).
3 Leakage from radiator core or header tank. This will require the radiator to be professionally repaired (see Chapter 3 for removal procedures) .
4 Engine drain plugs or water jacket core plugs leaking (see Chapter 2).

25 Internal coolant leakage

Note: *Internal coolant leaks can usually be detected by examining the oil. Check the dipstick and inside of the valve cover for water deposits and an oil consistency like that of a milkshake.*
1 Leaking cylinder head gasket. Have the cooling system pressure tested.
2 Cracked cylinder bore or cylinder head. Dismantle engine and inspect (Chapter 2).
3 Leaking intake manifold gasket (Chapter 2).

26 Coolant loss

1 Too much coolant in system (Chapter 1).
2 Coolant boiling away due to overheating (see Section 24).
3 Internal or external leakage (see Sections 24 and 25).
4 Faulty radiator cap. Have the cap pressure tested.

27 Poor coolant circulation

1 Inoperative water pump. A quick test is to pinch the top radiator hose closed with your hand while the engine is idling, then let it loose. You should feel the surge of coolant if the pump is working properly (Chapter 3).
2 Restriction in cooling system. Drain, flush and refill the system (Chapter 1). If necessary, remove the radiator (Chapter 3) and have it reverse flushed.
3 Water pump drivebelt defective or not adjusted properly (Chapter 1).
4 Thermostat sticking (Chapter 3).

Clutch

28 Fails to release (pedal pressed to the floor - shift lever does not move freely in and out of Reverse)

1 Improper linkage free play adjustment.
2 Clutch cable excessively stretched or damaged (Chapter 8).
3 Air in clutch hydraulic release system (Chapter 8).
4 Leaking clutch hydraulic release system (Chapter 8).
2 Clutch fork off ball stud.

3 Clutch plate warped or damaged (Chapter 8).

29 Clutch slips (engine speed increases with no increase in vehicle speed)

1 Linkage out of adjustment (Chapter 8).
2 Clutch plate oil soaked or lining worn. Remove clutch (Chapter 8) and inspect.
3 Clutch plate not seated. It may take 30 or 40 normal starts for a new one to seat.

30 Grabbing (chattering) as clutch is engaged

1 Oil on clutch plate lining. Remove (Chapter 8) and inspect. Correct any leakage source.
2 Worn or loose engine or transaxle mounts. These units move slightly when clutch is released. Inspect mounts and bolts.
3 Worn splines on clutch plate hub. Remove clutch components (Chapter 8) and inspect.
4 Warped pressure plate or flywheel. Remove clutch components and inspect.

31 Squeal or rumble with clutch fully engaged (pedal released)

1 Improper adjustment; no freeplay (Chapter 1).
2 Release bearing binding on transaxle bearing retainer. Remove clutch components (Chapter 8) and check bearing. Remove any burrs or nicks, clean and relubricate before reinstallation.
3 Weak linkage return spring. Replace the spring.

32 Squeal or rumble with clutch fully disengaged (pedal depressed)

1 Worn, defective or broken release bearing (Chapter 8).
2 Worn or broken pressure plate springs (or diaphragm fingers) (Chapter 8).

33 Clutch pedal travels to floor - no pressure or very little resistance

1 Clutch cable damaged or linkage binding.
2 Clutch hydraulic release system leaking or faulty (Chapter 8)
3 No fluid in clutch hydraulic release system reservoir (Chapter 1).
4 Broken release bearing or fork (Chapter 8).
5 Sticking clutch release diaphragm fingers (Chapter 8).

Manual transaxle

34 Noisy in Neutral with engine running

1   Input shaft bearing worn.
2   Damaged main drive gear bearing.
3   Worn countershaft bearings.
4   Worn or damaged countershaft endplay shims.

35 Noisy in all gears

1   Any of the above causes, and/or:
2   Insufficient lubricant (see checking procedures in Chapter 1).

36 Noisy in one particular gear

1   Worn, damaged or chipped gear teeth for that particular gear.
2   Worn or damaged synchronizer for that particular gear.

37 Slips out of high gear

1   Transaxle loose on clutch housing (Chapter 7).
2   Shift rods interfering with engine mounts or clutch lever (Chapter 7).
3   Shift rods not working freely (Chapter 7).
4   Damaged mainshaft pilot bearing.
5   Dirt between transaxle case and engine or misalignment of transaxle (Chapter 7).
6   Worn or improperly adjusted linkage (Chapter 7).

38 Difficulty in engaging gears

1   Clutch not releasing completely (see clutch adjustment in Chapter 8).
2   Loose, damaged or out of adjustment shift linkage. Make a thorough inspection, replacing parts as necessary (Chapter 7).

39 Oil leakage

1   Excessive amount of lubricant in transaxle (see Chapter 1 for correct checking procedures). Drain lubricant as required.
2   Side cover loose or gasket damaged.
3   Rear oil seal or speedometer oil seal in need of replacement (Chapter 7).

Automatic transaxle

Note: *Due to the complexity of the automatic transaxle, it is difficult for the home mechanic to properly diagnose and service this component. For problems other than the following, the vehicle should be taken to a dealer service department or reputable mechanic.*

40 General shift mechanism problems

1   Chapter 7 deals with checking and adjusting the shift linkage on automatic transaxles. Common problems which may be attributed to poorly adjusted linkage are:

Engine starting in gears other than Park or Neutral.
Indicator on shifter pointing to a gear other than the one actually being used.
Vehicle moves when in Park.

2   Refer to Chapter 7 to adjust the linkage.

41 Transaxle will not downshift with accelerator pedal pressed to the floor

Chapter 7 deals with adjusting the throttle valve (TV) cable to enable the transaxle to downshift properly.

42 Transaxle slips, shifts rough, is noisy or has no drive in forward or reverse gears

1   There are many probable causes for the above problems, but the home mechanic should be concerned with only one possibility - fluid level.
2   Before taking the vehicle to a repair shop, check the level and condition of the fluid, as described in Chapter 1. Correct fluid level as necessary or change the fluid and filter if needed. If the problem persists, have a professional diagnose the probable cause.

43 Fluid leakage

1   Automatic transaxle fluid is a deep red color. Fluid leaks should not be confused with engine oil, which can easily be blown by air flow to the transaxle.
2   To pinpoint a leak, first remove all built-up dirt and grime from around the transaxle Degreasing agents and/or steam cleaning will achieve this. With the underside clean, drive the vehicle at low speeds so air flow will not blow the leak far from its source. Raise the vehicle and determine where the leak is coming from. Common areas of leakage are:

a)   *Pan:* Tighten mounting bolts and/or replace pan gasket as necessary (see Chapters 1 and 7).
b)   *Filler pipe:* Replace the rubber seal where pipe enters transaxle case.
c)   *Transaxle oil lines:* Tighten connectors where lines enter transaxle case and/or replace lines.
d)   *Vent pipe:* Transaxle overfilled and/or water in fluid (see checking procedures, Chapter 1).

e)   *Speedometer connector:* Replace the O-ring where speedometer cable enters transaxle case (Chapter 7).

Driveaxles

44 Clicking noise in turns

Worn or damaged outer CV joint. Check for cut or damaged CV joint boots. Repair as necessary (Chapter 8).

45 Knock or clunk when accelerating from coasting

Worn or damaged inner CV joint. Check for cut or damaged CV joint boots. Repair as necessary (Chapter 8)

46 Shudder or vibration during acceleration

1   Worn or damaged inner or outer CV joints. Repair or replace as necessary (Chapter 8).
2   Sticking inner CV joint assembly. Correct or replace as necessary (Chapter 8).

Rear axle

47 Noise

1   Road noise. No corrective procedures available.
2   Tire noise. Inspect tires and check tire pressures (Chapter 1).
3   Rear wheel bearings loose, worn or damaged (Chapter 10).

Brakes

Note: *Before assuming that a brake problem exists, make sure that the tires are in good condition and inflated properly (see Chapter 1), that the front end alignment is correct and that the vehicle is not loaded with weight in an unequal manner.*

48 Vehicle pulls to one side during braking

1   Defective, damaged or oil contaminated disc brake pads on one side. Inspect as described in Chapter 9.
2   Excessive wear of brake pad material or disc on one side. Inspect and correct as necessary.
3   Loose or disconnected front suspension components. Inspect and tighten all bolts to the specified torque (Chapter 10).

4   Defective caliper assembly. Remove caliper and inspect for stuck piston or other damage (Chapter 9).

49   Noise (high-pitched squeal when the brakes are applied)

Disc brake pads worn out. The noise comes from the wear sensor rubbing against the disc (does not apply to all vehicles). Replace pads with new ones immediately (Chapter 9).

50   Excessive brake pedal travel

1   Partial brake system failure. Inspect entire system (Chapter 9) and correct as required.
2   Insufficient fluid in master cylinder. Check (Chapter 1), add fluid and bleed system if necessary (Chapter 9).
3   Rear brakes not adjusting properly. Make a series of starts and stops while the vehicle is in Reverse. If this does not correct the situation, remove drums and inspect self adjusters (Chapter 9).

51   Brake pedal feels spongy when depressed

1   Air in hydraulic lines. Bleed the brake system (Chapter 9).
2   Faulty flexible hoses. Inspect all system hoses and lines. Replace parts as necessary.
3   Master cylinder mounting bolts/nuts loose.
4   Master cylinder defective (Chapter 9).

52   Excessive effort required to stop vehicle

1   Power brake booster not operating properly (Chapter 9).
2   Excessively worn linings or pads. Inspect and replace if necessary (Chapter 9).
3   One or more caliper pistons or wheel cylinders seized or sticking. Inspect and rebuild as required (Chapter 9).
4   Brake linings or pads contaminated with oil or grease. Inspect and replace as required (Chapter 9).
5   New pads or shoes installed and not yet seated. It will take a while for the new material to seat against the drum (or rotor).

53   Pedal travels to the floor with little resistance

Little or no fluid in the master cylinder

reservoir caused by leaking wheel cylinder(s), leaking caliper piston(s), loose, damaged or disconnected brake lines. Inspect entire system and correct as necessary.

54   Brake pedal pulsates during brake application

1   Wheel bearings not adjusted properly or in need of replacement (Chapter 1).
2   Caliper not sliding properly due to improper installation or obstructions. Remove and inspect (Chapter 9).
3   Disc defective. Remove the disc (Chapter 9) and check for excessive lateral runout and parallelism. Have the disc resurfaced or replace it with a new one.

Suspension and steering systems

55   Vehicle pulls to one side

1   Tire pressures uneven (Chapter 1).
2   Defective tire (Chapter 1).
3   Excessive wear in suspension or steering components (Chapter 10).
4   Front end in need of alignment.
5   Front brakes dragging. Inspect brakes as described in Chapter 9.

56   Shimmy, shake or vibration

1   Tire or wheel out-of-balance or out-of-round. Have professionally balanced.
2   Loose, worn or out-of-adjustment wheel bearings (Chapter 10).
3   Shock absorbers and/or suspension components worn or damaged (Chapter 10).

57   Excessive pitching and/or rolling around corners or during braking

Defective struts/shock absorbers. Replace as a set (Chapter 10).
2   Broken or weak springs and/or suspension components. Inspect as described in Chapter 10.

58   Excessively stiff steering

1   Lack of fluid in power steering fluid reservoir (Chapter 1).
2   Incorrect tire pressures (Chapter 1).
3   Lack of lubrication at steering joints (Chapter 1).
4   Front end out of alignment.
5   See also section titled *Lack of power assistance.*

59   Excessive play in steering

1   Loose front wheel bearings (Chapter 1).
2   Excessive wear in suspension or steering components (Chapter 10).
3   Steering gearbox out of adjustment (Chapter 10).

60   Lack of power assistance

1   Steering pump drivebelt faulty or not adjusted properly (Chapter 1).
2   Fluid level low (Chapter 1).
3   Hoses or lines restricted. Inspect and replace parts as necessary.
4   Air in power steering system. Bleed system (Chapter 10).

61   Excessive tire wear (not specific to one area)

1   Incorrect tire pressures (Chapter 1).
2   Tires out of balance. Have professionally balanced.
3   Wheels damaged. Inspect and replace as necessary.
4   Suspension or steering components excessively worn (Chapter 10).

62   Excessive tire wear on outside edge

1   Inflation pressures incorrect (Chapter 1).
2   Excessive speed in turns.
3   Front end alignment incorrect (excessive toe in). Have professionally aligned.
4   Suspension arm bent or twisted (Chapter 10).

63   Excessive tire wear on inside edge

1   Inflation pressures incorrect (Chapter 1).
2   Front end alignment incorrect (toe-out). Have professionally aligned.
3   Loose or damaged steering components (Chapter 10).

64   Tire tread worn in one place

1   Tires out of balance.
2   Damaged or buckled wheel. Inspect and replace if necessary.
3   Defective tire (Chapter 10).

Chapter 1
Tune-up and routine maintenance

Contents

Specifications

Recommended lubricants and fluids

Note: *Listed here are manufacturer recommendations at the time this manual was printed. Manufacturers occasionally upgrade their fluid lubricant specifications so check with your local auto parts store for the most current fluid and lubricant recommendations.*

Engine oil type .... API grade SG or SG/CD multigrade and fuel efficient oil
Engine oil viscosity .... See accompanying chart

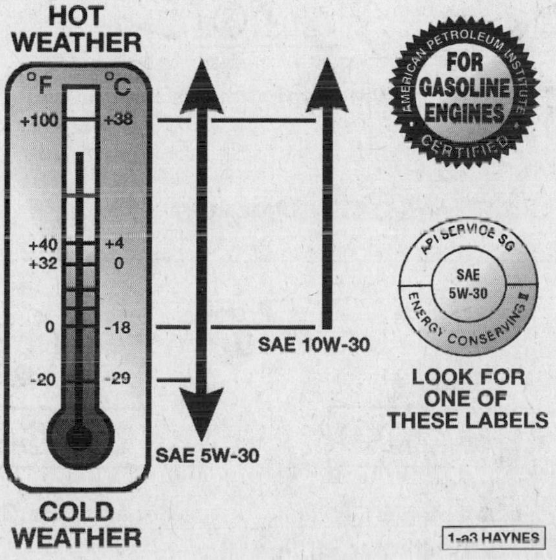

HOT WEATHER

°F   °C
+100 +38
+40   +4
+32   0
0   -18
-20   -29

SAE 10W-30

SAE 5W-30

COLD WEATHER

FOR GASOLINE ENGINES — AMERICAN PETROLEUM INSTITUTE CERTIFIED

API SERVICE SG
SAE 5W-30
ENERGY CONSERVING II

LOOK FOR ONE OF THESE LABELS

Engine oil viscosity chart - for best fuel economy and cold starting, select the lowest SAE viscosity grade for the expected temperature range

1-a3 HAYNES

Recommended lubricants and fluids (continued)

Coolant type	50/50 mixture of ethylene glycol-based antifreeze and water
Automatic transaxle fluid type	
1993 and earlier	Dexron type automatic transmission fluid
1994 and later	Dexron IIE or Dexron III
Manual transaxle lubricant type	
1982	80W-90 gear oil
1983	Dexron type automatic transmission fluid
1984, 1985	5W-30 engine oil
1986	Dexron type automatic transmission fluid
1987 on	5W-30 engine oil
Brake fluid type	DOT 3 brake fluid
Power steering fluid type	
1985 and earlier models	GM power steering fluid or equivalent
1986 and later models	GM power steering fluid or equivalent
Hydraulic clutch fluid type	DOT 3 brake fluid
Rear wheel bearing lubricant	NLGI No. 2 lithium base wheel bearing grease

Capacities*

Engine oil (**Note:** *When changing the oil filter, one additional quart of oil may be needed*)	
2.5L four-cylinder engine	3.0 qts
All others	4.0 qts
Automatic transaxle fluid (initial refill - after fluid and filter change	4.0 qts
Manual transaxle lubricant	3.0 qts
Cooling system	7.5 to 12.9 quarts (depending on engine and cooling system option)

* All capacities approximate. Add as necessary to bring to the appropriate level.

General

Radiator cap opening pressure	15 psi
Thermostat	
Starts to open	188 to 193-degrees F
Fully open	212-degrees F
Engine idle speed*	
Automatic transaxle	700 rpm
Manual transaxle	750 rpm
Drivebelt deflection	1/4 to 1/2 inch
Serpentine drive belt tension	Automatically adjusted

* Refer to the Vehicle Emission Control Information label in the engine compartment and follow the information on the label if it differs from that shown here.

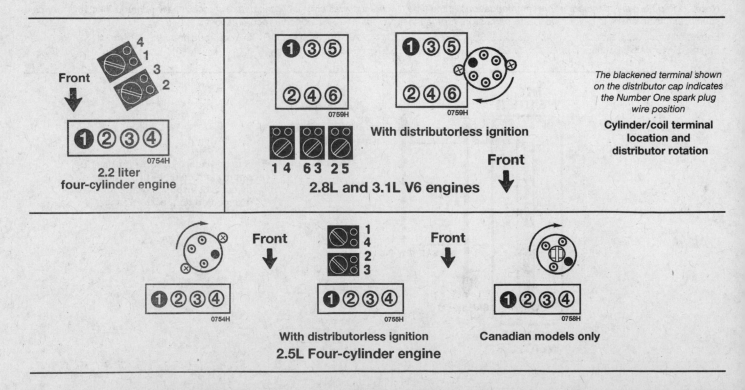

Front

2.2 liter four-cylinder engine

0754H

0759H

0759H

With distributorless ignition

1 4 6 3 2 5

2.8L and 3.1L V6 engines

Front

The blackened terminal shown on the distributor cap indicates the Number One spark plug wire position

Cylinder/coil terminal location and distributor rotation

Front

Front

0754H

0755H

0758H

With distributorless ignition   **Canadian models only**

2.5L Four-cylinder engine

Ignition system

Distributor direction of rotation...	Clockwise
Firing order	
2.2L/2.5L four-cylinder engines	1-3-4-2
2.8L and 3.1L V6 engines...	1-2-3-4-5-6
3.0L, 3.3L and 3.8L V6 engines......................................	1-6-5-4-3-2

Spark plug type and gap*	Type	Gap
Four-cylinder engines		
1982 through 1985, 1988 and 1989...................	AC R44TSX or equivalent	0.060 inch
1986, 1987	AC R43CTS6 or equivalent	0.060 Inch
1990, 1991	AC R43TS6 or equivalent	0.060 inch
1992 and 1993		
2.2L	AC R44LTSM or equivalent	0.045 inch
2.5L	AC R43TS6 or equivalent	0.060 inch
1994 and later	AC 41-908 or equivalent	0.060 inch
V6 engines		
1982, 1983		
2.8L...	AC R43CTS or equivalent	0.045 inch
3.0L...	AC R44TS8 or equivalent	0.080 inch
1984		
2.8L...	AC R43CTS or equivalent	0.045 inch
3.0L...	AC R44TSX or equivalent	0.060 inch
3.8L...	AC R45TS or equivalent	0.045 inch

Type I

**1985-1988 3.0L engines
Some 1986-1988 3.8L with
VIN code 3
1992 3.3L with VIN code N**

Type II

**1986-1988 3.8L with
VIN code 3**

**1985-1992 3.3L with
VIN code N
1988-1989 3.0L**

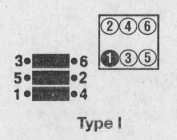

Type I

**1988-1991 3.8L with
VIN code C
Some 1990-1992 3.8L with
VIN code L**

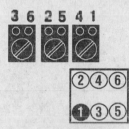

Type II

**1990-1993 3.8L with
VIN code L and 1
1993 3.3L with
VIN code N**

1984-1985 3.8L

**1984-1985 3.0L with
VIN code E**

Front

38005-1-00 HAYNES

The blackened terminal shown on the distributor cap indicates the Number One spark plug wire position

Cylinder/coil terminal location and distributor rotation

Ignition system (continued)

Spark plug type and gap*

	Type	Gap
V6 engines		
1985		
2.8L		
Carbureted	AC R43CTS or equivalent	0.045 inch
Fuel-injected	AC R42CTS or equivalent	0.045 inch
3.0L	AC R44TSX or equivalent	0.060 inch
3.8L	AC R45TS8 or equivalent	0.080 inch
1986		
2.8L		
Carbureted	AC R43CTS or equivalent	0.045 inch
Fuel-injected	AC R42CTS or equivalent	0.045 inch
3.8L	AC R44LTS or equivalent	0.045 inch
1987, 1988		
2.8L	AC R43LTSE or equivalent	0.045 inch
3.8L	AC R44LTS or equivalent	0.045 inch
1989 through 1991		
2.8L, 3.1L	AC R43LTSE or equivalent	0.045 inch
3.3L	AC R45LTS6 or equivalent	0.060 inch
1992 and 1993	AC 41-600 or equivalent	0.060 inch
1994 and 1995	AC R44LTSM6 or equivalent	0.060 inch
1996	AC 41-940 or equivalent	0.060 inch

Ignition timing*
Four-cylinder engine .... 8-degrees BTDC
V6 engines
 2.8L, 3.1L .... 10-degrees BTDC
 3.0L, 3.3L, 3.8L .... 15-degrees BTDC

Refer to the Vehicle Emission Control Information label in the engine compartment and follow the information on the label if it differs from that shown here.

Brakes

Disc brake pad minimum thickness. .... 1/8 inch
Drum brake shoe minimum thickness. .... 1/16 inch

Torque specifications

Ft-lbs (unless otherwise indicated)

Spark plugs
 1986 and earlier.. 84 to 180 in-lbs
 1987 to 1991 20
 1992 on .... 132 in-lbs
Automatic transaxle fluid pan bolts .... 120 in-lbs
Carburetor mounting nuts/bolts .... 120 in-lbs
TBI mounting nuts/bolts .... 156 in-lbs
Wheel lug nuts 100
Oxygen sensor.. 30

Typical V6 engine compartment component location

1	Coolant reservoir	6	Battery
2	Drive belt	7	Windshield washer reservoir
3	Engine oil fill cap	8	Brake master cylinder reservoir
4	Throttle body	9	Power steering fluid reservoir
5	Radiator hose		

10	Air filter housing
11	Automatic transaxle dipstick
12	Spark plug wires
13	Engine oil dipstick

1 Introduction and routine maintenance schedule

Introduction

This Chapter was designed to help the home mechanic maintain his or her vehicle for peak performance, economy, safety and long life.

On the following pages you will find a maintenance schedule, along with Sections which deal specifically with each item on the schedule. Included are visual checks, adjustments and component replacement procedures.

Servicing your vehicle using the time/mileage maintenance schedule and the sequenced Sections will give you a planned program of maintenance. Keep in mind that it is a full plan, and maintaining only a few items at the specified intervals will not give you the same results.

As you service your vehicle you will find that many of the procedures can, and should, be grouped together, due to the nature of the job at hand. Examples of this are as follows:

If the vehicle is raised for chassis lubrication, for example, it is an ideal time to check the exhaust system, suspension, steering and fuel system.

If the tires and wheels are removed, as during a routine tire rotation, check the brakes and wheel bearings at the same time.

If you must borrow or rent a torque wrench it is a good idea to service the spark plugs and check the carburetor or TBI mounting nut/bolt torque all in the same day to save time and money.

The first step of the maintenance plan is to prepare yourself before the actual work begins. Read through the appropriate Sections for all work that is to be performed. Gather together all the necessary parts and tools. If it appears that you could have a problem during a particular job, don't hesitate to seek advice from your local parts store or dealer service department.

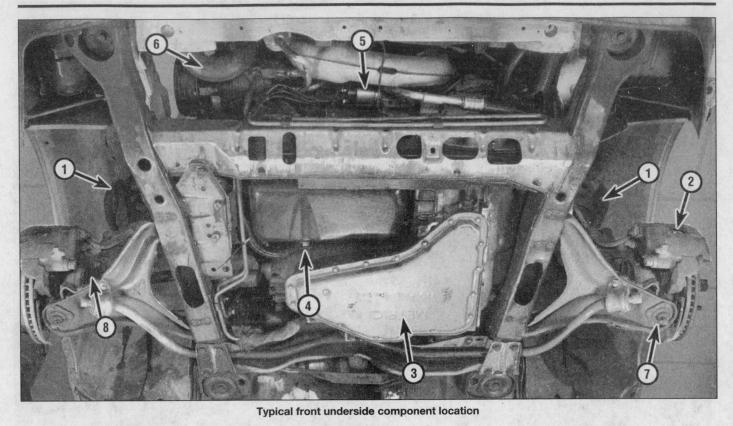

Typical front underside component location

1	Strut assembly	4	Engine oil drain plug	7	Lubrication fitting
2	Front brake caliper	5	Starter motor	8	Driveaxle boot
3	Automatic transaxle fluid pan	6	Radiator hose		

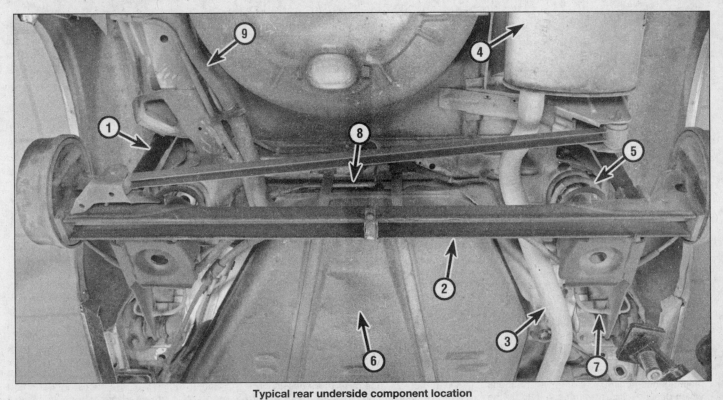

Typical rear underside component location

1	Shock absorber	4	Muffler	7	Brake hose
2	Axle assembly	5	Coil spring	8	Fuel line
3	Exhaust pipe	6	Fuel tank	9	Fuel filler hose

Routine maintenance intervals

The following recommendations are given with the assumption that the vehicle owner will be doing the maintenance or service work, as opposed to having it done by a dealer service department. The following are factory maintenance recommendations. The owner interested in keeping his or her vehicle in peak conditions at all times may wish to perform these operations more often. This can also enhance the resale value of the vehicle, and we encourage such owner initiative.

When the vehicle is new it should be serviced by a factory authorized dealer service department to protect the factory warranty. In many cases the initial maintenance check is done at no cost to the owner. **Note:** *The following maintenance intervals are based on recommendations by the manufacturer. In the interest of vehicle longevity, we recommend shorter intervals on certain operations, such as fluid and filter replacement.*

Every 250 miles or weekly, whichever comes first

Check the tires and tire pressures (Section 3)
Check the engine oil level (Section 4)
Check the engine coolant level (Section 4)
Check the windshield washer fluid level (Section 4)
Check the automatic transaxle fluid level (Section 4)

Every 3000 miles or 3 months, whichever comes first

Change the engine oil and oil filter (Section 16)

Every 5000 miles or 5 months, whichever comes first

Adjust the clutch pedal (Section 24)

Every 6000 miles or 6 months, whichever comes first

Check the power steering fluid level (Section 4)
Check the brake master cylinder fluid level (Section 4)
Check the manual transaxle oil level (Section 4)
Check and service the battery (Section 5)
Check and adjust (if necessary) the engine drivebelts (Section 6)
Check the cooling system (Section 7)
Check and replace (if necessary) the underhood hoses (Section 8)
Check and replace (if necessary) the windshield wiper blades (Section 9)
Check and lubricate the chassis components (Section 10)
Check the exhaust system (Section 11)
Check the steering and suspension components (Section 12)
Check the disc brake pads (Section 13)
Check the brake system (Section 13)
Check the operation of the choke (Section 14)
Check and adjust (if necessary) the engine idle speed (Section 15)
Check the tightness of the carburetor or TBI mounting nuts/bolts (Section 20)

Every 12000 miles or 12 months, whichever comes first

Check the drum brake linings (Section 13)
Check the parking brake (Section 13)
Check the fuel system components (Section 17)
Replace the fuel filter (Section 18)
Check the throttle linkage (Section 19)
Check the carburetor/Throttle Body Injection (TBI) mounting nut/bolt torque (Section 20)

Check the thermostatically-controlled air cleaner (THERMAC) for proper operation (Section 21)
Check the differential seals and driveaxle boots (Section 22)
Rotate the tires (Section 23)

Every 15000 miles or 15 months, whichever comes first

Check the wheel bearings (Section 27)
Change the automatic transaxle fluid and filter (if driven primarily in heavy city traffic, in hot climate regions, in hilly or mountainous areas or if used for frequent trailer pulling (Section 28)

Every 24000 miles or 24 months, whichever comes first

Check the EGR system (Section 32)
Check the EECS emissions system and replace the canister filter (Section 33)
Check and adjust (if necessary) the ignition timing (Section 34)
Check the (EFE) early fuel evaporation system (Section 37)
Check the engine compression (Chapter 2E)

Every 30000 miles or 30 months, whichever comes first

Inspect and clean (if necessary) the EGR valve (3.0, 3.3 and 3.8 liter engines) (Chapter 6)
Drain, flush and refill the cooling system (Section 26)
Change the automatic transaxle fluid and filter (except Dexron III) (Section 28)
Replace the air filter and PCV valve filter (Section 29)
Check the oxygen sensor (Chapter 6) and replace if necessary (Section 30)
Inspect and replace (if necessary) the PCV valve (Section 31)
Check the operation of the EGR valve (Section 32)
Replace the spark plugs (except platinum-tipped spark plugs) (Section 35)
Inspect and replace (if necessary) the spark plug wires, distributor cap and rotor (Section 36)

Every 48000 miles or 48 months, whichever comes first

Change the manual transaxle lubricant (Section 25)

Every 100,000 miles

Replace the spark plugs when using platinum-tipped spark plugs (Section 35)
Replace the transaxle fluid and filter when using Dexron III (Section 28)

2   Tune-up general information

The term tune-up is loosely used for any general operation that puts the engine back in its proper running condition. A tune-up is not a specific operation, but rather a combination of individual operations, such as replacing the spark plugs, adjusting the idle speed, setting the ignition timing, etc.

If, from the time the vehicle is new, the routine maintenance schedule (Section 1) is followed closely and frequent checks are made of fluid levels and high wear items, as suggested throughout this manual, the engine will be kept in relatively good running condition and the need for additional tune-ups will be minimized.

More likely than not, however, there will be times when the engine is running poorly due to lack of regular maintenance. This is even more likely if a used vehicle, which has not received regular and frequent maintenance checks, is purchased. In such cases an engine tune-up will be needed outside of the regular routine maintenance intervals.

The following series of operations are those most often needed to bring a poor running engine back into a proper state of tune.

Minor tune-up

Clean, inspect and test the battery
  (Section 5)
Check all engine-related fluids (Section 4)

Check the engine compression (See
  Chapter 2E)
Check and adjust the drivebelts
  (Section 6)
Replace the spark plugs (Section 35)
Inspect the distributor cap and rotor
  (Section 36)
Inspect the spark plug wires and coil wire
  (Section 36)
Check and adjust the idle speed
  (Section 15)
Check and adjust the timing (Section 34)
Replace the fuel filter (Section 18)
Check the PCV valve (Section 31)
Check the cooling system (Section 7)

Major tune-up

All items listed under Minor tune-up plus . . .

Check the EGR system (Chapter 6)
Check the ignition system (Chapter 5)
Check the charging system (Chapter 5)
Check the fuel system (Section 17)

3   Tire and tire pressure checks (every 250 miles or weekly)

Refer to illustrations 3.2, 3.3, 3.4a, 3.4b and 3.8

1   Periodic inspection of the tires may save you the inconvenience of being stranded with a flat tire. It can also provide you with vital information regarding possible problems in the steering and suspension systems before

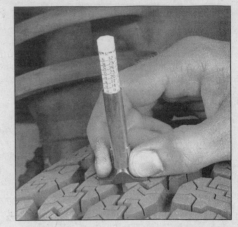

3.2 Use a tire tread depth indicator to monitor tire wear - they are available at auto parts stores and service stations and cost very little

major damage occurs.

2   Tires are equipped with 1/2-inch wide bands that will appear when tread depth reaches 1/16-inch, at which time the tires can be considered worn out. Tread wear can be monitored with a simple, inexpensive device known as a tread depth indicator **(see illustration)**.

3   Note any abnormal tire wear **(see illustration)**. Tread pattern irregularities such as cupping, flat spots and more wear on one side that the other are indications of front end

UNDERINFLATION

CUPPING

Cupping may be caused by:
● Underinflation and/or mechanical
  irregularities such as out-of-balance
  condition of wheel and/or tire,
  and bent or damaged wheel.
● Loose or worn steering tie-rod
  or steering idler arm.
● Loose, damaged or worn front
  suspension parts.

OVERINFLATION

**INCORRECT TOE-IN
OR EXTREME CAMBER**

**FEATHERING DUE
TO MISALIGNMENT**

3.3 This chart will help you determine the condition of the tires, the probable cause(s) of abnormal wear and the corrective action necessary

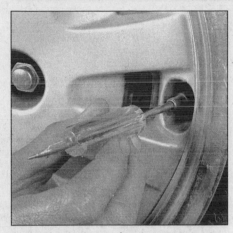

3.4a If a tire loses air on a steady basis, check the valve stem core first to make sure it's snug (special inexpensive wrenches are commonly available at auto parts stores

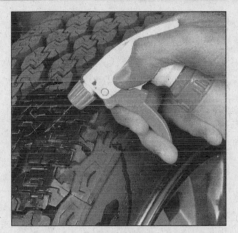

3.4b If the valve stem core is tight, raise the corner of the vehicle with the low tire and spray a soapy water solution onto the tread as the tire is turned slowly - leaks will cause small bubbles to appear

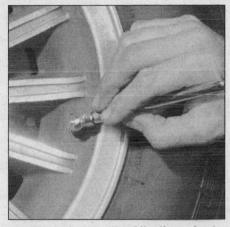

3.8 To extend the life of the tires, check the air pressure at least once a week with an accurate gauge (don't forget the spare)

alignment and/or balance problems. If any of these conditions are noted, take the vehicle to a tire shop or service station to correct the problem.

4   Look closely for cuts, punctures and embedded nails or tacks. Sometimes a tire will hold air pressure for a short time or leak down very slowly after a nail has embedded itself in the tread. If a slow leak persists, check the valve stem core to make sure it is tight (see illustration). Examine the tread for an object that may have embedded itself in the tire or for a "plug" that may have begun to leak (radial tire punctures are repaired with a plug that is installed in the puncture). If a puncture is suspected, it can be easily verified by spraying a solution of soapy water onto the puncture (see illustration). The soapy solution will bubble if there is a leak. Unless the puncture is unusually large, a tire shop or service station can usually repair the tire.

5   Carefully inspect the inner sidewall of each tire for evidence of brake fluid leakage. If you see any, inspect the brakes immediately.

6   Correct air pressure adds miles to the lifespan of the tires, improves mileage and enhances overall ride quality. Tire pressure cannot be accurately estimated by looking at a tire, especially if it's a radial. A tire pressure gauge is essential. Keep an accurate gauge in the glove compartment. The pressure gauges attached to the nozzles of air hoses at gas stations are often inaccurate.

7   Always check tire pressure when the tires are cold. Cold, in this case, means the vehicle has not been driven over a mile in the three hours preceding a tire pressure check. A pressure rise of four to eight pounds is not uncommon once the tires are warm.

8   Unscrew the valve cap protruding from the wheel or hubcap and push the gauge firmly onto the valve stem (see illustration). Note the reading on the gauge and compare the figure to the recommended tire pressure

shown in your owner's manual or on the tire placard on the passenger side door or door pillar. Be sure to reinstall the valve cap to keep dirt and moisture out of the valve stem mechanism. Check all four tires and, if necessary, add enough air to bring them to the recommended pressure.

9   Don't forget to keep the spare tire inflated to the specified pressure (refer to your owner's manual or the placard attached to the door pillar). Note that the pressure recommended for temporary (mini) spare tires is higher than for the tires on the vehicle.

4   Fluid level checks (every 250 miles or weekly)

1   There are a number of components on a vehicle which rely on the use of fluids to perform their job. During normal operation of the vehicle these fluids are used up and must be replenished before damage occurs. See *Recommended lubricants and fluids* at the beginning of this Chapter for the specific fluid to be used when addition is required. When checking fluid levels it is important to have the vehicle on a level surface.

Engine oil

Refer to illustration 4.4

2   The engine oil level is checked with a

dipstick, which is located at the side of the engine block. The dipstick travels through a tube and into the oil pan.

3   Preferably the oil level should be checked before the vehicle has been driven, or about 15 minutes after the engine has been shut off. If the oil is checked immediately after driving the vehicle, some of the oil will remain in the upper engine components, producing an inaccurate reading on the dipstick.

4   Pull the dipstick from the tube and wipe the oil from the end with a clean rag. Insert the clean dipstick all the way back into the oil pan and pull it out again. Observe the oil at the end of the dipstick. At its highest point, the level should be between the Add and Full marks (see illustration).

5   It takes one quart of oil to raise the level from the Add mark to the Full mark on the dipstick. Do not allow the level to drop below the add mark as engine damage due to oil starvation may occur. On the other hand, do not overfill the engine by adding oil above the full mark, since this may result in oil-fouled spark plugs, oil leaks or oil seal failures.

6   Oil is added to the engine after removing a twist-off cap located on the valve cover or through a raised tube near the front of the engine. The cap should be marked *Engine Oil* or *Oil*. An oil can spout or funnel will help reduce spills.

7   Checking the oil level can also be an important preventative maintenance step. If

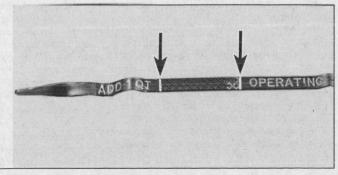

4.4 The oil level should be in the cross-hatched area - if it's below the ADD line, add enough oil to bring the level near the upper line (it takes one quart of oil to raise the level from the lower to upper mark)

ADD 1 QT   OPERATING

4.9 The engine coolant level should appear near the Full Hot mark with the engine at normal operating temperature

4.10   The radiator cap is removed by pushing down and rotating (arrows), but never remove the radiator cap while the engine is hot

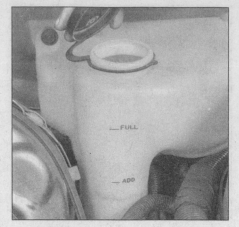

4.15 The windshield washer fluid level should be kept between the Full and Add marks

you find the oil level dropping abnormally, it is an indication of oil leakage or internal engine wear which should be corrected. The condition of the oil can also be checked along with the level. If there are water droplets in the oil, or if the oil looks like chocolate milk, component failure is indicated and the engine should be checked immediately. With the dipstick removed from the engine, take your thumb and index finger and wipe the oil up the dipstick, looking for small dirt or metal particles which will cling to the dipstick. This is an indication that the oil should be drained and fresh oil added (Sec-tion 16).

Engine coolant

Refer to illustrations 4.9 and 4.10
Warning: *Do not allow antifreeze to come in contact with your skin or painted surfaces of the vehicle. Rinse off spills immediately with plenty of water. Antifreeze is highly toxic if ingested. Never leave antifreeze lying around in an open container or in puddles on the floor; children and pets are attracted by it's sweet smell and may drink it. Check with local authorities about disposing of used antifreeze. Many communities have collection centers which will see that antifreeze is disposed of safely.*
8   All vehicles covered by this manual are equipped with a pressurized coolant recovery system. A white coolant reservoir attached to the inner fender panel is connected by a hose to the radiator cap. As the engine heats up during operation the expanding coolant is forced from the radiator, through the connecting tube and into the reservoir. As the engine cools the coolant is automatically drawn back into the radiator to keep the level correct.
9   The coolant level should be checked when the engine is hot. Observe the level of fluid in the reservoir, which should be at or near the Full Hot mark **(see illustration)**. If the system is completely cool you can also check the level in the radiator by removing the cap.

10   **Warning:** *Under no circumstances should the radiator cap or the coolant recovery reservoir cap be removed when the system is hot. Escaping steam and scalding liquid could cause serious personal injury.* In the case of the radiator, wait until the system has cooled completely, then wrap a thick cloth around the cap and turn it to the first stop **(see illustration)**. If any steam escapes, wait until the system has cooled further, then remove the cap. The coolant recovery cap may be removed after it is apparent that no further boiling is occurring in the recovery tank.
11   If only a small amount of coolant is required to bring the system up to the proper level, regular water can be used. However, to maintain the proper antifreeze/water mixture in the system, both should be mixed together to replenish a low level. High-quality antifreeze offering protection to -20-degrees F should be mixed with water in the proportion specified on the container. Do not allow antifreeze to come in contact with your skin or painted surfaces of the vehicle. Flush contacted areas immediately with plenty of water.
12   Coolant should be added to the reservoir until it reaches the Full Cold mark.
13   As the coolant level is checked, note the condition of the coolant. It should be relatively clear. If it is brown or a rust color, the system should be drained, flushed and refilled (see Section 26).
14   If the cooling system requires repeated additions to maintain the proper level, have the radiator cap checked for proper sealing. Also check for leaks in the system (cracked hoses, loose hose connections, leaking gaskets, etc.).

Windshield washer fluid

Refer to illustration 4.15
15   Fluid for the windshield washer system is located in a plastic reservoir located next to the coolant reservoir **(see illustration)**. The reservoir should be kept no more than two-

thirds full to allow for expansion should the fluid freeze. The use of a windshield washer fluid additive, available at auto parts stores, will help lower the freezing point of the fluid and will result in better cleaning of the windshield surface. Do not use antifreeze because it will cause damage to the vehicle's paint.
16   To prevent icing in cold weather, warm the windshield with the defroster before using the washer.

Battery electrolyte

Refer to illustration 4.17
17   All vehicles with which this manual is concerned are equipped with a maintenance-free battery which is permanently sealed (except for vent holes) and has no filler caps **(see illustration)**. Water does not have to be added to these batteries. If, however, the battery has been replaced with a traditional-style battery, remove the filler caps and check the level. It must be at or near the split ring. If the level is low, add distilled water. Install and securely retighten the caps. **Caution:** *Overfilling the cells may cause electrolyte to spill over during periods of heavy charging, causing corrosion or damage.*

4.17 All models covered by this manual were originally equipped with a maintenance-free battery

4.19 The brake fluid level can be checked without removing the cap

4.21 Be careful not to spill brake fluid on painted surfaces

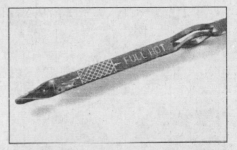

4.40 The automatic transaxle level should be kept within the marked areas, depending on whether the fluid is hot or cool when checked

4.43 Using a funnel to add fluid to the automatic transaxle

Brake fluid

Refer to illustrations 4.19 and 4.21

18 The brake master cylinder is mounted on the firewall (non-power brake models) or on the front of the power booster unit (power brake models) in the engine compartment.

19 The master cylinder reservoir incorporates a window which allows checking the fluid level without removal of the reservoir cover. The level should be maintained at 1/4-inch below the lowest edge of each reservoir **(see illustration)**.

20 If a low level is indicated, be sure to wipe the top of the reservoir cover with a clean rag to prevent contamination of the brake system before removing the cover.

21 When adding fluid, pour it carefully into the reservoir, taking care not to spill any onto surrounding painted surfaces **(see illustration)**. Be sure the specified fluid is used, since mixing different types of brake fluid can cause damage to the system. See *Recommended lubricants and fluids* or your owner's manual.

22 At this time the fluid and cylinder can be inspected for contamination. Normally the brake system will not need periodic draining and refilling, but if rust deposits, dirt particles or water droplets are seen in the fluid the system should be dismantled, drained and refilled with fresh fluid.

23 After filling the reservoir to the proper level, make sure the lid is properly seated to prevent fluid leakage and/or system pressure loss.

24 The brake fluid in the master cylinder will drop slightly as the brake shoes or pads at each wheel wear down during normal operation. If the master cylinder requires repeated replenishing to keep it at the proper level, this is an indication of leakage in the brake system, which should be corrected immediately. Check all brake lines and connections, along with the wheel cylinders and booster (see Section 13 for more information).

25 If, upon checking the master cylinder fluid level, you discover one or both reservoirs empty or nearly empty, the brake system should be bled (see Chapter 9).

Manual transaxle lubricant

1987 and earlier models

26 The manual transaxle lubricant level on these models is checked with the transaxle cold by removing a plug in the side of the transaxle case. Locate the plug and use a rag to clean the plug and the area around it, then remove the plug.

27 If lubricant immediately starts leaking out, thread the plug back into the transaxle. The level is correct. If there is no leakage, completely remove the plug and place your little finger inside the hole. The lubricant level should be just at the bottom of the plug hole.

28 If the transaxle needs more lubricant, use a syringe to squeeze the appropriate type into the plug hole until the proper level is reached.

29 Thread the plug back into the transaxle and tighten it securely.

30 Drive the vehicle a short distance, then check for leaks around the plug.

1988 and later models

31 All 1988 and later model transaxles are equipped with a dipstick for checking the lubricant level.

32 Check the lubricant level only when the engine is off, the vehicle is on a level surface and the transaxle is cool enough to touch without burning your fingers.

33 Remove the dipstick and wipe it off with a rag, then reinsert it and remove it again. Read the indicated level.

a) If the dipstick indicates FULL, and the transaxle is warm, the lubricant level is correct.

b) If the dipstick indicates C (cold) and the transaxle is cold, the lubricant level is correct.

c) If the dipstick indicates ADD, or below, add the proper type of lubricant (see Recommended lubricants and fluids at the front of this Chapter) to fill the transaxle. Be sure the lubricant level is between the FULL and C (cold) marks on the dipstick.

Automatic transaxle fluid

Refer to illustrations 4.40 and 4.43

34 The level of the automatic transaxle fluid should be carefully maintained. Low fluid level can lead to slipping or loss of drive, while overfilling can cause foaming and loss of fluid.

35 With the parking brake set, start the engine, then move the shift lever through all the gear ranges, ending in Park. The fluid level must be checked with the vehicle level and the engine running at idle. **Note:** *Incorrect fluid level readings will result if the vehicle has just been driven at high speeds for an extended period, in hot weather in city traffic, or if it's been pulling a trailer. If any of these conditions apply, wait until the fluid has cooled (about 30 minutes).*

36 With the transaxle at normal operating temperature, remove the dipstick, located on the left side of the engine compartment.

37 Wipe the fluid from the dipstick with a clean rag and push it back into the filler tube until the cap seats.

38 Carefully touch the end of the dipstick to determine the temperature of the fluid. It may be cool, warm or hot.

39 Wipe the fluid from the dipstick with a clean rag and push the dipstick back into the filler tube until the cap seats.

40 Pull the dipstick out and note the fluid level **(see illustration)**.

41 If the fluid felt cool or warm, the level should be between the dimples above the Full mark.

42 If the fluid felt hot, the level should be in the cross-hatched area near the Full mark.

43 Add just enough of the recommended fluid to fill the transmission to the proper level **(see illustration)**. It takes about one pint to

4.46 The power steering reservoir is located on the firewall or on the front of the engine

4.50 Checking of the power steering fluid level is done with the engine at normal operating temperature (the level should be near the Full Hot mark)

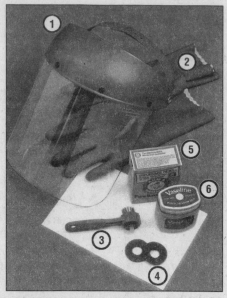

5.1 Tools and materials required for battery maintenance

raise the level from the Add mark to the Full mark with a hot transaxle, so add the fluid a little at a time and keep checking the level until it is correct.

44   The condition of the fluid should also be checked. If the fluid is a dark reddish-brown color, or if the fluid has a burned smell, the transaxle fluid should be changed. If you are in doubt about the condition of the fluid, purchase some new fluid and compare the two for color and smell.

Power steering fluid

Refer to illustrations 4.46 and 4.50

45   Unlike manual steering, the power steering system relies on fluid which may, over a period of time, require replenishing.

46   The fluid reservoir for the power steering pump will either be located near the front of the engine or on the engine compartment firewall **(see illustration)**.

47   For the check, the front wheels should be pointed straight ahead and the engine should be off.

48   Use a clean rag to wipe off the reservoir cap and the area around the cap. This will help prevent any foreign matter from entering the reservoir during the check.

49   Warm the engine to normal operating temperature.

50   Remove the dipstick, wipe it off with a clean rag, reinsert it, then withdraw it and read the fluid level **(see illustration)**. The level should be between the Add and Full Hot marks.

51   If additional fluid is required, pour the specified type directly into the reservoir, using a funnel to prevent spills.

52   If the reservoir requires frequent fluid additions, all power steering hoses, hose connections and the power steering pump should be checked for leaks.

Hydraulic clutch fluid

53   Check the fluid level in the reservoir at least once every month and add more fluid as required. The proper level is indicated by a step on the reservoir. **Caution:** *Be sure to clean the top and sides of the reservoir before removing the cover.*

5   Battery check, maintenance and charging (every 6000 miles or 6 months)

Check and maintenance

Refer to illustrations 5.1 and 5.7

Warning: *Certain precautions must be followed when checking and servicing the battery. Hydrogen gas, which is highly flammable, is always present in the battery cells, so keep lighted tobacco and all other flames and sparks away from it. The electrolyte inside the battery is actually dilute sulfuric acid, which will cause injury if splashed on your skin or in your eyes. It will also ruin clothes and painted surfaces. When removing the battery cables, always detach the negative cable first and hook it up last!*

1   Battery maintenance is an important procedure which will help ensure that you are not stranded because of a dead battery. Several tools are required for this procedure **(see illustration)**.

2   Before servicing the battery, always turn the engine and all accessories off and disconnect the cable from the negative terminal of the battery.

3   A sealed (sometimes called maintenance free) battery is standard equipment. The cell caps cannot be removed, no electrolyte checks are required and water cannot be added to the cells. However, if an aftermarket battery has been installed and it is a type that requires regular maintenance, the following procedures can be used.

4   Check the electrolyte level in each of the battery cells (see Section 4). It must be above the plates. There's usually a split-ring indicator in each cell to indicate the correct level. If the level is low, add distilled water only, then install the cell caps. **Caution:** *Overfilling the cells may cause electrolyte to spill over during periods of heavy charging, causing corrosion and damage to nearby components.*

5   If the positive terminal and cable clamp on your vehicle's battery is equipped with a rubber or plastic protector, make sure that it's not torn or damaged. It should completely cover the terminal.

6   The external condition of the battery

1   **Face shield/safety goggles** - *When removing corrosion with a brush, the acidic particles can easily fly up into your eyes*

2   **Rubber gloves** - *Another safety item to consider when servicing the battery - remember that's acid inside the battery!*

3   **Battery terminal/cable cleaner** - *This wire brush cleaning tool will remove all traces of corrosion from the battery and cable*

4   **Treated felt washers** - *Placing one of these on each terminal, directly under the cable end, will help prevent corrosion (be sure to get the correct type for side-terminal batteries)*

5   **Baking soda** - *A solution of baking soda and water can be used to neutralize corrosion*

6   **Petroleum jelly** - *A layer of this on the battery terminal bolts will help prevent corrosion*

should be checked periodically. Look for damage such as a cracked case.

7   Check the tightness of the battery cable terminals to ensure good electrical connections and inspect the entire length of each cable, looking for cracked or abraded insulation and frayed conductors **(see illustration)**.

8   If corrosion (visible as white, fluffy deposits) is evident, remove the cables from the terminals, clean them with a battery brush and reinstall them. Corrosion can be kept to a minimum by installing specially treated washers available at auto parts stores or by applying a layer of petroleum jelly or grease to the terminals and cable clamps after they are assembled.

9   Make sure the battery carrier is in good condition and that the hold-down clamp bolt is tight. If the battery is removed (see Chapter 5 for the removal and installation proce-

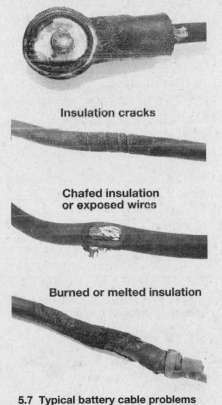

Terminal end corrosion or damage

Insulation cracks

**Chafed insulation
or exposed wires**

Burned or melted insulation

5.7 Typical battery cable problems

dure), make sure that no parts remain in the bottom of the carrier when it's reinstalled. When reinstalling the hold-down clamp, don't overtighten the bolt.

10   Corrosion on the carrier, battery case and surrounding areas can be removed with a solution of water and baking soda. Apply the mixture with a small brush, let it work, then rinse it off with plenty of clean water.

11   Any metal parts of the vehicle damaged by corrosion should be coated with a zinc-based primer, then painted.

12   Additional information on the battery and jump starting can be found in Chapter 5 and at the front of this manual.

Charging

13   Remove all of the cell caps (if equipped) and cover the holes with a clean cloth to prevent spattering electrolyte. Disconnect the negative battery cable and hook the battery charger leads to the battery posts (positive to positive, negative to negative), then plug in the charger. Make sure it is set at 12-volts if it has a selector switch.

14   If you're using a charger with a rate higher than two amps, check the battery regularly during charging to make sure it doesn't overheat. If you're using a trickle charger, you can safely let the battery charge overnight after you've checked it regularly for the first couple of hours.

15   If the battery has removable cell caps, measure the specific gravity with a hydrome-

ter every hour during the last few hours of the charging cycle. Hydrometers are available inexpensively from auto parts stores - follow the instructions that come with the hydrometer. Consider the battery charged when there's no change in the specific gravity reading for two hours and the electrolyte in the cells is gassing (bubbling) freely. The specific gravity reading from each cell should be very close to the others. If not, the battery probably has a bad cell(s).

16   Some batteries with sealed tops have built-in hydrometers on the top that indicate the state of charge by the color displayed in the hydrometer window. Normally, a bright-colored hydrometer indicates a full charge and a dark hydrometer indicates the battery still needs charging. Check the battery manufacturer's instructions to be sure you know what the colors mean.

17   If the battery has a sealed top and no built-in hydrometer, you can hook up a voltmeter across the battery terminals to check the charge. A fully charged battery should read 12.6-volts or higher.

18   Further information on the battery and jump starting can be found in Chapter 5 and at the front of this manual.

6   Drivebelt check and adjustment (every 6000 miles or 6 months)

Refer to illustrations 6.1, 6.4, 6.9a, 6.9b and 6.9c

1   The drivebelts, or V-belts as they are often called, are located at the front of the engine and play an important role in the overall operation of the vehicle and its components. Due to their function and material make-up, the belts are prone to failure after a period of time and should be inspected and adjusted periodically to prevent major engine damage **(see illustration)**.

2   The number of belts used on a particular vehicle depends on the accessories installed. Drivebelts are used to turn the generator/alternator, power steering pump, water pump and air-conditioning compressor. Depending on the pulley arrangement, more than one of these components may be driven by a single belt.

3   With the engine off, open the hood and

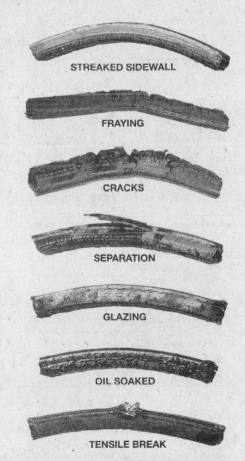

STREAKED SIDEWALL

FRAYING

CRACKS

SEPARATION

GLAZING

OIL SOAKED

TENSILE BREAK

6.1 Here are some of the more common problems associated with drivebelts (check the belts carefully to prevent an untimely breakdown

locate the various belts at the front of the engine. Using your fingers (and a flashlight, if necessary) , move along the belts checking for cracks and separation of the belt plies. Also check for fraying and glazing, which gives the belt a shiny appearance. Both sides of the belt should be inspected, which means you will have to twist the belt to check the underside.

4   The tension of each belt is checked by pushing on the belt at a distance halfway between the pulleys. Push firmly with your

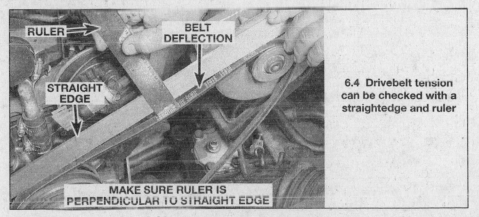

RULER

BELT DEFLECTION

STRAIGHT EDGE

MAKE SURE RULER IS PERPENDICULAR TO STRAIGHT EDGE

6.4 Drivebelt tension can be checked with a straightedge and ruler

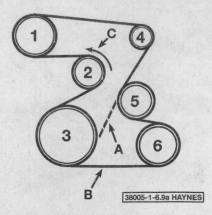

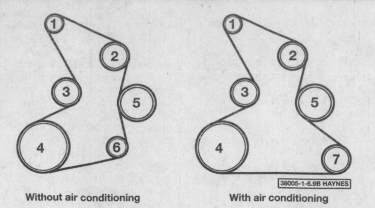

6.9a Serpentine drivebelt routing diagram - 2.2L and 2.5L four cylinder engine

1   Power steering pulley
2   Belt tensioner
3   Crankshaft pulley
4   Alternator pulley
5   Idler pulley
6   Air conditioning compressor pulley
A   Without air conditioning
B   With air conditioning
C   Tensioner - rotate in direction of
    arrow to remove or install belt

thumb and see how much the belt moves (deflects). A rule of thumb is that if the distance from pulley center to pulley center is between 7 and 11 inches, the belt should deflect 1/4-inch. If the belt travels between pulleys spaced 12 to 16 inches apart, the belt should deflect 1/2-inch **(see illustration)**.

5   If it is necessary to adjust the belt tension, either to make the belt tighter or looser, it is done by moving the belt-driven accessory on the bracket.

6   For each component there will be an adjusting bolt and a pivot bolt. Both bolts

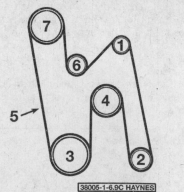

6.9c Serpentine drivebelt routing diagram - 3.0, 3.3 and 3.8L V6 engines

1   Alternator pulley
2   Air conditioning compressor
3   Crankshaft balancer
4   Water pump pulley
5   Serpentine belt
6   Belt tensioner
7   Power steering pump pulley

Without air conditioning   **With air conditioning**

6.9b Serpentine drivebelt routing diagram - 2.8/3.1L V6 engines

1   Alternator   5   Water pump
2   Power steering pump 6   Idler pulley
3   Belt tensioner   7   Air conditioning
4   Crankshaft pulley   compressor

must be loosened slightly to enable you to move the component.

7   After the two bolts have been loosened, move the component away from the engine to tighten the belt or toward the engine to loosen the belt. Hold the accessory in position and check the belt tension. If it is correct, tighten the two bolts until just snug, then recheck the tension. If the tension is all right, tighten the bolts.

8   It will often be necessary to use some sort of prybar to move the accessory while the belt is adjusted. If this must be done to gain the proper leverage, be very careful not to damage the component being moved or the part being pried against.

9   Later models are equipped with a single "serpentine" drivebelt, which powers all engine accessories **(see illustrations)**. This style belt requires no adjustment; it is handled by a spring loaded tensioner pulley. The belt should be inspected regularly for missing ribs and frayed plies. Cracks in the belt ribs do not necessarily indicate a faulty or damaged belt, since they will not impair belt performance.

10 To replace the belt, insert a half-inch drive breaker bar (some models require a 15 mm socket) into the tensioner and rotate the pulley counterclockwise, releasing belt tension.

11 Remove the drivebelt from the pulleys.

12 Install the new belt, starting with the bottom pulleys, then release the tensioner. Make sure the belt is properly centered on each pulley.

7   Cooling system check (every 6000 miles or 6 months)

Refer to illustrations 7.4a and 7.4b

1   Many major engine failures can be attributed to a faulty cooling system. If the vehicle is equipped with an automatic trans-

Check for a chafed area that could fail prematurely.

Check for a soft area indicating the hose has deteriorated inside.

Overtightening the clamp on a hardened hose will damage the hose and cause a leak.

Check each hose for swelling and oil-soaked ends. Cracks and breaks can be located by squeezing the hose.

7.4a Hoses, like drivebelts, have a habit of failing at the worst possible time - to prevent the inconvenience of a blown radiator or heater hose, inspect them carefully as shown here

7.4b Although this radiator hose appears to be in good condition, it should be periodically checked for cracks (more easily revealed when squeezed)

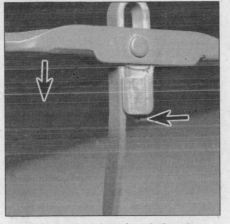

9.5 Press the tab and push the wiper down out of the hook in the end of the arm

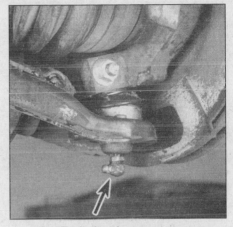

10.2 Typical replacement grease fitting (arrow)

mission, the cooling system also plays an important role in prolonging transmission life.

2   The cooling system should be checked with the engine cold. Do this before the vehicle is driven for the day or after it has been shut off for at least three hours.

3   Remove the radiator cap and thoroughly clean the cap, inside and out, with clean water. Also clean the filler neck on the radiator. All traces of corrosion should be removed.

4   Carefully check the upper and lower radiator hoses and the smaller diameter heater hoses. Inspect each hose along its entire length, replacing any hose which is cracked, swollen or shows signs of deterioration. Cracks may become more apparent if the hose is squeezed (see illustrations).

5   Make sure that all hose connections are tight. A leak in the cooling system will usually show up as white or rust colored deposits on the areas near the leak.

6   Use compressed air or a soft brush to remove bugs, leaves, etc. from the front of the radiator or air-conditioning condenser. Be careful not to damage the delicate cooling fins or cut yourself on them.

7   Finally, have the cap and system pressure tested. If you do not have a pressure tester, most gas stations and repair shops will do this for a minimal change.

8   Underhood hose check and replacement (every 6000 miles or 6 months)

Warning: *Replacement of air-conditioning hoses must be left to a dealer or air-conditioning specialist who can depressurize the system and perform the work safely. Never disconnect air conditioning hoses or components until the system has been depressurized.*

1   The high temperatures present under the hood can cause deterioration of rubber and plastic hoses.

2   Periodic inspection should be made for cracks, loose clamps and leaks. Some of the hoses are part of the emissions control systems and can affect the engine's performance.

3   Remove the air cleaner if necessary and trace the entire length of each hose. Squeeze each hose to check for cracks and look for swelling, discoloration and leaks.

4   If the vehicle has considerable mileage or if one or more of the hoses is suspect, it is a good idea to replace all of the hoses at one time.

5   Measure the length and inside diameter of each hose and obtain and cut the replacement to size. Since original equipment hose clamps are often good for only one use it is a good idea to replace them with screw-type clamps.

6   Replace each hose one at a time to eliminate the possibility of confusion. Hoses attached to the heater and radiator contain coolant, so newspapers or rags should be kept handy to catch the spills when they are disconnected.

7   After installation, run the engine until it reaches operating temperature, shut it off and check for leaks. After the engine has cooled, retighten all of the screw type clamps.

9   Wiper blade inspection and replacement (every 6000 miles or 6 months)

Refer to illustration 9.5

1   The windshield wiper and blade assembly should be inspected periodically for damage, loose components and cracked or worn blade elements.

2   Road film can build up on the wiper blades and affect their efficiency, so they should be washed regularly with a mild detergent solution.

3   The action of the wiping mechanism can loosen the bolts, nuts and fasteners so they

should be checked and tightened, as necessary, at the same time the wiper blades are checked.

4   If the wiper blade elements are cracked, worn or warped, they should be replaced with new ones.

5   Remove the wiper blade by raising the wiper arm and pushing the bottom of the blade towards the glass to disengage the arm from the blade. Lift the blade and remove it (see illustration).

6   Install the blade by inserting the pronged end of the arm into the blade slots and pulling the bottom of the blade towards the arm to lock it in place.

10   Chassis lubrication (every 6000 miles or 6 months)

Refer to illustrations 10.2 and 10.10

1   A grease gun and a cartridge filled with the proper grease (see *Recommended fluids and lubricants*) are usually the only equipment necessary to lubricate the chassis components. In some chassis locations plugs may be installed rather than grease fittings, in which case grease fittings will have to be installed.

2   The grease fittings are located at various locations under the vehicle (see illustration). Look under the vehicle to find these components and determine if grease fittings or solid plugs are installed. If there are plugs, remove them and thread grease fittings into the component. A dealer service department or auto parts store will be able to supply replacement fittings. Straight, as well as angled, fittings are available. **Note:** *Later models may not be equipped with grease fittings or provisions for them.*

3   For easier access under the vehicle raise it with a jack and place jackstands under the frame. Make sure the vehicle is securely supported by the stands.

4   Before proceeding, pump a little of the grease out of the nozzle of the grease gun to remove any dirt from the end of the gun.

10.10 Multi-purpose grease is used to lubricate the hood latch mechanism

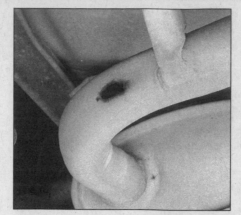

11.2 On light-colored exhaust pipes, leaks usually show up easily as brown or black stains - this stain around a small hole is indicative of a tailpipe needing replacement

Wipe the nozzle clean with a rag.

5   With the grease gun, plenty of clean rags and the diagram, crawl under the vehicle and begin lubricating the components.

6   Wipe the grease fitting clean and push the nozzle firmly over the fitting. Pump the trigger on the grease gun to force grease into the component. **Note:** *The tie-rod ends should be lubricated until the rubber boot is firm to the touch. Do not pump too much grease into these fittings as it could rupture the boot.* On the control arm balljoint fittings, continue pumping grease into the fitting until grease seeps out of the joint between the two components. If the grease seeps out around the grease gun nozzle, the fitting is clogged or the nozzle is not seated on the fitting. Resecure the gun nozzle to the fitting and try again. If necessary, replace the fitting.

7   Wipe the excess grease from the components and the grease fitting. Follow the same procedures for the remaining fittings.

8   While you are under the vehicle clean and lubricate the parking brake cable, the cable guides and levers. This can be done by smearing some of the chassis grease onto the cable and its related parts with your fingers. Place a few drops of light engine oil on the transmission shift linkage rods and swivels.

9   Lower the vehicle for the remaining lubrication procedures.

10   Open the hood and apply chassis grease to the hood latch mechanism **(see illustration).** If the hood has an inside release, have an assistant pull the release knob as you lubricate the cable at the latch.

11   Lubricate all the hinges (door, hood, liftgate) with a few drops of light engine oil.

12   The key lock cylinders should be lubricated with spray-on graphite dry lubricant, which is available at auto parts stores.

11   Exhaust system check (every 6000 miles or 6 months)

Refer to illustration 11.2

1   With the engine cold (at least three

hours after the vehicle has been driven) , check the complete exhaust system from its starting point at the engine to the end of the tailpipe. This should be done on a hoist where unrestricted access is available.

2   Check the pipes and connections for signs of leakage and corrosion, indicating a potential failure **(see illustration).** Make sure that all brackets and hangers are in good condition and tight.

3   Inspect the underside of the body for holes, corrosion, open seams, etc., which may allow exhaust gases to enter the passenger compartment. Seal all body openings with silicone or body putty.

4   Rattles and other noises can often be traced to the exhaust system, especially the mounts and hangers. Try to move the pipes, muffler and catalytic converter. If the components can come in contact with the body or suspension parts, secure the exhaust system with new mounts.

5   Check the running condition of the engine by inspecting inside the end of the tailpipe. The exhaust deposits here are an indication of engine state-of-tune. If the pipe is black and sooty or coated with white deposits, the engine is in need of a tune-up, including a thorough carburetor inspection and adjustment.

12   Suspension and steering check (every 6000 miles or 6 months)

1   Whenever the front of the vehicle is raised for service visually check the suspension and steering components for wear.

2   Indications of a fault in these systems are excessive play in the steering wheel before the front wheels react, excessive sway around corners, body movement over rough roads or binding at some point as the steering wheel is turned.

3   Before the vehicle is raised for inspection, test the shock absorbers by pushing down to rock the vehicle at each corner. If

you push down and the vehicle does not come back to a level position within one or two bounces, the shocks/struts are worn and must be replaced. As this is done, check for squeaks and noises coming from the suspension components. Information on suspension components can be found in Chapter 10.

4   Raise the front of the vehicle and support it securely on jackstands placed under the frame rails.

5   Check the wheel bearings (see Section 27).

6   Crawl under the vehicle and check for loose bolts, broken or disconnected parts and deteriorated rubber bushings on all suspension and steering components. Look for grease or fluid leaking from the steering gear. Check the power steering hoses and connections for leaks. Check the balljoints for wear.

7   Have an assistant turn the steering wheel from side-to-side and check the steering components for free movement, chafing and binding. If the steering does not react with the movement of the steering wheel, try to determine where the slack is located.

13   Brake check (every 6000 miles or 6 months)

Refer to illustrations 13.6a, 13.6b and 13.13
Warning: *The dust created by the brake system may contain asbestos, which is harmful to your health. Never blow it out with compressed air and don't inhale any of it. An approved filtering mask should be worn when working on the brakes. Do not, under any circumstances, use petroleum-based solvents to clean brake parts. Use brake system cleaner only!*
Note: *For detailed photographs of the brake system, see Chapter 9.*

1   The brakes should be inspected every time the wheels are removed or whenever a defect is suspected. Indications of a potential brake system defect are:

a)   *The vehicle pulls to one side when the brake pedal is depressed.*
b)   *Noises coming from the brakes when they are applied.*
c)   *Excessive brake pedal travel.*
d)   *Pulsating pedal.*
e)   *Leakage of fluid, usually seen on the inside of the tire or wheel.*

Disc brakes

2   Both front and rear disc brakes (if the rear is so equipped) can be visually checked without removing any parts except the wheels.

3   Raise the vehicle and place it securely on jackstands. Remove the wheels (see *Jacking and towing* at the front of the manual, if necessary).

4   The disc brake calipers, which contain the pads, are now visible. There is an outer pad and an inner pad in each caliper. All pads should be inspected.

5   The outer pads on the front wheels are

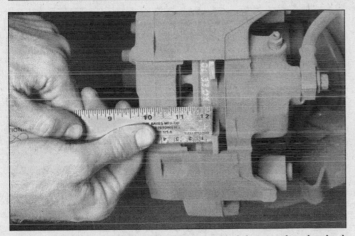

13.6a The amount of disc pad material remaining can be checked by looking through the opening in the caliper

13.6b The disc brake pads are equipped with wear indicators that contact the disc and make a squealing sound when the pad has worn to its limit

equipped with a wear sensor. This is a small, bent piece of metal which is visible from the inboard side of the brake caliper. When the pads wear to the danger limit the mental sensor rubs against the disc and makes a screeching sound.

6   Check the pad thickness by looking at each end of the caliper and through the inspection hole in the caliper body (see illustrations). If the wear sensor clip is very close to the disc, or if the lining material is 1/8-inch or less in thickness, the pads should be replaced. Keep in mind that the lining material is riveted or bonded to a metal backing shoe and the metal portion is not included in this measurement.

7   Remove the pads for further inspection or replacement if you are in doubt as to the condition of the pad.

8   Before installing the wheels, check for leakage around the brake hose connections leading to the caliper and damage (cracking, splitting, etc.) to the brake hose. Replace the hose or fittings as necessary, referring to Chapter 9.

9   Check the condition of the disc. Look for scoring, gouging and burned spots. If these conditions exist the disc should be removed for servicing (see Chapter 9).

Drum brakes

10   Using a scribe or chalk, mark the drum and hub so the drum can be reinstalled in the same position on the hub.

11   Remove and discard the retaining clip and pull the brake drum off the axle and brake assembly. If this proves difficult, make sure the parking brake is released, then squirt some penetrating oil around the center hub area. Allow the oil to soak in and try to pull the drum off again. If the drum still can't be pulled off, the brake shoes will have to be retracted. This is done by first removing the lanced knock-out in the backing plate with a hammer and chisel. With the lanced area punched in, pull the self-adjusting lever off the star wheel and use a small screwdriver to turn the wheel, which will move the shoes away from the drum.

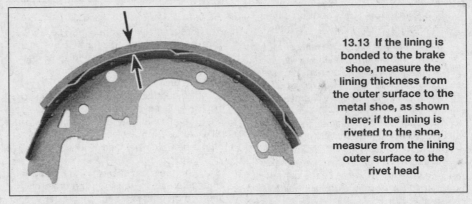

13.13 If the lining is bonded to the brake shoe, measure the lining thickness from the outer surface to the metal shoe, as shown here; if the lining is riveted to the shoe, measure from the lining outer surface to the rivet head

12   With the drum removed, clean the assembly with brake system cleaner.

13   Note the thickness of the lining material on the brake shoes (see illustration). If the material is worn to within 1/16-inch of the recessed rivets or metal backing, the shoes should be replaced. If the linings look worn, but you are unable to determine their exact thickness, compare them with a new set at an auto parts store. The shoes should also be replaced if they are cracked, glazed (shiny surface) or contaminated with brake fluid.

14   Check to see that all the brake assembly springs are connected and in good condition.

15   Check the brake components for signs of fluid leakage. Carefully pry back the rubber cups on the wheel cylinder, located at the top of the brake backing plate. Any leakage is an indication that the wheel cylinders should be overhauled immediately (see Chapter 9). Also check the hoses and connections for signs of leakage.

16   Clean the inside of the drum with brake system cleaner. Again, be careful not to breathe the asbestos dust.

17   Check the inside of the drum for cracks, scores, deep scratches and hard spots, which will appear as small discolored areas. If imperfections cannot be removed with fine emery cloth the drum must be taken to a machine shop for resurfacing.

18   After the inspection process, if all parts are found to be in good condition, reinstall the brake drum. Install the wheel and lower the vehicle to the ground.

Parking brake

19   The easiest way to check the operation of the parking brake is to park the vehicle on a steep hill with the parking brake set and the transmission in Neutral (stay in the car while performing this check). If the parking brake can't prevent the vehicle from rolling, it is in need of adjustment (see Chapter 9).

14   Carburetor choke check (every 6000 miles or 6 months)

1   The choke only operates when the engine is cold, so this check should be performed before the engine has been started for the day.

2   Open the hood and remove the top plate of the air cleaner assembly. It is held in place by a wing nut. If any vacuum hoses must be disconnected make sure you tag them to insure reinstallation in their original positions. Place the top plate and nut aside, out of the way of moving engine components.

3   Look at the top of the carburetor at the center of the air cleaner housing. You will notice a flat plate at the carburetor opening.

4   Have an assistant press the accelerator pedal to the floor. The plate should close

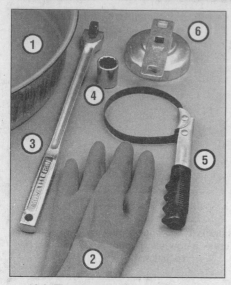

16.3 These tools are required when changing the engine oil and filter

1   **Drain pan** - *It should be fairly shallow in depth, but wide to prevent spills*
2   **Rubber gloves** - *When removing the drain plug and filter, you will get oil on your hands (the gloves will prevent burns)*
3   **Breaker bar** - *Sometimes the oil drain plug is tight, and a long breaker bar is needed to loosen it*
4   **Socket** - *To be used with the breaker bar or a ratchet (must be the correct size to fit the drain plug - six-point preferred)*
5   **Filter wrench** - *This is a metal band-type wrench, which requires clearance around the filter to be effective*
6   **Filter wrench** - *This type fits on the bottom of the filter and can be turned with a ratchet or breaker bar (different-size wrenches are available for different types of filters)*

completely. Start the engine while you observe the plate at the carburetor. **Warning:** *Do not position your face directly over the carburetor. The engine could backfire and cause serious burns.* When the engine starts the choke plate should open slightly.

5   Allow the engine to continue running at an idle speed. Every thirty seconds depress the throttle slightly. As the engine warms up to operating temperature the plate should slowly open, allowing more air to enter through the top of the carburetor.

6   After a few minutes the choke plate should be all the way open to the vertical position.

7   You will notice that the engine speed corresponds with the plate opening. With the plate completely closed, the engine should run at a fast idle. As the plate opens, the engine speed will decrease.

8   If a malfunction is detected during the above checks, see Chapter 4 for specific information related to adjusting and servicing choke components.

15   Engine idle speed check and adjustment (every 6000 miles or 6 months)

1   The engine idle speed is adjustable on some models and should be checked at the scheduled maintenance interval.

2   On those vehicles with provisions for idle speed adjustment, the specifications for such adjustments are shown on the *Vehicle Emissions Control Information* label. However, the adjustments must be made using calibrated test equipment. The adjustments should therefore be made by a dealer service department or other repair facility.

16   Engine oil and filter change (every 3000 miles or 3 months)

Refer to illustrations 16.3 and 16.14

1   Frequent oil changes may be the best form of preventative maintenance available to the home mechanic. When engine oil ages, it becomes diluted and contaminated, which leads to premature engine wear.

2   Although some sources recommend oil filter changes every other oil change, we feel that the minimal cost of an oil filter and the relative ease with which it is installed dictate that a new filter be used whenever the oil is changed.

3   The tools necessary for a oil and filter change are a wrench to fit the drain plug at the bottom of the oil pan, an oil filter wrench to remove the old filter, a container with at least a six-quart capacity to drain the old oil into and a funnel to help pour fresh oil into the engine **(see illustration)**.

4   In addition, you should have plenty of clean rags and newspapers handy to mop up any spills. Access to the underside of the vehicle is greatly improved if the vehicle can be lifted on a hoist, driven onto ramps or supported by jackstands. **Warning:** *Do not work under a vehicle which is supported only by a jack.*

5   If this is your first oil change on the vehicle, it is a good idea to crawl underneath and familiarize yourself with the locations of the oil drain plug and the oil filter. The engine and exhaust components will be hot during the actual work, so it is a good idea to figure out any potential problems before becoming involved with the procedure.

6   Allow the engine to warm up to normal operating temperature. If the new oil or any tools are needed, use this warm-up time to gather everything necessary for the job. The correct type of oil to buy for your application can be found in *Recommended lubricants and fluids* at the beginning of this manual.

7   With the engine oil warm (warm engine oil will drain better and more built-up sludge will be removed with the oil), raise and support the vehicle. Make sure it is firmly supported.

8   Move all necessary tools, rags and newspapers under the vehicle. Position the

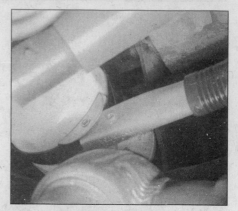

16.14 A strap-type oil filter wrench works well in hard-to-reach locations

drain pan under the drain plug. Keep in mind that the oil will initially flow from the pan with some force, so place the pan accordingly.

9   Being careful not to touch any of the hot exhaust components, use the wrench to remove the drain plug near the bottom of the oil pan. Depending on how hot the oil has become, you may want to wear gloves while unscrewing the plug the final few turns.

10   Allow the old oil to drain into the pan. It may be necessary to reposition the pan as the oil flow slows to a trickle.

11   After all the oil has drained wipe off the drain plug with a clean rag. Small metal particles may cling to the plug and would immediately contaminate the new oil.

12   Clean the area around the drain plug opening and reinstall the plug. Tighten the plug securely with the wrench.

13   Move the drain pan into position under the oil filter.

14   Use the filter wrench to loosen the oil filter. Chain or metal band-type filter wrenches may distort the filter canister, but this is of no concern as the filter will be discarded **(see illustration)**. On later models equipped with the 2.5L four-cylinder engine, an element-type filter in the oil pan replaces the spin-on type filter on the side of the engine block. Some of these engines have a separate drain plug to make draining the oil easier. Unscrew and remove the large oil filter access plug from the center of the oil pan, then reach up inside the hole with a pair of pliers, grasp the filter securely, pull it down using a twisting motion and remove it from the oil pan. Check the filter to make sure the rubber O-ring has come out with it. If it hasn't, reach up inside the pan opening and remove it.

15   Sometimes the oil filter is on so tight it cannot be loosened, or is positioned in an area which is inaccessible with a filter wrench. As a last resort you can punch a metal bar or long screwdriver directly through the sides of the canister and use it as a T-handle to turn the filter. If this becomes necessary be prepared for oil to spurt out of the canister as it is punctured.

16   Completely unscrew the old filter. Be careful, it is full of oil. Empty the filter into the drain pan.

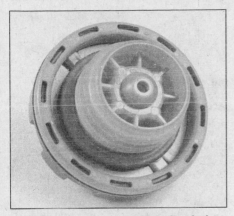

17.5 With today's sophisticated emissions systems, it is essential that the seal in the gas tank cap be checked regularly

17 Compare the old filter with the new one to make sure they are the same type.

18 Use a clean rag to remove all oil, dirt and sludge from the area where the oil filter mounts to the engine. Check the old filter to make sure the rubber gasket is not stuck to the engine mounting surface. If the gasket is stuck to the engine remove it.

19 Open one of the containers of oil and fill the filter half-full. Apply a light coat of oil around the full circumference of the rubber gasket of the oil filter,

20 Attach the filter to the engine following the tightening directions printed on the filter canister or packing box. Most filter manufacturers recommend against using a filter wrench due to the possibility of overtightening and damage to the seal. On later models equipped with a 2.5L four-cylinder engine, coat the new O-ring (included with the new filter) with clean engine oil and the slide it into position, all the way up in the filter opening. Coat the inside of the grommet on the top of the new filter with clean engine oil then slide the new oil filter up into the oil pan opening as far as possible without forcing it. Reinstall the plug, tighten it by hand until the gasket contacts the oil pan, then tighten it an additional 1/4-turn with a wrench.

21 Remove all tools, rags, etc. from under the vehicle, being careful not to spill the oil in the drain pan, then lower the vehicle.

22 Move to the engine compartment and locate the oil filler cap on the engine. Remove the cap.

23 Pour the new oil through the filler opening.

24 Pour three quarts of fresh oil into the engine. Wait a few minutes to allow the oil to drain into the pan, then check the level on the oil dipstick (see Section 4 if necessary). If the oil level is at or near the lower Add mark, start the engine and allow the new oil to circulate.

25 Run the engine for one minute then shut it off. Immediately look under the vehicle and check for leaks at the oil pan drain plug and around the oil filter. If either is leaking, tighten with a bit more force.

26 With the new oil circulated and the filter now completely full, recheck the level on the dipstick and add enough oil to bring the level to the Full mark on the dipstick.

27 During the first few trips after an oil change, make it a point to check frequently for leaks and proper oil level.

28 The old oil drained from the engine cannot be reused in its present state and should be disposed of. Oil reclamation centers, auto repair shops and gas stations will normally accept the oil, which can be refined and used again. After the oil has cooled, it can be drained into a suitable container (capped plastic jugs, topped bottles, milk cartons, etc.) for transport to one of these disposal sites.

17 Fuel system check (every 12000 miles or 12 months)

Refer to illustration 17.5

Warning: *Gasoline is extremely flammable, so take extra precautions when you work on any part of the fuel system. Don't smoke or allow open flames or bare light bulbs near the work area, and don't work in a garage where a natural gas-type appliance (such as a water heater or clothes dryer) with a pilot light is present. If you spill any fuel on your skin, rinse it off immediately with soap and water. When you perform any kind of work on the fuel system, wear safety glasses and have a Class B type fire extinguisher on hand.*

1 If your vehicle is equipped with fuel injection, refer to the *fuel pressure relief procedure* (see Chapter 4) before servicing any component of the fuel system. Also, remove the fuel tank cap to relieve the pressure in the tank.

2 The fuel system is under a small amount of pressure, so before any fuel lines are disconnected for servicing be prepared to catch the fuel as it spurts out. Plug all disconnected fuel lines immediately after disconnection to prevent the tank from emptying itself.

3 The fuel system is most easily checked with the vehicle raised on a hoist so the components underneath the vehicle are readily visible and accessible.

4 If the smell of gasoline is noticed while driving or after the vehicle has been in the sun, the system should be thoroughly inspected immediately.

5 Remove the gas filler cap and check for damage, corrosion and an unbroken sealing imprint on the gasket **(see illustration)**. Replace the cap with a new one if necessary.

6 With the vehicle raised, inspect the gas tank and filler neck for punctures, cracks or other damage. The connection between the filler neck and the tank is especially critical. Sometimes a rubber filler neck will leak due to loose clamps or deteriorated rubber, problems a home mechanic can usually rectify. **Warning:** *Do not, under any circumstances, try to repair a fuel tank yourself (except rubber components). A torch or even a spark can easily cause the fuel vapors to explode if the proper precautions are not taken.*

7 Check all rubber hoses and metal lines leading away from the fuel tank. Check for loose connections, deteriorated hoses, crimped lines and other damage. Follow the lines to the front of the vehicle, carefully inspecting them all the way. Repair or replace damaged sections as necessary.

8 If a fuel odor is still evident after the inspection, check the evaporative emissions control system (see Section 33).

18 Fuel filter replacement (every 12000 miles or 12 months)

Refer to illustrations 18.1 and 18.17

Warning: *Gasoline is extremely flammable, so take extra precautions when you work on any part of the fuel system. Don't smoke or allow open flames or bare light bulbs near the work area, and don't work in a garage where a natural gas-type appliance (such as a water heater or clothes dryer) with a pilot light is present. If you spill any fuel on your skin, rinse it off immediately with soap and water. When you perform any kind of work on the fuel system, wear safety glasses and have a Class B type fire extinguisher on hand.*

Carbureted models

1 On these models the fuel filter is located inside the fuel inlet at the carburetor. It is made of pleated paper and cannot be cleaned or reused **(see illustration)**.

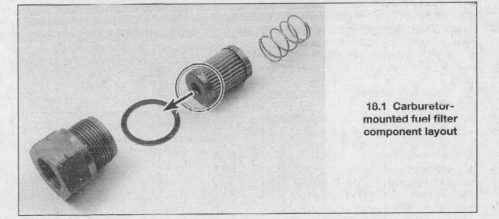

18.1 Carburetor-mounted fuel filter component layout

18.17 Typical frame-mounted fuel filter used with Multi-port Fuel Injection

19.1 Remove the accelerator cable retaining clips (arrows)

2   This job should be done with the engine cold (after sitting at least three hours). The necessary tools include open-end wrenches to fit the fuel line nuts. Flare nut wrenches, which wrap around the nut, should be used, if available, to prevent damage to the fittings, which are generally made of brass or aluminum. In addition, you will have to obtain a replacement filter. Make sure it is for your specific vehicle and engine. You will also need some clean rags.

3   Remove the air cleaner assembly. If vacuum hoses must be disconnected, be sure to note their positions and/or tag them so they can be reinstalled correctly.

4   Follow the fuel line from the fuel pump to the point where it enters the carburetor. The fuel pump is located low on the engine, at the right front. In most cases the fuel line will be metal all the way from the fuel pump to the carburetor.

5   Place some rags under the fuel inlet fittings to catch spilled fuel as the fittings are disconnected. Remove the fuel tank cap to relieve the pressure in the tank.

6   With the proper size wrench, hold the large nut immediately next to the carburetor body. Loosen the fitting at the end of the metal fuel line. A flare nut wrench on this fitting will help prevent slipping and possible damage. Make sure the larger nut next to the carburetor is held securely while the fuel line is disconnected.

7   After the fuel line is disconnected, move it aside for better access to the inlet filter nut. Do not crimp the fuel line.

8   Unscrew the fuel inlet filter nut which was previously held steady. As this fitting is drawn away from the carburetor body, be careful not to lose the thin washer-type gasket or the spring located behind the fuel filter.

9   Compare the old filter with the new one to make sure they are the same length and design.

10   Reinstall the spring in the carburetor body.

11   Place the new filter in position. The filter will have a rubber gasket and a check valve at one end, which should point away from the carburetor.

12   Install a new washer-type gasket on the fuel inlet filter nut. A gasket is usually supplied with the new filter. Install the nut in the carburetor. Make sure it is not cross-

threaded. Tighten it securely, but do not overtighten it, as the hole can strip easily, causing fuel leaks.

13   Hold the fuel inlet nut securely with a wrench while the fuel line is connected. Again, be careful not to cross-thread the fitting. Tighten the fitting securely.

14   Plug the vacuum hose which leads to the air cleaner snorkel motor so the engine can be started.

15   Start the engine and check carefully for leaks. If the fuel line connector leaks, disconnect it using the above procedures and check for stripped or damaged threads. If the fuel line fitting has stripped threads, remove the entire line and have a repair shop install a new fitting, or replace the line.

16   Reinstall the air cleaner assembly, connecting the hoses in their original positions.

Fuel-injected models

Warning: *Refer to the fuel pressure relief procedure in Chapter 4 before performing this procedure.*

Note: *If equipped with quick-connect fittings, see Chapter 4, Section 8.*

17   Fuel-injected models employ a stainless steel in-line fuel filter. On TBI engines it is located at the left rear of the engine, clamped to the cylinder head. On Multi-Port Fuel Injected models the filter is attached to the frame rail or on the rear crossmember in the engine compartment **(see illustration)**.

18   With the engine cold, place a container under the fuel filter.

19   Remove any bolts attaching the fuel filter bracket to the engine.

20   Remove the line from the top of the filter.

21   Unclamp and remove the fuel line from the bottom of the filter and remove the filter.

22   Install the new filter by reversing the removal procedure. Do not overtighten the fitting at the top of the fuel filter.

19   Accelerator cable check and maintenance (every 12000 miles or 12 months)

Refer to illustration 19.1

1   The accelerator linkage is a cable type and although there are no adjustments to the

linkage itself, periodic maintenance is necessary to assure its proper function **(see illustration)**.

2   Remove the air cleaner so the entire linkage is visible.

3   Check the entire length of the cable to make sure that it is not binding.

4   Check all the nylon bushings for wear, replacing them with new ones as necessary.

5   Lubricate the cable mechanisms with engine oil at the pivot points, but do not lubricate the cable itself.

20   Carburetor/Throttle Body Injection (TBI) mounting nut/bolt torque check (every 12,000 miles or 12 months)

1   The carburetor/TBI unit is attached to the top of the intake manifold by four nuts or bolts. These fasteners can sometimes work loose from vibration and temperature changes during normal engine operation and cause a vacuum leak.

2   To properly tighten the mounting nuts a torque wrench is necessary. If you do not own one, they can usually be rented on a daily basis.

3   Remove the air cleaner assembly, tagging each hose to be disconnected with a piece of numbered tape to make reassembly easier.

4   Locate the mounting nuts/bolts at the base of the carburetor/TBI unit. Decide what special tools or adapters will be necessary, if any, to tighten the fasteners with a socket and the torque wrench.

5   Tighten the nuts/bolts to the torque listed in this Chapter's Specifications. Do not overtighten them, as the threads could strip.

6   If you suspect that a vacuum leak exists at the bottom of the carburetor, obtain a length of hose about the diameter of fuel hose. Start the engine and place one end of the hose next to your ear as you probe around the base of the carburetor with the other end. You will hear a hissing sound if a leak exists.

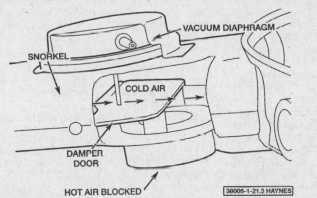

VACUUM DIAPHRAGM
SNORKEL
COLD AIR
DAMPER DOOR
HOT AIR BLOCKED

38005-1-21.3 HAYNES

21.3 Typical THERMAC assembly shown with the snorkel passage (damper door) open

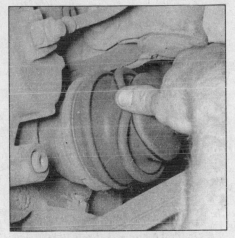

22.4 Check the driveaxle boot to make sure it is not cracked or loose

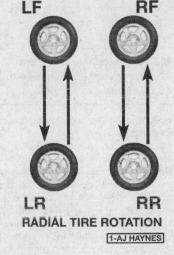

LF   RF

LR   RR

RADIAL TIRE ROTATION

1-AJ HAYNES

23.2 Tire rotation diagram

7   If, after the nuts/bolts are properly tightened, a vacuum leak still exists, the carburetor/TBI unit must be removed and a new gasket installed. See Chapter 4 for more information.

8   After tightening the fasteners, reinstall the air cleaner and return all hoses to their original positions.

21 Thermostatically controlled air cleaner (THERMAC) check (every 12000 miles or 12 months)

Refer to illustration 21.3

Note: *This procedure applies to carbureted and Throttle Body Injected models only.*

1   All carbureted and Throttle Body Injected engines are equipped with a thermostatically controlled air cleaner which draws air to the carburetor from different locations, depending upon engine temperature.

2   This is a visual check. If access is limited, a small mirror may have to be used.

3   Open the hood and locate the damper door inside the air cleaner assembly. It will be located inside the long snorkel of the metal air cleaner housing **(see illustration)**.

4   If there is a flexible air duct attached to the end of the snorkel, leading to an area behind the grille, disconnect it at the snorkel. This will enable you to look through the end of the snorkel and see the damper inside.

5   The check should be done when the engine is cold. Start the engine and look through the snorkel at the damper, which should move to a closed position. With the damper closed, air can't enter through the end of the snorkel, but instead enters the air cleaner through the flexible duct attached to the exhaust manifold and the heat stove passage.

6   As the engine warms up to operating temperature, the damper should open to allow air through the snorkel end. Depending on ambient temperature, this may take 10 to 15 minutes. To speed up this check you can reconnect the snorkel air duct, drive the vehicle, then check to see if the damper is completely open.

7   If the thermo-controlled air cleaner is not operating properly see Chapter 6 for more information.

22 Differential seal and driveaxle boot check (every 12000 miles or 12 months)

Refer to illustration 22.4

1   At the recommended intervals the transaxle output shaft seals and driveaxle boots should be inspected for leaks and damage.

2   Raise the front of the vehicle and support it securely on jackstands.

3   Check the differential seals located where the driveaxles exit from the transaxle. It may be necessary to clean this area before inspection. If there is any oil leaking from either of the driveaxle/transaxle junctions, the differential seals must be replaced (see Chapter 7B).

4   The driveaxle boots prevent dirt, water and other foreign material from entering and damaging the constant velocity (CV) joints. Inspect the condition of all four boots (two on each driveaxle) **(see illustration)**. Clean the boots using soap and water, as oil or grease will cause the boot material to deteriorate prematurely. If there is any damage or evidence of leaking lubricant they must be replaced as described in Chapter 8. Check the tightness of the boot clamps. If they are loose and can't be tightened, the clamp must be replaced.

23 Tire rotation (every 12000 miles or 12 months)

Refer to illustration 23.2

1   The tires should be rotated at the specified intervals and whenever uneven wear is noticed. With the vehicle raised and the tires removed, you can also check the brakes (see Section 13) and the wheel bearings (see Section 27).

2   Refer to the accompanying illustration of the preferred tire rotation patterns **(see illustration)**.

3   Refer to the information in *Jacking and towing* at the front of this manual for the proper procedures to follow when raising the vehicle and changing a tire. If the brakes are to be checked, do not apply the parking brake as stated. Make sure the tires are blocked to prevent the vehicle from rolling.

4   Preferably, the entire vehicle should be raised at the same time. This can be done on a hoist or by jacking up each corner and then lowering the vehicle onto jackstands placed under the frame rails. Always use four jackstands and make sure the vehicle is securely supported.

5   After rotation, check and adjust the tire pressures as necessary and be sure to check the lug nut tightness.

24 Clutch pedal adjustment (every 5000 miles or 5 months)

Refer to illustration 24.2

1   At the specified interval the clutch pedal must be adjusted to maintain a constant tension on the clutch self-adjusting mechanism cable.

2   Grasp the pedal and pull it up to the rubber stop, then depress the pedal slowly **(see**

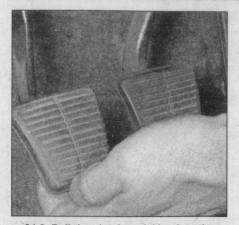

24.2 Pull the clutch pedal back to the stop, then depress it slowly to adjust the freeplay

illustration). **Note:** *Do not pull up on the pedal after it stops or the clutch linkage could be damaged.*

25 Manual transaxle lubricant change (every 48000 miles or 48 months)

1   Raise the vehicle and support it securely on jackstands.

2   Move a drain pan, rags, newspapers and wrenches under the transaxle.

3   Remove the transaxle drain plug at the bottom of the case and allow the oil to drain into the pan.

4   After the oil has drained completely, reinstall the plug and tighten it securely.

5   Remove the fill plug in the side of the transaxle case. Using a hand pump, syringe or funnel, fill the transaxle with the correct amount of the specified lubricant. Reinstall the fill plug and tighten it securely.

6   Lower the vehicle.

26 Cooling system servicing (draining, flushing and refilling) (every 30000 miles or 30 months)

Warning: *Do not allow antifreeze to come in contact with your skin or painted surfaces of the vehicle. Rinse off spills immediately with plenty of water. Antifreeze is highly toxic if ingested. Never leave antifreeze lying around in an open container or in puddles on the floor; children and pets are attracted by it's sweet smell and may drink it. Check with local authorities about disposing of used antifreeze. Many communities have collection centers which will see that antifreeze is disposed of safely.*

1   Periodically the cooling system should be drained, flushed and refilled to replenish the antifreeze mixture and prevent formation of rust and corrosion, which can impair the performance of the cooling system and

cause engine damage.

2   At the same time the cooling system is serviced, all hoses and the radiator cap should be inspected and, if necessary, replaced (see Section 7).

3   Since antifreeze is a corrosive and poisonous solution, be careful not to spill any of the coolant mixture on the vehicle's paint or your skin. If this happens, rinse immediately with plenty of clean water. Consult your local authorities about the dumping of antifreeze before draining the cooling system. In many areas reclamation centers have been set up to collect automobile oil and drained antifreeze/water mixtures, rather than allowing them to be added to the sewage system.

4   With the engine cold, remove the radiator cap.

5   Move a large container under the radiator to catch the coolant as it is drained.

6   Drain the radiator. Most models are equipped with a drain plug at the bottom. If this drain has excessive corrosion and cannot be turned easily, or if the radiator is not equipped with a drain, disconnect the lower radiator hose to allow the coolant to drain. Be careful that none of the solution is splashed on your skin or into your eyes.

7   If accessible, remove the two engine block drain plugs. There is usually one plug on each side of the engine about halfway back, on the lower edge near the oil pan rail. These will allow the coolant to drain from the engine itself.

8   Disconnect the hose from the coolant reservoir and remove the reservoir. Flush it out with clean water.

9   Place a garden hose in the radiator filler neck and flush the system until the water runs clear at all drain points.

10   In severe cases of contamination or clogging of the radiator, remove it (see Chapter 3) and reverse flush it. This involves inserting the hose in the bottom radiator outlet to allow the clear water to run against the normal flow, draining through the top. A radiator repair shop should be consulted if further cleaning or repair is necessary.

11   When the coolant is regularly drained and the system refilled with the correct antifreeze/water mixture, there should be no need to use chemical cleaners or descalers.

12   To refill the system reconnect the radiator hoses and install the drain plugs securely in the engine. Special thread-sealing tape, available at auto parts stores, should be used on the drain plugs. Install the reservoir and the overflow hose where applicable.

13   Fill the radiator to the base of the filler neck and then add more coolant to the reservoir until it reaches the Full Cold mark.

14   Run the engine until normal operating temperature is reached and, with the engine idling, add coolant to the Full Hot level. Install the radiator and reservoir caps.

15   Always refill the system with a mixture of high quality antifreeze and water in the proportion called for on the antifreeze container or in your owner's manual. Chapter 3 also contains information on antifreeze mixtures.

16   Keep a close watch on the coolant level and the various cooling system hoses during the first few miles of driving. Tighten the hose clamps and add more coolant as necessary.

27 Wheel bearing check (every 15000 miles or 15 months)

1   With the vehicle securely supported on jackstands. spin the wheels and check for noise, rolling resistance and freeplay. Grasp the top of the tire with one hand and the bottom of the tire with the other. Move the tire in and out. If it moves more than 0.005 inch, the bearings should be checked and, if necessary, replaced.

2   The wheel bearings on these models are of the sealed type which cannot be serviced and must be replaced with new ones if a fault develops. See Chapter 10 for the proper procedure.

28 Automatic transaxle fluid and filter change (every 30000 miles or 30 months)

Refer to illustrations 28.7, 28.9, 28.11 and 28.17

1   At the specified time intervals the automatic transaxle fluid should be changed and the filter replaced.

2   Since there is no drain plug, the transaxle oil pan must be removed to drain the fluid. Before beginning work, purchase the specified transmission fluid (see *Recommended lubricants and fluids* at the front of this Chapter) , and a new filter.

3   Other tools necessary for this job include jackstands to support the vehicle in a raised position, a drain pan capable of holding at least eight pints, newspapers and clean rags.

4   The fluid should be drained immediately after the vehicle has been driven. This will remove any built-up sediment better than if the fluid were cold. Because of this, it is wise to wear protective gloves. Fluid temperature can exceed 350-degrees in a hot transaxle.

5   After the vehicle has been driven to warm up the fluid. raise it and place it on jackstands for access underneath.

6   Move the necessary equipment under the vehicle, being careful not to touch any of the hot exhaust components.

7   Place the drain pan under the transaxle fluid pan and loosen, but do not remove, the bolts at one end of the pan **(see illustration)**.

8   Moving around the pan, loosen all the bolts a little at a time. Be sure the drain pan is in position, as fluid will begin dripping out. Continue in this manner until all of the bolts are removed except for one at each of the corners.

9   While supporting the pan, remove the remaining bolts and lower the pan **(see illustration)**. If necessary, use a screwdriver to

28.7 Begin the automatic transaxle drain pan removal by loosening the bolts at one end

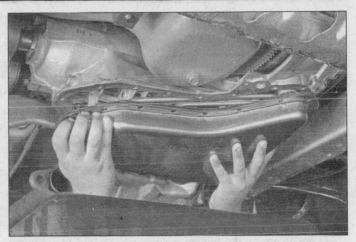

28.9 After draining the fluid, separate the fluid pan from the automatic transaxle

28.11 Remove the automatic transaxle filter by detaching the clip and pulling it straight down

28.17 Be sure to apply thread locking compound to the threads of bolt A

23   Check the fluid level to make sure it is just below the Add mark on the dipstick. Do not allow the fluid level to go above this point as the transaxle would then be overfilled, necessitating the removal of the pan to drain excess fluid.

24   Push the dipstick firmly back into its tube and let the engine idle, with the transaxle in Park, for three minutes. Check the fluid level again and add as necessary to bring the level to just above the add mark. Now drive the vehicle far enough to reach normal operating temperature in the transaxle. This should take just a few miles of highway driving, slightly less in the city. Park the vehicle on a level surface and check the fluid level on the dipstick with the engine idling and the transaxle in Park. The level should now be at the F mark on the dipstick. If not, add more fluid, a little at a time, to bring the level up to this point. Again, do not overfill.

break the gasket seal, but be careful not to damage the pan or transaxle gasket surfaces. Drain the remaining fluid into the drain pan. As this is done check the fluid for metal particles, which may be an indication of internal failure.

10   Now visible at the bottom of the transaxle is the filter/strainer.

11   Remove the filter and O-ring seal **(see illustration)**.

12   Thoroughly clean the transaxle fluid pan with solvent. Check for metal filings or foreign material. Dry with compressed air if available. It is important that all remaining gasket material be removed from the pan mounting flange. Use a gasket scraper or putty knife for this.

13   Clean the filter mounting surface on the valve body. Again, this surface should be smooth and free of any leftover gasket material.

14   Install the new filter with a new O-ring seal.

15   Press the new gasket into place on the pan, making sure all bolt holes line up.

16   Lift the pan up to the bottom of the

transaxle and install the mounting bolts. Tighten the bolts in a diagonal pattern working around the pan. Using a torque wrench, tighten the bolts in a criss-cross pattern to the torque listed in this Chapter's Specifications.

17   When reinstalling the pan on a 3-speed transaxle, you must apply thread locking compound to the threads of bolt A **(see illustration)** to prevent fluid leaks.

18   Lower the vehicle.

19   Open the hood and remove the transaxle fluid dipstick.

20   Add the specified amount and type of fluid to the transaxle through the filler tube. Use a funnel to prevent spills. It is best to add a little fluid at a time, continually checking the level with the dipstick. Allow the fluid time to drain into the pan.

21   With the selector lever in Park, apply the parking brake and start the engine without depressing the accelerator pedal (if possible). Do not race the engine - run it at idle only.

22   With the engine idling, check the level on the dipstick. Look under the vehicle for leaks around the transaxle oil pan mating surface.

29   Air filter and PCV filter replacement (every 30000 miles or 30 months)

Refer to illustrations 29.4a, 29.4b, 29.8a and 29.8b

1   At the specified intervals, the air filter and PCV filter should be replaced with new ones. A thorough program of preventative maintenance would call for the two filters to be inspected between changes.

2   On some models, the air filter is located inside the air cleaner housing on the top of the engine. On other models the air cleaner housing is located on the left side of the engine compartment. On some models the filter is replaced by removing the wing nut at the top of the air cleaner assembly and lifting off the top plate. On other models, spring clips must be released to lift the cover off of the housing.

3   While the top plate is off, be careful not to drop anything down into the carburetor

4   Lift the air filter element out of the hous

29.4a Removing the air filter element

29.4b On models with Multi-Port Fuel Injection, the air filter is located in a housing in the left side of the engine compartment (some are round like this one - others are square and plastic and have a flat, pleated filter element)

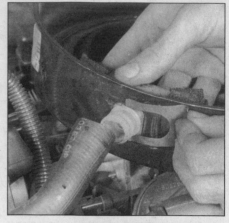

29.8a Removing the PCV filter housing retaining clip

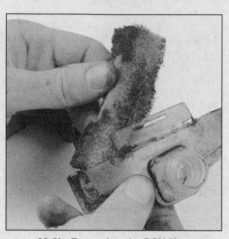

29.8b Removing the PCV filter

ing **(see illustrations)**. On models with a flat, pleated paper filter element, be sure to note which way the filter is installed.

5   Wipe out the inside of the air cleaner housing with a clean rag.

6   Place the new filter into the air cleaner housing. Make sure it seats properly in the bottom of the housing.

7   The PCV filter is also located inside the

air cleaner housing. Remove the top plate and air filter as described previously, then locate the PCV filter on the side of the housing.

8   Remove the PCV filter housing clip and remove the PCV filter **(see illustrations)**.

9   Install a new PCV filter and the air filter.

10   Install the top plate and any hoses which were disconnected.

---

30   Oxygen sensor replacement (every 30000 miles or 30 months)

Refer to illustration 30.1

1   The sensor is located in the exhaust manifold or exhaust pipe and is accessible from under the vehicle or in the engine compartment **(see illustration)**.

2   Since the oxygen sensor may be difficult to remove with the engine cold, begin by operating the engine until it has warmed to at least 120-degrees F.

3   Disconnect the oxygen sensor electrical connector.

4   Note the position of the silicone boot and carefully back out the oxygen sensor from the exhaust manifold. Be advised that excessive force may damage the threads. Inspect the oxygen sensor for damage. **Note:** *Special care must be taken when handling the oxygen sensor:*

a) *The oxygen sensor has a permanently attached pigtail and connector, which should not be removed from the sensor. Damage or removal of the pigtail or connector can adversely affect its operation*

b) *Grease, dirt and other contaminants should be kept away from the electrical connector and the louvered end of the sensor.*

c) *Do not use cleaning solvents of any kind on the oxygen sensor.*

d) *Do not drop or roughly handle the sensor.*

e) *The silicone boot must be installed in the correct position to prevent the boot from being melted and to allow the sensor to operate properly.*

5   A special anti-seize compound must be used on the threads of the oxygen sensor to aid in future removal. New or replacement sensors will have this compound already applied. but if for any reason an oxygen sensor is removed and then reinstalled, the threads must be coated before reinstallation.

6   Install the sensor and tighten it to the torque listed in this Chapter's Specifications.

7   Plug in the electrical connector.

---

31   Positive Crankcase Ventilation (PCV) valve check and replacement (every 30000 miles or 30 months)

Refer to illustrations 31.1 and 31.2

1   On some models the PCV valve is located in the valve cover. A hose runs from the valve to the carburetor base plate or intake manifold. On other models, the valve plugs into the intake manifold and is con-

30.1 The oxygen sensor (arrow) threads into the exhaust manifold

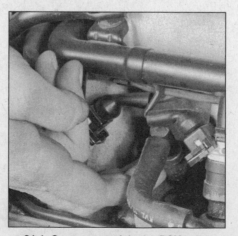

31.1 On some models the PCV valve plugs into the intake manifold

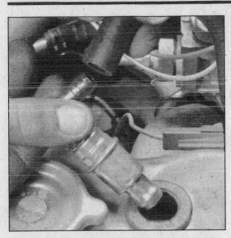

31.2 Removing the PCV valve from the valve cover

32.2 The EGR valve can be checked for free movement by pushing up on the diaphragm

33.2 The EECS canister is located at the front corner of the engine compartment

nected to the valve cover by a hose **(see illustration)**.

2   Pull the valve (with hose attached) from the rubber grommet in the valve cover **(see illustration)** or, on models with the valve mounted in the intake manifold, detach the PCV hose from its fitting on the valve cover.

3   Start the engine and bring it to normal operating temperature.

4   Place your finger over the end of the valve or hose. If the engine speed drops, the valve is working properly. If the speed doesn't drop the valve is faulty and should be replaced with a new one.

5   To replace the valve. pull it from the end of the hose or out of the manifold, noting its installed position and direction.

6   When purchasing a replacement PCV valve, make sure it is for your particular vehicle, model year and engine size. Compare the old valve with the new one to make sure they are the same. Push the valve into the end of the hose until it is seated.

7   Inspect the rubber grommet for damage and replace it with a new one if necessary.

8   Push the PCV valve and hose securely into position.

9   More information on the PCV system can be found in Chapter 6.

32 Exhaust Gas Recirculation (EGR) valve check (every 24000 miles or 24 months)

Refer to illustration 32.2

1   The EGR valve is located on the intake manifold. Most problems in the emissions control system are due to a stuck or corroded EGR valve.

2   With the engine cold to prevent burns, reach under the EGR valve and manually push on the diaphragm. Using moderate pressure, you should be able to press the diaphragm up and down inside the housing **(see illustration)**.

3   If the diaphragm does not move or moves only with much effort, replace the

EGR valve with a new one. If in doubt about the condition of the valve, compare the free movement of your EGR valve with a new valve.

4   See Chapter 6 for more information on the EGR system.

33 Evaporative Emissions Control System (EECS) check (every 24000 miles or 24 months)

Refer to illustration 33.2

1   The function of the Evaporative Emissions Control System is to capture fuel vapors from the fuel tank and carburetor and intake manifold before they can escape into the atmosphere, store them in a charcoal canister and then burn them during normal engine operation.

2   The most common symptom of a fault in the evaporative emissions system is a strong fuel odor in the engine compartment. If a fuel odor is detected, inspect the charcoal canister, located at the front corner of the engine compartment, and system hoses **(see illustration)**.

3   A simple check of system operation is to place your hand under the canister with the engine at normal operating temperature and slowly increase engine speed. If air can be felt being sucked into the bottom of the canister the system is operating properly.

4   The evaporative emissions control system is explained in more detail in Chapter 6.

34 Ignition timing check and adjustment (every 24000 miles or 24 months)

Refer to illustration 34.2

Note: *It is imperative that the procedures included on the Vehicle Emissions Control Information label be followed when adjusting the ignition timing. The label will include all information concerning preliminary steps to*

be performed before adjusting the timing as well as the timing specifications. Two different methods of timing are used. The conventional method and on some four-cylinder models the averaging method. The VECI label will tell you which method is used with your engine.

1   Locate the VECI label under the hood and read through and perform all preliminary instructions concerning ignition timing.

2   Locate the timing scale located beside the crankshaft pulley. The O or T mark represents Top Dead Center (TDC). The pointer plate will be marked in two-degree increments and should have the proper timing mark for your particular vehicle noted. If not, count back from the O or T mark the correct number of degrees BTDC (*Before* Top Dead Center), as noted on the VECI label, and mark the scale **(see illustration)**.

3   Locate the notch on the crankshaft balancer or pulley and mark it with chalk or a dab of paint so it will be visible under the timing light.

4   Start the engine, warm it up to the normal operating temperature and shut it off. Turn off all lights and other electrical loads.

5   With the ignition off, connect the pickup lead of the timing light to the number one

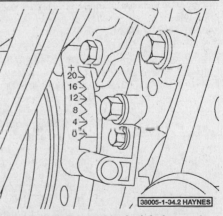

38005-1-34.2 HAYNES

34.2 Location of a typical timing scale

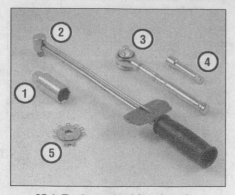

35.1 Tools required for changing spark plugs

1   *Spark plug socket - This will have special padding inside to protect the spark plug's porcelain insulator*
2   *Torque wrench - Although not mandatory, using this tool is the best way to ensure the plugs are tightened properly*
3   *Ratchet - Standard hand tool to fit the spark plug socket*
4   *Extension - Depending on model and accessories, you may need special extensions and universal joints to reach one or more of the plugs*
5   *Spark plug gap gauge - This gauge for checking the gap comes in a variety of styles. Make sure the gap for your engine is included*

35.5a Spark plug manufacturers recommend using a wire-type gauge when checking the gap - if the wire does not slide between the electrodes with a slight drag, adjustment is required

35.5b To change the gap, bend the side electrode only, as indicated by the arrows, and be very careful not to crack or chip the porcelain insulator surrounding the center electrode

spark plug wire. Connect the timing light power leads according to the manufacturer's instructions.
6   Start the engine, aim the timing light at the timing mark by the crankshaft pulley and note which timing mark the notch on the pulley is lining up with.
7   If the notch is not lining up with the correct mark. loosen the distributor hold-down bolt and rotate the distributor until the notch is lined up with the correct timing mark.
8   Retighten the hold-down bolt and recheck the timing.
9   Turn off the engine and disconnect the timing light. Reconnect the number one spark plug wire, if removed, and any other components which were disconnected.

Averaging method

10   The averaging method is used to bring the timing of each cylinder into alignment with the base timing specification. Models using the averaging method have a double-notched crankshaft pulley with the notch for the number one cylinder scribed across all three edges of the pulley. Another notch, scribed across only the center section of the pulley, is located 180-degrees away. The coil wire, instead of the number one spark plug wire, is used to trigger the timing light. Because the trigger signal is picked up at the coil wire, each spark firing causes a flash from the timing light. This makes the timing notch appear to jiggle since each firing is

indicated. Adjustment is accomplished by centering the total apparent notch width over the specified timing mark.
11   On electronic spark timing equipped models disconnect the four terminal EST plug at the distributor so the engine will operate in the bypass timing mode.
12   Connect the timing light, following the manufacturer's instructions. Be very careful not to tangle the wires in moving engine parts.
13   Clamp the timing light inductive pickup around the high tension coil wire. Peel back the protective plastic sheath on the wire when installing the timing light inductive pickup.
14   Loosen the distributor clamp nut sufficiently to allow the distributor to be rotated for adjustment.
15   Start the engine, aim the timing light at the timing tab and, if necessary, rotate the distributor to center the notch width over the specified mark. Remember that a slight jiggling of the pulley notch is normal.
16   Shut the engine off and tighten the distributor clamp nut, taking care not to move the distributor.
17   Recheck the timing and repeat the adjustment if necessary.
18   Plug in the EST connector, replace the plastic cover on the coil wire and remove the timing light. **Note:** *On some models it will be necessary to remove and replace the ECM 1 fuse to clear the trouble code memory.*

35   Spark plug replacement (every 30000 miles or 30 months)

Refer to illustrations 35.1, 35.5a, 35.5b and 35.10
1   In most cases, tools necessary for a spark plug replacement include a plug wrench or spark plug socket which fits onto a ratchet wrench (this special socket will be

insulated inside to protect the porcelain insulator) and a wire-type feeler gauge to check and adjust the spark plug gap **(see illustration)**.
2   The spark plugs are located on each side of V6 engines and on the front (radiator) side of four-cylinder engines.
3   The best procedure to follow when replacing the spark plugs is to purchase the new spark plugs beforehand, adjust them to the proper gap and then replace each plug one at a time. When buying the new spark plugs, it is important to obtain the correct plugs for your specific engine. This information can be found on the *Vehicle Emissions Control Information* label, located under the hood, or in the owner's manual. If differences exist between these sources, purchase the spark plug type specified on the label because the information was printed for your specific engine.
4   With the new spark plugs at hand, allow the engine to cool completely before attempting plug removal. During this time, each of the new spark plugs can be inspected for defects and the gaps can be checked.
5   The gap is checked by inserting the proper thickness gauge between the electrodes at the tip of the plug. The gap between the electrodes should be the same as that given in this Chapter's Specifications or on the *Vehicle Emissions Control Information* label. The wire should just touch each of the electrodes **(see illustration)**. If the gap is incorrect, use the notched adjuster on the feeler gauge body to bend the curved side electrode slightly until the proper gap is achieved **(see illustration)**. If the side electrode is not exactly over the center electrode, use the notched adjuster to align the two. Check for cracks in the porcelain insulator, indicating the spark plug should not be used.
6   With the engine cool, remove the spark plug wire from one spark plug. Do this by grabbing the boot at the end of the wire, not

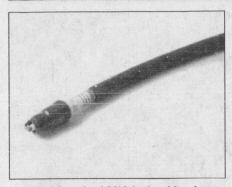

35.10 A length of 5/16-inch rubber hose eases the job of installing a spark plug in difficult to reach areas

36.3 Releasing the distributor cap hold-down latches

the wire itself. Sometimes it is necessary to use a twisting motion while the boot and plug wire are pulled free.

7   If compressed air is available, use it to blow any dirt or foreign material away from the spark plug area. A common bicycle pump will also work. The idea here is to eliminate the possibility of material falling into the cylinder as the spark plug is removed.

8   Place the spark plug wrench or socket over the plug and remove it from the engine by turning in a counterclockwise direction.

9   Compare the spark plug with those shown in the accompanying photos to get an indication of the overall running condition of the engine.

10   Due to the angle at which the spark plugs must be installed on most engines, installation will be simplified by inserting the end of the new spark plug into a 5/16-inch rubber hose, a few inches long **(see illustration)**. This procedure serves two purposes. The rubber hose gives you flexibility for establishing the proper angle of plug insertion in the head and, should the threads be improperly aligned, the rubber hose will slip on the spark plug when it meets resistance, preventing cross-threading into the head.

11   After installing the plug to the limit of the hose grip, tighten it with the socket. It is a

good idea to use a torque wrench for this to insure that the plug is seated correctly. The correct torque figure is included in this Chapter's Specifications.

12   Before pushing the spark plug wire onto the end of the plug, inspect it following the procedures outlined in Section 36.

13   Attach the plug wire to the new spark plug, again using a twisting motion on the boot until it is firmly seated on the spark plug. Make sure the wire is routed away from the exhaust manifold.

14   Allow the above procedure for the remaining spark plugs, replacing them one at a time to prevent mixing up the spark plug wires.

36   Spark plug wires, distributor cap and rotor check and replacement (every 30000 miles or 30 months)

Refer to illustrations 36.3, 36.4, 36.6, 36.7, 36.17a and 36.17b

1   Begin this procedure by making a visual check of the spark plug wires while the engine is running. In a darkened garage (do

this at night with the garage door open) start the engine and observe each plug wire. Be careful not to come into contact with any moving engine parts. If there is a break in the wire, you will see arcing or a small spark at the damaged area. If arcing is noticed, make a note to obtain new wires, then allow the engine to cool and check the distributor cap and rotor.

2   Disconnect the negative cable from the battery. **Caution:** *If the vehicle is equipped with a Delco Loc II audio system, make sure you have the correct activation code before disconnecting the battery. See the information at the front of this manual for the radio re-activation procedure.* At the distributor, disconnect the ECM connector and the coil connector (coil-in-cap models) or coil wire (models with a separately mounted coil).

3   Remove the distributor cap by placing a screwdriver on the slotted head of each latch. Press down on the latch and turn it 90-degrees to release the hooked end at the bottom **(see illustration)**. On some engines, due to restricted working room, a stubby screwdriver will work best. With all latches disengaged, separate the cap from the distributor with the spark plug wires still attached. **Note:** *Some models may use screws instead of latches.*

4   Inspect the cap for cracks and other damage. Closely examine the terminals on the inside of the cap for excessive corrosion **(see illustration)**. Slight pitting is normal. Deposits on the terminals may be removed with a small file.

5   If the inspection reveals damage to the cap, make a note to obtain a replacement for your particular engine, then examine the rotor.

6   The rotor is visible, with the cap removed, at the top of the distributor shaft. It is held in place by two screws. Remove the screws and the rotor **(see illustration)**.

7   Inspect the rotor for cracks and other damage. Carefully check the condition of the metal contact at the top of the rotor for excessive burning and pitting **(see illustra-**

36.4 Inspect the distributor cap for cracks and carbon tracks and the terminals (arrow) for corrosion and damage

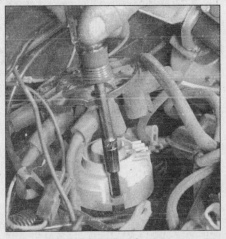

36.6 Removing the rotor

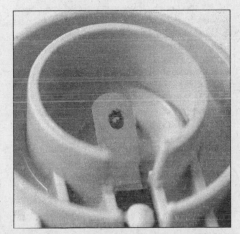

36.7 Close-up of the metal contact on this rotor reveals a normal wear pattern

36.17a Disengaging the spark plug wire retaining ring clip from the top of the distributor cap

36.17b Removing the plug wire retainer from the cap

tion). On coil-in-cap models, also check the top of the rotor for carbon tracks. This is a sign of moisture contamination due to a leaking seal between the distributor cap and the coil. The rotor and seal should be replaced with new ones if carbon tracks are visible.

8   If it is determined that a new rotor is required, make a note to that effect. If the rotor and cap are in good condition, reinstall them at this time. Be sure to apply a small dab of silicone lubricant to the terminals inside the cap before installing it. Note that the rotor has two raised pegs on the bottom and that it has a wide slot and a narrow slot. Make sure that the slots are correctly aligned and that the pegs are firmly seated with the rotor is installed.

9   If the cap must be replaced, do not reinstall it. Leave it off the distributor with the wires still connected.

10   If the spark plug wires are being replaced, now is the time to obtain a new set, along with a new cap and rotor as determined in the checks above. Purchase a wire set for your particular engine, pre-cut to the proper size, with the rubber boots already installed.

11   If the spark plug wires passed the check in Step 1, they should be checked further as follows.

12   Examine the wires one at a time to avoid mixing them up.

13   Disconnect the plug wire from the spark plug. A removal tool can be used for this, or you can grab the rubber boot, twist slightly and then pull the wire free. Do not pull on the wire itself, only on the rubber boot.

14   Inspect inside the boot for corrosion, which will look like a white crusty powder. Some models use a conductive white silicone lubricant, which should not be mistaken for corrosion.

15   Push the wire and boot back onto the end of the spark plug. It should be a tight fit on the plug end. If not, remove the wire and use pliers to carefully crimp the metal connector inside the wire boot until the fit is snug.

16   Using a clean rag, clean the entire length of the wire. Remove all built-up dirt and grease. As this is done, check for burns, cracks and any other form of damage. Bend the wires in several places to ensure that the conductive wire inside has not hardened.

17   The wires should be checked at the distributor cap (or coils, on models with a distributorless ignition system) in the same manner. On four-cylinder engines and later model V6 engines, remove the wire from the cap by pulling on the boot, again examining the wires one at a time, and reinstalling each one after examination. Apply new silicone lubricant before installation. On early models with V6 engines, the spark plug wire boots are connected to a circular retaining ring attached to the distributor cap. Release the locking tabs, turn the ring upside down and check all wire boots at the same time **(see illustrations)**.

18   If the wires appear to be in good condition, reinstall the retaining ring (some models) and make sure that all wires are secure at both ends. If the cap and rotor are also in good condition, the check is finished. Reconnect the wires at the distributor (or coil) and the battery.

19   If it was determined that new wires are required, obtain them at this time, along with a new cap and rotor if so determined by the checks above.

20   If a new cap is being installed on a coil-in-cap type distributor, the coil and cover from the cap being replaced should be transferred to the new cap.

21   Remove the three coil attaching screws and lift off the cover.

22   Remove the coil attaching screws, disconnect the leads and separate the coil from the distributor.

23   Attach the new coil to the cap by reversing Steps 21 and 22. Use a new seal between the coil and cap and be sure to lubricate the seal with multi-purpose grease.

24   Attach the rotor to the distributor. Make sure that the carbon brush is properly installed in the cap, as a side gap between the carbon brush and the rotor will cause rotor burn-through and/or damage to the distributor cap.

25   If new wires are being installed, replace them one at a time. **Note:** *It is important to replace wires one at a time, noting the routing as each wire is removed and installed, to maintain the correct firing order and to prevent cross-firing.*

26   Attach the cap to the distributor, reconnecting all wires disconnected earlier, then reconnect the battery cable.

37   Early Fuel Evaporation (EFE) system check (every 24000 miles or 24 months)

Refer to illustrations 37.1 and 37.13

1   The EFE system is designed to recirculate exhaust gases to help preheat the induction system, thereby improving cold engine driveability and, by reducing the time that the choke is closed, reducing exhaust emissions levels. There are two basic types of EFE systems. The first is a valve in the exhaust system, between the exhaust manifold and the exhaust pipe, which is called a vacuum servo type **(see illustration)**. The second type is an electrically heated unit located between the carburetor base and the intake manifold. The procedures which follow in this Section are concerned only with the first type. If you have the electrically heated type, see Chapter 6 for more information.

2   Locate the EFE valve and actuator, which is bolted to the exhaust manifold.

3   With the engine cold, have an assistant start it. Observe the movement of the actuator link. It should immediately be drawn into the diaphragm, closing the valve.

4   If the valve does not close it could be seized. Shut off the engine and apply penetrating oil to the shaft at the pivot points in the valve assembly, allow it to work, then restart the engine and observe the actuator link. If it still does not close, disconnect the vacuum hose at the actuator.

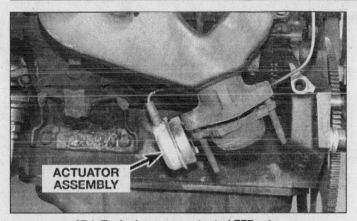

37.1 Typical vacuum-actuated EFE valve

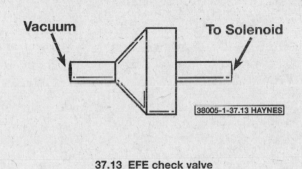

37.13 EFE check valve

5 Hold your thumb over the disconnected hose. If vacuum is felt, test the actuator and valve as follows.

6 Attach a piece of hose to the actuator vacuum outlet, apply vacuum to the hose, then quickly place your thumb over it. If the actuator holds vacuum, it is operating correctly and the valve is defective. See Chapter 6 and replace the valve assembly.

7 If the actuator does not hold vacuum, the actuator diaphragm is defective. See Chapter 6 and replace the actuator.

8 If no vacuum was felt at the disconnected vacuum source hose in Step 5, either the hose is crimped or plugged, or the EFE solenoid is not functioning properly.

9 Check the hose for cracks and restrictions and replace it as necessary. Because of its interrelationship with the ECM, the solenoid must be tested by a dealer service department.

10 With the hose again connected to the EFE actuator, continue to warm up the engine until it reaches normal operating temperature.

11 Make sure that the actuating link has moved the valve to the open position.

12 If the valve does not open, remove the hose from the actuator. If the valve opens, there is no air bleed for the valve actuator diaphragm, the electrical solenoid plunger is stuck in the cold mode or the engine is not reaching proper operating temperature. See Chapter 6 to replace the actuator diaphragm.

If the engine is not reaching proper operating temperature, check the thermostat (see Chapter 3). If the valve does not open with the hose removed from the actuator, it may be stuck closed by corrosion.

13 Check the EFE check valve located in the vacuum hose between the carburetor and the EFE solenoid **(see illustration)**.

14 Remove the check valve from the hose and apply vacuum to the tapered end. Air should flow freely through the valve.

15 Vacuum applied to the other (squared off) end of the valve should not flow through and should not leak down for at least one minute.

16 If the check valve fails either test, replace it with a new one.

Notes

Chapter 2 Part A
2.2L four-cylinder engine

Contents

Specifications

General

Cylinder numbers (drivebelt end-to-transaxle end)	1-2-3-4
Firing order	1-3-4-2

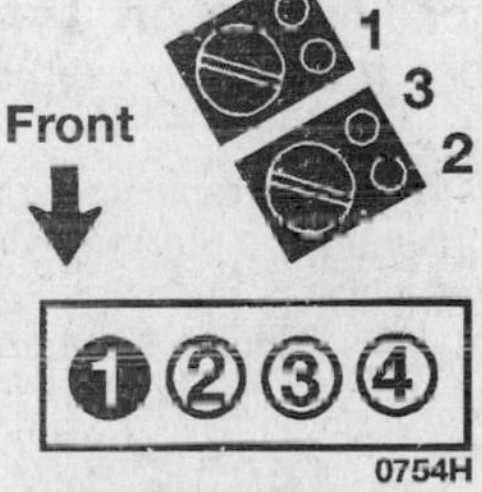

Torque specifications

Ft-lbs (unless otherwise indicated)

Camshaft sprocket bolt	
1995 and earlier	77
1996	95
Crankshaft pulley-to-hub bolts	37
Crankshaft pulley center bolt	77
Cylinder head bolts	
Step 1	
Short bolts	43
Long bolts	46
Step 2	Rotate all bolts an additional 90-degrees
Exhaust manifold fasteners	115 in-lbs
Flywheel bolts	54
Driveplate bolts	52
Intake manifold fasteners	
Upper	22
Lower	24
Oil pan nuts	89 in-lbs
Oil pump mounting bolt	32
Valve cover bolts	89 in-lbs
Rocker arm nuts	22
Timing chain cover bolts	97 in-lbs
Timing chain tensioner bolts	18

Front →

0754H

2.2 liter four-cylinder engine

Cylinder and coil terminal locations

3.6 Remove the rocker arm cover retaining bolts (arrows)

4.2 Loosen the nuts and pivot the rocker arms to one side if just the pushrods are being removed (otherwise, remove the nuts and lift off the pivot balls and rocker arms)

1   General information

This Part of Chapter 2 is devoted to in-vehicle repair procedures for the 2.2 liter four-cylinder overhead valve engine. These engines have cast iron blocks and cast aluminum pistons. The aluminum cylinder head has replaceable valve seats and guides. Stamped steel rocker arms and tubular pushrods actuate the valves.

All information concerning engine removal and installation and engine block and cylinder head overhaul can be found in Part E of this Chapter.

The following repair procedures are based on the assumption the engine is in the vehicle. If the engine has been removed from the vehicle and mounted on a stand, many of the steps outlined in this Part of Chapter 2 will not apply.

The Specifications included in this Part of Chapter 2 apply only to the procedures contained in this Part. Part E of Chapter 2 contains the Specifications necessary for cylinder head and engine block rebuilding.

2   Repair operations possible with the engine in the vehicle

Many major repair operations can be accomplished without removing the engine from the vehicle.

Clean the engine compartment and the exterior of the engine with some type of degreaser before any work is done. It'll make the job easier and help keep dirt out of the internal areas of the engine.

Depending on the components involved, it may be helpful to remove the hood to improve access to the engine as repairs are performed (refer to Chapter 11 if necessary). Cover the fenders to prevent damage to the paint. Special pads are available, but an old bedspread or blanket will also work.

If vacuum, exhaust, oil or coolant leaks develop, indicating a need for gasket or seal replacement, the repairs can generally be

made with the engine in the vehicle. The intake and exhaust manifold gaskets, timing chain cover gasket, oil pan gasket, crankshaft oil seals and cylinder head gasket are all accessible with the engine in place.

Exterior engine components, such as the intake and exhaust manifolds, the oil pan (and the oil pump), the water pump, the starter motor, the alternator and the fuel system components can be removed for repair with the engine in place.

Since the cylinder head can be removed without pulling the engine, valve component servicing can also be accomplished with the engine in the vehicle. Replacement of the timing chain and sprockets is also possible with the engine in the vehicle.

In extreme cases caused by a lack of necessary equipment, repair or replacement of piston rings, pistons, connecting rods and rod bearings is possible with the engine in the vehicle. However, this practice is not recommended because of the cleaning and preparation work that must be done to the components involved.

3   Valve cover - removal and installation

Refer to illustration 3.6

Removal

1   Remove the air cleaner assembly, tagging each hose to be disconnected with a piece of numbered tape to simplify installation.
2   Remove the breather hose from the valve cover.
3   Remove the spark plug wires from the spark plugs and from the valve cover clips.
4   Detach the control cable bracket at the intake plenum and valve cover.
5   Disconnect the cables at the throttle body.
6   Remove the valve cover bolts **(see illustration)**.
7   Detach the valve cover from the head.
Note: *If the cover is stuck to the cylinder*

head, use a block of wood and hammer to dislodge it. If that doesn't work, try to slip a flexible putty knife between the head and cover to break the gasket seal. Don't pry at the cover-to-head joint or damage to the sealing surfaces may occur (leading to oil leaks in the future).

Installation

8   The mating surfaces of the cylinder head and valve cover must be perfectly clean when the cover is installed. Use a gasket scraper to remove all traces of sealant or old gasket, then clean the mating surfaces with lacquer thinner or acetone (if there's sealant or oil on the mating surfaces when the cover is installed, oil leaks may develop). The head and cover are made of aluminum, so be extra careful not to nick or gouge the mating surfaces with the scraper.
9   Clean the mounting bolt threads with a die if necessary to remove any corrosion and restore damaged threads. Make sure the threaded holes in the head are clean - run a tap into them if necessary to remove corrosion and restore damaged threads.
10   Apply a thin coat of RTV-type sealant to the sealing flange on the cover and install a new gasket.
11   Place the valve cover on the cylinder head and install the mounting bolts. Tighten the bolts a little at a time to the torque listed in this Chapter's Specifications. Work from the center out in a spiral pattern.
12   Complete the installation by reversing the removal procedure.

4   Rocker arms and pushrods - removal, inspection and installation

Refer to illustrations 4.2, 4.4a and 4.4b

Removal

1   Refer to Section 3 and detach the valve cover from the cylinder head.
2   Beginning at the front of the cylinder head, loosen the rocker arm nuts **(see illus-**

4.4a The pushrods can be lifted straight out

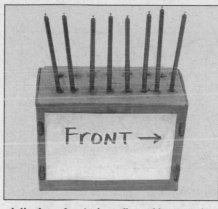

4.4b A perforated cardboard box can be used to store the pushrods to ensure they're reinstalled in their original locations - note the label indicating the front (drivebelt end) of the engine

tration). **Note:** *If the pushrods are the only items being removed, rotate the rocker arms to one side so the pushrods can be lifted out.*

3   Remove the nuts, the rocker arms and the pivot balls and store them in marked containers (they must be reinstalled in their original locations).

4   Remove the pushrods and store them separately to make sure they don't get mixed up during installation **(see illustrations)**.

5   If the pushrod guides must be removed for any reason, make sure they're marked so they can be reinstalled in their original locations.

Inspection

6   Check each rocker arm for wear, cracks and other damage, especially where the pushrods and valve stems contact the rocker arm faces.

7   Make sure the hole at the pushrod end of each rocker arm is open.

8   Check each rocker arm pivot area for wear, cracks and galling. If the rocker arms are worn or damaged, replace them with new ones and use new pivot balls as well.

9   Inspect the pushrods for cracks and excessive wear at the ends. Roll each pushrod across a piece of plate glass to see if it's bent (if it wobbles, it's bent).

Installation

10   Lubricate the lower ends of the pushrods with clean engine oil or moly-base grease and install them in their original locations. Make sure each pushrod seats completely in the lifter socket.

11   Apply moly-base grease to the ends of

the valve stems and the upper ends of the pushrods before positioning the rocker arms and installing the nuts.

12   Set the rocker arms in place, then install the pivot balls and nuts. Apply moly-base grease to the pivot balls to prevent damage to the mating surfaces before engine oil pressure builds up. Tighten the nuts to the torque listed in this Chapter's Specifications

5   Valve springs, retainers and seals - replacement

Refer to illustrations 5.4, 5.9 and 5.17

Note: *Broken valve springs and defective valve stem seals can be replaced without removing the cylinder head. Two special tools and a compressed air source are normally required to perform this operation, so read through this Section carefully and rent or buy the tools before beginning the job. If compressed air isn't available, a length of nylon rope can be used to keep the valves from falling into the cylinder during this procedure.*

1   Refer to Section 3 and remove the valve cover.

2   Remove the spark plug from the cylinder which has the defective component. If all of the valve stem seals are being replaced, all of the spark plugs should be removed.

3   Turn the crankshaft until the piston in the affected cylinder is at top dead center on the compression stroke (refer to Chapter 2,

Part E, for instructions). If you're replacing all of the valve stem seals, begin with cylinder number one and work on the valves for one cylinder at a time. Move from cylinder-to-cylinder following the firing order sequence (see this Chapter's Specifications).

4   Thread an adapter into the spark plug hole **(see illustration)** and connect an air hose from a compressed air source to it. Most auto parts stores can supply the air hose adaptor. **Note:** *Many cylinder compression gauges utilize a screw-in fitting that may work with your air hose quick-disconnect fitting.*

5   Remove the nut, pivot ball and rocker arm for the valve with the defective part and pull out the pushrod. If all of the valve stem seals are being replaced, all of the rocker arms and pushrods should be removed (refer to Section 4).

6   Apply compressed air to the cylinder. **Warning:** *The piston may be forced down by compressed air, causing the crankshaft to turn suddenly. If the wrench used when positioning the number one piston at TDC is still attached to the bolt in the crankshaft nose, it could cause damage or injury when the crankshaft moves.*

7   The valves should be held in place by the air pressure. If the valve faces or seats are in poor condition, leaks may prevent air pressure from retaining the valves - a "valve job" is necessary to correct this problem.

8   If you don't have access to compressed air, an alternative method can be used. Position the piston at a point just before TDC on the compression stroke, then feed a long piece of nylon rope through the spark plug hole until it fills the combustion chamber. Be sure to leave the end of the rope hanging out of the engine so it can be removed easily. Use a large ratchet and socket to rotate the crankshaft in the normal direction of rotation (clockwise) until slight resistance is felt.

9   Stuff shop rags into the cylinder head holes above and below the valves to prevent parts and tools from falling into the engine, then use a valve spring compressor to compress the spring. Remove the keepers with small needle-nose pliers or a magnet **(see illustration)**. **Note:** *A couple of different*

5.9 Once the spring is compressed, remove the keepers with a magnet or needle-nose pliers

5.4 This is what the air hose adapter that threads into the spark plug hole looks like - they're commonly available at auto parts stores

5.17 Keepers don't always stay in place, so apply a small dab of grease to each one, as shown here, before installation - it'll hold them in place on the valve stem as the spring is released

types of tools are available for compressing the valve springs with the head in place. The type shown here utilizes the rocker arm stud and nut for leverage, while the other type grips the lower spring coils and presses on the retainer as the knob is turned. Both types work very well, although the lever type is usually less expensive.

10   Remove the spring retainer and valve spring, then remove the valve guide seal. **Note**: If air pressure fails to hold the valve in the closed position during this operation, the valve face or seat is probably damaged. If so, the cylinder head will have to be removed for additional repair operations.

11   Wrap a rubber band or tape around the top of the valve stem so the valve won't fall into the combustion chamber, then release the air pressure. **Note**: If a rope was used instead of air pressure, turn the crankshaft slightly in the direction opposite normal rotation.

12   Inspect the valve stem for damage. Rotate the valve in the guide and check the end for eccentric movement, which would indicate the valve stem is bent.

13   Move the valve up-and-down in the guide and make sure it doesn't bind. If the valve stem binds, either the valve is bent or the guide is damaged. In either case, the head will have to be removed for repair.

14   Reapply air pressure to the cylinder to retain the valve in the closed position, then remove the tape or rubber band from the valve stem. If a rope was used instead of air pressure, rotate the crankshaft in the normal direction of rotation until slight resistance is felt.

15   Lubricate the valve stem with engine oil and install a new valve guide seal. **Note**: Intake and exhaust valve seals are different.

16   Install the spring in position over the valve.

17   Install the valve spring retainer. Compress the valve spring and carefully install the keepers in the groove. Apply a small dab of grease to the inside of each keeper to hold it in place if necessary **(see illustration)**.

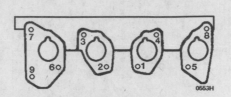

6.8 Intake manifold bolt tightening sequence

Remove the pressure from the spring tool and make sure the keepers are seated.

18   Disconnect the air hose and remove the adapter from the spark plug hole. If a rope was used in place of air pressure, pull it out of the cylinder.

19   Refer to Section 4 and install the rocker arm(s) and pushrod(s).

20   Install the spark plug(s) and hook up the wire(s).

21   Refer to Section 3 and install the valve cover.

22   Start and run the engine, then check for oil leaks and unusual sounds coming from the valve cover area.

6   Intake manifold - removal and installation

Refer to illustration 6.8

Note: This procedure may be easier with the engine rotated forward. To do this, remove the through-bolt from the engine mount strut at the engine bracket **(see Chapter 2C, illustration 17.27)**, pry the engine forward, using the bracket as a pry point, until the "slave hole" in the bottom of the strut aligns with the mount bracket hole. Then re-install the through-bolt. Reverse this procedure to return the engine to its original position.

1   Relieve the fuel pressure (see Chapter 4), then disconnect the negative battery cable from the battery. **Caution**: If the vehicle is equipped with a Delco Loc II audio system, make sure you have the correct activation code before disconnecting the battery. See the information at the front of this manual for the radio activation procedure.

2   Remove the upper intake manifold assembly (see Chapter 4).

3   Raise the front of the vehicle and support it securely on jackstands. Drain the coolant (refer to Chapter 1).

4   If necessary for clearance, remove the power steering pump (if equipped) and tie it aside in an upright position (see Chapter 10).

5   Remove the heater hose and coolant line retaining nut near the bottom of the intake manifold.

6   Remove the mounting nuts from the intake manifold.

7   Separate the intake manifold and gasket from the engine. Scrape all traces of gasket material off the intake manifold and head

gasket mating surfaces. When scraping, be careful not to scratch or gouge the delicate aluminum gasket surfaces on the head and manifold. Clean the surfaces with a rag soaked in lacquer thinner or acetone.

8   Installation is the reverse of removal. Be sure to use a new gasket. Tighten the nuts/bolts to the torque listed in this Chapter's Specifications **(see illustration)**.

9   Add coolant, run the engine and check for leaks and proper operation.

7   Exhaust manifold - removal and installation

Refer to illustration 7.11

Caution: Allow the engine to cool completely before beginning this procedure.

1   Disconnect the negative cable from the battery. **Caution**: If the vehicle is equipped with a Delco Loc II audio system, make sure you have the correct activation code before disconnecting the battery. See the information at the front of this manual for the radio activation procedure.

2   Unplug the oxygen sensor lead.

3   Remove the air cleaner and air duct assembly.

4   Remove the air-inlet resonator from the upper tie bar.

5   Remove the lower air duct.

6   Disconnect the upper engine mounting torque strut from the engine **(see Chapter 2C, illustration 17.27)**.

7   Remove the nuts and bolts and disconnect the engine strut bracket from the cylinder head.

8   Remove the drivebelt, the alternator and the alternator rear support bracket (see Chapters 1 and 5).

9   Remove the oil level dipstick and dipstick holder.

10   Raise the front of the vehicle, support it securely on jackstands and apply the parking brake. Block the rear wheels to keep the vehicle from rolling off the jackstands. Unbolt the exhaust pipe from the manifold. Lower the vehicle.

11   Remove the exhaust manifold-to-cylinder head nuts/bolts **(see illustration)**, pull the manifold off the engine and lift it out of the exhaust pipe flange. Remove and discard the gasket.

12   Scrape all traces of gasket material off the exhaust manifold and cylinder head mating surfaces. Be careful not to scratch or gouge the delicate aluminum cylinder head or exhaust leaks will develop. Wipe the surfaces clean with a rag soaked in lacquer thinner or acetone.

13   Clean all bolt and stud threads before installation. A wire brush can be used on the manifold mounting studs, while a tap works well when cleaning the cylinder head bolt holes.

14   If a new manifold is being installed, transfer the oxygen sensor from the old manifold to the new one.

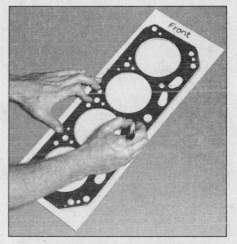

7.11 Remove the exhaust manifold retaining nuts (arrows)

8.11a To avoid mixing up the head bolts, use the new gasket to transfer the bolt hole pattern to a piece of cardboard, then punch holes in the cardboard to accept the bolts

15   Installation is the reverse of removal. Be sure to use a new gasket and tighten the nuts/bolts to the torque listed in this Chapter's Specifications. Work in a spiral pattern from the center out.

8   Cylinder head - removal and installation

Caution: *Allow the engine to cool completely before beginning this procedure.*

Note: *On vehicles with high mileage and during an engine overhaul, camshaft lobe height should be checked prior to cylinder head removal (see Chapter 2, Part E for instructions).*

Removal

Refer to illustrations 8.11a and 8.11b

1   Relieve the fuel pressure (see Chapter 4). Disconnect the cable from the negative battery terminal. **Caution:** *If the vehicle is equipped with a Delco Loc II audio system, make sure you have the correct activation code before disconnecting the battery. See the information at the front of this manual for the radio activation procedure.*

2   Remove the alternator and brackets as described in Chapter 5.

3   Remove the intake manifold as described in Section 6.

4   Remove the exhaust manifold as described in Section 7.

5   Unbolt the drivebelt tensioner bracket.

6   Unbolt the power steering pump (if equipped) and set it aside without disconnecting the hoses (see Chapter 10).

7   Disconnect any remaining wires, hoses, fuel and vacuum lines from the cylinder head. Be sure to label them to simplify reinstallation.

8   Disconnect the spark plug wires and remove the spark plugs. Be sure the plug wires are labeled to simplify reinstallation.

9   Remove the valve cover (see Section 3).

10   Remove the rocker arms and pushrods (see Section 4).

11   Using the new head gasket, outline the cylinders and bolt pattern on a piece of cardboard **(see illustration)**. Be sure to indicate the front of the engine for reference. Punch holes at the bolt locations. Loosen each of the cylinder head mounting bolts 1/4-turn at a time until they can be removed by hand **(see illustration)**. Store the bolts in the cardboard holder as they're removed - this will ensure they are reinstalled in their original locations, which is absolutely essential.

12   Lift the head off the engine. If it's stuck, don't attempt to pry it off - you could damage the sealing surfaces. Instead, use a hammer and block of wood to tap the head and break the gasket seal. Place the head on a block of wood to prevent damage to the gasket surface.

13   Remove the cylinder head gasket.

14   Refer to Chapter 2, Part E, for cylinder head disassembly and valve service procedures.

Installation

Refer to illustrations 8.17 and 8.21

15   If a new cylinder head is being installed,

transfer all external parts from the old cylinder head to the new one.

16   If not already done, thoroughly clean the gasket surfaces on the cylinder head and the engine block. Do not gouge or otherwise damage the soft aluminum gasket surfaces.

17   To get the proper torque readings, the threads of the head bolts must be clean **(see illustration)**. This also applies to the threaded holes in the engine block. Run a tap through the holes to ensure they are clean.

18   Place the gasket in position over the engine block dowel pins. Note any marks like "THIS SIDE UP" and install the gasket accordingly.

19   Carefully lower the cylinder head onto the engine, over the dowel pins and the gasket.

20   Install the bolts finger tight. Don't tighten any of the bolts at this time.

21   Tighten each of the bolts in 1/4-turn increments in the recommended sequence

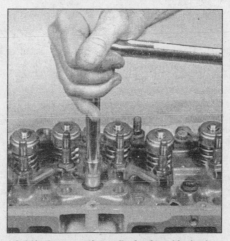

8.11b Loosen the cylinder head bolts in 1/4-turn increments to avoid warping the head

8.17 A die should be used to remove corrosion and sealant from the head bolt threads prior to installation

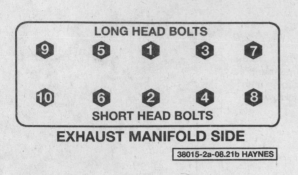

LONG HEAD BOLTS

| 9 | 5 | 1 | 3 | 7 |

| 10 | 6 | 2 | 4 | 8 |

SHORT HEAD BOLTS

EXHAUST MANIFOLD SIDE

38015-2a-08.21b HAYNES

8.21 Cylinder head bolt tightening sequence

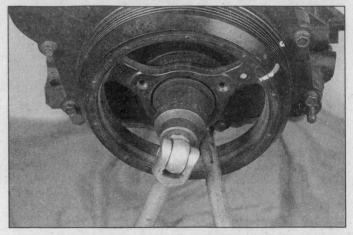

10.4a The crankshaft pulley can be held with a bar while the bolt is loosened or tightened

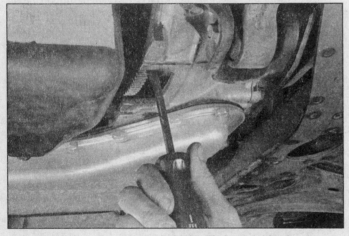

10.4b Have an assistant hold the ring gear with a large screwdriver as the pulley-to-crankshaft bolt is loosened/tightened

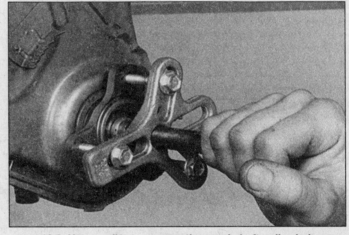

10.6 Use a puller to remove the crankshaft pulley hub

(see illustration). Note that the rear bolts have a different torque specification than the front bolts. Continue tightening in the recommended sequence until the torque (and angle of rotation) specified in this Chapter is reached. Mark each bolt with a felt-tip marker each time you tighten it to make sure none of the bolts have been left out of the sequence.

22   The remaining installation steps are the reverse of removal.

23   Be sure to refill the cooling system and change the oil and filter (see Chapter 1).

9   Hydraulic lifters - removal, inspection and installation

This procedure is essentially the same as for the 2.5L four-cylinder engine (see Chapter 2, Part B), except there's no pushrod cover to remove. You'll need a long magnetic tool, scribe or lifter removal tool, since you'll have to reach down into the cylinder block to remove the lifters.

10   Crankshaft pulley - removal and installation

Refer to illustrations 10.4a, 10.4b and 10.6

Removal

1   Remove the cable from the negative battery terminal. **Caution:** *If the vehicle is equipped with a Delco Loc II audio system, make sure you have the correct activation code before disconnecting the battery. See the information at the front of this manual for the radio activation procedure.*

2   Remove the drivebelt (see Chapter 1).

3   Raise the front of the vehicle and support it securely on jackstands. Remove the right front tire and the inner fender splash shield.

4   Remove the crankshaft pulley-to-crankshaft bolt **(see illustration)**. A breaker bar will probably be needed, since the bolt is very tight. If necessary, remove the lower bellhousing cover and insert a large screwdriver into the teeth of the flywheel/driveplate ring gear to prevent the crankshaft from turning **(see illustration)**.

5   Remove the three bolts that attach the pulley to the hub.

6   Using a puller, remove the crankshaft pulley or hub from the crankshaft **(see illustration)**.

Installation

7   Refer to Section 11 for the oil seal replacement procedure.

8   Apply a thin layer of clean multi-purpose grease to the seal contact surface of the hub.

9   Position the hub on the crankshaft and slide it through the seal until it bottoms against the crankshaft gear. Note that the slot (keyway) in the hub must be aligned with the Woodruff key in the end of the crankshaft. The pulley-to-crankshaft bolt can be used to press the hub into position.

10   Tighten the pulley-to-crankshaft bolt to the torque listed in this Chapter's Specifications.

11   The remaining installation steps are the reverse of removal.

12.5 The timing chain cover bolt locations

13.9 Align the camshaft and crankshaft sprocket timing marks with the tabs on the timing chain tensioner (arrows)

11 Crankshaft front oil seal - replacement

1 Remove the crankshaft pulley (see Section 10).

2 Pry the old oil seal out with a seal removal tool or a screwdriver. Be very careful not to nick or otherwise damage the crankshaft in the process. Wrap the screwdriver tip with vinyl tape to protect the crankshaft.

3 Apply a thin coat of RTV-type sealant to the outer edge of the new seal. Lubricate the seal lip with moly-base grease or clean engine oil.

4 Place the seal squarely in position in the bore and drive it into place with a seal driver.

5 If you don't have a seal driver, carefully tap the seal into place with a large socket or piece of pipe and a hammer. The outer diameter of the socket or pipe should be the same size as the seal outer diameter. Make sure the seal is seated completely in the bore.

6 Install the crankshaft pulley (see Section 10).

7 Reinstall the remaining parts in the reverse order of removal.

8 Start the engine and check for oil leaks at the seal.

12 Timing chain cover - removal and installation

Refer to illustration 12.5

1 Remove the crankshaft pulley (and hub, if equipped) as described in Section 10.

2 Remove the oil pan (see Section 15).

3 Remove the bolts holding the power steering pump and position it aside.

4 Remove the alternator bolts and position it aside.

5 Remove the drivebelt tensioner and bracket (see illustration 8.5) and the timing chain cover-to-block bolts, then detach the cover (see illustration).

6 Using a scraper and degreaser, remove all old gasket material from the sealing surfaces of the timing chain cover, engine block and oil pan.

13.10 Press the tensioner in and insert an appropriate size drill bit through the hole to retain the tensioner in the retracted position

7 If necessary, replace the front oil seal by carefully prying it out of the cover with a large screwdriver. Don't distort the cover.

8 Install the new seal with the spring side toward the inside of the cover. Drive the seal into place using a seal installation tool or a large socket and hammer. A block of wood will also work.

9 Use a thin coat of RTV-type sealant to position a new gasket on the timing chain cover.

10 Place the cover in position over the dowel pins on the block.

11 Install the bolts that secure the cover to the block, then tighten all of them to the torque listed in this Chapter's Specifications. Follow a criss-cross pattern to avoid distorting the cover.

12 Install the oil pan (see Section 15).

13 Complete the installation by reversing the removal procedure.

13 Timing chain and sprockets - inspection, removal and installation

Refer to illustrations 13.9, 13.10 and 13.11

9 Temporarily install the crankshaft pulley

13.11 Wedge a prybar against two bolts in the temporarily installed crankshaft hub to hold the crankshaft while loosening the camshaft sprocket bolt

hub and bolt. Rotate the crankshaft until the timing marks on the crankshaft and camshaft sprockets align with the tabs on the chain tensioner housing (see illustration). **Note:** *Before removing the timing chain tensioner, check it carefully. Measure the distance from the hole in the bracket to the unworn surface of the timing chain tensioner shoe. It should not exceed 5/16 inch (8 mm). If out of limits, replace the tensioner, timing chain and both sprockets. This excessive play in the gears and chain can only be removed by installing new parts.*

10 Push the spring back on the timing chain tensioner and insert an appropriate size drill bit into the hole to retain it in the retracted position (see illustration).

11 Use a prybar against two bolts in the crankshaft balancer hub (installed temporarily) to keep the engine from turning while removing the camshaft bolt (see illustration). Do not turn the camshaft in the process (if you do, realign the timing marks before the sprocket is removed).

12 Use two large screwdrivers to carefully pry the camshaft sprocket off the camshaft dowel pin (it may come off easily with no tools required), and remove the sprocket and chain.

Installation

13   Mesh the timing chain with the camshaft sprocket, then engage it with the crankshaft sprocket. The timing marks should be aligned as shown in **illustration 13.9**. **Note:** *If the crankshaft has been disturbed, turn it until the mark stamped on the crankshaft sprocket is pointing at the projection on the tensioner. If the camshaft was turned, install the sprocket temporarily and turn the camshaft until the timing marks align.*

14   Install the camshaft sprocket bolt and tighten it to the torque listed in this Chapter's Specifications.

15   Press the timing chain against the tensioner, pull out the pin retaining the spring and release the tensioner.

16   Lubricate the chain and sprocket with clean engine oil. Rotate the engine through two complete revolutions and check the alignment of the timing marks again.

17   Install the timing chain cover, using a new gasket and tighten the cover bolts to the torque listed in this Chapter's Specifications.

18   Install the oil pan.

19   The remaining installation steps are the reverse of removal.

14 Camshaft and bearings - removal, inspection and installation

Due to the fact the engine is mounted transversely in the vehicle, there isn't enough room to remove the camshaft with the engine in place. Therefore, the procedure is covered in Chapter 2, Part E.

15 Oil pan - removal and installation

Refer to illustration 15.22

1   Warm up the engine, then drain the oil and remove the oil filter (see Chapter 1).

2   Detach the cable from the negative battery terminal. **Caution:** *If the vehicle is equipped with a Delco Loc II audio system, make sure you have the correct activation code before disconnecting the battery. See the information at the front of this manual for the radio activation procedure.*

3   Remove the air cleaner and air-duct assembly.

4   Remove the drivebelt (see Chapter 1).

5   Disconnect the upper engine mounting strut from the engine bracket.

6   Support the engine from above with a hoist or an engine support fixture.

7   Loosen the right front wheel lug nuts, then raise the vehicle and support it securely on jackstands.

8   Remove the right front wheel and tire.

9   Remove the right-side engine splash shield.

10   Remove the exhaust pipe and catalytic converter.

11   On air conditioned models, remove the air conditioner brace at the starter and compressor bracket.

12   Remove the starter and bracket (see Chapter 5).

13   Remove the lower bellhousing cover.

14   On air conditioned models, remove the air conditioner brace.

15   Remove the four right support bolts. Lower the support slightly to gain clearance for oil pan removal.

16   Remove the oil filter extension (automatic transaxle equipped models only).

17   Remove the bolts and nuts securing the oil pan to the engine block.

18   Tap on the pan with a soft-face hammer to break the gasket seal, then detach the oil pan from the engine.

19   Using a gasket scraper, remove all traces of old gasket and/or sealant from the engine block and oil pan. Make sure the threaded bolt holes in the block are clean. Wash the oil pan with solvent and dry it thoroughly.

20   Check the gasket flanges for distortion, particularly around the bolt holes. If necessary, place the pan on a block of wood and use a hammer to flatten and restore the gasket surfaces. Clean the mating surfaces with lacquer thinner or acetone.

21   Place a 2 mm diameter bead of RTV sealant on the oil pan-to-block sealing flanges and the oil pan-to-front cover surface.

22   Apply a thin coat of RTV sealant to the ends of the rear oil pan seal down to the ears. Press the oil pan seal into position **(see illustration)**.

23   Carefully place the oil pan against the block.

24   Install the bolts/nuts and tighten them in 1/4-turn increments to the torque listed in this Chapter's Specifications. Start with the bolts closest to the center of the pan and work out in a spiral pattern. Don't overtighten them or leakage may occur.

25   Reinstall components removed for access to the oil pan.

26   Add oil and install a new filter, run the engine and check for oil leaks.

16 Oil pump - removal and installation

1   Remove the oil pan (see Section 15).

2   Place a large drain pan under the engine.

3   Unbolt the pump from the rear main bearing cap.

4   Lower the pump and extension shaft from the engine.

5   Before installation, prime the pump with engine oil. Pour oil into the pick-up while the pump extension shaft is turned.

6   Attach the pump, extension shaft and retainer to the main bearing cap. While aligning the pump with the dowel pins at the bottom of the main bearing cap, align the top end of the extension shaft with the lower end of the oil pump drive. When aligned properly, it should slip into place easily.

7   Install the pump mounting bolt and tighten it to the torque listed in this Chapter's Specifications.

8   Install the oil pan and add oil (see Section 15).

17 Flywheel/driveplate - removal and installation

Refer to illustrations 17.3 and 17.4

1   Raise the vehicle and support it securely on jackstands, then refer to Chapter 7 and remove the transaxle. If it's leaking, now would be a very good time to replace the front pump seal/O-ring (automatic transaxle only).

2   Remove the pressure plate and clutch disc (Chapter 8 - manual transaxle equipped vehicles). Now is a good time to check/replace the clutch components and pilot bearing.

3   If there is no dowel pin, make some marks on the flywheel/driveplate and crankshaft to ensure correct alignment during reinstallation **(see illustration)**.

15.22 Remove the oil pan mounting bolts (arrows; not all the bolts are visible in this photo)

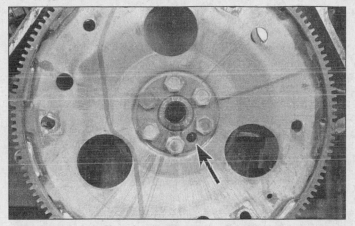

17.3 Most flywheels and driveplates have locating dowels (arrow) - if the one you're working on doesn't, make some marks to ensure correct installation

17.4 A large screwdriver wedged in the starter ring gear teeth or one of the holes in the driveplate can be used to keep the flywheel/driveplate from turning as the mounting bolts are removed

4   Remove the bolts that secure the flywheel/driveplate to the crankshaft **(see illustration)**. If the crankshaft turns, wedge a screwdriver through the openings in the driveplate (automatic transaxle) or against the flywheel ring gear teeth (manual transaxle). Since the flywheel is fairly heavy, be sure to support it while removing the last bolt.

5   Remove the flywheel/driveplate from the crankshaft.

6   Clean the flywheel to remove grease and oil. Inspect the friction surface for cracks, rivet grooves, burned areas and score marks. Light scoring can be removed with emery cloth. Check for cracked and broken ring gear teeth. Lay the flywheel on a flat surface and use a straightedge to check for warpage.

7   Clean and inspect the mating surfaces of the flywheel/driveplate and the crankshaft. If the crankshaft rear seal is leaking, replace it before reinstalling the flywheel/driveplate.

8   Position the flywheel/driveplate against the crankshaft. Be sure to align the dowel or marks made during removal. Before installing the bolts, apply thread locking compound to the threads.

9   Keep the flywheel/driveplate from turning as described above while you tighten the bolts to the torque listed in this Chapter's Specifications.

10   The remainder of installation is the reverse of the removal procedure.

18   Rear main oil seal - replacement

1   Remove the flywheel/driveplate (see Section 17).

2   Using a thin screwdriver or seal removal tool, carefully remove the oil seal from the engine block. Be very careful not to damage the crankshaft surface while prying the seal out.

3   Clean the bore in the block and the seal contact surface on the crankshaft. Check the seal contact surface on the crankshaft for scratches and nicks that could damage the new seal lip and cause oil leaks - if the

crankshaft is damaged, the only alternative is a new or different crankshaft. Inspect the seal bore for nicks and scratches. Carefully smooth it with a fine file if necessary, but don't nick the crankshaft in the process.

4   A special tool is recommended to install the new oil seal. Lubricate the oil seal lips. Slide the seal onto the mandril until the dust lip bottoms squarely against the collar of the tool. **Note:** *If the special tool isn't available, carefully work the seal lip over the crankshaft and tap it into place with a hammer and blunt punch.*

5   Align the dowel pin on the tool with the dowel pin hole in the crankshaft and attach the tool to the crankshaft by hand-tightening the bolts.

6   Turn the tool handle until the collar bottoms against the case, seating the seal.

7   Loosen the tool handle and remove the bolts. Remove the tool.

8   Check the seal and make sure it's seated squarely in the bore.

9   Install the flywheel/driveplate (see Section 17).

10   Install the transaxle.

19   Engine mounts - check and replacement

1   Engine mounts seldom require attention, but broken or deteriorated mounts should be replaced immediately or the added strain placed on the driveline components may cause damage or wear.

Check

2   During the check, the engine must be raised slightly to remove the weight from the mounts.

3   Raise the vehicle and support it securely on jackstands, then position a jack under the engine oil pan. Place a large block of wood between the jack head and the oil pan, then carefully raise the engine just enough to take the weight off the mounts. **Warning:** *DO NOT*

place any part of your body under the engine when it's supported only by a jack!

4   Check the mounts to see if the rubber is cracked, hardened or separated from the metal plates. Sometimes the rubber will split right down the center.

5   Check for relative movement between the mount plates and the engine or frame (use a large screwdriver or prybar to attempt to move the mounts). If movement is noted, lower the engine and tighten the mount fasteners.

6   Rubber preservative should be applied to the mounts to slow deterioration.

Replacement

7   Disconnect the negative battery cable from the battery. **Caution:** *If the vehicle is equipped with a Delco Loc II audio system, make sure you have the correct activation code before disconnecting the battery. See the information at the front of this manual for the radio activation procedure.* Raise the vehicle and support it securely on jackstands (if not already done).

Lower mount

8   Remove the through-bolt from the engine bracket end of the upper mount strut and rotate the strut out of the way (see Chapter 2C, **illustration 17.27**).

9   Raise the engine slightly with a jack or hoist. Remove the fasteners and detach the mount from the frame bracket.

10   Remove the mount-to-block bracket bolts/nuts and detach the mount.

Upper mount strut

11   Disconnect the negative battery cable from the battery and remove the bolts and nuts from the strut and the brace. **Caution:** *If the vehicle is equipped with a Delco Loc II audio system, make sure you have the correct activation code before disconnecting the battery. See the information at the front of this manual for the radio activation procedure.*

12   Installation is the reverse of removal. Use thread locking compound on the threads and be sure to tighten everything securely.

Notes

Chapter 2 Part B
2.5L four-cylinder engine

Contents

Specifications

General
Cylinder numbers (drivebelt end-to-transaxle end)	1-2-3-4
Firing order	1-3-4-2
Direction distributor rotor rotates	Clockwise

Torque specifications
Ft-lbs (unless otherwise indicated)

Oil pan bolts	89 in-lbs
Oil screen support bolt	37
Oil pump-to-block bolt	22
Oil pump cover bolt	
1987 and earlier models	10
1988 and later models	89 in-lbs
Force balancer assembly-to-block bolts	
1988 and earlier	
Short bolts	
Step 1	108 in-lbs
Step 2	Turn an additional 75 degrees
Long bolts	
Step 1	108 in-lbs
Step 2	Turn an additional 90 degrees

Front

Front

With distributorless ignition
2.5L Four-cylinder engine

Canadian models only

Cylinder/coil terminal location and distributor rotation

The blackened terminal shown on the distributor cap indicates the Number One spark plug wire position

Torque specifications (continued)

Ft-lbs (unless otherwise indicated)

Force balancer assembly-to-block bolts (continued)

1989

Short bolts

Step 1 15

Step 2 .... Turn an additional 60 degrees

Long bolts

Step 1 .... 132 in-lbs

Step 2 .... Turn an additional 90 degrees

1990

Short bolts

Step 1 .... 132 in-lbs

Step 2 .... Turn an additional 75 degrees

Long bolts

Step 1 .... 132 in-lbs

Step 2 .... Turn an additional 90 degrees

1991 and later

Short bolts

Step 1 .... 108 in-lbs

Step 2 .... 132 in-lbs, then turn an additional 75-degrees

Long bolts

Step 1 .... 108 in-lbs

Step 2 .... 132 in-lbs, then turn an additional 90 degrees

Pushrod cover bolts .... 89 in-lbs

Harmonic balancer bolts

1990 and earlier 200

1991 and later 162

Driveplate-to-crankshaft bolts

1987 and earlier 63

1988 and later 55

Flywheel-to-crankshaft bolts

1990 and earlier 70

1991 and later 55

Intake manifold bolts

1990 and earlier 29

1991 and later 25

Exhaust manifold bolts

1990 and earlier 44

1991 and later

Bolts 1, 2 and 3 **(see illustration 6.13)** 37

Bolts 4, 5, 6 and 7 28

Timing cover bolts .... 89 in-lbs

Rocker arm bolts

1987 and earlier 20

1988 and later 24

Cylinder head bolts (see illustration 7.24)

1985 and earlier 85

1986 and 1987

Step 1 18

Step 2

All but bolt 9 22

Bolt 9 29

Step 3

All but bolt 9 .... Turn an additional 120 degrees

Bolt 9 .... Turn an additional 90 degrees

1988 and later

Step 1 18

Step 2

All but bolt 9 26

Bolt 9 18

Step 3 (all bolts) .... Turn an additional 90 degrees

Valve cover bolts .... 50 in-lbs

Camshaft thrust plate bolts .... 90 in-lbs

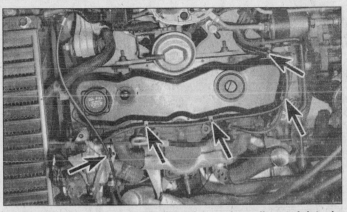

2.3 The PCV valve can be pulled out of the rubber grommet in the valve cover (leave the hose attached to the valve)

2.4 Disconnect all four spark plug wire retainer clips and detach the throttle cable from the exhaust manifold bracket (arrows)

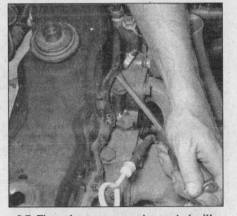

2.6 Remove the valve cover bolts (manifold shown removed for clarity)

2.7 The valve cover may be sealed with RTV - if you have to pry it off the head, try to avoid bending the flange

2.8 Remove the old sealant from the valve cover flange and the cylinder head with a gasket scraper, then clean the mating surfaces with lacquer thinner or acetone

1 General information

The Sections in this Part of Chapter 2 are devoted to in-vehicle repair procedures for the 2.5 liter four-cylinder engine. Information concerning engine removal, engine block and cylinder head servicing can be found in Part E of this Chapter.

The repair procedures are based on the assumption that the engine is still installed in the vehicle. Therefore, if this information is being used during a complete engine overhaul, with the engine already out of the vehicle and on a stand, many of the steps included here will not apply.

The specifications included apply only to the engine and procedures found here. For specifications regarding engines other than the 2.5 liter four-cylinder engine, see Part A, C or D, whichever applies. Part E contains the specifications necessary for engine block and cylinder head rebuilding.

2 Valve cover - removal and installation

Refer to illustrations 2.3, 2.4, 2.6, 2.7, 2.8 and 2.9

1   Remove the air cleaner assembly, tagging each hose as it is disconnected with a piece of numbered tape to simplify installation.
2   Disconnect the throttle cable from the fuel injection assembly, making careful note of the exact locations of the cable components and hardware to ensure correct reinstallation.
3   Remove the PCV valve from the valve cover **(see illustration)**.
4   Remove the spark plug wires from the spark plugs, referring to the removal technique described in Chapter 1, then remove the wires and retaining clips from the valve cover **(see illustration)**. Be sure to label each wire before removal to ensure that all wires are reinstalled correctly.
5   Loosen the fuel injection mounting nuts and bolts to provide clearance for removal of the EGR valve, then remove the EGR valve (see Chapter 6, if necessary).
6   Remove the valve cover bolts **(see illustration)**.
7   Remove the valve cover. **Note:** *If the cover sticks to the cylinder head, use a block of wood and a hammer to dislodge it. If the cover still will not come loose, pry on it carefully, but do not distort the sealing flange surface* **(see illustration)**.
8   Prior to reinstallation of the cover, clean all dirt, oil and old gasket material from the sealing surfaces of the cover and cylinder head with a scraper and a degreaser, such as

acetone or lacquer thinner **(see illustration)**. **Note:** *Aerosol gasket removal solvents are available at auto parts stores and may prove helpful.*
9   If the cover was sealed with RTV (no gasket) (1990 and earlier models), apply a continuous 3/16-inch diameter bead of RTV-type sealant to the sealing flange of the cover. Be sure to apply the sealant inside of the bolt holes **(see illustration)**.

2.9 On 1990 and earlier models, apply a continuous 3/16-inch bead of RTV-type sealant (arrow) to the valve cover flange (make sure it is applied to the inside of the bolt holes as shown)

3.5 The pushrod cover is held in place with four nuts (arrows) (manifold shown removed for clarity)

3.7 Don't forget to install new rubber sealing washers around the pushrod cover mounting studs or oil will leak past the studs

3.8 Install the pushrod cover while the sealant is still tacky - be sure the semi-circular cutout (arrow) is facing down

4.4 This is what the air hose adapter that threads into the spark plug hole looks like - they're commonly available at auto parts stores

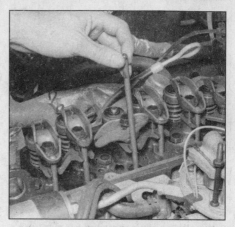

4.5a Loosen the rocker arm bolt, rotate the rocker arm to one side and lift out the pushrod

10   If the cover was sealed with a gasket (1991 and later models), install the new gasket with no RTV sealant.

11   Place the valve cover on the cylinder head while the sealant (if used) is still wet and install the mounting bolts. Tighten the bolts from the center out, a little at a time, to the torque listed in this Chapter's Specifications.

12   Complete installation by reversing the removal procedure.

3   Pushrod cover - removal and installation

Refer to illustrations 3.5, 3.7 and 3.8

1   Rotate the steering shaft until the gear stub shaft clamp bolt is accessible. Remove the bolt and disconnect the shaft from the stub.

2   Raise the vehicle and support it securely on jackstands.

3   Support the engine cradle with a jack, then remove the two rear engine support cradle bolts.

4   Remove the two exhaust pipe flex joint bolts. Lower the support cradle between four

and six inches for access to the pushrod cover bolts.

5   Remove the pushrod cover nuts **(see illustration)** and lift off the cover. If the gasket seal is difficult to break, tap on the cover gently with a rubber hammer. Do not pry on the cover.

6   Using a scraper and degreaser, clean the sealing surfaces on the cover and engine block to remove all oil and old gasket material. **Note:** *Aerosol gasket removal solvents are available at auto parts stores and may prove helpful.*

7   Prior to installation of the cover apply a continuous 3/16-inch (5 mm) bead of RTV-type sealant to the mounting flange of the pushrod cove. Also be sure to install new rubber sealing washers on the pushrod cover mounting studs **(see illustration).**

8   With the sealant still wet, place the cover in position on the block and install the cover nuts **(see illustration).** Tighten the nuts gradually, following a crisscross pattern, to the torque listed in this Chapter's Specifications.

9   Install the cradle and exhaust pipe, lower the vehicle and reconnect the steering shaft.

4   Valve train components - replacement (cylinder head installed)

Refer to illustrations 4.4, 4.5a, 4.5b, 4.5c, 4.9a, 4.9b, 4.10, 4.17a and 4.17b

Note: *Broken valve springs and defective valve stem seals can be replaced without removing the cylinder heads. Two special tools and a compressed air source are normally required to perform this operation, so read through this Section carefully and rent or buy the tools before beginning the job. If compressed air isn't available, a length of nylon rope can be used to keep the valves from falling into the cylinder during this procedure.*

1   Refer to Section 2 and remove the valve cover from the cylinder head.

2   Remove the spark plug from the cylinder which has the defective component. If all of the valve stem seals are being replaced, all of the spark plugs should be removed.

3   Turn the crankshaft until the piston in the affected cylinder is at top dead center on the compression stroke (refer to Chapter 2E). If you're replacing all of the valve stem seals,

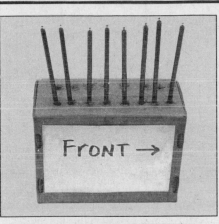

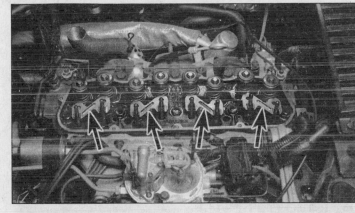

4.5c If they're removed, make sure the pushrod guides (arrows) are kept in order also

4.5b If more than one pushrod is being removed, store them in a perforated cardboard box to prevent mix-ups during installation - note the label on the box indicating the front (drivebelt end) of the engine

begin with cylinder number one and work on the valves for one cylinder at a time. Move from cylinder-to-cylinder, following the firing order sequence (see the Specifications).

4   Thread an adapter into the spark plug hole **(see illustration)** and connect an air hose from a compressed air source to it. Most auto parts stores can supply the air hose adapter. **Note:** *Many cylinder compression gauges utilize a screw-in fitting that may work with your air hose quick-disconnect fitting.*

5   Loosen the rocker arm nut and pivot the rocker arm aside for the valve with the defective part and pull out the pushrod **(see illustration)**. If all of the valves are being worked on, all of the rocker arms and pushrods should be removed. Store the pushrods so they can be returned to their original locations with the same end facing down **(see illustration)**. If necessary, also remove the pushrod guides **(see illustration)**.

6   Apply compressed air to the cylinder. **Warning:** *The piston may be forced down by compressed air, causing the crankshaft to turn suddenly. If the wrench used when positioning the number one piston at TDC is still attached to the bolt in the crankshaft nose, it could cause damage or injury when the crankshaft moves.*

7   The valves should be held in place by the air pressure. If the valve faces or seats are in poor condition, leaks may prevent air pressure from retaining the valves - refer to the alternative procedure below.

8   If you don't have access to compressed air, an alternative method can be used. Position the piston at a point just before TDC on the compression stroke, then feed a long piece of nylon rope through the spark plug hole until it fills the combustion chamber. Be sure to leave the end of the rope hanging out of the engine so it can be removed easily. Use a large ratchet and socket to rotate the crankshaft in the normal direction of rotation until slight resistance is felt.

9   Stuff shop rags into the cylinder head holes above and below the valves to prevent

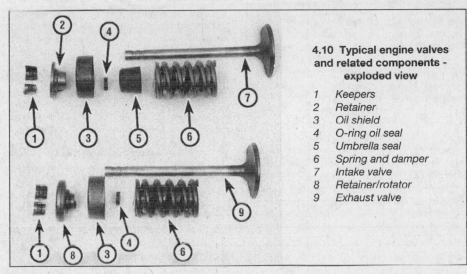

4.9a After the valve spring has been compressed, the keepers can be removed with needle-nose pliers or a magnet

4.9b Using a lever-type valve spring compressor to compress a valve spring - note that a rocker arm bolt has been reinstalled to be used for leverage

4.10 Typical engine valves and related components - exploded view

1   Keepers
2   Retainer
3   Oil shield
4   O-ring oil seal
5   Umbrella seal
6   Spring and damper
7   Intake valve
8   Retainer/rotator
9   Exhaust valve

parts and tools from falling into the engine, then use a valve spring compressor to compress the spring. Remove the keepers with small needle-nose pliers or a magnet **(see illustration)**. **Note:** *A couple of different types of tools are available for compressing the valve springs with the head in place. One type grips the lower spring coils and presses on the retainer as the knob is turned, while the other type, shown here* **(see illustration)**,

utilizes the rocker arm stud and nut for leverage. Both types work very well, although the lever type is usually less expensive.

10   Remove the spring retainer, shield and valve spring, then remove the seal **(see illustration)**. **Note:** *If air pressure fails to hold the valve in the closed position during this operation, the valve face or seat is probably damaged. If so, the cylinder head will have to be removed for additional repair operations.*

4.17a Make sure the O-ring seal under the retainer is seated in the groove and not twisted before installing the keepers

4.17b Put a small dab of grease on the inside of each keeper before assembly - it'll hold them in place until the spring is released

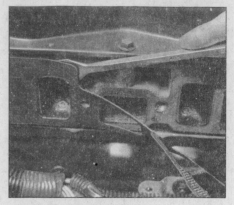

5.11 Remove the old intake manifold gasket with a scraper - don't leave any material on the mating surfaces

11   Wrap a rubber band or tape around the top of the valve stem so the valve won't fall into the combustion chamber, then release the air pressure. **Note**: *If a rope was used instead of air pressure, turn the crankshaft slightly in the direction opposite normal rotation.*

12   Inspect the valve stem for damage. Rotate the valve in the guide and check the end for eccentric movement, which would indicate that the valve is bent.

13   Move the valve up-and-down in the guide and make sure it doesn't bind. If the valve stem binds, either the valve is bent or the guide is damaged. In either case, the head will have to be removed for repair.

14   Reapply air pressure to the cylinder to retain the valve in the closed position, then remove the tape or rubber band from the valve stem. If a rope was used instead of air pressure, rotate the crankshaft in the normal direction of rotation until slight resistance is felt.

15   Lubricate the valve stem with engine oil.

16   Install the spring and shield in position over the valve.

17   Install the valve spring retainer. Compress the valve spring and carefully install the O-ring seal **(see illustration)**, then install the keepers. Apply a small dab of grease to the inside of each keeper to hold it in place **(see illustration)**.

18   Remove the pressure from the spring tool and make sure the keepers are seated.

19   Disconnect the air hose and remove the adapter from the spark plug hole. If a rope was used in place of air pressure, pull it out of the cylinder.

20   Install the rocker arm(s) and pushrod(s).

21   Install the spark plug(s) and hook up the wire(s).

22   Install the valve cover.

23   Start and run the engine, then check for oil leaks and unusual sounds coming from the valve cover area.

5   Intake manifold - removal and installation

Refer to illustrations 5.11, 5.16a and 5.16b

1   Disconnect the cable from the negative battery terminal. **Caution**: *If the vehicle is equipped with a Delco Loc II audio system, make sure you have the correct activation code before disconnecting the battery. See the information at the front of this manual for the radio re-activation procedure.*

2   Remove the air cleaner assembly, tagging each hose as it is disconnected with a piece of numbered tape to simplify reinstallation.

3   Remove the PCV valve and hose.

4   Drain the cooling system (refer to Chapter 1).

5   Label and disconnect the fuel line, vacuum lines and electrical connectors from the

fuel injection assembly. When disconnecting the fuel line be prepared to catch some fuel, then plug the fuel line to prevent contamination.

6   Disconnect the fuel injection throttle linkage, making careful note of how it is installed.

7   Disconnect the cruise control linkage (if so equipped).

8   Disconnect the coil wire, remove the two retaining screws and one bolt, then remove the coil.

9   Remove the coolant hoses from the manifold.

10   Remove the manifold retaining bolts and separate the manifold from the cylinder head. Do not pry between the manifold and head, as damage to the gasket sealing surfaces may result.

11   Remove the manifold gasket with a scraper **(see illustration)**.

12   If the intake manifold is to be replaced with another, transfer all components still attached to the old manifold to the new one.

13   Before installing the manifold, clean the cylinder head and manifold gasket surfaces. All gasket material and sealing compound must be removed prior to installation. Gasket removal solvents are available at auto parts stores and may prove helpful. After the gasket material and sealing compound is removed, wipe the gasket surfaces clean with a rag soaked in lacquer thinner or acetone.

14   Apply a thin bead of RTV-type sealant to

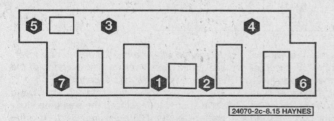

5.16a On models through 1990, tighten the intake manifold mounting bolts a little at a time, in the order shown, until they are all at the torque listed in this Chapter's Specifications

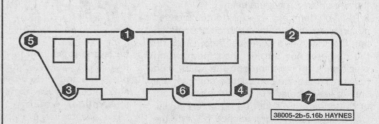

5.16b Use this intake manifold bolt tightening sequence on 1991 and later models

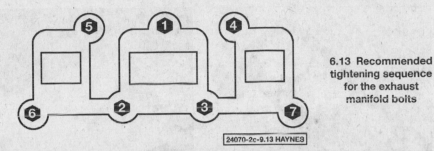

6.13 Recommended tightening sequence for the exhaust manifold bolts

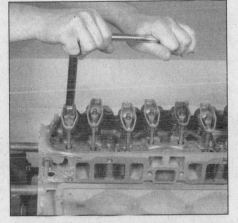

7.11 Use a socket and ratchet to remove the rocker arm nuts

7.12 Remove the pushrods with your fingers and store them in order so they can be reinstalled in the same holes with the same end facing up

the intake manifold and cylinder head mating surfaces. Make certain that the sealant will not spread into the air or coolant passages when the manifold is installed.

15   Place a new intake manifold gasket on the manifold, hold the manifold in position against the cylinder head and install the mounting bolts finger tight.

16   Tighten the mounting bolts a little at a time in the sequence shown until they are all at the torque listed in this Chapter's Specifications (see illustrations).

17   Install the remaining components in the reverse order of removal.

18   Fill the radiator with coolant, start the engine and check for leaks. Adjust the ignition timing and idle speed as necessary (Chapter 1).

6   Exhaust manifold - removal and installation

Refer to illustration 6.13

Warning: *The engine must be completely cool before beginning this procedure.*

1   If the vehicle is equipped with air conditioning, carefully examine the routing of the hoses and the mounting of the compressor. You may be able to remove the exhaust manifold without disconnecting the system. If you are in doubt, take the vehicle to a GM dealer or automotive air conditioning shop to have the system depressurized. Caution: *Do not, under any circumstances, disconnect any air conditioning system lines while the system is under pressure.*

2   Remove the cable from the negative battery terminal. Caution: *If the vehicle is equipped with a Delco Loc II audio system, make sure you have the correct activation code before disconnecting the battery. See the information at the front of this manual for the radio re-activation procedure.*

3   Remove the air cleaner assembly, tagging each hose as it is disconnected with a piece of numbered tape to simplify reinstallation.

4   Disconnect and remove the torque strut located between the engine mount bracket and cylinder head.

5   Raise the vehicle and support it securely on jackstands.

6   Remove the oxygen sensor (see Chapter 6).

7   Label the four spark plug wires, then disconnect them and secure them out of the way.

8   Disconnect the exhaust pipe from the exhaust manifold. You may have to apply penetrating oil to the fastener threads, as they are usually corroded. The exhaust pipe can be hung from the frame with a piece of wire.

9   Remove the exhaust manifold end bolts first, then remove the center bolts and separate the exhaust manifold from the engine.

10   Remove the exhaust manifold gasket.

11   Before installing the manifold, clean the gasket mating surfaces on the cylinder head and manifold. All leftover gasket material and carbon deposits must be removed.

12   Place a new exhaust manifold gasket in position on the cylinder head, then place the manifold in position and install the mounting bolts finger tight.

13   Tighten the mounting bolts a little at a time, in the sequence shown in the accompanying illustration, until all of the bolts are at the torque listed in this Chapter's Specifications (see illustration).

14   Lower the vehicle.

15   Install the remaining components in the reverse order of removal, using new gaskets wherever one has been removed.

16   Start the engine and check for exhaust leaks between the manifold and cylinder head and between the manifold and exhaust pipe.

7   Cylinder head - removal and installation

Refer to illustrations 7.11, 7.12, 7.14a, 7.14b, 7.14c, 7.15, 7.16, 7.23 and 7.24

Removal

1   Drain the cooling system (Chapter 1) and remove the air cleaner assembly.

2   Remove the intake manifold as described in Section 5.

3   Remove the exhaust manifold as described in Section 6.

4   Remove the bolts that secure the alternator bracket to the cylinder head.

5   If so equipped, unbolt the air conditioning compressor and swing it out of the way for clearance. Normally, you won't have to disconnect any air conditioning hoses or lines. Caution: *Do not disconnect any of the air conditioning hoses or lines unless the system has been depressurized by a dealer service department or automotive air conditioning shop. Otherwise, personal injury may occur.*

6   Disconnect all electrical and vacuum lines from the cylinder head. Be sure to label the lines to simplify reinstallation.

7   Remove the upper radiator hose.

8   Disconnect the spark plug wires and remove the spark plugs. Be sure to label the plug wires to simplify reinstallation.

9   Remove the valve cover. To break the gasket seal it may be necessary to strike the cover with your hand or a rubber hammer. Do not pry between the sealing surfaces. Refer to Section 2 if necessary.

10   When disassembling the valve mechanisms, keep all of the components separate so they can be reinstalled in their original positions. A cardboard box or rack, numbered to correspond to the engine cylinders, can be used for this purpose.

11   Remove each of the rocker arm nuts and separate the rocker arms and pivots from the cylinder head (see illustration).

12   Remove the pushrods (see illustration).

13   If the ignition coil is mounted separately from the distributor, disconnect the wires and remove the coil.

14   Loosen each of the cylinder head mounting bolts one turn at a time until they

7.14a Loosen the cylinder head mounting bolts

7.14b To avoid mixing up the head bolts, use a new gasket to transfer the bolt hole pattern to a piece of cardboard, then punch holes to accept the bolts. . .

7.14c . . .and push each bolt through the matching hole in the cardboard

7.15 If the head is stuck, pry it up at the overhang just behind and below the thermostat housing

7.16 Once the head is off, stuff the cylinders with clean shop rags to prevent debris from falling into them and scrape off the old gasket material with a gasket scraper

can be removed **(see illustrations)**. Note the length and position of each bolt to ensure correct reinstallation.

15   Lift the head off of the engine. If it is stuck to the engine block, try using a hammer and block of wood to tap the head and break the gasket seal. If this does not work, pry carefully at the casting overhang **(see illustration)**. Place the head on a block of wood to prevent damage to the gasket surface.

16   Using a scraper, remove all traces of the cylinder head gasket from the head and block **(see illustration)**. Gasket removal solvents are available at auto parts stores and may prove helpful. After all material is removed, clean the gasket surfaces with a rag soaked in lacquer thinner or acetone.

17   Refer to Chapter 2E for cylinder head disassembly and valve service procedures.

Installation

18   If a new cylinder head is being installed, transfer all external parts from the old cylinder head to the new one.

19   Using a scraper, thoroughly clean the gasket surfaces on the cylinder head and the engine block. Do not gouge or otherwise

damage the gasket surfaces. **Note:** *Aerosol gasket removal solvents are often available at auto parts stores and may prove helpful.* After all gasket material is removed, wipe the gasket surfaces clean with a rag soaked in lacquer thinner or acetone.

20   To get the proper torque readings, the threads of the head bolts must be clean. This also applies to the threaded holes in the engine block. Run a tap through the holes to ensure that they are clean.

21   Place the new gasket in position over the engine block dowel pins.

22   Carefully lower the cylinder head onto the engine, over the dowel pins and the gasket.

23   Coat the threads of each cylinder head bolt and install the bolts finger tight. Do not tighten any of the bolts at this time **(see illustration)**.

24   Tighten each of the bolts a little at a time in the sequence shown in the accompanying illustration. Continue tightening in this sequence until the proper torque reading is obtained (see the Specifications). As a final check, work around the head in a front-to-rear sequence to make sure none of the bolts

7.23 The cylinder head mounting bolts should be coated with sealant (arrows) before installation

have been left out of the sequence. Note that later model head bolts are torqued in steps. Tighten all bolts to the torque listed in each step before proceeding to the next step.

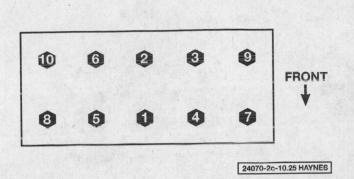

FRONT ↓

24070-2c-10.25 HAYNES

7.24 Cylinder head bolt positions and bolt tightening sequence

8.7a Pushrod cover stud locknuts (arrows) - manifold removed for clarity

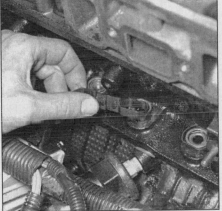

8.7b Remove the lifter guide - if you're removing more than one guide, keep them in order to prevent mix-ups during installation

8.8a On engines that haven't accumulated a lot of sludge and varnish, the lifters can usually be removed by hand

8.8b If the lifters are stuck, remove them with a special tool like the one shown here

25   The remaining steps are the reverse of the removal procedure. Run the engine and check for leaks.

8   Hydraulic lifters - removal, inspection and installation

Refer to illustrations 8.7a, 8.7b, 8.8a, 8.8b, 8.9, 8.10a, 8.10b, 8.10c, 8.10d and 8.10e

1   A noisy valve lifter can be isolated when the engine is idling. Place a length of hose or tubing near the position of each valve while listening at the other end of the tube. Another method is to remove the valve cover and, with the engine idling, place a finger on each of the valve spring retainers, one at a time. If a valve lifter is defective, it will be evident from the shock felt at the retainer as the valve seats.

2   A common cause of a noisy valve lifter is a piece of dirt trapped between the plunger and the lifter body.

3   Remove the valve cover as described in Section 2.

4   Remove the intake manifold as described in Section 5.

5   Remove the pushrod cover as described in Section 3.

6   Loosen the rocker arm bolt and rotate the rocker arm away from the pushrod.

7   Remove the pushrod. On later models with roller lifters, remove the retainers and guides (see illustrations). If the roller lifters are not marked to show which end faces the drivebelt end of the engine, mark them. Roller lifters must be reinstalled so the roller rotates the same direction as it originally did.

8   If the lifters are relatively clean (not a lot of carbon and varnish build-up below the bores), they can sometimes be pulled out by hand or with the pointed end of a bent scribe hooked under the lifter retainer (see illustration). If the lifters are stuck, special tools designed to grip and remove the lifters are manufactured by many tool companies and are widely available (see illustration).

8.9 If you're removing more than one lifter, keep them in order in a clearly labeled box

9   The lifters should be kept in order for reinstallation in their original positions (see illustration).

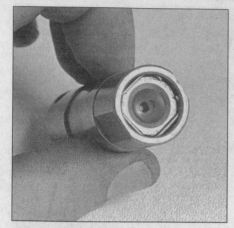

8.10a Check the pushrod seat (arrow) in the top of each lifter for wear

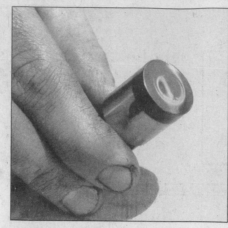

8.10b If the bottom of any lifter is worn concave, scratched or galled, replace the entire set with new lifters

8.10c If the lifters are pitted or rough, they shouldn't be reused

10   Inspect each lifter to identify excessive wear and damage **(see illustrations)**. If they are worn, damaged or stuck, replace them as a set, along with a new camshaft (see Section 16). **Caution:** *Never replace only the lifters or only the camshaft, since accelerated wear to the components may result. Reassemble used components only when the original lifters can be replaced in the same position on the original camshaft.*

11   When installing the lifters, make sure they are replaced in their original bores. Coat them with moly-base grease or engine assembly lube.

12   Do not forget, during installation of roller type lifters, to position the lifter guides and retainers and tighten the studs before installing the pushrods.

13   The remaining installation steps are the reverse of removal.

8.10d The foot of each lifter should be slightly convex - the side of another lifter can be used as a straightedge to check it; if it appears flat, it is worn and must not be reused

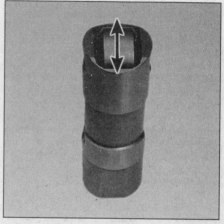

8.10e The roller on roller lifters must turn freely - check for wear and excessive play as well

9   Oil pump driveshaft - removal and installation

Refer to illustration 9.6

Note: *This procedure does not apply to 1987 and later models with force balancers. These models are most easily identified by the oil filter in the bottom of the oil pan. On models without force balancers, the oil filter is on the side of the engine block.*

1   Rotate the steering shaft until the clamp bolt is accessible, remove the bolt and disconnect the shaft from the steering gear stub shaft (Chapter 10).

2   Raise the vehicle and support it securely on jackstands.

3   Support the engine.

4   Remove the two rear engine cradle bolts and lower the cradle for access.

5   Remove the oil filter.

6   Remove the oil pump driveshaft cover plate bolts **(see illustration)**.

7   Remove the bushing.

8   Remove the shaft and gear assembly.

9   Thoroughly clean the sealing surfaces on the engine block and cover plate.

10   Inspect the gear teeth to see if they are chipped or cracked.

11   Install the oil pump driveshaft in the block and turn it until it engages with the camshaft drive gear in the oil pump body.

12   Apply a 1/16-inch (1.5 mm) diameter bead of RTV-type sealant to the cover plate so that it completely seals around the oil pump driveshaft hole in the block, as shown **(see illustration 9.6)**.

13   Install the cover plate mounting bolts and tighten them to the specified torque.

14   Complete the installation by reversing the removal procedure.

9.6 The oil pump driveshaft retainer plate is located on the engine block, just below the pushrod cover and just above the oil filter

10.18 During installation, the rubber tips on the front oil pan gasket should be pressed into the holes In the timing chain cover (1984 and earlier models)

11.2 Remove the oil pump flange mounting bolts

10 Oil pan - removal and installation

Refer to illustration 10.18

Removal

Warning: *The air conditioning system is under high pressure. DO NOT disassemble any part of the system (hoses, compressor, line fittings, etc.) until after the system has been depressurized by a dealer service department or automotive air conditioning shop.*

1 Disconnect the cable from the negative battery terminal. **Caution:** *If the vehicle is equipped with a Delco Loc II audio system, make sure you have the correct activation code before disconnecting the battery. See the information at the front of this manual for the radio re-activation procedure.*

2 Raise the vehicle, place it securely on jackstands and drain the engine oil. Remove the oil filter. Refer to Chapter 1 if necessary.

3 If necessary, remove the coolant reservoir.

4 Disconnect the engine mounting torque strut (sometimes called a "dogbone" because of its shape) from its mounting bracket on the engine by removing the through-bolt and nut. Move the strut down so it's well out of the way of the bracket.

5 Remove the air cleaner and duct assembly (see Chapter 4).

6 On models so equipped, remove the serpentine drivebelt (see Chapter 1).

7 On 1988 and earlier models, if necessary for clearance, disconnect the power steering pump and bracket and set the pump aside without disconnecting the hoses. Keep the pump upright so no fluid spills.

8 Remove the air conditioning compressor and support brace (if equipped) (see Chapter 3). Set the compressor aside without disconnecting the refrigerant lines (see *Warning* above).

9 Remove the cradle-to-front engine mount nuts.

10 Disconnect the exhaust pipe at the exhaust manifold and the rear transaxle mount.

11 Disconnect the starter and remove the flywheel inspection cover.

12 Remove the upper alternator bracket, if necessary for clearance.

13 Support the engine with a hoist.

14 If necessary for clearance (mostly on earlier models), remove the lower alternator bracket and engine support bracket.

15 Remove the oil pan bolts and separate the oil pan from the block. **Note:** *On later models with RTV sealant instead of a gasket, the pan may be difficult to remove. If so, try striking the side of the pan with a rubber mallet. If this does not work, try running a sharp knife between the block and pan to cut the RTV seal. Be careful not to damage the gasket mating surfaces.*

Installation

16 Clean the pan with solvent and, using a scraper, remove all old sealant and gasket material from the block and pan sealing surfaces. Gasket removal solvents are available at many auto parts stores and may prove helpful. If the flange where the pan mates to the block is bent, straighten it with a block of wood and a hammer.

1984 and earlier models

17 Install the rear pan oil seal in the groove in the rear main bearing cap and apply a small quantity of RTV-type sealant to the depressions where the seal meets the block.

18 Install the front pan oil seal on the timing cover, pressing the tips into the holes in the cover **(see illustration)**.

19 Using a light coat of RTV sealant as a retainer, install the pan side gaskets. Apply a 1/8-inch diameter by 1/4-inch long bead of RTV-type sealant at the parting lines of the front seal and side gaskets.

1985 and later models

20 Apply a continuous bead of RTV sealant to the oil pan. Make sure you run the bead to the inner side of the bolt holes.

All models

21 Attach the oil pan to the block. The bolts that secure the pan to the timing cover should be installed last. They are installed at an angle into holes which will line up as the rest of the pan bolts are tightened.

22 After all bolts are installed, tighten them to the torque listed in this Chapter's Specifications. Use a criss-cross pattern and work up to the final torque in three or four steps.

23 The remaining steps are the reverse of the removal procedure.

11 Oil pump (models without force balancers) - removal and installation

Refer to illustration 11.2

Note: *This procedure does not apply 1987 and later models with force balancer assemblies (these are most easily identified by the oil filter in the oil pan, instead of on the side of the engine). See Section 13 to remove the oil pump on force-balancer-equipped models.*

1 Remove the oil pan (refer to Section 10).

2 Remove the two oil pump flange mounting bolts and the nut from the main bearing cap bolt **(see illustration)**.

3 Lift out the oil pump and screen as an assembly.

4 To install the pump, align the shaft so it mates with the oil pump driveshaft tang, then install the pump on the block, over the oil pump driveshaft lower bushing. No gasket is used. The oil pump should slide easily into place. If not, remove it and relocate the slot.

5 Install the mounting bolts and nut and tighten them to the specified torque.

6 Reinstall the oil pan (refer to Section 10).

12 Force balancer/oil pump assembly - removal and installation

Removal

Note: *To remove the oil pump only, It is not necessary to remove the entire force balancer/oil pump assembly. To remove only the oil pump, see Section 13.*

1   Some 1987 and all 1988 and later model 2.5L engines are equipped with a force balancer. The assembly consists of two eccentrically weighted shafts and gears which are counter-rotated by a concentric gear on the crankshaft at twice crankshaft speed, dampening engine vibration. The oil filter, a pick-up screen and gerotor type oil pump are also integral parts of the assembly, so the oil pump removal procedure in Section 11 does not apply. The oil pump is driven from the back side of one of the balancers.

2   The balancer-equipped engine can be distinguished by the element-type oil filter located in the oil pan.

3   The force balancer/oil pump assembly must be removed to disassemble the engine for overhaul.

4   Remove the oil pan (see Section 10).

5   Position the number 1 piston at TDC on the compression stroke (see Chapter 2E).

6   Unbolt the balancer assembly. and remove it from the engine. **Warning:** *The assembly is heavy, so support it carefully before removing the bolts and be careful not to drop it!*

Installation

1987 through 1990 models

7   Position the crankshaft by measuring from the engine block to the first cut of the double notch on the reluctor ring. The distance should be 1 - 11/16-inches. If it isn't, turn the crankshaft until it is.

8   Mount the balancer with the counterweights parallel and pointing AWAY from the crankshaft. Tighten the bolts to the torque listed in this Chapter's Specifications.

1991 and later models

9   Rotate the crankshaft until the number 4 counterweight is EXACTLY at Bottom Dead Center. **Note:** *When installing the balancer, the housing end without dowel pins must continuously remain in contact with the engine block surface. If it loses contact, the gears may loose their proper engagement and damage may occur to either the crankshaft or balancer gears.*

10   Install the balancer onto the engine block with the balance weights EXACTLY at Bottom Dead Center (plus or minus 1/2 gear tooth).

11   Install the balancer bolts and hand tighten evenly.

12   Tighten all bolts a little at a time, to the torque listed in this Chapter's Specifications.

All models

13   Rotate the crankshaft four times and check for clearance between the fourth counterweight and the balancer weights.

14   Install the oil pan.

15   Install a new oil filter and add oil (see Chapter 1). Run the engine and check for leaks.

13   Oil pump/pressure regulator valve (models with force balancers) - removal, inspection, and installation

Removal

Note: *It isn't necessary to remove the force balancer assembly to service the oil pump or pressure regulator valve.*

1   Remove the oil pan (see Section 10).

2   Remove the restrictor (if equipped).

3   Remove the oil pump cover assembly and oil pump gears or, on later models, the gerotor assembly.

4   **Warning:** *The pressure regulator valve is under pressure. Exercise caution when unscrewing the plug or removing the pin, as bodily injury may result.* Remove the pressure regulator valve plug (or pin) and spring, then remove the valve itself. If the valve is stuck, clean the valve and pump housing with carburetor cleaner or solvent.

5   Remove any sludge, oil or varnish from the parts with carburetor cleaner or solvent. If the varnish on any of the parts is difficult to remove, allow them to soak for awhile.

Inspection

6   Inspect all parts for the presence of foreign material. If you find evidence of contamination, determine its source.

7   Inspect the oil pump pocket and oil pump cover assembly for cracks, scoring, and casting imperfections.

8   Inspect the pressure regulator valve for scoring and sticking. Remove burrs with a fine oil stone.

9   Inspect the pressure regulator valve spring for distortion and loss of tension. If you have any doubt regarding the condition of the spring, replace it.

10   Clean the screen assembly and inspect it for damage.

11   Inspect the pump gears for chipping, galling, and wear.

12   We recommend replacing the oil pump gears (or gerotor assembly on later models) whenever they are removed, since they are so critical to proper engine lubrication.

Installation

13   Lubricate all internal parts with engine oil.

14   To assure priming and avoid engine damage, pack all pump cavities with petroleum jelly.

15   Install the oil pump gears.

16   Install the oil pump cover assembly.

17   Install the pressure regulator valve and spring.

18   Install the pressure regulator plug or pin. Make sure it's properly secured.

19   Install the oil pump cover assembly and tighten the bolts securely.

20   Install the restrictor (if equipped) and a new filter.

21   Install the oil pan.

14.4 Remove the crankshaft hub bolt

22   Fill the crankcase to the correct level with clean engine oil.

23   Remove the oil pressure sending unit and install an oil pressure gauge in its place.

24   Start the engine and note the oil pressure. If it doesn't build up quickly, remove the oil pan and examine the pump. If necessary, disassemble the pump and repack all cavities with petroleum jelly. Running the engine without oil pressure will cause extensive damage.

14   Crankshaft pulley hub and front oil seal - removal and installation

Refer to illustrations 14.4, 14.6 and 14.10

1   Remove the cable from the negative battery terminal. **Caution:** *If the vehicle is equipped with a Delco Loc II audio system, make sure you have the correct activation code before disconnecting the battery. See the information at the front of this manual for the radio re-activation procedure.*

2   Loosen the accessory drivebelt tension adjusting bolts, as necessary, and remove the drivebelts (see Chapter 1). Tag each belt as it is removed to simplify reinstallation.

3   Remove the right front inner fender splash shield.

4   Remove the flywheel/driveplate access cover and wedge a large screwdriver into the ring gear teeth to keep the engine from turning, then loosen the hub bolt. A breaker bar will probably be necessary, since the bolt is very tight **(see illustration)**.

5   Mark the position of the pulley in relation to the hub. Remove the bolts and separate the pulley from the hub.

6   Using a puller, remove the hub from the crankshaft **(see illustration)**.

7   If you're replacing the front seal with the cover installed, carefully pry the oil seal out of the front cover with a large screwdriver. Be careful not to distort the cover.

8   Install the new seal with the helical lip toward the engine. Drive the seal into place using a seal installation tool or a large socket

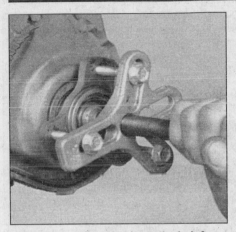

14.6 Use a puller to remove the hub from the crankshaft

14.10 Use the pulley hub bolt to press the hub onto the crankshaft

15.7 Remove the timing gear cover mounting bolts

and hammer. If there is enough room, a block of wood and hammer can also be used.

9 Apply a thin layer of multi-purpose grease to the seal contact surface of the hub.

10 Position the pulley hub on the crankshaft and slide it through the seal until it bottoms against the crankshaft gear. Note that the slot in the hub must be aligned with the Woodruff key in the end of the crankshaft. The hub-to-crankshaft bolt can also be used to press the hub into position **(see illustration)**.

11 Install the crank pulley on the hub, noting the alignment marks made during removal. The pulley-to-hub bolts should be coated with thread locking compound whenever they are removed and installed.

12 Tighten the hub-to-crankshaft bolt to the torque listed in this Chapter's Specifications.

13 The remaining installation steps are the reverse of removal. Tighten the drivebelts to the proper tension (refer to Chapter 1).

15 Timing gear cover- removal and installation

Refer to illustrations 15.7 and 15.13

1 Remove the crankshaft pulley hub as described in Section 14.

2 Remove the lower alternator bracket.

3 Remove the front engine mount-to-cradle nuts.

4 Raise the engine sufficiently with a jack to allow removal of the engine support bracket and mount assembly.

5 Remove the mounting bracket-to-engine block bolts and remove the support bracket and mount as an assembly.

6 Remove the oil pan-to-timing gear cover bolts.

7 Remove the timing cover-to-block bolts **(see illustration)**.

8 Using a sharp knife, cut the oil pan front gasket (RTV only is used on later models) flush with the engine block at both sides.

9 Remove the cover and the attached portion of the oil pan gasket.

10 Remove the cover gasket.

11 Using a scraper and degreaser, remove all dirt and old gasket material from the sealing surfaces of the timing gear cover, engine block and oil pan. Gasket removal solvents are available at auto parts stores and may prove helpful.

12 Remove the front oil seal by carefully prying it out of the timing gear cover with a large screwdriver. Do not distort the cover.

13 Install the new seal with the helical lip toward the inside of the cover. Drive the seal into place using a seal installation tool or a large socket and hammer. A block of wood will also work **(see illustration)**.

1984 and earlier models

14 Prior to installing the cover, install a new front oil pan gasket. Cut the ends off of the gasket, as shown in the accompanying illustration, and attach it to the cover by pressing the rubber tips into the holes provided.

15 Apply a thin coat of RTV-type gasket sealant to the timing gear cover gasket and place it in position on the cover.

16 Apply a bead of RTV-type sealant to the joint between the oil pan and engine block.

1985 and later models

17 On 1985 and later models, RTV sealant only is used to seal the front cover and oil pan.

18 Apply a 3/8-inch (wide) by 3/16-inch (thick) bead of RTV sealant to the joint at the oil pan and timing gear cover **(see illustration)**.

19 Apply a 1/4-inch (wide) by 1/8-inch (thick) bead of RTV sealant to the timing gear cover at the block mating surfaces.

All models

20 Lubricate the pulley hub seal with clean engine oil.

21 Insert the hub through the cover seal and place the cover in position on the block as the hub slides onto the crankshaft. This will ensure that the seal is centered evenly around the hub.

22 Install the oil pan-to-cover bolts and

15.13 Use a block of wood and hammer to install the oil seal

partially tighten them.

23 Install the bolts that secure the cover to the block, then tighten all of the mounting bolts to the torque listed in this Chapter's Specifications.

24 Complete the installation by reversing the removal procedure.

16 Camshaft and timing gears - removal and installation

Since the engine is mounted transversely in the engine compartment, there is not room to remove the camshaft and timing gears with the engine in the vehicle. Refer to Chapter 2, Part E for the camshaft inspection, removal and installation procedures.

17 Flywheel/driveplate and rear main oil seal - removal and installation

Refer to illustrations 17.5 and 17.8

1 The rear main oil seal can be replaced without removal of the oil pan or crankshaft.

17.5 Carefully pry the oil seal out with a screwdriver - don't nick or scratch the crankshaft or the new seal will be damaged and leaks will develop

17.8 Tap around the outer edge of the new seal with a hammer and a punch to seat it squarely in the bore

2   Refer to Chapter 7, follow all precautionary notes and remove the transaxle.

3   If equipped with a manual transmission, remove the pressure plate and clutch disc (see Chapter 8).

4   Remove the flywheel or driveplate mounting bolts and separate it from the crankshaft.

5   Using a screwdriver or prybar, carefully remove the oil seal from the block **(see illustration)**.

6   Using solvent, thoroughly clean the block-to-seal mating surfaces, then dry them with compressed air. **Warning:** *Wear eye protection when using compressed air.*

7   Apply a light coat of engine oil to the lip and outside surface of the new seal.

8   Carefully work the lip of the new seal over the crankshaft, then gently tap the seal into place with a hammer and punch **(see illustration)**.

9   Install the flywheel or driveplate and tighten the bolts to the torque listed in this Chapter's Specifications.

10   If equipped with a manual transaxle, reinstall the clutch disc and pressure plate.

11   Reinstall the transaxle as described in Chapter 7.

18   Engine and transaxle mounts - check and replacement

Check (engine and transaxle mounts)

1   If the rubber mounts have become hard, split or separated from the metal backing, they must be replaced. Applying rubber preservative to the mounts will help slow deterioration. To check the mounts, raise the vehicle, place it securely on jackstands, then raise the engine or transaxle slightly with a jack (just enough to take the weight off the mount) - see Step 3. Check the following:

a) *Check the mounts to see if the rubber is cracked, hardened or separated from the metal plates. Sometimes the rubber will split right down the center.*

b) *Check for relative movement between the mount plates and the engine/transaxle or frame (use a large screwdriver or prybar to attempt to move the mounts). If movement is noted, lower the engine and tighten the mount fasteners.*

Engine mount removal and installation

2   Raise the vehicle and support it securely on jackstands.

3   Support the engine with a jack. If you must position the jack head under the oil pan, place a large wood block between the jack head and oil pan to prevent pan dents and possible oil starvation. **Warning:** *Never position any part of your body under the engine when it's supported only by a jack.*

4   Remove the mount-to-chassis nuts.

5   On air-conditioning-equipped models, remove the forward torque strut bolts at the radiator support panel.

6   Remove the two upper mount-to-engine support bracket nuts and lift the mount from the vehicle. **Warning:** *When removing the mount, use a long screwdriver or similar tool so there's no chance of your hands being injured if the jack should fail.*

7   Installation is the reverse of removal.

Front transaxle mount removal and installation

8   Raise the vehicle and support it securely on jackstands.

9   Support the transaxle with a jack. **Warn-** *ing: Never position any part of your body under the transaxle or engine when it's supported only by a jack.*

10   Remove the mount-to-chassis nuts.

11   Remove the mount-to-transaxle support bracket nut and lift the mount from the vehicle. **Warning:** *When removing the mount, use a long screwdriver or similar tool so there's no chance of your hands being injured if the jack should fail.*

12   Install the new mount and tighten the nut.

13   Install the mount-to-chassis nuts.

14   Remove the jack supporting the transaxle and lower the vehicle.

Rear transaxle mount removal and installation

15   Raise the vehicle and support it securely on jackstands.

16   Place a jackstand under the rear cradle, remove the bolts and lower the cradle.

17   Remove the upper mount bolts and the cradle-to-mount nuts.

18   Raise the engine with a jack sufficiently to allow removal of the mount. If you must position the jack head under the oil pan, place a large wood block between the jack head and oil pan to prevent pan dents and possible oil starvation. **Warning:** *Never position any part of your body under the engine when it's supported only by a jack. When removing the mount, use a long screwdriver or similar tool so there's no chance of your hands being injured if the jack should fail.*

19   Install the new mount and install the upper mount bolts.

20   Remove the jack supporting the engine.

21   Raise the cradle into position and install the bolts.

22   Install the lower mount-to-cradle nuts.

23   Lower the vehicle.

Chapter 2 Part C
2.8L and 3.1L V6 engines

Contents

Specifications

General

Cylinder numbers (drivebelt end-to-transaxle end)	
Front bank (radiator side)	2-4-6
Rear bank	1-3-5
Firing order	1-2-3-4-5-6

Torque specifications

Ft-lbs (unless otherwise indicated)

Camshaft sprocket bolts	
1991 and earlier	18
1994 and later	81
Rear camshaft cover bolts	84 in-lbs
Cylinder head bolts	
1985 and earlier	68
1986 and later	
Step 1	33
Step 2	Turn an additional 90-degrees
Crankshaft pulley bolts	25
Vibration damper bolt	75
Engine mounting bracket bolts	80
Engine mount strut bracket bolt	
1990 and earlier	35
1991 and later	41
Exhaust manifold mounting bolts	
1990 and earlier	25
1991 and later	18
Flywheel/driveplate mounting bolts	
1991 and earlier	50
1994 and later	61

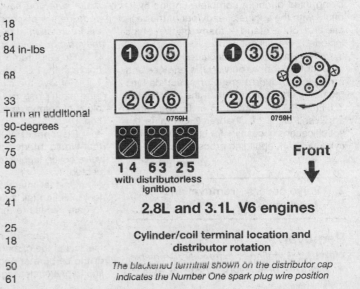

1 4 63 25
with distributorless ignition

Front ↓

2.8L and 3.1L V6 engines

Cylinder/coil terminal location and distributor rotation

The blackened terminal shown on the distributor cap indicates the Number One spark plug wire position

Torque specifications (continued)   Ft-lbs (unless otherwise indicated)

Front cover mounting bolts
  Small bolts
    1986 and earlier 15
    1987 through 1991.. 20
    1994 and later 15
  Large bolts
    1986 and earlier 25
    1987 through 1991.. 28
    1994 and later 35
Intake manifold mounting bolts
  1986 and earlier 23
  1987 through 1991
    Step 1 15
    Step 2 24
  1994 and later .... 115 in-lbs
Oil pan mounting bolts/nuts
  1991 and earlier
    Small bolts .... 96 in-lbs
    Large bolts 18
  1994 and later
    Bottom bolts 18
    Side bolts 37
  Nuts (if equipped) .... 96 in-lbs
Oil pump mounting bolt 30
Oil pump cover bolts .... 96 in-lbs
Valve cover bolts .... 96 in-lbs
Rocker arm nuts
  1987 through 1995 18
  1996
    Step 1 .... 89 in-lbs
    Step 2 .... Tighten an additional 30 degrees
Timing chain tensioner bolts... 15

---

1   General information

The following Sections in this Part of Chapter 2 are devoted to in-vehicle repair procedures for the 2.8 liter and 3.1 liter V6 engines. All information concerning engine removal and installation and cylinder block and cylinder head servicing can be found in Part E of this Chapter.

The repair procedures are based on the assumption that the engine is still installed in the vehicle. Therefore, if this information is being used during a complete engine overhaul - with the engine already out of the vehicle and on a stand - many of the Steps included here will not apply.

The Specifications included in this Part of Chapter 2 apply only to the engines and procedures found here. For specifications regarding engines other than the 2.8 liter and 3.1 liter V6, see Part A, B or D, whichever applies. Part E of Chapter 2 contains the specifications necessary for engine block and cylinder head rebuilding procedures.

2   Valve covers - removal and installation

Removal

Warning: *Gasoline is extremely flammable, so take extra precautions when you work on*

any part of the fuel system. Don't smoke or allow open flames or bare light bulbs near the work area, and don't work in a garage where a natural gas-type appliance (such as a water heater or clothes dryer) with a pilot light is present. If you spill any fuel on your skin, rinse it off immediately with soap and water. When you perform any kind of work on the fuel system, wear safety glasses and have a Class B type fire extinguisher on hand.

1   Disconnect the cable from the negative battery terminal. **Caution:** *If the vehicle is equipped with a Delco Loc II audio system, make sure you have the correct activation code before disconnecting the battery. See the information at the front of this manual for the radio re-activation procedure.*

2   On carbureted models, disconnect the hoses at the PCV valve and label them.

3   Remove the air cleaner assembly, tagging each hose to be disconnected with a piece of numbered tape to simplify reinstallation.

4   Disconnect all other wires and hoses that would interfere with the removal of the valve cover, tagging them as they are disconnected.

5   On fuel injected models, remove any fuel injection (air induction) parts necessary to gain access to the valve cover bolts and cover.

6   On carbureted models, disconnect the fuel line at the carburetor, plugging the fitting at the carburetor and the disconnected fuel line to prevent leakage and contamination.

Front cover

7   Drain the coolant from the radiator (see Chapter 1).

8   Loosen the coolant tube hose clamp below the thermostat housing, then disconnect the other end of the hose at the water pump.

9   Unbolt the coolant tube bracket and move it aside.

10   Remove the vent tube from the valve cover to the air inlet hose.

11   Unbolt the engine mount strut from the bracket on the cylinder head, loosen but do not remove the through bolt on the opposite end at the radiator support, then swing the bracket up and forward, out of the way.

12   Remove the strut bracket from the cylinder head.

Rear cover

13   On automatic transaxle-equipped models, disconnect the throttle valve (TV) cable from the carburetor or fuel injection throttle body.

14   Remove the bolts retaining the air management valve (if equipped).

15   If equipped, disconnect the carburetor controls at the carburetor, then remove them from the support bracket.

16   Remove the carburetor - if equipped - (see Chapter 4).

17   Detach the brake booster vacuum line from the bracket.

18   Remove the serpentine drivebelt (see Chapter 1).

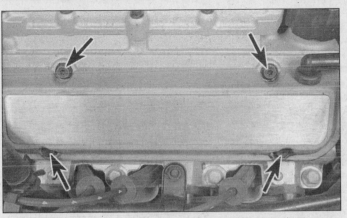

2.23a Removing the valve cover bolts (1986 and earlier models)

2.23b Valve cover mounting bolt locations on 1987 and later models - note that many of these later valve covers are secured by Torx bolts

19 Mark the wires to the alternator with pieces of numbered tape, then disconnect the wires. Remove the rear alternator brace and detach the alternator.

20 Remove the alternator bracket.

Both covers

Refer to illustrations 2.23a and 2.23b

21 Mark the spark plug wires with tape to facilitate reassembly, then disconnect the wires and lay them out of the way.

22 Move aside any wires and hoses that may interfere with valve cover removal.

23 Remove the valve cover bolts **(see illustrations)**.

24 Remove the valve cover(s). **Note:** *If the cover sticks to the cylinder head, use a block of wood and a hammer to dislodge it. If the cover still will not come loose, pry on it carefully, but do not distort the sealing flange surface.*

Installation

25 Clean the valve cover and cylinder head mating surfaces with a scraper and solvent or degreaser. Be sure to remove all traces of old gasket material and sealant.

1986 and earlier models

26 Apply a continuous 3/16-inch diameter bead of RTV-type sealant to the flange of the cover. Be sure to apply the sealant inner side of the bolt holes.

1987 and later models

27 Apply a 3 mm dab of RTV sealant to the intake manifold-to-cylinder head notch at each end of the engine.

28 Install a new valve cover gasket. It may be helpful to "glue" the gasket to the valve cover using a small amount of sealant. Make sure the bolt holes in the gasket line up with the holes in the cover.

All models

29 Place the valve cover on the cylinder head while the sealant is still wet and install the mounting bolts. Tighten the bolts a little at a time to the torque listed in this Chapter's Specifications.

30 Complete the job by reversing the removal procedure. Run the engine and check for leaks.

3 Valve train components - replacement (cylinder head installed)

This procedure is essentially the same as for the 2.5L four-cylinder engine. Follow the procedure in Chapter 2, Part B, except note that the valve seals, which are pressed onto the valve guide protrusion on the cylinder head, are removed differently. GM recommends using a special valve seal removal tool to avoid seal damage, although a pair of pliers will work, since the old seal is always discarded. Install the new seal before installing the spring and retainer, and note that intake and exhaust valve seals are different.

4 Intake manifold - removal and installation

Warning: *Gasoline is extremely flammable, so take extra precautions when you work on any part of the fuel system. Don't smoke or allow open flames or bare light bulbs near the work area, and don't work in a garage where a natural gas-type appliance (such as a water heater or clothes dryer) with a pilot light is present. If you spill any fuel on your skin, rinse it off immediately with soap and water. When you perform any kind of work on the fuel system, wear safety glasses and have a Class B type fire extinguisher on hand.*

Removal

Refer to illustration 4.30

1 If the vehicle is equipped with air conditioning, carefully examine the routing of the hoses and the mounting of the compressor. You may be able to remove the intake manifold without disconnecting the system (this may involve unbolting the A/C compressor

and setting it aside, without disconnecting the lines). If you are in doubt, take the vehicle to a dealer service department or automotive air conditioning shop to have the system depressurized. Do not, under any circumstances, disconnect the hoses while the system is under pressure.

2 On fuel-injected models, relieve the fuel system pressure (see Chapter 4).

3 Disconnect the cable from the negative battery terminal. **Caution:** *If the vehicle is equipped with a Delco Loc II audio system, make sure you have the correct activation code before disconnecting the battery. See the information at the front of this manual for the radio re-activation procedure.*

4 Drain the coolant from the radiator (Chapter 1).

5 On carbureted and TBI models, remove the air cleaner assembly, tagging each hose to be disconnected with a piece of numbered tape to simplify reinstallation. On multi-port fuel-injected models, disconnect the air intake duct at the throttle body.

6 Label and disconnect all electrical wires and vacuum hoses at the carburetor or throttle body.

7 On carbureted models, disconnect the fuel line at the carburetor. Have an approved gasoline container ready to catch some fuel, then plug the fuel line to prevent contamination.

8 On fuel-injected models, disconnect the fuel inlet and return lines at the throttle body or fuel rail (see Chapter 4).

9 Disconnect the throttle cable and, if equipped, the cruise control cable and automatic transaxle downshift cable. Make careful note of how the cables were installed.

10 On multi-point fuel-injected models, remove the throttle body (see Chapter 4).

11 Disconnect the spark plug wires at the spark plugs, referring to the removal technique described in Chapter 1.

12 Disconnect the wires at the coil, again using numbered pieces of tape to label them.

13 If equipped, remove the distributor cap and the attached spark plug wires (refer to Chapter 5).

4.30 Using a large screwdriver or prybar to break the intake manifold gasket seal

4.34 Apply a 3/16-inch bead of RTV sealant (arrows) to the front and rear ridges of the engine block (1987 and later models shown, but earlier models require sealant at the same locations)

14   If equipped, remove the distributor (refer to Chapter 5).

15   Remove the power brake pipe and bracket.

16   Move the power brake tube/hose aside so it will not interfere with the removal of the manifold.

17   On multi-port fuel-injected models, remove the serpentine drivebelt (see Chapter 1), then remove the power steering pump without disconnecting the hoses and set it aside, being careful not to spill any fluid (see Chapter 10).

18   On multi-port fuel-injected models, remove the alternator and bracket (see Chapter 5).

19   Remove the solenoid/hose bracket.

20   On multi-port fuel-injected models, remove the EGR valve, then remove the upper intake plenum (see Chapter 4).

21   On multi-port fuel-injected models, remove the fuel rail (see Chapter 4).

22   Remove the mounting bolts from the left valve cover, then remove the cover.

23   Remove the AIR pump and bracket.

24   Remove the bolts from the right valve cover, then remove the cover.

25   Remove the upper radiator hose from the manifold.

26   Disconnect the heater hose at the manifold.

27   Make sure that all wires, vacuum hoses and coolant hoses that would interfere with manifold removal have been disconnected.

28   If the manifold is to be replaced with a new one, the external components remaining on the manifold must be removed for transfer to the new manifold. These components may be removed either before or after the manifold has been separated from the engine. On most models these components include: Carburetor choke assembly and carburetor studs or bolts (Refer to Chapter 4 for details), Coolant switch, EGR valve (use a new gasket when installing), emissions system TVS valve.

29   Remove the manifold mounting bolts.

30   Separate the manifold from the engine by prying with a suitable bar (do not pry

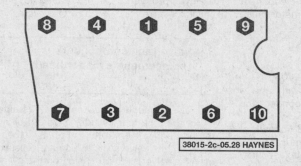

4.39 Intake manifold bolt tightening sequence

38015-2c-05.28 HAYNES

between the mating surfaces) or tapping the manifold with a hammer and wooden block to loosen it **(see illustration)**.

Installation

Refer to illustrations 4.34 and 4.39

31   If a new manifold is being installed, transfer the external components from the old manifold to the new one.

32   On 1987 and later models, loosen the rocker arms and withdraw the pushrods. Store the pushrods separately to ensure reinstallation in the same positions.

33   Before installing the manifold, place clean, lint-free rags in the engine cavity and clean the engine block, cylinder head and manifold gasket surfaces. All gasket material and sealant must be removed prior to installation (a gasket scraper is very helpful). Remove all dirt and gasket remnants from the engine cavity.

34   Clean the gasket sealing surfaces with degreaser, then apply a 3/16-inch diameter bead of RTV-type sealant to the engine block end ridges only **(see illustration)**.

35   Install the new intake gaskets on the cylinder heads. Notice that the gaskets are normally marked *Right* and *Left*. Be sure to use the correct gasket on each cylinder head.

36   On 1987 and later models, install the pushrods in their original locations and reposition the rocker arms on the pushrods. Tighten the rocker arm nuts to the torque

listed in this Chapter's Specifications.

37   Hold the gaskets in place by extending the bead of RTV 1/4-inch onto the gasket ends. On 1986 and earlier models, the new gaskets will have to be cut so they can be installed behind the pushrods.

38   Carefully lower the intake manifold into position, making sure that you do not disturb the gaskets.

39   Install the intake manifold mounting bolts and tighten them following the sequence illustrated. Tighten the bolts a little at a time until they are all at the torque listed in this Chapter's Specifications **(see illustration)**.

40   Install the remaining components in the reverse order of removal.

41   Fill the radiator with coolant, start the engine and check for leaks. Adjust the ignition timing and idle speed as necessary (refer to Chapter 1).

5   Hydraulic lifters - removal, inspection and installation

This procedure is essentially the same as for the 2.5L four-cylinder engine. Refer to Chapter 2, Part B for the procedure, but follow the procedures in this Part for valve cover and intake manifold removal and installation. On 1986 and earlier models, be sure to adjust the valve lash after re-assembly (see the next Section). On 1987 and later models, tighten

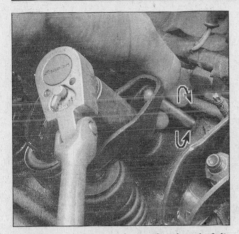

6.5 Determining at what point drag is felt on the pushrod by rotating it as the nut is tightened

8.8a Loosen the rocker arm nuts

8.8b When removing the pushrods, be sure to store them separately to ensure reinstallation in their original positions

the rocker arm nuts to the torque listed in this Chapter's Specifications. Keep in mind that a noisy lifter on 1986 and earlier models could be due to incorrect valve lash adjustment.

6   Valve lash - adjustment (1986 and earlier models)

Refer to illustration 6.5
Note: *1987 and later models have rocker arms that are secured by locking nuts - the valve lash is pre-set and cannot be adjusted.*
1   Disconnect the cable from the negative battery terminal. **Caution:** *If the vehicle is equipped with a Delco Loc II audio system, make sure you have the correct activation code before disconnecting the battery. See the information at the front of this manual for the radio re-activation procedure.*
2   If the valve covers are still on the engine, refer to Section 2 and remove them.
3   If the valve train components have been serviced just prior to this procedure, make sure that the components are completely reassembled.
4   Rotate the crankshaft until the number one piston is at Top Dead Center (TDC) on the compression stroke (see Chapter 2E).
5   Start with the number one cylinder intake valve. Back off the rocker arm nut until play is felt at the pushrod, then turn it back in until all play is removed. This can be determined by rotating the pushrod while tightening the nut. Just when a slight drag is felt when rotating the pushrod, all lash has been removed. Now tighten the nut an additional 3/4 turn **(see illustration).**
6   Adjust the number one, five and six cylinder intake valves and the number one, two and three cylinder exhaust valves, with the crankshaft in this position, using the method just described.
7   Rotate the crankshaft until the number four piston is at TDC on the compression stroke and adjust the number two, three and four cylinder intake valves and the number

four, five and six cylinder exhaust valves.
8   Refer to Section 2 and install the valve covers.

7   Exhaust manifolds - removal and installation

Warning: *The engine must be completely cool before beginning this procedure.*
1   Remove the cable from the negative battery terminal. **Caution:** *If the vehicle is equipped with a Delco Loc II audio system, make sure you have the correct activation code before disconnecting the battery. See the information at the front of this manual for the radio re-activation procedure.*
2   Remove the air cleaner assembly, labeling all hoses.

Rear manifold

3   Disconnect the air injection reactor (AIR) bracket.
4   Raise the front of the vehicle and support it securely on jackstands. Block the rear wheels to keep the vehicle from rolling.
5   Remove the bolts attaching the exhaust pipe to the exhaust manifold, then separate the pipe from the manifold.
6   Remove the jackstands and lower the vehicle.
7   Disconnect the oxygen sensor pigtail electrical connector.
8   Disconnect the air management hose at the check valve.
9   Disconnect the spark plug wires from the spark plugs, labeling them as they are disconnected to simplify installation.
10   Remove the exhaust manifold mounting bolts and separate the manifold from the engine.
11   Installation is the reverse of the removal procedure. Before installing the manifold, be sure to thoroughly clean the mating surfaces on the manifold and cylinder head.

Front manifold

12   Disconnect the crossover pipe.
13   On models equipped with Multi-Point

Fuel Injection, remove the air conditioning compressor mounting bolts, secure the compressor aside (without disconnecting the refrigerant lines) and remove the compressor mounting bracket.
14   Remove the bolts retaining the exhaust pipe to the manifold, then disconnect the pipe from the manifold.
15   Remove the four bolts and one nut accessible at the rear of the manifold.
16   Disconnect and label any wires that will interfere with the removal of the manifold.
17   Remove the remaining manifold bolts and separate the manifold and heat shield from the engine.
18   Installation is the reverse of the removal procedure. Be sure to thoroughly clean the cylinder head and manifold surfaces before installing the manifold.

8   Cylinder heads - removal and installation

Refer to illustrations 8.8a, 8.8b, 8.10 and 8.15
1   Remove the exhaust crossover pipe (see Section 7).
2   Raise the vehicle and place it securely on jackstands.
3   Locate the engine block drain plugs, remove them and drain the coolant (the plug on the left side is just above the oil filter).
4   Disconnect the exhaust pipe from the rear exhaust manifold, then remove the jackstands and lower the vehicle.
5   Remove the alternator and bracket and the air injection reactor (AIR) pump and brackets, then remove the AIR system Air Management valve and hose (see Chapter 6).
6   Remove the oil dipstick tube assembly from the left side of the engine, then remove the cruise control servo bracket (if equipped).
7   Remove the intake manifold (refer to Section 4) and exhaust manifolds (Section 7).
8   Loosen the rocker arm nuts enough to allow removal of the pushrods, then remove the pushrods **(see illustrations).**

8.10 Use a tool such as a breaker bar inserted into an exhaust port to break the gasket seal on the cylinder head

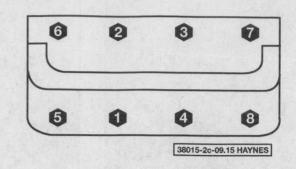

38015-2c-09.15 HAYNES

8.15 Recommended tightening sequence for the cylinder head mounting bolts

9   Loosen the head bolts in a sequence opposite to the one used for tightening (**see illustration 8.15**).

10   Remove the cylinder heads. To break the gasket seal, insert a bar into one of the exhaust ports, then carefully lift on the tool (**see illustration**).

11   If a new cylinder head is being installed, transfer the various components, such as the manifold, brackets and coolant temperature sensor, from the old head. Before installing the new head, use a gasket scraper to clean the gasket surfaces of both the head and the engine block and make sure they're free of nicks and scratches. Also, the threads in the block and on the head bolts must be completely clean, as any dirt or sealant in the threads will affect bolt torque. Taps and dies can be used to clean the bolt holes and bolts. Gasket removal solvents are commonly available at auto parts stores and may prove helpful.

12   Place the gaskets in position over the locating dowels, with the note *This Side Up* visible.

13   Position the cylinder heads over the gaskets.

14   Coat the cylinder head bolts with an appropriate sealant and install the bolts.

15   Tighten the bolts in the proper sequence (**see illustration**) to the specified torque. Work up to the final torque in two steps.

16   Install the pushrods, making sure the lower ends are in the lifter seats, place the rocker arm ends over the pushrods and install the rocker arms. On 1986 and earlier models, install the rocker arm nuts loosely. On 1987 and later models, tighten the rocker arm nuts to the torque listed in this Chapter's Specifications.

17   The remaining installation Steps are the reverse of those for removal. On 1986 and earlier models, adjust the valve lash (refer to Section 6) before installing the valve covers.

9   Oil pan - removal and installation

Note: *Most of the Steps in this procedure will not be required if the engine has been*

removed from the vehicle. The pan can simply be unbolted and removed, cleaned and installed as indicated.

1   Disconnect the cable from the negative battery terminal. **Caution:** *If the vehicle is equipped with a Delco Loc II audio system, make sure you have the correct activation code before disconnecting the battery. See the information at the front of this manual for the radio re-activation procedure.*

2   Raise the vehicle and support it on jackstands.

3   Drain the engine oil.

4   If equipped with an automatic transmission, remove the converter shroud.

5   If equipped with a manual transmission, remove the flywheel cover.

6   Remove the starter (refer to Chapter 5). On 1987 and later models, if the engine is equipped with an AIR pump, remove it (see Chapter 6).

7   Support the engine with a hoist.

8   Remove the front engine mount and the engine mount-to-block bracket (see Section 17). Disconnect the exhaust pipe from the rear exhaust manifold.

9   Remove the oil pan bolts. On 1994 and later models, remove the oil pan side bolts. Note the different sizes used and their locations.

10   Raise the engine and remove the oil pan.

11   Before installing the pan, make sure that the sealing surfaces on the pan, block and front cover are clean and free of oil. If the old pan is being reinstalled, make sure that all sealant has been removed from the pan sealing flange and from the blind attaching holes. Gasket removal solvents are available at auto parts stores and may prove helpful. Make sure all bolts are clean and that the pan sealing flanges are straight. To straighten a bent pan flange, support the flange from below on a piece of 1-by-4 wood and tap on the top of the pan flange with a hammer.

1986 and earlier models

12   With all the sealing surfaces clean, place a 1/8-inch bead of RTV-type sealant on the oil pan sealing flange. Make sure you run the

bead to the inner side of the bolt holes or oil leaks will develop at the bolt holes.

1987 and later models

13   1987 and later models use a special one-piece neoprene gasket. Apply a bead of RTV sealant to the front of the gasket, where it contacts the front cover, and to the rear main bearing cap, where the gasket tabs insert into the groove, then install the gasket on the pan carefully so it does not fall out of position when installed.

All models

14   Lift the pan into position and install all bolts finger tight. Tighten the bolts, working from the center out, to the torques listed in this Chapter's Specifications. Do not take more than five minutes from the time the sealant is applied to the time the bolts are torqued, otherwise the sealant will not bond properly to the block.

15   Install the front engine mount and engine mount bracket. Lower the front of the engine onto the mount and install the retaining nuts. Tighten the nuts securely.

16   Follow the removal steps in reverse order. Fill the crankcase with the correct grade and quantity of oil, start the engine and check for leaks.

10   Oil pump - removal and installation

Refer to illustration 10.2

1   Remove the oil pan (refer to Section 9).

2   Remove the pump-to-rear main bearing cap bolt and separate the pump and extension shaft from the engine (**see illustration**).

3   Considering the relatively reasonable cost of a new oil pump compared with the potential of major engine damage if the oil pump malfunctions, we recommend replacing the oil pump any time it's removed. Inspect the extension shaft for any wear in the areas where it fits into the distributor drive gear and oil pump. Also inspect the shaft for twisting damage. Replace it if

10.2 Remove the oil pump-to-rear main bearing cap bolt

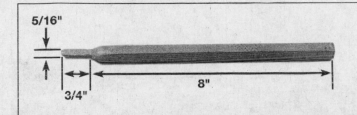
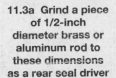

11.3a Grind a piece of 1/2-inch diameter brass or aluminum rod to these dimensions as a rear seal driver

11.3b Drive each end of the seal into the groove until it feels tightly packed

11.5 Measure the amount that the seal has been driven up into the groove - here a small screwdriver was used with a sleeve of masking tape (arrow) to serve as a depth indicator

there's any wear or damage. Again, we recommend replacing the shaft as a matter of course whenever it's removed, since shaft failure means a complete loss in oil pressure.

4   To install the pump, move it into position and align the top end of the hexagonal extension shaft with the hexagonal socket in the lower end of the distributor drive gear. The distributor drives the oil pump, so it is essential that this alignment is correct.

5   Install the oil pump-to-rear main bearing cap bolt and tighten it to the torque listed in this Chapter's Specifications.

6   Reinstall the oil pan.

11   Rear main oil seal - replacement

1982 and 1983 models

Refer to illustrations 11.3a, 11.3b and 11.5
Note: *Special tools, as noted in the Steps which follow, are required for this procedure. In most cases they can be obtained from an auto parts store or tool rental shop.*

1   Although the crankshaft must be removed to install a new seal, the upper portion of the seal can be repaired with the crankshaft in place.

2   Remove the oil pan and oil pump (Sections 9 and 10), then unbolt and remove the rear main bearing cap.

3   Insert the special seal tool or equivalent **(see illustration)**. Drive the old seal gently back into the groove, packing it tight. It will pack in to a depth of 1/4 to 3/4-inch **(see illustration)**.

4   Repeat the procedure on the other end of the seal.

5   Measure the amount that the seal was driven up into the groove on one side and add 1/16-inch. Remove the old seal from the main bearing cap. Use the main bearing cap as a fixture and cut off a piece of the old seal to the predetermined length. Repeat this process for the other side **(see illustration)**.

6   Place a drop of sealant on each end of these pieces and then pack them into the

upper groove to fill the gap made previously.

7   Trim the remaining material perfectly flush with the block.

8   Be careful not harm the bearing surface. If necessary place a thin piece of shim stock between the seal and the crankshaft, to protect the crankshaft, and trim the seal against the shim stock.

9   Install a new seal in the main bearing cap.

10   Apply a thin, even coat of anaerobic-type gasket sealant to the areas of the rear main bearing cap that mate with the engine block (indicated in the illustration in Chapter 2, Part E). **Caution:** *Do not get any sealant on the bearing or seal faces.*

11   Tighten the rear main bearing cap bolts to the torque specified in Chapter 2, Part E.

12   Install the oil pump and oil pan.

1984 and 1985 models

Refer to illustrations 11.17, 11.20, 11.21 and 11.24

13   These models use a two-piece (180-degree) neoprene lip-type seal. Always replace both halves of the seal. While replacement of this seal is much easier with the engine removed from the vehicle, the job can be done with the engine in place.

14   Remove the oil pan and oil pump as described previously in this Chapter.

15   Remove the rear main bearing cap from the engine.

16   Using a screwdriver, pry the lower half of the oil seal from the bearing cap.

17   To remove the upper half of the seal, use a small hammer and a brass pin punch to roll the seal around the crankshaft journal.

Tap one end of the seal with the hammer and punch (be careful not to strike the crankshaft) until the other end of the seal protrudes enough to pull it out with pliers **(see illustration)**.

18   Remove all sealant and foreign material from the main bearing cap. Do not use an abrasive cleaner for this.

19   Inspect the components for nicks, scratches and burrs at all sealing surfaces. Remove any defects with a fine file or deburring tool.

11.17 Drive in one end of the upper seal half until the other end protrudes, then pull the seal (arrow) all the way out with a pair of pliers

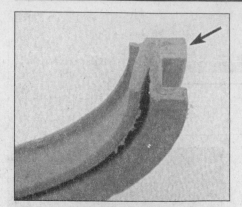

11.20 A very thin coat of RTV-type gasket sealant should be applied to the area shown on 1984 and 1985 rear main bearing seals (avoid getting sealant on the seal lips)

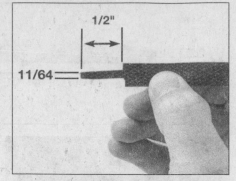

11.21 A "shoehorn" guide for the rear seal can be made from a thin piece of plastic, brass or shim stock

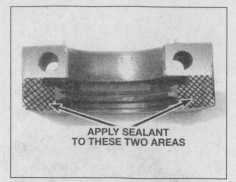

11.24 Apply anaerobic sealant to the areas shown on the rear main bearing cap of 1984 and 1985 models prior to installation (do not get sealant in the grooves or on the seal)

20   Apply a very thin coat of RTV-type gasket sealant to the outer surface of the upper seal as shown in the accompanying illustration. Do not get any sealant on the seal lips **(see illustration)**.

21   Included in the purchase of the rear main oil seal should be a small plastic installation tool. If not, a tool may be fashioned from an old feeler gauge blade **(see illustration)**.

22   With the upper half of the seal positioned so that the seal lip faces toward the front of the engine and the small dust lip faces toward the flywheel, install the seal by rolling it around the crankshaft using the installation tool as a shoehorn for protection against being damaged by the engine block's sharp corner.

23   Apply sealing compound as described in Step 20 to the other half of the seal and install it in the bearing cap.

24   Apply a 1/32-inch bead of anaerobic sealant to the cap between the rear main oil seal end and oil pan rear seal groove. Be sure to keep the sealant off the rear main oil seal and bearing and out of the drain slot **(see illustration)**.

25   Just before installing the cap, apply a light coat of moly-based grease or engine assembly lube to the crankshaft surface that will contact the seal.

26   Install the rear main bearing cap and tighten the bolts to the torque specified in Chapter 2, Part E.

27   Install the oil pump and oil pan.

1986 and later models

Refer to illustration 11.31

28   Beginning in 1986, a 360-degree (one-piece) lip-type seal is utilized, which allows the oil pan to remain in place when performing this operation.

29   Remove the transmission (refer to Chapter 7).

30   Remove the flywheel or driveplate (see Chapter 2, Part A).

31   Pry out the old seal, taking care not to mar the crankshaft or seal bore surfaces. Inspect the crankshaft for scratches, burrs and nicks on the sealing surface **(see illustration)**.

32   Press the new seal into place with a special seal installer if available. If the installer is not available tap around the outer edge of the new seal with a hammer and punch to seat it squarely in the bore.

33   Install the flywheel or driveplate.

If equipped with a manual transaxle, reinstall the clutch disc and pressure plate.

34   Reinstall the transaxle (see Chapter 7).

12   Vibration damper - removal and installation

Refer to illustrations 12.5 and 12.7

1   Disconnect the negative cable at the battery. **Caution:** *If the vehicle is equipped with a Delco Loc II audio system, make sure you have the correct activation code before disconnecting the battery. See the information at the front of this manual for the radio re-activation procedure.*

2   Loosen the accessory drivebelt adjusting bolts as necessary, then remove the drivebelts, tagging each one as it is removed to simplify reinstallation.

3   Raise the vehicle and support it securely on jackstands.

4   Remove the inner fender splash shield for access.

5   Remove the accessory drivebelt pulley **(see illustration)**.

6   Remove the center bolt from the vibration damper. The crankshaft will probably

11.31 On 1986 and later models, use a screwdriver to pry the rear main seal from the bore (be careful not to scratch the crankshaft sealing surface or the edge of the bore)

12.5 Four bolts secure the crankshaft pulley

12.7 Use a puller to remove the vibration damper

13.25 Front cover bolt locations (1987 and later models)

rotate, since the bolt is very tight. Wedge a large screwdriver into the ring gear teeth on the flywheel/driveplate to keep the crankshaft from rotating.

7   Attach a puller to the damper. Draw the damper off the crankshaft, being careful not to drop it as it breaks free **(see illustration)**. A common gear puller should not be used to draw the damper off, as it may separate the outer portion of the damper from the hub. Use only a puller which bolts to the hub.

8   Before installing the damper, coat the front cover seal area on the damper with moly-base grease.

9   Place the damper in position over the key on the crankshaft. Make sure the damper keyway lines up with the key.

10   Using a damper installation tool available at most auto parts stores, push the damper onto the crankshaft. The special tool distributes the pressure evenly around the hub.

11   Remove the installation tool and install the damper retaining bolt. Tighten the bolt to the torque listed in this Chapter's Specifications.

12   Follow the removal procedure in the reverse order for the remaining components.

13   Adjust the drivebelts (refer to Chapter 1).

13   Crankcase front cover - removal and installation

1   Disconnect the cable from the negative battery terminal. **Caution:** *If the vehicle is equipped with a Delco Loc II audio system, make sure you have the correct activation code before disconnecting the battery. See the information at the front of this manual for the radio re-activation procedure.*

1986 and earlier models

2   If equipped with air conditioning, remove the compressor, mounting bracket and air injection reactor (AIR) pump and bracket. Do not disconnect any of the air

conditioning system hoses without having the system depressurized by a GM dealer or air conditioning technician.

3   Remove the water pump as described in Chapter 3.

4   Raise the vehicle and support it securely on jackstands, then, remove the vibration damper, as described in Section 12.

5   Remove the oil pan-to-front cover bolts.

6   Lower the vehicle.

7   Remove the front cover mounting bolts and separate the cover from the engine.

8   Using a scraper, clean all oil, dirt and old gasket material from the sealing surfaces of the front cover and block. Be very careful not to scratch or gouge the delicate aluminum gasket surfaces on the front cover. Gasket removal solvents are available at auto parts stores and may prove helpful. Wipe the surfaces clean with a rag soaked in lacquer thinner or acetone. Replace the front cover oil seal as described in Section 14.

9   On models which do not use a gasket, apply a continuous 3/32-inch (2 mm) bead of RTV-type sealant to both mating surfaces of the front cover. Also apply sealant to the areas surrounding the coolant passages. On models which use a gasket, apply a 7/64-inch (3 mm) bead of RTV-type sealant to the oil pan contact surface of the cover.

10   Place the front cover in position on the engine block and install the mounting bolts.

11   Tighten the bolts to the specified torque within five minutes.

12   The remaining installation procedures are the reverse of removal.

1987 and later models

Refer to illustration 13.25

13   Open the drain valve at the bottom of the radiator and drain the cooling system (see Chapter 1).

14   Remove the serpentine belt and tensioner (see Chapter 1).

15   Unbolt the alternator and position it aside.

16   Unbolt the power steering pump and

move it aside. It is not necessary to disconnect the power steering hoses.

17   Raise the vehicle and support it on jackstands.

18   Remove the inner fender splash shield for access.

19   Remove the vibration damper (refer to Section 12).

20   Drain the engine oil and remove the oil pan (refer to Section 9).

21   Remove the lower front cover bolts.

22   Lower the vehicle.

23   Disconnect the radiator hose at the water pump.

24   Disconnect the heater hose, bypass and overflow hoses, and position them aside.

25   Remove the remaining front cover bolts and separate the cover from the engine block **(see illustration)**. If the cover sticks, break it loose with a soft-face hammer, but do not pry between the sealing surfaces.

26   Clean all traces of old gasket material from the front cover and engine block mating surfaces.

27   Install a new front cover gasket and apply RTV-type sealant to the bottom ends of the gasket, where the gasket meets the oil pan.

28   Place the front cover in position and install the upper mounting bolts.

29   Once again, raise the vehicle and support it on jackstands.

30   Install the lower cover mounting bolts and tighten them to the torque listed in this Chapter's Specifications.

31   Tighten the upper bolts to the specified torque.

32   Install the crankshaft damper pulley.

33   Lower the vehicle.

34   Reconnect the heater hose, radiator hose, and bypass and overflow hoses.

35   Install the power steering pump.

36   Install the alternator.

37   Install the belt tensioner and serpentine belt.

38   Fill the cooling system with the proper antifreeze solution (refer to Chapter 1). Do not install the cooling system pressure cap at this time.

14.7 Driving the seal out of the front cover

14.9 Install the front cover oil seal with a wood block and hammer

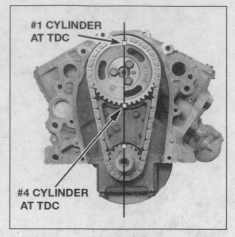

#1 CYLINDER AT TDC

#4 CYLINDER AT TDC

15.9 Proper alignment of the camshaft and crankshaft timing marks

39   Reconnect the battery cable and start the engine. Allow it to run until the upper radiator hose becomes warm to the touch, indicating that the thermostat has opened.
40   Stop the engine and check the coolant level. Add coolant as necessary, install the pressure cap and check for leaks.

14   Front cover oil seal - replacement

Refer to illustrations 14.7 and 14.9
Note: *Always inspect the seal contact area on the vibration damper as part of this procedure. If there is a groove on the damper (caused by wear from contacting the seal), the new seal will probably leak. Auto parts stores may stock sleeves to fit over the damaged area, restoring a flat contact surface. If a sleeve is not available, the only alternative is a new vibration damper.*

With front cover installed on engine

Note: *This method is not preferred, since it is more difficult to perform. However, it saves much time and effort if the front cover does not need to be removed.*
1   With the vibration damper removed (Section 12), pry the old seal out of the crankcase front cover with a seal removal tool or screwdriver. Be careful not to damage the surface of the crankshaft or the seal bore. If you're using a screwdriver, it's a good idea to wrap the tip in tape to prevent damaging the crankshaft or seal bore.
2   Coat the inside and outside diameter of the new seal with engine oil. Place the new seal in position with the open end of the seal (seal lip) toward the engine.
3   Drive the seal into the cover until it is seated. If available, use a seal driver of the proper size. These tools are designed to exert even pressure around the entire circumference of the seal as it is hammered into place. A section of large-diameter pipe or a large socket can also be used. Be careful not

to distort the front cover.
4   Install all components previously removed. Run the engine and check for leaks.

With front cover removed from engine

5   This method is preferred, as the cover can be supported while the old seal is removed and the new one is installed.
6   Remove the crankcase front cover (refer to Section 13).
7   Using a large screwdriver, pry the old seal out of the front cover. Alternatively, support the cover and drive the seal out from the rear **(see illustration)**. Be careful not to damage the cover.
8   Coat the inside (lip) and outside circumference of the new seal with engine oil. With the front of the cover facing up, place the new seal in position with the open (lip) end of the seal toward the inside of the cover.
9   Using a wooden block and hammer, drive the new seal into the cover until it is completely seated **(see illustration)**.
10   Install the cover by reversing the removal procedure. Run the engine and check for leaks.

15   Timing chain and sprockets - inspection, removal and installation

Refer to illustrations 15.9, 15.10 and 15.13
1   Disconnect the cable from the negative battery terminal. **Caution:** *If the vehicle is equipped with a Delco Loc II audio system, make sure you have the correct activation code before disconnecting the battery. See the information at the front of this manual for the radio re-activation procedure.*
2   Remove the vibration damper (refer to Section 12).
3   Remove the crankcase front cover (refer to Section 13).
4   Before removing the chain and sprockets, visually inspect the teeth on the sprock-

ets for signs of wear and the chain for looseness. Check the condition of the timing chain tensioners.
5   If either or both sprockets show any signs of wear (edges on the teeth of the camshaft sprocket not "square", bright blue areas on the teeth of either sprocket, chipping, pitting, etc.), they should be replaced with new ones. Wear in these areas is very common.
6   Failure to replace a worn timing chain may result in erratic engine performance, loss of power and lowered gas mileage.
7   If any one component requires replacement, all related components, including the tensioners, should be replaced as well.
8   If it is determined that the timing components require replacement, proceed as follows. **Note:** *Considering how time consuming it is to change the chain and sprockets, we recommend doing so whenever they are removed.*
9   Rotate the crankshaft until the marks on the camshaft and crankshaft are in exact alignment (this can be done by re-installing the vibration damper bolt into the end of the crankshaft and using a socket and breaker bar to turn it). At this point the number one and four pistons will be at top dead center with the number four piston in the firing position (verify by checking the position of the rotor in the distributor or, on models with direct ignition, by removing the number four spark plug and feeling for compression at the spark plug hole as the crankshaft is rotated). Do not attempt to remove either sprocket or the timing chain until this is done and do not turn the crankshaft or camshaft after the sprockets and chain are removed **(see illustration)**.
10   Remove the three camshaft sprocket retaining bolts and lift the camshaft sprocket and timing chain off the front of the engine **(see illustration)**. It may be necessary to tap the sprocket with a soft-face hammer to dislodge it.
11   If it is necessary to remove the crankshaft sprocket, it can be withdrawn from the crankshaft with a puller.

15.10 Use a screwdriver to hold the camshaft sprocket in place while you loosen the mounting bolts

15.13 Lubricate the thrust surface of the camshaft sprocket

12 Push the crankshaft sprocket onto the nose of the crankshaft, aligning it with the key, until it seats against the shoulder.

13 Lubricate the thrust (rear) surface of the camshaft sprocket with moly-base grease or engine assembly lube **(see illustration)**. Install the timing chain over the camshaft sprocket with slack in the chain hanging down over the crankshaft sprocket.

14 With the timing marks aligned, slip the chain over the crankshaft sprocket and then draw the camshaft sprocket into place with the three retaining bolts. Do not hammer or attempt to drive the camshaft sprocket into place, as it could dislodge the Welch plug at the rear of the engine.

15 With the chain and both sprockets in place, check again to ensure that the timing marks on the two sprockets are properly aligned. If not, remove the timing chain and cam sprocket, turn the camshaft enough to change the chain position on the crankshaft sprocket one tooth, reinstall the chain and camshaft sprocket and check the timing mark alignment. Repeat as necessary until the marks are in alignment.

16 Lubricate the chain with engine oil and install the remaining components in the reverse order of removal.

16 Camshaft - removal and installation

Since the engine must be removed from the vehicle for this procedure, the procedure is covered in Chapter 2, Part E. If your vehicle is a 1986 or earlier model, be sure to adjust the valve lash (Section 6) after the engine is reassembled.

17 Engine and transaxle mounts - check and replacement

Refer to illustration 17.27

1 Mounts seldom require attention, but broken or deteriorated mounts should be replaced immediately or the added strain placed on the driveline components may cause damage or wear.

Check

2 During the check, the engine must be raised slightly to remove the weight from the mounts.

3 Raise the vehicle and support it securely on jackstands, then position a jack under the engine oil pan. Place a large block of wood between the jack head and the oil pan, then carefully raise the engine just enough to take the weight off the mounts. **Warning:** *DO NOT place any part of your body under the engine when it's supported only by a jack!*

4 Check the mounts to see if the rubber is cracked, hardened or separated from the metal plates. Sometimes the rubber will split right down the center.

5 Check for relative movement between the mount plates and the engine or frame (use a large screwdriver or pry bar to attempt to move the mounts). If movement is noted, lower the engine and tighten the mount fasteners.

6 Rubber preservative should be applied to the mounts to slow deterioration.

Replacement

Engine mount

7 Remove the engine mount retaining nuts from below the cradle mounting bracket.

8 Raise the engine slightly, using a hoist or a jack with a wood block under the oil pan, then remove the mount-to-engine bracket nuts and remove the mount. The engine should be raised only enough to provide clearance. **Warning:** *DO NOT place any part of your body under the engine when it's supported only by a jack!*

9 Install the new mount and lower the engine into place. Install the nuts and tighten them securely.

Front transaxle mount

10 Lift the transaxle sufficiently to take the weight off the mounts. **Warning:** *DO NOT place any part of your body under the*

transaxle when it's supported only by a jack!

11 Remove the crossmember-to-mount nuts.

12 Remove the bracket-to-transaxle bolts and remove the mount and bracket assembly.

13 Remove the mount-to-bracket nuts.

14 Install the new mount on the transaxle bracket and the mount assembly on the transaxle.

15 Align the crossmember-to-transaxle studs with the holes as the transaxle is lowered into position.

16 Check the alignment of the transaxle mounts, adjusting as necessary.

17 Install the mount-to-crossmember nuts. Tighten nuts securely.

Rear transaxle mount

18 Remove the crossmember-to-mount nuts.

19 Remove the mount-to-transaxle bracket nut.

20 Remove the left rear cradle-to-body mount nuts.

21 Pry the cradle down and block it in position with 2 by 4 wood blocks.

22 Raise the transaxle with a jack and remove the mount.

23 Install the mount with the stud through the transaxle bracket. Install the nut finger tight.

24 Align the crossmember-to-mount studs with the holes as the transaxle is lowered.

25 Install the cradle-to-body mount bolt and tighten to the specified torque.

26 Install the mount-to-crossmember nuts and tighten to the specified torque.

Engine strut

27 Remove the strut-to-bracket bolts and lift the strut out of the bracket and radiator support **(see illustration)**.

28 Place the strut in position and install the bolts. Tighten the bolts to the specified torque.

17.27 Remove the strut mounting bolts (arrows)

Notes

Chapter 2 Part D
3.0L, 3.3L and 3.8L V6 engines

Contents

Specifications

General

Firing order	1-6-5-4-3-2
Cylinder numbers (drivebelt end-to-transaxle end)	
Front bank	1-3-5
Rear bank	2-4-6

Type I

1985-1988 3.0L engines
Some 1986-1988 3.8L with VIN code 3
1992 3.3L with VIN code N

Type II

1986-1988 3.8L with VIN code 3

1985-1992 3.3L with VIN code N
1988-1989 3.0L

The blackened terminal shown on the distributor cap indicates the Number One spark plug wire position

Cylinder/coil terminal location and distributor rotation

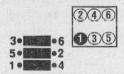

Type I

1988-1991 3.8L with VIN code C
Some 1990-1992 3.8L with VIN code L

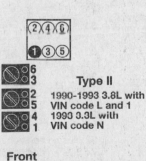

Type II

1990-1993 3.8L with VIN code L and 1
1990 3.3L with VIN code N

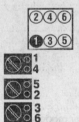

1984-1985 3.8L

1984-1985 3.0L with VIN code E

Front

Oil pump service limits
All 1984 and earlier models and 1985 3.8L engine
Gear length	0.8835 to 0.8720 inch
Gear diameter	1.666 to 1.664 inches
Gear pocket depth	
Through 1989	0.8697 to 0.8677 inch
1990 and later	0.461 to 0.4625 inch
Gear pocket diameter	
Through 1989	1.674 to 1.671 inches
1990 and later	3.508 to 3.512 inches
Gear lash	0.0015 to 0.003 inch
Side clearance	0.003 to 0.005 inch
End clearance	
Through 1989	0.002 to 0.006 inch
1990 and later	0.001 to 0.0035 inch
Cover warpage limit	0.001 inch

All 1986 and later models and 1985 3.0L engine
Outer gear-to-housing clearance	0.008 to 0.015 inch
Inner gear-to-outer gear clearance	0.006 inch
Gear end clearance	0.001 to 0.0035 inch
Pump cover warpage limit	0.002 inch

Torque specifications
Ft-lbs (unless otherwise indicated)

Crankshaft balancer bolt	
Through 1990	200 to 225
1991	105 plus an additional 56-degrees rotation
1992 and later	110 plus an additional 76-degrees rotation
Cylinder head bolts	
Through 1985	80
1986 and later 3.0L and 3.8L engines	
Step 1	25
Step 2	Turn an additional 90-degrees. (**Caution:** *If a torque value of 60 ft-lbs is attained, continue to the next Step. Do not continue to tighten the bolt*)
Step 3	Turn an additional 90-degrees
3.3L engine	
Step 1	35
Step 2	Turn an additional 130-degrees
Step 3 (four center bolts only)	Turn an additional 30-degrees
Driveplate or flywheel-to-crankshaft bolts	
Through 1989	60
1990 and 1991	84 in-lbs plus an additional 90-degrees rotation
1992 and later	11 plus an additional 50-degrees rotation
Oil pan bolts	144 in-lbs
Oil pump	
Cover bolts	120 in-lbs
Pressure regulator retainer bolt	35
Pump housing-to-cylinder block bolt (**earlier models**)	96 in-lbs
Timing chain cover bolts	
Through 1985	30
1986 and later	22
Intake manifold bolts	
Carbureted models	45
Fuel-injected models through 1987	32
1988 through 1990 (all models)	10
1991 and later (all models)	88 in-lbs
Exhaust manifold bolts	
Through 1990	25
1991	41
1992 and 1993	38
1994 and later	144 in-lbs
Timing chain sprocket-to-camshaft bolts	
Through 1987	20
1988 through 1990	26
1991	52 plus an additional 110-degrees rotation
1992 and later	74 plus an additional 105-degrees rotation
Valve cover-to-cylinder head	
Bolts	60 in-lbs
Nuts	96 in-lbs

Torque specifications (continued)

	Ft-lbs (unless otherwise indicated)
Rocker arm shaft or old style pedestal bolts	
Through 1985	30
1986 and later	28
Timing chain dampener bolt	
Through 1991	168 in-lbs
1992 and later	16
New style pedestal bolts	
Step 1	11
Step 2	Turn an additional 110-degrees rotation

1   General information

This Part of Chapter 2 is devoted to in-vehicle repair procedures for the 3.0, 3.3 and 3.8 liter V6 engines.

Information concerning engine removal and installation, as well as engine block and cylinder head overhaul, is in Part E of this Chapter.

The following repair procedures are based on the assumption that the engine is installed in the vehicle. If the engine has been removed from the vehicle and mounted on a stand, many of the steps included in this Part of Chapter 2 will not apply.

The Specifications included in this Part of Chapter 2 apply only to the engine and procedures in this Part. The Specifications necessary for rebuilding the block and cylinder heads are found in Part E.

2   Repair operations possible with the engine in the vehicle

Many major repair operations can be accomplished without removing the engine from the vehicle.

Clean the engine compartment and the exterior of the engine with some type of pressure washer before any work is done. A clean engine will make the job easier and will help keep dirt out of the internal areas of the engine.

Depending on the components involved, it may be a good idea to remove the hood to improve access to the engine as repairs are performed (refer to Chapter 11 if necessary).

If vacuum, exhaust, oil or coolant leaks develop, indicating a need for gasket or seal replacement, the repairs can generally be made with the engine in the vehicle. The intake and exhaust manifold gaskets, oil pan gasket and cylinder head gaskets are all accessible with the engine in place.

Exterior engine components such as the intake and exhaust manifolds, the oil pan, the oil pump, the water pump, the starter motor, the alternator, the distributor and the fuel injection system can be removed for repair with the engine in place. The timing chain and sprockets can also be replaced with the engine in the vehicle, but the camshaft cannot be removed.

Since the cylinder heads can be removed without pulling the engine, valve component servicing can also be accomplished with the engine in the vehicle.

In extreme cases caused by a lack of necessary equipment, repair or replacement of piston rings, pistons, connecting rods and rod bearings is possible with the engine in the vehicle. However, this practice is not recommended because of the cleaning and preparation work that must be done to the components involved.

3   Valve covers - removal and installation

Refer to illustrations 3.9 and 3.23

Removal - right side (rear) cover

1   Disconnect the negative battery cable from the battery. **Caution:** *If the vehicle is equipped with a Delco Loc II audio system, make sure you have the correct activation code before disconnecting the battery. See the information at the front of this manual for the radio re-activation procedure.*

2   On carbureted models, remove the air cleaner assembly.

3   If necessary for clearance, remove the power steering pump, tensioner brace and brackets, setting the pump aside without disconnecting the hoses (see Chapter 10).

4   On early models, remove the PCV pipe, hot air tube and any emissions system hoses or electrical wires which will interfere with removal.

5   Remove the throttle cables and bracket (Chapter 4).

6   Remove the spark plug wires from the spark plugs (Chapter 1). Be sure to label each wire before removal to ensure correct reinstallation.

7   On models without a distributor, remove the ignition coil module and wiring (Chapter 5) and the EGR solenoid, wiring and vacuum hoses (Chapter 6).

8   On fuel-injected models, drain at least three quarts of coolant from the radiator (Chapter 1).

9   On fuel-injected models, disconnect the coolant hoses at the throttle body (**see illustration**). **Note:** *You may have to remove the throttle body to gain access to the hose clamp screws (see Chapter 4).*

10   Remove the valve cover mounting nuts or bolts.

11   Detach the valve cover. **Note:** *If the cover sticks to the cylinder head, use a block of wood and a hammer to dislodge it. If the cover still won't come loose, pry on it carefully, but don't distort the sealing flange.*

Removal - left-side (front) cover

12   Disconnect the negative battery cable from the battery. **Caution:** *If the vehicle is equipped with a Delco Loc II audio system, make sure you have the correct activation code before disconnecting the battery. See the information at the front of this manual for the radio re-activation procedure.*

13   On carbureted models, remove the air cleaner assembly (see Chapter 4).

14   Disconnect the engine mounting torque strut and the engine lifting bracket.

15   If necessary for clearance, remove the alternator (see Chapter 5).

16   Remove the spark plug wire harness cover, if equipped.

17   Remove the spark plug wires from the spark plugs (Chapter 1). Be sure to label each wire before removal to ensure correct reinstallation.

18   On later models, remove the PCV tube from the cover.

19   Remove the valve cover mounting nuts.

20   Detach the valve cover. **Note:** *If the cover sticks to the cylinder head, use a block of wood and a hammer to dislodge it. If the cover still won't come loose, pry on it carefully, but don't distort the sealing flange.*

Installation - both covers

21   The mating surfaces of each cylinder head and valve cover must be perfectly clean when the covers are installed. Use a gasket scraper to remove all traces of sealant or old gasket, then clean the mating surfaces with lacquer thinner or acetone (if there's sealant

3.9 On fuel-injected models, you may have to remove the throttle body to gain access to the hose clamp screws (arrows)

or oil on the mating surfaces when the cover is installed, oil leaks may develop). Most valve covers are made of aluminum, so be extra careful not to nick or gouge the mating surfaces with the scraper.

22   Clean the mounting nut stud threads with a die to remove any corrosion and restore damaged threads.

23   Place the valve cover and new gasket in position, then install the bolts or the new rubber grommets, washers and mounting nuts **(see illustration)**. Tighten the nuts in several steps to the torque listed in this Chapter's Specifications.

24   On fuel-injected models, reinstall the coolant hoses and refill the engine with coolant (rear cover only).

25   Complete the installation by reversing the removal procedure. Start the engine and check carefully for oil leaks at the valve cover-to-head joints.

4   Valve springs, retainers and seals - replacement

This procedure is essentially the same as for the 2.2L four-cylinder engine. Refer to Chapter 2, Part A, except note that many models use a valve seal only on the intake valve. Also note that the rocker arm shafts on earlier models must be removed (see the next Section) before the springs can be compressed.

5   Rocker arms and pushrods - removal, inspection and installation

Removal

Refer to illustrations 5.2 and 5.3

1   Refer to Section 3 and detach the valve covers from the cylinder heads.

2   Loosen the rocker arm pedestal bolts or shaft bolts and detach the bolts and shafts (earlier models) or pedestals, rocker arms and pedestal retainers (later models) **(see illustration)**. On models with rocker arm shafts, loosen the three bolts on each shaft a little at a time, working from the center out. Store each set of valve components separately in a marked plastic bag to ensure that they're reinstalled in their original locations.

3   Remove the pushrods and store them separately to make sure they don't get mixed up during installation **(see illustration)**. Also keep track of which end of the pushrod faces up, since the wear patterns at the pushrod ends must match their respective lifter and rocker arm.

Inspection

Refer to illustration 5.4

4   Check each rocker arm for wear, cracks and other damage, especially where the pushrods and valve stems contact the rocker arm. On earlier models with rocker arm

shafts, remove the nylon retainers with pliers **(see illustration)** and slide the rocker arms off the shafts. Keep track of the rocker arm positions, since they must be returned to the same locations. Put the rocker arms (along with their pedestals, if equipped) in separate labeled bags.

5   Check the pedestal or rocker-shaft seat in each rocker arm and the pedestal faces or rocker shaft wear areas. Look for galling, stress cracks and unusual wear patterns. If the rocker arms are worn or damaged, replace them with new ones and install new pedestals or shafts as well.

6   Make sure the hole at the pushrod end of each rocker arm is open.

7   Inspect the pushrods for cracks and excessive wear at the ends. Roll each pushrod across a piece of plate glass to see if it's bent (if it wobbles, it's bent).

Installation

Refer to illustration 5.10

8   Lubricate the lower end of each pushrod with clean engine oil or moly-base grease and install them in their original locations. Make sure each pushrod seats completely in the lifter socket.

9   Apply moly-base grease to the ends of

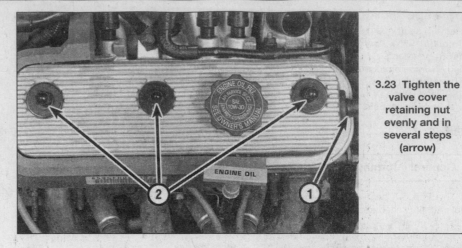

3.23 Tighten the valve cover retaining nut evenly and in several steps (arrow)

5.2 Loosen the pedestal bolts (old style shown)

5.3 A perforated cardboard box can be used to store the pushrods to ensure that they're reinstalled in their original locations - note the label indicating the front (drive belt end) of the engine

the valve stems and the upper ends of the pushrods.

10   Apply moly-base grease to the pedestal faces or rocker shaft contact areas to prevent

5.4 Remove the rocker arm retainers only if you have to inspect the shaft - the plastic retainers will probably break, so make sure you have new ones on hand

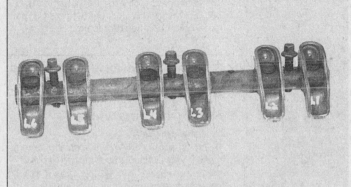

5.10 Reinstall the rockers (numbered with paint before removal) to the shaft in their original sequence

6.13a Some vacuum lines are equipped with fittings that prevent mixing them up during installation (fuel-injected model shown)

damage to the mating surfaces before engine oil pressure builds up. Install the rocker arm components. On earlier models, note that the intake and exhaust rocker arms are different and are marked "R" and "L" **(see illustration)**; after installing the rocker arms, install new nylon retainers. On all models, tighten the bolts to the torque listed in this Chapter's Specifications. As the bolts are tightened, make sure the pushrods engage properly in the rocker arms.

11   Install the valve covers.

6   Intake manifold - removal and installation

Warning: *Gasoline is extremely flammable, so take extra precautions when you work on any part of the fuel system. Don't smoke or allow open flames or bare light bulbs near the work area, and don't work in a garage where a natural gas-type appliance (such as a water heater or clothes dryer) with a pilot light is present. If you spill any fuel on your skin, rinse it off immediately with soap and water. When you perform any kind of work on the fuel system, wear safety glasses and have a Class B type fire extinguisher on hand.*

Removal

Refer to illustrations 6.13a, 6.13b and 6.15

1   On fuel-injected models, relieve the fuel system pressure (Chapter 4).

2   Disconnect the negative battery cable from the battery. **Caution:** *If the vehicle is equipped with a Delco Loc II audio system, make sure you have the correct activation code before disconnecting the battery. See the information at the front of this manual for the radio re-activation procedure.*

3   On carbureted models, remove the air cleaner assembly, tagging each hose to be disconnected with a piece of numbered tape to simplify reinstallation.

4   On fuel-injected models, remove the mass airflow sensor and the air intake duct (Chapter 4).

5   On fuel-injected models, remove the PCV valve from the intake manifold.

6   Remove the throttle (and cruise control - when equipped) cable(s) from the manifold bracket.

7   Remove the transaxle TV cable from the manifold bracket (automatic transaxle only) (Chapter 7).

8   If it will interfere with manifold removal, remove the alternator and brackets (Chapter 5).

9   Drain the cooling system (Chapter 1).

10   On fuel-injected models, remove the spark plug wires that will interfere with manifold removal.

11   On fuel-injected models, disconnect the ignition module assembly (Chapter 5) and set it aside.

12   Disconnect the upper radiator and coolant hoses at the manifold and, if equipped, throttle body.

13   Label and disconnect the fuel and vacuum lines **(see illustrations)** and electrical leads at the manifold and carburetor or throttle body. When disconnecting fuel line fittings, be prepared to catch some fuel, then cap the fittings to prevent contamination.

14   On fuel-injected models, remove the fuel rail and injectors (Chapter 4).

15   Remove the manifold mounting bolts and separate the manifold from the engine **(see illustration)**. Do not pry between the manifold and heads, as damage to the gasket sealing surfaces may result. If you're

6.13b Removing the vacuum line bracket nut (fuel-injected models)

6.15 Note the locations of the mounting studs prior to manifold removal

6.16 Use a gasket scraper to remove all traces of sealant and old gasket material from the head and manifold mating surfaces

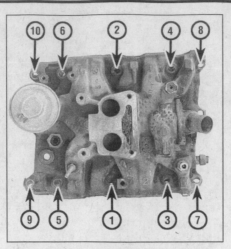

6.20a Intake manifold bolt tightening sequence (carbureted models)

installing a new manifold, transfer the EGR valve and all fittings and sensors to the new manifold.

Installation

Refer to illustrations 6.16, 6.20a and 6.20b
Note: *The mating surfaces of the cylinder heads, block and manifold must be perfectly clean when the manifold is installed. Gasket removal solvents in aerosol cans are available at most auto parts stores and may be helpful when removing old gasket material that's stuck to the heads and manifold (since the manifold is made of aluminum, aggressive scraping can cause damage). Be sure to follow the directions printed on the container.*

16   Use a gasket scraper to remove all traces of sealant and old gasket material **(see illustration)**, then clean the mating surfaces with lacquer thinner or acetone. If there's old sealant or oil on the mating surfaces when the manifold is installed, oil or vacuum leaks

may develop. Use a vacuum cleaner to remove any gasket material that falls into the intake ports or the lifter valley.

17   Use a tap of the correct size to chase the threads in the bolt holes, then use compressed air (if available) to remove the debris from the holes. **Warning:** *Wear safety glasses or a face shield to protect your eyes when using compressed air.*

18   If steel manifold gaskets are used, apply RTV sealant to both sides of the gaskets before positioning them on the heads. Apply RTV sealant to the ends of the new manifold-to-block seals, then install them. Make sure the pointed end of the seal fits snugly against both the head and block.

19   Carefully lower the manifold into place and install the mounting bolts finger tight.

20   Tighten the mounting bolts in three stages, following the recommended sequence **(see illustrations)**, until they're all at the specified torque.

21   Install the remaining components in the reverse order of removal.

22   Change the oil and filter (Chapter 1).

23   Fill the cooling system (Chapter 1), start the engine and check for leaks.

7   Exhaust manifolds - removal and installation

Right (rear) manifold

Refer to illustration 7.8
Note: *On some early models, clearance may make it very difficult to unbolt and remove the rear manifold, If this is the case, it may be necessary to remove the upper engine mounting strut, disconnect the rear of the engine cradle and lower it with a jack (see the transaxle removal and installation procedure in Chapter 7, Part B for more information on the engine cradle).*

1   Disconnect the negative battery cable.
Caution: *If the vehicle is equipped with a Delco Loc II audio system, make sure you have the correct activation code before disconnecting the battery. See the information at the front of this manual for the radio re-activation procedure.*

2   Allow the engine to cool completely, then drain the coolant and remove the heater hoses and tubing above the exhaust manifold.

3   Remove the two nuts attaching the crossover pipe to the rear exhaust manifold.

4   Disconnect the spark plug wires from the rear plugs (Chapter 1).

5   On earlier models, If necessary for clearance, remove the alternator (see Chapter 5).

6   If necessary for clearance, unbolt the power steering pump without removing the hoses and hold it to one side with a wire (Chapter 10).

7   On models without a distributor (direct ignition), remove the ignition module bracket nuts.

8   Remove the manifold heat shield and coolant tube brackets **(see illustration)**.

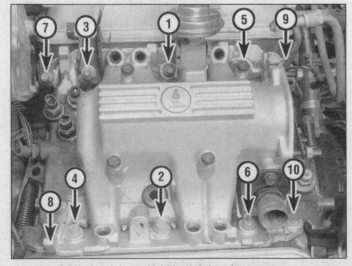

6.20b   Intake manifold bolt tightening sequence (fuel-injected models)

7.8   Manifold mounting details (shown here with engine removed for clarity) - note the oxygen sensor wire connector (arrow)

7.24a When removing the nut, the stud may turn and distort the heat shield, so . . .

7.24b . . . hold the stud with a pair of pliers while loosening the nut

8.3 Remove the bolts holding the brackets to the cylinder head (arrows) - later model shown

8.11 Pry the cylinder head loose at the rear corner to avoid damage to the gasket sealing surfaces

9   Set the parking brake, block the rear wheels and raise the front of the vehicle, supporting it securely on jackstands.

10   Working under the vehicle, remove the two exhaust pipe-to-manifold bolts. You may have to apply penetrating oil to the fastener threads - they're usually corroded.

11   Disconnect the oxygen sensor wire (the sensor is threaded into the manifold), then lower the vehicle.

12   Remove the bolts and detach the manifold from the head.

13   Clean the mating surfaces to remove all traces of old sealant, then check for warpage and cracks. Warpage can be checked with a precision staightedge held against the mating flange. If a feeler gauge thicker than 0.030-inch can be inserted between the straightedge and flange surface, take the manifold to an automotive machine shop for resurfacing.

14   Place the manifold in position and install the bolts finger tight.

15   Starting in the middle and working out toward the ends, tighten the mounting bolts a little at a time until all of them are at the torque listed in this Chapter's Specifications.

16   Install the remaining components in reverse order of removal.

17   Start the engine and check for exhaust leaks between the manifold and cylinder head and between the manifold and exhaust pipe.

Left (front) manifold

Refer to illustrations 7.24a and 7.24b

18   Disconnect the negative battery cable. **Caution:** *If the vehicle is equipped with a Delco Loc II audio system, make sure you have the correct activation code before disconnecting the battery. See the information at the front of this manual for the radio re-activation procedure.*

19   Remove the cooling fan (Chapter 3).

20   Unbolt the crossover pipe from the manifold.

21   Remove the dipstick tube hold-down nut and wiggle the dipstick tube out of the block.

22   Remove the spark plug wire cover and

wires (Chapter 1).

23   Remove the spark plugs to prevent breaking them.

24   Unbolt the heat shield. If turning the nuts causes the studs to turn and bend the shield **(see illustration)**, keep the stud from turning with a thin 14 mm open end wrench or a pair of vise-grip pliers **(see illustration)**.

25   Unbolt and remove the exhaust manifold.

26   Follow Steps 13 through 17 above.

8   Cylinder heads - removal and installation

Removal

Refer to illustrations 8.3 and 8.11

1   Disconnect the negative battery cable at the battery. **Caution:** *If the vehicle is equipped with a Delco Loc II audio system, make sure you have the correct activation code before disconnecting the battery. See the information at the front of this manual for the radio re-activation procedure.*

2   Remove the intake manifold as described in Section 6.

3   When removing the left (front) cylinder head, remove the dipstick tube retaining nut and wiggle the tube out of the block. Remove the bolts holding the brackets to the head **(see illustration)**.

4   When removing the right cylinder head, remove the power steering pump and brackets (Chapter 10).

5   Disconnect all wires and vacuum hoses from the cylinder head(s). Be sure to label them to simplify reinstallation.

6   Disconnect the spark plug wires and remove the spark plugs (Chapter 1). Be sure to label the plug wires to simplify reinstallation.

7   Detach the exhaust manifolds from the cylinder heads (Section 7).

8   Remove the valve covers (Section 3).

9   Remove the rocker arms and pushrods (Section 5).

10   Loosen the head bolts in 1/4-turn incre-

ments until they can be removed by hand. Work from bolt-to-bolt in a pattern that's the reverse of the tightening sequence shown in illustration 8.20. Remove the bolts. **Note:** *On models where the head bolts are angle torqued (the final tightening step(s) are measured in degrees of rotation - see the Specifications), NEW BOLTS MUST BE USED when installing the head(s)! Discard the old bolts.*

11   Lift the head(s) off the engine. If resistance is felt, don't pry between the head(s) and block as damage to the mating surfaces will result. Recheck for head bolts that may have been overlooked, then use a hammer and block of wood to tap the head(s) and break the gasket seal. Be careful because there are locating dowels in the block which position each head. As a last resort, pry each head up at the rear corner only and be careful not to damage anything **(see illustration)**. After removal, place the head(s) on blocks of wood to prevent damage to the gasket surfaces.

12   Refer to Chapter 2, Part E, for cylinder head disassembly, inspection and valve service procedures.

8.14 The cylinder head and block mating surfaces must be perfectly clean to ensure a good gasket seal

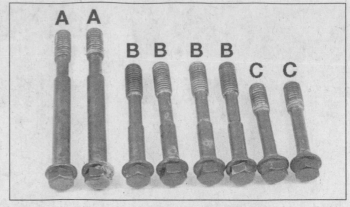

8.19 The head bolts are different lengths and must be installed in the correct locations (refer to illustration 8.20)

A:	1 and 3	C:	5 and 8
B:	2, 4, 6 and 7		

8.20 Cylinder head bolt tightening sequence

9.1a The guide plate is held in place by two bolts (arrows)

Installation

Refer to illustrations 8.14, 8.19 and 8.20

Note: *On later models, the manufacturer recommends using a special torque angle meter to obtain accurate final head bolt torques. Check the Specifications to see if your engine requires the bolts to be angle torqued (the final torque(s) are listed in degrees), then, if needed, obtain this special tool before proceeding.*

13   The mating surfaces of the cylinder heads and block must be perfectly clean when the heads are installed.

14   Use a gasket scraper to remove all traces of carbon and old gasket material, then clean the mating surfaces with lacquer thinner or acetone. If there's oil on the mating surfaces when the heads are installed, the gaskets may not seal correctly and leaks may develop. When working on the block, it's a real good idea to cover the lifter valley with shop rags to keep debris out of the engine. Use a shop rag or vacuum cleaner to remove any debris that falls into the cylinders **(see illustration)**.

15   Check the block and head mating surfaces for nicks, deep scratches and other damage. If damage is slight, it can be removed with a file; if it's excessive, machining may be the only alternative.

16   Use a tap of the correct size to chase the threads in the head bolt holes. Dirt, corrosion, sealant and damaged threads will affect torque readings.

17   Position the new gaskets over the dowel pins in the block. If steel gaskets are used, apply RTV sealant. Install "non-retorquing" type gaskets dry (no sealant), unless the manufacturer states otherwise. Some gaskets are marked TOP or THIS SIDE UP because they must be installed a certain way.

18   Carefully position the heads on the block without disturbing the gaskets.

19   Remember to use NEW head bolts - don't reinstall the old ones - and apply sealant to the threads and the undersides of the bolt heads. Install the bolts in the correct locations - three different lengths are used **(see illustration)**.

20   Tighten the bolts in the sequence shown **(see illustration)** to the torque listed in this Chapter's Specifications. **Note:** *Later models require angle torquing. First tighten all bolts to the base torque specification (Step 1 in the Specifications), then complete torquing by tightening the bolts the number of degrees of rotation listed in the subsequent Step(s). To obtain accurate results, we recommend using a special torque angle meter.*

21   The remaining installation steps are the reverse of removal.

22   Change the oil and filter (Chapter 1).

9   Hydraulic lifters - removal, inspection and installation

Refer to illustration 9.1a and 9.1b

This procedure is essentially the same as for the 2.5L four-cylinder engine. Follow the procedure in Chapter 2, Part B, but follow the procedures in this Chapter for valve cover and intake manifold removal and installation.

9.1b The lifter guides slip over the lifters

10.7 The crankshaft balancer is attached to the end of the crankshaft - the bolt is very tight, so use a large breaker bar and six-point socket to remove it

11.9 Timing chain cover bolt locations (later model shown)

Note that models with roller lifters have lifter guides and a guide retainer that must be removed before the lifters can be removed **(see illustrations).**

10   Crankshaft balancer - removal and installation

Refer to illustration 10.7
Note: *The engine balancer, which is essentially the same as a vibration dampener, is serviced as an assembly. Do not attempt to separate the pulley from the balancer hub.*

1   Disconnect the negative cable from the battery. **Caution:** *If the vehicle is equipped with a Delco Loc II audio system, make sure you have the correct activation code before disconnecting the battery. See the information at the front of this manual for the radio re-activation procedure.*
2   Loosen the lug nuts on the right front wheel.
3   Raise the vehicle and support it securely on jackstands.
4   Remove the right front wheel.
5   Remove the right front fender liner (Chapter 11).
6   Remove the drivebelt(s) (Chapter 1).
7   Remove the flywheel cover plate and position a large screwdriver in the ring gear teeth to keep the crankshaft from turning while an assistant removes the crankshaft balancer bolt **(see illustration).** The bolt is normally quite tight, so use a large breaker bar and a six-point socket.
8   Pull the balancer off the crankshaft by hand. Leave the Woodruff key in place in the end of the crankshaft.
9   Installation is the reverse of removal. Be sure to apply moly-base grease to the seal contact surface on the back side of the balancer (if it isn't lubricated, the seal lip could be damaged and oil leakage would result).
10   Tighten the crankshaft bolt to the torque listed in this Chapter's Specifications.

11   Timing chain cover - removal and installation

Refer to illustrations 11.9, 11.10 and 11.12
1   Disconnect the negative battery cable from the battery. **Caution:** *If the vehicle is equipped with a Delco Loc II audio system, make sure you have the correct activation code before disconnecting the battery. See the information at the front of this manual for the radio re-activation procedure.*
2   Drain the coolant (Chapter 1).
3   Drain the oil (Chapter 1).
4   Remove the lower radiator hose and the heater return hose at the timing chain cover.
5   Remove the water pump (Chapter 3).
6   Remove the crankshaft balancer from the front of the crankshaft (Section 10).
7   On models without a distributor (distributorless ignition system), remove the crankshaft sensor (Chapter 5).
8   Remove the timing chain cover-to-oil pan bolts.
9   Remove the timing chain cover-to-

engine block bolts **(see illustration).**
10   Separate the cover from the front of the engine. Inside the cover is a spring and button that controls camshaft end play. If it's missing, look for it in the oil pan **(see illustration).**
11   Use a gasket scraper to remove all traces of old gasket material and sealant from the cover and engine block. The cover is made of aluminum, so be careful not to nick or gouge it. Clean the gasket sealing surfaces with lacquer thinner or acetone.
12   Check the camshaft thrust surface in the cover for excessive wear **(see illustration).** If it's worn, a new cover will be required.
13   On later models where the oil pump is mounted to the back of the front cover, the oil pump cover must be removed and the cavity packed with petroleum jelly as described in Section 13 before the cover is installed.
14   Apply a thin layer of RTV sealant to both sides of the new gasket, then position the gasket on the engine block (the dowel pins should keep it in place). Make sure the spring and button are in place in the end of the

11.10 Once the timing cover has been removed, remove the camshaft button from the end of the camshaft

11.12 The camshaft thrust surface on this cover is worn away (arrow), which means that a new cover must be installed

12.6 Use a cold chisel and hammer to separate the seal from the cover - drive the chisel into the joint, but don't distort the cover

12.7a Clean the bore, then apply grease or oil to the outer edge of the new seal and drive it squarely into the cover with a large socket . . .

12.7b . . . or a block of wood and hammer - DO NOT damage the seal in the process!

camshaft, then attach the cover to the engine. The oil pump drive must engage with the distributor gear.

15   Apply thread sealant to the bolt threads, then install them finger tight. On models so equipped, install the crankshaft position sensor, but leave its bolts finger tight until Step 16. Tighten the other bolts, following a criss-cross pattern when tightening them and working up to the specified torque in three steps to avoid warping the cover.

16   Use a special tool (available at most auto parts stores) to position the crankshaft position sensor on the timing cover. Tighten the bolts to the torque listed in this Chapter's Specifications for the timing chain cover.

17   The remainder of installation is the reverse of removal.

18   Add oil and coolant, start the engine and check for leaks.

12 Crankshaft front oil seal - replacement

Note: *The crankshaft front oil seal can be replaced with the timing chain cover in place. However, due to the limited amount of room available, you may conclude that the procedure would be easier if the cover were removed from the engine first. If so, refer to Section 11 for the cover removal and installation procedure.*

Timing chain cover in place

1   Remove the crankshaft balancer (Section 10).

2   Use a small cold chisel and a hammer to remove the seal from the cover. Carefully drive the chisel under the outer flange of the seal at several points until the seal can be pryed out. Be very careful not to distort the cover!

3   Apply clean engine oil or multi-purpose grease to the outer edge of the new seal, then install it in the cover. Drive the seal into

place with a large socket and a hammer (if a large socket isn't available, a piece of pipe will also work). Make sure the seal enters the bore squarely and seats completely.

4   Install the crankshaft balancer (Section 10).

Timing chain cover removed

Refer to illustrations 12.6, 12.7a and 12.7b

5   Remove the timing chain cover as described in Section 11.

6   Use a small cold chisel and a hammer to remove the seal from the cover. Carefully drive the chisel under the outer flange of the seal at several points until the seal can be pryed out **(see illustration)**. Be very careful not to distort the cover!

7   Apply clean engine oil or multi-purpose grease to the outer edge of the new seal, then install it in the cover. Drive the seal into place with a large socket and a hammer (if a large socket isn't available, a piece of pipe or even a large block of wood will also work) **(see illustrations)**. Make sure the seal enters the bore squarely and seats completely.

8   Reinstall the timing chain cover.

13 Oil pump - removal, inspection and installation

All 1984 and earlier models and 1985 3.8L models

Removal

1   Remove the oil filter.

2   Remove the oil pump cover-to-timing chain cover attaching bolts.

3   Lift out the cover, oil pump drive and driven gears as an assembly.

4   Do not attempt to remove the oil filter bypass valve and spring - they are staked in place.

Inspection

Refer to illustrations 13.6, 13.7a, 13.7b, 13.10a, 13.10b and 13.11

5   Clean all components thoroughly in solvent.

6   Inspect all components for wear and scoring and the bypass valve for cracks, nicks and warping **(see illustration)**.

7   Measure the oil pump gears as shown **(see illustrations)**.

8   Measure the gear pocket as shown.

9   Install the oil pump gears and shaft in

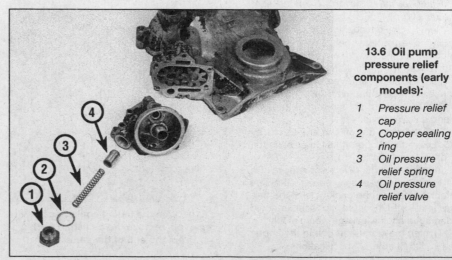

13.6 Oil pump pressure relief components (early models):

1   *Pressure relief cap*
2   *Copper sealing ring*
3   *Oil pressure relief spring*
4   *Oil pressure relief valve*

13.7a With a micrometer or precision caliper, measure the gear thickness (early models) . . .

13.7b . . and width, then compare your measurements to the Specifications (early models)

13.10a Measure the depth of the oil pump cavity (early models)

13.10b Check the gear tip clearance in the pump body (early models)

13.11 Lay a straightedge across the pump body and measure the clearance between the gears and gasket surface (early models) (end clearance)

13.20 On later models, the oil pump cover is attached to the inside of the timing chain cover - a T-30 Torx driver is required for removal of the screws

13.26 Measuring the outer gear-to-housing clearance with a feeler gauge (later models)

the oil pump body section of the timing chain cover.

10 Measure the gear lash and side clearance at several points as shown (see illustrations).

11 Place a ruler over the gears and measure the clearance between the ruler edge and gasket surface as shown (see illustration).

12 Check the pump cover flatness by placing a ruler across the face and measuring with a feeler gauge between the ruler edge and cover surface.

13 Compare the measurements to specifications. replacing any worn or damaged components with new ones. Note: Considering that a malfunctioning oil pump will cause severe engine damage, we recommend replacing the oil pump gears whenever they are removed. Also, replace the cover and body if there's any doubt to their condition.

Installation

14 Remove the gears and pack the pump cavity with petroleum jelly.

15 Install the gears so that petroleum jelly is forced into every cavity. Failure to follow this procedure could cause the pump to "lose its prime" when the engine is started, causing

damage to the engine.

16 Install the cover, using a new gasket, and install the oil filter. Add oil as necessary.

All 1986 and later models and 1985 3.0L models

Refer to illustrations 13.20, 13.26 and 13.27

Removal

17 Remove the oil filter (Chapter 1).

18 Remove the oil filter adapter, pressure regulator valve and spring (Section 14).

19 Remove the timing chain cover (Section 11).

20 Remove the oil pump cover-to-timing chain cover bolts with a T-30 Torx bit (see illustration).

21 Lift out the cover and oil pump gears as an assembly.

Inspection

22 Clean the parts with solvent and dry them with compressed air (if available).

23 Inspect all components for wear and score marks. Replace any worn out or damaged parts.

24 Refer to Section 14 for pressure regulator valve information.

25 Reinstall the gears in the timing chain cover.

26 Measure the outer gear-to-housing clearance with a feeler gauge (see illustration).

13.27 Measuring the inner gear-to-outer gear clearance with a feeler gauge (later models)

14.3 Carefully pull the oil filter adapter away from the timing cover, the pressure regulator (arrow) is spring loaded which may spring out when the adapter is removed

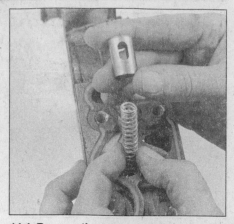

14.4 Remove the pressure regulator valve and spring, then check the valve for wear and damage

27   Measure the inner gear-to-outer gear clearance at several points (see illustration).
28   Use a dial indicator or straightedge and feeler gauges to measure the gear end clearance (distance from the gear to the gasket surface of the cover).
29   Check for pump cover warpage by laying a precision straightedge across the cover and trying to slip a feeler gauge between the cover and straightedge.
30   Compare the measurements to the Specifications. Replace all worn or damaged components with new ones.

Installation

31   Remove the gears and pack the pump cavity with petroleum jelly.
32   Install the gears - make sure petroleum jelly is forced into every cavity. Failure to do so could cause the pump to lose its prime when the engine is started, causing damage from lack of oil pressure.
33   Install the pump cover, using a new GM gasket only - its thickness is critical for maintaining the correct clearances.
34   Install the pressure regulator spring and valve.
35   Install the timing chain cover.
36   Install the oil filter and check the oil level. Start and run the engine and check for correct oil pressure, then look carefully for oil leaks at the timing chain cover.

14   Oil filter adapter and pressure regulator valve - removal and installation

Refer to illustrations 14.3, 14.4 and 14.6
Note: This procedure applies only to models with the oil pump mounted to the back of the timing chain cover (all 1986 and later models and 1985 3.0L models).
1   Remove the oil filter (Chapter 1).
2   Remove the timing chain cover (Section 11).
3   Remove the four bolts holding the oil filter adapter to the timing chain cover (see

illustration). The cover is spring loaded, so remove the bolts while keeping pressure on the cover, then release the spring pressure carefully.
4   Remove the pressure regulator valve and spring (see illustration). Use a gasket scraper to remove all traces of the old gasket.
5   Clean all parts with solvent and dry them with compressed air (if available). Check for wear, score marks and valve binding.
6   Installation is the reverse of removal. Be sure to use a new gasket. Caution: If a new timing chain cover is being installed on the engine, make sure the oil pressure relief valve supplied with the new cover is used. If the old style relief valve is installed in a new cover, oil pressure problems will result (see illustration).
7   Tighten the bolts to the specified torque.
8   Run the engine and check for oil leaks.

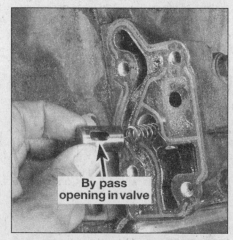

By pass opening in valve

14.6 If the timing chain cover is replaced with a new one, be sure to use the correct pressure relief valve - an early valve will not work in a later timing chain cover! (early model shown; later models use a solid valve)

15   Timing chain and sprockets - removal and installation

Refer to illustrations 15.1 and 15.4

Removal

1   Remove the timing chain cover (Section 11), then slide the shim or oil slinger off the nose of the crankshaft (see illustration).
2   The timing chain should be replaced with a new one if the total free play midway between the sprockets exceeds one inch. Failure to replace the timing chain may result in erratic engine performance, loss of power and lowered gas mileage.
3   Temporarily install the crankshaft balancer bolt and turn the bolt to align the timing marks on the crankshaft and camshaft sprockets directly opposite each other (see illustration 15.1).
4   Remove the camshaft sprocket bolts (see illustration). Try not to turn the camshaft in the process (if you do, realign the

15.1 The marks on the crankshaft and camshaft sprockets must be aligned opposite each other as shown here (the mark on the camshaft sprocket is a dimple - the one on the crankshaft sprocket is a circle)

15.4 Remove the two camshaft sprocket bolts (arrows)

16.6 Use some RTV sealant to hold the new gasket in place, then install the oil pan before the RTV cures

timing marks after the bolts are out).

5   Use two large screwdrivers to alternately pry the camshaft sprocket and then the crankshaft sprocket forward and remove the camshaft sprocket and timing chain.

6   Remove the crankshaft sprocket.

7   Detach the spring, then remove the bolt and separate the timing chain dampener from the block.

8   Clean the timing chain and sprockets with solvent and dry them with compressed air (if available).

9   Inspect the components for wear and damage. Look for teeth that are deformed, chipped, pitted, polished or discolored.

Installation

Note: *If the crankshaft has been disturbed, turn it until the O stamped on the crank sprocket is exactly at the top. If the camshaft was turned, install the sprocket temporarily and turn the camshaft until the timing mark is at the bottom, opposite the mark on the crank sprocket* **(see illustration 15.1)**.

10   Attach the dampener assembly to the block and install the spring. Assemble the timing chain on the sprockets, then slide the sprocket and chain assembly onto the shafts with the timing marks aligned as shown in illustration 15.1. Hold the dampener out of the way, against spring pressure, as the chain/sprocket assembly is installed.

11   Install the camshaft sprocket bolts and tighten them to the specified torque.

12   Install the camshaft thrust button and spring. Hold it in place with grease.

13   Lubricate the chain and sprocket with clean engine oil. Install the timing chain cover (Section 11).

16 Oil pan - removal and installation

Refer to illustration 16.6

1   Disconnect the cable from the negative battery terminal. **Caution:** *If the vehicle is equipped with a Delco Loc II audio system, make sure you have the correct activation code before disconnecting the battery. See the information at the front of this manual for*

the radio re-activation procedure.

2   Raise the vehicle, place it securely on jackstands and drain the engine oil (refer to Chapter 1 if necessary).

3   Remove the flywheel inspection cover.

4   Remove the bolts and stiffener plates and carefully separate the oil pan from the block. Don't pry between the block and the pan or damage to the sealing surfaces may result and oil leaks may develop. Instead, tap the pan with a soft-face hammer to break the gasket seal.

5   Clean the pan with solvent and remove all old sealant and gasket material from the block and pan mating surfaces. Gasket removal solvents are available at auto parts stores and may prove helpful. Clean the mating surfaces with lacquer thinner or acetone and make sure the bolt holes in the block are clear. Check the oil pan flange for distortion, particularly around the bolt holes. If necessary, place the pan on a block of wood and use a hammer to flatten and restore the gasket surface.

6   Some models have a gasket, while others use RTV sealant to seal the oil pan. On models that have a gasket, always use a new gasket whenever the oil pan is installed **(see illustration)**. On models that use RTV sealant, apply a 1/8-inch diameter bead of sealant to the oil pan flange, inboard of the bolt holes.

7   Place the oil pan in position on the block and install the bolts. Don't forget the stiffener plates (if used).

8   After the bolts are installed, tighten them to the specified torque. Starting at the center, follow a criss-cross pattern and work up to the final torque in three steps.

9   The remaining steps are the reverse of the removal procedure.

10   Refill the engine with oil, run it until normal operating temperature is reached and check for leaks.

17 Oil pump pipe and screen assembly - removal and installation

1   Remove the oil pan (Section 16).

2   Unbolt the oil pump pipe and screen assembly and detach it from the engine.

3   Clean the screen and housing assembly

with solvent and dry it with compressed air, if available. **Note:** *If the oil screen is damaged or has metal chips in it, replace it. An abundance of metal chips indicates a major engine problem which must be corrected.*

4   Make sure the mating surfaces of the pipe flange and the engine block are clean and free of nicks and install the pump and screen assembly with a new gasket.

5   Install the oil pan (Section 16).

6   Refill the engine with oil before running it.

18 Rear main oil seal - replacement

1990 and earlier models

Refer to illustrations 18.3, 18.6, 18.7, 18.10 and 18.13

Note: *Braided fabric seals inserted into grooves in the engine block and main bearing cap are used to seal against oil leakage around the crankshaft. The upper rear main bearing oil seal can be replaced only with the crankshaft removed (Chapter 2, Part D) but it can be repaired with the crankshaft in place. Two piece rubber seals are available from aftermarket suppliers. Several special tools are required for this procedure.*

1   Remove the oil pan (Section 16).

2   Remove the rear main bearing cap.

3   Using the special tool, drive the upper seal gently back into the groove in the engine

18.3 Packing the seal into the engine block groove with the special tool (arrow)

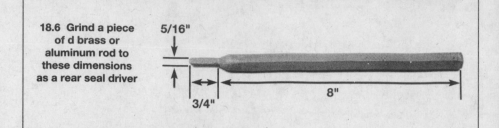

18.6 Grind a piece of d brass or aluminum rod to these dimensions as a rear seal driver

5/16"

3/4"

8"

18.10 Rear main bearing cap oil seal installation details (earlier models)

NEOPRENE COMPOSITION SEAL

APPLY SEALER TO THESE TWO AREAS

18.13 Sealant applied to the parting line of the main bearing cap (earlier models)

18.7 Measure the amount that the seal has been driven up into the groove - here a small screwdriver was used with a sleeve of masking tape (arrow) to serve as a depth indicator

21   Check the seal and make sure it's seated squarely in the bore.
22   Install the flywheel or driveplate.
If equipped with a manual transaxle, reinstall the clutch disc and pressure plate.
23   Reinstall the transaxle (see Chapter 7).

19   Flywheel/driveplate - removal and installation

This procedure is essentially the same as for the 2.2L four-cylinder engine. Follow the procedure in Part A, but use the specifications listed at the front of this Chapter.

20   Engine and transaxle mounts - check and replacement

This procedure is essentially the same as for the 2.8L and 3.1L V6 engines. Refer to Part C for the procedure.

block, packing it tight. It will pack in to a depth of between 1/4-inch and 3/4-inch **(see illustration)**.
4   Repeat the procedure on the other end of the seal.
5   Measure how far the seal was driven up in the groove on each side and add 1/16-inch. Remove the old seal from the main bearing cap. Use the main bearing cap as a fixture and cut two pieces of the old seal to the predetermined lengths.
6   Grind a piece of brass or aluminum to the dimensions shown **(see illustration)**.
7   Using the packing tool, work the short pieces of the previously cut seal into the engine block groove. Lubricate the seal with oil to ease installation **(see illustration)**.
8   Remove the guide tool.
9   Place a new seal in the main bearing cap groove with both ends projecting above the parting surface of the cap.
10   Use the handle of a hammer or similar tool to force the seal into the groove until it projects no more than 1/16-inch. Cut the ends of the seal flush with the surface of the cap with a single-edge razor blade **(see illustration)**.
11   Soak the neoprene seals which fit into the side grooves in the bearing cap in light oil or kerosene for one or two minutes.
12   Install the neoprene seals in the groove between the bearing cap and the block. The seals are slightly undersize and swell in the presence of heat and oil. They are slightly longer than the groove in the bearing cap and must be cut to fit.
13   Apply a small amount of RTV sealant to

the joint where the bearing cap meets the block to help eliminate oil leakage. A very thin coat is all that's necessary **(see illustration)**.
14   Install the main bearing cap on the block. Force the seals up into the bearing cap with a blunt instrument to be sure of a good seal at the upper parting line. Install the bolts and tighten them to the torque listed in the Chapter 2, Part E Specifications.
15   Install the oil pan.

1991 and later models

Refer to illustrations 18.18 and 18.20
16   Remove the transaxle (see Chapter 7).
17   Remove the flywheel or driveplate (see the next Section).
18   Using a thin screwdriver or seal removal tool, carefully remove the oil seal from the engine block **(see illustration)**. Be very careful not to damage the crankshaft surface while prying the seal out.
19   Clean the bore in the block and the seal contact surface on the crankshaft. Check the seal contact surface on the crankshaft for scratches and nicks that could damage the new seal lip and cause oil leaks - if the crankshaft is damaged, the only alternative is a new or different crankshaft. Inspect the seal bore for nicks and scratches. Carefully smooth it with a fine file if necessary, but don't nick the crankshaft in the process.
20   Press the new seal into place with a special seal installer if available. If the installer is not available tap around the outer edge of the new seal with a hammer and punch to seat it squarely in the bore.

18.18 Carefully pry the old oil seal out (later models)

Chapter 2 Part E
General engine overhaul procedures

Contents

Specifications

2.2 liter four-cylinder engine

General
Displacement	134 cubic inches
Cylinder compression pressure	
Minimum	100 psi
Maximum variation between cylinders	30-percent
Oil pressure (minimum)	15 psi at 1200 rpm

Cylinder head
Warpage limit	0.005 inch

Valves and related components
Valve face angle	45-degrees
Valve seat	
Angle	46-degrees
Width	
Intake	0.049 to 0.059 inch
Exhaust	0.063 to 0.075 inch
Runout	0.002 inch
Margin width	1/32 inch minimum
Valve stem-to-guide clearance	
Intake	0.0011 to 0.0026 inch
Exhaust	0.0014 to 0.003 inch
Valve spring free length	1.89 inch
Valve spring installed height	1.637 inch

Crankshaft and connecting rods
Crankshaft endplay	0.002 to 0.008 inch
Connecting rod side clearance (endplay)	0.004 to 0.015 inch
Main bearing journal	
Diameter	2.4945 to 2.4954 inch
Taper/out-of-round limits	0.0002 inch
Main bearing oil clearance	0.0006 to 0.0019 inch
Connecting rod journal	
Diameter	1.9983 to 1.9994 inch
Taper/out-of-round limits	0.0002 inch
Connecting rod bearing oil clearance	0.001 to 0.0031 inch

2.2 liter four-cylinder engine (continued)

Engine block
Cylinder bore
    Diameter .... 3.5036 to 3.5043 inch
    Out-of-round limit .... 0.0005 inch
    Taper limit (maximum) .... 0.0005 inch
Block deck warpage limit .... 0.005 inch (**Note:** *If more than 0.010 inch must be removed, replace the block*)

Pistons and rings
Piston-to-bore clearance .... 0.0007 to 0.0017 inch
Piston ring side clearance
    Compression rings .... 0.0019 to 0.0027 inch
    Oil control ring .... 0.0019 to 0.0082 inch
Piston ring end gap
    Compression rings .... 0.010 to 0.020 inch
    Oil control ring .... 0.010 to 0.050 inch

Camshaft
Lobe lift
    1993 and earlier
        Intake .... 0.259 inch
        Exhaust .... 0.250 inch
    1994 and later
        Intake .... 0.288 inch
        Exhaust .... 0.288 inch
Bearing journal diameter .... 1.867 to 1.869 inch
Bearing oil clearance .... 0.001 to 0.0039 inch

Torque specifications
Ft-lbs (unless otherwise indicated)

Main bearing cap bolts
    1993 66
    1994 and later 70
Connecting rod cap nuts 38
Camshaft thrust plate-to-block bolts .... 108 in-lbs

Note: *Refer to Part A for additional torque specifications.*

2.5 liter four-cylinder engine

General
Cylinder compression pressure .... Lowest reading should be within 70 percent of highest reading. No cylinder should measure less than 100 psi.

Oil pressure
    Through 1987 .... 36 to 41 psi at 2000 rpm
    1988 through 1990 .... 50 psi at 2000 rpm
    1991 and later .... 26 psi at 800 rpm

Cylinder head warpage limit
0.005 inch

Valves and related components
Valve margin width .... 1/32-inch minimum
Valve face angle 45-degrees
Valve seat angle 46-degrees
Valve stem diameter
    Through 1985
        Intake .... 0.3425 to 0.3418 inch
        Exhaust .... 0.3418 to 0.3425 inch
Valve stem diameter
    1986 and later
        Intake .... 0.313 to 0.314 inch
        Exhaust .... 0.312 to 0.313 inch
Stem-to-guide clearance
    Through 1990 (intake and exhaust) .... 0.0012 to 0.003 inch
    1991 and 1992
        Intake .... 0.001 to 0.0028 inch
        Exhaust .... 0.0013 to 0.0041 inch
Valve seat width
    Intake .... 0.035 to 0.075 inch
    Exhaust .... 0.058 to 0.105 inch

Valve spring installed height
    Through 1985 .... 1.69 inch
    1986 and 1987 .... 1.440 inch
    1988 and later .... 1.679 inch

Crankshaft and connecting rods

Crankshaft endplay.. 0.0005 to 0.010 inch
Connecting rod endplay (side clearance)................. 0.006 to 0.024 inch
Main bearing journal diameter.................................. 2.300 inch
Main bearing oil clearance.. 0.0005 to 0.0026 inch
Connecting rod bearing journal diameter................ 2.000 inches
Connecting rod bearing oil clearance
    Through 1990 .... 0.0005 to 0.0026 inch
    1991 and later .... 0.0005 to 0.003 inch
Crankshaft journal taper/out-of-round limit............. 0.0005 inch

Engine block

Cylinder bore diameter .... 4.000 inch
Out-of-round limit
    Through 1987 .... 0.0014 inch
    1988 .... 0.001 inch
    1989 and 1990 .... 0.002 inch
    1991 and later .... 0.001 inch
Taper limit.. 0.0005 inch

Pistons and rings

Compression ring side clearance .... 0.003 inch
Oil control ring side clearance .... 0.015 to 0.055 inch
Piston diameter (measured 1 - 1/8 inch down from piston top)
    Through 1991 .... 3.9971 to 3.9975 inches
    1992 and later .... 3.998 to 4.00 inches
Piston-to-bore clearance
    Top .... 0.0025 to 0.0033 inch
    Bottom.. 0.0017 to 0.0041 inch
Piston pin diameter
    Through 1990 .... 0.938 to 0.942 inch
    1991 and later .... 0.927 to 0.928 inch
Piston ring end gap
    Top ring .... 0.010 to 0.026 inch
    Second ring .... 0.009 to 0.019 inch
    Oil ring .... 0.015 to 0.055 inch

Camshaft

Lobe lift (intake and exhaust)
    Through 1985 .... 0.398 inch
    1986 through 1989 .... 0.232 inch
    1990 and later .... 0.248 inch
Bearing journal diameter... 1.869 inch
Bearing oil clearance .... 0.0007 to 0.0027 inch
Camshaft thrust plate (end) clearance...................... 0.0015 to 0.0050 inch

Torque specifications

                                                               Ft-lbs
Main bearing cap bolts 70
Connecting rod cap nuts 32

Refer to Part B of this Chapter for additional torque specifications.

2.8 and 3.1 liter V6 engines

General

Cylinder compression pressure................................. Lowest reading should be within 70 percent of highest reading.
                                                                  No cylinder should measure less than 100 psi.
Oil pressure... 40 psi minimum at 2500 rpm

Cylinder head warpage limit.................................. 0.005 inch

Valves and related components

Valve face angle.. 45-degrees
Valve seat angle... 46-degrees

2.8 and 3.1 liter V6 engines (continued)

Valve seat runout
Through 1985	0.002 inch maximum
1986 and later	0.001 inch maximum

Stem-to-guide clearance
Through 1987	0.001 to 0.0028 inch
1988 and later	0.001 to 0.0027 inch

Valve margin width .... 1/32-inch minimum

Valve seat width

Through 1985
Intake	0.049 to 0.059 inch
Exhaust	0.063 to 0.075 inch

1986 and later
Intake	0.061 to 0.073 inch
Exhaust	0.067 to 0.079 inch

Valve spring installed height
1991 and earlier	1.57 inches
1994 and later	1.70 inches

Valve spring free length
1991 and earlier	1.91 inches
1994 and later	1.89 inches

Crankshaft and connecting rods

Crankshaft endplay
Through 1985	0.002 to 0.007 inch
1986 and 1987	0.0024 to 0.0083 inch
1988 through 1990	0.0016 to 0.0031 inch
1991 and later	0.0024 to 0.0083 inch

Connecting rod endplay (side clearance)
Through 1987	0.006 to 0.017 inch
1988 through 1991	0.014 to 0.027 inch
1994 and later	0.007 to 0.017 inch

Main bearing journal diameter
Through 1985	2.4937 to 2.4946 inches
1986 and later	2.6473 to 2.6483 inches

Main bearing oil clearance
1987 and earlier	0.0016 to 0.0030 inch
1988 through 1991	0.0012 to 0.0027 inch
1994 and later	0.008 to 0.0025 inch

Connecting rod bearing journal diameter .... 1.9983 to 1.9994 inches
Crankshaft journal taper/out-of-round limit .... 0.0002 inch

Connecting rod bearing oil clearance
1987 and later	0.0015 to 0.0036 inch
1988 through 1991	0.0011 to 0.0034 inch
1994 and later	0.0007 to 0.0024 inch

Engine block

Cylinder bore diameter
Through 1987	3.504 to 3.507 inches
1988 through 1990	3.5033 to 3.546 inches
1991 and later	3.5046 to 3.5053 inches

Out-of-round limit .... 0.0005 inch
Taper limit .... 0.0008 inch

Pistons and rings

Compression ring side clearance

Top ring
Through 1985	0.0019 to 0.0028 inch
1986 through 1989	0.001 to 0.003 inch
1990 and later	0.002 to 0.0035 inch

Second ring
Through 1985	0.0016 to 0.0037 inch
1986 through 1990	0.001 to 0.003 inch
1991 and later	0.002 to 0.0035 inch

Piston-to-bore clearance .... 0.0006 to 0.0028 inch

Piston ring end gap (compression rings only)
Top ring	0.010 to 0.020 inch
Second ring	0.020 to 0.028 inch

Camshaft

Lobe lift

Intake

Through 1985..	0.231 inch
1986 through 1991...	0.2626 inch
1994 and later..	0.2727 inch

Exhaust

Through 1985..	0.262 inch
1986 through 1991...	0.2732 inch
1994 and later..	0.2727 inch

Bearing journal diameter

Through 1985..	1.868 to 1.870 inch
1986 through 1991...	1.86798 to 1.8815 inch
1994 and later..	1.868 to 1.869 inches
Bearing oil clearance	0.001 to 0.004 inch

Torque specifications

Ft-lbs (unless otherwise indicated)

Main bearing cap bolts

1991 and earlier...	74

1994 and later

Step 1...	37
Step 2...	Tighten an additional 77-degrees

Connecting rod cap nuts

1991 and earlier...	37

1994 and later

Step 1...	15
Step 2...	Tighten an additional 75-degrees

Note: *Refer to Part C for additional torque specifications.*

3.0, 3.3 and 3.8 liter V6 engines

General

Cylinder compression pressure.....................................	Lowest reading should be within 70 percent of highest reading. No cylinder should measure less than 100 psi.
Oil pressure...	30 psi minimum at 2000 rpm

Cylinder head warpage limit ....

0.005 inch

Valves and related components

Valve margin width	1/32-inch minimum
Stem-to-guide clearance	0.0015 to 0.0035 inch

Intake valve

Head diameter..	1.715 to 1.705 inches
Face angle..	45-degrees
Seat angle	46-degrees
Seat width	0.062 inch
Seat runout limit	0.002 inch
Stem diameter...	0.3412 to 0.3401 inch

Exhaust valve

Head diameter..	1.505 to 1.495 inches
Face angle..	45-degrees
Seat angle	46-degrees
Seat width	0.074 to 0.104 inch
Seat runout limit	0.002 inch
Stem diameter...	0.3412 to 0.3405 inch

Valve springs

Free length	1.981 to 2.03 inches
Installed height	1.690 to 1.720 inches

Crankshaft and connecting rods

Crankshaft endplay at thrust bearing	0.003 to 0.011 inch
Connecting rod journal diameter	2.2487 to 2.2495 inches
Connecting rod journal runout and taper limits...............	0.0003 inch
Connecting rod bearing oil clearance............................	0.0008 to 0.0028 inch

Connecting rod bearing side clearance

Through 1985..	0.005 to 0.026 inch
1986 through 1988...	0.003 to 0.015 inch
1991 and later...	0.003 to 0.015 inch

3.0, 3.3 and 3.8 liter V6 engines (continued)

Main bearing journal diameter	
Through 1985	2.4995 inches
1986 through 1988	2.4988 to 2.4998 inches
1991 and later	2.4988 to 2.4998 inches
Main bearing-to-journal (oil) clearance	
Through 1991	0.0003 to 0.0018 inch
1992 and later	0.0008 to 0.0022 inch

Engine block

Cylinder bore diameter	
Through 1988	3.80 inch
1989 and later (3.3L)	3.700 inch
Out-of-round limit	0.0005 inch
Taper limit	0.0005 inch

Pistons and rings

Piston ring end gap - top and second (compression) rings only	
Through 1985	0.013 to 0.023 inch
1986 through 1988	0.010 to 0.020 inch
1989 and 1990	0.0013 to 0.0031 inch
1991 and later	0.010 to 0.025 inch
Piston ring side clearance - top and second (compression) rings only	
Through 1985	0.003 to 0.005 inch
1986 through 1988	0.001 to 0.003 inch
1989 and later	0.0013 to 0.0031 inch
Piston-to-bore clearance	
Top of bore..	0.001 to 0.002 inch
Bottom of bore	0.0015 to 0.035 inch
Piston diameter measuring point	
Through 1988	In-line with piston pin
1989 through 1990	1.65 inch down from top of piston
1991 and later	1.73 inch down from top of piston

Camshaft

Bearing journal diameter..	1.785 to 1.786 inch
Bearing oil clearance	0.0005 to 0.0044 inch
Lobe lift	
Intake	0.250 inch
Exhaust..	0.255 inch

Torque specifications

	Ft-lbs (unless otherwise indicated)
Main bearing cap bolts	
Through 1988	100
1989 and later	
Step 1..	26
Step 2..	Tighten an additional 45-degrees
Connecting rod cap nuts	
Through 1988	45
1989 and later	
Step 1..	20
Step 2..	Tighten an additional 50-degrees

Note: *Refer to Part D for additional torque specifications.*

1   General information

Included in this portion of Chapter 2 are the general overhaul procedures for the cylinder head and internal engine components. The information ranges from advice concerning preparation for an overhaul and the purchase of replacement parts to detailed, step-by-step procedures covering removal and installation of internal engine components and the inspection of parts.

The following Sections have been written based on the assumption that the engine has been removed from the vehicle. For information concerning in-vehicle engine repair, as well as removal and installation of the external components necessary for the overhaul, see Part A, B, C or D of Chapter 2 (depending on engine type) and Section 8 of this Part.

The specifications included here are only those necessary for the inspection and overhaul procedures which follow. Refer to Part A, B, C or D for additional specifications related to the various engines covered in this manual.

2   Compression check

Refer to illustration 2.4

1   A compression check will tell you what mechanical condition the engine is in. Specifically, it can tell you if the compression is down due to leakage caused by worn piston rings, defective valves and seats or a blown head gasket.

Note: *The engine must be at normal operating temperature and the battery must be fully charged for this check.*

2.4 Using a compression gauge to check cylinder compression

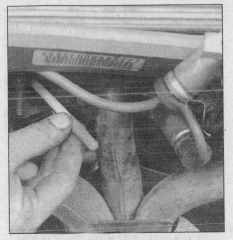

3.6 On engines with direct ignition and no timing marks, a plastic pen inserted into the spark plug hole can be used to find TDC

2   Begin by cleaning the area around the spark plugs before you remove them. This will keep dirt from falling into the cylinders while you are performing the compression test.

3   Disconnect the coil wire from the distributor or the small-wire electrical connector from the direct ignition system coil pack. Block the throttle and choke valve (if equipped) open. On fuel-injected models, remove the fuse marked EFI or INJ/COIL from the fuse block. On models with Throttle Body Injection (TBI), remove the ECM fuse.

4   With the compression gauge in the number one spark plug hole, crank the engine over at least four compression strokes and observe the gauge **(see illustration)**. The compression should build up quickly in a healthy engine. Low compression on the first stroke, which does not build up during successive strokes, indicates leaking valves, a blown head gasket or a cracked head. Record the highest gauge reading obtained.

5   Repeat the procedure for the remaining cylinders. The lowest compression reading should not be less than 70% of the highest reading. No reading should be less than 100 psi.

6   If the readings are below normal, pour a couple of teaspoons of engine oil (a squirt can works great for this) into each cylinder, through the spark plug hole, and repeat the test.

7   If the compression increases after the oil is added, the piston rings are worn. If the compression does not increase significantly, the leakage is occurring at the valves or head gasket. Leakage past the valves may be caused by burned valve seats or faces or warped, cracked or bent valves.

8   If two adjacent cylinders have equally low compression, there is a strong possibility that the head gasket between them is blown. The appearance of coolant in the combustion chambers or the crankcase would verify this condition.

9   If the compression is higher than normal, the combustion chambers are probably coated with carbon deposits. If that it the case, the cylinder head(s) should be removed and decarbonized.

10   If compression is down or varies greatly between cylinders, it would be a good idea to have a leak-down test performed by an automotive repair shop. This test will pinpoint exactly where the leakage is occurring and how severe it is.

3   Top Dead Center (TDC) for number one piston - locating

Refer to illustration 3.6

Note: *The following procedure is based on the assumption that the distributor is correctly installed. If you are trying to locate TDC to install the distributor correctly, piston position must be determined by feeling for compression at the number one spark plug hole, then aligning the ignition timing marks as described in Step 8.*

1   Top Dead Center (TDC) is the highest point in the cylinder that each piston reaches as it travels up-and-down when the crankshaft turns. Each piston reaches TDC on the compression stroke and again on the exhaust stroke, but TDC generally refers to piston position on the compression stroke.

2   Positioning the piston(s) at TDC is an essential part of many procedures such as valve train component removal and distributor removal.

3   Before beginning this procedure, be sure to place the transaxle in Neutral and apply the parking brake or block the rear wheels. Also, disable the ignition system by detaching the coil wire from the center terminal of the distributor cap and grounding it on the block with a jumper wire (models with a distributor) or disconnecting the small-wire electrical connector from the coil pack (models with direct ignition). Remove the spark plugs (see Chapter 1).

4   When looking at the drivebelt end of the engine, normal crankshaft rotation is clock-wise. In order to bring any piston to TDC, the crankshaft must be turned with a socket and ratchet attached to the bolt threaded into the center of the lower drivebelt pulley (vibration damper) on the crankshaft.

5   Have an assistant turn the crankshaft with a socket and ratchet as described above while you hold a finger over the number one spark plug hole. **Note:** *See the Specifications for the engine you are working on for the number one cylinder location.*

6   When the piston approaches TDC, air pressure will be felt at the spark plug hole. Have your assistant stop turning the crankshaft when the timing marks at the crankshaft pulley are aligned. **Note:** *On models with no distributor (direct ignition systems), there may be no timing marks. After you feel pressure, stop turning the crankshaft, then insert a plastic pen into the spark plug hole (see illustration). As the piston rises, the pen will be pushed out. Note the point where the pen stops moving out - this is TDC.*

7   If the timing marks are bypassed, turn the crankshaft two complete revolutions clockwise until the timing marks are properly aligned.

8   After the number one piston has been positioned at TDC on the compression stroke, TDC for any of the remaining pistons can be located by turning the crankshaft one-half turn (180-degrees) on four-cylinder engines or one-third turn (120-degrees) on V6 engines to get to TDC for the next cylinder in the firing order.

4   Engine overhaul - general information

Refer to illustrations 4.4a and 4.4b

It is not always easy to determine when, or if, an engine should be completely overhauled, as a number of factors must be considered.

High mileage is not necessarily an indication that an overhaul is needed, while low mileage does not preclude the need for an overhaul. Frequency of servicing is probably the most important consideration. An engine that has had regular and frequent oil and filter changes, as well as other required maintenance, will most likely give many thousands of miles of reliable service. Conversely, a neglected engine may require an overhaul very early in its life.

Excessive oil consumption is an indication that piston rings and/or valve guides are in need of attention. Make sure, however, that oil leaks are not responsible before deciding that the rings and guides are bad. Have a compression or leak-down test performed by an experienced tune-up mechanic to determine the extent of the work required.

If the engine is making obvious knocking or rumbling noises, the connecting rod and/or main bearings are probably at fault. Check the oil pressure with a gauge, installed in place of the oil pressure sending unit, and compare it to the Specifications. **Note:** *The*

4.4a On later 2.8L/3.1L V6 engines, the oil pressure sending unit is located just behind the oil filter adapter (arrow)

4.4b On 3.0L, 3.3L and 3.8L V6 engines, the oil pressure sending unit is located just above the oil filter (arrow)

oil pressure sending unit on most models is near the oil filter (see illustrations). If it is extremely low, the bearings and/or oil pump are probably worn out.

Loss of power, rough running, excessive valve train noise and high fuel consumption rates may also point to the need for an overhaul, especially if they are all present at the same time. If a complete tune-up does not remedy the situation, major mechanical work is the only solution.

An engine overhaul involves restoring the internal parts to the specifications of a new engine. During an overhaul, the piston rings are replaced and the cylinder walls are reconditioned (rebored or honed). If a rebore is done, new pistons are also required. The main and connecting rod bearings are replaced with new ones and, if necessary, the crankshaft may be reground to restore the journals. Generally, the valves are serviced as well, since they are usually in less-than-perfect condition at this point. While the engine is being overhauled, other components, such as the carburetor, distributor, starter and alternator can be rebuilt as well. The end result should be a like-new engine that will give many thousands of trouble-free miles.

Before beginning the engine overhaul, read through the entire procedure to familiarize yourself with the scope and requirements of the job. Overhauling an engine is not difficult, but it is time consuming. Plan on the vehicle being tied up for a minimum of two weeks, especially if parts must be taken to an automotive machine shop for repair or reconditioning. Check on availability of parts and make sure that any necessary special tools and equipment are obtained in advance. Most work can be done with typical hand tools, although a number of precision measuring tools are required for inspecting parts to determine if they must be replaced. Often an automotive machine shop will handle the inspection of parts and offer advice concerning reconditioning and replacement. **Note:** *Always wait until the engine has been completely disassembled and all components, especially the engine block, have been*

inspected before deciding what service and repair operations must be performed by an automotive machine shop. Since the block's condition will be the major factor to consider when determining whether to overhaul the original engine or buy a rebuilt one, never purchase parts or have machine work done on other components until the block has been thoroughly inspected. As a general rule, time is the primary cost of an overhaul, so it does not pay to install worn or sub-standard parts.

As a final note, to ensure maximum life and minimum trouble from a rebuilt engine, everything must be assembled with care in a spotlessly clean environment.

5   Engine rebuilding alternatives

The do-it-yourselfer is faced with a number of options when performing an engine overhaul. The decision to replace the engine block, piston/connecting rod assemblies and crankshaft depends on a number of factors, with the primary consideration being the condition of the block. Other considerations are cost, access to machine shop facilities, parts availability, time required to complete the project and experience.

Some of the rebuilding alternatives include:

Individual parts - If the inspection procedures reveal that the engine block and most engine components are in reusable condition, purchasing individual parts may be the most economical alternative. The block, crankshaft and piston/connecting rod assemblies should all be inspected carefully. Even if the block shows little wear, the cylinder bores should receive a finish hone; a job for an automotive machine shop.

Master kit (crankshaft kit) - This rebuild package usually consists of a reground crankshaft and a matched set of pistons, connecting rods and bearings. The pistons will already be installed on the connecting rods. These kits are commonly available for standard cylinder bores, as well as

for engine blocks which have been bored to a regular oversize.

Short block - A short block consists of an engine block with a crankshaft, camshaft and piston/connecting rod assemblies already installed. All new bearings are incorporated and all clearances will be correct. Depending on where the short block is purchased, a guarantee may be included. The existing valve train components, cylinder head and external parts can be bolted to the short block with little or no machine shop work necessary.

Long block - A long block consists of a short block plus an oil pump, oil pan, cylinder head and valve train components, timing sprockets and chain and timing chain cover. All components are installed with new bearings, seals and gaskets incorporated throughout. The installation of manifolds and external parts is all that is necessary. Some form of guarantee is usually included with the purchase.

Give careful thought to which alternative is best for you and discuss the situation with local automotive machine shops, auto parts dealers or dealership parts personnel before ordering or purchasing replacement parts.

6   Engine removal - methods and precautions

If it has been decided that an engine must be removed for overhaul or major repair work, certain preliminary steps should be taken.

Locating a suitable work area is extremely important. A shop is, of course, the most desirable place to work. Adequate work space, along with storage space for the vehicle, is very important. If a shop or garage is not available, at the very least a flat, level, clean work surface made of concrete or asphalt is required.

Cleaning the engine compartment and engine prior to removal will help keep tools clean and organized.

An engine hoist or A-frame will also be necessary. Make sure that the equipment is rated in excess of the combined weight of the engine and its accessories. Safety is of primary importance, considering the potential hazards involved in lifting the engine out of the vehicle.

If the engine is being removed by a novice, a helper should be available. Advice and aid from someone more experienced would also be helpful. There are many instances when one person cannot simultaneously perform all of the operations required when lifting the engine out of the vehicle.

Plan the operation ahead of time. Arrange for or obtain all the tools and equipment you will need prior to beginning the job. Some of the equipment necessary to perform engine removal and installation safely and with relative ease are, in addition to an engine hoist, a heavy-duty floor jack, complete sets

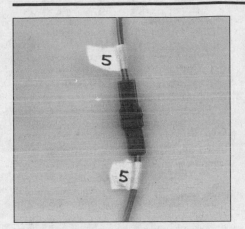

7.5 Label each hose and electrical connection with pieces of numbered tape before disconnecting them

7.11 Use a wire or rope to tie the power steering pump out of the way - make sure to keep the pump in an upright position

7.12 Unbolt the air conditioning compressor from the engine and tie it out of the way with a wire or rope

of wrenches and sockets as described in the front of this manual, wooden blocks and plenty of rags and cleaning solvent for mopping up the inevitable spills. If the hoist is to be rented, make sure that you arrange for it in advance and perform beforehand all of the operations possible without it. This will save you money and time.

Plan for the vehicle to be out of use for a considerable amount of time. A machine shop will be required to perform some of the work which the do-it-yourselfer cannot accomplish due to a lack of special equipment. These shops often have a busy schedule, so it would be wise to consult them before removing the engine in order to accurately estimate the amount of time required to rebuild or repair components that may need work.

Always use extreme caution when removing and installing the engine. Serious injury can result from careless actions. Plan ahead. Take your time and a job of this nature, although major, can be accomplished successfully.

7   Engine - removal and installation

Warning 1: *Gasoline is extremely flammable, so take extra precautions when you work on any part of the fuel system. Don't smoke or allow open flames or bare light bulbs near the work area, and don't work in a garage where a natural gas-type appliance (such as a water heater or clothes dryer) with a pilot light is present. If you spill any fuel on your skin, rinse it off immediately with soap and water. When you perform any kind of work on the fuel system, wear safety glasses and have a Class B type fire extinguisher on hand.*

Warning 2: *The air conditioning system is under high pressure! Have a dealer service department or automotive air conditioning shop discharge the system before disconnecting any air conditioning system hoses or fittings.*

Note: *Read through the following Steps carefully and familiarize yourself with the procedure before beginning work.*

Removal

Refer to illustrations 7.5, 7.11, 7.12 and 7.19

1   Refer to Chapter 4 and relieve the fuel system pressure (fuel-injected models only), then disconnect the negative cable from the battery.

2   Cover the fenders and cowl and remove the hood (see Chapter 11). Special pads are available to protect the fenders, but an old bedspread or blanket will also work.

3   Remove the air cleaner assembly.

4   Drain the cooling system (see Chapter 1).

5   Label the vacuum lines, emissions system hoses, wiring connectors, ground straps and fuel lines, to ensure correct reinstallation, then detach them. Pieces of masking tape with numbers or letters written on them work well **(see illustration)**. If there's any possibility of confusion, make a sketch of the engine compartment and clearly label the lines, hoses and wires. Photographs may also help.

6   Label and detach all coolant hoses from the engine.

7   Disconnect the engine mounting torque strut from the bracket on the engine, loosen the through-bolt at the other end of the strut and rotate the strut out of the way.

8   Remove the drivebelts (see Chapter 1).

9   Disconnect the fuel lines running from the engine to the chassis (see Chapter 4). Plug or cap all open fittings/lines.

10   Disconnect the throttle linkage (and TV

linkage/speed control cable, if equipped) from the engine (see Chapter 4).

11   On power-steering-equipped models, unbolt the power steering pump (see Chapter 10). Leave the lines/hoses attached and make sure the pump is kept in an upright position in the engine compartment **(see illustration)** (use wire or rope to restrain it out of the way).

12   On air conditioned models, unbolt the compressor (see Chapter 3) and set it aside **(see illustration)**. Do not disconnect the hoses unless absolutely necessary. See Warning 2 at the beginning of this Section.

13   Drain the engine oil (Chapter 1) and remove the filter.

14   Remove the starter motor (see Chapter 5).

15   Remove the alternator (see Chapter 5).

16   Unbolt the exhaust system from the engine (see Chapter 4).

17   If you're working on a vehicle with an automatic transaxle, refer to Chapter 7 and remove the torque converter-to-driveplate fasteners.

18   Support the transaxle with a jack. Position a block of wood between them to prevent damage to the transaxle. Special transmission jacks with safety chains are available - use one if possible.

19   Attach an engine sling or a length of chain to the lifting brackets on the engine **(see illustration)**.

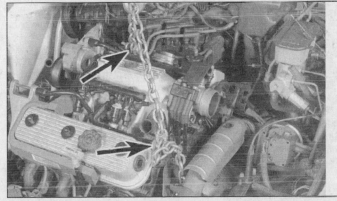

7.19 Attach the chain or hoist cable to the engine brackets (arrows) - 3.8L V6 engine shown

20   Roll the hoist into position and connect the sling to it. Take up the slack in the sling or chain, but don't lift the engine. **Warning:** *DO NOT place any part of your body under the engine when it's supported only by a hoist or other lifting device.*

21   Remove the transaxle-to-engine block bolts.

22   Remove the engine mount-to-frame bolts.

23   Recheck to be sure nothing is still connecting the engine to the transaxle or vehicle. Disconnect anything still remaining.

24   Raise the engine slightly. Carefully separate it from the transaxle. If you're working on a vehicle with an automatic transaxle, be sure the torque converter stays in the transaxle (clamp a pair of vise-grips to the housing to keep the converter from sliding out). If you're working on a vehicle with a manual transaxle, the input shaft must be completely disengaged from the clutch. Slowly raise the engine out of the engine compartment. Check carefully to make sure nothing is hanging up.

25   Remove the flywheel/driveplate and mount the engine on an engine stand.

Installation

26   Check the engine and transaxle mounts. If they're worn or damaged, replace them.

27   If you're working on a manual transaxle-equipped vehicle, install the clutch and pressure plate (see Chapter 8). Now is a good time to install a new clutch.

28   Carefully lower the engine into the engine compartment - make sure the engine mounts line up.

29   Align the engine with the transaxle bellhousing and carefully slide them together. Make sure the dowel pins line up and the transaxle input shaft (manual transaxle models) slides into the clutch friction disc.

30   Install the transaxle-to-engine bolts and tighten them securely. **Caution:** *DO NOT use the bolts to force the transaxle and engine together!*

31   Reinstall the remaining components in the reverse order of removal.

32   Add coolant, oil, power steering and transmission fluid as needed.

33   Run the engine and check for leaks and proper operation of all accessories, then install the hood and test drive the vehicle.

34   Have the air conditioning system recharged and leak tested.

8   Engine overhaul disassembly sequence

1   It is much easier to disassemble and work on the engine if it is mounted on a portable engine stand. These stands can often be rented for a reasonable fee from an equipment rental yard. Before the engine is mounted on a stand, the flywheel/driveplate should be removed from the engine (refer to Chapter 8).

2   If a stand is not available, it is possible to disassemble the engine with it blocked up on a sturdy workbench or on the floor. Be careful not to tip or drop the engine when working without a stand.

3   If you are going to obtain a rebuilt engine, all external components must come off your old engine to be transferred to the replacement engine, just as they will if you are doing a complete engine overhaul yourself. These include:

> *Alternator and brackets*
> *Emissions control components*
> *Distributor or coil pack, spark plug wires and spark plugs*
> *Thermostat and housing cover*
> *Water pump*
> *Carburetor/fuel injection components*
> *Intake and exhaust manifolds*
> *Oil filter*
> *Fuel pump*
> *Engine mounts*
> *Flywheel or driveplate*

Note: *When removing the external components from the engine, pay close attention to details that may be helpful or important during installation. Note the installed position of gaskets, seals, spacers, pins, washers, bolts and other small items.*

4   If you are obtaining a short block, which consists of the engine block, crankshaft, pistons and connecting rods all assembled, then the cylinder head, oil pan and oil pump will have to be removed as well. See *Engine rebuilding alternatives* for additional information regarding the different possibilities to be considered.

5   If you are planning a complete overhaul, the engine must be disassembled and the components removed in the following order:

> *Valve cover*
> *Intake and Exhaust manifolds*
> *Rocker arms and pushrods*
> *Valve lifters*
> *Cylinder head*
> *Timing chain cover*
> *Timing chain/sprockets/gears*
> *Camshaft*
> *Oil pan*
> *Oil pump*
> *Piston/connecting rod assemblies*
> *Crankshaft*

6   Before beginning the disassembly and overhaul procedures, make sure the following items are available:

> *Common hand tools*
> *Small cardboard boxes or plastic bags for storing parts*
> *Gasket scraper*
> *Ridge reamer*
> *Vibration damper puller*
> *Micrometers*
> *Small hole gauges*
> *Telescoping gauges*
> *Dial indicator set*
> *Valve spring compressor*
> *Cylinder surfacing hone*
> *Piston ring groove cleaning tool*
> *Electric drill motor*
> *Tap and die set*

> *Wire brushes*
> *Cleaning solvent*

9   Camshaft and timing gears - removal, inspection and installation

Camshaft lobe lift check

With cylinder head(s) installed

Refer to illustration 9.3

1   In order to determine the extent of cam lobe wear, the lobe lift should be checked prior to camshaft removal. Refer to Part A, B, C or D and remove the valve cover(s).

2   Position the number one piston at TDC on the compression stroke (see Section 3).

3   Beginning with the number one cylinder valves, loosen the rocker arm nuts and pivot the rocker arms sideways. **Note:** *This will not be possible on engines with shaft-mounted rocker arms. On these engines, mount the dial indicator plunger on the rocker arm, directly over the pushrod.* Mount a dial indicator on the engine and position the plunger against the top of the first pushrod. The plunger must be directly in line with the pushrod **(see illustration).**

4   Zero the dial indicator, then very slowly turn the crankshaft in the normal direction of rotation (clockwise) until the indicator needle stops and begins to move in the opposite direction. The point at which it stops indicates maximum cam lobe lift.

5   Record this figure for future reference, then reposition the piston at TDC on the compression stroke.

6   Move the dial indicator to the remaining number one cylinder push rod and repeat the check. Be sure to record the results for each valve.

7   Repeat the check for the remaining valves. Since each piston must be at TDC on the compression stroke for this procedure, work from cylinder-to-cylinder, following the firing order sequence.

8   After the check is complete, compare the results to this Chapter's Specifications. If

9.3 The dial indicator plunger must be positioned directly above and in-line with the pushrod (use a short length of vacuum hose to hold the plunger over the pushrod end, if you encounter difficulty keeping the plunger on the pushrod)

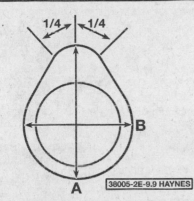

9.9 To verify camshaft lobe lift, measure the major (A) and minor (B) diameters of each lobe with a micrometer or vernier caliper - subtract each minor diameter from the major diameter to arrive at the lobe lift

9.14 On the 2.5L four-cylinder engine, turn the crankshaft until the holes in the gear are aligned with the thrust plate bolts, then remove them with a ratchet and socket

9.15 On all except 2.5L four-cylinder engines, thread long bolts into the sprocket bolt holes to use as a handle when removing and installing the camshaft

camshaft lobe lift is less than specified, cam lobe wear has occurred and a new camshaft should be installed.

With cylinder head(s) removed

Refer to illustration 9.9

9   If the cylinder heads have already been removed, an alternate method of lobe measurement can be used. Remove the camshaft, as described below. Using a micrometer, measure the lobe at its highest point. Then measure the base circle perpendicular (90-degrees) to the lobe **(see illustration)**. Do this for each lobe and record the results.

10   Subtract the base circle measurement from the lobe height. The difference is the lobe lift. See Step 8 above.

Removal

Refer to illustrations 9.14, 9.15 and 9.17,

11   Refer to the appropriate Sections in Part A, B, C or D and remove the timing chain/gear cover, chain and sprockets (if equipped), hydraulic lifters and pushrods.

12   On carbureted models, remove the fuel pump and pushrod (see Chapter 4).

13   On models so equipped, remove the distributor (see Chapter 5).

14   Remove the camshaft thrust plate-to-block bolts. On 2.5L models, you can access these bolts through the holes in the camshaft gear **(see illustration)**.

15   On 2.5L models, slide out the camshaft and gear together as an assembly. On all other models, thread long bolts into the camshaft sprocket bolt holes to use as a handle when removing the camshaft from the block **(see illustration)**.

16   Carefully pull the camshaft out. Support the cam near the block so the lobes don't nick or gouge the bearings as it's withdrawn.

17   When reinstalling the camshaft, be sure to coat the bearing journals and lobes, as well as the wear surfaces of all other valve train components, with moly-base grease or engine assembly lube. Again, install the camshaft very carefully to avoid damaging

9.17 Align the timing marks as shown here when installing the camshaft on the 2.5L four-cylinder engine

the camshaft bearings. The remainder of installation is the reverse of removal. On 2.5L four-cylinder engines, be sure to align the timing gear marks **(see illustration)**.

Inspection

Camshaft

Refer to illustration 9.19

18   After the camshaft has been removed from the engine, cleaned with solvent and dried, inspect the bearing journals for uneven wear, pitting and evidence of seizure. If the journals are damaged, the bearing inserts in the block are probably damaged as well. Both the camshaft and bearings will have to be replaced.

19   Measure the bearing journals with a micrometer **(see illustration)** to determine if they're excessively worn or out-of-round.

20   Check the camshaft lobes for heat discoloration, score marks, chipped areas, pitting and uneven wear. If the lobes are in good condition, and if the lobe lift measurements are as specified, the camshaft can be reused.

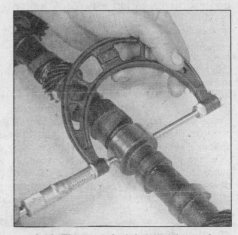

9.19 The camshaft bearing journal diameter is subtracted from the bearing inside diameter to obtain the oil clearance, which must be as listed in this Chapter's Specifications

Camshaft bearings

21   Check the bearings in the block for wear and damage. Look for galling, pitting and discolored areas.

22   The inside diameter of each bearing can be determined with a telescoping gauge and outside micrometer or an inside micrometer. Subtract the camshaft bearing journal diameters from the corresponding bearing inside diameters to obtain the bearing oil clearance. If it's excessive, new bearings will be required regardless of the condition of the originals.

23   Camshaft bearing replacement requires special tools and expertise that place it outside the scope of the home mechanic. Take the block to an automotive machine shop to ensure the job is done correctly.

Gears (2.5L engine only)

24   Check the camshaft drive and driven gears for cracks, missing teeth and excessive wear. If the teeth are highly polished, pitted and galled, or if the outer hardened surface of

10.3a Use a valve spring compressor to compress the springs, then remove the keepers from the valve stem with a magnet or small needle-nose pliers

10.3b If you can't pull the valve through the guide, deburr the edge of the stem end and the area around the top of the keeper groove with a file or whetstone

11.12 Check the cylinder head gasket surface for warpage by trying to slip a feeler gauge under the straightedge (see this Chapter's Specifications for the maximum warpage allowed and use a feeler gauge of that thickness)

the teeth is flaking off, new parts will be required. If one gear is worn or damaged, replace both gears as a set. Never install one new and one used gear. **Note:** *We recommend replacing the gears as a set whenever they are removed. The camshaft gear must be pressed off the camshaft by an automotive machine shop.*

25   Check the end clearance with a feeler gauge and compare it to the Specifications. If it's less than the minimum specified, the spacer ring should be replaced. If it's excessive, the thrust plate must be replaced. In either case, the gear will have to be pressed off the camshaft, so take the parts to an automotive machine shop.

10   Cylinder head - disassembly

Refer to illustrations 10.3a and 10.3b
Note: *New and rebuilt cylinder heads are commonly available for most engines at dealerships and auto parts stores. Due to the fact that some specialized tools are necessary for the disassembly and inspection procedures, and replacement parts may not be readily available, it may be more practical and economical for the home mechanic to purchase a replacement head rather than taking the time to disassemble, inspect and recondition the original head.*

1   Cylinder head disassembly involves removal of the intake and exhaust valves and their related components. If they are still in place, remove the nuts or bolts and pivot balls, then separate the rocker arms and/or shafts from the cylinder head. Label the parts or store them separately so they can be reinstalled in their original locations.
2   Before the valves are removed, arrange to label and store them, along with their related components, so they can be kept separate and reinstalled in the same valve guides. Measure the valve spring installed height (see Section 13) for each valve and compare it to the Specifications. If it is

greater than specified, the valves will require servicing. Tell the automotive machine shop who does this work about this out-of-spec condition.
3   Compress the valve spring with a spring compressor and remove the keepers **(see illustration)**. Carefully release the valve spring compressor and remove the retainer, the shield (if so equipped), the springs, the valve guide seal and/or O-ring seal, any spring seat shims and the valve from the head. If the valve binds in the guide (won't pull through), push it back into the head and deburr the area around the keeper groove with a fine file or whetstone **(see illustration)**.
4   Repeat the procedure for the remaining valves. Remember to keep together all the parts for each valve so they can be reinstalled in the same locations.
5   Once the valves have been removed and safely stored, the head should be thoroughly cleaned and inspected. If a complete engine overhaul is being done, finish the engine disassembly procedures before beginning the cylinder head cleaning and inspection process.

11   Cylinder head - cleaning and inspection

1   Thorough cleaning of the cylinder head and related valve train components, followed by a detailed inspection, will enable you to decide how much valve service work must be done during the engine overhaul.

Cleaning

2   Scrape away all traces of old gasket material and sealing compound from the head gasket, intake manifold and exhaust manifold sealing surfaces.
3   Remove any built-up scale around the coolant passages.
4   Run a stiff wire brush through the oil holes to remove any deposits that may have formed in them.

5   It is a good idea to run a tap into each of the threaded holes to remove any corrosion and thread sealant that may be present. If compressed air is available, use it to clear the holes of the debris produced by this operation.
6   Clean the exhaust and intake manifold stud threads with a die. Clean the rocker arm pivot bolt or stud threads with a wire brush.
7   Clean the cylinder head with solvent and dry it thoroughly. Compressed air will speed the drying process and ensure that all holes and recessed areas are clean. **Note:** *Decarbonizing chemicals are available and may prove very useful when cleaning cylinder heads and valve train components. They are very caustic and should be used with caution. Be sure to follow the instructions on the container.*
8   Clean the rocker arms, pivot balls and pushrods with solvent and dry them thoroughly. Compressed air will speed the drying process and can be used to clean out the oil passages.
9   Clean all the valve springs, keepers, retainers, shields and spring seat shims with solvent and dry them thoroughly. Do the components from one valve at a time to avoid mixing up the parts.
10   Scrape off any heavy deposits that may have formed on the valves, then use a motorized wire brush to remove deposits from the valve heads and stems. Again, make sure the valves do not get mixed up.

Inspection

Refer to illustrations 11.12, 11.14a, 11.14b, 11.19, 11.20, 11.21a and 11.21b

Cylinder head

11   Inspect the head very carefully for cracks, evidence of coolant leakage or other damage. If cracks are found, a new cylinder head should be obtained.
12   Using a straightedge and feeler gauge,

11.14a Use a small-hole gauge to determine the inside diameter of the valve guides (the gauge is then measured with a micrometer)

11.14b A dial indicator can also be used to determine the valve stem-to-guide clearance (the reading must be divided by two to obtain the actual clearance

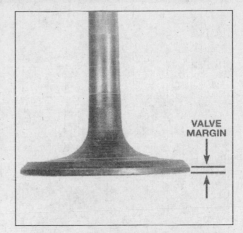

11.19 The margin width on each valve must be as specified (if no margin exists, the valve must be replaced)

check the head gasket mating surface for warpage **(see illustration)**. If the warpage exceeds 0.006-inch over the length of the head, it can be resurfaced at an automotive machine shop.

13 Examine the valve seats in each of the combustion chambers. If they are pitted, cracked or burned, the head will require valve service that is beyond the scope of the home mechanic.

14 Measure the inside diameter of the valve guides (at both ends and the center of each guide) with a small hole gauge and a 0-to-1-inch micrometer **(see illustration)**. Record the measurements for future reference. These measurements, along with the valve stem diameter measurements, will enable you to compute the valve stem-to-guide clearances. These clearances, when compared to the Specifications, will be one factor that will determine the extent of valve service work required. The guides are measured at the ends and at the center to determine if they are worn in a bellmouth pattern (more wear at the ends). If they are, guide reconditioning or replacement is necessary. As an alternative to using a small-hole gauge and micrometer, use a dial indicator to measure the lateral movement of each valve stem with the valve in the guide and approximately 1/16-inch off the seat **(see illustration)**.

Rocker arm components

15 Check the rocker arm faces, where they contact the pushrod ends and valve stems, for pits, wear and rough spots. Check the pivot contact areas as well.

16 Inspect the pushrod ends for scuffing and excessive wear. Roll the pushrod on a flat surface, such as a piece of glass, to determine if it is bent.

17 Any damaged or excessively worn parts must be replaced with new ones.

Valves

18 Carefully inspect each valve face for cracks, pits and burned spots. Check the

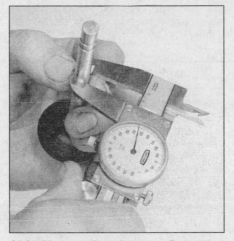

11.20 Measure the valve stem diameter at three points

valve stem and neck for cracks. Rotate the valve and check for any obvious indication that it is bent. Check the end of the stem for pits and excessive wear. The presence of any of these conditions indicates the need for valve service by a properly equipped shop.

19 Measure the width of the valve margin on each valve and compare it to Specifications. Any valve with a margin narrower than specified will have to be replaced with a new one **(see illustration)**.

20 Measure the valve stem diameter **(see illustration)**. **Note:** *The exhaust valves used in the 2.5L four-cylinder engine have tapered stems and are approximately 0.001-inch larger at the tip end than at the head end.* By subtracting the stem diameter from the corresponding valve guide diameter, the valve stem-to-guide clearance is obtained. Compare the results to the Specifications. If the stem-to-guide clearance is greater than specified, the guides will have to be reconditioned and new valves may have to be installed, depending on the condition of the old valves.

11.21a Measure the free length of each valve spring with a dial or vernier caliper

11.21b Check each valve spring for squareness

Valve components

21 Check each valve spring for wear and pits on the ends. Measure the free length and compare it to the Specifications **(see illustration)**. Any springs that are shorter than specified have sagged and should not be reused. Stand the spring on a flat surface and check it for squareness **(see illustration)**.

22 Check the spring retainers and keepers for obvious wear and cracks. Any question-

13.6 Measuring valve spring installed height

13.7 Checking the valve stem seals for leakage (models with O-ring type seals)

14.2 A special tool is required to remove the ridge from the top of each cylinder (do it before removing the piston)

able parts should be replaced with new ones, as extensive damage will occur in the event of failure during engine operation.

23   If the inspection process indicates that the valve components are in generally poor condition and worn beyond the limits specified, which is usually the case in an engine that is being overhauled, reassemble the valves in the cylinder head and refer to Section 12 for valve servicing recommendations.

24   If the inspection turns up no excessively worn parts, and if the valve faces and seats are in good condition, the valve train components can be reinstalled in the cylinder head without major servicing. Refer to the appropriate Section for cylinder head reassembly procedures.

12   Valves - servicing

1   Because of the complex nature of the job and the special tools and equipment needed, servicing of the valves, the valve seats and the valve guides (commonly known as a "valve job") is best left to a professional.

2   The home mechanic can remove and disassemble the head, do the initial cleaning and inspection, then reassemble and deliver the head to a dealer service department or an automotive machine shop for the actual valve servicing.

3   The dealer service department, or automotive machine shop, will remove the valves and springs, recondition or replace the valves and valve seats, recondition the valve guides, check and replace the valve springs, spring retainers and keepers (as necessary), replace the valve seals with new ones, reassemble the valve components and make sure the installed spring height is correct. The cylinder head gasket surface will also be resurfaced if it is warped.

4   After the valve job has been performed by a professional, the head will be in like-new condition. When the head is returned, be sure to clean it again to remove any metal particles and abrasive grit that may still be pre-

sent from the valve service or head resurfacing operations. Use compressed air, if available, to blow out all the oil holes and passages.

13   Cylinder head - reassembly

Refer to illustrations 13.6 and 13.7

1   Regardless of whether or not the head was sent to an automotive repair shop for valve servicing, make sure it is clean before beginning reassembly.

2   If the head was sent out for valve servicing, the valves and related components will already be in place. Begin the reassembly procedure with Step 6.

3   Install new seals on each of the valve guides. Using a hammer and a deep socket, gently tap each seal into place until it is properly seated on the guide. Do not twist or cock the seals during installation or they will not seal properly on the valve stems.

4   Install the valves, taking care not to damage the new valve stem oil seals, drop the valve spring shim(s) around the valve guide boss and set the valve spring, cap and retainer in place.

5   Compress the spring with a valve compressor tool and install the valve locks. Release the compressor tool, making sure the locks are seated properly in the valve stem upper groove. If necessary, grease can be used to hold the locks in place while the compressor tool is released.

6   Double-check the installed valve spring height. If it was correct before reassembly it should still be within the specified limits. If it is not, install an additional valve spring seat shims (available from your dealer) to bring the height to within the specified limit **(see illustration)**.

7   On models equipped with O-ring-type seals, check the seals with a vacuum pump and adapter **(see illustration)**. A properly installed oil seal should not leak vacuum.

8   Install the rocker arms and tighten the nuts to the specified torque. Be sure to lubri-

cate the ball pivots with moly-base grease or engine assembly lube.

14   Piston/connecting rod assembly - removal

Refer to illustrations 14.2, 14.6 and 14.8

1   Prior to removal of the piston/connecting rod assemblies, the engine should be positioned upright.

2   Using a ridge reamer, completely remove the ridge at the top of each cylinder. Follow the manufacturer's instructions provided with the ridge reaming tool **(see illustration)**. Failure to remove the ridge before attempting to remove the piston/connecting rod assemblies will result in piston breakage.

3   After the cylinder wear ridges have been removed, turn the engine upside-down.

4   Before the connecting rods are removed, check the endplay. Mount a dial indicator with its stem in line with the crankshaft and touching the side of the number one connecting rod cap.

5   Push the connecting rod backward, as far as possible, and zero the dial indicator. Next, push the connecting rod all the way to the front and check the reading on the dial indicator. The distance that it moves is the endplay. If the endplay exceeds the service limit, a new connecting rod will be required. Repeat the procedure for the remaining connecting rods.

6   An alternative method is to slip feeler gauges between the connecting rod and the crankshaft throw until the play is removed **(see illustration)**. The endplay is then equal to the total thickness of the feeler gauges.

7   Check the connecting rods and connecting rod caps for identification marks. If they are not plainly marked, identify each rod and cap, using a small punch to make the appropriate number of indentations to indicate the cylinders they are associated with.

8   Loosen each of the connecting rod cap nuts approximately 1/2-turn. Remove the

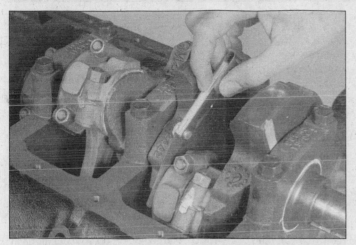

14.6 Checking connecting rod endplay with a feeler gauge

14.8 To prevent damage to the crankshaft journals and cylinder walls, slip sections of hose over the rod bolts before removing the pistons

15.1 Checking crankshaft endplay with a dial indicator

15.3 Checking crankshaft endplay with a feeler gauge

15.4 Use a centerpunch or number stamping dies to mark the main bearing caps to ensure installation in their original locations on the block - make the punch marks near one of the bolt heads

number one connecting rod cap and bearing insert. Do not drop the bearing insert out of the cap. Slip a short length of plastic or rubber hose over each connecting rod cap bolt to protect the crankshaft journal and cylinder wall when the piston is removed **(see illustration)** and push the connecting rod/piston assembly out through the top of the engine. Use a wooden tool to push on the upper bearing insert in the connecting rod. If resistance is felt, double-check to make sure that all of the ridge was removed from the cylinder.

9 Repeat the procedure for the remaining cylinders. After removal, reassemble the connecting rod caps and bearing inserts in their respective connecting rods and install the cap nuts finger-tight. Leaving the old bearing inserts in place until reassembly will help prevent the connecting rod bearing surfaces from being accidentally nicked or gouged.

15 Crankshaft - removal

Refer to illustrations 15.1, 15.3 and 15.4

1 Before the crankshaft is removed check

the endplay. Mount a dial indicator with the stem in line with the crankshaft and just touching one of the crank throws **(see illustration)**.

2 Push the crankshaft all the way to the rear and zero the dial indicator. Next, pry the crankshaft to the front as far as possible and check the reading on the dial indicator. The distance that it moves is the endplay. If it is greater than specified, check the crankshaft thrust surfaces for wear. If no wear is apparent, new main bearings should correct the endplay.

3 If a dial indicator is not available, feeler gauges can be used. Gently pry or push the crankshaft all the way to the front of the engine. Slip feeler gauges between the crankshaft and the front face of the thrust main bearing **(see illustration)** to determine the clearance, which is equivalent to crankshaft endplay.

4 Loosen each of the main bearing cap bolts 1/4-turn at a time, until they can be removed by hand. Check the main bearing caps to see if they are marked as to their locations. They are usually numbered consecutively from the front of the engine to the rear. If they are not, mark them with number

stamping dies or a center-punch **(see illustration)**. Most main bearing caps have a cast-in arrow, which points to the front of the engine.

5 Gently tap the caps with a soft-face hammer, then separate them from the engine block. If necessary, use the main bearing cap bolts as levers to remove the caps. Try not to drop the bearing insert if it comes out with the cap.

6 Carefully lift the crankshaft out of the engine. It is a good idea to have an assistant available, since the crankshaft is quite heavy. With the bearing inserts in place in the engine block and in the main bearing caps, return the caps to their respective locations on the engine block and tighten the bolts finger-tight.

16 Engine block - cleaning

Refer to illustrations 16.1a, 16.1b and 16.10

1 Remove the soft plugs from the engine block. To do this, knock the plugs into the

16.1a A hammer and large punch can be used to drive the soft plugs into the block

16.1b Using pliers to remove a soft plug from the block

16.10 A large socket on an extension can be used to force the new soft plugs into their bores

block, using a hammer and punch, then grasp them with large pliers and pull them back through the holes **(see illustrations)**.

2   Using a gasket scraper, remove all traces of gasket material from the engine block. Be very careful not to nick or gouge the gasket sealing surfaces.

3   Remove the main bearing caps and separate the bearing inserts from the caps and the engine block. Tag the bearings according to which cylinder they are removed from and whether they were in the cap or the block, then set them aside.

4   Remove the threaded oil gallery plugs from the front and back of the block.

5   If the engine is extremely dirty, it should be taken to an automotive machine shop to be steam cleaned or hot tanked. Any bearings left in the block, such as the camshaft bearings, will be damaged by the cleaning process, so plan on having new ones installed while the block is at the machine shop.

6   After the block is returned, clean all oil holes and oil galleries one more time. Brushes for cleaning oil holes and galleries are available at most auto parts stores. Flush the passages with warm water until the water runs clear, dry the block thoroughly and wipe all machined surfaces with a light, rust preventative oil. If you have access to compressed air, use it to speed the drying process and to blow out all the oil holes and galleries.

7   If the block is not extremely dirty or sludged up, you can do an adequate cleaning job with warm soapy water and a stiff brush. Take plenty of time and do a thorough job. Regardless of the cleaning method used, be very sure to thoroughly clean all oil holes and galleries, dry the block completely and coat all machined surfaces with light oil.

8   The threaded holes in the block must be clean to ensure accurate torque readings during reassembly. Run the proper-size tap into each of the holes to remove any rust, corrosion, thread sealant or sludge and to restore any damaged threads. If possible,

use compressed air to clear the holes of debris produced by this operation. Now is a good time to thoroughly clean the threads on the head bolts and the main bearing cap bolts as well.

9   Reinstall the main bearing caps and tighten the bolts finger-tight.

10   After coating the sealing surfaces of the new soft plugs with a non-hardening gasket sealant, such as Permatex no. 2, install them in the engine block **(see illustration)**. Make sure they are driven in straight and seated properly or leakage could result. Special tools are available for this purpose, but equally good results can be obtained using a socket with an outside diameter that will just slip into the soft plug and a hammer.

11   If the engine is not going to be reassembled right away, cover it with a large plastic trash bag to keep it clean.

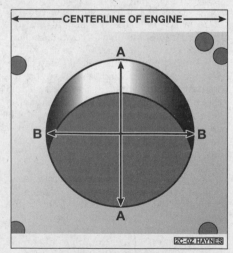

17.4a Measure the diameter of each cylinder at a right angle to engine centerline (A), and parallel to the engine centerline (B) - out-of-round is the difference between A and B; taper is the difference between A and B at the top of the cylinder and A and B at the bottom of the cylinder

17 Engine block - inspection

Refer to illustrations 17.4a, 17.4b, 17.4c, 17.7a and 17.7b

1   Thoroughly clean the engine block as described in Section 16 and double-check to make sure that the ridge at the top of each cylinder has been completely removed.

2   Visually check the block for cracks, rust and corrosion. Look for stripped threads in the threaded holes. It is also a good idea to have the block checked for hidden cracks by an automotive machine shop that has the special equipment to do this type of work. If defects are found, have the block repaired, if possible, or replaced.

3   Check the cylinder bores for scuffing and scoring.

4   Using an expansion gauge and micrometer, measure each cylinder's diameter at the top (just under the ridge), center and bottom of the cylinder bore, parallel to the crankshaft axis **(see illustrations)**. Next, measure each

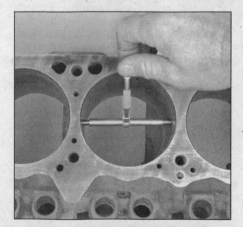

17.4b The ability to "feel" when the telescoping gauge is at the correct point will be developed over time, so work slowly and repeat the check until you're satisfied the bore measurement is accurate

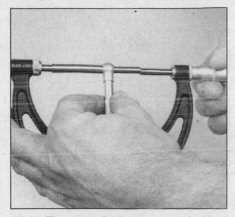

17.4c The gauge is then measured with a micrometer to determine the bore size

17.7a If this is the first time you've ever honed cylinders, you'll get better results with a "bottle brush" hone than you will with a traditional spring-loaded hone

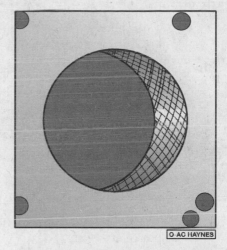

17.7b The cylinder hone should leave a smooth, crosshatch pattern with the lines intersecting at approximately a 60-degree angle

cylinder's diameter at the same three locations across the crankshaft axis. Compare the results to the Specifications. If the cylinder walls are badly scuffed or scored, or if they are out-of-round or tapered beyond the limits given in the Specifications, have the engine block rebored and honed at an automotive machine shop. If a rebore is done, oversize pistons and rings will be required.

5 If the cylinders are in reasonably good condition and not worn to the outside of the limits, and if the piston-to-cylinder clearances can be maintained properly, then they do not have to be rebored. Honing is all that is necessary.

6 Before honing the cylinders, install the main bearing caps, without the bearings, and tighten the bolts to the specified torque.

7 To perform the honing operation you will need the proper-size hone (with fine stones), plenty of light oil or honing oil, some rags and an electric drill motor. Mount the hone in the drill motor, compress the stones and slip the hone into the first cylinder (see illustration). Lubricate the cylinder thoroughly, turn on the drill and move the hone up and down in the cylinder at a pace which will produce a fine crosshatch pattern on the cylinder walls, with the crosshatch lines intersecting at approximately a 60-degree angle (see illustration). Be sure to use plenty of lubricant and do not take off any more material than is absolutely necessary to produce the desired finish. Do not withdraw the hone from the cylinder while it is running. Instead, shut off the drill and continue moving the hone up and down in the cylinder until it comes to a complete stop, then compress the stones and withdraw the hone. Wipe the oil out of the cylinder and repeat the procedure on the remaining cylinders. If you do not have the tools or do not desire to perform the honing operation, most automotive machine shops will do it for a reasonable fee.

8 After the honing job is complete, chamfer the top edges of the cylinder bores with a small file so the rings will not catch when the pistons are installed.

9 The entire engine block must be thor-

oughly washed again with warm, soapy water to remove all traces of the abrasive grit produced during the honing operation. Be sure to run a brush through all oil holes and galleries and flush them with running water. After rinsing, dry the block and apply a coat of light rust preventative oil to all machined surfaces. Wrap the block in a plastic trash bag to keep it clean and set it aside until reassembly.

18 Piston/connecting rod assembly - inspection

Refer to illustrations 18.4, 18.10 and 18.11

1 Before the inspection process can be carried out, the piston/connecting rod assemblies must be cleaned and the original piston rings removed from the pistons. **Note:** *Always use new piston rings when the engine is reassembled.*

2 Using a piston ring installation tool, carefully remove the rings from the pistons. Do not nick or gouge the pistons in the process.

3 Scrape all traces of carbon from the top (or crown) of the piston. A hand-held wire brush or a piece of fine emery cloth can be used once the majority of the deposits have been scraped away. Do not, under any circumstances, use a wire brush mounted in a drill motor to remove deposits from the pistons. The piston material is soft and will be eroded away by the wire brush.

4 Use a piston ring groove cleaning tool to remove any carbon deposits from the ring grooves. If a tool is not available, a piece broken off an old ring will do the job. Be very careful to remove only the carbon deposits. Do not remove any metal and do not nick or scratch the sides of the ring grooves (see illustration).

5 Once the deposits have been removed, clean the piston/rod assemblies with solvent and dry them thoroughly. Make sure that the

oil return holes in the back sides of the ring grooves are clear.

6 If the pistons are not damaged or worn excessively, and if the engine block is not rebored, new pistons will not be necessary. Normal piston wear appears as even, vertical wear on the piston thrust surfaces and slight looseness of the top ring in its groove. New piston rings, on the other hand, should always be used when an engine is rebuilt.

7 Carefully inspect each piston for cracks around the skirt, at the pin bosses and at the ring lands.

8 Look for scoring and scuffing on the thrust faces of the skirt, holes in the piston crown and burned areas at the edge of the crown. If the skirt is scored or scuffed, the engine may have been suffering from overheating or abnormal combustion, which caused excessively high operating temperatures. The cooling and lubrication systems should be checked thoroughly. A hole in the piston crown is an indication that abnormal combustion (preignition) was occurring.

18.4 The piston ring grooves can be cleaned with a special tool, as shown here, or a piece of a broken piston ring

18.10 Check the piston ring side clearance with a feeler gauge at several points around the groove

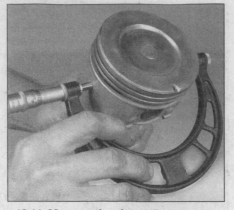

18.11 Measure the piston diameter at a 90-degree angle to the piston pin at the specified point on the skirt (see the Specifications)

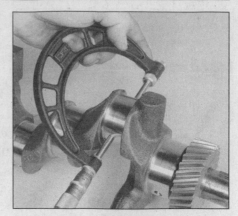

19.2 Measure the diameter of each crankshaft journal at several points to detect taper and out-of-round conditions

Burned areas at the edge of the piston crown are usually evidence of spark knock (detonation). If any of the above problems exist, the causes must be corrected or the damage will occur again.

9   Corrosion of the piston (evidenced by pitting) indicates that coolant is leaking into the combustion chamber or the crankcase. Again, the cause must be corrected or the problem may persist in the rebuilt engine.

10   Measure the piston ring side clearance by laying a new piston ring in each ring groove and slipping a feeler gauge between the ring and the edge of the ring groove (see illustration). Check the clearance at four locations around each groove. Be sure to use the correct ring for each groove; they are different. If the side clearance is greater than specified, new pistons will have to be used.

11   Check the piston-to-bore clearance by measuring the bore (see Section 17) and the piston diameter. Make sure that the pistons and bores are correctly matched. Measure the piston across the skirt (see illustration). Subtract the piston diameter from the bore diameter to obtain the clearance. If it is greater than specified, the block will have to be rebored and new pistons and rings installed. Check the piston-to-rod clearance by twisting the piston and rod in opposite directions. Any noticeable play indicates that there is excessive wear, which must be corrected. The piston/connecting rod assemblies should be taken to an automotive machine shop to have new piston pins installed and the pistons and connecting rods rebored.

12   If the pistons must be removed from the connecting rods, such as when new pistons must be installed, or if the piston pins have too much play in them, they should be taken to an automotive machine shop. While they are there, have the connecting rods checked for bend and twist, as automotive machine shops have special equipment for this purpose. Unless new pistons or connecting rods must be installed, do not disassemble the pistons from the connecting rods.

13   Check the connecting rods for cracks and other damage. Temporarily remove the

rod caps, lift out the old bearing inserts, wipe the rod and cap bearing surfaces clean and inspect them for nicks, gouges or scratches. After checking the rods, replace the old bearings, slip the caps into place and tighten the nuts finger tight.

19   Crankshaft - inspection

Refer to illustration 19.2

1   Clean the crankshaft with solvent and dry it thoroughly. Be sure to clean the oil holes with a stiff brush and flush them with solvent. Check the main and connecting rod bearing journals for uneven wear, scoring, pitting or cracks. Check the remainder of the crankshaft for cracks and damage. Automotive machine shops are equipped with Magnaflux machines to check the crankshaft for cracks that may not be visible to the eye.

2   Using a micrometer, measure the diameter of the main and connecting rod journals (see illustration) and compare the results to the Specifications. By measuring the diameter at a number of points around the journal's circumference you will be able to determine whether or not the journal is out of round. Take the measurement at each end of the journal, near the crank counterweights, to determine whether the journal is tapered.

3   If the crankshaft journals are damaged, tapered, out-of-round or worn beyond the limits given in the Specifications, have the crankshaft reground by a reputable automotive machine shop. Be sure to use the correct undersize bearing inserts if the crankshaft is reconditioned.

20   Main and connecting rod bearings - inspection

Refer to illustration 20.3

1   Even though the main and connecting rod bearings should be replaced with new ones during the engine overhaul, the old bearings should be retained for close exami-

nation, as they may reveal valuable information about the condition of the engine.

2   Bearing failure occurs primarily because of lack of lubrication, the presence of dirt or other foreign particles, overloading the engine and corrosion. Regardless of the cause of bearing failure, it must be corrected before the engine is reassembled to prevent it from happening again.

3   When examining the bearings, remove them from the engine block, the main bearing caps, the connecting rods and the rod caps and lay them out on a clean surface in the same general position as their location in the engine. This will enable you to match any bearing problems with the corresponding crankshaft journal (see illustration).

4   Dirt and other foreign particles get into the engine in a variety of ways. It may be left in the engine during assembly, or it may pass through filters or breathers. It may get into the oil, and from there into the bearings. Metal chips from machining operations and normal engine wear are often present. Abrasives are sometimes left in engine components after reconditioning, especially when parts are not thoroughly cleaned using the proper cleaning methods. Whatever the source, these foreign objects often end up embedded in the soft bearing material and are easily recognized. Large particles will not embed in the bearing and will score or gouge the bearing and shaft. The best prevention for this cause of bearing failure is to clean all parts thoroughly and keep everything spotlessly clean during engine assembly. Frequent and regular engine oil and filter changes are also recommended.

5   Lack of lubrication (or lubrication breakdown) has a number of interrelated causes. Excessive heat (which thins the oil), overloading (which squeezes the oil from the bearing face) and oil leakage or throwoff (from excessive bearing clearances, worn oil pump or high engine speeds) all contribute to lubrication breakdown. Blocked oil passages, which usually are the result of misaligned oil holes in a bearing shell, will also oil-starve a bearing and destroy it. When lack of lubrication is the

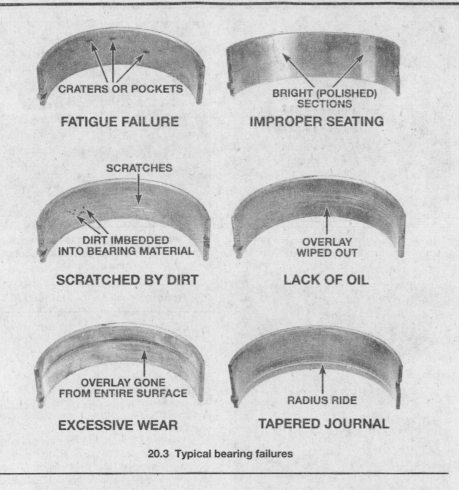

FATIGUE FAILURE — CRATERS OR POCKETS

IMPROPER SEATING — BRIGHT (POLISHED) SECTIONS

SCRATCHED BY DIRT — SCRATCHES — DIRT IMBEDDED INTO BEARING MATERIAL

LACK OF OIL — OVERLAY WIPED OUT

EXCESSIVE WEAR — OVERLAY GONE FROM ENTIRE SURFACE

TAPERED JOURNAL — RADIUS RIDE

20.3 Typical bearing failures

cause of bearing failure, the bearing material is wiped or extruded from the steel backing of the bearing. Temperatures may increase to the point where the steel backing turns blue from overheating.

6   Driving habits can have a definite effect on bearing life. Full-throttle, low-speed operation (or *lugging* the engine) puts very high loads on bearings, which tends to squeeze out the oil film. These loads cause the bearings to flex, which produces fine cracks in the bearing face (fatigue failure). Eventually the bearing material will loosen in pieces and tear away from the steel backing. Short-trip driv-

ing leads to corrosion of bearings because insufficient engine heat is produced to drive off the condensed water and corrosive gases. These products collect in the engine oil, forming acid and sludge. As the oil is carried to the engine bearings, the acid attacks and corrodes the bearing material.

7   Incorrect bearing installation during engine assembly will lead to bearing failure as well. Tight-fitting bearings leave insufficient bearing oil clearance and will result in oil starvation. Dirt or foreign particles trapped behind a bearing insert result in high spots on the bearing which can lead to failure.

21 Piston rings - installation

Refer to illustrations 21.3a, 21.3b, 21.9a, 21.9b and 21.12

1   Before installing the new piston rings, the ring end gaps must be checked. It is assumed that the piston ring side clearance has been checked and verified correct (Section 18).

2   Lay out the piston/connecting rod assemblies and the new ring sets so the ring sets will be matched with the same piston and cylinder during the end gap measurement and engine assembly.

3   Insert the top ring into the cylinder and square it up with the cylinder walls by pushing it in with the top of the piston, until it is near the bottom of ring travel in the cylinder. To measure the end gap, slip a feeler gauge between the ends of the ring **(see illustrations)**. Compare the measurement to the Specifications.

4   If the gap is larger or smaller than specified, double-check to make sure that you have the correct rings before proceeding.

5   If the gap is too small, it must be enlarged or the ring ends may come in contact with each other during engine operation, which can cause serious damage to the engine. The end gap can be increased by filing the ring ends very carefully with a fine file. Mount the file in a vise equipped with soft jaws, slip the ring over the file with the ends contacting the file face and slowly move the ring to remove material from the ends. When performing this operation, file only from the outside in.

6   Excess end gap is not critical unless it is greater than 0.040-inch. Again, double-check to make sure you have the correct rings for your engine.

7   Repeat the procedure for the rest of the rings. Remember to keep rings, pistons and cylinders matched up.

8   Once the ring end gaps have been checked, the rings can be installed on the pistons.

9   The oil control ring (lowest one on the piston) is installed first. It is composed of three separate components. Slip the spacer/expander into the groove **(see illus-**

21.3a Use the piston to square up the ring in the cylinder prior to checking the ring end gap

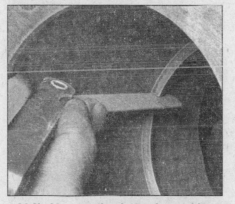

21.3b Measure the ring end gap with a feeler gauge

21.9a Installing the spacer/expander in the oil control ring groove

21.9b Do not use a piston ring tool when installing the oil ring side rails

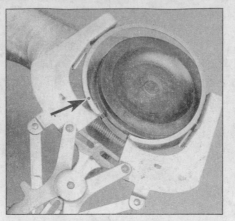

21.12 Installing the compression rings with a ring expander - the mark (arrow) must face up

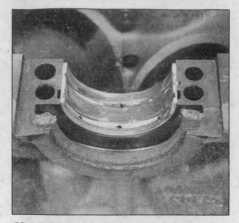

22.1 When correctly installed, the ends of the rope-type seal should extend out of the block

22.2 Seat the seal in the groove, but do not depress it below the bearing surface (the seal must contact the crankshaft journal)

22.3a Trim the ends flush with the block . . .

22 Rear main oil seal - installation

Rope-type seal

Refer to illustrations 22.1, 22.2, 22.3a, 22.3b, 22.4, 22.5, 22.6a and 22.6b

1   Lay one seal section on edge in the seal groove in the block and push it into place with your thumbs. Both ends of the seal should extend out of the block slightly **(see illustration)**.

2   Seat it in the groove by rolling a large socket or piece of bar stock along the entire length of the seal **(see illustration)**. As an alternative, push the seal very carefully into place with a wooden hammer handle.

3   Once you are satisfied that the seal is completely seated in the groove, trim off the excess on the ends with a single-edge razor blade or razor knife. The seal ends must be flush with the block-to-cap mating surfaces **(see illustrations)**. Make sure that no seal fibers get caught between the block and cap.

4   Repeat the entire procedure to install the other half of the seal in the bearing cap. Apply a thin film of engine assembly lube to the edge of the seal where it contacts the crankshaft **(see illustration)**.

tration), then install the lower side rail **(see illustration)**. Do not use a piston ring installation tool on the oil ring side rails, as they may be damaged. Instead, place one end of the side rail into the groove between the spacer/expander and the ring land, hold it firmly in place and slide a finger around the piston while pushing the rail into the groove. Next, install the upper side rail in the same manner.

10   After the three oil ring components have been installed, check to make sure that both the upper and lower side rails can be turned smoothly in the ring groove.

11   The number two (middle) ring is installed next. It should be stamped with a mark so it can be readily distinguished from the top ring. **Note:** *Always follow the instructions printed on the ring package or box - different manufacturers may use different approaches.* Do not mix up the top and middle rings, as they have different cross sections.

12   Use a piston ring installation tool and make sure that the identification mark is facing the top of the piston, then slip the ring into the middle groove on the piston **(see**

illustration). Do not expand the ring any more than is necessary to slide it over the piston.

13   Install the number one (top) ring in the same manner. Make sure the identifying mark is facing up.

14   Repeat the procedure for the remaining pistons and rings. Be careful not to confuse the number one and number two rings.

22.3b . . .but leave the inner edge (arrow) protruding slightly

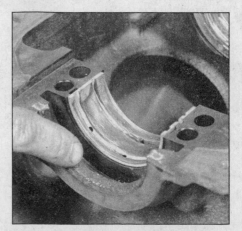

22.4 Lubricate the seal with assembly lube or moly-base grease

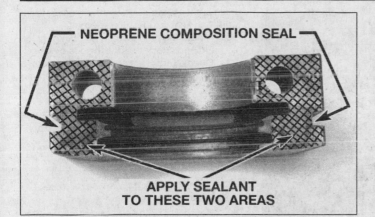

22.5 Applying the composition seals and sealer to the 3.0L, 3.3L and 3.8L V6 engine rear main bearing cap

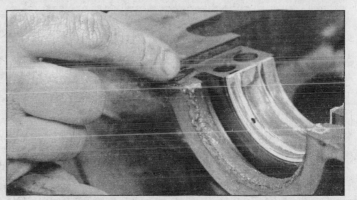

22.6a When applying the sealant, be sure it gets into the corner and onto the vertical cap-to-block mating surface or oil leaks will result

5   On 3.0, 3.3 and 3.8 liter V6 engines install the neoprene seals in the bearing cap groove as shown **(see illustration)**. These seals are slightly undersize, but swell in the presence of oil and heat so that after the engine is run they will seal effectively. The seals are also slightly longer than the bearing cap grooves, but must not be cut to length. Soak the seals for two minutes in kerosene or light oil prior to installation.

6   During final installation of the crankshaft, after the main bearing oil clearances have been checked with Plastigage as described in Section 23, apply a thin, even film of anaerobic-type gasket sealant to the areas of the rear main bearing cap.**(see illustrations)**. **Caution:** *Do not get any sealant on the bearing or seal faces.*

Neoprene lip-type seal

Refer to illustration 22.8

7   Inspect the bearing cap and engine block mating surfaces and seal grooves for nicks, burrs and scratches. Remove any defects with a fine file or deburring tool.

8   Install one seal section in the block with the lip facing the front of the engine. Leave one end protruding from the block 3/8-inch and make sure it is completely seated. **Note:** *Apply a very thin coat of RTV type gasket sealant to the outer surface of the seal as shown in the accompanying illustration. Do not get any sealant on the seal lip* **(see illustration)**.

9   Repeat the procedure to install the remaining seal half in the rear main bearing cap. In this case, leave the opposite end of the seal protruding from the cap the same distance the block seal is protruding from the block.

10   Prior to final installation of the crankshaft, lubricate the seal lips with moly-base grease or engine assembly lube.

One-piece seal

11   Later models are equipped with a one-piece, lip-type seal. The crankshaft must be in place and the main bearing caps installed before the seal is installed. See Part A, B, C or D (depending on which engine you have) for the procedure.

22.6b Anaerobic type sealant should be used where the rear main cap touches the engine block

23   Crankshaft - installation and main bearing oil clearance check

Refer to illustrations 23.10 and 23.14

1   Crankshaft installation is generally one of the first steps in engine reassembly. It is assumed at this point that the engine block and crankshaft have been cleaned, inspected and repaired or reconditioned.

2   Position the engine with the bottom facing up.

3   Remove the main bearing cap bolts and lift out the caps. Lay them out in the proper order to help ensure that they are installed correctly.

4   If they are still in place, remove the old bearing inserts from the block and the main bearing caps. Wipe the main bearing surfaces of the block and caps with a clean, lint-free cloth. They must be kept spotlessly clean.

5   Clean the back sides of the new main bearing inserts and lay one bearing half in each main bearing saddle in the block. Lay the other bearing half from each bearing set in the corresponding main bearing cap. Make sure the tab on the bearing insert fits into the recess in the block or cap. Do not hammer

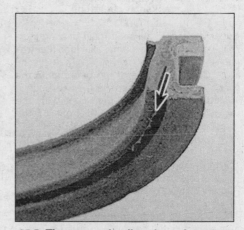

22.8 The rear main oil seal may have two lips - the oil seal (arrow) must point toward the front of the engine, which means that the dust seal will face out, toward the rear of the engine

the bearing into place and do not nick or gouge the bearing faces. No lubrication should be used at this time.

6   The flanged thrust bearing must be installed in the number two cap and saddle (3.0L, 3.3L and 3.8L V6 engines), the number three cap and saddle (2.8L and 3.1L V6 engines), the number five cap and saddle (2.5L four-cylinder engines) or the number four cap and saddle (2.2L four-cylinder engines).

7   Clean the faces of the bearings in the block and the crankshaft main bearing journals with a clean, lint-free cloth. Check or clean the oil holes in the crankshaft, as any dirt here can go only one way - straight into the new bearings.

8   Once you are certain that the crankshaft is clean, carefully lay it in position (an assistant would be very helpful here) in the main bearings.

9   Before the crankshaft can be permanently installed, the main bearing oil clearance must be checked.

10   Trim several pieces of the appropriate size of Plastigage slightly shorter than the width of the main bearings and place one

23.10 Lay the Plastigage strips (arrow) on the main bearing journals, parallel to the crankshaft centerline

23.14 Compare the width of the crushed Plastigage to the scale on the envelope to determine the main bearing oil clearance (always take the measurement at the widest point of the Plastigage); be sure to use the correct scale - standard and metric ones are included

piece on each crankshaft main bearing journal, parallel with the journal axis **(see illustration)**.

11 Clean the faces of the bearings in the caps and install the caps in their respective positions (do not mix them up) with the arrows pointing toward the front of the engine. Do not disturb the Plastigage.

12 Starting with the center main and working out toward the ends, tighten the main bearing cap bolts, in three steps, to the torque listed in this Chapter's Specifications. Do not rotate the crankshaft at any time during this operation.

13 Remove the bolts and carefully lift off the main bearing caps. Keep them in order. Do not disturb the Plastigage or rotate the crankshaft. If any of the main bearing caps are difficult to remove, tap them gently from side-to-side with a soft-face hammer to loosen them.

14 Compare the width of the crushed Plastigage on each journal to the scale printed on the Plastigage container to obtain the main bearing oil clearance **(see illustration)**. Check the Specifications to make sure it is correct.

15 If the clearance is not correct, double-check to make sure you have the right size bearing inserts. Also, make sure that no dirt or oil is between the bearing inserts and the main bearing caps or the block when the clearance was measured.

16 Carefully scrape all traces of the Plasti-

gage material off the main bearing journals and the bearing faces. Do not nick or scratch the bearing faces.

17 Carefully lift the crankshaft out of the engine. Clean the bearing faces in the block, then apply a thin, uniform layer of moly-base grease or engine assembly lube to each of the bearing surfaces. Be sure to coat the thrust flange faces as well as the journal face of the thrust bearing.

18 Lubricate the rear main bearing oil seal where it contacts the crankshaft with moly-base grease or engine assembly lube. Note that on four-cylinder engines and later V6 engines a 360 degree lip-type seal is utilized and is installed after the crankshaft is in place (refer to Parts A, B, C or D of this Chapter).

19 If you are working on an engine with a two-piece seal, refer to Section 22 and apply anaerobic-type gasket sealant to the rear main bearing cap as described there. Make sure the crankshaft journals are clean, then lay the crankshaft back in place in the block. Clean the faces of the bearings in the caps, then apply a thin, uniform layer of moly-base grease to each of the bearing faces. Install the caps in their respective positions with the arrows pointing toward the front of the engine. Install the bolts and tighten them to the specified torque, starting with the center

main and working out toward the ends. Work up to the final torque in three steps.

20 Rotate the crankshaft a number of times by hand and check for any obvious binding.

21 Check the crankshaft endplay with a feeler gauge or a dial indicator as described in Section 15.

24 Piston/connecting rod assembly - installation and bearing oil clearance check

Refer to illustrations 24.5, 24.8, 24.10, 24.12 and 24.14

1 Before installing the piston/connecting rod assemblies the cylinder walls must be perfectly clean, the top edge of each cylinder must be chamfered, and the crankshaft must be in place.

2 Remove the connecting rod cap from the end of the number one connecting rod. Remove the old bearing inserts and wipe the bearing surfaces of the connecting rod and cap with a clean, lint-free cloth (they must be kept spotlessly clean). Slip pieces of rubber hose over the connecting rod bolts to prevent crankshaft damage.

3 Clean the back side of the new upper bearing half, then lay it in place in the connecting rod. Make sure that the tab on the bearing fits into the recess in the rod. Do not hammer the bearing insert into place and be very careful not to nick or gouge the bearing face. Do not lubricate the bearing at this time.

4 Clean the back side of the other bearing insert and install it in the rod cap. Again, make sure the tab on the bearing fits into the recess in the cap, and do not apply any lubricant. It is critically important that the mating surfaces of the bearing and connecting rod are perfectly clean and oil-free when they are assembled.

5 Position the piston ring gaps as shown, **(see illustration)**, then slip a section of plastic or rubber hose over the connecting rod cap bolts.

6 Lubricate the piston and rings with clean

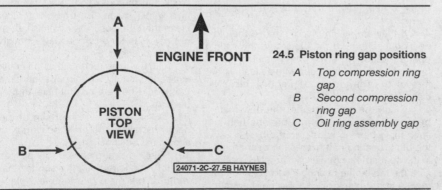

A ↓ ↑ A

ENGINE FRONT

PISTON TOP VIEW

B → ← C

24071-2C-27.5B HAYNES

24.5 Piston ring gap positions

A *Top compression ring gap*
B *Second compression ring gap*
C *Oil ring assembly gap*

24.8 The notch or arrow on each piston must face the front (drivebelt end) of the engine

24.10 If resistance is encountered when tapping the piston/connecting rod assembly into the block, stop immediately and make sure the rings are fully compressed

24.12 Position the Plastigage strip on the bearing journal, parallel to the journal axis

24.14 The crushed Plastigage is compared to the scale printed on the container to obtain the bearing oil clearance

engine oil and attach a piston ring compressor to the piston. Leave the skirt protruding about 1/4-inch to guide the piston into the cylinder. The rings must be compressed as far as possible.

7   Rotate the crankshaft until the number one connecting rod journal is as far from the number one cylinder as possible (bottom dead center), and apply a coat of engine oil to the cylinder walls.

8   With the notch on top of the piston facing to the front of the engine **(see illustration)**, slip the piston/connecting rod assembly into the number one cylinder bore and rest the bottom edge of the ring compressor on the engine block. Tap the top edge of the ring compressor to make sure it is contacting the block around its entire circumference.

9   Clean the number one connecting rod journal on the crankshaft and the bearing faces in the rod.

10   Carefully tap on the top of the piston with the end of a wooden hammer handle **(see illustration)** while guiding the end of the connecting rod into place on the crankshaft journal. The piston rings may try to pop out of the ring compressor just before entering the cylinder bore, so keep some pressure on the ring compressor. Work slowly, and if any resistance is felt as the piston enters the cylinder, stop immediately. Find out what is hanging up and fix it before proceeding. Do not, for any reason, force the piston into the cylinder, as you will break a ring and/or the piston.

11   Once the piston/connecting rod assembly is installed, the connecting rod bearing oil clearance must be checked before the rod cap is permanently bolted in place.

12   Cut a piece of the appropriate size Plastigage slightly shorter than the width of the connecting rod bearing and lay it in place on the number one connecting rod journal, parallel with the journal axis. It must not cross the oil hole in the journal **(see illustration)**.

13   Clean the connecting rod cap bearing face, remove the protective hoses from the connecting rod bolts and install the rod cap

in place. Make sure the mating mark on the cap is on the same side as the mark on the connecting rod. Install the nuts and tighten them to the torque listed in this Chapter's Specifications, working up to it in three steps. Do not rotate the crankshaft at any time during this operation.

14   Remove the rod cap, being careful not to disturb the Plastigage. Compare the width of the crushed Plastigage to the scale printed on the Plastigage container to obtain the oil clearance **(see illustration)**. Compare it to the Specifications to make sure the clearance is correct. If the clearance is not correct, double-check to make sure that you have the correct-size bearing inserts. Also, recheck the crankshaft connecting rod journal diameter and make sure that no dirt or oil was between the bearing inserts and the connecting rod or cap when the clearance was measured.

15   Carefully scrape all traces of the Plastigage material off the rod journal and bearing face. Be very careful not to scratch the bearing - use your fingernail or a piece of hardwood. Make sure the bearing faces are perfectly clean, then apply a uniform layer of moly-base grease or engine assembly lube to both of them. You will have to push the piston into the cylinder to expose the face of the bearing insert in the connecting rod. Be sure to slip the protective hoses over the rod bolts first.

16   Slide the connecting rod back into place on the journal, remove the protective hoses from the rod cap bolts, install the rod cap and tighten the nuts to the torque listed in this Chapter's Specifications. Again, work up to the torque in three steps.

17   Repeat the entire procedure for the remaining piston/connecting rod assemblies. Keep the back sides of the bearing inserts and the inside of the connecting rod and cap perfectly clean when assembling them. Make sure you have the correct piston for the cylinder and that the notch on the piston faces to the front of the engine when the piston is installed. Remember, use plenty of oil to lubricate the piston before installing the ring compressor. Also, when installing the rod caps for the final time, be sure to lubricate

the bearing faces adequately.

18   After all the piston/connecting rod assemblies have been properly installed, rotate the crankshaft a number of times by hand and check for any obvious binding.

19   As a final step, the connecting rod endplay must be checked. Refer to Section 14 for this procedure. Compare the measured endplay to the Specifications to make sure it is correct.

25 Engine overhaul - reassembly sequence

Before beginning engine reassembly, make sure you have all the necessary new parts, gaskets and seals as well as the following items on hand:

> Common hand tools
> A 1/2-inch drive torque wrench
> Piston ring installation tool
> Piston ring compressor
> Short lengths of rubber hose to fit over
>   rod bolts
> Plastigage
> Feeler gauges
> A fine-tooth file
> New engine oil
> Engine assembly lube or moly-base
>   grease
> RTV-type gasket sealant
> Anaerobic-type gasket sealant
> Thread locking compound

2   In order to save time and avoid problems, engine reassembly must be done in the following order.

> Rear main oil seal (two-piece seal only)
> Crankshaft and main bearings
> Piston rings
> Piston/connecting rod assemblies
> Oil pump
> Oil pan
> Camshaft
> Timing chain/sprockets or gears
> Timing chain/gear cover
> Valve lifters
> Cylinder heads and pushrods

Intake and exhaust manifolds
Oil filter
Pre-oil the engine (2.8 and 3.1 liter
   V6 engines only - Section 26)
Valve covers
Fuel pump
Water pump
Rear main oil seal (one-piece seals)
Flywheel/driveplate
Carburetor/fuel injection components
Thermostat and housing cover
Distributor (if equipped), spark plug wires
   and spark plugs
Emissions control components
Alternator

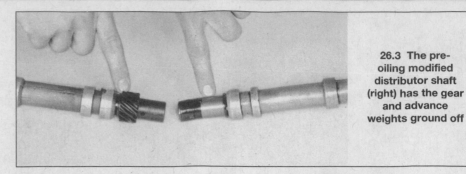

26.3 The pre-oiling modified distributor shaft (right) has the gear and advance weights ground off

26 Pre-oiling the engine after overhaul (2.8L and 3.1L V6 engines only)

Refer to illustrations 26.3, 26.4 and 26.5

1   After an overhaul it is a good idea to pre-oil the engine before it is installed and initially started. This will reveal any problems with the lubrication system at a time when corrections can be made easily and without major engine damage. Pre-oiling the engine will also allow the parts to be lubricated thoroughly in a normal fashion, but without the heavy loads associated with the combustion process placed upon them.
2   The engine should be assembled completely with the exception of the distributor and the valve covers.
3   A modified distributor will be needed for this procedure. This pre-oil tool is a distributor body with the bottom gear ground off and the advance weight assembly removed from the top of the shaft **(see illustration)**.
4   Place the pre-oiler into the distributor shaft access hole at the rear of the intake manifold and make sure the bottom of the shaft mates with the oil pump. Clamp the modified distributor into place just as you would an ordinary distributor. Now attach an electric drill motor to the top of the shaft **(see illustration)**.

5   With the oil filter installed, all oil ways plugged (oil-pressure sending unit at rear of block) and the crankcase full of oil as shown on the dipstick, rotate the pre-oiler with the drill. Make sure the rotation is in a clockwise direction. Soon, oil should start to flow from the rocker arms, signifying that the oil pump and lubrication system are functioning **(see illustration)**. It may take two or three minutes for oil to flow to all of the rocker arms. Allow the oil to circulate through the engine for a few minutes, then shut off the drill motor.
6   Check for oil leaks at the filter and all gasket and seal locations.
7   Remove the pre-oil tool, then install the distributor and rocker arm covers.

27 Initial start-up and break-in after overhaul

1   Once the engine has been properly installed in the vehicle, double check the engine oil and coolant levels.
2   With the spark plugs out of the engine and the coil high-tension lead grounded to the engine block, crank the engine over until oil pressure registers on the gauge (if so equipped) or until the oil light goes off.
3   Install the spark plugs, hook up the plug wires and the coil high tension lead.
4   Make sure the carburetor choke plate is closed, then start the engine. It may take a few moments for the gasoline to reach the carburetor, but the engine should start with-

out a great deal of effort.
5   As soon as the engine starts it should be set at a fast idle to ensure proper oil circulation and allowed to warm up to normal operating temperature. While the engine is warming up, make a thorough check for oil and coolant leaks.
6   Shut the engine off and recheck the engine oil and coolant levels. Restart the engine and check the ignition timing and the engine idle speed (refer to Chapter 1). Make any necessary adjustments.
7   Drive the vehicle to an area with minimum traffic, accelerate at full throttle from 30 to 50 mph, then allow the vehicle to slow to 30 mph with the throttle closed. Repeat the procedure 10 or 12 times. This will load the piston rings and cause them to seat properly against the cylinder walls. Check again for oil and coolant leaks.
8   Drive the vehicle gently for the first 500 miles (no sustained high speeds) and keep a constant check on the oil level. It is not unusual for an engine to use oil during the break-in period.
9   At approximately 500 to 600 miles, change the oil and filter, retorque the cylinder head bolts and recheck the valve clearances (if applicable).
10   For the next few hundred miles, drive the vehicle normally. Do not either pamper it or abuse it.
11   After 2000 miles, change the oil and filter again and consider the engine fully broken in.

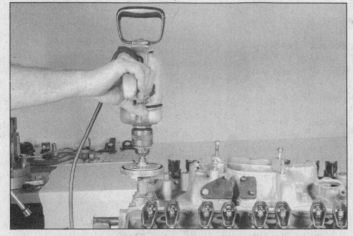

26.4 A drill motor connected to the modified distributor drives the oil pump

26.5 Oil will flow out of the holes in the rocker arms if the lubrication system is functioning properly

Chapter 3
Cooling, heating and air conditioning systems

Contents

Specifications

General

Radiator cap pressure cap rating	15 psi
Thermostat rating	195-degrees F
Refrigerant type	
1993 and earlier	R-12
1994 and later	R-134a

Torque specifications

Ft-lbs (unless otherwise indicated)

Thermostat housing bolts	
2.2L and 2.5L four-cylinder engines, 2.8/3.1L V6 engines	17
3.0/3.8L V6 engines	88 in-lbs
3.3L V6 engine	20
Water pump mounting bolts	
2.2L four-cylinder engine	18
2.5L four-cylinder engine	
1986 and earlier	21
1987 on	24
2.8L V6 engine (1986 and earlier)	16
2.8/3.1L V6 engines (1987 on)	89 in-lbs
3.3L V6 engine	
Water pump-to-block bolts	22
Water pump-to-front cover bolts	134 in-lbs plus an additional 80-degrees rotation
3.0/3.8L V6 engines	
Long bolts	97 in-lbs
Short bolts	29
Water pump pulley bolts	
2.2 liter engine	22
3.0/3.8L V6 engines	115 in-lbs
All others	120 to 180 in-lbs

Component location

Typical V6 engine heating air conditioning system

1	Radiator cap	4	Upper radiator hose	7	Accumulator
2	Radiator	5	Thermostat housing	8	Evaporator line connection
3	Cooling fan	6	Water pump	9	Blower motor

1   General information

Engine cooling system

All vehicles covered by this manual employ a pressurized engine cooling system with thermostatically controlled coolant circulation. An impeller type water pump mounted on the front of the block pumps coolant through the engine. The coolant flows around each cylinder and toward the rear of the engine. Cast-in coolant passages direct coolant around the intake and exhaust ports, near the spark plug areas and in close proximity to the exhaust valve guide inserts.

During warm up, the closed thermostat prevents coolant from circulating through the radiator. When the engine reaches normal operating temperature, the thermostat opens and allows hot coolant to travel through the radiator, where it is cooled before returning to the engine.

The aluminum radiator is of the crossflow type, with tanks on either side of the core.

The cooling system is sealed by a pressure type radiator cap. This raises the boiling point of the coolant and the higher boiling point of the coolant increases the cooling efficiency of the radiator. If the system pressure exceeds the cap pressure relief value, the excess pressure in the system forces the spring-loaded valve inside the cap off its seat and allows the coolant to escape through the overflow tube into a coolant reservoir. When the system cools, the excess coolant is automatically drawn from the reservoir back into the radiator.

The coolant reservoir serves as both the point at which coolant is added to the cooling system to maintain the proper fluid level and as a holding tank for overheated coolant.

This type of cooling system is known as a closed design because coolant that escapes past the pressure cap is saved and reused.

Heating system

The heating system consists of a blower fan and heater core located under the dashboard, the inlet and outlet hoses connecting the heater core to the engine cooling system and the heater/air conditioning control head on the dashboard. Hot engine coolant is circulated through the heater core at all times. When the heater mode is activated, a flap opens to expose the heater box to the passenger compartment. A fan switch on the control head activates the blower motor, which forces air through the core, heating the air.

Air conditioning system

The air conditioning system consists of a condenser mounted in front of the radiator, an evaporator mounted under the dash, a

3.9 Some thermostat covers are secured by two fasteners, others by three

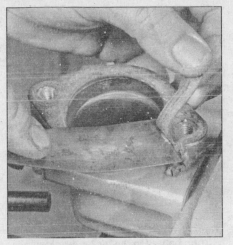

3.10 Remove all traces of gasket material from the thermostat housing and cover

3.11 Some models use a rubber gasket around the circumference of the thermostat

compressor mounted on the engine, a filter-drier (accumulator) which contains a high pressure relief valve and the plumbing connecting all of the above.

A blower fan forces the warmer air of the passenger compartment through the evaporator core (sort of a radiator-in-reverse), transferring the heat from the air to the refrigerant. The liquid refrigerant boils off into low pressure vapor, taking the heat with it when it leaves the evaporator.

2   Antifreeze – general information

Warning: *Do not allow antifreeze to come in contact with your skin or painted surfaces of the vehicle. Rinse off spills immediately with plenty of water. Antifreeze is highly toxic if ingested. Never leave antifreeze lying around in an open container or in puddles on the floor; children and pets are attracted by it's sweet smell and may drink it. Check with local authorities about disposing of used antifreeze. Many communities have collection centers which will see that antifreeze is disposed of safely.*

The cooling system should be filled with a water/ethylene glycol based antifreeze solution which will prevent freezing down to at least -20-degrees F. It also provides protection against corrosion and increases the coolant boiling point.

The cooling system should be drained, flushed and refilled at least every other year (see Chapter 1). The use of antifreeze solutions for periods of longer than two years is likely to cause damage and encourage the formation of rust and scale in the system. If your tap water is "hard", use distilled water with the antifreeze.

Before adding antifreeze to the system, check all hose connections, because antifreeze tends to leak through very minute openings. Engines don't normally consume coolant, so if the level goes down, find the cause and correct it.

The exact mixture of antifreeze-to-water which you should use depends on the relative weather conditions The mixture should contain at least 50-percent antifreeze, but should never contain more than 70-percent antifreeze. Consult the mixture ratio chart on the antifreeze container before adding coolant. Hydrometers are available at most auto parts stores to test the ratio of antifreeze to water.

3   Thermostat - check and replacement

Refer to illustrations 3.9, 3.10, 3.11 and 3.12

Warning 1: *DO NOT remove the radiator cap, drain the coolant or replace the thermostat until the engine has cooled completely.*

Warning 2: *When working in the vicinity of the electric cooling fan, disconnect the negative battery cable from the battery to prevent the fan from coming on accidentally.*

Caution: *If the vehicle is equipped with a Delco Loc II audio system, make sure you have the correct activation code before disconnecting the battery. See the information at the front of this manual for the radio re-activation procedure.*

Check

1   Before assuming the thermostat is to blame for a cooling system problem, check the coolant level (see Chapter 1), drivebelt tension (see Chapter 1) and temperature gauge (or light) operation.

2   If the engine seems to be taking a long time to warm up (based on heater output or temperature gauge operation), the thermostat is probably stuck open. Replace the thermostat with a new one.

3   If the engine runs hot, use your hand to check the temperature of the upper radiator hose. If the hose isn't hot, but the engine is, the thermostat is probably stuck closed, preventing the coolant inside the engine from

escaping to the radiator. Replace the thermostat. **Caution:** *Don't drive the vehicle without a thermostat. The computer may stay in open loop and emissions and fuel economy will suffer.*

4   If the upper radiator hose is hot, it means the coolant is flowing and the thermostat is open. Consult the *Troubleshooting* section at the front of this manual for cooling system diagnosis.

Replacement

5   Disconnect the negative battery cable from the battery and drain the cooling system (see Chapter 1). If the coolant is relatively new or in good condition, save it and reuse it.

6   Follow the upper radiator hose to the engine to locate the thermostat cover.

7   Loosen the hose clamp, then detach the hose from the fitting. If the hose sticks, grasp it near the end with a pair of large adjustable pliers and twist it to break the seal, then pull it off. If the hose is old or deteriorated, cut it off and install a new one.

8   If the outer surface of the large fitting that mates with the hose is severely deteriorated (corroded, pitted, etc.) it may be damaged further by hose removal. If it is, the thermostat cover will have to be replaced.

9   Detach any hoses or electrical connectors that may interfere with removal of the thermostat cover. Remove the bolts/nuts and detach the thermostat cover **(see illustration)**. If the cover is stuck, tap it with a soft-face hammer to jar it loose. Be prepared for some coolant to spill as the gasket seal is broken.

10   Note how it's installed, then remove the thermostat. Clean all gasket material from the mating surfaces of the thermostat housing and cover **(see illustration)**. Clean both mating surfaces with lacquer thinner or acetone.

11   Some models are equipped with a rubber gasket around the circumference of the thermostat **(see illustration)**. If the vehicle you are working on is equipped with this type of thermostat, replace the rubber gasket.

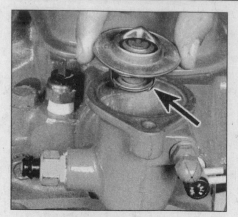

3.12 When installing the thermostat, make sure the spring end (arrow) is directed into the engine

12   Install the new thermostat in the housing **(see illustration)**. Make sure the thermostat is installed the correct way - the spring end is normally directed into the engine.
13   If there was a gasket under the thermostat cover, install a new one. If the thermostat was equipped with a rubber gasket, apply a bead of RTV sealant to the mating flange of the cover. Install the cover and tighten the bolts to the torque listed in this Chapter's Specifications.
14   The remaining steps are the reverse of removal.
15   Refill the cooling system (see Chapter 1).
16   Start the engine and allow it to reach normal operating temperature, then check for leaks and proper thermostat operation (as described in Step 3).

4   Engine cooling fan - check, removal and installation

Refer to illustrations 4.1 and 4.6
Caution: *When working in the vicinity of the electric fan, disconnect the negative battery cable from the battery to prevent the fan from coming on accidentally. If the vehicle is equipped with a Delco Loc II audio system, make sure you have the correct activation code before disconnecting the battery. See the information at the front of this manual for the radio re-activation procedure.*

Check

Note: *Before checking any electrical component or system, check the fuses first (see Chapter 12).*
1   To test the fan motor, unplug the electrical connector at the motor and use jumper wires to connect the fan directly to the battery **(see illustration)**. If the fan still doesn't work, replace the motor.

1986 and earlier models

2   If the motor tested OK, the fault lies in the coolant fan switch, the relay or the wiring which connects the components. Plug in the electrical connector.

4.1 The fan motor can be tested by running fused jumper wires directly from the battery to the motor terminals

3   On four-cylinder models the coolant fan switch is mounted on the left end (driver's side) of the cylinder head, on the front. On V6 models it's mounted on the intake manifold, near the distributor. Unplug the electrical connector from the switch and, using a jumper wire, connect it to a good ground. If the fan now works, the coolant fan switch is defective.
4   If it still doesn't work, the relay or the wiring that connects the components is defective. Carefully check all wiring and connections. If no obvious problems are found, further diagnosis should be done by a dealer service department or other repair shop.

1987 and later models

5   The electric cooling fan on these models is controlled by the Electronic Control Module (ECM) and the coolant sensor. If the fan is inoperative, check to see if any trouble codes are stored in the computer. If a problem with the coolant temperature sensor is indicated, check the sensor and its circuit. If no trouble codes are stored, have the diagnosis performed by a dealer service department or other qualified repair shop.

Removal and installation

6   Remove the fan frame-to-radiator bolts.
7   Lift the retaining tabs and unplug the fan connector.
8   Lift the fan assembly from the engine compartment.
9   If you're installing a new fan or fan motor, remove the nut that retains the fan to the motor. **Note:** *This nut may have left-hand threads. Check the hub of the fan for marks that indicate which way to loosen the nut.*
10   Installation is the reverse of removal.

5   Radiator - removal, servicing and installation

Warning 1: *Some models covered by this manual are equipped with airbags. Always disable the airbag system before working in the vicinity of the impact sensors, steering column or instrument panel to avoid the possibility of accidental deployment of the airbag(s),* which could cause personal injury (see Chapter 12 for the airbag disarming procedure).
Warning 2: *The engine must be completely cool before beginning this procedure. Also, when working in the vicinity of the electric fan, disconnect the negative battery cable from the battery to prevent the fan from coming on accidentally.*
Note: *Radiators used on later models are aluminum and plastic (an aluminum core with plastic side tanks) The drain fitting is located on the lower part of one of the tanks and can be repaired. Radiator repairs should be performed by a dealer service department or radiator repair shop.*

Removal

1   Refer to the Warning in Section 2.
2   Disconnect the cable from the negative battery terminal. **Caution:** *If the vehicle is equipped with a Delco Loc II audio system, make sure you have the correct activation code before disconnecting the battery. See the information at the front of this manual for the radio re-activation procedure.*
3   Drain the cooling system (see Chapter 1).
4   Disconnect the engine forward strut bracket from the radiator, loosen the bolt and swing the bracket to the rear.
5   Disconnect the forward headlight harness from the frame and unplug the cooling fan electrical connector.
6   Remove the cooling fan assembly (see Section 4).
7   Scribe a line around the hood latch on the radiator support to mark its location, then remove the latch.
8   Detach the radiator hoses from the radiator, disconnect the coolant recovery hose, and on automatic transaxle models, disconnect and plug the fluid cooler lines.
9   Remove the bolts from the radiator mounting panel (or on some models the radiator-to-radiator support bolts) and lift the radiator from the engine compartment. On air-conditioned models, lift the driver's side of the radiator first, so the radiator neck will clear the compressor.

Servicing

10   Carefully examine the radiator for evidence of leaks and damage. It is recommended that any necessary repairs be performed by a radiator repair shop.
11   With the radiator removed, brush accumulations of insects and leaves from the fins and examine and replace, if necessary, any hoses or clamps which have deteriorated.
12   The radiator can be flushed as described in Chapter 1.
13   Replace the radiator cap with a new one of the same rating, or if the cap is relatively new, have it tested by a service station.

Installation

14   If you are installing a new radiator, transfer the fittings from the old unit to the new one.

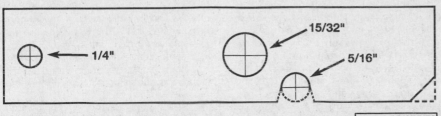

7.5a Here's a template for the 2.8L V6 timing chain cover holder, shown in actual size

15 Installation is the reverse of removal. When setting the radiator in the chassis, make sure that it seats securely in the lower rubber mounting pads.

16 After installing the radiator, refill it with the proper coolant mixture (see Chapter 1), then start the engine and check for leaks.

6 Water pump - check

1 A failure in the water pump can cause overheating and serious engine damage, as a defective pump will not circulate coolant through the engine.

2 There are two ways to check the operation of the water pump while it is installed on the engine. If the pump is defective, it should be replaced with a new or rebuilt unit.

3 Water pumps are equipped with weep or vent holes. If a pump seal failure occurs, coolant will leak from the weep holes. In most cases it will be necessary to use a flashlight from under the vehicle to see evidence of leakage from this point on the pump body.

4 If the water pump shaft bearings fail, there may be a squealing sound emitted from the front of the engine while it is running. Shaft wear can be felt if the water pump pulley is forced up and down. Do not mistake

drivebelt slippage, which also causes a squealing sound, for water pump failure.

7 Water pump - removal and installation

Refer to illustrations 7.5a, 7.5b, 7.6a and 7.6b

Warning: *The engine must be completely cool before beginning this procedure. Also, when working in the vicinity of the electric cooling fan, disconnect the negative battery cable from the battery to prevent the fan from coming on accidentally.*

Caution: *If the vehicle is equipped with a Delco Loc II audio system, make sure you have the correct activation code before disconnecting the battery. See the information at the front of this manual for the radio re-activation procedure.*

Removal

1 Refer to the Warning in Section 2.

2 Drain the cooling system (see Chapter 1).

3 Remove the accessory drivebelts, alternator, air conditioning compressor and other components which could interfere with removal.

4 On models that have hoses attached to the water pump, loosen the hose clamps and

7.5b Here's the holder bolted in place on the right cylinder head (this applies to 1986 and earlier 2.8L V6 models only). Note the 1/4 x 1-inch bolt inserted at the left side of the holder and secured with a nut - it serves as a spacer

disconnect the hoses from the pump. Remove the water pump pulley bolts and the pulley. Wedge a screwdriver between two bolts to prevent the pulley from turning as the bolts are loosened. Loosen all of the bolts before removing any of them.

5 On 1986 and earlier 2.8L V6 engines, care must be taken when removing the water pump bolts because they pass through the timing chain cover. Removal of the bolts can break the case seal and allow coolant to enter the crankcase To prevent this, before removing the water pump, secure the timing chain cover to the block with a clamping device shown in the accompanying illustration **(see illustration)**.

6 Remove the retaining bolts/nuts and lift the water pump from the engine **(see illustrations)**. If the pump is stuck, jar it loose with a soft-faced hammer or a block of wood. Don't pry between the pump and the engine, as damage to the sealing surfaces may

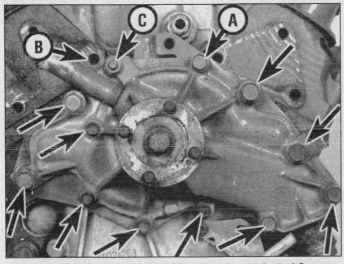

7.6a On 1986 and earlier 2.8L V6 engines in which stud C goes through both the timing cover and the water pump, remove the water pump mounting bolts (arrows) after using bolt A to attach the tool mentioned to the right cylinder head at hole B

7.6b The mounting bolts are located around the perimeter of the pump (arrows) - later 2.8/3.1L V6 engines

result. On some models it may be necessary to unbolt the right side engine mount from the cradle (subframe) and raise the engine slightly to obtain enough clearance to remove the water pump.

Installation

Note: *If the water pump has a pressed-on pulley, take the pump to a dealer service department or other repair shop to have the pulley pressed off and transferred to the new pump. Don't pry or hammer on the pulley as damage may occur.*

7   Remove all traces of old gasket material and sealant from the water pump mating surface on the engine (and on the water pump if the same one is to be reinstalled).

8   On 1986 and earlier 2.5L and 2.8L engines, apply a 1/8-inch bead of RTV sealant on the pump mating surface. Coat the threads of the retaining bolts with thin film of RTV sealant to prevent leaks. While the sealant is still wet, install the pump and mounting bolts. Tighten the bolts to the torque listed in this Chapter's Specifications in a criss-cross pattern.

9   On all other models, install a new gasket and position the water pump on the engine. Coat the threads of the retaining bolts with a thin film of RTV sealant to prevent leaks. Install the bolts and tighten them to the torque listed in this Chapter's Specifications in a criss-cross pattern. If you're working on a 1987 or later 2.8L or 3.1L V6 engine, be sure the locators on the pump and gasket are vertical.

10   Install the pulley and tighten the bolts to the torque listed in this Chapter's Specifications.

11   Connect the hoses to the water pump (where applicable) and tighten the hose clamps securely.

12   The remainder of installation is the reverse of the removal procedure. Refill the cooling system with the proper coolant mixture (see Chapter 1).

13   Connect the battery negative cable, start the engine and run it until normal operating temperature is reached, then check for leaks.

8   Coolant temperature sending unit - check and replacement

1   The coolant temperature indicator system is composed of a light mounted in the instrument panel and a coolant temperature sending unit located in a water passage, usually in the cylinder head or engine block. If a temperature gauge is included in the instrument cluster, the temperature sending unit is replaced by a transducer.

2   **Caution:** *Since the ignition key will be in the On position for some of the diagnostic steps, be especially careful to stay clear of the electric cooling fan blades.*

3   If overheating occurs, check the coolant level in the system and then make sure that the wiring between the light or gauge and the sending unit is secure.

4   When the ignition switch is turned on and the starter motor is turning, the indicator light should be on (overheated engine indication). If the light is not on, the bulb may be burned out, the ignition switch may be faulty or the circuit may be open.

5   As soon as the engine starts, the light should go out and remain out unless the engine overheats. Failure of the light to go out may be due to grounded wiring between the light and the sending unit, a defective sending unit or a faulty ignition switch.

6   To test the circuit, unplug the electrical connector and, using a jumper wire, connect the wiring harness to a good ground. With the ignition On, the indicator light should be glowing. If it does but the engine has been overheating and the light hasn't been coming on, replace the sending unit. If the light does not glow, there is a break in the wire or a burned-out bulb.

7   If the sending unit is to be replaced, it is simply unscrewed and a replacement installed. Make sure that the engine is cool before removing the defective sending unit here will be some coolant loss, so check the level after the replacement has been installed.

9   Heater core - replacement

Warning: *Some models covered by this manual are equipped with airbags. Always disable the airbag system before working in the vicinity of the impact sensors, steering column or instrument panel to avoid the possibility of accidental deployment of the airbag(s), which could cause personal injury (see Chapter 12 for the airbag disarming procedure).*

Warning: *The engine must be completely cool before beginning this procedure.*

1   Drain the cooling system (see Chapter 1).

2   Working in the engine compartment, loosen the hose clamps and disconnect the heater hoses from the heater core tubes at

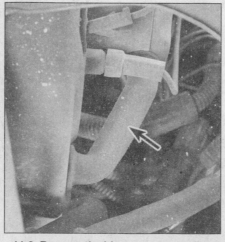

11.2 Remove the blower motor cooling tube (arrow)

the firewall. Plug the ends of the heater core tubes to prevent spillage when it is removed.

3   Working inside the vehicle, remove the right side under-dash panel.

4   Remove the heater floor outlet duct.

5   Remove the screws and clips that secure the heater core cover, then remove the cover.

6   Remove the heater core retaining straps and remove the heater core from the housing. Be careful not to spill any coolant as this is done.

7   Installation is the reverse of the removal procedure. Refill the cooling system with the proper coolant mixture (see Chapter 1). Run the engine and check for leaks.

10   Heater and air conditioner control assembly - removal and installation

Warning: *Some models covered by this manual are equipped with airbags. Always disable the airbag system before working in the vicinity of the impact sensors, steering column or instrument panel to avoid the possibility of accidental deployment of the airbag(s), which could cause personal injury (see Chapter 12 for the airbag disarming procedure).*

1   Remove the trim panel around the heater and air conditioner control assembly (see Chapter 11).

2   Remove the screws on each side of the control assembly.

3   Pull the control out of the dash then label and unplug the vacuum and electrical connectors **(see illustration)**. **Note:** *Do not disconnect the individual vacuum lines - disconnect the entire vacuum connector.*

4   Carefully pry the cable housing and cable retaining clips off with a small screwdriver.

5   Installation is the reverse of removal.

11   Heater and air conditioner blower motor - removal and installation

Refer to illustrations 11.2 and 11.4

Warning: *Some models covered by this manual are equipped with airbags. Always disable the airbag system before working in the vicinity of the impact sensors, steering column or instrument panel to avoid the possibility of accidental deployment of the airbag(s), which could cause personal injury (see Chapter 12 for the airbag disarming procedure).*

1   Working in the engine compartment, disconnect the wires from the blower motor.

2   Detach the blower motor cooling tube **(see illustration)**.

3   Remove the screws and separate the motor/fan assembly from the housing. **Note:** *On some models it may be necessary to remove the power steering pump to provide clearance for blower removal.*

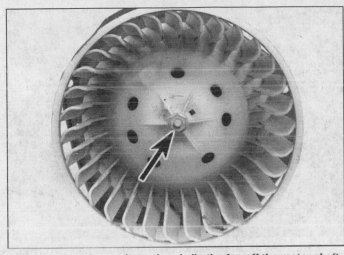

11.4 Remove the nut (arrow) and slip the fan off the motor shaft

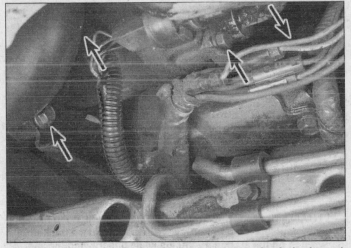

13.8 Remove air conditioning compressor mounting bolts (arrow)

4   Remove the retaining nut and slide the fan off the motor shaft **(see illustration)**.

5   Before installing the blower motor, apply a strip of weatherstrip caulking compound to the perimeter of the opening in the blower motor housing.

6   Installation is the reverse of removal. Be sure to attach the cooling hose to the motor.

12   Air conditioning system - check and maintenance

Warning: *The air conditioning system is under high pressure. Do not loosen any fittings or remove any components until after the system has been discharged. Air conditioning refrigerant should be properly discharged into an EPA-approved container at a dealer service department or an automotive air conditioning repair facility. Always wear eye protection when disconnecting air conditioning system fittings.*

Caution: *There are two types of refrigerants used on the models covered by this manual. 1993 and earlier models use R-12 refrigerant, while 1994 and later models use the new "environmentally friendly" R-134a refrigerant. The two refrigerants (and their appropriate refrigerant oils) are not compatible and must never be mixed or components will be damaged.*

1   The following maintenance checks should be performed on a regular basis to ensure that the air conditioner continues to operate at peak efficiency. **Note:** *Long term non-use can cause hardening, and subsequent failure, of the seals.*

a)   *Check the compressor drivebelt. If it's worn or deteriorated, replace it (see Chapter 1).*

b)   *Check the drivebelt tension and, if necessary, adjust it (see Chapter 1)*

c)   *Check the system hoses. Look for cracks, bubbles, hard spots and deterioration. Inspect the hoses and all fittings for oil bubbles and seepage. If there's*

any evidence of wear, damage or leaks, replace the hose(s).

d)   *Inspect the condenser fins for leaves, bugs and other debris. Use a "fin comb" or compressed air to clean the condenser.*

e)   *Make sure the system has the correct refrigerant charge.*

f)   *Check the evaporator housing drain tube for blockage.*

2   Because of the complexity of the air conditioning system and the special equipment necessary to service it, in-depth troubleshooting and repairs are not included in this manual. For more complete information on the air conditioning system, refer to the *Haynes Automotive Heating and Air Conditioning Manual.*

3   The most common cause of poor cooling is simply a low system refrigerant charge. If a noticeable drop in cool air output occurs, one of the following quick checks will help you determine if the refrigerant level is low.

4   Warm the engine up to normal operating temperature.

5   Place the air conditioning temperature selector at the coldest setting and put the blower at the highest setting. Open the doors (to make sure the air conditioning system doesn't cycle off as soon as it cools the passenger compartment).

6   With the compressor engaged - the clutch will make an audible click and the center of the clutch will rotate - inspect the sight glass, if equipped. If the refrigerant looks foamy, it's low. Have the system charged by a dealer service department or other qualified repair shop.

7   If there's no sight glass, feel the inlet and outlet pipes at the compressor. One side should be much colder than the other. If there's no perceptible difference between the two pipes, there's something wrong with the compressor or the system. It might be a low charge - it might be something else. Take the vehicle to a dealer service department or other qualified repair shop.

13   Air conditioning compressor - removal and installation

Refer to illustration 13.8

Warning: *The air conditioning system is under high pressure. DO NOT loosen any hose or line fittings or remove any components until after the system has been depressurized by a dealer service department or other repair shop. Always wear eye protection when disconnecting air conditioning system fittings.*

Note: *The accumulator and expansion tube (Sections 14 and 15) should be replaced whenever a new compressor is installed.*

Removal

1   Have the system discharged (see the Warning above).

2   Disconnect the negative battery cable from the battery. **Caution:** *If the vehicle is equipped with a Delco Loc II audio system, make sure you have the correct activation code before disconnecting the battery. See the information at the front of this manual for the radio re-activation procedure.*

3   Set the parking brake and block the rear wheels. Raise the front of the vehicle and support it securely on jackstands.

4   Remove the right under-vehicle splash shield.

5   Remove the drivebelt (see Chapter 1). On some models it may also be necessary to remove the oil filter to provide clearance for compressor removal.

6   Disconnect the compressor clutch electrical connector.

7   Disconnect the refrigerant lines from the rear of the compressor. Plug the open fittings to prevent entry of dirt and moisture.

8   Unbolt the compressor from its mounting brackets and lower it from the vehicle **(see illustration).**

Installation

9   If a new compressor is being installed, follow the directions with the new compres-

14.4 On some models the accumulator is located along the left side of the engine compartment - be sure to use a back-up wrench on the stationary fittings while unscrewing the line fittings (arrows)

14.5 Loosen the accumulator bracket retaining bolt (arrow)

sor regarding the draining of excess oil prior to installation.

10   The clutch may have to be transferred from the original to the new compressor.

11   Installation is the reverse of removal. Replace all O-rings with new ones made specifically for air conditioning system use and lubricate them with refrigerant oil.

12   Have the system evacuated, recharged and leak tested by the shop that discharged it.

14 Air conditioning accumulator - removal and installation

Refer to illustrations 14.4 and 14.5

Warning: *The air conditioning system is under high pressure. DO NOT loosen any hose or line fittings or remove any components until after the system has been depressurized by a dealer service department or other repair shop. Always wear eye protection when disconnecting air conditioning system fittings.*

Note: *Whenever the accumulator is replaced, the expansion tube should also be replaced (see Section 15).*

Removal

1   Have the system discharged (see the Warning above).

2   Disconnect the negative battery cable from the battery. **Caution:** *If the vehicle is equipped with a Delco Loc II audio system, make sure you have the correct activation code before disconnecting the battery. See the information at the front of this manual for the radio re-activation procedure.*

3   On some models it may be necessary to remove the air cleaner housing for access to the accumulator.

4   Disconnect the refrigerant lines from the accumulator **(see illustration)**. Use a back-up wrench to avoid twisting the tubing. Plug the open fittings to prevent the entry of dirt and moisture.

5   Loosen the mounting bracket bolts **(see illustration)** and remove the accumulator.

Installation

6   If a new accumulator is being installed, remove the Schrader valve and pour the oil out into a measuring cup, noting the amount. Add fresh refrigerant oil to the new accumulator equal to the amount removed from the old unit, plus one ounce.

7   The remainder of installation is the reverse of removal.

8   Have the system evacuated, recharged and leak tested by the shop that discharged it.

15 Air conditioning expansion tube - replacement

Warning: *The air conditioning system is under high pressure. DO NOT loosen any hose or line fittings or remove any components until after the system has been depressurized by a dealer service department or other repair shop. Always wear eye protection when disconnecting air conditioning system fittings.*

Note: *Whenever the expansion tube is replaced, the accumulator should also be replaced (see Section 14).*

1   Have the system discharged (see the Warning above).

2   Disconnect the negative battery cable from the battery. **Caution:** *If the vehicle is equipped with a Delco Loc II audio system, make sure you have the correct activation code before disconnecting the battery. See the information at the front of this manual for the radio re-activation procedure.*

3   If you're working on a 1986 or earlier model, loosen the refrigerant line fitting at the evaporator inlet pipe. Separate the line from the inlet pipe.

4   If you're working on a 1987 or later model, loosen the refrigerant line fitting at the condenser outlet pipe.

5   Using needle-nose pliers, remove the expansion tube.

6   Installation is the reverse of removal. Be sure to insert the expansion tube with the shorter screen end in first.

7   Have the system evacuated, recharged and leak tested by the shop that discharged it.

16 Air conditioning evaporator - removal and installation

Warning: *The air conditioning system is under high pressure. DO NOT loosen any hose or line fittings or remove any components until after the system has been depressurized by a dealer service department or other repair shop. Always wear eye protection when disconnecting air conditioning system fittings.*

1   Have the system discharged (see the Warning above).

2   Disconnect the negative battery cable from the battery. **Caution:** *If the vehicle is equipped with a Delco Loc II audio system, make sure you have the correct activation code before disconnecting the battery. See the information at the front of this manual for the radio re-activation procedure.*

3   On models with carburetors or Throttle Body Injection, remove the air cleaner housing.

4   Detach any wiring harness clips on the evaporator/blower housing and move the wiring harness aside.

5   If the vehicle you are working on has a vacuum tank near the evaporator/blower housing, remove it.

6   On some models it may be necessary to remove the power steering pump to provide adequate clearance for removal of the evaporator/blower housing (see Chapter 10).

7   Disconnect the fittings at the evaporator inlet and the low pressure line at the accumulator inlet.

8   Remove the screws that attach the

evaporator/blower housing to the firewall. Detach the housing from the firewall.

9   Remove the evaporator from the case.

10   Installation is the reverse of removal. If a new evaporator is being installed, add three ounces of refrigerant oil into it prior to installation.

11   Before installing the evaporator/heater case to the firewall, apply a bead of caulking compound to the perimeter of the case-to-firewall mating surface.

12   Have the system evacuated, recharged and leak tested by the shop that discharged it.

17.5 Pull the condenser core carefully until it is free of the rubber insulators (arrows)

17   Air conditioning condenser - removal and installation

Warning 1: *Some models covered by this manual are equipped with airbags. Always disable the airbag system before working in the vicinity of the impact sensors, steering column or instrument panel to avoid the possibility of accidental deployment of the airbag(s), which could cause personal injury (see Chapter 12 for the airbag disarming procedure).*

Warning 2: *The air conditioning system is under high pressure. DO NOT loosen any hose or line fittings or remove any components until after the system has been depressurized by a dealer service department or other repair shop. Always wear eye protection when disconnecting air conditioning system fittings.*

Removal

1   Have the system discharged (see the Warning above).

2   Disconnect the negative battery cable from the battery. **Caution:** *If the vehicle is equipped with a Delco Loc II audio system, make sure you have the correct activation code before disconnecting the battery. See the information at the front of this manual for the radio re-activation procedure.*

3   Disconnect the refrigerant lines from the condenser. Be sure to use a backup wrench on the condenser fittings to avoid twisting the line.

4   Remove the grille center support.

5   Remove the condenser mounting bolts **(see illustration)**.

6   Remove the engine support strut and

the radiator support. Tilt the radiator back and lift out the condenser. Be careful not to bend the fins on either the radiator or condenser. If the original condenser is to be reinstalled, plug the line fittings to prevent dirt and moisture from entering.

Installation

7   If a new condenser is being installed, pour one ounce of refrigerant oil into it prior to installation.

8   Reinstall the components in the reverse order of removal. Be sure any rubber mounting pads that may have been present during removal are properly located.

9   Have the system evacuated, recharged and leak tested by the shop that discharged it.

Notes

Chapter 4
Fuel and exhaust systems

Contents

Specifications

General

Minimum idle speed adjustment (see Section 15)	600 +/- 25 rpm
Fuel injector resistance	
TBI	1.2 to 1.6 ohms
MPFI	
All except 3.8L V6	11.8 to 12.6 ohms
3.8L V6	14.3 to 14.7 ohms

Fuel pressure (at idle)

Throttle Body Injection (TBI)	9 to 13 psi
Multi-Port Fuel Injection (MPFI)	
3.8L V6 engine	
Regulator vacuum hose connected	Approximately 25 to 35 psi
Regulator vacuum hose disconnected	Pressure should increase by 5 to 10 psi
All others	
Regulator vacuum hose connected	Approximately 30 to 44 psi
Regulator vacuum hose disconnected	Pressure should increase by 5 to 10 psi

Torque specifications

	Ft-lbs (unless otherwise indicated)
Mechanical fuel pump mounting bolts/nuts	15 to 22
Carburetor mounting bolts/nuts	120 in-lbs
TBI unit mounting bolts/nuts	156 in-lbs
Exhaust pipe-to-manifold nuts	15 to 22
Throttle body (MPFI) mounting bolts/nuts	10 to 18
Air intake plenum mounting bolts/nuts	
V6 engines	16
2.2L four-cylinder engine	22
Injector retainer screws (2.2L four-cylinder engine)	31 in-lbs

Component location

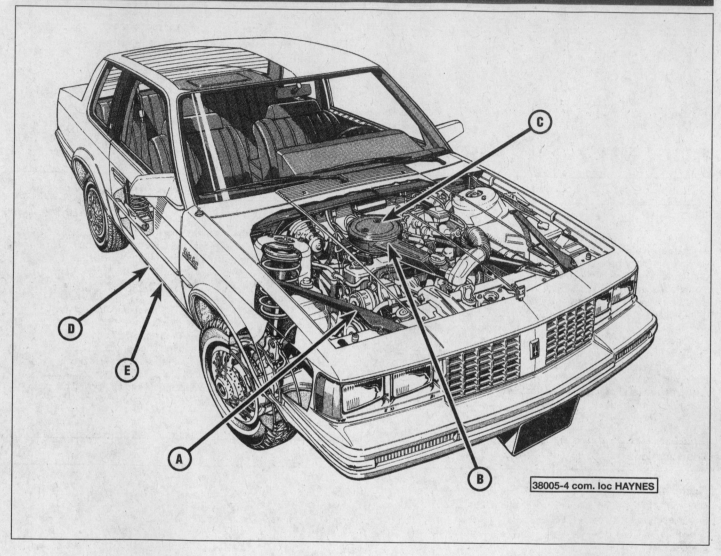

38005-4 com. loc HAYNES

1   General information

The fuel system consists of a rear mounted fuel tank, a mechanically operated fuel pump (carbureted engines) or an electric fuel pump (fuel-injected engines), a carburetor or fuel injection system and an air cleaner.

Models equipped with Throttle Body Injection utilize one injector, centrally mounted in a carburetor-like housing. The injector is an electric solenoid, with fuel delivered to the injector at a constant pressure level. To maintain the fuel pressure at a constant level, excess fuel is returned to the fuel tank.

Models equipped with Multi-Port Fuel Injection utilize one injector per cylinder. The injectors are mounted on the intake manifold, above each intake port. The throttle body serves only to control the amount of air enter-

ing the engine. Because each cylinder is equipped with an injector mounted immediately adjacent to the intake valve, much better control of the fuel/air mixture is possible.

The exhaust system includes a catalytic converter, muffler, related emissions equipment and associated pipes and hardware.

2   Fuel pressure relief procedure

Refer to illustration 2.4
Warning: *Gasoline is extremely flammable, so take extra precautions when you work on any part of the fuel system. Don't smoke or allow open flames or bare light bulbs near the work area. and don't work in a garage where a natural gas-type appliance (such as a water heater or clothes dryer) with a pilot light is present. If you spill any fuel on your skin, rinse*

2.4 Remove the cap to gain access to the Schrader valve for connecting a fuel pressure gauge (V6 engines)

Component location

A Typical mechanical fuel pump used on carbureted models, typically located on the lower front side of the engine block

Note: *Some later model carbureted models use an electric (in-tank) fuel pump*

B Typical E2SE carburetor located under the air cleaner (carbureted models)

C The fuel injector(s) are located under the air cleaner in the throttle body (TBI models)

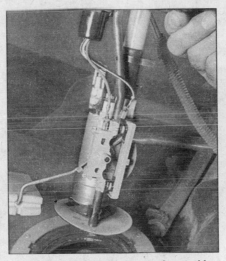

D Typical electric fuel pump located in the fuel tank (fuel-injected models)

E The fuel filter is typically located in the rear of the car behind the fuel tank (fuel-injected models)

it off immediately with soap and water. When you perform any kind of work on the fuel system, wear safety glasses and have a Class B type fire extinguisher on hand.

Note: *After the fuel pressure has been relieved, it's a good idea to lay a shop towel over any fuel connection to be disassembled, to absorb the residual fuel that may leak out when servicing the fuel system.*

1   Before servicing any fuel system component, you must relieve the fuel pressure to minimize the risk of fire or personal injury.

2   Remove the fuel filler cap - this will relieve any pressure built up in the tank.

3   On models with Throttle Body Injection, remove the fuel pump fuse and run the engine until it stalls, then crank the engine for three seconds. Disconnect the cable from the negative terminal of the battery. **Caution:** *If the vehicle is equipped with a Delco Loc II audio system, make sure you have the correct activation code before disconnecting the battery. See the information at the front of this manual for the radio re-activation procedure.*

4   On models with Port Fuel Injection, use one of the two following methods:

a) *Disconnect the fuel pump electrical connector at the fuel tank (lower the tank if necessary). Run the engine until it stops, then engage the starter again for another three seconds. With the ignition turned*

Off, reconnect the fuel tank electrical connector, then disconnect the cable from the negative terminal of the battery (read the Caution in Step 3).

b) *Loosen the fuel filler cap. Attach fuel pressure gauge to the Schrader valve on the fuel rail (see illustration). Place the gauge bleeder hose in an approved fuel container. Open the valve on the gauge to relieve pressure, then disconnect the cable from the negative terminal of the battery.*

5   Unless this procedure is followed before servicing fuel lines or connections, fuel spray (and possible injury) may occur.

3   Fuel pump/fuel system pressure - check

Warning: *Gasoline is extremely flammable, so take extra precautions when you work on any part of the fuel system. Don't smoke or allow open flames or bare light bulbs near the work area, and don't work in a garage where a natural gas-type appliance (such as a water heater or clothes dryer) with a pilot light is present. If you spill any fuel on your skin, rinse it off immediately with soap and water. When you perform any kind of work on the fuel system, wear safety glasses and have a Class B type fire extinguisher on hand.*

Note: *The following checks assume the fuel filter is in good condition. If you doubt its condition, install a new one (see Chapter 1).*

1   Check that there is adequate fuel in the fuel tank. If you doubt the reading on the gauge, insert a long wooden dowel at the filler opening; it will serve as a dipstick.

Carbureted models

Preliminary check

2   If you suspect insufficient fuel delivery, first inspect all fuel lines to ensure that the problem is not simply a leak in a line.

3   If there are no leaks evident in the fuel lines, inspect the fuel pump itself. The following checks will tell you if the fuel pump is leaking and whether it is pumping fuel.

4   Remove the air cleaner housing.

Fuel pump output check

5   Hook up a remote starter switch in accordance with the manufacturer's instructions. If you don't have a remote starter switch, you will need an assistant to help you with this and the following procedure.

6   Trace the fuel outlet line from the pump to the carburetor and detach it at the carburetor.

7   Detach the wires from the primary terminals of the ignition coil (see Chapter 5).

8   Place a metal container under the open end of the fuel pump outlet line. If the line is metal and you can't get a can under the end of it, attach a length of fuel hose to the end of the line and place it in the can.

9   Direct the fuel pump outlet line into the container while cranking the engine for a few seconds with the remote starter (or while an assistant cranks the engine with the ignition key).

10   If fuel is emitted in well defined spurts, the pump is operating satisfactorily. If fuel dribbles or trickles out the hose, the pump is defective. Replace it (see Section 6).

Fuel-injected models

Fuel pump operational check

11   Set the parking brake and have an assistant turn the ignition switch to the On position while you listen at the fuel pump. You should hear a whirring sound, lasting for a couple of seconds. Start the engine. The whirring sound should now be continuous (although harder to hear with the engine running). if there is no whirring sound, either the fuel pump or the fuel pump circuit is defective. Proceed to Step 21.

Pressure check

12   Relieve the fuel pressure (see Section 2).

13   If you're working on a TBI-equipped model, remove the air cleaner assembly.

14   If you're working on a TBI-equipped model, remove the fuel line from the TBI unit and attach a fuel pressure gauge between the fuel feed line and the throttle body using a T-fitting. To do this you'll need a short section of metal fuel line with a fitting just like the one you unscrewed from the TBI unit, which must be threaded into the TBI unit. Clamp the lines securely to make sure there will not be any leaks.

15   If you're working on a model with port fuel injection, connect a fuel pressure gauge to the Schrader valve on the fuel rail **(see illustration 2.4).**

16   Start the engine. With the engine idling, measure the fuel pressure. It should be as listed in this Chapter's Specifications. On models with port fuel injection, detach the vacuum hose from the fuel pressure regulator - the fuel pressure reading should immediately increase. Compare the pressure with the value listed in this Chapter's Specifications. If the pressure doesn't rise when the hose is disconnected, the fuel pressure regulator is faulty. Reconnect the vacuum hose.

17   If the fuel pressure is too high, check for a pinched or clogged fuel return hose or pipe. If the fuel return line is not obstructed, replace the fuel pressure regulator.

18   If the pressure is lower than specified, inspect the fuel filter - make sure it's not clogged. Look for a pinched or clogged fuel hose between the fuel tank and the fuel injection assembly. If the fuel feed line is OK, pinch the fuel return hose with a pair of pliers. If the pressure rises, replace the fuel pressure regulator.

19   If there are no problems with any of the above listed components, check the fuel pump (see below).

Fuel pump check

20   If you suspect a problem with the fuel pump, verify the pump actually runs. Remove the fuel filler cap and place your ear next to the opening. Have an assistant turn the ignition switch to ON - you should hear a brief whirring noise as the pump comes on and pressurizes the system. Have the assistant start the engine. This time you should hear a constant whirring sound from the pump (but it's more difficult to hear with the engine running).

21   If the pump does not come on (makes no sound), check the fuses. If the fuses are OK, proceed to the next step.

22   Raise the rear of the vehicle and support it securely on jackstands. Disable the ignition system by disconnecting the primary wires from the ignition coil (see Chapter 5). If the vehicle is equipped with a distributorless ignition system, detach the electrical connector from the ignition module/coil pack.

23   Locate the electrical connector to the fuel pump. It may be necessary to lower the tank slightly to provide access to the connector.

24   Unplug the electrical connector and probe the fuel pump feed wire with a test light. Have an assistant turn the ignition key to On - the test light should glow for about two seconds, then go off.

25   Have the assistant turn the ignition key to Start - the test light should glow as long as the engine is cranking.

26   If voltage is available, replace the fuel pump (see Section 6).

27   If no voltage is available, trace the fuel pump harness back and look for an open or short circuit condition. If no problem is found with the wiring harness, have the problem diagnosed by a dealer service department or other repair shop.

4   Fuel tank - removal and installation

Refer to illustration 4.8

Warning: *Gasoline is extremely flammable, so take extra precautions when you work on any part of the fuel system. Don't smoke or allow open flames or bare light bulbs near the work area, and don't work in a garage where a natural gas-type appliance (such as a water heater or clothes dryer) with a pilot light is present. If you spill any fuel on your skin, rinse it off immediately with soap and water. When you perform any kind of work on the fuel system, wear safety glasses and have a Class B type fire extinguisher on hand.*

Note: *Don't begin this procedure until the fuel gauge indicates the tank is empty or nearly empty. If the tank must be removed when it's full (for example, if the fuel pump malfunctions), siphon any remaining fuel from the tank prior to removal.*

1   Unless the vehicle has been driven far enough to completely empty the tank, it's a good idea to siphon the residual fuel out before removing the tank from the vehicle. **Warning:** *DO NOT start the siphoning action by mouth! Use a siphoning kit, available at most auto parts stores.*

2   Relieve the fuel pressure (see Section 2).

3   Detach the cable from the negative terminal of the battery. **Caution:** *If the vehicle is equipped with a Delco Loc II audio system, make sure you have the correct activation code before disconnecting the battery. See the information at the front of this manual for the radio re-activation procedure.*

4   Raise the vehicle and place it securely on jackstands.

5   Locate the electrical connector for the electric fuel pump and fuel gauge sending unit in front of the tank, and unplug it. If the vehicle doesn't have a connector, see Step 9.

6   Disconnect the fuel feed and return lines, the vapor return line and the filler neck

4.8 Remove the fuel tank mounting strap bolts (arrows)

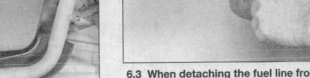

6.3 When detaching the fuel line from the mechanical fuel pump, hold the inside fitting with one wrench while turning the outside fitting with another

and vent tubes.

7 Support the fuel tank with a floor jack.

8 Disconnect both fuel tank retaining straps **(see illustration)**.

9 Lower the tank enough to disconnect the wires and ground strap from the fuel pump/fuel gauge sending unit, if you haven't already done so.

10 Remove the tank from the vehicle.

11 Installation is the reverse of removal.

5 Fuel tank cleaning and repair - general information

1 All repairs to the fuel tank or filler neck should be carried out by a professional who has experience in this critical and potentially dangerous work. Even after cleaning and flushing of the fuel system, explosive fumes can remain and ignite during repair of the tank.

2 If the fuel tank is removed from the vehicle, it should not be placed in an area where sparks or open flames could ignite the fumes coming out of the tank. Be especially careful inside garages where a natural gas-type appliance is located, because the pilot light could cause an explosion.

6 Fuel pump - removal and installation

Warning: *Gasoline is extremely flammable, so take extra precautions when you work on any part of the fuel system. Don't smoke or allow open flames or bare light bulbs near the work area, and don't work in a garage where a natural gas-type appliance (such as a water heater or clothes dryer) with a pilot light is present. If you spill any fuel on your skin, rinse it off immediately with soap and water. When you perform any kind of work on the fuel system, wear safety glasses and have a Class B type fire extinguisher on hand.*

Mechanical pump (carbureted models)

Refer to illustrations 6.3 and 6.4

Note: *Some later model carbureted models use an electric (in-tank) fuel pump.*

1 The fuel pump is a sealed unit and cannot be rebuilt.

2 Disconnect the cable from the negative terminal of the battery.

3 Detach the fuel inlet hose, the outlet line and the vapor return hose (if equipped). Hold the fitting on the pump with a back-up wrench as the outlet line is disconnected **(see illustration)**. Also, if possible, use a flare-nut wrench on the fuel line fitting.

4 Remove the two mounting bolts and detach the fuel pump **(see illustration)**. As the pump is removed, the pushrod may fall out - be sure to retrieve it.

5 Remove the gasket and mounting plate.

6 Remove all traces of old gasket and sealant with a scraper, then clean the block mounting surface with lacquer thinner or acetone.

7 Apply a dab of heavy grease to the pushrod to hold it in place as the pump is installed.

8 Position the new gasket, the mounting

plate and the pump on the block, then install the bolts and tighten them to the torque listed in this Chapter's Specifications.

9 Reattach the inlet hose, the outlet line and the vapor return hose to the pump. Be sure to tighten the fitting on the outlet line and the clamps on the hoses securely.

10 Start the engine and check for fuel leaks at the hose and line connections.

Electric pump (fuel-injected models)

Refer to illustrations 6.15 and 6.18

11 Relieve the fuel pressure (see Section 2).

12 Disconnect the cable from the negative battery terminal. **Caution:** *If the vehicle is equipped with a Delco Loc II audio system, make sure you have the correct activation code before disconnecting the battery. See the information at the front of this manual for the radio re-activation procedure.*

13 Remove the fuel tank (see Section 4).

14 The fuel pump/sending unit assembly is located inside the fuel tank. It is held in place by a cam lock ring mechanism consisting of an inner ring with three locking cams and an outer ring with three tangs. The outer ring is welded to the tank and can't be turned.

15 To unlock the fuel pump/sending unit

6.4 Remove the fuel pump mounting bolts (arrows)

6.15 Use a brass punch to tap the lock ring counterclockwise until the tabs align with the recess areas of the fuel tank

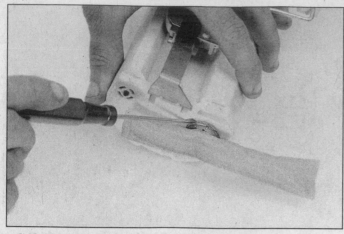

6.18 Inspect the fuel strainer for dirt; if too dirty to be cleaned carefully pry the fuel strainer from the inlet pipe

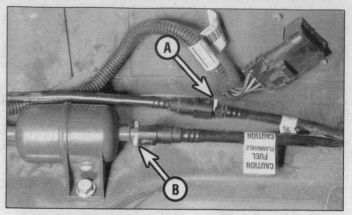

8.8a Some late models are equipped with fuel lines that can be disconnected by pinching the tabs and separating each connector

A	Fuel return line	B	Fuel feed line

assembly, turn the inner ring counterclockwise using a hammer and a BRASS punch or hard-wood dowel until the locking cams are free of the tangs **(see illustration). Warning:** *Do not use a steel punch to knock the lock rings loose - a spark could cause an explosion!*

16   Lift the fuel pump/sending unit assembly from the fuel tank. **Caution:** *The fuel level float and sending unit are delicate. Do not bump them against the tank during removal or the accuracy of the sending unit may be affected.*

17   Inspect the condition of the rubber gasket around the mouth of the lock ring mechanism. If it is dried, cracked or deteriorated, replace it.

18   Inspect the strainer on the lower end of the fuel pump **(see illustration)**. If it is dirty, remove it, clean it with a suitable solvent and blow it out with compressed air. If it is too dirty to be cleaned, replace it.

19   If it is necessary to separate the fuel pump and sending unit, remove the pump from the sending unit by pulling the fuel pump assembly into the rubber connector and sliding the pump away from the bottom support. Care should be taken to prevent damage to the rubber insulator and fuel strainer during removal. After the pump assembly is clear of the bottom support, pull it out of the rubber connector.

20   Insert the fuel pump/sending unit assembly into the fuel tank.

21   Turn the inner lock ring clockwise until the locking cams are fully engaged with the retaining tangs. **Note:** *If you have installed a new O-ring type rubber gasket, it may be necessary to push down on the inner lock ring until the locking cams slide under the retaining tangs.*

22   Install the fuel tank (see Section 4).

7   Fuel level sending unit - check and replacement

Warning: *Gasoline is extremely flammable, so take extra precautions when you work on*

any part of the fuel system. Don't smoke or allow open flames or bare light bulbs near the work area, and don't work in a garage where a natural gas-type appliance (such as a water heater or clothes dryer) with a pilot light is present. If you spill any fuel on your skin, rinse it off immediately with soap and water. When you perform any kind of work on the fuel system, wear safety glasses and have a Class B type fire extinguisher on hand.*

Check

1   Raise the vehicle and support it securely on jackstands.

2   Disconnect the electrical connector for the fuel pump/level sending unit. With the ignition key in the On position, the needle on the fuel level gauge should deflect to the maximum full position.

3   Using a jumper wire, ground the wire to the fuel level sending unit (it's usually the pink or purple wire). The needle on the gauge should now read empty.

4   If the gauge responds properly to these checks, the harness and gauge are OK. Replace the fuel level sending unit. If the gauge does not operate as described, the problem lies in the wiring harness to the gauge, or the gauge itself.

Replacement

5   Follow the procedure described in Section 6, beginning with Step 11, to remove the fuel level sending unit (and on fuel-injected models, the fuel pump). On fuel-injected models, transfer the fuel pump to the new sending unit.

8   Fuel lines and fittings - general information

Refer to illustrations 8.8a, 8.8b and 8.8c
Warning: *Gasoline is extremely flammable, so take extra precautions when you work on any part of the fuel system. Don't smoke or allow open flames or bare light bulbs near the work area, and don't work in a garage where*

a natural gas-type appliance (such as a water heater or clothes dryer) with a pilot light is present. If you spill any fuel on your skin, rinse it off immediately with soap and water. When you perform any kind of work on the fuel system, wear safety glasses and have a Class B type fire extinguisher on hand.*

1   Always relieve the fuel pressure before servicing fuel lines or fittings (see Section 2), and be sure to disconnect the cable from the negative terminal of the battery. **Caution:** *If the vehicle is equipped with a Delco Loc II audio system, make sure you have the correct activation code before disconnecting the battery. See the information at the front of this manual for the radio re-activation procedure.*

2   The fuel feed and return lines extend from the fuel tank to the engine compartment. The lines are secured to the underbody with clip and screw assemblies. The lines must be occasionally inspected for leaks, kinks and dents.

3   If evidence of dirt is found in the system or fuel filter during disassembly, the lines should be disconnected and blown out. Check the fuel strainer on the fuel gauge sending unit (see Section 6) for damage and deterioration.

Steel tubing

4   If replacement of a fuel line or emission line is called for, use welded steel tubing meeting GM specification 124-M or its equivalent.

5   Don't use copper or aluminum tubing to replace steel tubing. These materials cannot withstand normal vehicle vibration.

6   Because fuel lines used on fuel injected vehicles are under high pressure, they require special consideration.

7   Most fuel lines have threaded fittings with O-rings. Any time the fittings are loosened to service or replace components:

a)   Use a backup wrench while loosening and tightening the fittings.

b)   Check all O-rings for cuts, cracks and deterioration. Replace any that appear worn or damaged.

8.8b On quick-connect fuel lines, use the special fuel line disconnect tools and push them into the connector (arrows) to separate the fuel lines

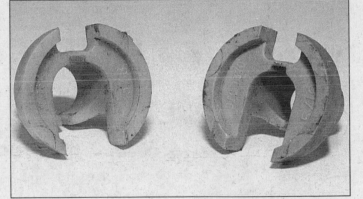

8.8c 3/8 and 5/16-inch fuel line disconnect tools

c) *If the lines are replaced, always use original equipment parts, or parts that meet the GM standards specified in this Section.*

Quick-connect fuel line fittings - removal and installation

8   New quick-connect fuel line fittings were introduced on 1989 and later models **(see illustration)**. A special tool, available at your local auto parts store, is required to disconnect them **(see illustration)**.

9   To separate the fuel lines, relieve the fuel system pressure (see Section 2) and insert the fuel line separator tool into the fitting and pull the lines apart.

10   To reattach quick-connect fittings, push the line into the fitting as far as possible, then pull back on it to verify that the connection is secure. **Warning:** *The line must be pushed in and pulled back to verify proper connector engagement - DO NOT rely on an audible click or visual verification to check the assembly of the quick-connect fittings.*

Rubber hose

Warning: *Never use rubber hose to replace metal line on a fuel-injected vehicle - use original equipment fuel line (or equivalent line*

meeting GM standards) only!

11   When a rubber hose is being replaced, use reinforced, fuel resistant hose (GM Specification 6163-M) with the word *Fluoroelastomer* imprinted on it. Hose(s) not clearly marked like this could fail prematurely and could fail to meet Federal emission standards. Hose inside diameter must match line outside diameter.

12   Don't use rubber hose within four inches of any part of the exhaust system or within ten inches of the catalytic converter. Metal lines and rubber hoses must never be allowed to chafe against the frame. A minimum of 1/4-inch clearance must be maintained around a line or hose to prevent contact with the frame or other components.

9   Carburetor - removal and installation

Refer to illustrations 9.3 and 9.7

Warning: *Gasoline is extremely flammable, so take extra precautions when you work on any part of the fuel system. Don 't smoke or allow open flames or bare light bulbs near the work area, and don 't work in a garage where a natural gas-type appliance (such as a water heater or clothes dryer) with a pilot light is present. If you spill any fuel on your skin, rinse*

it off immediately with soap and water. When you perform any kind of work on the fuel system, wear safety glasses and have a Class B type fire extinguisher on hand.

Removal

1   Remove the fuel tank cap to relieve the pressure in the tank.

2   Detach the cable from the negative battery terminal, then remove the air cleaner. **Caution:** *If the vehicle is equipped with a Delco Loc II audio system, make sure you have the correct activation code before disconnecting the battery. See the information at the front of this manual for the radio re-activation procedure.*

3   Mark and disconnect all hoses, vacuum lines and electrical connectors from the carburetor. Unscrew the fuel line from the carburetor inlet fitting, using a back-up wrench on the fitting to prevent the line from twisting **(see illustration)**.

4   Disconnect the accelerator linkage and cruise control linkage (if so equipped).

5   Disconnect the downshift cable (automatic transaxle models).

6   Remove the carburetor mounting nuts and/or bolts and separate the carburetor from the manifold.

7   Remove the gasket and/or Early Fuel Evaporation (EFE) heater and insulator **(see illustration)**.

9.3 Be sure to use a back-up wrench on the inlet fitting when disconnecting the fuel line from the carburetor

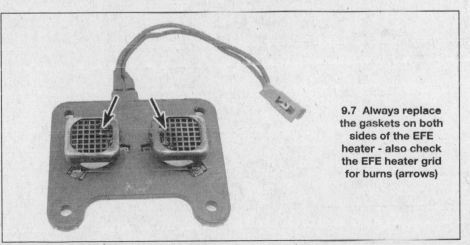

9.7 Always replace the gaskets on both sides of the EFE heater - also check the EFE heater grid for burns (arrows)

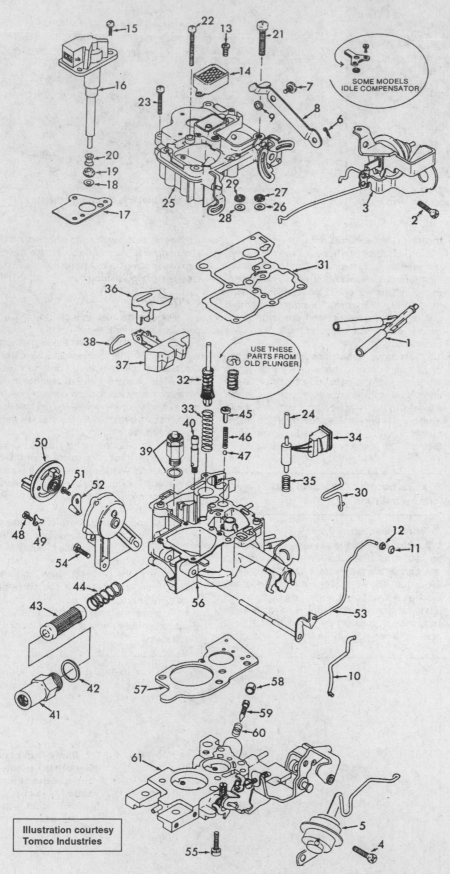

10.6 Exploded view of the E2SE carburetor

1   Vacuum break hose
2   Primary vacuum break attaching screw
3   Primary vacuum break assembly
4   Secondary vacuum break attaching screw
5   Secondary vacuum break assembly
6   Pump rod retaining clip
7   Pump lever screw
8   Pump lever
9   Washer
10 Pump rod
11 Choke rod retainer
12 Choke rod bushing
13 Vent stack screw
14 Vent stack
15 Screw
16 Mixture control solenoid
17 Gasket
18 Seal retainer
19 Seal
20 Spacer
21 Bowl cover screw (large)
22 Bowl cover screw
23 Bowl cover screw
24 Throttle Position Sensor plunger
25 Air horn assembly
26 Plunger seal retainer
27 Plunger seal
28 Pump seal retainer
29 Pump stem seal
30 Fast idle cam rod
31 Air horn gasket
32 Accelerator pump assembly
33 Pump return spring
34 Throttle Position Sensor (TPS)
35 TPS spring
36 Float bowl insert
37 Float
38 Float hinge pin
39 Fuel inlet valve and gasket
40 Primary metering jet
41 Fuel inlet nut
42 Fuel inlet nut gasket
43 Fuel filter
44 Fuel filter spring
45 Pump discharge ball and spring retainer
46 Pump discharge spring
47 Pump discharge ball
48 Choke retainer screw
49 Retainer
50 Choke cover assembly
51 Choke lever screw
52 Choke lever
53 Choke shaft and rod assembly
54 Choke housing screw
55 Throttle body screw
56 Float bowl assembly
57 Throttle body gasket
58 Plug
59 Idle mixture screw
60 Spring
61 Throttle body assembly

SOME MODELS
IDLE COMPENSATOR

USE THESE
PARTS FROM
OLD PLUNGER

**Illustration courtesy
Tomco Industries**

Installation

8   Installation is the reverse of the removal procedure, but the following points should be noted:

a) *By filling the carburetor bowl with fuel, the initial start-up will be easier and less drain on the battery.*
b) *New gaskets should be used.*
c) *Tighten the mounting bolts to the torque listed in this Chapter's Specifications.*
c) *Idle speed and mixture settings should be checked and, if necessary, adjusted.*

10 Carburetor - diagnosis, overhaul and adjustments

Warning: *Gasoline is extremely flammable, so take extra precautions when you work on any part of the fuel system. Don't smoke or allow open flames or bare light bulbs near the work area, and don't work in a garage where a natural gas-type appliance (such as a water heater or clothes dryer) with a pilot light is present. If you spill any fuel on your skin, rinse it off immediately with soap and water. When you perform any kind of work on the fuel system, wear safety glasses and have a Class B type fire extinguisher on hand.*

Diagnosis

1   A thorough road test and check of carburetor adjustments should be done before any major carburetor service work. Specifications for some adjustments are listed on the *Vehicle Emissions Control Information* (VECI) label found in the engine compartment.

2   Carburetor problems usually show up as flooding, hard starting, stalling, severe backfiring and poor acceleration. A carburetor that's leaking fuel and/or covered with wet looking deposits definitely needs attention.

3   Some performance complaints directed at the carburetor are actually a result of loose, out-of-adjustment or malfunctioning engine or electrical components. Others develop when vacuum hoses leak, are disconnected or are incorrectly routed. The proper approach to analyzing carburetor problems should include the following items:

a) *Inspect all vacuum hoses and actuators for leaks and correct installation.*
b) *Tighten the intake manifold and carburetor mounting bolts evenly and securely.*
c) *Perform a cylinder compression test (see Chapter 2).*
d) *Clean or replace the spark plugs as necessary (see Chapter 1).*
e) *Check the spark plug wires (see Chapter 1).*
f) *Inspect the ignition primary wires.*
g) *Check the ignition timing (see Chapter 1).*
h) *Check the fuel pressure (see Section 3).*
i) *Check the thermo-sensor assembly in the air cleaner for proper operation (see Chapter 6).*

j) *Check/replace the air filter element (see Chapter 1).*
k) *Check the PCV system (see Chapters 1 and 6).*
l) *Check/replace the fuel filter (see Chapter 1). Also, the strainer in the tank could be restricted.*
m) *Check for a plugged exhaust system.*
n) *Check EGR valve operation (see Chapter 6).*
o) *Check the choke - it should be completely open at normal engine operating temperature (see Chapter 1).*
p) *Check for fuel leaks and kinked or dented fuel lines.*
q) *Check accelerator pump operation with the engine off (remove the air cleaner cover and operate the throttle as you look into the carburetor throat - you should see a stream of gasoline enter the carburetor).*
r) *Check for incorrect fuel or bad gasoline.*
s) *Check the valve clearances (if applicable) and camshaft lobe lift (see Chapters 1 and 2).*
t) *Have a dealer service department or repair shop check the electronic engine and carburetor controls.*

4   Diagnosing carburetor problems may require that the engine be started and run with the air cleaner off. While running the engine without the air cleaner, backfires are possible. This situation is likely to occur if the carburetor is malfunctioning, but just the removal of the air cleaner can lean the fuel/air mixture enough to produce an engine backfire. **Warning:** *Don't position any part of your body, especially your face, directly over the carburetor during inspection and servicing procedures. Wear eye protection!*

Overhaul

Refer to illustrations 10.6 and 10.7

5   If you are going to overhaul the carburetor yourself, first obtain a good quality carburetor rebuild kit (which will include all necessary gaskets, internal parts, instructions and a parts list). You will also need some carburetor cleaner and a means of blowing out the

internal passages of the carburetor with air.

6   Because carburetor designs are constantly modified by the manufacturer in order to meet emissions regulations, it isn't feasible for us to do a step-by-step overhaul of each type. You'll receive a detailed set of instructions with any quality carburetor overhaul kit. They will apply in a more specific manner to the carburetor on your vehicle **(see illustration)**.

7   An alternative is to obtain a new or rebuilt carburetor. They are readily available from dealers and auto parts stores. Make sure the exchange carburetor is identical to the original. A number is cast into the side of the carburetor **(see illustration)**. It will aid in determining the exact type of carburetor you have. When obtaining a rebuilt carburetor or a rebuild kit, take time to make sure that the kit or carburetor matches your application exactly. Seemingly insignificant differences can make a large difference in the performance of your engine.

8   If you choose to overhaul your own carburetor, allow enough time to disassemble the carburetor carefully, soak the necessary parts in the cleaning solvent (usually for at least one-half day or according to the instructions listed on the carburetor cleaner) and reassemble it, which will usually take much longer than disassembly. When disassembling the carburetor, match each part with the illustration in the carburetor kit and lay the parts out in order on a clean work surface.

Adjustments

9   Because there are a number of different configurations for Federal, California and Canadian carburetors and because a considerable number of special tools and tuning equipment is necessary to adjust these carburetors, it is impossible to include a detailed step-by-step procedure outlining every adjustment. Aside from idle speed adjustment and other adjustments shown in the carburetor overhaul kit, do not attempt to adjust the carburetor on your vehicle. If adjustments are needed other than those listed above, take the vehicle to a professional mechanic.

10.7 Location of the carburetor identification number

11.2 To detach the throttle cable at the pedal, pull the spring cup (arrow) toward the end of the cable and slide the cable out of the slot

11.6a If your vehicle has this type of retainer, pop off the retaining clip from the throttle lever arm

11.6b If your vehicle has this type of retainer, push the cable end forward and lift up to detach it from the throttle lever arm

11   Accelerator cable - removal and installation

Refer to illustrations 11.2, 11.6a and 11.6b

Removal

1   Detach the screws and the clip retaining the lower instrument panel trim and lower the trim (if necessary).
2   Detach the accelerator cable from the accelerator pedal **(see illustration)**.
3   Squeeze the accelerator cable cover tangs and push the cable through the firewall into the engine compartment.
4   Remove the cable clamp attaching screws and the cable clamp (if equipped).
5   Detach the routing clip (if equipped) and the accelerator cable.
6   Detach the accelerator cable-to-throttle lever retainer and detach the accelerator cable from the throttle body lever **(see illustrations)**.
7   Squeeze the accelerator cable retaining tangs and push the cable through the accelerator cable bracket.

Installation

8   Installation is the reverse of removal. **Note:** *To prevent possible interference, flexible components (hoses, wires, etc.) must not be routed within two inches of moving parts, unless routing is controlled.*
9   Operate the accelerator pedal and check for any binding condition by completely opening and closing the throttle.
10   At the engine compartment side of the firewall, apply sealant around the accelerator cable.

12   Fuel injection systems - general information

Some models employ fuel injection in place of the conventional carburetor. Two types of fuel injection are used. Throttle Body Injection (TBI) and Multi-Port Fuel Injection (MPFI). Fuel injection provides optimum mixture ratios at all stages of combustion. Combined with its immediate response characteristics, Fuel injection permits the engine to run on the leanest possible air/fuel mixture, which greatly reduces exhaust gas emissions.

The fuel injection system is controlled directly by the vehicle's Electronic Control Module (ECM), which automatically adjusts the air/fuel mixture in accordance with engine load and performance.

Throttle Body Injection (TBI)

The main component of the TBI system is the Throttle Body Injection (TBI) unit, which is mounted on the intake manifold just like a carburetor. The TBI unit is made up of two major assemblies: the throttle body and the fuel metering assembly.

The throttle body contains a single throttle valve, controlled by the accelerator pedal, similar to a carburetor. Attached to the exterior of the body are the Throttle Position Sensor (TPS), which sends throttle position information to the ECM, and the Idle Air Control (IAC) assembly, which is used by the ECM to maintain a constant idle speed during normal engine operation.

The fuel metering assembly contains the fuel pressure regulator and the single fuel injector. The regulator dampens the pulsations of the fuel pump and maintains a steady pressure at the injector. The fuel injector is controlled by the ECM through an electrically operated solenoid. The amount of fuel injected into the intake manifold is varied by the length of time the injector plunger is held open.

Multi-Port Fuel Injection (MPFI)

Multi-Port Fuel Injection (MPFI) consists of an air intake manifold, the throttle body, the injectors, the fuel rail assembly, an electric fuel pump and attendant plumbing.

Air is drawn through the air cleaner and throttle body. A Mass Air Flow (MAF) sensor mounted between the air cleaner and the throttle body measures the mass (weight) of air passing through the manifold and compensates for temperature and pressure variations.

While the engine is running, the fuel constantly circulates through the fuel rail, which removes vapors and keeps the fuel cool while maintaining sufficient pressure to the injectors under all running conditions.

As with TBI, the operation of the MPFI injection system is controlled by the ECM so that it works in conjunction with the rest of the vehicle functions to provide optimum driveability and emissions control.

Because the MPFI system meters fuel and air precisely, it is important to the proper operation of the vehicle that the fuel and air filters be changed at the specified intervals.

Both systems

The ECM controlling both types of fuel injection systems has a learning capability for certain performance conditions. If the battery is disconnected, part of the ECM memory is erased, which makes it necessary to "reteach" the computer. This is done by thoroughly warming up the engine and operating the vehicle at part throttle, stop and go and idle conditions.

A fuel pump relay is used to control the electric fuel pump operation. When the ignition is turned on, the fuel pump relay immediately supplies current to the fuel pump to pressurize the fuel system. If the engine doesn't start after two seconds, the fuel pump will automatically shut off. If the fuel pump relay fails, the fuel pump will still operate after the ECM receives pulses from the distributor or about four pounds of oil pressure has built up, depending on the model.

The throttle stop screw, used to regulate the minimum idle speed, is adjusted at the factory and sealed with a plug to discourage unnecessary readjustment.

13.9 Measure the resistance of the injectors with an ohmmeter

14.4a Disconnect the IAC electrical connection (arrow) - Model 300 TBI unit shown

14.4b Disconnect the TPS electrical connection (arrow) - Model 700 TBI unit shown

13 Fuel injection system - check

Warning: *Gasoline is extremely flammable, so take extra precautions when you work on any part of the fuel system. Don't smoke or allow open flames or bare light bulbs near the work area, and don't work in a garage where a natural gas-type appliance (such as a water heater or clothes dryer) with a pilot light is present. If you spill any fuel on your skin, rinse it off immediately with soap and water. When you perform any kind of work on the fuel system, wear safety glasses and have a Class B type fire extinguisher on hand.*
Note: *The following procedure is based on the assumption that the fuel pump is working and the fuel pressure is adequate (see Section 3).*

Preliminary checks

1   Check all electrical connectors that are related to the system. Loose electrical connectors and poor grounds can cause many problems that resemble more serious malfunctions.
2   Check to see that the battery is fully charged, as the control unit and sensors depend on an accurate supply voltage in order to properly meter the fuel.
3   Check the air filter element - a dirty or partially blocked filter will severely impede performance and economy (see Chapter 1).
4   If a blown fuse is found, replace it and see if it blows again. If it does, search for a grounded wire in the harness to the fuel pump.

Multi-Port Fuel Injection only

Refer to illustration 13.9
5   Check the air intake duct from the Mass Air Flow (MAF) sensor (if equipped) to the intake manifold for leaks, which will result in an excessively lean mixture. Also check the condition of the vacuum hoses connected to the intake manifold.
6   Remove the air intake duct from the throttle body and check for dirt, carbon or

other residue build-up in the throttle body, particularly around the throttle plate. If it's dirty, clean it with carburetor cleaner and a toothbrush.
7   With the engine running, place a screwdriver (or stethoscope) against each injector, one at a time, and listen through the handle for a clicking sound, indicating operation.
8   If an injector isn't functioning (not clicking), purchase a special injector test light (sometimes called a "noid" light) and install it into the injector electrical connector. Start the engine and check to see if the noid light flashes. If it does, the injector is receiving proper voltage. If it doesn't flash, further diagnosis should be performed by a dealer service department or other repair shop.
9   With the engine OFF and the fuel injector electrical connectors disconnected, measure the resistance of each injector **(see illustration)**. Compare your measurement to the injector resistance values listed in this Chapter's Specifications.
10   The remainder of the system checks can be found in Section 17 and Chapter 6.

TBI systems only

11   Set the parking brake, remove the air cleaner top plate and, with the engine idling in Park, observe the operating fuel injector. The spray pattern should be even and conical in shape. The spray should touch the throttle body bore.

a)   *If the spray is weak or uneven, the injector is clogged or faulty. Gasoline additives designed to clean fuel injectors can sometimes clear a clogged injector. If not, a dealer service department or other qualified shop has more effective cleaning equipment.*

b)   *If an injector is not operating at all, check its electrical connector. If the connection is good and the injector is receiving voltage, but the injector still doesn't work, the injector is faulty.*

12   Turn the engine off and observe the injector. There shouldn't be any leakage or dripping. If the injector does drip, either the

injector seals are faulty or the injector itself is defective. Usually a problem like this will result in a hard-starting condition and/or a puff of smoke as the engine is started.

14 Throttle Body Injection (TBI) unit - removal and installation

Refer to illustrations 14.4a and 14.4b
Warning: *Gasoline is extremely flammable, so take extra precautions when you work on any part of the fuel system. Don't smoke or allow open flames or bare light bulbs near the work area, and don't work in a garage where a natural gas-type appliance (such as a water heater or clothes dryer) with a pilot light is present. If you spill any fuel on your skin, rinse it off immediately with soap and water. When you perform any kind of work on the fuel system, wear safety glasses and have a Class B type fire extinguisher on hand.*
Note: *The fuel injector, pressure regulator, throttle position sensor and the idle air control valve can be replaced without removing the throttle body assembly.*

Removal

1   Relieve the fuel system pressure (see Section 2).
2   Disconnect the cable from the negative terminal of the battery. **Caution:** *If the vehicle is equipped with a Delco Loc II audio system, make sure you have the correct activation code before disconnecting the battery. See the information at the front of this manual for the radio re-activation procedure.*
3   Remove the air cleaner housing.
4   Unplug the electrical connectors from the idle air control valve, throttle position sensor and the fuel injector **(see illustrations)**.
5   Remove the wiring harness and insulating grommet from the throttle body.
6   Disconnect the accelerator cable and return spring, transmission control and cruise control cables, if equipped.
7   Using pieces of numbered tape, mark all

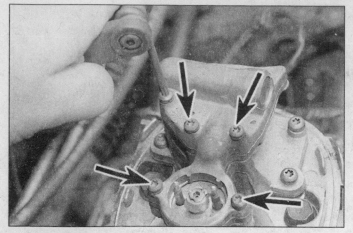

15.6 Fuel meter cover-to-fuel meter body screw locations

15.8 The fuel pressure regulator is installed in the fuel meter cover and pre-adjusted at the factory - don't remove the four retaining screw (arrows) or you may damage the regulator

of the vacuum hoses to the throttle body and disconnect them.

8   Disconnect the fuel inlet and return lines. Use a backup wrench on the inlet and return fitting nuts to prevent damage to the throttle body and fuel lines. Remove the O-rings on the ends of the fuel lines and discard them (be sure to install new ones during reassembly). Later models use quick-connect fuel lines - refer to Section 8 for the disconnection procedure.

9   Remove the TBI assembly mounting bolts/nuts and lift the unit from the intake manifold. It's a good idea to stuff a rag into the intake manifold opening to prevent foreign matter from falling in. Remove all old gasket material from the intake manifold and the underside of the throttle body unit.

Installation

10   Installation is the reverse of the removal procedure. Be sure to install a new throttle body-to-intake manifold gasket, new fuel line O-rings and tighten the mounting bolts/nuts to the torque listed in this Chapter's Specifications.

11   Turn the ignition switch to the On position (don't start the engine) and check for fuel leaks.

12   Check to see if the accelerator pedal is free by depressing the pedal to the floor and releasing it with the ignition switch off.

---

15   Model 300 Throttle Body Injection (TBI) unit (1986 and earlier models) - component check and replacement

---

Warning: *Gasoline is extremely flammable, so take extra precautions when you work on any part of the fuel system. Do not smoke or allow open flames or bare light bulbs near the work area, and don't work in a garage where a natural gas-type appliance (such as a water heater or clothes dryer) with a pilot light is present. If you spill any fuel on your skin, rinse*

15.9a The best way to remove the fuel injector is to pry on it with a screwdriver, using a second screwdriver as a fulcrum

it off immediately with soap and water. When you perform any kind of work on the fuel system, wear safety glasses and have a Class B type fire extinguisher on hand.

Note: *Because of its relative simplicity, a throttle body assembly does not need to be removed from the intake manifold nor completely disassembled for component replacement. However, for the sake of clarity, the following procedures are shown with the TBI unit removed from the vehicle.*

1   Relieve the fuel pressure (see Section 2).

2   Detach the cable from the negative terminal of the battery.

3   Remove the air cleaner housing assembly, adapter and gaskets.

Fuel meter cover and fuel injector

Refer to illustrations 15.6, 15.8, 15.9a, 15.9b, 15.11, 15.12, 15.18, 15.19 and 15.20

Check

4   Refer to Section 13 for the fuel injector checking procedure. Also check for stored trouble codes in the ECM (see Chapter 6).

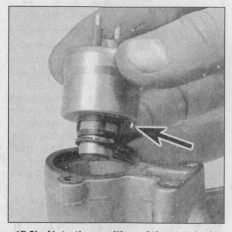

15.9b Note the position of the terminals on top and the dowel pin on the bottom of the injector in relation to the fuel meter body when you lift the injector out of the body

Disassembly

5   Remove the injector electrical connector (on top of the TBI unit) by squeezing the two tabs together and pulling straight up.

6   Unscrew the five fuel meter cover retaining screws and lockwashers securing the fuel meter cover to the fuel meter body. Note the location of the two short screws **(see illustration)**.

7   Remove the fuel meter cover. **Caution:** *Do not immerse the fuel meter cover in solvent. It might damage the pressure regulator diaphragm and gasket.*

8   The fuel meter cover contains the fuel pressure regulator, which is pre-set and plugged at the factory. If a malfunction occurs, it cannot be serviced, and must be replaced as a complete assembly. **Warning:** *Do not remove the screws securing the pressure regulator to the fuel meter cover* **(see illustration)**. *It has a large spring under heavy compression inside.*

9   With the old fuel meter cover gasket in place to prevent damage to the casting, care-

15.11 Carefully peel away the old fuel meter outlet passage gasket and fuel meter cover gasket with a razor blade

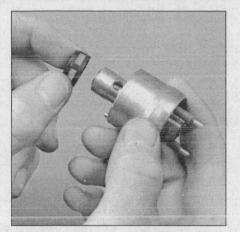

15.12 Gently rotate the fuel injector filter back and forth and pull it off the nozzle

15.18 Make sure that the lug is aligned with the groove in the bottom of the fuel injector cavity

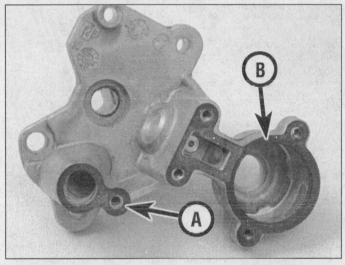

15.19 Position the fuel outlet passage gasket (A) and the fuel meter cover gasket (B) properly

15.20 Install a new dust seal into the recess of the fuel meter body

fully pry the injector from the fuel meter body with a screwdriver until it can be lifted free **(see illustrations)**. **Caution:** *Use care in removing the injector to prevent damage to the electrical connector terminals, the injector fuel filter, the O-ring and the nozzle.*

10   The fuel meter body should be removed from the throttle body if it needs to be cleaned. To remove it, remove the fuel feed and return line fittings and the Torx screws that attach the fuel meter body to the throttle body.

11   Remove the old gasket from the fuel meter cover and discard it. Remove the large O-ring and steel back-up washer from the upper counterbore of the fuel meter body injector cavity **(see illustration)**. Clean the fuel meter body thoroughly in carburetor cleaner and blow it dry.

12   Remove the small O-ring from the nozzle end of the injector. Carefully rotate the injector fuel filter back and forth and remove the filter from the base of the injector **(see illustration)**. Gently clean the filter in solvent

and allow it to drip dry. It is too small and delicate to dry with compressed air. **Caution:** *The fuel injector itself is an electrical component. Do not immerse it in any type of cleaning solvent.*

13   The fuel injector is not serviceable. If it is malfunctioning, replace it as an assembly.

Reassembly

14   Install the clean fuel injector nozzle filter on the end of the fuel injector with the larger end of the filter facing the injector so that the filter covers the raised rib at the base of the injector. Use a twisting motion to position the filter against the base of the injector.

15   Lubricate a new small O-ring with automatic transmission fluid. Push the O-ring onto the nozzle end of the injector until it presses against the injector fuel filter.

16   Insert the steel backup washer in the top counterbore of the fuel meter body injector cavity.

17   Lubricate a new large O-ring with automatic transmission fluid and install it directly

over the backup washer. Be sure the O-ring is seated properly in the cavity and is flush with the top of the fuel meter body casting surface. **Caution:** *The back-up washer and large O-ring must be installed before the injector or improper seating of the large O-ring could cause fuel to leak.*

18   Install the injector in the cavity in the fuel meter body, aligning the raised lug on the injector base with the cast-in notch in the fuel meter body cavity. Push straight down on the injector with both thumbs **(see illustration)** until it is fully seated in the cavity. **Note:** *The electrical terminals of the injector should be approximately parallel to the throttle shaft.*

19   Install a new fuel outlet passage gasket on the fuel meter cover and a new fuel meter cover gasket on the fuel meter body **(see illustration)**.

20   Install a new dust seal into the recess on the fuel meter body **(see illustration)**.

21   Install the fuel meter cover onto the fuel meter body, making sure that the pressure regulator dust seal and cover gaskets are in place.

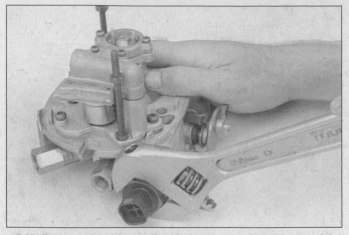

15.27 Remove the IAC valve with a large wrench, but be careful - it's a delicate device

15.28 Distance A should be less than 1-1/8 inch for either type of Idle Air Control valve - if it isn't, determine which kind of valve you have and adjust it accordingly

22   Apply a thread locking compound to the threads of the fuel meter cover attaching screws. Install the screws (the two short screws go next to the injector) and tighten them securely. **Note:** *Service repair kits include a small vial of thread locking compound with directions for use. If this material is not available, use Loctite 262 or equivalent. Do not use a higher strength locking compound than recommended, as this may prevent subsequent removal of the attaching screws or cause breakage of the screwhead if removal becomes necessary.*

23   Plug in the electrical connector to the injector.

24   Install the air cleaner.

Idle Air Control (IAC) valve

Refer to illustrations 15.27 and 15.28

Check

25   Refer to Chapter 6 and check for trouble codes stored in the ECM. If the IAC valve is malfunctioning, a trouble code indicating this condition would most likely have been set.

Removal

26   Unplug the electrical connector at the IAC valve.

27   Remove the IAC valve with a wrench on the hex surface only **(see illustration)**.

Installation

28   Before installing a new IAC valve, measure the distance the valve is extended **(see illustration)**. The measurement should be made from the motor housing to the end of the cone. The distance should be no greater than 1-1/8 inch. If the cone is extended too far, damage may occur to the valve when it is installed.

29   Identify the replacement IAC valve as either a Type I (with a collar at the electrical connector end) or a Type II (without a collar) **(as shown in illustration 15.28)**. If the measured dimension "A" is greater than 1-1/8 inch, the distance must be reduced as follows:

Type I -Exert firm pressure on the valve to retract it (a slight side-to-side movement may be helpful).

Type II - Compress the retaining spring of the valve while turning the valve in a clockwise direction. Return the spring to its original position with the straight portion of the spring aligned with the flat surface of the valve.

30   Install the new IAC valve to the throttle body. Use the new gasket supplied with the assembly.

31   Plug in the electrical connector.

32   Install the air cleaner.

33   Start the engine and allow it to reach normal operating temperature. The Electronic Control Module (ECM) will reset the idle speed when the vehicle is driven above 35 mph.

Minimum idle speed adjustment

Refer to illustration 15.35

Note: *This adjustment should be performed only when the throttle body has been replaced. The engine should be at normal operating temperature before making the adjustment.*

34   Remove the air cleaner housing.

35   Remove the plug covering the idle stop screw by piercing it with an awl, then applying leverage **(see illustration)**.

36   Plug any vacuum ports as required by the VECI label.

37   With the IAC valve connected, ground the diagnostic terminal of the ALDL connector (see Chapter 6). Turn the ignition to On but don't start the engine. Wait at least 30 seconds to allow the IAC calce pintle to extend and seat in the throttle body. Disconnect the IAC valve electrical connector. Remove the jumper wire from the ALDL connector and start the engine.

38   Adjust the idle stop screw to obtain the specified idle speed in Park.

39   Turn the ignition off and reconnect the IAC valve electrical connector.

40   Unplug any plugged vacuum ports and reconnect the hoses.

41   Install the air cleaner housing.

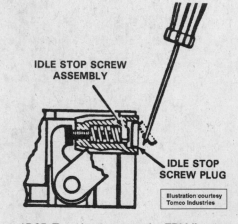

IDLE STOP SCREW ASSEMBLY

IDLE STOP SCREW PLUG

Illustration courtesy Tomco Industries

15.35 To gain access to the TBI idle stop screw, pierce the metal plug with a sharp object and pry it from the throttle body (this is not a routine tune-up adjustment and should only be performed when the TBI unit is replaced and the idle speed is then incorrect)

42   Disconnect the cable from the negative terminal of the battery for at least ten seconds. This will erase any stored trouble codes that may have been set by unplugging the IAC valve and running the engine. **Caution:** *If the vehicle is equipped with a Delco Loc II audio system, make sure you have the correct activation code before disconnecting the battery. See the information at the front of this manual for the radio re-activation procedure.*

Throttle Position Sensor (TPS)

Refer to illustration 15.48

General information and check

43   The Throttle Position Sensor (TPS) is connected to the throttle shaft on the TBI unit. As the throttle valve angle is changed (as the accelerator pedal is moved), the output of the TPS also changes. At a closed throttle position, the output of the TPS is

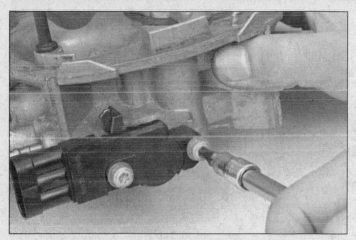

15.48 The Throttle Position Sensor (TPS) is mounted to the side of the TDI with two Torx screws

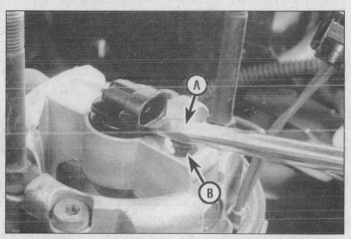

16.5 Pry the injector out of the fuel meter body using one screwdriver as a fulcrum (B) and another as a lever (A)

below 1.25-volts. As the throttle valve opens, the output increases so that, at wide-open throttle, the output voltage is approximately 5-volts.

44 A broken or loose TPS can cause intermittent bursts of fuel from the injector and an unstable idle, because the ECM thinks the throttle is moving. If a problem with the TPS sensor or circuit develops, a trouble code most likely will be set (see Chapter 6).

45 Connect a digital voltmeter from the TPS electrical connector center terminal "B" to outside terminal "C" (you'll have to fabricate jumper wires for terminal access).

46 With the ignition on and the engine off, TPS voltage should be between 0.45 and 1.25 volts. If it's more than specified, check and, if necessary, adjust the minimum idle speed before condemning the TPS.

47 The TPS is not adjustable. If the TPS malfunctions, it must be replaced as a unit.

Replacement

48 Unscrew the two Torx screws **(see illustration)** and remove the TPS.

49 Install the new TPS and tighten the screws securely. **Note:** *Make sure the tang on the lever is properly engaged with the stop on the TBI.*

50 Install the air cleaner assembly.

51 Attach the cable to the negative terminal of the battery.

16   Model 700 Throttle Body Injection (TBI) unit (1987 and later models - component check and replacement

Warning: *Gasoline is extremely flammable, so take extra precautions when you work on any part of the fuel system. Do not smoke or allow open flames or bare light bulbs near the work area, and don't work in a garage where a natural gas type appliance (such as a water heater or clothes dryer) with a pilot light is*

present. If you spill any fuel on your skin, rinse it off immediately with soap and water. When you perform any kind of work on the fuel system, wear safety glasses and have a Class B type fire extinguisher on hand.

Fuel injector

Check

1 Refer to Section 13 for the fuel injector checking procedure. Also check for stored trouble codes in the ECM (see Chapter 6).

Replacement

Refer to illustration 16.5

2 Disconnect the negative battery cable. **Caution:** *If the vehicle is equipped with a Delco Loc II audio system, make sure you have the correct activation code before disconnecting the battery. See the information at the front of this manual for the radio re-activation procedure.*

3 Unplug the electrical connector from the fuel injector.

4 Remove the injector retainer screw and the retainer.

5 Using one screwdriver as a fulcrum on the fuel meter body, place another screwdriver tip under the ridge on the fuel injector opposite the electrical connector end and gently pry the injector out **(see illustration).**

6 If the injector is to be reused, replace the upper and lower O-rings on the injector and in the fuel injector cavity. Install the upper O-ring in the groove on the injector and the lower O-ring flush against the filter element.

7 Install the injector assembly in the fuel meter body by pushing it straight down. Make sure the connector end is facing in the direction of the opening in the fuel meter body for the wire harness grommet.

8 Install the injector retainer and screw. Use a thread locking compound on the retainer screw (Loctite 262 or equivalent).

9 Reconnect the negative battery cable. Pressurize the fuel system by turning the ignition key to the On position, then inspect the

area around the injector for leaks.

10 Plug the electrical connector into the injector and start the engine to check for correct operation.

Pressure regulator assembly

Check

11 Refer to Section 3 and perform the fuel pressure checks, which will diagnose a malfunctioning fuel pressure regulator.

Replacement

12 Underneath the pressure regulator cover assembly is a large spring which is highly compressed. Repairs to this component should be performed by a dealer service department or other repair shop due to the possibility of personal injury. Also, the tension on this spring affects fuel pressure and is set at the factory - any tampering with this component would be in violation of Federal law.

Idle Air Control valve

Check

13 Refer to Chapter 6 and check for trouble codes stored in the ECM. If the IAC valve is malfunctioning, a trouble code indicating this condition would most likely have been set.

Replacement

Refer to illustrations 16.18a and 16.18b

14 Disconnect the negative battery cable. **Caution:** *If the vehicle is equipped with a Delco Loc II audio system, make sure you have the correct activation code before disconnecting the battery. See the information at the front of this manual for the radio re-activation procedure.*

15 Remove the air cleaner and unplug the electrical connector from the IAC valve.

16 Remove the two valve retaining screws and pull the valve out of the throttle body.

17 If the same valve is to be reinstalled, be sure to use a new O-ring.

18 Before installing the valve, measure the distance from the end of the pintle to the

16.18a The Idle Air Control valve pintle must not extend more than 1-1/8 inch - also, replace the O-ring if it is brittle

    A   Distance of pintle extension
    B   O-ring

16.18b To reduce the IAC valve pintle extension, grasp the valve and depress the pintle using a slight side-to-side motion

16.30 The Throttle Position Sensor mounts to the side of the throttle body and is not adjustable

mounting flange **(see illustration)**. If the distance exceeds 1-1/8 inch, reduce that distance by pushing the pintle into the valve assembly with a slight side-to-side motion **(see illustration)**. If this is not done, the valve will be damaged during installation.

19   Position the valve on the throttle body and install the screws. Plug in the electrical connector to the valve.

20   No adjustment of the IAC valve is necessary, as it is automatically reset by the ECM.

Minimum idle speed adjustment

21   Refer to Section 15, Steps 34 through 42 for this adjustment.

Throttle Position Sensor (TPS)

General information and check

22   The Throttle Position Sensor (TPS) is connected to the throttle shaft on the TBI unit. As the throttle valve angle is changed (as the accelerator pedal is moved), the output of the TPS also changes. At a closed throttle position, the output of the TPS is below 1.25-volts. As the throttle valve opens, the output increases so that, at wide-open throttle, the output voltage is approximately 5-volts.

23   A broken or loose TPS can cause intermittent bursts of fuel from the injector and an unstable idle, because the ECM thinks the throttle is moving. If a problem with the TPS sensor or circuit develops, a trouble code most likely will be set (see Chapter 6).

24   Connect a digital voltmeter from the TPS electrical connector terminal "C" (dark blue wire) to terminal "B" (black wire) (you'll have to fabricate jumper wires for terminal access).

25   With the ignition on and the engine off, TPS voltage should be between 0.45 and 1.25 volts. If it's more than specified, check and, if necessary, adjust the minimum idle speed before condemning the TPS.

26   The TPS is not adjustable. If the TPS malfunctions, it must be replaced as a unit.

Replacement

Refer to illustration 16.30

27   Disconnect the cable from the negative battery terminal. **Caution:** *If the vehicle is equipped with a Delco Loc II audio system, make sure you have the correct activation code before disconnecting the battery. See the information at the front of this manual for the radio re-activation procedure.*

28   Remove the air cleaner housing.

29   Unplug the electrical connector from the throttle position sensor.

30   Remove the two sensor mounting screws and pull the sensor from the throttle body **(see illustration)**.

31   To install the TPS, align the slot in the rear of the sensor with the throttle shaft and insert the sensor into the throttle body. Install the mounting screws and tighten them securely. This style TPS is not adjustable.

32   The remainder of installation is the reverse of the removal procedure.

17 Multi-Port Fuel Injection (MPFI) - component check, removal and installation

Warning: *Gasoline is extremely flammable, so take extra precautions when you work on any part of the fuel system. Do not smoke or allow open flames or bare light bulbs near the work area, and don't work in a garage where a natural gas-type appliance (such as a water heater or clothes dryer) with a pilot light is present. If you spill any fuel on your skin, rinse it off immediately with soap and water. When you perform any kind of work on the fuel system, wear safety glasses and have a Class B type fire extinguisher on hand.*

Throttle body

Check

Refer to illustration 17.2

1   Detach the air intake duct from the throttle body and move the duct out of the way.

2   Have an assistant depress the throttle

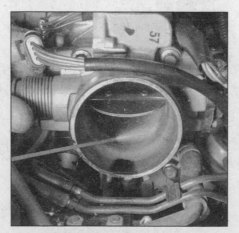

17.2 Clean the throttle body with carburetor cleaner to remove sludge deposits

17.5a Disconnect the IAC electrical connection (arrow) - 2.8/3.1L engine shown

17.5b Disconnect the TPS electrical connection (arrow) - 2.8/3.1L engine shown

17.5c To detach the throttle body from the plenum, remove these two bolts (arrows)

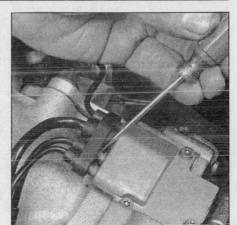

17.6 Using a small screwdriver, pry the vacuum harness connector from the throttle body

17.8 On some models you can't see the two coolant hoses attached to the throttle body until you unbolt the throttle body from the plenum and turn it over

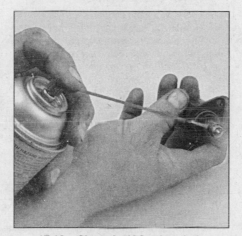

17.16a Clean the IAC valve pintle with carburetor spray to remove carbon deposits

17.16b Spray carburetor cleaner into the IAC valve housing and check for clogged air passages in the air intake plenum

pedal while you watch the throttle valve. Check that the throttle valve moves smoothly when the throttle is moved from closed (idle position) to fully open (wide open throttle). **Note:** *Spray carburetor cleaner into the throttle body, especially around the shaft area, to free-up any binding caused by the accumulation of carbon deposits or sludge buildup* **(see illustration).**

3   Wiggle the throttle lever while watching the throttle shaft inside the bore. If it appears worn (loose), replace the throttle body unit.

Removal

Refer to illustrations 17.5a, 17.5b, 17.5c, 17.6 and 17.8

4   Disconnect the cable from the negative terminal of the battery. **Caution:** *If the vehicle is equipped with a Delco Loc II audio system, make sure you have the correct activation code before disconnecting the battery. See the information at the front of this manual for the radio re-activation procedure.*

5   Unplug the Idle Air Control (IAC) valve and the Throttle Position Sensor (TPS) electrical connectors **(see illustrations).**

6   Mark and disconnect any vacuum hoses connected to the throttle body **(see illustration).** Also detach the breather hose, if equipped.

7   Disconnect the accelerator cable from the throttle lever, then detach the cable housing from its bracket.

8   Loosen the clamps and disconnect the coolant hoses from the underside of the throttle body. Be prepared for some coolant spillage and plug the ends of the hoses. **Note:** *On some models you can't get to these hoses until after the throttle body has been unbolted from the plenum* **(see illustration).**

9   Detach the air intake duct.

10   Remove the throttle body bolts and detach the throttle body.

Installation

11   Clean off all traces of old gasket material from the throttle body and the plenum.

12   Install the throttle body and a new gasket and tighten the bolts to the torque listed in this Chapter's Specifications.

13   The rest of the procedure is the reverse of removal. Be sure to check the coolant level (see Chapter 1) and add, if necessary.

Idle Air Control (IAC) valve

Check

Refer to illustrations 17.16a and 17.16b

14   The idle air control valve (IAC) controls the engine idle speed. This output actuator is mounted on the throttle body and is controlled by voltage pulses sent from the ECM (computer). The IAC valve pintle moves in or out allowing more or less intake air into the system according to the engine conditions. To increase idle speed, the ECM retracts the IAC valve pintle away from the seat and allows more air to bypass the throttle bore. To decrease idle speed, the ECM extends the IAC valve pintle towards the seat, reducing the air flow.

15   To check the IAC valve, unplug the electrical connector and, using an ohmmeter, measure the resistance across terminals A and B, then terminals C and D. Each resistance check should indicate 20 ohms or greater. If not, replace the IAC valve.

16   Next, remove the valve (see Step 17) and inspect it:

a) *Check the pintle for excessive carbon*

17.18 You'll need a Torx driver to remove the IAC valve retaining screw on some models (arrows)

17.32 If you plan to install the same TPS, be sure to make an alignment mark between the TPS and the throttle body

17.34 The TPS lever (A) must mate with the TPS drive lever (B) when you attach the TPS to the throttle body

deposits. If necessary, clean it with carburetor cleaner spray **(see illustration)**. *Also clean the IAC valve housing to remove any deposits* **(see illustration)**.

b) *Next, apply battery voltage to the IAC valve terminals (one at a time) while holding the valve against a good ground. Make sure the valve pintle extends and retracts with the voltage signal. If there is no movement from the valve, replace it with a new one.*

Removal

Refer to illustration 17.18

17   Unplug the electrical connector from the Idle Air Control (IAC) valve.

18   Unscrew the valve or remove the two IAC valve attaching screws and withdraw the valve **(see illustration)**.

19   Check the condition of the rubber O-ring. If it's hardened or deteriorated, replace it. On models equipped with a gasket, remove the gasket.

20   Clean the sealing surface and the bore of the idle air/vacuum signal housing assembly to ensure a good seal. **Caution:** *The IAC valve itself is an electrical component and must not be soaked in any liquid cleaner, as damage may result.*

21   Before installing the IAC valve, the position of the pintle must be checked. If the pintle is extended too far, damage to the assembly may occur.

Installation

22   Measure the distance from the flange or gasket mounting surface of the IAC valve to the tip of the pintle **(see illustration 16.18a)**.

23   If the distance is greater than 1-1/8 inch, reduce it by applying firm hand pressure on the pintle **(see illustration 16.18b)** to retract it (a slight side-to-side motion may help).

24   Position the new O-ring or gasket on the IAC valve. Lubricate the O-ring with a light film of engine oil. If the IAC valve is the screw-in type, apply a light film of RTV sealant to the threads of the valve.

25   Install the IAC valve and tighten the

valve or the mounting screws securely.

26   Plug in the electrical connector at the IAC valve assembly. **Note:** *No adjustment is made to the IAC assembly after reinstallation. The IAC resetting is controlled by the ECM when the engine is started.*

Throttle Position Sensor (TPS)

Check

27   Check for stored trouble codes in the ECM (see Chapter 6).

28   To check the operation of the TPS, connect the positive probe of a high-impedance digital voltmeter to the terminal of the TPS with the dark-blue wire and the negative probe to the TPS ground wire, which will either be black or black with an orange stripe. Turn the ignition switch to the On position (don't start the engine). With the throttle in the closed (idle) position, the voltmeter should indicate approximately 0.45 to 1.25 volts. Now open the throttle completely and check the voltmeter - it should read approximately 4.5 volts.

29   If the TPS doesn't respond as described, replace it.

Replacement

Refer to illustrations 17.32 and 17.34

Note: *Only Throttle Position Sensors with slotted mounting holes are adjustable.*

30   Unplug the electrical connector from the TPS.

31   If the TPS is located on the underside of the throttle body, remove the throttle body as described in Steps 4 through 10.

32   If you intend to install the same TPS, scribe or paint an alignment mark between the TPS and the throttle body **(see illustration)**. If you're installing a new TPS, you'll have to set it with a voltmeter.

33   Remove the TPS screws and detach the TPS from the throttle body.

34   Installation is the reverse of removal. Be sure to install the TPS onto the throttle body with the throttle valve in the closed position. Make sure the TPS lever lines up with the TPS drive lever on the throttle shaft **(see**

illustration). On models that don't have a lever, make sure the slot in the TPS aligns with the end of the throttle shaft.

35   Install the screws and retainers. Tighten the screws finger-tight at this time.

36   Plug in the electrical connector to the TPS and connect a high-impedance digital voltmeter as described in Step 28. Turn the ignition to the On position and, with the throttle shaft in the closed position, rotate the TPS to obtain a voltmeter reading of 0.55 +/- 0.05 volts. Tighten the TPS mounting screws and recheck the voltmeter reading to verify that the adjustment has not changed.

37   If the throttle body was removed, reinstall it (see Steps 11 through 13).

Air intake plenum (2.2L, 2.8L and 3.1L engines only)

Refer to illustration 17.44

Note: *This component is sometimes referred to as the upper intake manifold.*

Removal

38   Disconnect the cable from the negative terminal of the battery. **Caution:** *If the vehicle is equipped with a Delco Loc II audio system, make sure you have the correct activation code before disconnecting the battery. See the information at the front of this manual for the radio re-activation procedure.*

39   Detach the air intake duct from the throttle body.

40   Disconnect the accelerator cable, transmission control cable and cruise control cable (if equipped) from the throttle lever. Unbolt the accelerator cable bracket and position the bracket and cables aside.

41   Detach any hoses and electrical connectors from the throttle body and plenum. If necessary, mark them with pieces of numbered tape to avoid confusion during reassembly.

42   On V6 models, remove the EGR valve (see Chapter 6). On 2.2L four-cylinder models, unscrew the EGR tube fitting.

43   If necessary, remove the bolts which

17.44 Location of the plenum mounting bolts (arrows) - 2.8L V6 engine

17.51 Use a back-up wrench when disconnecting the fuel lines

17.53a Before removing the injector electrical connectors, label the connectors according to cylinder number

secure the plastic spark plug wire shield and detach the shield.

44   Remove the plenum bolts and lift the plenum from the intake manifold (see illustration). If the plenum sticks, use a block of wood and a hammer to dislodge it. Don't pry between the sealing flanges, as this will damage the machined surfaces and could cause vacuum leaks to develop.

45   Remove all traces of old gasket material from the plenum and intake manifold mating surfaces. It's a good idea to stuff rags into the intake manifold openings to prevent debris from falling in.

Installation

46   Install the new gasket(s) and set the plenum into position.

47   Install the plenum bolts and tighten them to the torque listed in this Chapter's Specifications in a criss-cross pattern.

48   The remainder of installation is the reverse or removal.

Fuel rail and injectors

Note: Refer to Section 13 for the injector checking procedure.

V6 engines

Refer to illustrations 17.51, 17.53a, 17.53b, 17.54a, 17.54b, 17.55, 17.56a, 17.56b and 17.57

Warning: *Before any work is performed on the fuel lines, fuel rail or injectors, the fuel system pressure must be relieved (see Section 2).*

49   Detach the negative battery cable from the battery. **Caution:** *If the vehicle is equipped with a Delco Loc II audio system, make sure you have the correct activation code before disconnecting the battery. See the information at the front of this manual for the radio re-activation procedure.*

50   Remove the plenum following the procedure described earlier in this Section (2.8L and 3.1L engines only).

51   Using a backup wrench, disconnect the fuel lines at the fuel rail (see illustration). If you're working on a 1985 or 1986 2.8L V6 engine, disconnect the cold start valve tube from the fitting on the fuel rail.

52   Detach the vacuum line at the fuel pressure regulator.

53   Label and unplug the injector electrical

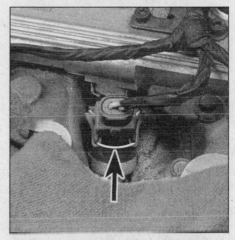

17.53b To remove the connector, push in the retaining clip and pull up

connectors (see illustrations).

54   Remove the fuel rail retaining bolts (see illustrations).

55   Carefully remove the fuel rail with the

17.54a To remove the fuel rail assembly, remove the retaining bolts (arrows) (1987 and later 2.8L/3.1L V6 shown)

17.54b To detach the fuel rail from the plenum, remove the nut (A) that attaches the alternator bracket to the right front fuel rail mounting bolt, then remove the four fuel rail bolts (B) - 3.0 and 3.3L engines

17.55 Use a gentle side-to-side rocking motion while pulling straight up to release the injectors from their bores in the intake manifold

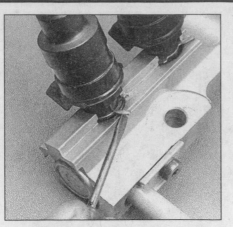

17.56A To remove an injector that is retained by a retaining clip, rotate the tang of the clip with a screwdriver until the clip is released, then pull the injector out of the fuel rail

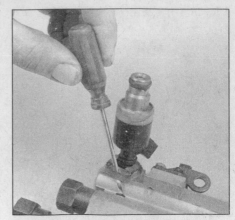

17.56b To remove an injector that is retained by a spring clip, simply pry off the clip with a small screwdriver, then pull the injector from the fuel rail

injectors **(see illustration)**. **Caution:** *Use care when handling the fuel rail assembly to avoid damaging the injectors..* **Note:** *An identification number is stamped on the side of the fuel rail assembly. Refer to this number if servicing or parts replacement is required.*

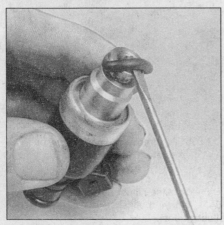

17.57 If you plan to use the same injectors, be sure to replace the O-rings with new ones

56   To remove the fuel injectors on 1985 and 1986 2.8L engines, rotate the injector retaining clip and pull the injector from the fuel rail **(see illustration)**. On all other models spread open the end of the injector clip slightly and remove it from the fuel rail, then extract the injector **(see illustration)**.

57   Remove the injector O-ring seals **(see illustration)**.

58   Install the new O-ring seal(s), as required, on the injector(s) and lubricate them with a light film of engine oil.

59   Install the injectors on the fuel rail.

60   Secure the injectors with the retainer clips.

61   Installation is the reverse of the removal procedure.

2.2L four-cylinder engine

Refer to illustrations 17.65, 17.67 and 17.68

Warning: *Relieve the fuel system pressure before beginning this procedure.*

Note: *The fuel rail on this engine is integral with the lower intake manifold.*

62   Detach the negative battery cable from the battery. **Caution:** *If the vehicle is*

equipped with a Delco Loc II audio system, make sure you have the correct activation code before disconnecting the battery. See the information at the front of this manual for the radio re-activation procedure.

63   Remove the air intake plenum (see Step 38).

64   Remove the fuel pressure regulator (see the procedure beginning with Step 87). **Caution:** *Failure to do this will result in a large amount of fuel draining into the cylinders when the injectors are removed. Be prepared for fuel spillage.*

65   Remove the injector retainer screws and retainer **(see illustration)**. **Caution:** *Don't try to remove the injectors along with the retainer. Slide the retainer off the injectors far enough to completely disengage the injectors from the slots in the retainer.*

66   Disconnect the electrical connectors from the injectors.

67   Remove the injectors from the lower intake manifold **(see illustration)**. Be sure to check the injector mounting holes for O-rings that may have fallen off the injectors.

68   If the original injectors are being installed, be sure to use new O-rings **(see illustration)**.

17.65 Remove the injector retainer bolts using a Torx driver, then detach the retainer

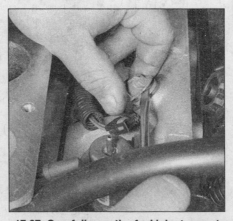

17.67 Carefully pry the fuel injectors out of the manifold

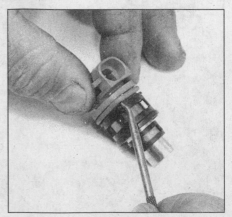

17.68 Remove the upper O-ring using a curved pick or screwdriver (the lower O-ring has already been removed)

17.79a A Torx driver is needed to remove the fuel pressure regulator mounting screws

17.79b Separate the fuel rail(s) from the regulator

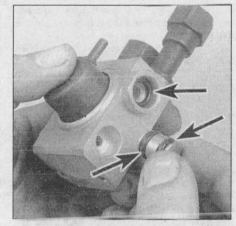

17.80 Always replace all O-rings when installing the regulator

69   Before installing the injectors, apply a light film of engine oil to the O-rings.
70   Install the injectors in their holes, using a twisting motion. Plug in the electrical connectors.
71   Install the injector retainer, making sure each injector properly fits into its retaining slot. Apply a non-hardening thread locking compound to the retainer screws and tighten the screws to the torque listed in this Chapter's Specifications.
72   The remainder of installation is the reverse of removal. **Caution:** *Because these injectors are the bottom-feed type, it is important to make sure that they are properly seated inside the intake manifold before starting the engine. If they are not seating correctly, fuel pressure inside the fuel rail portion of the intake manifold will force excessive amounts of fuel into the cylinders and possibly damage the engine. To check the seal, refer to Section 3 and check the fuel pressure with the ignition key ON (don't start the engine). If the fuel system holds pressure (gauge remains steady), the fuel system is sealed properly and the engine can be started safely.*

Fuel pressure regulator
Check
73   Refer to Section 3 for the fuel pressure checking procedure.

Replacement
2.8L/3.1L V6 engines
Refer to illustrations 17.79a, 17.79b and 17.80
74   Relieve the fuel system pressure (see Section 2).
75   Disconnect the cable from the negative terminal of the battery. **Caution:** *If the vehicle is equipped with a Delco Loc II audio system, make sure you have the correct activation code before disconnecting the battery. See the information at the front of this manual for the radio re-activation procedure.*
76   Remove the fuel rail following the procedure described earlier in this Section.
77   **Note:** *The manufacturer states that the fuel pressure regulator on 1985 and 1986 2.8L V6 engines is not serviceable. Check with your local auto parts store regarding the availability of placement parts.*
78   Unscrew the two fuel line fittings from the pressure regulator assembly.

79   Remove the pressure regulator mounting screws **(see illustration)** and separate the two fuel rails from the pressure regulator assembly **(see illustration)**.
80   Reassembly is the reverse of disassembly. Be sure to replace all gaskets and seals **(see illustration)**, otherwise a dangerous fuel leak may develop. When installing the seals, lubricate them with a light film of engine oil.

3.0L, 3.3L and 3.8L V6 engines
Refer to illustrations 17.83 and 17.84
81   Relieve the fuel system pressure (see Section 2).
82   Disconnect the cable from the negative terminal of the battery. **Caution:** *If the vehicle is equipped with a Delco Loc II audio system, make sure you have the correct activation code before disconnecting the battery. See the information at the front of this manual for the radio re-activation procedure.*
83   Detach the vacuum hose from the regulator **(see illustration)**.
84   Detach the fuel return line from the bottom of the regulator **(see illustration)**. Some models use a threaded fitting. On other models, the return line is secured by a screw. On this type of return line, be sure to install a new O-ring during reassembly.

17.83 To remove the fuel pressure regulator from the fuel rail, detach the vacuum hose (A), unscrew the fuel return line fitting (B) and remove the mounting bolts (C)

17.84 Use a back-up wrench when disconnecting the fuel return line fitting at the pressure regulator

85   Remove the pressure regulator mounting bolt(s) and detach the regulator from the fuel rail.

86   Installation is the reverse of removal. Be sure to use a new O-ring on the regulator and lubricate it with a light film of engine oil. If the regulator is equipped with a filter screen, make sure it's clean.

2.2L four-cylinder engine

87   Relieve the fuel system pressure (see Section 2).

88   Disconnect the cable from the negative terminal of the battery. **Caution:** *If the vehicle is equipped with a Delco Loc II audio system, make sure you have the correct activation code before disconnecting the battery. See the information at the front of this manual for the radio re-activation procedure.*

89   Detach the vacuum hose from the regulator.

90   Detach the fuel return line from the bottom of the regulator. Be sure to hold the regulator with a wrench while unscrewing the fitting.

91   Remove the regulator securing screw and detach the regulator from the lower intake manifold.

92   Installation is the reverse of removal. Be sure to use new O-rings on the regulator and return line and lubricate them with a light film of engine oil. If the regulator is equipped with a filter screen, make sure it's clean.

Cold start valve (1985 and 1986 2.8L V6 engines only)

93   Relieve the fuel system pressure (see Section 2).

94   Disconnect the cable from the negative terminal of the battery. **Caution:** *If the vehicle is equipped with a Delco Loc II audio system, make sure you have the correct activation code before disconnecting the battery. See the information at the front of this manual for the radio re-activation procedure.*

95   Remove the air intake plenum by following the procedure earlier in this Section.

96   Remove the cold start valve retaining bolt.

97   Unscrew the cold start tube fitting from the fuel rail.

98   Remove the valve.

99   Remove the valve from the tube and body assembly by bending the tab back and unscrewing the valve.

100 If the same valve is to be reinstalled, be sure to install new O-rings on each end of the valve and also on the end of the tube that connects to the fuel rail.

101 Turn the cold start valve completely into the tube and body assembly.

102 Turn the valve back one full turn, so the electrical connector is pointing up.

103 Bend the tang on the body forward to limit rotation of the valve.

104 Lubricate the O-rings with a light film of engine oil, then reinstall the valve by reversing the removal procedure.

---

18 Exhaust system components - general information, removal and installation

Refer to illustration 18.2

Warning: *The vehicle's exhaust system generates very high temperatures and should be allowed to cool down completely before any of the components are touched. Be especially careful around the catalytic converter, where the highest temperatures are generated.*

1   Replacement of exhaust system components is basically a matter of removing the heat shields, disconnecting the component and installing a new one. The heat shields and exhaust system hangers must be rein-

18.3 Check the crossover pipe for cracks in the flanges and the lead seal (arrow)

stalled in the original locations or damage could result. Due to the high temperatures and exposed locations of the exhaust system components, rust and corrosion can freeze parts together. Penetrating oils are available to help loosen frozen fasteners. However, in some cases it may be necessary to cut the pieces apart with a hacksaw or cutting torch. The latter method should be employed only by persons experienced in this work.

Crossover pipe

2   Remove the bolts or nuts securing the crossover pipe to the exhaust manifolds. Remove the crossover pipe.

3   Inspect the flanges and sealing areas of the pipe for cracks and carbon deposits, which would indicate leakage **(see illustration)**.

4   Installation is the reverse of removal. Tighten the fasteners evenly and securely.

Chapter 5
Engine electrical systems

Contents

Component location

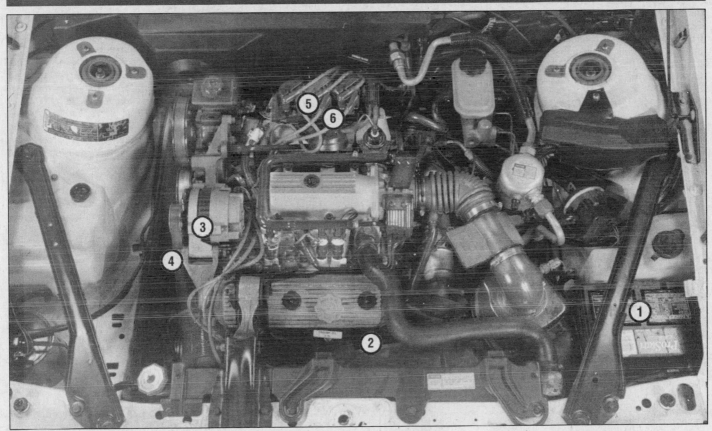

Typical V6 engine electrical system

1	Battery	3	Alternator	5	DIS coil pack (mounted	6	DIS ignition module
2	Starter	4	Crankshaft sensor		on the ignition module)		

1   Ignition system - general information

Warning: *Because of the very high voltage generated by the ignition system, extreme care should be taken whenever an operation involving ignition components is performed. This not only includes the distributor, coil(s), module and spark plug wires, but related items that are connected to the systems as well, such as the plug connections, tachometer and testing equipment.*

Early models are equipped with High Energy Ignition (HEI) systems, consisting of an ignition switch, battery, coil, primary (low tension) and secondary (high tension) wiring circuits, a distributor and spark plugs. Later models are equipped with a distributorless ignition system (either DIS or C3I - see below for further information).

High Energy Ignition (HEI) distributor

HEI equipped vehicles use a special HEI distributor with Electronic Spark Timing (EST). Some HEI distributors combine all the ignition components into one unit with the ignition coil in the distributor cap. On other HEI distributors, the coil is mounted separately.

All spark timing changes in the HEI/EST distributor are carried out by the Electronic Control Module (ECM), which monitors data from various engine sensors, computes the desired spark timing and signals the distributor to change the timing accordingly. No vacuum or mechanical advance is used.

Electronic Spark Control (ESC)

Some engines are equipped with an Electronic Spark Control (ESC), which uses a knock sensor in connection with the ECM to control spark timing to allow the engine to have maximum spark advance without spark knock. This improves drivability and fuel economy.

Direct Ignition System (DIS)

All distributorless four-cylinder and 2.8L and 3.1L V6 models use a distributorless ignition system called the Direct Ignition System (DIS). It use a "waste spark" method of spark distribution. Each cylinder is paired with its opposing cylinder in the firing order (1-4, 2-3 on a four, 1-4, 2-5, 3-6 on a V6) so that one cylinder on compression fires simultaneously with its opposing cylinder on exhaust. Since the cylinder on exhaust requires very little of the available voltage to fire its plug, most of the voltage is used to fire the cylinder on compression.

The DIS system includes a coil pack, an ignition module, a crankshaft reluctor ring, a magnetic crankshaft sensor and the ECM. The ignition module is located under the coil pack and is connected to the ECM.

The magnetic crankshaft sensor pro-

2.2 Remove the two brace bolts (arrows) and swing the brace in the direction shown

trudes through the engine block, within about 0.050-inch of the crankshaft reluctor ring. The reluctor ring is a special disc cast into the crankshaft, which acts as a signal generator for the ignition timing.

The system uses Electronic Spark Timing (EST) and control wires from the ECM, just like conventional distributor systems. The ECM controls timing using crankshaft position, engine rpm, engine temperature and manifold absolute pressure (MAP) sensing.

Computer Controlled Coil Ignition (C3I) system

The Computer Controlled Coil Ignition (C3I) distributorless ignition system is used on later 3.0L and all 3.3L and 3.8L V6 models. It is very similar to the DIS system, consisting of the ECM, ignition module, ignition coils, a "Hall effect" camshaft position sensor, the crankshaft position sensor and the connecting wires. On 3.0L and 3.3L models, the crank and cam sensor functions are combined into one dual sensor, called a combination sensor, which is mounted at the harmonic balancer.

Two types of module/coil assemblies are commonly used. They can be distinguished by the configuration of their coil towers: Type I module/coil assemblies have evenly spaced towers, with three on either side; Type IIs have all six towers (two per coil) placed on one side. The wiring harness and sensors, however, are interchangeable between either type.

The C3I system uses a waste spark method spark distribution. Each cylinder is paired with its opposite cylinder, i.e. 1-4, 5-2, 3-6. The spark occurs simultaneously in the cylinder coming up on compression and the cylinder coming up on exhaust.

The cylinder, on exhaust, requires very little of the available voltage to fire the spark plug. The remaining high voltage can then be used, as required, by the cylinder on compression.

The spark distribution is accomplished by a signal from the crank sensor, which is used by the ignition module to determine the proper time to trigger the next ignition coil. This signal is also processed by the C3I module into the reference signal used by the ECM.

The C3I system uses the electronic spark timing (EST) signal from the crankshaft, just like a HEI distributor ignition system equipped with EST, to control spark timing.

Timing is controlled by the ECM using the following inputs:

Crankshaft position
Engine speed (rpm)
Engine temperature
Amount of air entering the intake (mass air flow sensor)

2   Battery - removal and installation

Refer to illustration 2.2
Warning: *Hydrogen gas is produced by the battery, so keep open flames and lighted cigarettes away from it at all times. Always wear eye protection when working around a battery. Rinse off spilled electrolyte immediately with large amounts of water.*

1   The battery is located at the left front of the engine compartment.

Removal

2   Move the body brace (if equipped) out of the way **(see illustration).**
3   Detach the cables from the negative and positive terminals of the battery. **Caution 1:** *To prevent arcing, disconnect the negative (-) cable first, then remove the the positive (+) cable.* **Caution 2:** *If the vehicle is equipped with a Delco Loc II audio system, make sure you have the correct activation code before disconnecting the battery. See the information at the front of this manual for the radio re-activation procedure.*
4   Remove the hold-down clamp bolt and the clamp from the battery carrier.
5   Carefully lift the battery from the carrier. **Warning:** *Always keep the battery in an upright position to reduce the likelihood of electrolyte spillage. If you spill electrolyte on your skin, rinse it off immediately with large amounts of water.*

Installation

Note: *The battery carrier and hold-down clamp should be clean and free from corrosion before installing the battery. Make certain that there are no parts in the carrier before installing the battery.*
6   Set the battery in position in its carrier. Don't tilt it.
7   Install the hold-down clamp and bolt. The bolt should be snug, but overtightening it may damage the battery case.
8   Install both battery cables, positive first, then the negative. **Note:** *The battery terminals and cable ends should be cleaned prior*

to connection (see Chapter 1).

9   Reposition the body brace and install the bolts.

3   Battery - emergency jump starting

Refer to the booster battery (jump) starting procedure at the front of this manual.

4   Battery cables - check and replacement

1   Periodically inspect the entire length of each battery cable for damage, cracked or burned insulation and corrosion. Poor battery cable connections can cause starting problems and decreased engine performance.
2   Check the cable-to-terminal connections at the ends of the cables for cracks, loose wire strands and corrosion. The presence of white, fluffy deposits under the insulation at the cable terminal connection is a sign the cable is corroded and should be replaced. Check the terminals for distortion, missing mounting bolts or nuts and corrosion.
3   If only the positive cable is to be replaced, be sure to disconnect the negative cable from the battery first. **Caution:** *If the vehicle is equipped with a Delco Loc II audio system, make sure you have the correct activation code before disconnecting the battery. See the information at the front of this manual for the radio re-activation procedure.*
4   Disconnect and remove the cable. Make sure the replacement cable is the same length and diameter.
5   Clean the threads of the starter or ground connection with a wire brush to remove rust and corrosion. Apply a light coat of petroleum jelly to the threads to ease installation and prevent future corrosion.
6   Attach the cable to the starter or ground connection and tighten the mounting nut securely.
7   Before connecting the new cable to the battery, make sure it reaches the terminals without having to be stretched.
8   Connect the positive cable first, followed by the negative cable. Tighten the nuts and apply a thin coat of petroleum jelly to the terminal and cable connection.

5   Ignition system - check

Refer to illustration 5.2
Warning: *Because of the very high voltage generated by the ignition system, extreme care should be taken whenever an operation is performed involving ignition components. This not only includes the distributor, coil(s), control module and spark plug wires, but related items that are connected to the sys-*

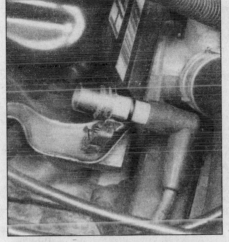

5.2 To use a calibrated ignition tester (available at most auto parts stores), simply disconnect a spark plug wire, attach the wire to the tester, clip the tester to a convenient ground (like a valve cover bolt) and operate the starter - if there's enough power to fire the plug, sparks will be visible between the electrode tip and the tester body

tem as well, such as the plug connections, tachometer and any test equipment.
1   If the engine turns over but won't start, disconnect the spark plug wire from any spark plug and attach it to a calibrated ignition tester (available at most auto parts stores).
2   Connect the clip on the tester to a bolt or metal bracket on the engine **(see illustration)** If you're unable to obtain a calibrated ignition tester, remove the wire from one of the spark plugs and, using an insulated tool, hold the end of the wire about 1/4-inch from a good ground.
3   Crank the engine and watch the end of the tester or spark plug wire to see if bright blue, well-defined sparks occur. If you're not using a calibrated tester, have an assistant crank the engine for you. **Warning:** *Keep clear of drivebelts and other moving engine components that could injure you.*
4   If sparks occur, sufficient voltage is reaching the plug to fire it (repeat the check at the remaining plug wires to verify the wires, distributor cap and rotor [if equipped] or other coils [distributorless systems] are OK). However, the plugs themselves may be fouled, so remove them and check them as described in Chapter 1.
5   On distributor (HEI) systems, if no sparks or intermittent sparks occur, remove the distributor cap and check the cap and rotor as described in Chapter 1. If moisture is present, dry out the cap and rotor, then reinstall the cap.
6   On distributor systems with a separate coil, if there's still no spark, detach the coil secondary wire from the distributor cap and hook it up to the tester (reattach the plug wire to the spark plug), then repeat the spark

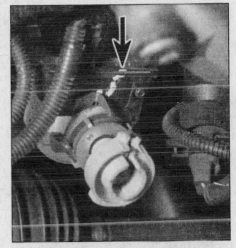

6.4 Mark the position of the rotor to the distributor before removing the distributor - also mark the relationship of the distributor to the engine block

check. Again, if you don't have a tester, hold the end of the wire about 1/4-inch from a good ground. If sparks occur now, the distributor cap, rotor or plug wire(s) may be defective.
7   On all models, if no sparks occur, check the spark plug wires and the wire connections at the coil(s) to make sure they're clean and tight. Check for voltage to the coil. Make any necessary repairs, then repeat the check again.
8   On distributor systems with a separate coil, if there's still no spark, the coil-to-cap wire may be bad (check the resistance with an ohmmeter - it should be 7000 ohms per foot or less). If a known good wire doesn't make any difference in the test results, the ignition module may be defective.

6   HEI distributor - removal and installation

Removal

Refer to illustrations 6.4 and 6.5
1   Disconnect the cable from the negative battery terminal. **Caution:** *If the vehicle is equipped with a Delco Loc II audio system, make sure you have the correct activation code before disconnecting the battery. See the information at the front of this manual for the radio re-activation procedure.*
2   Remove the coil wire or small wire electrical connections from the distributor cap.
3   Remove the distributor cap (see Chapter 1).
4   Note the position of the rotor and the distributor-to-block alignment. Make an alignment mark on the distributor to indicate the position of the rotor **(see illustration)**. Also make a mark to indicate distributor-to-block relationship.
5   Remove the distributor hold-down

6.5 The distributor hold-down clamp and bolt must be removed before the distributor can be removed from the engine (four-cylinder engine shown)

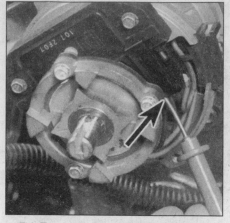

7.4 To check the module for voltage, insert the voltmeter probe into the module positive terminal (arrow)

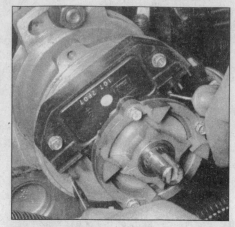

7.6 With a test light connected at terminal "P," check the voltage with the meter probe at the "C" terminal

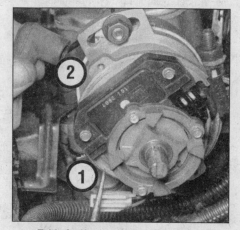

7.11 As the test light probe (1) is removed, check for a spark at the coil wire (2)

clamp bolt and clamp **(see illustration)**. Remove the distributor from the engine. **Caution:** *Do not turn the crankshaft while the distributor is removed from the engine. If the crankshaft is turned, the position of the rotor will be altered and the engine will have to be re-timed.*

Installation (crankshaft not turned after distributor removal)

6   Insert the distributor into the engine in exactly the same relation to the block in which it was removed. To mesh the gears, it may be necessary to turn the rotor slightly. At this point the distributor may not seat down against the block completely. This is due to the lower end of the distributor shaft not mating properly with the oil pump shaft. **Note:** *On four-cylinder models the distributor mates with the camshaft.* If this is the case, check again to make sure the distributor is aligned with the block in the same position it was in before removal and that the rotor is correctly aligned with the distributor body. The gear on the distributor shaft is engaged with the gear on the camshaft, and this relationship cannot change as long as the distributor is not lifted from the engine. Use a socket and breaker bar on the crankshaft bolt to turn the engine over in the normal direction of rotation. The rotor will turn, but the oil pump shaft will not because the two shafts are not engaged. When the proper alignment is reached the distributor will drop down over the oil pump shaft, and the distributor body will seat properly against the block.
7   Install the hold-down clamp and tighten the bolt securely.
8   Install the distributor cap and coil wire.
9   Connect the cable to the negative terminal of the battery.

Installation (crankshaft turned after distributor removal)

10   Remove the number one spark plug.

11   Place your finger over the spark plug hole while turning the crankshaft in the normal direction of rotation with a wrench on the pulley bolt at the front of the engine.
12   When you feel compression, continue turning the crankshaft slowly until the timing mark on the crankshaft pulley is aligned with the "0" on the engine timing indicator.
13   Position the rotor to point at the number one distributor terminal.
14   Insert the distributor into the engine in exactly the same relation to the block in which it was removed. To mesh the gears, it may be necessary to turn the rotor slightly. If the distributor does not seat fully against the block it is because the oil pump shaft has not seated in the distributor shaft. Make sure the distributor drive gear is fully engaged with the camshaft gear, then use a socket on the crankshaft bolt to turn the engine over in the normal direction of rotation until the two shafts engage and the distributor seats against the block.
15   Install the hold-down clamp and tighten the bolt securely.
16   Install the distributor cap and coil wire.
17   Connect the cable to the negative terminal of the battery.

7   Ignition module and distributorless ignition system sensors - check and replacement

HEI (distributor) ignition system

Note: *It is not necessary to remove the distributor to check or replace the module.*

Check

Refer to illustrations 7.4, 7.6 and 7.11
1   Disconnect the tachometer (if so equipped) at the distributor.
2   Check for a spark at the coil and spark plug wires (Section 5).
3   If there is no spark, remove the distributor cap. Remove the ignition module from the distributor but leave the connector plugged in.
4   With the ignition switch turned On, check for voltage at the module positive terminal **(see illustration)**.
5   If the reading is less than ten volts, there is a fault in the wire between the module positive (+) terminal and the ignition coil positive connector or the ignition coil and primary circuit-to-ignition switch.
6   If the reading is ten volts or more, check the "C" terminal on the module **(see illustration)**.
7   If the reading is less than one volt, there is an open or grounded lead in the distributor-to-coil "C" terminal connection or ignition coil or an open primary circuit in the coil itself.
8   If the reading is one to ten volts, replace the module with a new one and check for a spark (Section 5). If there is a spark the module was faulty and the system is now operating properly. If there is no spark, there is a fault in the ignition coil.
9   If the reading in Step 4 is 10 volts or more, unplug the pickup coil connector from

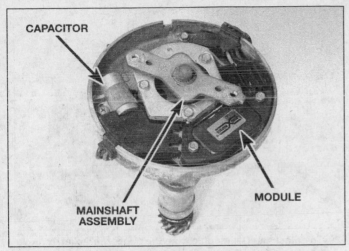

7.16 Silicone lubricant applied to the distributor base in the area under the ignition module dissipates heat and prevents module failure

7.23 Unbolt and unplug the connector from the right end of the C3I ignition coil/module assembly

the module. Check the "C" terminal voltage with the ignition switch On and watch the voltage reading as a test light is momentarily (five seconds or less) connected between the battery positive (+) terminal and the module "P" terminal **(see illustration 7.6)**.

10   If there is no drop in voltage, check the module ground and, if it is good, replace the module with a new one.

11   If the voltage drops, check for spark at the coil wire as the test light is removed from the module terminal. If there is no spark, the module is faulty and should be replaced with a new one. If there is a spark, the pick-up coil or connections are faulty or not grounded **(see illustration)**.

Replacement
Refer to illustration 7.16

12   Detach the cable from the negative terminal of the battery. **Caution:** *If the vehicle is equipped with a Delco Loc II audio system, make sure you have the correct activation code before disconnecting the battery. See the information at the front of this manual for the radio re-activation procedure.*

13   Remove the distributor cap and rotor (see Chapter 1).

14   Remove both module attaching screws and lift the module up and away from the distributor.

15   Disconnect both electrical leads from the module. Note that the leads cannot be interchanged.

16   Do not wipe the grease from the module or the distributor base if the same module is to be reinstalled. If a new module is to be installed, a package of silicone grease will be included with it. Wipe the distributor base and the new module clean, then apply the silicone grease on the face of the module and on the distributor base where the module seats **(see illustration)**. This grease is necessary for heat dissipation.

17   Install the module and attach both electrical leads.

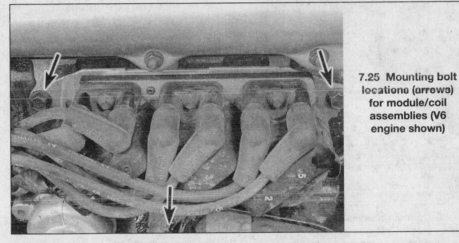

7.25 Mounting bolt locations (arrows) for module/coil assemblies (V6 engine shown)

18   Install the distributor rotor and cap (see Chapter 1).

19   Attach the cable to the negative terminal of the battery.

Distributorless ignition systems (DIS and C3I)
Check

20   Because of the complex nature of these systems and their interrelationship with the engine management system, complete troubleshooting is beyond the scope of the home mechanic. Check for trouble codes (see Chapter 6), check the spark plug wires and spark plugs (see Chapter 1), check for a loose electrical connection at the coils, perform a basic ignition system check (see Section 5) and check the coils (see Section 9). If you are not able to identify the problem, take the vehicle to a dealer service department or other qualified shop for complete diagnosis.

Ignition module replacement
Refer to illustrations 7.23, 7.25, 7.28 and 7.29

21   Detach the cable from the negative terminal of the battery. **Caution:** *If the vehicle is equipped with a Delco Loc II audio system,*

make sure you have the correct activation code before disconnecting the battery. See the information at the front of this manual for the radio re-activation procedure.

22   Clearly label, then disconnect, all spark plug wires from the DIS or C3I assembly. **Note:** *On 2.8L and 3.1L engines, it may be necessary to remove the engine cooling fan (see Chapter 3) and raise the vehicle to gain access to the DIS assembly, which is located on the front side of the engine.* **Warning:** *Always support the vehicle securely on jackstands when it's raised.*

23   Unbolt or unplug the electrical connector at the module **(see illustration)**

24   If equipped, detach the vacuum lines and the electrical connector from the EGR valve solenoid on the left end of the coil/module assembly.

25   Unbolt and remove the DIS or C3I and support bracket assembly **(see illustration)**. **Caution:** *On 2.5L four-cylinder models, lift off the assembly very carefully, since the crankshaft position sensor, which protrudes into the engine block, is attached to the bottom of the assembly.*

26   Using a Torx screwdriver or bit (most models), remove the coil-to-module attach-

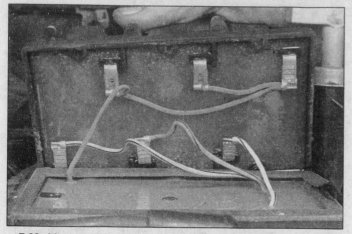

7.28 After removing the screws that hold the coil and module assemblies together, label, then detach, the wires from the module

7.29 To detach the C3I module from the support bracket, remove the three nuts

7.32 On most models, the electrical connector for the crankshaft sensor is located near the starter motor

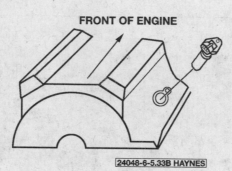

FRONT OF ENGINE

24048-6-5.33B HAYNES

7.37 The 2.8L/3.1L V6 engine crankshaft sensor (arrow) is bolted to the firewall side of the engine block

7.38 The camshaft sensor is located near the water pump (arrow)

ing screws.

27   Separate the coil and module assemblies.

28   Open the coil and module halves as shown **(see illustrations)**. Label, then detach, the wires between the module and the coil assemblies from the spade terminals on the underside of the coils.

29   Unbolt the module **(see illustration)** from the support bracket.

30   Installation is the reverse of removal. Be sure to attach the wires of the new module to the coil assembly spade terminals in exactly the same order in which they were removed.

Crankshaft or combination sensor replacement

3.0L, 3.3L and 3.8L V6 models

Refer to illustration 7.32

31   Remove the crankshaft balancer (vibration damper) (see Chapter 2, Part D).

32   Disconnect the electrical connector for the sensor **(see illustration)**.

33   Unbolt and remove the sensor.

34   Check the interrupter rings on the back of the crankshaft balancer for damage and

bends. Replace the balancer as an assembly if any problems exist. A special tool which fits over the end of the crankshaft should be used to check the interrupter rings and adjust the new sensor.

35   Installation is the reverse of removal. Before tightening the mounting bolts, adjust the sensor with the special tool.

2.5L four-cylinder models

36   The crankshaft sensor is attached to the bottom of the DIS assembly. After carefully lifting the assembly off the engine block (see Steps 21 through 25 above), unbolt the sensor from the bottom of the base plate. Installation is the reverse of removal.

2.2L four-cylinder and 2.8L/3.1L V6 models

Refer to illustration 7.37

37   Unplug the electrical connector, remove the bolt and carefully lift the sensor out of the engine block **(see illustration)**.

Camshaft sensor replacement (3.8L models only)

Refer to illustration 7.38

38   The sensor is located just below the water pump pulley, towards the front of the

vehicle **(see illustration)**. Disconnect the electrical connector, remove the bolt and detach the sensor. Installation is the reverse of removal.

8   Ignition pickup coil (HEI systems) - check and replacement

Refer to illustrations 8.5a, 8.5b, 8.9 and 8.10

Check

1   Detach the cable from the negative terminal of the battery. **Caution:** *If the vehicle is equipped with a Delco Loc II audio system, make sure you have the correct activation code before disconnecting the battery. See the information at the front of this manual for the radio re-activation procedure.*

2   Remove the distributor cap and rotor (see Chapter 1).

3   Remove the distributor from the engine (see Section 6). **Note:** *This Step is necessary on most models, since it is difficult to gain access to the pick-up coil wires in the distributor. If access on your vehicle is relatively*

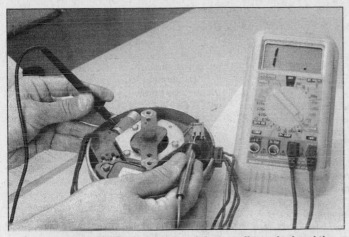

8.5a Connect the ohmmeter to a pick-up coil terminal and the distributor body. If continuity is indicated, there is a short from the pick-up coil wiring to the distributor body

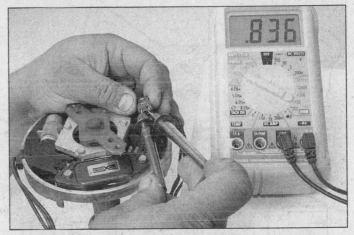

8.5b Connect the ohmmeter to the pick-up coil terminals as shown and measure the resistance of the pick-up coil. It should be between 500 and 1,500 ohms

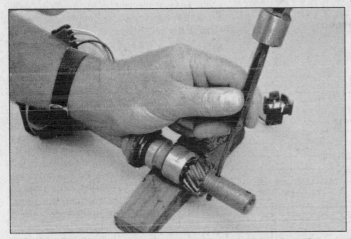

8.9 To remove the distributor shaft assembly, place the distributor assembly in a soft-jawed vise and knock out the roll pin with a punch and hammer

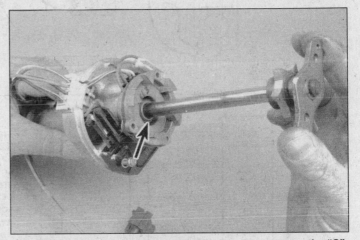

8.10 Remove the shaft from the distributor, then remove the "C" clip (arrow) to remove the pickup coil assembly

unrestricted, this Step may not be necessary.

4   Detach the pickup coil wires from the module.

5   Connect one lead of an ohmmeter to the terminal of the pickup coil lead and the other to ground as shown **(see illustrations)**. Flex the leads by hand to check for intermittent opens. The ohmmeter should indicate infinite resistance at all times. If it doesn't, the pickup coil is defective and must be replaced.

6   Connect the ohmmeter leads to both terminals of the pickup coil wires. Flex the wires by hand to check for intermittent opens. The ohmmeter should read one steady value between 500 and 1500 ohms as the leads are flexed by hand. If it doesn't, the pickup coil is defective and must be replaced.

Replacement

7   Remove distributor, if not already done, then remove the spring from the distributor shaft.

8   Mark the distributor gear drive and shaft so that they can be reassembled in the same position.

9   Carefully mount the distributor in a soft-jawed vise and, using a hammer and punch, remove the roll pin from the distributor shaft and gear **(see illustration)**. Pull the shaft out of the distributor body. **Caution:** *If the shaft binds when being pulled out, you may need to lightly sand the lower shaft area so it will pull through without binding.*

10   To remove the pick up coil, remove the thin "C" clip **(see illustration)**. **Note:** *On some models, you may have to unbolt a shield to gain access to the "C" clip.*

11   Lift the pickup coil assembly straight up and remove it from the distributor.

12   Reassembly is the reverse of disassembly.

13   Installation is the reverse of removal.

9   Ignition coil - removal, testing and installation

1   Disconnect the cable from the negative terminal of the battery. **Caution:** *If the vehicle*

is equipped with a Delco Loc II audio system, make sure you have the correct activation code before disconnecting the battery. See the information at the front of this manual for the radio re-activation procedure.

HEI (distributor) ignition systems

Removal

2   On models with a separately mounted coil, unplug the coil high tension wire and both electrical leads from the coil.

3   Remove both mounting nuts and remove the coil from the engine.

4   On models with the coil in the distributor cap, remove the coil cover screws and lift off the cover. **Note:** *If you are just checking the coil, it is not necessary to remove the coil from the cap. Refer to the checking procedure below.*

5   Push the coil electrical leads through the top of the hood with a small screwdriver.

6   Remove the coil mounting screws and lift the coil, with the leads, from the cap.

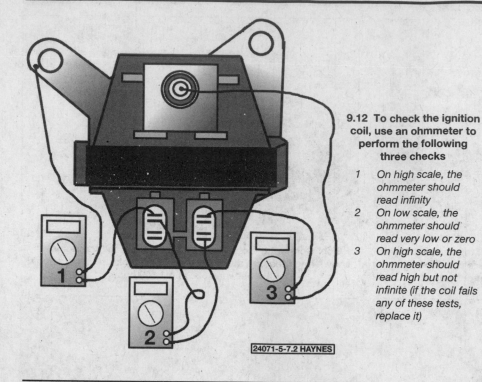

9.12 HAYNES

9.12 To check the ignition coil, use an ohmmeter to perform the following three checks

1   On high scale, the ohmmeter should read infinity
2   On low scale, the ohmmeter should read very low or zero
3   On high scale, the ohmmeter should read high but not infinite (if the coil fails any of these tests, replace it)

24071-5-7.2 HAYNES

Check

Coil-in cap models

7   It is not necessary to remove the coil from the distributor cap on coil-in-cap models to test the coil.

8   Disconnect the negative cable from the battery. **Caution:** *If the vehicle is equipped with a Delco Loc II audio system, make sure you have the correct activation code before disconnecting the battery. See the information at the front of this manual for the radio re-activation procedure.*

9   Remove the distributor cap and turn it over so the coil electrical connectors are visible.

10   Connect an ohmmeter to the two outer coil terminals. It should indicate zero resistance. If it doesn't, replace the coil.

11   Connect the ohmmeter between one of the outer terminals and the central coil-to-rotor contact with the ohmmeter on the high scale. Repeat the test using the other terminal. If both terminals show infinite resistance, replace the coil.

Models with a separately mounted coil

Refer to illustration 9.12

12   On models with a separately mounted

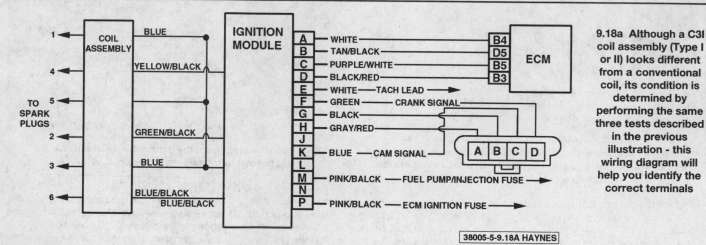

9.18a Although a C3I coil assembly (Type I or II) looks different from a conventional coil, its condition is determined by performing the same three tests described in the previous illustration - this wiring diagram will help you identify the correct terminals

38005-5-9.18A HAYNES

9.18b Test #2: Using the low scale, check the resistance between the positive terminal and the negative terminal

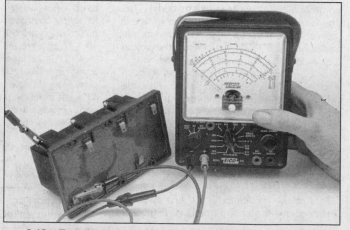

9.18c Test #3: Using the high scale, check the resistance between the negative terminal of the coil and the high tension tower terminal - it should be infinite

coil, check the coil for opens and grounds by performing the following three tests with an ohmmeter **(see illustration)**.

13 Using the ohmmeter's high scale, hook up the ohmmeter leads as illustrated (see test #1 in illustration 9.12). The ohmmeter should indicate a very high, or infinite, resistance value. If it doesn't, replace the coil.

14 Using the low scale, hook up the leads as illustrated (see test #2 in illustration 9.12). The ohmmeter should indicate a very low, or zero, resistance value. If it doesn't, replace the coil.

15 Using the high scale, hook up the leads as illustrated (see test #3 in illustration 9.12). The ohmmeter should not indicate an infinite resistance. If it does, replace the coil.

Installation

16 Installation of the coil is the reverse of the removal procedure.

Distributorless (DIS and C3I) ignition systems

Removal

17 Refer to Section 7 and remove the DIS or C3I coil/module assembly, then separate the coils from the module/bracket.

Check

Refer to illustrations 9.18a, 9.18b and 9.18c

18 The three-test checking procedure for the DIS coil is the same as the one outlined above for the HEI-type coil. However, the primary terminals are not marked; study the accompanying photos and wiring diagram before attempting to check the coil **(see illustrations)**.

Installation

19 Installation is the reverse of removal. Be careful when inserting the module/coil assembly to avoid damage to the sensor.

---

10 Hall effect switch (HEI systems) - check and replacement

Refer to illustration 10.2

1 Some HEI distributors are equipped with a Hall effect switch which is located above the pickup coil assembly. The Hall effect switch is used in place of the R terminal of the HEI distributor to send engine RPM information to the ECM.

2 Test the switch by connecting a 12-volt power supply and voltmeter as shown **(see illustration)**. Check the polarity markings carefully before making any connections.

3 When the feeler gauge is not inserted as shown, the voltmeter should read less than 0.5 volts. If the reading is more, the Hall effect switch is faulty and must be replaced by a new one.

4 With the feeler gauge inserted, the voltmeter should read within 0.5 volts of battery voltage. Replace the switch with a new one if the reading is more.

5 Remove the Hall effect switch by unplugging the connector and removing the retaining screws.

6 Installation is the reverse of removal.

---

11 Charging system - general information and precautions

Caution: *If the vehicle is equipped with a Delco Loc II audio system, make sure you have the correct activation code before disconnecting the battery. See the information at the front of this manual for the radio re-activation procedure.*

The charging system consists of a belt-driven alternator with an integral voltage regulator and the battery. These components work together to supply electrical power for the ignition system, the lights and all accessories.

There are two types of alternators used. Earlier vehicles use the SI type and later models are equipped with the CS type. There are two types of CS alternators in use, the CS-130 and the CS-144. All types use a conventional pulley and fan.

To determine which type of alternator is fitted to your vehicle, look at the fasteners employed to attach the two halves of the alternator housing. All CS models use rivets instead of screws. CS alternators are rebuildable once the rivets are drilled out. However, we don't recommend this practice. For all intents and purposes, CS types should be considered non-serviceable and, if found to be faulty, should be exchanged as cores for new or rebuilt units.

The purpose of the voltage regulator is to limit the alternator's voltage to a preset value. This prevents power surges, circuit overloads, etc., during peak voltage output. On all models with which this manual is concerned, the voltage regulator is contained within the alternator housing.

The charging system does not ordinarily require periodic maintenance. The drivebelts, electrical wiring and connections should, however, be inspected at the intervals suggested in Chapter 1.

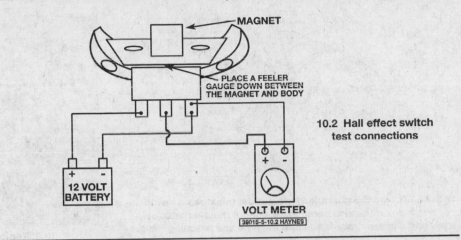

10.2 Hall effect switch test connections

Take extreme care when making circuit connections to a vehicle equipped with an alternator and note the following. When making connections to the alternator from a battery, always match correct polarity. Before using arc welding equipment to repair any part of the vehicle, disconnect the wires from the alternator and the battery terminal. Never start the engine with a battery charger connected. Always disconnect both battery leads before using a battery charger.

The charging indicator light on the dash lights when the ignition switch is turned on and goes out when the engine starts. If the light stays on or comes on once the engine is running, a charging system problem has occurred. See Section 12 for the proper diagnosis procedure for each type of alternator.

---

12 Charging system - check

Refer to illustration 12.5

1 If a malfunction occurs in the charging circuit, do not immediately assume that the alternator is causing the problem. First check the following items:

a) *The battery cables where they connect to the battery. Make sure the connections are clean and tight.*

b) *The battery electrolyte specific gravity. If it is low, charge the battery.*

c) *Check the external alternator wiring and connections. They must be in good condition.*

d) *Check the drivebelt condition and tension (Chapter 1).*

e) *Make sure the alternator mounting bolts are tight.*

f) *Run the engine and check the alternator for abnormal noise (may be caused by a loose drive pulley, loose mounting bolts, worn or dirty bearings, defective diode or defective stator).*

2 Using a voltmeter, check the battery voltage with the engine off. It should be approximately 12 volts.

3 Start the engine and check the battery voltage again. It should now be approximately 14 to 15 volts.

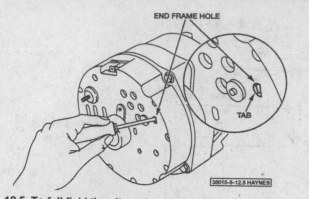

END FRAME HOLE

TAB

38015-5-12.5 HAYNES

12.5 To full field the alternator, ground the tab located inside the test hole on the end frame (backside) of the alternator by inserting a screwdriver blade into the hole and touching the tab and the case at the same time

13.2 Remove the alternator electrical connectors

4   Locate the test hole in the back of the alternator. **Note:** *If there is no test hole, your vehicle is equipped with a newer CS type alternator. Further testing of this type of alternator must be done by a dealer or automotive electrical shop.*

5   Ground the tab that is located inside the hole by inserting a screwdriver blade into the hole and touching the tab and the case at the same time **(see illustration). Caution:** *Do not run the engine with the tab grounded any longer than necessary to obtain a voltmeter reading. If the alternator is charging, it is running unregulated during the test. This condition may overload the electrical system and cause damage to the components.*

6   The reading on the voltmeter should be 15 volts or higher with the tab grounded in the test hole.

7   If the voltmeter indicates low battery voltage, the alternator is faulty and should be replaced with a new one (Section 13).

8   If the voltage reading is 15 volts or higher and a no charge condition is present, the regulator or field circuit is the problem. Remove the alternator (Section 13) and have it checked further by an auto electric shop.

13   Alternator - removal and installation

Refer to illustration 13.2

1   Detach the cable from the negative terminal of the battery. **Caution:** *If the vehicle is equipped with a Delco Loc II audio system, make sure you have the correct activation code before disconnecting the battery. See the information at the front of this manual for the radio re-activation procedure.*

2   Clearly label, if necessary, then unplug and unbolt the electrical connectors from the alternator **(see illustration).**

3   Remove the drivebelt (see Chapter 1).

4   Remove the alternator mounting bolts and remove the alternator.

5   Installation is the reverse of removal.

14.2 Mark the drive end frame and rectifier end frame assemblies with a scribe or paint before separating the two halves

14   Alternator brushes - replacement

Refer to illustrations 14.2, 14.3a, 14.3b, 14.4, 14.5, 14.6, 14.7 and 14.10

Note: *The following procedure applies only to SI type alternators. CS types have riveted housings and cannot be disassembled.*

1   Remove the alternator from the vehicle (Section 15).

2   Scribe or paint marks on the front and

14.3a With the through bolts removed, carefully separate the drive end frame and the rectifier end frame

rear end frame housings of the alternator to facilitate reassembly **(see illustration).**

3   Remove the four through-bolts holding the front and rear end frames together, then separate the drive end frame from the rectifier end frame **(see illustrations).**

4   Remove the bolts holding the stator to the rear end frame and separate the stator from the end frame **(see illustration).**

5   Remove the nuts attaching the diode

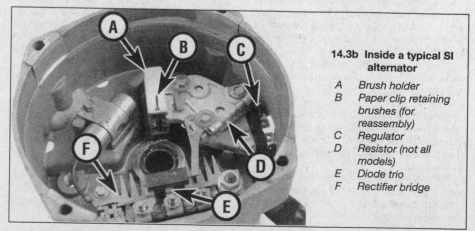

14.3b Inside a typical SI alternator

A   Brush holder
B   Paper clip retaining brushes (for reassembly)
C   Regulator
D   Resistor (not all models)
E   Diode trio
F   Rectifier bridge

14.4 After removing the bolts holding the stator assembly to the end frame, remove the stator

14.5 Remove the nuts attaching the diode trio to the rectifier bridge and remove the trio

14.6 After removing the screws that attach the brush holder and the resistor (if equipped) to the end frame, remove the brush holder

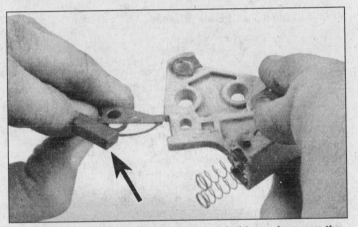

14.7 Slip the brush retainer off the brush holder and remove the brushes (arrow)

trio to the rectifier bridge and remove the trio **(see illustration)**.

6   Remove the screws attaching the resistor (not used on all models) and brush holder to the end frame and remove the brush holder **(see illustration)**.

14.10 To hold the brushes in place during reassembly, insert a paper clip through the hole in the end frame nearest to the rotor shaft

7   Remove the brushes from the brush holder by slipping the brush retainer off the brush holder **(see illustration)**.

8   Remove the springs from the brush holder.

9   Installation is the reverse of the removal procedure, noting the following:

10   When installing the brushes in the brush holder, install the brush closest to the end frame first. Slip the paper clip through the rear of the end frame to hold the brush, then insert the second brush and push the paper clip in to hold both brushes while reassembly is completed **(see illustration)**. The paper clip should not be removed until the front and rear end frames have been bolted together.

15   Starting system - general information

Caution: *If the vehicle is equipped with a Delco Loc II audio system, make sure you have the correct activation code before disconnecting the battery. See the information at the front of this manual for the radio re-activation procedure.*

The starting system is composed of a starting motor, solenoid and battery. The battery supplies the electrical energy to the solenoid, which then completes the circuit to the starting motor, which does the actual work of cranking the engine.

The solenoid and starting motor are mounted together at the lower front side of the engine. No periodic lubrication or maintenance is required.

The electrical circuitry of the vehicle is arranged so that the starter motor can only be operated when the clutch pedal is depressed (manual transaxle) or the transaxle selector lever is in Park or Neutral (automatic transaxle).

Never operate the starter motor for more than 15 seconds at a time without pausing to allow it to cool for at least two minutes.

Excessive cranking can cause overheating, which can seriously damage the starter.

16   Starter motor - testing in vehicle

Refer to illustration 16.6

1   If the starter motor does not turn at all when the switch is operated, make sure that the shift lever is in Neutral or Park (automatic

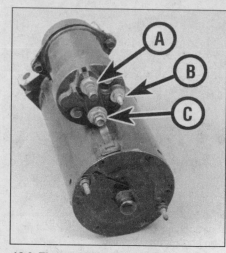

16.6 There are three terminals on the end of the typical starter solenoid

A *Battery terminal*
B *Switch terminal (S)*
C *Motor terminal (M)*

transaxle) or that the clutch pedal is depressed (manual transaxle).

2   Make sure that the battery is charged and that all cables, both at the battery and starter solenoid terminals, are secure.

3   If the starter motor spins but the engine is not cranking, the overrunning clutch in the starter motor is slipping and the motor must be removed from the engine for replacement.

4   If, when the switch is actuated, the starter motor does not operate at all but the solenoid clicks, then the problem lies with either the battery, the main solenoid contacts or the starter motor itself. **Note:** *Before diagnosing starter problems, make sure that the battery is fully charged.*

5   If the solenoid plunger cannot be heard when the switch is actuated, the solenoid itself is defective or the solenoid circuit is open.

6   To check the solenoid, connect a jumper lead between the battery (+) and the "S" terminal on the solenoid **(see illustration)**. If the starter motor now operates, the solenoid is OK and the problem is in the ignition switch, neutral start switch or in the wiring.

7   If the starter motor still does not operate, remove the starter/solenoid assembly for disassembly, testing and repair.

8   If the starter motor cranks the engine at an abnormally slow speed, first make sure that the battery is charged and that all terminal connections are tight. If the engine is partially seized, or has the wrong viscosity oil in it, it will crank slowly.

9   Run the engine until normal operating temperature is reached, then disconnect the

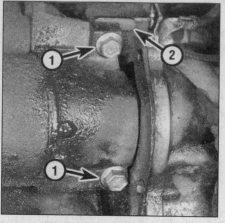

17.4 Typical starter motor installation details

1 *Starter bolts*
2 *Shim*

coil wire from the distributor cap and ground it on the engine.

10   Connect a voltmeter positive lead to the starter motor terminal of the solenoid and then connect the negative lead to ground.

11   Crank the engine and take the voltmeter readings as soon as a steady figure is indicated. Do not allow the starter motor to turn for more than 15 seconds at a time. A reading of 9 volts or more, with the starter motor turning at normal cranking speed, is normal. If the reading is 9 volts or more but the cranking speed is slow, the motor is faulty. If the reading is less than 9 volts and the cranking speed is slow, the solenoid contacts are probably burned.

17   Starter motor - removal and installation

Refer to illustration 17.4

1   Disconnect the negative battery cable. **Caution:** *If the vehicle is equipped with a Delco Loc II audio system, make sure you have the correct activation code before disconnecting the battery. See the information at the front of this manual for the radio re-activation procedure.*
Note: *On certain models, access to the starter is gained by removing the front exhaust manifold and moving the air conditioning condenser hose from the compressor out of the way. If this is the case, be sure to have the air conditioning system discharged prior to starting the job.*

2   Raise the front of the vehicle and support it securely on jackstands. Remove dust covers if equipped.

3   From under the vehicle, disconnect the

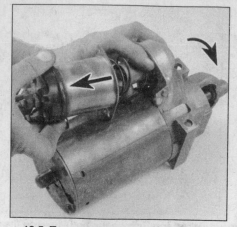

18.5 To remove the solenoid housing from the starter motor, remove the screws and turn it clockwise

solenoid wire and battery cable from the terminals on the rear of the solenoid.

4   Remove the starter motor bolts **(see illustration)**.

5   Remove the starter motor. Note the location of the spacer shim(s).

6   Installation is the reverse of removal. Be sure to install the spacer shim(s) in exactly the same location.

18   Starter solenoid - removal and installation

Refer to illustration 18.5

1   Disconnect the cable from the negative terminal of the battery. **Caution:** *If the vehicle is equipped with a Delco Loc II audio system, make sure you have the correct activation code before disconnecting the battery. See the information at the front of this manual for the radio re-activation procedure.*

2   Remove the starter motor (Section 17).

Removal

3   Disconnect the strap from the solenoid to the starter motor terminal.

4   Remove the two screws which secure the solenoid to the starter motor.

5   Twist the solenoid in a clockwise direction to disengage the flange from the starter body **(see illustration)**.

Installation

6   To install, first make sure the return spring is in position on the plunger, then insert the solenoid body into the starter housing and turn the solenoid counterclockwise to engage the flange.

7   Install the two solenoid screws and connect the motor strap.

Chapter 6
Emissions and engine control systems

Contents

1 General information

Refer to illustrations 1.1a, 1.1b and 1.1c

To prevent pollution of the atmosphere from burned and evaporating gases, a number of emissions control systems are incorporated on the vehicles covered by this manual. The combination of systems used depends on the year in which the vehicle was manufactured, the locality to which it was originally delivered and the engine type **(see illustrations)**. The major systems incorporated on the vehicles with which this manual is concerned include the:

Air Injection Reaction (AIR)/PULSAIR or Air Management (AM) system
Fuel Control System
Electronic Spark Control (ESC) system
Electronic Spark Timing (EST) system
Early Fuel Evaporation (EFE) system
Exhaust Gas Recirculation (EGR) system
Evaporative Emissions Control (EECS) system
Transmission Converter Clutch (TCC)
Positive Crankcase Ventilation (PCV) system
Thermostatic Air Cleaner (THERMAC)
Catalytic converter

All of these systems are linked, directly or indirectly, to the Computer Command Control System (CCCS).

The Sections in this Chapter include general descriptions, checking procedures (where possible) and component replacement procedures (where applicable) for each of the systems listed above.

Before assuming that an emissions control system is malfunctioning, check the fuel and ignition systems carefully. In some cases special tools and equipment, as well as specialized training, are required to accurately diagnose the causes of a rough running or difficult to start engine. If checking and servicing become too difficult, or if a procedure is beyond the scope of the home mechanic, consult your dealer service department. This does not necessarily mean, however, that the emissions control systems are particularly difficult to maintain and repair. You can quickly and easily perform many checks and do most (if not all) of the regular maintenance at home with common tune up and hand tools. **Note:** *The most frequent cause of emissions system problems is simply a loose or broken vacuum hose or wiring connection. Therefore, always check the hose and wiring*

Component location

1.1a Emissions control system and related component locations - typical 3.3L V6 engine

1　Fuel injectors (three of six)
2　Idle air control valve (IAC)
3　Exhaust gas recirculation valve (EGR)
4　Fuel vapor canister
5　Exhaust oxygen sensor
6　Positive Crankcase Ventilation (PCV) valve

7　EGR vacuum solenoid
8　Throttle position switch (TPS)
9　Knock (ESC) sensor
10　Coolant temperature sensor
11　Camshaft sensor(A), Crankshaft sensor (B)
12　System power

13　ECM harness ground
14　Manifold air temperature sensor (MAT)
15　Mass air flow sensor (MAF)
16　Fuel pressure regulator
17　Vehicle Emission Control Information label (VECI)

1 Fuel injectors (three of six)

2 Idle air control valve (IAC)

Component location

3 Exhaust gas recirculation valve (EGR)

4 Fuel vapor canister

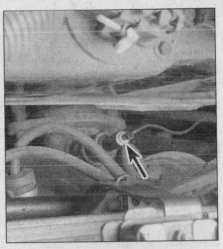

5 Exhaust oxygen sensor

6 Positive Crankcase Ventilation (PCV) valve

7 EGR vacuum solenoid

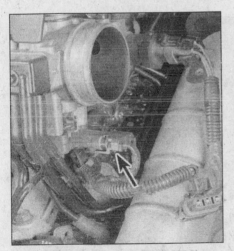

8 Throttle position switch (TPS)

9 Knock (ESC) sensor

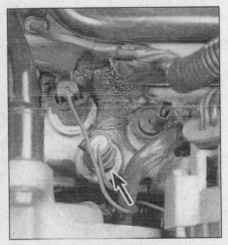

10 Coolant temperature sensor

Component location

11 Camshaft sensor(A), Crankshaft sensor (B)

12 System power

13 ECM harness ground

14 Manifold air temperature sensor (MAT)

15 Mass air flow sensor (MAF)

16 Fuel pressure regulator

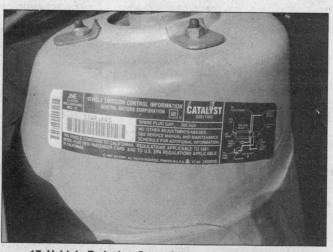

17 Vehicle Emission Control Information (VECI) label

Component location

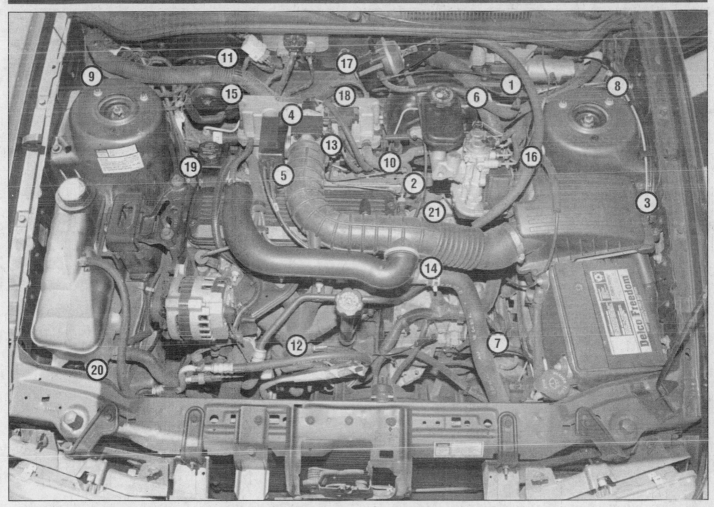

1.1b Emissions control system and related component locations - typical 2.2L MPFI four-cylinder engine

1	ECM power fuse	8	Cooling fan relay	15	Vehicle speed sensor
2	ECM harness ground	9	A/C compressor relay	16	P/N switch
3	Fuel pump test connector	10	Direct ignition system assembly	17	P/S pressure switch
4	Fuel injector solenoid	11	Manifold pressure sensor (MAP)	18	MAT sensor
5	Idle air control valve	12	Exhaust oxygen sensor	19	Crankcase vapor canister
6	Fuel pump relay	13	Throttle position switch	20	Fuel vapor canister
7	TCC solenoid connector	14	Coolant temperature sensor	21	Exhaust gas recirculation valve

connections first.

Pay close attention to any special precautions outlined in this Chapter. It should be noted that the illustrations of the various systems may not exactly match the system installed on your particular vehicle due to changes made by the manufacturer during production or from year to year.

A *Vehicle Emissions Control Information* (VECI) label is located in the engine compartment of all vehicles with which this manual is concerned **(see illustration)**. This label contains important emissions specifications and setting procedures, as well as a vacuum hose schematic with emissions components identi-

fied. When servicing the engine or emissions systems, the VECI label in your particular vehicle should always be checked for up-to-date information. **Note:** *Because of a federally mandated extended warranty which covers the emission control system components (and any components which have a primary purpose other than emission control but have significant effects on emissions), check with your dealer about warranty coverage before working on any emission related systems.*

Unless otherwise noted, procedures in this Chapter referring to carbureted models also apply to fuel injected models. Because of their more precise fuel/air management,

fuel injected engines use simpler emissions systems which do not use all of the systems described previously.

The number of emissions control system components on later model fuel injected vehicles has actually decreased due to the high efficiency of the new fuel injection and ignition systems. No longer needed are the AIR pump (most models), early fuel evaporation (EFE) system (except for TBI models), dual bed catalytic converter (although a single bed or monolithic converter is still used) and many of the confusing thermal vacuum switches, valves and hoses as installed on the carbureted engines.

Component location

1.1c Emissions control system and related component locations - typical 2.8/3.1L MPFI V6 engine

1	ECM harness ground	12	Fuel vapor canister sensor	23	A/C low pressure switch (mounted in compressor)
2	Fuel pump test connector	13	Manifold pressure sensor (MAP)		
3	Fuel pump/ECM fuse	14	Exhaust oxygen sensor	24	A/C high pressure switch (mounted in compressor)
4	Fuel injector	15	Throttle position sensor (TPS)		
5	Idle air control motor	16	Coolant temperature sensor	25	Crankcase vent valve (PCV)
6	Fuel pump relay	17	Crankshaft sensor	26	Engine temperature switch (telltale)
7	Transaxle converter clutch connector	18	Knock (ESC) sensor	27	Engine temperature sensor (gauge)
8	Direct ignition system (DIS)	19	MAT sensor	28	Oil pressure switch (telltale)
9	Engine cooling fan relay	20	P/N switch	29	Oil pressure sensor (gauge)
10	Exhaust gas recirculation valve (EGR)	21	P/S pressure switch	30	Fuel pressure connector
11	A/C compressor relay	22	A/C pressure fan switch	31	Vehicle speed sensor

2 Self-diagnosis system and trouble codes

Note: 1995 and earlier models are equipped with the OBD I self diagnosis system, while 1996 models are equipped with the OBD II self diagnosis system. 1994 and later models require the use of a Scan tool to access trou-

ble codes. However, many of the information sensor checks and replacement procedures do apply to both systems. Because 1994 and later systems require a special SCAN tool to access the trouble codes, have the vehicle diagnosed by a dealer service department or other qualified automotive repair facility if the proper SCAN tool is not available. 1994 V6 models and all 1996 models utilize five-digit

trouble codes. These "generic" trouble codes listed in the following table do not include the manufacturer's specific trouble codes. Consult a dealer service department or other qualified repair shop for additional information. Refer to the troubleshooting tips in the beginning of this manual and the information described in Section 4 to gain some insight to the most likely causes of a problem.

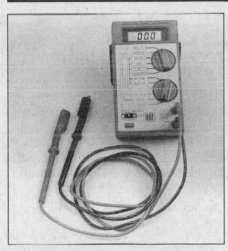

£.1 Digital multimeters can be used for testing all types of circuits; because of their high impedance, they are much more accurate than analog meters for measuring millivolts in low-voltage computer circuits

Diagnostic tool information

Refer to illustrations 2.1, 2.2 and 2.4

1   A digital multimeter is a necessary tool for checking fuel injection and emission related components **(see illustration)**. A digital volt-ohmmeter is preferred over the older style analog multimeter for several reasons. The analog multimeter cannot display the volts-ohms or amps measurement in hundredths and thousandths increments. When working with electronic circuits which are often very low voltage, this accurate reading is most important. Another good reason for the digital multimeter is the high impedance circuit. The digital multimeter is equipped with a high resistance internal circuitry (10 million ohms). Because a voltmeter is hooked up in parallel with the circuit when testing, it is vital that none of the voltage being measured should be allowed to travel the parallel path set up by the meter itself. This dilemma does not show itself when measuring larger amounts of voltage (9 to 12 volt circuits) but if you are measuring a low voltage circuit such as the oxygen sensor signal voltage, a fraction of a volt may be a significant amount when diagnosing a problem.

2   Hand-held scanners are the most powerful and versatile tools for analyzing engine management systems used on later model vehicles **(see illustration)**. Unfortunately, they are the most expensive. Early model scanners handle codes and some diagnostics for many OBD I systems. Each brand scan tool must be examined carefully to match the year, make and model of the vehicle you are working on. Often interchangeable cartridges are available to access the particular manufacturer: Ford, GM, Chrysler, etc.). Some manufacturers will specify by continent; Asia, Europe, USA, etc.

3   With the arrival of the federally mandated emission control system (OBD II), a specially designed scanner must also be

2.2 Scanners like the Actron Scantool and the AutoXray XP240 are powerful diagnostic aids - programmed with comprehensive diagnostic information, they can tell you just about anything you want to know about your engine management system, but they are expensive

developed. At this time, several manufacturers plan to release OBD II scan tools for the home mechanic. Ask the parts salesperson at a local auto parts store for additional information concerning dates and costs. **Note:** *Although 1994 and 1995 OBDI and 1996 OBD II codes cannot be accessed without a Scan tool, follow the simple component checks in Section 4.*

4   Another type of code reader is available at parts stores **(see illustration)**. These tools simplify the procedure for extracting codes from the engine management computer by simply "plugging in" to the diagnostic connector on the vehicle wiring harness and are much less expensive (however, they will not work on models that require the use of a scan tool to extract codes).

General description

5   The electronically controlled fuel and emissions system is linked with many other related engine management systems. It consists mainly of sensors, output actuators and an Electronic Control Module (ECM) or Powertrain Control Module (PCM) (see Section 1). Completing the system are various other components which respond to commands from the ECM/PCM.

6   In many ways, this system can be compared to the central nervous system in the human body. The sensors (nerve endings) constantly gather information and send this data to the ECM/PCM (brain), which processes the data and, if necessary, sends out a command for some type of vehicle change (limbs).

7   Here's a specific example of how one portion of this system operates: An oxygen sensor, mounted in the exhaust manifold and protruding into the exhaust gas stream, constantly monitors the oxygen content of the exhaust gas as it travels through the exhaust pipe. If the percentage of oxygen in the exhaust gas is incorrect, an electrical signal is sent to the ECM/PCM. The ECM/PCM takes this information, processes it and then sends a command to the fuel injectors, telling it to change the fuel/air mixture. To be effective, all this happens in a fraction of a second, and it goes on continuously while the engine is running. The end result is a fuel/air mixture which is constantly kept at a predetermined ratio, regardless of driving conditions.

Obtaining trouble codes

Refer to illustrations 2.11a and 2.11b

8   One might think that a system which uses exotic electrical sensors and is controlled by an on-board computer would be difficult to diagnose. This is not necessarily the case.

9   The On Board Diagnostic (OBD) system has a built-in self-diagnostic system, which indicates a problem by turning on a "SERVICE ENGINE SOON" light on the instrument panel when a fault has been detected. **Note:** *Since some of the trouble codes do not set the CHECK ENGINE or SERVICE ENGINE SOON light, it is a good idea to access the OBD system and look for any trouble codes that may have been recorded and need tending.*

10   Perhaps more importantly, the ECM/PCM will recognize this fault, in a particular system monitored by one of the various information sensors, and store it in its memory in the form of a trouble code. Although the trouble code cannot reveal the exact cause of the malfunction, it greatly facilitates diagnosis as you or a dealer mechanic can "tap into" the ECM/PCM's memory and be directed to the problem area.

11   To retrieve this information from the ECM on 1993 and earlier models, you must use a short jumper wire to ground a diagnostic terminal. The terminal is part of an electri-

2.4 Trouble code tools simplify the task of extracting the trouble codes

**2.11a The 12-pin Assembly Line Data Link (ALDL)
terminal identification**

A   Ground   *B   Diagnostic TEST terminal*

2.11b The 16 pin ALDL found on models equipped with OBD II

cal connector called the Assembly Line Data Link (ALDL) **(see illustrations)**. The ALDL is located just under the dashboard, next to the steering column. On some models a small rectangular plate is used to cover the connector and must be pried off to provide access to the terminals. With the electrical connector exposed, push one end of the jumper wire into the diagnostic TEST terminal and the other end into the GROUND terminal. Turn the ignition to the On position - *not* the Start position. The CHECK ENGINE light should flash Trouble Code 12, indicating that the diagnostic system is working. Code 12 will consist of one flash, followed by a short pause, and then two flashes in quick succession. After a longer pause, the code will repeat itself two more times. If no other codes have been stored, Code 12 will continue to repeat itself until the jumper wire is disconnected. If additional Trouble Codes have been stored, they will follow code 12. Again, each Trouble Code will flash three times before moving on. The ECM can also be checked for stored codes on carbureted models with the engine running. Completely remove the jumper wire from the diagnostic and ground terminals, start the engine and then plug the jumper wire back in. With the engine running, all stored trouble codes will flash. However, Code 12 will flash only if there is a fault in the distributor reference circuit. **Note:** *1994 and 1995 models with a 12-pin diagnostic connector do not have a terminal B present in the connector. On these models a scan tool is required to access trouble codes.*

12   On 1994 and later models, a scan tool must be connected to the Assembly Line

Data Link (ALDL). The scan tool is a hand held digital computer scanner that interfaces with the on-board computer. The scan tool is a very powerful tool; it not only reads the trouble codes but also displays the actual operating conditions of the sensors and actuators. Scan tools are expensive, but they are necessary to accurately diagnose a modern computerized fuel-injected engine. Scan tools are available from auto parts stores and specialty tool companies.

13   It should be noted that the self-diagnosis feature built into this system does not detect all possible faults. If you suspect a problem with the On Board Diagnostic (OBD) system, but the CHECK ENGINE or SERVICE ENGINE SOON light has not come on and no trouble codes have been stored, and performing the checks described in Section 4 doesn't pinpoint a problem, take the vehicle to a dealer service department or other qualified repair shop for diagnosis.

14   Furthermore, when diagnosing an engine performance, fuel economy or exhaust emissions problem (which is not accompanied by a CHECK ENGINE or SERVICE ENGINE SOON light) do not automatically assume the fault lies in this system. Perform all standard troubleshooting procedures, as indicated elsewhere in this manual, before turning to the On Board Diagnostic (OBD) system.

15   Finally, since this is an electronic system, you should have a basic knowledge of automotive electronics before attempting any diagnosis. Damage to the ECM/PCM, Programmable Read Only Memory (PROM) calibration unit or related components can easily occur if care is not exercised.

Clearing trouble codes

16   To clear the trouble codes from the ECM's memory on a 1993 or earlier model, unplug the ECM electrical pigtail at the positive battery cable and wait at least 30 seconds before plugging it back in. If the vehicle you are working on does not have this connector, disconnect the cable from the negative terminal of the battery for at least 30 seconds. **Caution 1:** *To prevent damage to the ECM, the ignition switch must be turned OFF when disconnecting or connecting power to the ECM.* **Caution 2:** *If the vehicle is equipped with a Delco Loc II audio system, make sure you have the correct activation code before disconnecting the battery. See the information at the front of this manual for the radio reactivation procedure.*

17   To clear the codes from the ECM/PCM memory on 1994 and later models, install the SCAN tool, scroll the menu for the function that describes "CLEARING CODES" and follow the prescribed method for that particular SCAN tool or momentarily remove the PCM/IGN fuse from the fuse box for 30 seconds. Clearing codes may also be accomplished by removing the fusible link (main power fuse) located near the battery positive terminal (see Chapter 12) or by disconnecting the cable from the positive terminal (+) of the battery. **Caution:** *If the vehicle is equipped with a Delco Loc II audio system, make sure you have the correct activation code before disconnecting the battery. See the information at the front of this manual for the radio reactivation procedure.*

18   Disconnecting the power to the ECM/PCM to clear the memory can be an important diagnostic tool, especially on intermittent problems.

19   **Note:** *Not all codes apply to all models.*

2-digit trouble codes

Code	Code definition
12	Diagnostic mode
13	Oxygen sensor or circuit
14	Coolant sensor or circuit/high temperature indicated
15	Coolant sensor or circuit/low temperature indicated
16	System voltage out of range
19	Crankshaft position sensor or circuit
21	Throttle Position Sensor (TPS) or circuit - voltage high
22	Throttle Position Sensor (TPS) or circuit - voltage low
23	Mixture Control (M/C) solenoid or circuit (carbureted models)

Code	Code definition
23	Manifold Air Temperature (MAT) sensor or circuit (1990 and earlier models)
23	Intake Air Temperature (IAT) sensor circuit (fuel-injected models)
24	Vehicle Speed Sensor (VSS) or circuit
25	Manifold Air Temperature (MAT) sensor or circuit - high temperature indicated (1990 and earlier models)
25	Intake Air Temperature (IAT) sensor or circuit - high temperature indicated (1991 and later models)
26	Quad Driver module circuit
27	Quad Driver module circuit
28	Quad Driver module circuit
29	Quad Driver module circuit
31	Park/Neutral Position (PNP) switch circuit
32	BARO sensor or circuit (carbureted models)
32	EGR circuit (fuel-injected models)
33	Manifold Absolute Pressure (MAP) sensor signal voltage high
33	Mass Air Flow (MAF) sensor or circuit - excessive airflow indicated
34	Manifold Absolute Pressure (MAP) sensor signal voltage low
34	Mass Air Flow (MAF) sensor signal - low airflow indicated
35	Idle Speed Control (ISC) switch or circuit (shorted) (carbureted models)
35	Idle Air Control (IAC) valve or circuit
38	Brake switch circuit
39	Torque Converter Clutch (TCC) circuit
41	No distributor signals to ECM, or faulty ignition module (carbureted models)
41	Cylinder select error - MEM-CAL or ECM problem (fuel-injected models)
41	Cam sensor circuit (3.8L engine)
42	Bypass or Electronic Spark Timing (EST) circuit
43	Low voltage at ECM terminal L (carbureted models)
43	Knock sensor circuit
44	Oxygen sensor or circuit - lean exhaust detected
45	Oxygen sensor or circuit - rich exhaust detected
46	Power steering pressure switch circuit
48	Misfire diagnosis
51	PROM, MEM-CAL or ECM problem
52	CALPAK or ECM problem
53	EGR fault (carbureted models only)
53	System over-voltage (ECM over 17.7 volts)
54	Mixture Control (M/C) solenoid or circuit (carbureted models)
54	Fuel pump circuit (1986 and later models)
55	Oxygen sensor circuit or ECM
55	Fuel lean monitor (2.2L engine)
61	Oxygen sensor signal faulty (possible contaminated sensor)
62	Transaxle gear switch signal circuits
63	Manifold Absolute Pressure (MAP) sensor voltage high (low vacuum detected)
64	Manifold Absolute Pressure (MAP) sensor voltage low (high vacuum detected)
66	Air conditioning pressure sensor or circuit

5-digit trouble codes

Code	Code definition
P0101	Mass Air Flow (MAF) sensor error
P0102	Mass Air Flow (MAF) sensor circuit - low frequency detected
P0103	Mass Air Flow (MAF) sensor - high frequency detected
P0106	Manifold Absolute Pressure (MAP) sensor performance fault
P0107	Manifold Absolute Pressure (MAP) sensor circuit low input
P0108	Manifold Absolute Pressure (MAP) sensor circuit high input
P0112	Intake Air Temperature (IAT) sensor circuit low input
P0113	Intake Air Temperature (IAT) sensor circuit high input

5-digit trouble codes (continued)

Code	Code definition
P0117	Engine Coolant Temperature (ECT) sensor circuit low input
P0118	Engine Coolant Temperature (ECT) sensor circuit high input
P0121	Throttle Position Sensor (TPS) range/performance fault
P0122	Throttle Position Sensor (TPS) circuit low input
P0123	Throttle Position Sensor (TPS) circuit high input
P0125	Engine Coolant Temperature (ECT) takes too long to enter closed loop
P0131	Upstream heated O2 sensor circuit low voltage (Bank 1, Sensor 1)
P0132	Upstream heated O2 sensor circuit high voltage (Bank 1, Sensor 1)
P0133	Upstream heated O2 sensor slow response (lazy sensor) (Bank 1, Sensor 1)
P0134	Upstream heated O2 sensor insufficient activity (Bank 1, Sensor 1)
P0135	Upstream heated O2 sensor - heater circuit fault (Bank 1, Sensor 1)
P0137	Downstream heated O2 sensor circuit low voltage (Bank 1, Sensor 2)
P0138	Downstream heated O2 sensor circuit high voltage (Bank 1, Sensor 2)
P0140	Downstream heated O2 sensor insufficient activity (Bank 1, Sensor 2)
P0141	O2 sensor heater circuit fault (Bank 1, Sensor 2)
P0171	System Adaptive fuel too lean
P0172	System Adaptive fuel too rich
P0191	Injector Pressure sensor system performance
P0192	Injector Pressure sensor circuit low input
P0193	Injector Pressure sensor circuit high input
P0300	Cylinder misfire detected (random)
P0301	Cylinder number 1 misfire detected
P0302	Cylinder number 2 misfire detected
P0303	Cylinder number 3 misfire detected
P0304	Cylinder number 4 misfire detected
P0305	Cylinder number 5 misfire detected
P0306	Cylinder number 6 misfire detected
P0321	Crankshaft Position sensor circuit fault
P0325	Knock sensor circuit fault
P0326	Knock sensor circuit performance
P0327	Knock sensor noise channel - low voltage
P0335	Crankshaft Position sensor circuit
P0336	Crankshaft reference signal circuit
P0341	Camshaft Position sensor circuit
P0342	Camshaft Position sensor circuit
P0401	Exhaust Gas Recirculation (EGR) system flow insufficient
P0420	Three Way Catalyst (TWC) system - low efficiency
P0441	EVAP system - no flow during purge cycle
P0351	COP ignition coil 1 primary circuit fault
P0352	COP ignition coil 2 primary circuit fault
P0353	COP ignition coil 3 primary circuit fault
P0354	COP ignition coil 4 primary circuit fault
P0400	EGR flow fault
P0401	EGR insufficient flow detected
P0402	EGR excessive flow detected
P0420	Catalyst system efficiency below threshold (Bank 1)
P0421	Catalyst system efficiency below threshold (Bank 1)
P0430	Catalyst system efficiency below threshold (Bank 2)
P0431	Catalyst system efficiency below threshold (Bank 2)
P0441	EVAP incorrect purge flow
P0443	EVAP VMV circuit fault
P0452	EVAP fuel tank pressure sensor low input
P0453	EVAP fuel tank pressure sensor high input
P0502	VSS circuit low input

P0503......................	VSS circuit range performance
P0506......................	IAC system rpm lower than expected
P0507......................	IAC system rpm higher than expected
P0530......................	A/C refrigerant pressure sensor circuit
P0560......................	System voltage out of range
P0600......................	PCM serial data communication link fault
P0601......................	PCM memory problem
P0602......................	PCM control module programming error
P0650......................	Quad driver module circuit
P0703......................	TCC brake switch input circuit fault
P0705......................	Transaxle Range sensor circuit malfunction
P0706......................	Transaxle Range sensor performance
P0712......................	Transaxle fluid temperature sensor circuit low input
P0713......................	Transaxle fluid temperature sensor circuit high Input
P0740......................	TCC circuit fault
P0755......................	Shift solenoid circuit fault

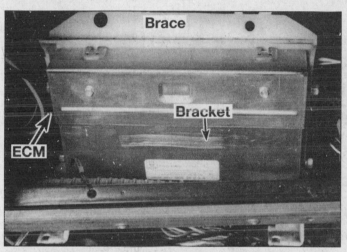

3.4a Typical Electronic Control Module (ECM) mounting details

3.4b To remove the Electronic Control Module (ECM) from the vehicle, remove the glove box to gain access to the mounting bolts (typical)

3   Electronic Control Module (ECM)

ECM replacement

Refer to illustration 3.4a and 3.4b

Caution: *The ignition switch must be turned off when pulling out or plugging in the connectors to prevent damage to the ECM.*

1   The Electronic Control Module (ECM) is located under the instrument panel.

2   Disconnect the negative battery cable from the battery. **Caution:** *If the vehicle is equipped with a Delco Loc II audio system, make sure you have the correct activation code before disconnecting the battery. See the information at the front of this manual for the radio re-activation procedure.*

3   Remove the glove box to gain access to the ECM.

4   Remove the retaining bolts **(see illustration)** and carefully slide the ECM out far enough to unplug the electrical connector.

5   Unplug the electrical connectors from the ECM.

6   Installation is the reverse of removal.

PROM, CALPAK or MEM-CAL replacement

Refer to illustration 3.8

7   To allow one model of ECM to be used for many different vehicles, a device called a PROM (Programmable Read-Only Memory), CALPAK (calibration pack) or MEM-CAL (memory and calibration) is used. Some models use a combination of two of these. This device is located inside the ECM and contains information on the vehicle's weight, engine, transaxle, axle ratio, etc. One ECM part number can be used by many GM vehicles but the PROM, CALPAK or MEM-CAL is very specific and must be used only in the vehicle for which it was designed. For this reason, it's essential to check the latest parts book and Service Bulletin information for the correct part number when replacing one of these components. A replacement ECM doesn't come with a PROM, CALPAK or MEM-CAL. It (or they) must be carefully removed from the old ECM and installed in the new ECM.

8   Remove the access cover **(see illustration)**.

3.8 A typical electronic control module (ECM) - the PROM, CALPAK or MEM-CAL unit is located under the access cover

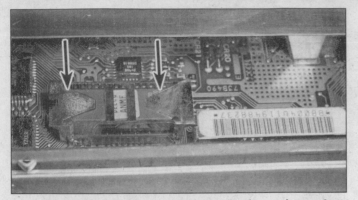

3.9 Using two fingers, push the retaining clips (arrows) away from the MEM-CAL and simultaneously grasp it at both ends and lift it up, out of the socket

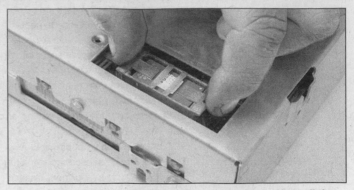

3.10 To install the MEM-CAL, press only on the ends until the retaining clips snap into the ends of the MEM-CAL - make sure the notches in the MEM-CAL are aligned with the small notches in the socket

MEM-CAL

Refer to illustrations 3.9 and 3.10

9   To remove a MEM-CAL, push both retaining clips back away from the MEM-CAL **(see illustration)**. At the same time, grasp the unit at both ends and lift it up out of the socket. Don't remove the MEM-CAL cover itself. **Caution:** *Use of unapproved removal or installation methods may damage the MEM-CAL or socket.*

10   To install the MEM-CAL, press only on the ends. The small notches in the MEM-CAL must be aligned with the small notches in the MEM-CAL socket. Press on the ends of the MEM-CAL until the retaining clips snap into the ends of the MEM-CAL. Don't press on the middle of the MEM-CAL - press only on the ends **(see illustration)**.

PROM/CALPAK

Refer to illustrations 3.12 and 3.13

11   To remove a PROM or CALPAK, a special removal tool should be used. These usually are supplied when a replacement ECM is purchased. **Caution:** *Removal without this tool or with any other type of tool may cause damage.* Grasp the PROM carrier at the narrow ends. Gently rock the carrier from end-to-end while carefully pulling up.

12   Note the reference end of the PROM/-CALPAK carrier **(see illustration)** before setting it aside.

13   Position the PROM or CALPAK and carrier assembly squarely over the socket with the small notched end of the carrier aligned with the small notch in the socket. Press on the carrier until it seats firmly in the socket **(see illustration)**. **Caution:** *Don't press on the PROM or CALPAK - press only on the carrier. Also, if the unit is installed backwards, it will be destroyed when the ignition switch is turned on.*

Final installation

14   The remainder of the installation is the reverse of removal.

15   Once the new MEM-CAL is installed in the the old ECM (or the old unit is installed in the new ECM), check the installation to verify it has been installed properly by doing the fol-

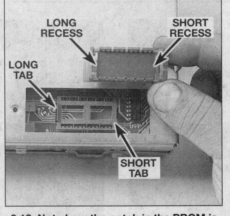

3.12 Note how the notch in the PROM is matched up with the smaller notch in the carrier

lowing test:

a) *Turn the ignition switch on.*
b) *Enter the diagnostics mode at the ALDL (see Section 2).*
c) *Allow code 12 to flash four times to verify that no other codes are present. This indicates the PROM, CALPAK or MEM-CAL is properly installed and the ECM is functioning properly.*

16   If trouble codes 41, 42, 43, 51 or 52 occur, or if the Service Engine Soon light is on constantly but isn't flashing any codes, the unit is either not completely seated or it's defective. If it's not seated, press firmly on the ends once again.

---

4   Information sensors

Note 1: *See the component location illustrations in Section 2 for the location of the following information sensors.*
Note 2: *After performing any checking procedure to any of the information sensors, be sure to clear the ECM of all trouble codes by disconnecting the cable from the negative terminal of the battery for at least ten seconds.*

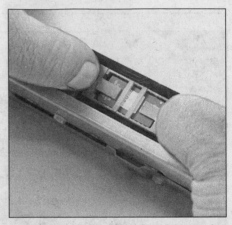

3.13 Press only on the ends of the carrier - pressure on the area in between could result in bent or broken pins or damage to the PROM

Caution: *If the vehicle is equipped with a Delco Loc II audio system, make sure you have the correct activation code before disconnecting the battery. See the information at the front of this manual for the radio re-activation procedure.*

Engine coolant temperature sensor

Refer to illustrations 4.2 and 4.3

General description and check

1   The coolant sensor is a thermistor (a resistor which varies the value of its voltage output in accordance with temperature changes). A failure in the coolant sensor circuit should set either a Code 14 or a Code 15. These codes indicate a failure in the coolant temperature circuit, so the appropriate solution to the problem will be either repair of a wire or replacement of the sensor. The sensor can also be checked with an ohmmeter, by measuring its resistance when cold, then warming up the engine and taking another measurement. If the difference in resistance readings is not approximately 500 ohms, the sensor is probably bad.

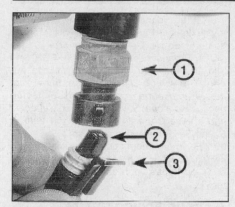

4.2 A typical engine coolant temperature sensor (1) electrical connector (2) has a locking tab (3) that must be released to unplug the connector

Replacement

2 To remove the sensor, release the locking tab **(see illustration)**, unplug the electrical connector, then carefully unscrew the sensor. **Caution:** *Handle the coolant sensor with care. Damage to this sensor will affect the operation of the entire fuel injection system.*

3 Before installing the new sensor, wrap the threads with Teflon sealing tape to prevent leakage and thread corrosion **(see illustration)**.

4 Installation is the reverse of removal.

Manifold Absolute Pressure (MAP) sensor

Refer to illustrations 4.5 and 4.7

General description

5 The Manifold Absolute Pressure (MAP) sensor **(see illustration)** monitors the intake manifold pressure changes resulting from changes in engine load and speed and converts the information into a voltage output. The ECM uses the MAP sensor to control fuel delivery and ignition timing.

Check

6 A failure in the MAP sensor circuit should set a Code 33, 34, 63 or 64, but the

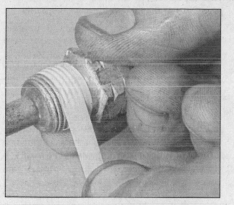

4.3 To prevent coolant leakage, be sure to wrap the temperature sensor threads with Teflon tape before installation

operation of the sensor can also be checked using a high-impedance digital voltmeter. Unplug the electrical connector from the sensor and, using jumper wires, connect terminals A and C (the two outside terminals) to their corresponding terminals in the electrical connector. Connect the positive lead of the voltmeter to terminal B (the center terminal) of the sensor and the negative lead to ground. With the ignition On (engine not running) the voltage reading should be about 4.5 to 5 volts. Start the engine and let it warm up. The reading should now be different from the original reading, and should fluctuate with changes in engine rpm. If it doesn't, check the vacuum hose for breaks or

blockage. If the hose is OK, the sensor is probably bad.

Replacement

7 To replace the sensor, detach the vacuum hose, unplug the electrical connector and remove the mounting screws **(see illustration)**. Installation is the reverse of removal.

Manifold Air Temperature (MAT) sensor or Intake Air Temperature (IAT) sensor

Refer to illustration 4.10

General description

8 This sensor, located in the intake manifold air cleaner housing or air duct, is a thermistor (a resistor which changes the value of its voltage output as the temperature changes). The ECM uses the this signal to delay EGR until the manifold air temperature reaches 40-degrees F.

Check

9 A failure in the MAT/IAT sensor circuit should set either a Code 23 or a Code 25. The sensor can also be checked with an ohmmeter, by measuring its resistance when cold, then warming it up (a hair dryer can be used for this) and taking another measurement. If the difference in resistance readings is not approximately 500 ohms, the sensor is probably bad.

Replacement

10 To remove a MAT/IAT sensor, unplug

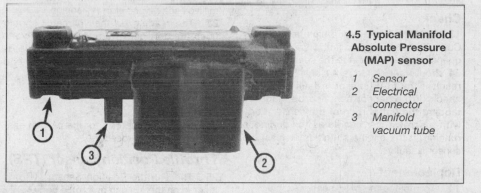

4.5 Typical Manifold Absolute Pressure (MAP) sensor

1 *Sensor*
2 *Electrical connector*
3 *Manifold vacuum tube*

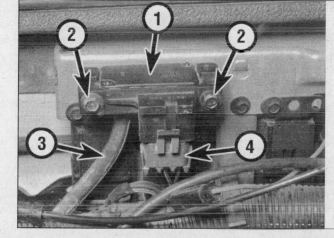

4.7 Typical MAP sensor installation details

1 *MAP sensor*
2 *Mounting screws*
3 *Vacuum line*
4 *Electrical connector*

4.10 Removing an IAT sensor from the air cleaner housing (air cleaner removed from engine for clarity) (typical)

4.12 Typical Mass Air Flow (MAF) sensor installation details (arrow)

the electrical connector and remove the sensor with a wrench **(see illustration)**.

11　Installation is the reverse of removal.

Mass Air Flow (MAF) sensor

Refer to illustration 4.12

General description

12　The Mass Air Flow (MAF) sensor, Which is located in a housing between the air cleaner housing and the intake duct **(see illustration)**, measures the amount of air entering the engine. The ECM uses this information to control fuel delivery. A large quantity of air indicates acceleration, while a small quantity indicates deceleration or idle.

Check

13　If the sensor fails at a high frequency, a Code 33 should set and if it fails at a low frequency or power is lost to the sensor, a Code 34 should set. A Code 44 or 45 may also result if the MAF sensor is faulty. A quick check of the sensor can also be made by tapping the flat portion of the sensor body with a screwdriver handle as the engine is running. If the engine stumbles or dies, the sensor is faulty.

Replacement

14　To replace the MAF sensor, unplug the electrical connector, loosen the clamps and detach the sensor from the air ducts.

15　Installation is the reverse of removal.

Oxygen sensor

General description

16　The oxygen sensor is mounted in the exhaust system where it can monitor the oxygen content of the exhaust gas stream. By monitoring the voltage output of the oxygen sensor, the ECM will know what fuel mixture command to give the mixture control solenoid (carbureted models) or fuel injector(s).

17　The oxygen sensor produces no voltage when it's below its normal operating temperature of about 600-degrees F. During this initial period before warm-up, the ECM operates in open loop mode.

18　If the engine reaches normal operating temperature and/or has been running for two or more minutes, and if the oxygen sensor is producing a steady signal voltage between 0.35 and 0.55-volt, even though the TPS indicates the engine isn't at idle, the ECM will set a Code 13.

19　A delay of two minutes or more between engine start-up and normal operation or the sensor, followed by a low voltage signal or a short in the sensor circuit, will cause the ECM to set a Code 44. If a high voltage signal occurs, The ECM will set a Code 45.

20　When any of the above codes occur, the ECM operates in the open loop mode - that is it controls fuel delivery in accordance with a programmed default value instead of feedback information from the oxygen sensor.

Check

21　An open in the oxygen sensor circuit should set a Code 13. A low voltage in the circuit should set a Code 44. A high voltage in the circuit should set a Code 45. Codes 44 and 45 may also be set as a result of fuel system problems.

22　The sensor can also be checked with a high-impedance digital voltmeter. Warm up the engine to normal operating temperature, then turn the engine off. Unplug the oxygen sensor electrical connector and connect the positive probe of the voltmeter to the sensor side of the connector. **Caution:** *Don't let the sensor wire or the voltmeter lead touch the exhaust pipe or manifold.* Ground the negative probe of the meter, turn the meter to the millivolt setting and start the engine.

23　The reading on the voltmeter should fluctuate between 100 and 1,000 millivolts (0.1 and 1.0 volts). If the meter reading doesn't fluctuate, the sensor is probably bad (although a fuel system problem could be the cause).

Replacement

24　Refer to Chapter 1 for the oxygen sensor replacement procedure.

Throttle Position Sensor (TPS)

25　The Throttle Position Sensor (TPS) is located on the TBI unit or throttle body.

26　By monitoring the output voltage from the TPS, the ECM can determine fuel delivery based on throttle valve angle (driver demand). A broken or loose TPS can cause intermittent bursts of fuel from the injector and an unstable idle because the ECM thinks the throttle is moving.

27　A problem in any of the TPS circuits will set either a Code 21 or 22. Once a trouble code is set, the ECM will use an artificial default value for TPS and some vehicle performance will return.

28　Checking and replacement procedures for the TPS are contained in Chapter 4.

Park/Neutral (P/N) switch

29　The Park/Neutral (P/N) switch, located on the rear upper part of the automatic transaxle, indicates to the ECM when the transaxle is in Park or Neutral. This information is used for Transaxle Converter Clutch (TCC), Exhaust Gas Recirculation (EGR) and Idle Air Control (IAC) valve operation. **Caution:** *The vehicle should not be driven with the Park/Neutral switch disconnected because idle quality will be adversely affected and a false Code 24 (failure in the Vehicle Speed Sensor circuit) may be set.*

30　For more information regarding the P/N switch, which is part of the Neutral start and back-up light switch assembly, see Chapter 7B.

Air conditioning (A/C) On Signal

31　This signal tells the ECM the A/C selector switch is in the On position and the high side low pressure switch is closed. The ECM uses this information to turn on the A/C and adjust the idle speed when the air conditioning system is working. If this signal isn't available to the ECM, idle may be rough, especially when the A/C compressor cycles.

32　Diagnosis of the circuit between the A/C On signal and the ECM should be left to a dealer service department or other repair shop.

Vehicle Speed Sensor (VSS)

33　The Vehicle Speed Sensor (VSS) sends a pulsing voltage signal to the ECM, which the ECM converts to miles per hour. This sensor controls the operation of the Torque Converter Clutch (TCC) system.

Crankshaft sensor

34　The crankshaft sensor sends a signal to the ECM to tell it both engine rpm and crankshaft position. See Chapter 5 for further information.

5　Fuel control system (carbureted models)

General description

1　The function of this system is to control the flow of fuel through the carburetor idle and main metering circuits. The major components of the system are the mixture control (M/C) solenoid and the oxygen sensor.

2　The M/C solenoid changes the fuel/air mixture by allowing more or less fuel to flow through the carburetor. The M/C solenoid, located in the carburetor air horn, is in turn controlled by the Electronic Control Module (ECM), which provides a ground for the solenoid. When the solenoid is energized, the fuel flow through the carburetor is reduced, providing a leaner mixture. When the ECM removes the ground path, the solenoid de-energizes and allows more fuel flow.

3　The ECM determines the proper fuel mixture required by monitoring a signal sent by the oxygen sensor, located in the exhaust stream. When the mixture is too lean, the oxygen sensor voltage is low and the ECM commands a richer mixture. Conversely, when the mixture is rich, the oxygen sensor voltage is higher and the ECM commands a leaner mixture.

Check

Oxygen sensor

4   Make sure that the oxygen sensor has been replaced at the proper maintenance interval (see Chapter 1).
5   Refer to Section 4 for the oxygen sensor checking procedure.

Mixture Control (M/C) solenoid

6   Check the electrical connectors and wires leading to the mixture control solenoid for looseness, fraying and other damage. Repair or replace any damaged wiring as necessary.
7   Check the mixture control solenoid for apparent physical damage. Replace it if damage is found.

Component replacement

Oxygen sensor

8   To replace the sensor, refer to Chapter 1.

Mixture control solenoid

9   If the M/C solenoid has been determined to be faulty, the carburetor will have to be at least partially disassembled to replace it (see Chapter 4, illustration 10.6). See Chapter 4 for general information and alternative suggestions to carburetor rebuilding.

---

6   Electronic Spark Timing (EST) system

---

1   Electronic Spark Timing is used on all engines with which this manual is concerned. The EST distributor contains no vacuum or centrifugal advance, depending on commands from the ECM instead. The ECM receives a reference pulse from the distributor, indicating both engine rpm and crankshaft position, determines the proper spark advance for the engine operating conditions and sends an EST pulse to the distributor. **Note:** *On later models, the ECM controls spark advance by receiving information from the crankshaft sensor and sending an EST pulse to the DIS module.*
2   Under normal operating conditions, the ECM will always control the spark advance. However, under certain conditions, such as cranking or setting base timing, the distributor can operate independent of ECM control. This condition is called Bypass mode and is determined by the bypass lead from the ECM to the distributor. When the bypass lead voltage is over two volts, the ECM will control the spark. Disconnecting the four terminal EST connector, or grounding the bypass lead, will cause the engine to operate in the bypass mode.

7.3 Typical Electronic Spark Control (ESC) knock sensor (arrow) located on the engine block

3   For further information (and checking and component replacement procedures) regarding the EST distributor, refer to Chapter 5.

---

7   Electronic Spark Control (ESC) system

Refer to illustration 7.3

General description

1   Irregular octane levels in modern gasoline can cause detonation in an engine. Detonation is sometimes referred to as "spark knock."
2   The Electronic Spark Control (ESC) system is designed to retard spark timing up to 20-degrees to reduce spark knock in the engine. This allows the engine to use maximum spark advance to improve driveability and fuel economy.
3   The ESC knock sensor, which is located on the engine block **(see Illustration)**, sends a voltage signal of 8 to 10-volts to the ECM when no spark knock is occurring and the ECM provides normal advance. When the knock sensor detects abnormal vibration (spark knock), the ESC module turns off the circuit to the ECM and the voltage at the ECM drops to zero volts. The ECM then retards the timing until spark knock is eliminated.
4   Failure of the ESC knock sensor signal or loss of ground at the ESC module will cause the signal to the ECM to remain high. This condition will result in the ECM controlling the EST as if no spark knock is occurring. Therefore, no retard will occur and spark knock may become severe under heavy engine load conditions. At this point, the ECM will set a Code 43.
5   Loss of the ESC signal to the ECM will cause the ECM to constantly retard EST. This will result in sluggish performance and cause the ECM to set a Code 43.

Check

6   Connect a timing light in accordance with the tool manufacturer's instructions. Start the engine and allow it to reach normal operating temperature.
7   With an assistant pointing the timing light at the timing marks, tap on the engine block with a hammer in the area of the ESC (knock) sensor. The ignition timing should retard noticeably each time the hammer strikes the block. If the timing retards, the system is operating properly.
8   If the timing does not retard, stop the engine and unplug the electrical connector from the sensor.
9   Using a digital voltmeter set on the 2-volt AC scale, probe the knock sensor single wire terminal with the positive probe and ground the negative probe to the engine block. Tap on the engine block with a hammer near the knock sensor and check for a small AC signal generated by the sensor as it detects the knock. If no signal is detected, the knock sensor is not functioning; replace the ESC knock sensor. If a signal is detected, the knock signal is functioning properly, the ESC module or the ECM may be defective; have further diagnosis performed by a dealership service department or other qualified repair facility.

ESC sensor replacement

10   Disconnect the electrical connector from the ESC sensor.
11   Unscrew the ESC sensor from the block.
12   Installation is the reverse of the removal procedure.

---

8   Air Injection Reaction (AIR/PULSAIR) system

Refer to illustrations 8.22, 8.23, 8.29, 8.33 and 8.42

General description

Note: *If your engine is equipped with an air pump, your concern in this Section will be with the AIR system. If no air pump is present, refer to the procedures involving the PULSAIR system.*

AIR system

1   The AIR system helps reduce hydrocarbons and carbon monoxide levels in the exhaust by injecting air into the exhaust ports of each cylinder during cold engine operation, or directly into the catalytic convertor during normal operation. It also helps the catalytic converter reach proper operating temperature quickly during warm-up.
2   The AIR system uses an air pump to force the air into the exhaust stream. An air management valve, controlled by the vehicle's Electronic Control Module (ECM) directs the air to the correct location, depending on engine temperature and driving conditions. During certain situations, such as decelera-

8.22 The air pump pulley is retained by three bolts

8.23 Removing the AIR pump filter (remove it as shown - do not insert any tool behind the filter to pry it off, as damage to the pump may occur)

8.29 Loosen the clamp then remove the hose from the AIR system check valve

tion, the air is diverted to the air cleaner to prevent backfiring from too much oxygen in the exhaust stream. One-way check valves are also used in the AIR system's air lines to prevent exhaust gases from being forced back through the system.

3   The following components are utilized in the AIR system: an engine driven air pump; air control, switching and divert management valves; air flow and control hoses; check valves; and a dual bed catalytic converter.

PULSAIR system

4   This system performs some of the same functions as the AIR system, but utilizes exhaust pressure pulses to draw air into the exhaust system. Fresh air that is filtered by the air cleaner is supplied to the system on a command from the ECM.

5   Components utilized in the system include the PULSAIR valve and external tubes and hoses.

6   The PULSAIR system's operation begins with the engine's firing, creating a pulsating flow of exhaust gases which are of positive or negative pressure. The pressure or vacuum is transmitted through the external tubes to the PULSAIR valve, which reacts as follows:

7   If the pressure is positive, the disc in the valve is forced to the closed position and no exhaust gas is allowed to flow past the valve and into the air supply.

8   If there is negative pressure (vacuum) present in the exhaust system at the valve, the disc will open, allowing fresh air to mix with the exhaust gases.

9   The disc, due to the inertia of the system, ceases to follow the pressure pulsations at high engine rpm. At this point the disc remains closed, preventing any further flow of fresh air.

Check

AIR system

10   Because of the complexity of this system it is difficult for the home mechanic to make a proper diagnosis. If the system is suspected of not operating properly, individ-

ual components can be checked.

11   Begin any inspection by carefully checking all hoses, vacuum lines and wires. Be sure they are in good condition and that all connections are tight and clean. Also make sure the pump drivebelt is in good condition and properly adjusted.

12   To check the pump, allow the engine to reach normal operating temperature and run it at about 1500 rpm. Locate the hose running from the air pump and squeeze it to feel the pulsations. Have an assistant increase the engine speed and check for a parallel increase in air flow. If this is observed as described, the pump is functioning properly. If it is not operating in this manner, a faulty pump is indicated.

13   The check valve can be inspected by first removing it from the air line. Attempt to blow through it from both directions. Air should only pass through it in the direction of normal air flow. If it is either stuck open or stuck closed the valve should be replaced.

14   To check the air management valve disconnect the vacuum signal line at the valve. With the engine running see if vacuum is present in the line. If not, the line is clogged.

15   To check the deceleration valve plug the air cleaner vacuum source. With the engine running at the specified idle speed remove the small deceleration valve signal hose from the manifold vacuum source, then reconnect the signal hose and listen for air flow through the ventilation pipe and into the deceleration valve. There should also be a noticeable engine speed drop when the signal hose is reconnected. If the air flow does not continue for at least one second, or the engine speed does not drop noticeably, check the deceleration valve hoses for restrictions and leaks. If no restrictions or leaks are found replace the deceleration valve.

PULSAIR system

16   A simple, functional test of this system can be performed with the engine running. Disconnect the rubber hose from the air valve

and hold your hand over the valve's inlet hole. With the engine idling there should be a steady stream of air being sucked into the valve. Have an assistant apply throttle, and as the engine gains speed, see if the suction increases. If this does not occur, the lines are leaking or restricted or the check valves are sticking. Also make sure that air is not being blown out of the air valve, as this is also an indication that the check valves are sticking open. Service or replace the components as necessary. If other PULSAIR problems are suspected, have a dealer or repair shop diagnose the problems, as they might relate to the ECM/engine control system.

Component replacement (AIR system)

Drivebelt

17   Loosen the pump mounting bolt and the pump adjustment bracket bolt.

18   Move the pump in until the belt can be removed.

19   Install the new belt and adjust it (see Chapter 1)

AIR pump pulley and filter

20   Compress the drivebelt to keep the pulley from turning and loosen the pulley bolts.

21   Remove the drivebelt as described above.

22   Remove the mounting bolts and lift off the pulley (see illustration).

23   If the fan-like filter must be removed, grasp it firmly with needle-nose pliers and pull it from the pump (see illustration). **Note:** *Do not insert a screwdriver between the filter and pump housing as the edge of the housing could be damaged. The filter will usually be distorted when pulled off. Be sure no fragments fall into the air intake hose.*

24   The new filter is installed by placing it in position on the pump, placing the pulley over it and tightening the pulley bolts evenly to draw the filter into the pump. Do not attempt to install a filter by pressing or hammering it into place. **Note:** *It is normal for the new filter to have an interference fit with the pump*

8.33 Removing a hose from the AIR management valve

8.42 AIR system deceleration valve (arrow) (some V6 engines)

housing and, upon initial operation, it may squeal until worn in.

25 Install the drivebelt and, while compressing the belt, tighten the pulley bolts securely.

26 Adjust the drivebelt tension (see Chapter 1).

Hoses and tubes

27 To replace any tube or hose always note how it is routed first, either with a sketch or with numbered pieces of tape.

28 Remove the defective hose or tube and replace it with a new one of the same material and size and tighten all connections.

Check valve

29 Disconnect the pump outlet hose at the check valve **(see illustration)**.

30 Remove the check valve from the pipe assembly, using a back-up wrench to hold the stationary fitting on the pipe to prevent twisting the assembly

31 Install a new valve after making sure that it is a duplicate of the part removed, then tighten all connections.

Air management valve

32 Disconnect the negative battery cable at the battery. **Caution:** *If the vehicle is equipped with a Delco Loc II audio system, make sure you have the correct activation code before disconnecting the battery. See the information at the front of this manual for the radio re-activation procedure.*

33 Disconnect the vacuum signal line from the valve. Also disconnect the air hoses **(see illustration)** and electrical connectors.

34 If the mounting bolts are retained by tabbed lock washers, bend the tabs back, then remove the mounting bolts and lift the valve off the adapter or bracket.

35 Installation is the reverse of the removal procedure. Be sure to use a new gasket when installing the valve.

Air pump

36 Remove the air management valve and adapter, if so equipped.

37 If the pulley must be removed from the

pump it should be done prior to removing the drivebelt (see Step 20).

38 If the pulley is not being removed, remove the drivebelt.

39 Remove the pump mounting bolts and separate the pump from the engine.

40 Installation is the reverse of the removal procedure. **Note:** *Do not tighten the pump mounting bolts until all components are installed.*

41 Following installation adjust the drivebelt tension as described in Chapter 1.

Deceleration valve

42 Disconnect the vacuum hoses from the valve **(see illustration)**.

43 Remove the screws retaining the valve to the engine bracket (if present) and remove the valve.

44 Install a new valve and reconnect all hoses.

Component replacement (PULSAIR system)

45 Remove the air cleaner and disconnect the negative cable from the battery. **Caution:** *If the vehicle is equipped with a Delco Loc II audio system, make sure you have the correct activation code before disconnecting the battery. See the information at the front of this manual for the radio re-activation procedure.*

46 Disconnect the hose from the PULSAIR valve.

47 Disconnect the support bracket.

48 Remove the PULSAIR solenoid and bracket from the PULSAIR unit.

49 Loosen the nuts that secure the air tubes to the cylinder head and remove the assembly. Due to the high temperature at this area, these connections may be difficult to loosen. Penetrating oil applied to the threads of the nuts may help.

50 Before installing, apply a light coat of oil to the ends of the air tubes and anti seize compound to the threads of the attaching nuts.

51 Installation is the reverse of the removal procedure.

9 Early Fuel Evaporation (EFE) system

Refer to illustrations 9.6, 9.21 and 9.25

General description

Servo type

Note: *If your vehicle is equipped with vacuum servo-type EFE system, refer to Chapter 1 for a general description of the system.*

Electrically heated type

1 This unit provides rapid heat to the intake air supply on carbureted and some throttle body injection engines by means of a ceramic heater grid. The grid is integral with the carburetor/TBI base gasket and located under the primary bore.

2 The components involved in the EFE's operation include the heater grid, a relay, electrical wires and connectors and the ECM.

3 The EFE heater unit is controlled by the vehicle's Electronic Control Module (ECM) through a relay. The ECM senses the coolant temperature level and applies voltage to the heater unit only when the engine temperature is below a predetermined level. At normal operating temperatures the heater unit is off.

4 If the EFE heater is not coming on, poor cold engine performance will be experienced. If the heater unit is not shutting off when the engine is warmed up the engine will run as if it is out of tune due to the constant flow of hot air through the carburetor or TBI.

Check

Servo type

5 To check the operation of the EFE/TVS (thermal vacuum switch), allow the engine temperature to fall below 80-degrees F.

6 Disconnect and label the vacuum hoses, then detach the hoses from the switch **(see illustration)**. Attach a length of vacuum hose to one of the ports.

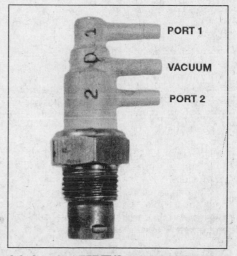

PORT 1

VACUUM

PORT 2

9.6 A typical EFE/TVS switch employed in servo-type EFE systems, typically located in the intake manifold

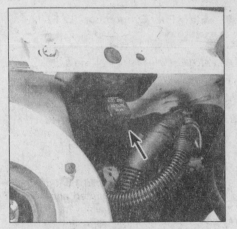

9.21 Typical EFE relay location

9.25 Removing the EFE system heater element

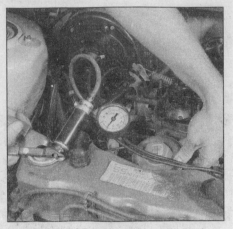

10.6 The EGR valve diaphragm can be checked using a vacuum pump

7   Blow into the hose. Air should flow through the valve.
8   Warm up the engine to normal operating temperature.
9   Blow into the hose again. No air should flow through the valve.
10   If the condition in either Step 9 or 10 is not met, replace the valve with a new one.
11   For other checking procedures for the servo type EFE system, refer to Chapter 1.

Electrically heated type

12   If the EFE system is suspected of malfunctioning while the engine is cold, first check all electrical wires and connectors to be sure they are clean, tight and in good condition.
13   With the ignition switch in the On position, use a circuit tester or voltmeter to check that current is reaching the relay. If not, there is a problem in the wiring leading to the relay, in the ECM's thermo switch or the ECM itself.
14   With the engine cold and the ignition switch On, disconnect the heater unit electrical connector and use a test light or voltmeter to see if current is reaching the heater unit. If so, use an ohmmeter connected to the terminals of the electrical connector to check for continuity of the heater unit. If continuity exists, the system is probably operating correctly in the cold engine mode.
15   If current is not reaching the heater unit, but is reaching the relay, replace the relay.
16   To check that the system turns off at normal engine operating temperature, first allow the engine to warm up thoroughly. With the engine idling, disconnect the heater unit electrical connector and use a test light or voltmeter to check for current at the heater unit.
17   If current is reaching the heater unit, the relay is stuck closed or the ECM is faulty.
18   For confirmation of the ECM's condition, check for trouble codes (see Section 2) or have the system checked by a dealer service department or other repair shop.

Component replacement

Heater relay

19   Disconnect the battery negative cable.

Caution: *If the vehicle is equipped with a Delco Loc II audio system, make sure you have the correct activation code before disconnecting the battery. See the information at the front of this manual for the radio re-activation procedure.*
20   Remove the relay bracket from the passenger's side inner fender panel next to the blower motor.
21   Unplug the electrical connectors, remove the retaining bolts and lift the relay from the vehicle **(see illustration)**.
22   Installation is the reverse of removal.

Heater element

23   Remove the carburetor or TBI unit (see Chapter 4).
24   Unplug the EFE heater electrical connector.
25   Remove the EFE heater assembly **(see illustration)**.
26   Installation is the reverse of removal.

---

10   Exhaust Gas Recirculation (EGR) system

General description (non-digital EGR system)

1   An EGR system is used on all engines with which this manual is concerned. The system meters exhaust gases into the engine induction system through passages cast into the intake manifold. From there the exhaust gases pass into the fuel/air mixture for the purpose of lowering combustion temperatures, thereby reducing the amount of oxides of nitrogen (NOx) formed.
2   The amount of exhaust gas admitted is regulated by a vacuum or backpressure controlled (EGR) valve in response to engine operating conditions. The EGR valve, in turn, is under the control of the ECM.
3   Common engine problems associated with the EGR system are rough idling or stalling at idle, rough engine performance during light throttle application and stalling during deceleration.

Check
Refer to illustration 10.6
4   Refer to Chapter 1 for EGR valve checking procedures.
5   If the EGR valve appears to be in proper operating condition, carefully check all hoses connected to the valve for breaks, leaks or kinks. Replace or repair the valve/hoses as necessary.
6   With the engine idling at normal operating temperature, disconnect the vacuum hose from the EGR valve and connect a vacuum pump. When vacuum is applied the engine should stumble or die, indicating the vacuum diaphragm is operating properly **(see illustration)**. **Note:** *Some models use a backpressure-type EGR valve. On models so equipped, backpressure must be created in the exhaust system before the vacuum pump will actuate the valve. To create backpressure, have an assistant hold a thick, folded-up towel against the end of the exhaust pipe while you apply vacuum to the valve.* **Warning:** *Be careful while doing this, since the exhaust gases will heat up the towel considerably. Don't restrict the exhaust system any longer than necessary to perform this test.* Replace the EGR valve with a new one if the test does not affect the idle.
7   Due to the interrelationship of the EGR system and the ECM, further checks of the system should be made by referring to Section 2 or having the system checked by a dealer service department or other repair shop.

Component replacement
Refer to illustrations 10.9 and 10.16
Warning: *Wait until the engine is completely cool before beginning these procedures.*

EGR valve
8   Disconnect the vacuum hose at the EGR valve.
9   Remove the nuts or bolts which secure the valve to the intake manifold or adapter **(see illustration)**.
10   Lift the EGR valve from the engine.

10.9 Removing the EGR valve mounting bolts

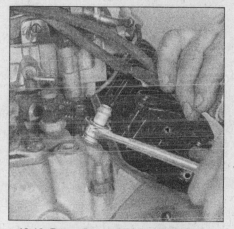

10.16 Removing the EGR TVS from the manifold (some V6 engines)

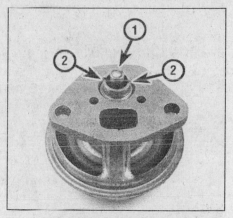

10.17 EGR valves which can be disassembled for cleaning are identified by wrench slots on the pintle (1) and punch marks on the seat (2)

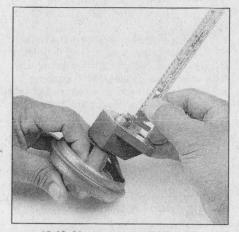

10.19 Measuring the EGR valve seat height

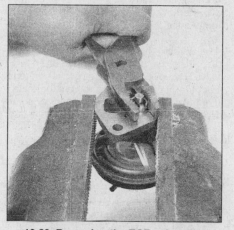

10.20 Removing the EGR valve seat

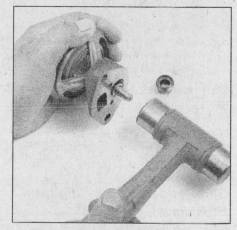

10.30 Deposits can be removed from the EGR pintle seating area by tapping the end of the pintle lightly with a soft-face hammer

11 Clean the mounting surfaces of the EGR valve. Remove all traces of gasket material.
12 Place the new EGR valve, with a new gasket, on the intake manifold or adapter and tighten the attaching nuts or bolts.
13 Connect the vacuum signal hose.

TVS (some V6 engines)

14 Drain sufficient coolant from the radiator to bring the level below the bottom of the TVS. The TVS is usually located at the front of the intake manifold.
15 Remove the hoses from the valve, labeling them to ensure proper installation.
16 Prepare the new TVS by wrapping the threads with Teflon tape. Remove the TVS and replace it with the new one (see illustration). Refill the cooling system (see Chapter 1).

Cleaning

EGR valve

Refer to illustrations 10.17, 10.19, 10.20, 10.30 and 10.31

17 Some 3.0L and 3.8L V6 engines use an EGR valve which can be disassembled for cleaning at the specified intervals. This valve can be identified by two alignment punch marks and wrench slots on the pintle seat (see illustration).
18 Clean the seat, base and threads and note the location of the punch marks for reassembly to the same position.
19 Measure and record the distance from the base surface to the shoulder of the seat as shown (see illustration).
20 Place the valve securely in a vise and unscrew the seat (see illustration). Because the pintle seat is staked in place, it may be necessary to work it back and forth to remove it. A suitable thread penetrant will also help ease removal .
21 With the valve in an upright position, use a pair of pliers to remove the pintle, taking care not to contact the sealing surface.
22 To clean the shaft opening, insert a suitable size drill into the opening in one inch increments, slowly turning it in a clockwise direction. The shaft depth is approximately two inches. Pull the drill bit directly out without turning it and repeat the procedure. The bit will bottom at a depth of about two inches. Tap the valve lightly to dislodge foreign material from the shaft opening.
23 Clean the hole in the pintle with a suitable size drill bit.

24 Clean the inside of the pintle with a suitable tool. Take care not to damage the snapring. Brush or use compressed air to blow out the particles. If compressed air is used, do not blow air directly into the shaft opening.
25 Place the pintle over the end of the shaft and force it down until the locking ring can be felt snapping into position.
26 Screw the seat into the base until the punch marks are aligned in their original positions and the base depth measurement made in Step 19 is reached.
27 Stake the seat in place at the three original staking locations.
28 On all other EGR valves, inspect the valve pintle for deposits.
29 Depress the valve diaphragm and check for deposits around the valve seating area.
30 Hold the valve securely and tap lightly on the round pintle with a soft-face hammer to remove any deposits from the valve seat (see illustration). Make sure to empty any loose particles from the valve. Depress the valve diaphragm again and inspect the valve seating area, repeating the cleaning operation as necessary.

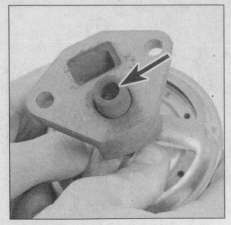

10.31 Check the EGR valve pintle where it extends into the exhaust passage for free movement and clean this area of deposits (arrow)

31   Use a wire brush to carefully clean deposits from the pintle (see illustration).
32   Remove any deposits from the valve outlet using a screwdriver.

EGR passages

33   With the EGR valve removed, inspect the passages for excessive deposits.
34   It is a good idea to place a rag securely in the passage opening to keep debris from entering. Clean the passages by hand, using a drill bit.

General description (digital EGR valve)

Refer to illustration 10.36

35   The digital EGR valve feeds small amounts of exhaust gas back into the intake manifold and then into the combustion chamber.
36   The digital EGR valve is designed to accurately supply EGR to an engine, independent of intake manifold vacuum. The valve controls EGR flow from the exhaust to the intake manifold through three orifices, which increment in size, to produce seven combinations. When a solenoid is energized, the armature, with attached shaft and swivel pintle, is lifted, opening the orifice. The flow accuracy is dependent on metering orifice size only, which results in improved control (see illustration).
37   The digital EGR valve is opened by the ECM, grounding each solenoid circuit. This activates the solenoid, raises the pintle, and allows exhaust gas flow into the intake manifold. The exhaust gas then moves with the air/fuel mixture into the combustion chamber.

Check

38   A special "scan" tool is needed to check this valve and should be left to a dealer service department or other repair shop.

Replacement

39   Disconnect the electrical connector

10.36 Typical digital EGR valve (arrow)

from the EGR valve.
40   Remove the two mounting bolts and remove the EGR valve from the intake manifold.
41   Remove the EGR valve and gasket.
42   Clean the mounting surface of the EGR valve. Remove all traces of gasket material from the intake manifold and from the valve if it is to be reinstalled. Clean both mating surfaces with a cloth dipped in lacquer thinner or acetone.
43   Install a new gasket and the EGR valve and tighten the bolts securely.
44   Connect the electrical connector onto the EGR valve.

---

11   Evaporative Emissions Control System (EECS)

Refer to illustration 11.2

General description

1   This system is designed to trap and

store fuel that evaporates from the carburetor and fuel tank which would normally enter the atmosphere and contribute to hydrocarbon (HC) emissions.
2   The system consists of a charcoal-filled canister and lines running to and from the canister. These lines include a vent line from the gas tank, a vent line from the carburetor float bowl or injection unit, an idle purge line into the vehicle's induction system and a vacuum line to the manifold (see illustration). In addition, there is a purge valve in the canister. The CCCS/ECM controls the vacuum to the purge valve with an electrically operated solenoid. The fuel tank cap is also an integral part of the system.
3   An indication that the system is not operating properly is a strong fuel odor.

Check

4   Maintenance and replacement of the charcoal canister filter is covered in Chapter 1.
5   Check all lines in and out of the canister for kinks, leaks and breaks along their entire lengths. Repair or replace as necessary.
6   Check the gasket in the gas cap for signs of drying, cracking or breaks. Replace the gas cap with a new one if defects are found.
7   Due to its interrelationship with the ECM/self-diagnosis system, other system checks should be made by referring to Section 2 or having the system checked by a dealer service department or other repair shop.

Component replacement

8   Replacement of the canister filter is covered in Chapter 1.
9   When replacing any line running to or from the canister, make sure the replacement line is a duplicate of the one you are replacing. These lines are often color coded to denote their particular usage.

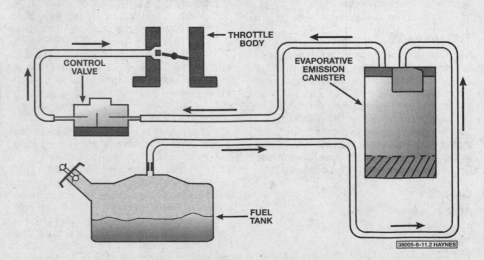

11.2 Details of a typical EECS system

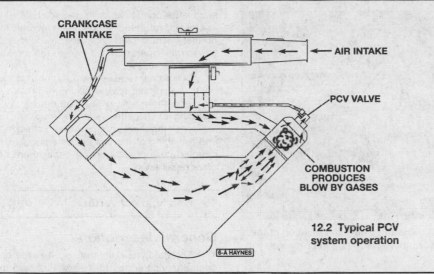

12.2 Typical PCV system operation

13.6 Vacuum applied to the vacuum motor should actuate the damper door

12 Positive Crankcase Ventilation (PCV) system

Refer to illustration 12.2

General description

1   The positive crankcase ventilation system reduces hydrocarbon emissions by circulating fresh air through the crankcase to pick up blow-by gases, which are then rerouted through the carburetor to be burned in the engine.
2   The main components of this system are vacuum hoses and a PCV valve, which regulates the flow of gases according to engine speed and manifold vacuum (see illustration).

Check and component replacement

3   Checking the system and PCV valve replacement are covered in Chapter 1.

13 Thermostatic Air Cleaner (THERMAC)

Refer to illustrations 13.6, 13.9a, 13.9b and 13.17

General description

1   The thermostatic air cleaner (THERMAC) system is provided to improve engine efficiency and reduce hydrocarbon emissions during the initial warm-up period by maintaining a controlled air temperature at the carburetor. This temperature control of the incoming air allows leaner fuel mixture calibrations.
2   The system uses a damper assembly, located in the snorkel of the air cleaner housing, to control the ratio of cold and warm air directed into the carburetor. This damper is controlled by a vacuum motor which is, in turn, modulated by a temperature sensor in the air cleaner. On some engines a check valve is used in the sensor, which delays the

opening of the damper flap when the engine is cold and the vacuum signal is low.
3   It is during the first few miles of driving, depending on outside temperature, that this system has its greatest effect on engine performance and emissions output. When the engine is cold, the damper flap blocks off the air cleaner inlet snorkel, allowing only warm air from around the exhaust manifold to enter the carburetor or TBI unit. Gradually, as the engine warms up, the flap opens the snorkel passage, increasing the amount of cold air allowed in. Once the engine reaches normal operating temperature, the flap opens completely, allowing only cold, fresh air to enter.
4   Because of this cold engine-only function, it is important to periodically check this system to prevent poor engine performance when cold or overheating of the fuel mixture once the engine has reached operating temperatures. If the air cleaner valve sticks in the no-heat position, the engine will run poorly, stall and waste gas until it has warmed up on its own. A valve sticking in the heat position causes the engine to run as if it is out of tune due to the constant flow of hot air to the carburetor or TBI unit.

Check

5   Refer to Chapter 1 for maintenance and checking procedures for this system. If problems were encountered in the system's per-

formance while performing the routine maintenance checks, refer to the procedures which follow.
6   If the damper door did not close off snorkel air when the cold engine was first started, disconnect the vacuum hose at the snorkel vacuum motor and place your thumb over the hose end, checking for vacuum. If there is vacuum going to the motor, check that the damper door and link are not frozen or binding within the air cleaner snorkel. If a vacuum pump is available, disconnect the vacuum hose and apply vacuum to the motor to make sure the damper door actuates (see illustration). Replace the vacuum motor if the application of vacuum does not open the door and the hose routing is correct but the damper door moves freely.
7   If there was no vacuum going to the motor in the above test, check the hoses for cracks, crimps and proper connection. If the hoses are clear and in good condition, replace the temperature sensor inside the air cleaner housing.

Component replacement

Air cleaner vacuum motor

8   Remove the air cleaner assembly from the engine and disconnect the vacuum hose from the motor.
9   Drill out the two spot welds which secure the vacuum motor retaining strap to the snorkel tube (see illustrations).

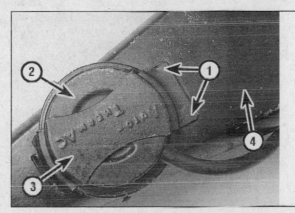

13.9a Components involved in removing the THERMAC vacuum motor on a typical carbureted model

1 Spot welds
2 Motor assembly
3 Retaining strap
4 Snorkle

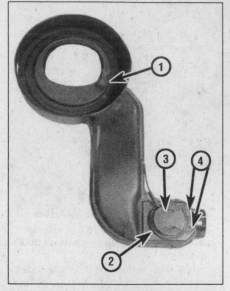

13.9b Components involved in removing the THERMAC vacuum motor on a typical TBI-equipped model

1   *Sensor*
2   *Motor assembly*
3   *Retaining strap*
4   *Spot welds*

10   Remove the motor attaching strap.

11   Lift up the motor, cocking it to one side to unhook the motor linkage at the control damper assembly.

12   To install the new motor, drill a 7/64-inch hole in the snorkel tube at the center of the retaining strap.

13   Insert the vacuum motor linkage into the control damper assembly.

14   Using the sheet metal screw supplied with the motor service kit, attach the motor and retaining strap to the snorkel. Make sure the sheet metal screw does not interfere with the operation of the damper door. Shorten the screw if necessary.

15   Connect the vacuum hose to the motor and install the air cleaner assembly .

Air cleaner temperature sensor

16   Remove the air cleaner from the engine and disconnect the vacuum hoses at the sensor.

13.17 Carefully note the position of the sensor before removing the retaining clip

17   Carefully note the position of the sensor. The new sensor must be installed in exactly the same position **(see illustration)**.

18   Pry up the tabs on the sensor retaining clip and remove the sensor and clip from the air cleaner.

19   Install the new sensor with a new gasket in the same position as the old one.

20   Press the retaining clip onto the sensor. Do not damage the control mechanism in the center of the sensor.

21   Connect the vacuum hoses and attach the air cleaner to the engine.

14   Transmission Converter Clutch (TCC)

1   Toward optimizing the efficiency of the emissions control network, the ECM controls an electric solenoid mounted in the automatic transaxle of vehicles so equipped. When the vehicle reaches a specified speed, the ECM energizes the solenoid and allows the torque converter to lock-up and mechanically couple the engine to the transmission, under which conditions emissions are at their minimum. However, because of other operating condition demands (deceleration, passing, idle, etc.), the transmission must also function in its normal, fluid-coupled mode. When

such latter conditions exist, the solenoid de-energizes, returning the torque converter to normal operation. The converter also returns to normal operation whenever the brake pedal is depressed.

2   Due to the requirement of special diagnostic equipment for the testing of this system, and the possible requirement for dismantling of the automatic transmission to replace components of this system, checking and replacing of the components should be handled by a dealer service department or other repair shop.

15   Catalytic converter

General description

1   The catalytic converter is an emission control device added to the exhaust system to reduce pollutants from the exhaust gas stream. There are two types of converters used. One converter contains pellets coated with the three way catylists while the monolithic converter contains a honeycomb mesh which is also coated with three catylists. The coating on the three way catalyst contains platinum and rhodium, which lowers the levels of oxides of nitrogen (NOx) as well as hydrocarbons (HC) and carbon monoxide (CO) emissions.

Check

2   The test equipment for a catalytic converter is expensive and highly sophisticated. If you suspect the converter is malfunctioning, take it to a dealer service department or authorized emissions inspection facility for diagnosis and repair.

3   Whenever the vehicle is raised for service of underbody components, check the converter for leaks, corrosion and other damage. If damage is discovered, the converter should be replaced.

Replacement

4   Because the converter is welded to the exhaust system, converter replacement requires removal of the exhaust pipe assembly (see Chapter 4). Take the vehicle, or the exhaust system, to a dealer service department or a muffler shop.

Chapter 7 Part A
Manual transaxle

Contents

Specifications

Torque specifications

	Ft-lbs (unless otherwise indicated)
Clutch cover housing bolts	120 in-lbs
Shift control retaining nuts	20
Strut bracket-to-transaxle bolts	35
Strut bracket mounting stud nut	30
Strut bolts	30
Suspension support bolts	75
Transaxle ground cable stud nut	30
Transaxle-to-engine bolts	55
Transaxle mount-to-engine bolts	40
Transaxle mount-to-side frame	
Bolts	40
Nuts	23

1 General information

The manual transaxle combines the transmission and differential assemblies into one compact unit. These models are equipped with four-speed transaxles.

Shifting is accomplished by a floor-mounted shifter, which is connected to the transaxle shift levers by cable assemblies.

2 Transaxle shift cables - removal and installation

Removal

1   Disconnect the battery negative cable. **Caution**: *If the vehicle is equipped with a Delco Loc II audio system, make sure you have the correct activation code before disconnecting the battery. See the information at* the front of this manual for the radio re-activation procedure.

2   Disconnect the retaining clips and cables at the transaxle.

3   Remove the console and shift boot (Chapter 11).

4   Disconnect the cables and remove the shift control lever assembly (Section 3).

5   Remove the left front sill plate and pull the carpet back sufficiently to gain access to the cables.

6   Remove the shift cable cover screws from the floor pan and remove the cables from the vehicle.

Installation

7   Route the cables into position and install the cable cover and attaching screws.
8   Place the carpet in position and install the sill plate.
9   From under the vehicle, route the cables to the transaxle.
10   In the engine compartment, connect the cables and retainers to the transaxle levers.
11   In the passenger compartment, connect the cables to the shift lever and install the console and shifter boot.
12   Adjust the shift linkage (Section 4).
13   Connect the battery negative cable.

---

3   Shift control lever - removal and installation

Removal

1   Disconnect the battery negative cable.
Caution: *If the vehicle is equipped with a Delco Loc II audio system, make sure you have the correct activation code before dis-connecting the battery. See the information at the front of this manual for the radio re-activa-tion procedure.*
2   In the engine compartment, loosen the shift cables at the transaxle levers.
3   Remove the console and shifter boot.
4   Disconnect the cables from the control lever.
5   Unbolt and remove the control lever.

Installation

6   Place the control lever in position and install the attaching nuts, tightening to the specified torque.
7   Connect the cables to the control assembly
8   Install the console and shifter boot.
9   Connect the battery negative cable.

---

4   Transaxle shift linkage - adjustment

1   Disconnect the battery negative cable.
Caution: *If the vehicle is equipped with a Delco Loc II audio system, make sure you have the correct activation code before dis-connecting the battery. See the information at the front of this manual for the radio re-activa-tion procedure.*
2   Place the transaxle in first gear.
3   Loosen the cable attaching nuts at the transaxle levers.
4   Remove the console trim plate, slide the shifter boot up the handle and then remove the console.
5   With the shifter pulled to the left and held against the stop (first gear position), insert a yoke clip or suitable shim so that it is snug enough to hold the lever.
6   Insert a 5/32 inch or No. 22 drill bit into the alignment hole at the side of the shifter assembly.
7   Install a yoke clip or suitable shim between the tower and carrier.
8   To remove any lash from the transaxle, rotate the lever while tightening the nut.
9   Remove the drill bit or yoke clip from the shifter assembly and install the shifter boot and retainer.
10   Lubricate the moving parts of the shift mechanism with white lithium base grease, using a stiff bristle brush.
11   Connect the battery negative cable and road test the vehicle to check the shifting operation. It may be necessary to repeat the adjustment procedure to completely remove looseness or misalignment from the linkage.

Chapter 7 Part B
Automatic transaxle

Contents

Specifications

Torque specifications

	Ft-lbs (unless otherwise indicated)
Shifter assembly retaining nuts	18
Shifter cover screws	132 in-lbs
Shifter cable bracket-to transaxle bolt	20
Shifter cable-to-transaxle lever pin nut	15
Shifter lever to-transaxle nut	20
Transaxle-to-engine bolts	55
TV cable-to-transaxle bolt	
Through 1990	108 in-lbs
1991	84 in-lbs
1992 and later	72 in-lbs

1 General information

Due to the complexity of the clutches and the hydraulic control system, and because of the special tools and expertise required to perform an automatic transmission overhaul, it should not be undertaken by the home mechanic. Therefore, the procedures in this Chapter are limited to general diagnosis, routine maintenance and adjustment and transmission removal and installation.

If the transmission requires major repair work it should be left to a dealer service department or an automotive or transmission repair shop. You can, however, remove and install the transmission yourself and save the expense, even if the repair work is done by a transmission specialist.

Adjustments that the home mechanic may perform include those involving the throttle valve cable, the shift linkage and the neutral safety switch. **Caution:** *Never tow a disabled vehicle at speeds greater than 30 mph or distances over 50 miles unless the front wheels are off the ground. Failure to observe this precaution may result in severe transmission damage caused by lack of lubrication.*

2 Diagnosis - general

Note 1: *Automatic transaxle malfunctions may be caused by five general conditions: poor engine performance, improper adjust-* ments, hydraulic malfunctions, mechanical malfunctions or malfunctions in the computer or its signal network. Diagnosis of these problems should always begin with a check of the easily repaired items: fluid level and condition (see Chapter 1), shift linkage adjustment (see Section 3) and throttle linkage adjustment (see Section 4). Next, perform a road test to determine if the problem has been corrected or if more diagnosis is necessary. If the problem persists after the preliminary tests and corrections are completed, additional diagnosis should be done by a dealer service department or transmission repair shop. Refer to the Troubleshooting section at the front of this manual for transaxle problem diagnosis.
Note 2: A common problem on TCC-equipped models is engine stalling after cruising. For more information, see Troubleshooting at the front of this manual, under the heading Engine Stalls.

Preliminary checks

1 Drive the vehicle to warm the transaxle to normal operating temperature.
2 Check the fluid level as described in Chapter 1:
a) If the fluid level is unusually low, add enough fluid to bring the level within the designated area of the dipstick, then check for external leaks.
b) If the fluid level is abnormally high, drain off the excess, then check the drained fluid for contamination by coolant. The presence of engine coolant in the automatic transmission fluid indicates that a failure has occurred in the internal radiator walls that separate the coolant from the transmission fluid (see Chapter 3).
c) If the fluid is foaming, drain it and refill the transaxle, then check for coolant in the fluid or a high fluid level.

3 Check the engine idle speed. **Note:** *If the engine is malfunctioning, do not proceed with the preliminary checks until it has been repaired and runs normally.*
4 Check the throttle valve (TV) cable for freedom of movement. Adjust it if necessary (see Section 4). **Note:** *The throttle valve cable may function properly when the engine is shut off and cold, but it may malfunction once the engine is hot. Check it cold and at normal engine operating temperature.*
5 Inspect the shift control cable (see Section 3). Make sure that it's properly adjusted and that the linkage operates smoothly.

Fluid leak diagnosis

6 Most fluid leaks are easy to locate visually. Repair usually consists of replacing a seal or gasket. If a leak is difficult to find, the following procedure may help.
7 Identify the fluid. Make sure it's transmission fluid and not engine oil or brake fluid (automatic transmission fluid is a deep red color).
8 Try to pinpoint the source of the leak. Drive the vehicle several miles, then park it over a large sheet of cardboard. After a

4.3a Typical TV cable routing (3.8L V6 engine shown)

A   Cable link end   B   Cable adjuster

4.3b Details of the TV cable adjuster assembly

A TV cable	C Release tab	E Slider
B Locking lugs	D Cable casing	

minute or two, you should be able to locate the leak by determining the source of the fluid dripping onto the cardboard.

9   Make a careful visual inspection of the suspected component and the area immediately around it. Pay particular attention to gasket mating surfaces. A mirror is often helpful for finding leaks in areas that are hard to see.

10   If the leak still cannot be found, clean the suspected area thoroughly with a degreaser or solvent, then dry it.

11   Drive the vehicle for several miles at normal operating temperature and varying speeds. After driving the vehicle, visually inspect the suspected component again.

12   Once the leak has been located, the cause must be determined before it can be properly repaired. If a gasket is replaced but the sealing flange is bent, the new gasket will not stop the leak. The bent flange must be straightened.

13   Before attempting to repair a leak, check to make sure that the following conditions are corrected or they may cause another leak.

Note: *Some of the following conditions cannot be fixed without highly specialized tools and expertise. Such problems must be referred to a transmission shop or a dealer service department.*

Gasket leaks

14   Check the pan periodically. Make sure the bolts are tight, no bolts are missing, the gasket is in good condition and the pan is flat (dents in the pan may indicate damage to the valve body inside).

15   If the pan gasket is leaking, the fluid level or the fluid pressure may be too high, the vent may be plugged, the pan bolts may be too tight, the pan sealing flange may be warped, the sealing surface of the transaxle housing may be damaged, the gasket may be damaged or the transaxle casting may be cracked or porous. If sealant instead of gasket material has been used to form a seal

between the pan and the transaxle housing, it may be the wrong sealant.

Seal leaks

16   If a transaxle seal is leaking, the fluid level or pressure may be too high, the vent may be plugged, the seal bore may be damaged, the seal itself may be damaged or improperly installed, the surface of the shaft protruding through the seal may be damaged or a loose bearing may be causing excessive shaft movement.

17   Make sure the dipstick tube seal is in good condition and the tube is properly seated. Periodically check the area around the speedometer gear or sensor for leakage. If transmission fluid is evident, check the O-ring for damage. Also inspect the side gear shaft oil seals for leakage.

Case leaks

18   If the case itself appears to be leaking, the casting is porous and will have to be repaired or replaced.

19   Make sure the oil cooler hose fittings are tight and in good condition.

Fluid comes out vent pipe or fill tube

20   If this condition occurs, the transaxle is overfilled, there is coolant in the fluid, the case is porous, the dipstick is incorrect, the vent is plugged or the drain back holes are plugged.

---

3   Shift linkage - check and adjustment

---

1   The shift linkage must be maintained in proper adjustment so that the shifter detents always correspond with the transaxle detents. If the linkage is not kept in adjustment, an internal leak in the transaxle could result, causing slippage.

2   Apply the parking brake and block the wheels to prevent the vehicle from rolling.

3   If equipped, loosen the nut retaining the

shift cable to the transaxle shift lever. If there's no nut, pry the cable off the lever **(see illustration 5.4)**.

4   Place the console shift lever in Neutral.

5   Place the transaxle lever in the Neutral position. This is accomplished by rotating the lever clockwise from the Park position, through Park, Reverse and into Neutral.

6   If equipped, tighten the attaching nut securely. The shift lever must be held out of the Park position during tightening.

7   If there is not an attaching nut (later models), hold the transaxle shift lever in position, re-attach the cable and push the locking tab on the shift cable to automatically adjust the cable. An assistant may be necessary.

8   Make sure the engine will start in the Park and Neutral positions only.

9   If the engine can be started in any of the drive positions, as indicated by the shifter inside the vehicle, see Section 5 for the neutral safety switch adjustment procedure or have the vehicle examined by a dealer service department or other repair shop.

---

4   Throttle valve (TV) cable - adjustment and replacement

---

1   The throttle valve cable controls the transaxle line pressure and consequently the shift feel and timing, as well as the part throttle and detent downshifts.

2   The TV cable is attached to the link at the throttle lever and bracket at the transaxle and to the throttle lever on the carburetor or throttle body on the engine.

Adjustment

Refer to illustrations 4.3a, 4.3b and 4.7

3   Whenever the TV cable has been disconnected from the carburetor/throttle body, it must be adjusted after installation **(see illustrations)**.

4   The freeness of the TV cable can be checked by pulling the upper end of the cable. The cable should travel a short dis-

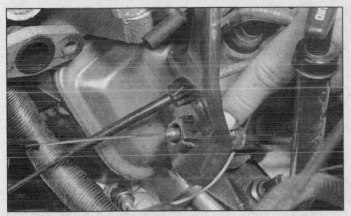

4.7 To adjust the TV cable, press down on the re-adjust tab, move the slider back against the fitting until it stops, release the re-adjust tab and rotate the throttle lever toward the wide-open position until you hear a click

4.13 Use needle-nose pliers to compress the TV cable tangs, then push the housing back through the bracket

tance with light resistance due to the small coiled return spring. Pull the cable farther out to move the lever into contact with the plunger, thus compressing the heavier TV spring. When released, the cable should return to the closed position, verifying that the cable, TV lever and bracket and the TV plunger are moving freely.

5   The engine must be off during adjustment.

6   Remove the air cleaner, labeling all hoses as they are removed to simplify installation.

7   Depress and hold down the metal readjusting tab at the engine end of the TV cable **(see illustration)**.

8   While holding the tab down, move the slider until it stops against the fitting.

9   Release the readjustment tab.

10   Rotate the throttle lever to the maximum travel stop position. The cable will ratchet through the slider and automatically readjust itself.

11   Road test the vehicle. If delayed or only full-throttle shifts still occur, have the vehicle checked by a dealer service department or transmission shop.

Replacement

Refer to illustrations 4.13, 4.15 and 4.16

12   Disconnect the TV cable from the throttle lever at the carburetor or throttle body.

13   Disconnect the TV cable housing from the bracket by compressing the tangs and pushing the housing back through the bracket **(see illustration)**.

14   Disconnect any clips or straps retaining the cable to the transaxle.

15   Remove the bolt retaining the cable housing to the transaxle **(see illustration)**.

16   Pull up on the cover until the end of the cable can be seen, then disconnect it from the transaxle TV link **(see illustration)**. Remove the cable from the vehicle.

17   To install the cable, connect it to the transaxle TV link and install the bolt. Tighten the bolt securely and push the cover securely over the cable. Route the cable to the top of

4.15 Remove the TV cable bolt (arrow) and pull up on the cable until it's out of the transaxle

4.16 Hold the transaxle TV link with needle-nose pliers and slide the cable link off the pin

the engine, push the housing through the bracket until it clicks into place, then connect the TV cable to the throttle lever. Adjust the cable (see above).

5   Neutral start and back-up light switch - replacement and adjustment

Replacement

Refer to illustrations 5.4, 5.6, and 5.7

1   Disconnect the negative cable from the battery. **Caution:** *If the vehicle is equipped with a Delco Loc II audio system, be sure you have the correct code before disconnecting the battery. See the information at the front of this manual for the radio re-activation procedure.*

2   Set the parking brake firmly and shift the transaxle into Neutral.

3   On 1985 and earlier models, where the switch is mounted to the floor shifter, remove the shift indicator from around the shift lever in the passenger compartment (see Chap-

5.4 On some models, there's no nut securing the shift cable to the lever at the transaxle - pry up on the nylon connector with a screwdriver to disconnect it

ter 11, if necessary).

4   On 1986 and later models, disconnect the shift cable at the transaxle shift lever under the hood **(see illustration)**.

5.6 If the neutral start switch is on the transaxle, trace the wires from the switch to the connector (arrow) and unplug it

5.7 Remove the neutral start switch bolts (arrows) (the type that's mounted on the transaxle is shown)

6.4 The rubber-type differential seal (arrow) can be pried out of the housing with a screwdriver; be careful not to damage the splines of the axleshaft (transaxle removed for clarity)

5   On 1985 and earlier models, disconnect the electrical connector at the switch mounted on the floor shift.

6   On 1986 and later models, trace the wire harness from the neutral start switch to the connector **(see illustration)** and unplug it.

7   Remove the screws or bolts **(see illustration)** and detach the switch.

8   On 1985 and earlier models, align the carrier tang on the new switch with the tang slot, set the switch loosely in place and loosely install the screws. Adjust the switch (see below). The remainder of installation is the reverse of removal.

9   On 1986 and later models, line up the flats on the shift shaft with the flats in the new switch and lower the switch onto the shaft. If the switch is new and the shaft hasn't moved, tighten the bolts. If the switch requires adjustment, leave the bolts loose and follow the procedure below. The remainder of installation is the reverse of removal.

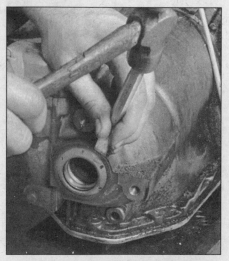

6.5 Dislodge the metal-type differential seal by working around the outer circumference with a chisel and hammer (transaxle removed for clarity)

Adjustment

10   Loosen the switch mounting bolts, then insert a 3/32-inch drill bit into the adjustment hole in the switch.

11   On 1985 and earlier models, rotate the switch until the adjustment hole on the switch is aligned with the carrier tang hole. The drill bit should slide in to a depth of about 5/8-inch.

12   On 1986 and later models, rotate the switch until the drill bit can be felt dropping into the switch, indicating that it's now in the Neutral position. Tighten the switch bolts.

13   The remainder of installation is the reverse of removal. Connect the negative battery cable and verify that the engine will start only in Neutral or Park.

6   Driveaxle oil seal replacement

Refer to illustrations 6.4 and 6.5

1   Oil leaks frequently occur due to wear of the driveaxle oil seals. Replacement of these seals is relatively easy, since the repairs can usually be performed without removing the transaxle from the vehicle.

2   The driveaxle oil seals are located at the sides of the transaxle, where the driveaxles are attached. If leakage at the seal is suspected, raise the vehicle and support it securely on jackstands. If the seal is leaking, fluid will be found on the sides of the transaxle.

3   Refer to Chapter 8 and remove the driveaxles.

4   On rubber-type seals, use a screwdriver or prybar to carefully pry the oil seal out of the transaxle bore. Be careful not to damage the splines on the output shaft **(see illustration)**. If the oil seal cannot be removed with a screwdriver or pry bar, a special oil seal removal tool (available at auto parts stores) will be required.

5   On metal-type seals, use a hammer and chisel to pry up the outer lip of the seal to dislodge it so it can be pried out of the housing

(see illustration).

6   Compare the old seal to the new one to be sure it's the correct one.

7   Coat the outside and inside diameters of the new seal with a small amount of transmission fluid.

8   Using a large section of pipe or a large deep socket as a drift, install the new oil seal. Drive it into the bore squarely and make sure it's completely seated.

9   Install the driveaxle(s). Be careful not to damage the lip of the new seal.

7   Transaxle - removal and installation

Refer to illustrations 7.8a, 7.8b, 7.13, 7.28 and 7.29
Note: *This procedure applies to both automatic and manual transaxles.*

Removal

1   Disconnect the battery negative cable. **Caution:** *If the vehicle is equipped with a Delco Loc II audio system, make sure you have the correct activation code before disconnecting the battery. See the information at the front of this manual for the radio re-activation procedure*

2   Remove the air cleaner assembly. Drain the transaxle fluid (or lubricant) and remove the filter (automatic transaxle only). On automatic transaxle models, replace the transaxle fluid pan.

3   Disconnect the TV cable (see Section 4).

4   Disconnect the shift linkage at the transaxle. On manual transaxle models, also disconnect the clutch cable or release cylinder at the transaxle.

5   Remove the shift linkage bracket. On automatic transaxle models, also disconnect the vacuum line from the vacuum modulator on the transaxle.

6   Loosen but do not remove the left front

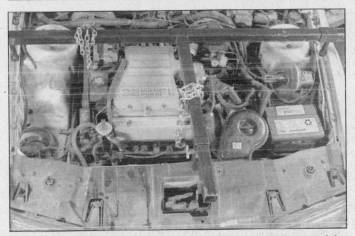

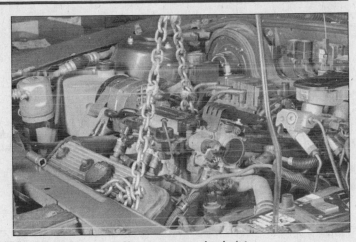

7.8a The engine must be supported from above with a special fixture such as this (2.8L engine shown). . .

7.8b . . .or an engine hoist

wheel lug nuts.

7 Raise the vehicle to provide sufficient clearance for lowering the transaxle and support it securely on jackstands.

8 There are two principal ways of supporting the weight of the engine during the removal of the cradle and transaxle. A special support fixture can be obtained which rests on the shock towers or cowl and radiator support **(see illustration)**, or an engine hoist can be used **(see illustration)**. If the engine support fixture is being used, install it at this time. If the engine hoist is being used to support the engine, the hood must be removed to gain sufficient clearance (see Chapter 11).

9 Disconnect any vacuum or electrical connectors attached to the transaxle which might interfere with the removal of the transaxle.

10 Remove the left front wheel.

11 Remove the strut shock and bracket from the transaxle.

12 Disconnect the speedometer cable or speed sensor electrical connector from the transaxle.

13 On automatic transaxle models, disconnect the oil cooler lines at the transaxle **(see illustration)**.

14 Remove the starter and torque converter splash shields.

15 On automatic transaxle models, mark the relationship of the torque converter to the driveplate to aid in installation.

16 On automatic transaxle models, remove the bolts securing the torque converter to the driveplate.

17 Disengage the driveaxles from the transaxle and insert a plug into the transaxle bore to reduce fluid leakage (Chapter 8). **Caution:** *Care must be taken not to overextend the CV joints and boots whenever the suspension is disconnected.* After disconnecting the driveaxles, the left axle can be removed from the transaxle and supported with a wire. The right axle can be removed as the transaxle is lowered from the vehicle.

18 Disconnect the steering intermediate shaft from the stub shaft on the steering gear by removing the pinch bolt (see Chapter 10).

19 Place a jack with a block of wood as a cushion under the oil pan to support the engine. **Warning:** *Do not place any part of your body under the engine when it's supported only by a jack.*

20 If equipped, remove the bracket supporting the power steering pressure and

return lines.

21 Remove the steering gear mounting bolts (see Chapter 10, if necessary).

22 If equipped, remove the driveline vibration damper.

23 Remove the bolts attaching the stabilizer bar to the left lower control arm (see Chapter 10, if necessary).

24 Disconnect the left lower balljoint from the steering knuckle (see Chapter 10).

25 Remove the stabilizer bar reinforcements and bushings from the right and left sidemembers.

26 Use a 1/2-inch drill bit to drill through the spot welds located between the left rear mounting holes of the stabilizer bar.

27 Disconnect the engine and transaxle mounts from the cradle.

28 Remove the bolts connecting the front crossmember to the right sidemember **(see illustration)**.

29 Remove the bolts securing the left engine cradle section to the body **(see illustration)**. Discard the bolts and use new ones on reassembly.

30 Carefully lower the left cradle section from the vehicle. It may be necessary to pull or carefully pry the section loose.

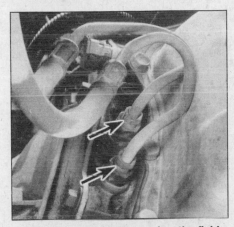

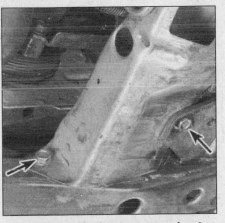

7.13 On automatic transaxles, the fluid cooler lines must be disconnected from the transaxle (arrows)

7.28 Remove the front crossmember-to-side crossmember retaining bolts (arrows)

7.29 Remove the engine cradle retaining bolts (arrow) (left side rear shown)

31   Firmly support the transaxle on a transmission jack. Safety chains should be used.
32   Remove the transaxle-to-engine supports and transaxle mounts. It may be necessary to lift the transaxle slightly to remove the rear support.
33   Remove the transaxle-to-engine bolts and remove the transaxle by sliding it away from the engine and lowering it from the vehicle. Be very careful not to let the torque converter fall out of the bellhousing (automatic transaxle models).
34   On manual transaxle models, inspect the clutch components (see Chapter 8).

Installation

35   Raise the transaxle into position and carefully guide the right driveaxle into the bore.

36   With the transaxle in position, install two four-inch-long bolts in the top transaxle-to-engine bolt holes to use as guide pins when drawing the transaxle into place. Align the torque converter to the driveplate (or align the input shaft on manual transaxle models) and slide the transaxle toward the engine.
37   Install the transaxle-to-engine mounting bolts, tightening to the torque listed in this Chapter's Specifications.
38   Refer to Chapter 11 for the installation procedure of the partial cradle.
39   The rest of the installation procedure is the reverse of the removal procedure with the following notes:

a) *Make sure the transaxle-to-engine bolts and torque converter-to-driveplate bolts are torqued to the proper Specifications*

(see the front of this Chapter). On manual transaxle models, refer to the Specifications in Chapter 7, Part A.
b) *After raising the left cradle section into position and loosely installing the mounting bolts, insert a 1/2-inch bolt through the hole drilled at the spot weld. This will maintain correct alignment as the cradle is bolted into place. After installing the stabilizer bar bushings, remove the bolt.*
c) *The suspension alignment should be checked by a dealer or automotive alignment shop.*
d) *On automatic transaxle models, adjust the TV cable (Section 4).*
e) *Refill the transaxle with the correct fluid or lubricant (Chapter 1).*

Chapter 8
Clutch and driveaxles

Contents

Specifications

Clutch
Fluid type	See Chapter 1
Disc runout	0.020 inch maximum
Slave cylinder pushrod travel	3/8-inch minimum

Driveaxles
Inner CV joint boot length (see illustration 12.3u)
1990 and earlier models (dimension A)	
Tripot design	5-1/16 inches
Ball-and-cage design	5-1/4 inches
1991, 1992, 1995 and 1996 models (dimension A)	4-29/32 inches
1993 and 1994 models (dimension B)	8-7/64 inches

Torque specifications
	Ft-lbs (unless otherwise indicated)
Clutch release lever bolt	30 to 45
Clutch pedal-to-mounting bracket bolt	20 to 25
Clutch pedal-to-locking pawl bolt	44 in-lbs
Clutch pressure plate-to-flywheel bolts	14 to 18
Clutch master cylinder mounting nuts	15 to 25
Clutch slave cylinder mounting nuts	14 to 20
Driveaxle/hub nut	
Initial	70
Final	
1982	225
1983 through 1992	185
1993 through 1995	103 plus an additional 20-degrees rotation
1996	107
Wheel lug nuts	See Chapter 1

1 General information

The information in this Chapter deals with the components from the rear of the engine to the drive wheels, except for the transaxle, which is covered in the previous Chapter. For the purposes of this Chapter, these components are grouped into two categories: clutch and driveaxles. Separate sections within this Chapter offer general descriptions and checking procedures for each of these groups.

Since many of the procedures covered in this Chapter involve working under the vehicle, make sure it is firmly supported on sturdy jackstands or on a hoist where the vehicle can easily be raised and lowered.

2   Clutch - description and check

Refer to illustration 2.1

1   All models with a manual transaxle use a single dry plate, diaphragm spring type clutch **(see illustration)**. The clutch disc has a splined hub which allows it to slide along the splines of the transaxle input shaft. The clutch disc and flywheel are held in contact by pressure exerted by the diaphragm spring in the pressure plate.

2   The clutch release system is operated by hydraulic pressure on some models, while on others a mechanical system is used. The hydraulic release system consists of the clutch pedal, a master cylinder, the hydraulic line, a slave cylinder which actuates the clutch release lever and the clutch release (or throwout) bearing. The mechanical release system includes the clutch pedal with adjuster mechanism, a clutch cable which actuates the clutch release lever and the release bearing.

3   When pressure is applied to the clutch pedal to release the clutch, hydraulic or mechanical pressure is exerted against the outer end of the clutch release lever. As the lever pivots, the shaft fingers push against the release bearing. The bearing pushes against the fingers of the diaphragm spring of the pressure plate assembly, which in turn releases the clutch plate.

4   Other than to replace components with obvious damage, some preliminary checks should be performed to diagnose a clutch system failure.

a)   *The first check should be of the fluid level in the clutch master cylinder. If the fluid level is low, add fluid as necessary and inspect the hydraulic clutch system for leaks. If the master cylinder reservoir has run dry, bleed the system as described in Section 4 and re-test the clutch operation.*

b)   *To check "clutch spin down time," run the engine at normal idle speed with the transaxle in Neutral (clutch pedal up - engaged). Disengage the clutch (pedal down), wait nine seconds and shift the transaxle into Reverse. No grinding noise should be heard. A grinding noise would most likely indicate a problem in the pressure plate or the clutch disc.*

c)   *To check for complete clutch release, run the engine (with the parking brake on to prevent movement) and hold the clutch pedal approximately 1/2-inch from the floor. Shift the transaxle between 1st gear and Reverse several times. If the shift is not smooth, component failure is indicated. On vehicles with a hydraulic release system, measure the slave cylinder pushrod travel. With the clutch pedal depressed completely the slave cylinder pushrod should extend 7/16-inch minimum. If the pushrod doesn't meet this requirement, check the fluid level in the clutch master cylinder.*

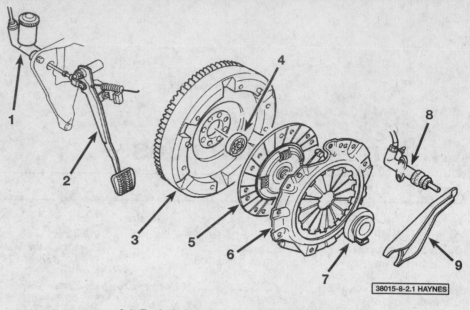

2.1 Exploded view of the clutch components

1	Clutch master cylinder	6	Clutch cover
2	Clutch pedal	7	Clutch release bearing
3	Flywheel	8	Clutch slave cylinder
4	Pilot bearing (if equipped)	9	Clutch release lever
5	Clutch disc		

d)   *Visually inspect the clutch pedal bushing at the top of the clutch pedal to make sure there is no sticking or excessive wear.*

e)   *On vehicles with mechanical release systems, a clutch pedal that is difficult to operate is most likely caused by a faulty clutch cable. Check the cable where it enters the casing for fraying, rust or other signs of corrosion. If it looks good, lubricate the cable with penetrating oil. If pedal operation improves, the cable is worn out and should be replaced.*

3   Clutch hydraulic release system - removal and installation

Refer to illustrations 3.4 and 3.5

Note: *The hydraulic clutch release system is serviced as a complete unit and has been bled of air from the factory, as individual components are not available separately. Other than replacing the entire system, bleeding the system of air is the only service procedure that may become necessary. There are no provisions for adjustment of clutch pedal height or freeplay.*

Removal

Four-cylinder engine

1   Disconnect the cable from the negative battery terminal.

2   Remove the left side under-dash panel.

3   Remove the clutch master cylinder pushrod retaining clip and slide the pushrod off of the pedal pin.

3.4 Remove the clutch master cylinder retaining nuts (arrows)

4   If the system is equipped with a remote fluid reservoir, disconnect the hose at the clutch master cylinder and plug it. Remove the two master cylinder mounting nuts **(see illustration)**.

5   Remove the clutch slave cylinder mounting nuts and detach the slave cylinder, the hydraulic line and the master cylinder from the vehicle as a unit **(see illustration)**.

V6 engine

6   Remove the air intake duct from the air cleaner.

7   Disconnect the battery cables from the battery, negative cable first.

8   Remove the left fender brace above the battery.

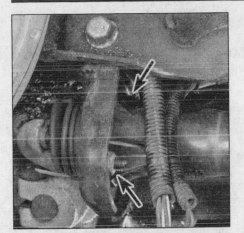

3.5 Remove the clutch slave cylinder retaining nuts (arrows)

9   Remove the battery from the vehicle (see Chapter 5).
10   Using pieces of numbered tape, mark the electrical connectors at the air cleaner and the Mass Air Flow sensor then disconnect the connectors.
11   Remove the PCV pipe clamp from the air intake duct and the air intake duct clamp at the throttle body.
12   Remove the Mass Air Flow sensor mounting bolt and the air cleaner bracket mounting bolts then remove the air cleaner, the Mass Air Flow sensor and the air intake duct as an assembly (see Chapter 6).
13   Remove the two bolts retaining the windshield washer bottle to the left inner fender well then remove the bottle.
14   If your vehicle is equipped with cruise control, unbolt the servo bracket nuts from the left strut tower and reposition the servo assembly.
15   Remove the left side under-dash panel.
16   Remove the clutch master cylinder pushrod retaining clip and slide the pushrod off of the pedal pin.
17   If the system is equipped with a remote fluid reservoir, disconnect the hose at the clutch master cylinder and plug it. Remove the two master cylinder mounting nuts (see illustration 3.4).
18   Remove the clutch slave cylinder mounting nuts and detach the slave cylinder, the hydraulic line and the master cylinder from the vehicle as a unit (see illustration 3.5).

Installation (all models)

19   Install the new slave cylinder into the support bracket and insert the pushrod into the cup on the clutch release lever. Tighten the nuts evenly, a little at a time until the specified torque is reached. **Note:** *Do not remove the plastic strap that holds the pushrod in position. It is designed to break off the first time the clutch pedal is depressed.*
20   Mount the clutch master cylinder to the firewall and install the nuts. Tighten the nuts evenly, a little at a time, to the specified torque. If the vehicle is equipped with a

remote fluid reservoir, reconnect the hose to the clutch master cylinder.
21   Remove the plastic pedal restrictor from the master cylinder pushrod. Coat the inside of the pushrod bushing with multi-purpose grease, connect the pushrod to the brake pedal pin and install the retaining clip. If the vehicle is equipped with cruise control, check to see that the disengage switch on the clutch pedal bracket is in contact with the clutch pedal when the pedal is at rest. If it is not, adjust it accordingly.
22   Pump the clutch pedal several times to break the slave cylinder retaining strap. Leave the remaining plastic button under the pushrod in place.
23   The remainder of the installation is the reverse of the removal procedure.

4   Clutch hydraulic release system - bleeding

1   If it becomes necessary to bleed the hydraulic release system, clean and remove the reservoir cap and fill the reservoir with the recommended fluid. Open the bleed screw on the slave cylinder body and allow the fluid to drip into a container (do not depress the clutch pedal). When it is apparent that there are no more bubbles at the bleed screw opening and a steady stream of fluid is flowing out, close the bleed screw. Re-check the fluid reservoir, topping it up if necessary. The system should now be free of air.
2   To confirm this, measure the slave cylinder pushrod travel, as described in Section 2.

5   Clutch cable - removal, installation and adjustment

Removal

1   Pull the clutch pedal rearward and support it against the bumper stop so that the adjuster pawl is released.
2   Disconnect the clutch cable from the release lever at the transaxle, taking care not to let it snap rearward, which could damage the adjusting mechanism.
3   Remove the left side under-dash panel.
4   Disconnect the clutch cable from the tangs of the detent, lift the locking pawl away from the detent and carefully slide the cable forward between the detent and pawl.
5   Remove the windshield washer reservoir.
6   In the engine compartment, pull the clutch cable out to disengage it from the firewall. Be prepared to retrieve the insulators, dampener and washers, which may separate during removal.
7   Disconnect the cable from the mounting bracket on the transaxle and remove it from the vehicle.
8   Inspect the cable and replace it if it's frayed, worn, damaged or kinked.

Installation and adjustment

9   Connect the cable into both of the insulators and the damper and washers. Lubricating the rear insulator with a small amount of light oil will ease the installation into the pedal mounting bracket.
10   Inside the passenger compartment, route the cable casing into the rubber isolator on the pedal bracket and then attach the cable end to the detent. Make sure the cable is routed underneath the pawl and into the detent cable groove.
11   Install the under-dash panel.
12   Hold the clutch pedal upward against the bumper stop to release the pawl from the detent and install the other end of the cable to the release lever and transaxle mount bracket.
13   Install the windshield washer reservoir.
14   Lift the clutch pedal up several times to allow the mechanism to adjust the cable length, then depress it several times to mesh the pawl with the detent teeth.

6   Clutch release bearing - removal and installation

Refer to illustrations 6.4, 6.6a and 6.6b

Removal

1   Disconnect the negative cable from the battery.
2   On vehicles with hydraulic release systems, remove the under-dash panel and disconnect the clutch master cylinder pushrod from the clutch pedal pin.
3   Remove the transaxle (see Chapter 7A).
4   Remove the clutch release bearing from the clutch fork. Place a mark on the release bearing pad and the release fork so the bearing can be returned to its original position if it is to be re-used (see illustration). Remove the bearing retaining spring from the release fork holes and remove the bearing.
5   Hold the center of the bearing and spin

6.4 Before removing the release bearing from the transaxle, index the bearing pad to the clutch release fork (arrow)

6.6a A small brush makes it easier to lubricate the fork ends

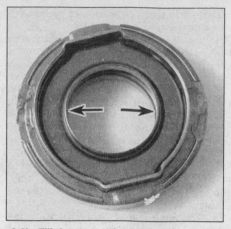

6.6b Fill the groove in the inner diameter of the release bearing with lithium-base grease (arrows)

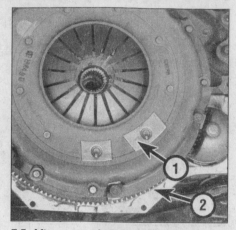

7.5 After removal of the transmission, this will be the view of the clutch components

1   *Pressure plate assembly (clutch disc inside)*
2   *Flywheel*

the outer portion. If the bearing doesn't turn smoothly or if it's noisy, replace it with a new one. Wipe the bearing with a clean rag and inspect it for damage, wear or cracks. Do not immerse the bearing in solvent - it is sealed for life and to do so would ruin it.

Installation

6   Lubricate the clutch fork ends where they contact the bearing lightly with white lithium base grease. Pack the inner diameter of the bearing with this grease (see illustrations).
7   Install the release bearing on the transaxle retainer so that both of the fork tangs fit into the outer diameter of the bearing groove. Be sure the bearing pads are resting on the fork ends with the previously inscribed marks aligned, then install the retaining spring. The spring must be fully seated in the retaining groove and both ends secured in the clutch fork holes.
8   Install the transaxle, making sure that the clutch lever does not move toward the flywheel until the transaxle is bolted to the engine.
9   On models with hydraulic release systems, reconnect the clutch master cylinder pushrod and install the under-dash cover.
10   Check the clutch operation. Adjust the clutch cable and depress the pedal slowly several times to mesh the pawl with the detent teeth (mechanically actuated systems).

---

7   Clutch components - removal, inspection and installation

Refer to illustrations 7.5, 7.9, 7.11 and 7.13
Warning: *Dust produced by clutch wear and deposited on clutch components may contain asbestos, which is hazardous to your health. DO NOT blow it out with compressed air and DO NOT inhale it. DO NOT use gasoline or petroleum-based solvents to remove the dust. Brake system cleaner should be used to flush the dust into a drain pan. After*

the clutch components are wiped clean with a rag, dispose of the contaminated rags and cleaner in a covered container.

Removal

1   Access to the clutch components is normally accomplished by removing the transaxle, leaving the engine in the vehicle. If, of course, the engine is being removed for major overhaul, then the opportunity should always be taken to check the clutch for wear and replace worn components as necessary. The following procedures assume that the engine will stay in place.
2   Remove the left side under-dash panel and disconnect the clutch master cylinder pushrod from the clutch pedal (hydraulic release systems).
3   Referring to Chapter 7 Part A, remove the transaxle from the vehicle. Remove the release bearing (see Section 6).
4   To support the clutch disc during removal, install a clutch alignment tool through the middle of the clutch.
5   If the pressure plate is to be re-used, mark the relationship of the pressure plate-to-flywheel so it can be installed in the same

position (see illustration).
6   Turning each bolt a little at a time, loosen the pressure plate-to-flywheel bolts. Work in a criss-cross pattern, again, loosening only a little at a time until all spring pressure is relieved. Support the pressure plate and completely remove the bolts, followed by the pressure plate and clutch disc.

Inspection

7   Ordinarily, when a fault is found in the clutch system, it can be attributed to wear of the clutch driven plate assembly (clutch disc). However, all components should be inspected at this time.
8   Inspect the flywheel for cracks, heat checking, grooves or other signs of obvious defects. If the imperfections are slight, a machine shop can machine the surface flat and smooth, which is highly recommended regardless of the surface appearance. Refer to Chapter 2 for the flywheel removal and installation procedure.
9   Inspect the facing on the clutch disc. There should be at least 1/16-inch of lining

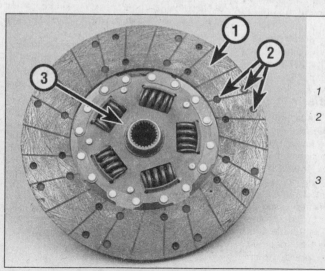

7.9 The clutch disc

1   *Facing - this will wear down in use*
2   *Rivets - these secure the facing and will damage the flywheel or pressure plate if allowed to contact the surfaces*
3   *Markings - "Flywheel side" or similar*

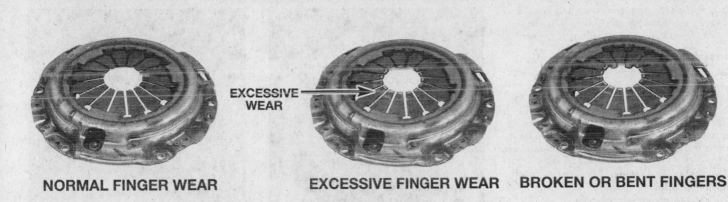

NORMAL FINGER WEAR   **EXCESSIVE FINGER WEAR**   **BROKEN OR BENT FINGERS**

7.11 Replace the pressure plate if excessive wear is noted

above the rivet heads. Check for loose rivets, distortion, cracks, broken springs or any other obvious damage **(see illustration)**. As mentioned above, ordinarily the disc is replaced as a matter of course, so if in doubt about the quality, replace it with a new one.

10 Ordinarily, the release bearing is also replaced along with the clutch disc (see Section 6).

11 Check the machined surfaces of the pressure plate **(see illustration)**. If the surface is grooved or otherwise damaged, take it to a machine shop for possible machining or replacement. Also check for obvious damage, distortion, cracking, etc. Light glazing can be removed with sandpaper or emery cloth. If a new pressure plate is indicated, new or factory-rebuilt units are available.

Installation

12 Before installation, carefully wipe clean the flywheel and pressure plate machined surfaces. It is important that no oil or grease is on these surfaces or the facing of the clutch disc. Handle these parts only with clean hands.

13 Position the clutch disc and pressure plate with the clutch disc held in place with

7.13 Center the clutch disc in the pressure plate with an alignment tool

an alignment tool **(see illustration)**. Make sure the disc is installed properly (most replacement discs will be marked "flywheel side" or similar. If not marked, install the disc with the damper springs toward the transaxle).

14 Tighten the pressure plate-to-flywheel bolts only finger tight, working around the pressure plate.

15 Center the clutch disc by inserting the alignment tool through the splined hub and into the bore on the crankshaft (if not already done). Tighten the pressure plate-to-flywheel bolts a little at a time, working in a criss-cross pattern to prevent distorting the cover. After all of the bolts are snug, tighten them to the torque listed in this Chapter's Specifications. Remove the alignment tool.

16 Using high temperature grease, lubricate the inner groove of the release bearing (see Section 6). Also place grease on the fork fingers.

17 Install the clutch release bearing as described in Section 6.

18 Install the transaxle and all components that were removed previously.

19 Adjust the shift linkage as outlined in Chapter 7 Part A.

8 Clutch pedal - removal and installation

Mechanically actuated clutch

Removal

1 Pull back on the clutch pedal and support it in the raised position. Disconnect the clutch cable from the release lever at the transaxle.

2 Remove the left side under-dash panel then remove the starter safety switch from the pedal and bracket (see Section 9).

3 Disconnect the clutch cable from the tangs of the detent, lift the pawl away and slide the cable between the detent and pawl.

4 Remove the pivot bolt. Remove the spring, pawl and spacer from the pedal

assembly.

5 Remove the detent spacer, bushings, spring and pawl.

6 Clean the parts and inspect for wear or damage. Replace both the pawl and detent if the teeth on either are damaged or worn.

Installation

7 Position the detent spring in the side of the detent and install the detent into the clutch pedal opening, hooking the spring onto the pedal.

8 Install the bushings onto the pedal assembly.

9 Install the pawl, spring, spacer and pivot mounting bolt, tightening to the specified torque.

10 Attach the clutch pedal to the mounting bracket and install the pivot bolt and nut. Both the pivot and pawl bolts must be installed as shown.

11 Check the pawl and detent for proper operation to make sure the pawl disengages when pulled to the upper position and the detent rotates freely in both directions.

12 Attach the cable end to the pawl, making sure to route the cable underneath the pawl and into the detent cable groove.

13 Install the starter safety switch.

14 Hold the clutch pedal up against the bumper stop and release the pawl from the detent.

15 Check the clutch pedal mechanism for proper operation and adjust the cable length by lifting the pedal. Depress the pedal slowly several times so the pawl meshes properly with the detent teeth.

16 Install the under-dash panel.

Hydraulically actuated clutch

Removal

17 Remove the left side under-dash panel.

18 Remove the starter safety switch from the pedal and bracket (see Section 9).

19 Remove the clutch master cylinder pushrod retaining clip and slide the pushrod off of the pedal pin.

20 Remove the clutch pedal pivot bolt and

pull the pedal from the mounting bracket. Extract the bushings and spacer and inspect them for wear, replacing them as necessary.

Installation

21   Lubricate the spacer and bushings with multi-purpose grease and install them on the clutch pedal. Position the pedal in the bracket and install the pivot bolt.

22   Lubricate the master cylinder pushrod bushing with multi-purpose grease, slide it onto the pedal pin and install the retaining clip.

23   Install and adjust the starter safety switch (see Section 9).

24   Install the under-dash panel.

9   Starter safety switch - check and replacement

Check

1   The starter safety switch is mounted on the clutch pedal support and allows the vehicle to be started only with the clutch pedal fully depressed. Place the shift lever in Neutral, depress the clutch pedal and turn the ignition key to the start position. The engine should only crank over when the pedal is depressed.

2   Remove the under-dash panel and unplug the electrical connector from the starter safety switch. Connect the leads of an ohmmeter to the terminals on the switch. There should only be continuity through the switch when the pedal is pushed down. If the switch doesn't operate as described, replace it.

Replacement

3   Disconnect the negative cable at the battery.

4   Remove the left side under-dash panel to gain access to the top of the clutch pedal.

5   At the top of the clutch pedal is a small rod which passes through the pedal. Remove the clip from the end of this rod.

6   Remove the screw which secures the starter safety switch to the clutch pedal support bracket.

7   Unplug the electrical connector from the switch and remove the switch.

8   Install the new switch in the reverse order of removal. Test to be sure that the vehicle can be started only when the clutch pedal is fully depressed. Be sure to perform this test with the shift lever placed in Neutral.

10   Driveaxles - general information and inspection

1   Power is transmitted from the transaxle to the wheels through a pair of driveaxles. The inner end of each driveaxle is splined into the differential side gears, or onto a splined intermediate axleshaft. The outer ends of the

11.5 To hold the hub/disc while breaking loose the driveaxle hub nut, jam a punch into the cooling vanes of the disc

driveaxles are splined to the axle hubs and locked in place by a large nut.

2   The inner ends of the driveaxles are equipped with sliding constant velocity joints, which are capable of both angular and axial motion. The inner joint assemblies consist of a tripot or ball-and-cage bearing and a joint housing (outer race) in which the joint is free to slide in and out as the driveaxle moves up and down with the wheel. The inner joints can be disassembled, cleaned, inspected and repacked, but they cannot be overhauled. If any parts are damaged, an inner joint must be replaced as a unit.

3   The outer CV joints are the crossgroove," or "ball-and-cage," type. The outer joints are capable of angular but not axial movement. The outer joints can be disassembled, cleaned, inspected and repacked, but they cannot be overhauled. If any parts are damaged, an outer joint must be replaced as a unit.

4   The boots should be inspected periodically for damage and leaking lubricant. Torn CV joint boots must be replaced immediately or the joints can be damaged. Boot replacement involves removal of the driveaxle (see Section 11). **Note:** *Some auto parts stores carry "split" type replacement boots, which can be installed without removing the driveaxle from the vehicle. This is a convenient alternative; however, the driveaxle should be removed and the CV joint disassembled and cleaned to ensure the joint is free from contaminants such as moisture and dirt which will accelerate CV joint wear.* The most common symptom of worn or damaged CV joints, besides lubricant leaks, is a clicking noise in turns, a clunk when accelerating after coasting and vibration at highway speeds. To check for wear in the CV joints and driveaxle shafts, grasp each axle (one at a time) and rotate it in both directions while holding the CV joint housings, feeling for play indicating worn splines or sloppy CV joints. Also check the driveaxle shafts for cracks, dents and distortion.

11.6 Using a brass punch, strike the end of the driveaxle sharply with a hammer; when it breaks free, it will move noticeably

11   Driveaxle - removal and installation

Removal

Refer to illustrations 11.5, 11.6, 11.9 and 11.10

1   Disconnect the cable from the negative terminal of the battery. **Caution:** *If the stereo in your vehicle is equipped with an anti-theft system, make sure you have the correct activation code before disconnecting the battery.*

2   Set the parking brake.

3   Loosen the front wheel lug nuts, raise the vehicle and support it securely on jackstands.

4   Remove the wheel.

5   Remove the driveaxle/hub nut and washer. To prevent the disc/hub from turning, wedge a long punch into the brake disc cooling vanes and allow it to rest against the caliper anchor **(see illustration)**.

6   To loosen the driveaxle from the hub splines, tap the end of the driveaxle with a soft-faced hammer or a hammer and a brass punch **(see illustration)**. **Note:** *Don't attempt to push the end of the driveaxle through the hub yet. Applying force to the end of the driveaxle, beyond just breaking it loose from the hub, can damage the driveaxle or transaxle.* If the driveaxle is stuck in the hub splines and won't move, it may be necessary to remove the brake disc (see Chapter 9) and push it from the hub with a two-jaw puller after Step 8 is performed.

7   Place a drain pan underneath the transaxle to catch the lubricant that will spill out when the driveaxles are removed.

8   Separate the strut from the steering knuckle (see Chapter 10).

9   Pull out on the steering knuckle and detach the driveaxle from the hub **(see illustration)**. Don't let the driveaxle hang by the inner CV joint after the outer end has been detached from the steering knuckle, as the inner joint could become damaged. Support

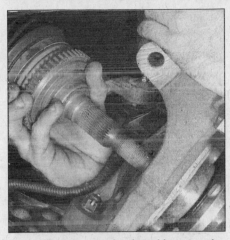

11.9 Pull the steering knuckle out and slide the end of the driveaxle out of the hub

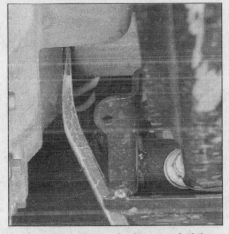

11.10 To separate the inner end of the driveaxle from the transaxle, pry on the CV joint housing like this with a large screwdriver or prybar - you may need to give the prybar a sharp rap with a hammer

12.3a Cut off the boot seal retaining clamps, using wire cutters or a chisel and hammer

the outer end of the driveaxle with a piece of wire, if necessary.

10   Carefully pry the inner CV joint out of the transaxle **(see illustration)** or off the splined end of the intermediate shaft (right driveaxle only, on vehicles so equipped).

11   Refer to Chapter 7 for the driveaxle oil seal replacement procedure.

Installation

12   Installation is the reverse of the removal procedure, but with the following additional points:

a) Seat the inner CV joint in the differential side gear by positioning the end of a large screwdriver in the groove in the CV joint housing and tapping it into position with a hammer. Once this has been done pull out on the joint housing to make sure the retaining ring has seated.

b) Tighten the strut-to-knuckle bolts/nuts to the torque listed in the Chapter 10 Specifications.

c) Install a new driveaxle/hub nut and tighten it to the torque listed in this Chapter's Specifications.

d) Install the wheel and lug nuts, lower the vehicle and tighten the lug nuts to the torque listed in the Chapter 1 Specifications.

e) Check the transaxle lubricant and add, if necessary, to bring it to the proper level (see Chapter 1).

12   Driveaxle boot - replacement

Note: If the CV joint boots must be replaced, explore all options before beginning the job. Complete rebuilt driveaxles are available on an exchange basis, which eliminates much time and work. Whichever route you choose to take, check on the cost and availability of parts before disassembling the vehicle.

1   Remove the driveaxle (see Section 11).

2   Place the driveaxle in a vise lined with

rags to avoid damage to the axleshaft. Check the CV joint for excessive play in the radial direction, which indicates worn parts. Check for smooth operation throughout the full range of motion for each CV joint. If a boot is torn, disassemble the joint, clean the components and inspect for damage due to loss of lubrication and possible contamination by foreign matter.

Inner CV joint

Refer to illustrations 12.3a through 12.3w

Note: Some models use a "ball-and-cage" type inner CV joint instead of the usual tripot design. Aside from a wire retainer ring which must be removed before the ball-and-cage assembly can be removed from the CV joint housing, this unit is similar in construction to the outer CV joint, which is covered in the sequence beginning with illustration 12.4a.

3   To replace the inner boot, refer to the accompanying illustrations **(see illustrations 12.3a through 12.3w).**

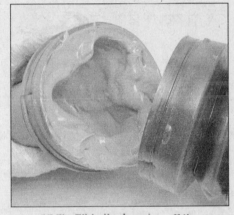

12.3b Slide the housing off the spider assembly

Outer CV joint

Refer to illustrations 12.4a through 12.4t

4   Refer to the accompanying illustrations and perform the outer CV joint boot replacement procedure **(see illustrations 12.4a through 12.4t).**

12.3c On models with a ball-and-cage inner joint, pry out the wire ring bearing retainer with a screwdriver

12.3d Slide the boot towards the center of the driveaxle

12.3e Spread the ends of the stop ring apart and slide it towards the center of the shaft

12.3f Slide the spider (or ball-and-cage) assembly back to expose the retaining ring and pry off the ring

12.3g Carefully tap the spider (or ball-and-cage) off the axleshaft with a brass punch

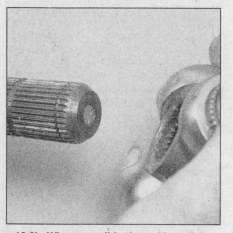

12.3h When you slide the spider off the driveaxle, hold the bearings in place with your hand; even better, use tape or a cloth wrapped around the spider bearing assembly to retain them

12.3i Slide the stop ring and the boot off the axleshaft

12.3j Clean all of the old grease out of the housing and spider assembly, then remove each bearing, one at time

12.3k Carefully disassemble each section of the spider assembly, clean the needle bearings with solvent and inspect the rollers, spider cross, bearings and housing for scoring, pitting and other signs of abnormal wear

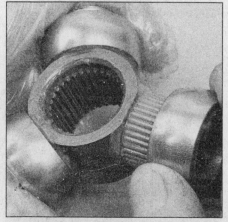

12.3l Apply a coat of CV joint grease to the inner bearing surfaces to hold the needle bearings in place and slide the bearing over them

12.3m Wrap the axleshaft splines with tape to avoid damaging the boot, then slide the small clamp and boot onto the axleshaft

12.3n Remove the tape and slide the stop ring onto the axleshaft, past the groove in which it seats

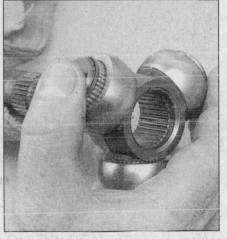

12.3o Install the spider assembly with the recess in the counterbore facing the end of the driveaxle

12.3p On ball-and-cage type inner joints, the small-diameter side of the cage must face the center of the axleshaft

12.3q Use a screwdriver to install the retaining ring, then slide the spider (or ball-and cage) assembly against it and install the stop ring in its groove

12.3r Pack the housing with half of the grease furnished with the new boot and place the remainder in the boot

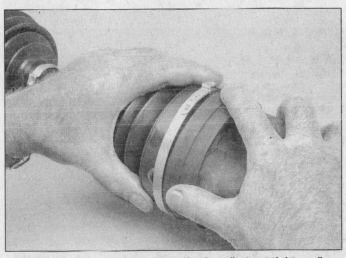

12.3s With the retaining clamps in place (but not tightened), install the joint housing

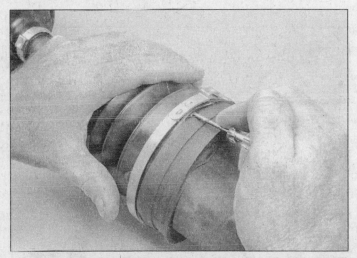

12.3t Seat the boot in the housing and axle seal grooves - a small screwdriver can make the job easier (make sure the boot isn't dimpled, stretched or out of shape)

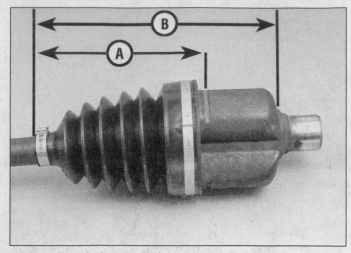

12.3u Adjust the length of the joint to the dimension listed in this Chapter's Specifications

A   *Measure here on all except 1993 and 1994 models*
B   *Measure here on 1993 and 1994 models*

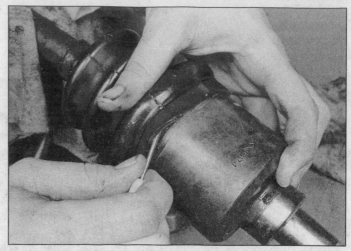

12.3v Equalize the pressure inside the boot by inserting a *dull* screwdriver between the boot and the outer race . . .

12.3w . . . then secure the boot clamps with special pliers (available at auto parts stores)

12.4a Cut off the band retaining the boot to the shaft, then slide the boot toward the center of the shaft

12.4b On models with a retaining ring, tap around the circumference of the retaining ring to remove it from the housing

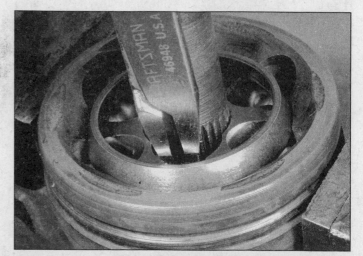

12.4c Remove the snap-ring, slide the joint off the shaft and remove the old boot

12.4d Press down on the inner race far enough to allow a ball bearing to be removed - if it's difficult to tilt, gently tap the cage and inner race with a brass punch and hammer

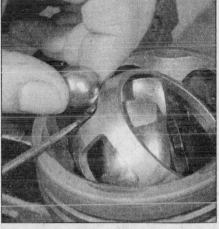

12.4e Pry the balls out of the cage, one at a time

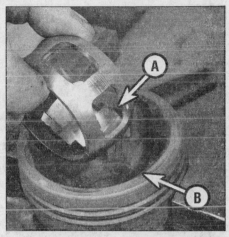

12.4f Tilt the inner race and cage 90-degrees, then align the windows in the cage (A) with the lands of the housing (B) and rotate the inner race up and out of the outer race

12.4g Align the inner race lands with the cage window and rotate the inner race out of the cage

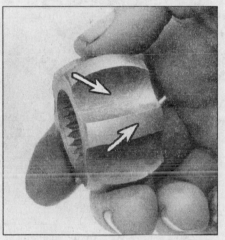

12.4h After cleaning the components with solvent, check the inner race lands and grooves for pitting and score marks

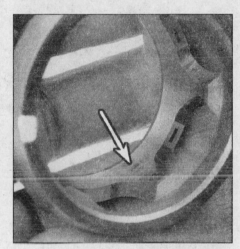

12.4i Check the cage for cracks, pitting and score marks - shiny spots are normal and don't affect operation

12.4j With the race and cage tilted at 90-degrees, lower the assembly into the housing

12.4k Rotate the assembly by gently tapping with a hammer and brass punch, then . . .

12.4l . . . press the balls into the cage windows, repeating until all of the balls are installed

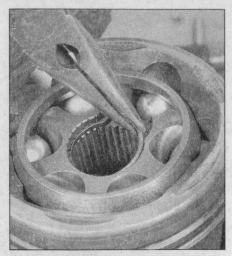

12.4m Use needle-nose pliers to lower a new snap-ring into the groove . . .

12.4n . . . then seat it into the groove with snap-ring pliers

12.4o Apply grease through the splined hole, then insert a wooden dowel (with a diameter slightly less than that of the axle) through the splined hole and push down - the dowel will force the grease into the joint - repeat until the bearing is completely packed

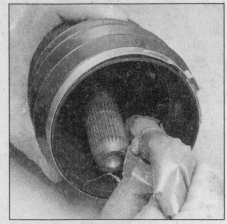

12.4p Install the small clamp and the boot on the driveaxle and apply grease to the inside of the axle boot until . . .

12.4q . . . the level is up to the end of the axle

12.4r Position the CV joint assembly on the driveaxle, aligning the splines, then use a soft-face hammer to drive the joint onto the driveaxle until the snap-ring is seated in the groove

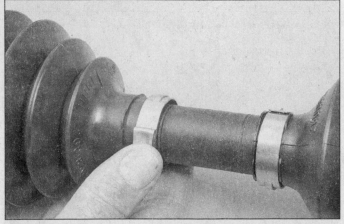

12.4s Seat the inner end of the boot in the groove and install the retaining clamp, then do the same on the other end of the boot - equalize the pressure in the boot (see illustration 12.3v), then tighten the boot clamps with the special tool (see illustration 12.3w)

12.4t On models with a retaining ring, carefully tap around the circumference of the retaining ring to install it on the housing

Chapter 9 Brakes

Contents

Specifications

Front disc brakes
Minimum (discard) thickness	Cast into disc
Disc runout (maximum)	0.004 inch
Disc thickness variation (maximum)	0.0005 inch

Rear drum brakes
Maximum (discard) diameter	Cast into drum
Drum taper (maximum)	0.003 inch

Rear disc brakes
Discard thickness	Cast into disc
Disc runout	0.004 inch
Disc thickness variation limit	0.0005 inch

Torque specifications
Ft-lbs (unless otherwise indicated)

Brake pedal-to-bracket bolt	25
Brake booster nuts	20
Caliper mounting bolts	
1990 and earlier	25 to 28
1991 on	38
Brake hose-to-caliper banjo bolt	
1990 and earlier	18 to 30
1991 on	33
Master cylinder-to-booster	
1990 and earlier	16
1991 on	20
Proportioner valve-to-master cylinder	
1990 and earlier	18 to 30
1991 on	20
Switch piston-to-master cylinder	24 to 48 in-lbs
Parking brake lever-to-rear brake caliper nut	35
Rear brake caliper bridge bolts (1989 and later)	74
Rear brake caliper mounting bolts	
1988 and earlier	30 to 45
1989 and later	74
Wheel lug nuts	See Chapter 1

Component location

Typical front disc brake assembly

1 *Front disc*	2 *Caliper*	3 *Outer brake pad*	4 *Brake hose*

1   General information

Conventional (non-ABS) system

All vehicles covered by this manual are equipped with hydraulically operated front and rear brake systems. All front brake systems are disc type, while the rear brakes are either disc or drum type.

All brakes are self-adjusting. The front and rear disc brakes automatically compensate for pad wear, while the rear drum brakes incorporate an adjustment mechanism which is activated as the brakes are applied when the vehicle is driven in reverse.

The hydraulic system consists of separate front and rear circuits. The master cylinder has separate reservoirs for the two cir-

cuits, and in the event of a leak or failure in one hydraulic circuit, the other circuit will remain operative. A visual warning of circuit failure, air in the system, or other pressure differential conditions in the brake system is given by a warning light activated by a failure warning switch in the master cylinder.

The proportioner valves are designed to provide better front to rear braking balance with heavy brake application. These valves allow more pressure to be applied to the front brakes (under certain braking operations) due to the fact the rear of the vehicle is lighter and does not require as much braking force.

The parking brake mechanically operates the rear brakes only. It is activated by a pedal mounted on the left kick panel.

The power brake booster, located in the engine compartment on the firewall, uses engine manifold vacuum and atmospheric

pressure to provide assistance to the hydraulically operated brakes.

After completing any operation involving the disassembly of any part of the brake system, always test drive the vehicle to check for proper braking performance before resuming normal driving. Test the brakes while driving on a clean, dry, flat surface. Conditions other than these can lead to inaccurate test results. Test the brakes at various speeds with both light and heavy pedal pressure. The vehicle should stop evenly without pulling to one side or the other. Avoid locking the brakes because this slides the tires and diminishes braking efficiency and control.

Tires, vehicle load and front end alignment are factors which also affect braking performance.

Torque values given in the Specifications section are for dry, unlubricated fasteners.

Component location

Typical rear brake drum assembly

1	Primary shoe	4	Actuating link	6	Hold-down spring	8	Adjusting screw
2	Secondary shoe	5	Actuating lever	7	Return spring	9	Hold-down spring
3	Return spring					10	Return spring

Anti-lock Brake System (ABS)

This system is available as an option. It is designed to reduce lost traction while braking. The system is similar to the non-ABS system except for the controller (computer) and related wiring, speed sensors and the hydraulic pump which replaces the master cylinder and power brake booster.

Anti-lock braking occurs only when a wheel is about to lock up (lose traction). Input signals from the wheel speed sensors to the computer are used to determine when a wheel is about to loose traction during braking. Hydraulic pressure will be reduced for the wheel about to lose traction. Diagnosis of this system is beyond the scope of the home mechanic. **Note:** *The ABS system is equipped with a self-diagnosis system similar to the engine codes. However, it is necessary to use a Tech 1 Diagnostic Computer (#94-00101A) linked into the ALDL for access to these codes. Any failures in the ABS system should be repaired by a dealer service department or other repair shop.*

2   Disc brake pads (front) - replacement

Refer to illustrations 2.5 and 2.6a through 2.6l

Warning: *Disc brake pads must be replaced on both front wheels at the same time - never replace the pads on only one wheel. Also, the dust created by the brake system may contain asbestos, which is harmful to your health. Never blow it out with compressed air and do*

2.5 A large C-clamp can be used to compress the piston into the caliper for removal. Note: *Wash the brake assembly with brake system cleaner before proceeding*

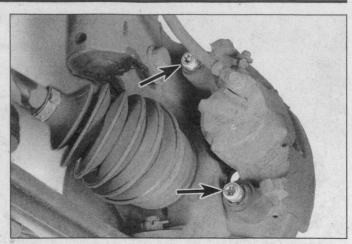

2.6a Remove the brake caliper mounting bolts (arrows) (early models have Allen head bolts, later models have Torx head bolts)

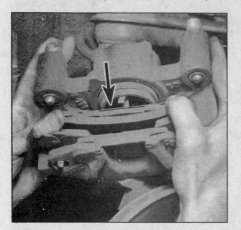

2.6b Remove the inner pad by snapping it out of the piston in the direction shown (arrow)

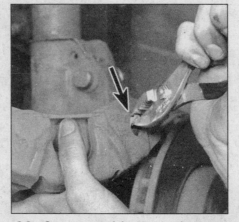

2.6c On some models, remove the outer pad by bending the tabs (arrow) straight out with pliers . . .

2.6d . . . then dislodge the pad from the caliper with a hammer

2.6e On other models, pry the ends of the retaining clip out of the holes in the caliper

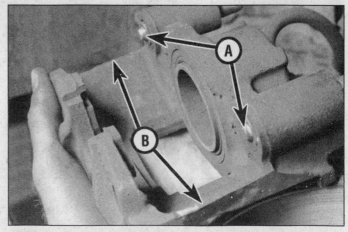

2.6f Inspect the caliper bolts and bushings (A) for damage and the contact surfaces (B) for corrosion

not inhale any of it. An approved filtering mask should be worn whenever servicing the brake system. Do not, under any circumstances, use petroleum-based solvents to clean brake parts. Use brake system cleaner only.

1   Remove the cover from the brake fluid reservoir, siphon off about two ounces of the

fluid into a container and discard it.

2   Loosen the wheel lug nuts, raise the vehicle and support it securely on jackstands.

3   Remove the front wheel, then reinstall three wheel lug nuts (flat side toward the disc) to hold the disc in place. Work on one brake assembly at a time, using the assem-

bled brake for reference if necessary.

4   Inspect the disc carefully as outlined in Section 8. If machining is necessary, follow the information in that Section to remove the disc, at which time the pads can be removed from the calipers as well.

5   Push the piston back into its bore, using

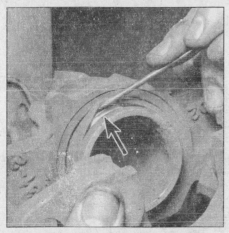

2.6g Carefully peel back the edge of the piston boot and check for corrosion and leaking fluid

2.6h Snap the inner pad retainer spring into the new pad in the direction shown (arrow)

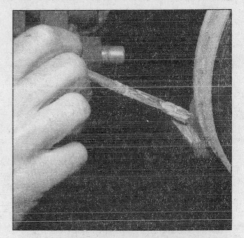

2.6i Lightly lubricate the lower steering knuckle contact surface with high-temperature grease

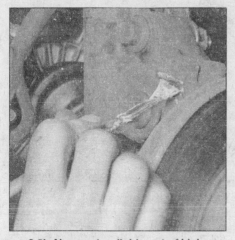

2.6j Also apply a light coat of high-temperature grease to the upper steering knuckle contact surface

2.6k Place the pads in position and snap the inner pad into place in the piston (arrow)

2.6l After installing the caliper, tighten the bolts to the torque listed in this Chapter's Specifications. On models with tabs that protrude through the caliper frame, insert a large screwdriver between the outer pad flange and the disc hat to seat the pad and then bend the tabs over with a hammer - on other models, make sure the ends of the retaining clip on the outer pad fit into the holes in the caliper frame

a large C-clamp **(see illustration)**. As the piston is depressed to the bottom of the caliper bore, the fluid in the master cylinder will rise. Make sure it does not overflow. If necessary, siphon off more of the fluid as directed in Step 1.

6   Follow the accompanying illustrations, beginning with 2.6a, for the actual pad replacement procedure. Be sure to stay in order and read the caption under each illustration.

7   When reinstalling the caliper, be sure to tighten the mounting bolts to the torque listed in this Chapter's Specifications. After the job has been completed, firmly depress the brake pedal a few times to bring the pads into contact with the disc. Test the brakes to confirm proper operation before driving the vehicle in traffic.

---

3   Disc brake caliper (front) - removal and installation

Refer to illustration 3.9
Warning: *The dust created by the brake sys-*

tem may contain asbestos, which is harmful to your health. Never blow it out with compressed air and do not inhale any of it. An approved filtering mask should be worn whenever servicing the brake system. Do not, under any circumstances, use petroleum-based solvents to clean brake parts. Use brake system cleaner only.

Removal

1   Remove the cover from the brake fluid reservoir and siphon off two thirds of the fluid into a container and discard it.

2   Loosen the wheel lug nuts, raise the front of the vehicle and support it securely on jackstands. Remove the front wheels.

3   Reinstall two lug nuts, flat side against the disc, to hold the disc in place.

4   Bottom the piston in the caliper bore. This is accomplished by pushing on the caliper, although it may be necessary to carefully use a flat prybar or a C-clamp **(see illustration 2.5)**.

5   If the caliper is to be removed from the vehicle, remove the brake hose inlet fitting

bolt and disconnect the fitting.

6   Remove the two mounting bolts **(see illustration 2.6a)** and detach the caliper from the steering knuckle. If the caliper is not to be removed from the vehicle, hang it out of the way with a piece of wire so the brake hose will not be damaged.

Installation

7   Inspect the mounting bolts for excessive corrosion.

8   Place the caliper in position over the disc and mounting bracket, install the bolts and tighten them to the torque listed in this Chapter's Specifications.

9   Check to make sure the clearance between the caliper and the bracket stops is

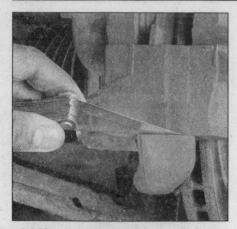

3.9 Measure the clearance between the caliper and bracket stops at the top and bottom

between 0.005 and 0.012 inch **(see illustration)**.

10   Connect the inlet fitting (if removed) and install the bolt (using new sealing washers), tightening it to the torque listed in this Chapter's Specifications. It will be necessary to bleed the brakes (see Section 15) if the fitting was disconnected.

11   Install the wheels and lower the vehicle. Depress the brake pedal a few times to bring the pads into contact with the disc.

---

4   Disc brake caliper (front) - overhaul

Refer to illustrations 4.4a, 4.4b, 4.5, 4.6, 4.10, 4.11, 4.12 and 4.13
Warning: *The dust created by the brake system may contain asbestos, which is harmful to your health. Never blow it out with compressed air and do not inhale any of it. An approved filtering mask should be worn whenever servicing the brake system. Do not, under any circumstances, use petroleum-based solvents to clean brake parts. Use*

4.4a Exploded view of the front disc brake caliper

1	Mounting bolt	5	Inner pad	9	Piston
2	Sleeve	6	Wear sensor	10	Piston seal
3	Bushing	7	Pad retainer	11	Bleeder screw
4	Outer pad	8	Dust boot	12	Caliper housing

brake system cleaner only.
Note: *If an overhaul is indicated, (usually because of fluid leakage) explore all options before beginning the job. New and factory*

rebuilt calipers are available on an exchange basis, which makes this job quite easy. If you decide to rebuild the calipers, make sure rebuild kits are available before proceeding.

1   Refer to Section 3 and remove the caliper.

2   Refer to Section 2 and remove the brake pads.

3   Clean the exterior of the brake caliper with brake system cleaner. Never use gasoline, kerosene or petroleum-based solvents. Place the caliper on a clean workbench.

4   Place a wooden block or shop rag in the caliper as a cushion, then use compressed air to remove the piston from the caliper **(see illustrations)**. Use only enough air pressure to ease the piston out of the bore. If the piston is blown out, even with the cushion in place, it may be damaged. **Warning:** *Never place your fingers in front of the piston in an attempt to catch or protect it when applying compressed air, as serious injury could occur.*

5   Carefully pry the dust boot out of the caliper bore **(see illustration)**.

6   Using a wood or plastic tool, remove the piston seal from the groove in the caliper

---

4.4b With the caliper padded to catch the piston, use compressed air to force the piston out of its bore (make sure your hands or fingers are not between the piston and caliper)

4.5 Carefully pry the dust boot out of the caliper, taking care not to scratch the bore

4.6 The piston seal should be removed with a wooden or plastic tool to avoid damage to the bore and seal groove - a pencil will do the job

4.10 Position the seal in the caliper bore making sure it isn't twisted

bore **(see illustration)**. Metal tools may cause bore damage.

7   Remove the caliper bleeder valve, then remove and discard the sleeves and bushings from the caliper ears. Discard all rubber parts.

8   Clean the remaining parts with brake system cleaner.

9   Carefully examine the piston for nicks and burrs and loss of plating. If surface defects are present, parts must be replaced. Check the caliper bore in a similar way, but light polishing with crocus cloth is permissible to remove light corrosion and stains. Discard the mounting bolts if they are corroded or damaged.

10   When assembling, lubricate the piston bore and seal with clean brake fluid. Position the seal in the caliper bore groove **(see illustration)**.

11   Lubricate the piston with clean brake fluid, then install a new boot in the piston groove with the fold toward the open end of the piston **(see illustration)**.

12   Insert the piston squarely into the caliper bore, then apply force to bottom the piston in the bore **(see illustration)**.

13   Position the dust boot in the caliper

counterbore, then use a drift to drive it into position **(see illustration)**. Make sure the boot is seated evenly below the caliper face.

14   Install the bleeder valve.

15   The remainder of the installation procedure is the reverse of the removal procedure. Always use new sealing washers when connecting the brake hose and bleed the system as described in Section 15.

5   Disc brake caliper (rear) - removal and installation

Warning: *The dust created by the brake system may contain asbestos, which is harmful to your health. Never blow it out with compressed air and do not inhale any of it. An approved filtering mask should be worn whenever servicing the brake system. Do not, under any circumstances, use petroleum-based solvents to clean brake parts. Use brake system cleaner only.*

1   Remove the cover from the brake fluid reservoir and siphon off two-thirds of the fluid into a container and discard it.

2   Loosen the rear wheel lug nuts, raise the

rear of the vehicle and place it securely on jackstands. Release the parking brake handle.

3   Remove the wheel, then reinstall one lug nut, flat side against the disc, to hold the disc in place. Work on one brake assembly at a time, using the assembled brake for reference, if necessary.

1988 and earlier models

Refer to illustrations 5.10 and 5.16

Removal

4   Loosen the tension on the parking brake cable by loosening the nuts at the equalizer (see Section 13).

5   Remove the cable, damper and spring from the cable lever.

6   Hold the lever and remove the nut, then remove the lever, lever seal and anti-friction washer from the caliper actuator screw.

7   Position a C-clamp on the caliper housing. **Note**: *Make sure the C-clamp does not contact the actuator screw.*

8   Tighten the C-clamp until the piston bottoms in the cylinder bore, then remove the clamp.

9   Reinstall the anti-friction washer, lever

4.11 Install the new dust boot in the piston groove with the folds facing the open end of the piston

4.12 Install the piston squarely in the caliper bore

4.13 Using a hammer and seal driver to seat the boot into the caliper bore

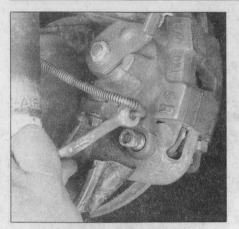

5.10 Disconnect the brake line from the caliper

seal (with the sealing bead against the housing), lever and nut on the actuating screw.

10 Loosen the brake line nut (using a flare nut wrench, if available), then disconnect the brake line from the caliper **(see illustration)**. **Note:** *If you are removing the caliper to replace the brake pads or for access to other components, don't disconnect the brake line.* If the brake line is seized, remove the banjo fitting bolt, banjo fitting and copper washers in order to free the line.

11 To prevent fluid loss and contamination, plug the openings in the caliper and brake line.

12 Remove the caliper mounting bolts.

13 Remove the caliper from the vehicle.

Installation

14 Installation is the reverse of removal. Always use a new lever seal and lubricate it with silicone grease before installing it. Also use a new anti-friction washer. If the banjo fitting was removed, use new copper washers when reinstalling it.

15 When installing the parking brake lever on the actuator screw hex, install the lever pointing down, then rotate the lever toward the front of the vehicle and hold it while installing the retaining nut. Tighten the nut to the torque listed in this Chapter's Specifications, then rotate the lever back against the stop on the caliper.

16 After connecting the parking brake cable **(see illustration)**, tighten it at the equalizer until the lever starts to move off the caliper stop, then loosen the adjustment until the lever just moves back against the stop. Depress the brake pedal a few times to bring the pads into contact with the disc.

17 If the brake line was disconnected, fill the master cylinder and bleed the hydraulic system (see Section 15).

1989 and later models

Removal

18 Remove the brake pads (see Section 6). Detach the parking brake cable and return spring from the parking brake lever. Loosen the cable adjuster at the equalizer, if necessary (see Section 13).

19 If you're removing the caliper for overhaul, remove the bolt which secures the brake hose fitting. If you're removing the caliper for access to other components, skip this step. Plug the fitting to prevent fluid loss and contamination.

20 Remove the caliper mounting bolts with a No. 55 Torx driver. **Note:** *Don't confuse the mounting bolts with the bridge bolts.*

21 Detach the caliper housing from the mounting bracket and the disc. If you're unbolting the caliper to service suspension components, hang the caliper with a wire hook from the suspension. Don't let it hang by the brake hose.

22 Remove the sleeves and sleeve bolts.

23 Inspect the mounting bolts and sleeves for corrosion. Inspect the sleeve boots for cuts, nicks and deterioration. If you find any corrosion or damage, replace the bolts, sleeves and sleeve boots.

Installation

24 Lubricate the outside of the sleeves and the inside of the mounting bolt holes in the caliper housing with silicone grease.

25 Install one sleeve boot in the groove in the mounting bolt hole of the caliper housing.

26 Push the sleeve into the mounting bolt hole, through the installed sleeve boot, about half-way into the hole.

27 Install the second sleeve boot in the groove at the other end of the mounting bolt hole.

28 Push in the sleeve to seat the sleeve boots in the grooves of the sleeve.

29 Repeat Steps 25 through 28 for the other sleeve.

30 Slide the caliper housing over the disc onto the mounting bracket. Install the caliper mounting bolts and tighten them to the torque listed in this Chapter's Specifications.

31 If you detached the brake hose, reattach it and tighten the fitting bolt to the torque listed in this Chapter's Specifications, using new copper washers on either side of the fitting.

32 Install the brake pads (see Section 6). Depress the brake pedal a few times to bring the pads into contact with the disc.

33 If you detached the brake hose, bleed the caliper following the procedure in this Chapter.

34 Check the brake fluid level and add fluid, if necessary (see Chapter 1).

35 Attach the parking brake cable and return spring to the parking brake lever.

36 Adjust the parking brake cable as described later in this Chapter.

---

6 Disc brake pads (rear) - replacement

Warning: *Disc brake pads must be replaced on both rear wheels at the same time - never replace the pads on only one wheel. Also, the dust created by the brake system may contain asbestos, which is harmful to your health. Never blow it out with compressed air and do not inhale any of it. An approved filtering*

5.16 Pull firmly on the cable and engage it with the parking brake lever. Finally, bleed the brakes, have an assistant depress the brake pedal firmly, then bend the ears of the outer pad against the caliper (see illustration 2.6l)

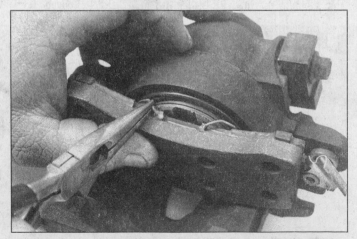

6.9 Rear brake pad installation details (make sure the dampening spring is installed correctly, and the D-notch in the piston face and D-tab on the inner brake pad engage with each other)

mask should be worn whenever servicing the brake system. Do not, under any circumstances, use petroleum-based solvents to clean brake parts. Use brake system cleaner only.

1988 and earlier models

Refer to illustration 6.8

1   Remove the brake caliper (see Section 5).
2   Remove the brake pads from the caliper.
3   Remove the sleeves and bushings from the caliper ears.
4   Using a small screwdriver, remove the flexible two-way check valve from the end of the caliper piston.
5   If leakage is noted at the caliper assembly, refer to Section 7 and overhaul the caliper.
6   Lubricate the new sleeves and bushings with silicone grease and install them in the caliper ears. Lubricate a new two-way check valve with silicone grease and install it in the caliper piston end.
7   Retract the piston in the caliper bore by engaging the tips of a pair of needle-nose pliers with the notches in the piston face and turning the piston until it bottoms in the bore.
8   Position the inner pad in the caliper. Make sure the D-shaped tab on the pad engages with the D-shaped notch in the piston. If the tab and notch do not line up, use a pair of needle-nose pliers to turn the piston until they do.
9   With the tab and notch properly aligned, install the inner pad in the caliper, with the wear sensor positioned so it is at the leading edge. Slide the edge of the plate under the ends of the dampening spring **(see illustration)** and snap the assembly into place against the piston, making sure the plate lies flat against the piston. **Note**: *If the assembly fails to lie flat, recheck the alignment of the D-shaped notch and tab.*
10   Install the outer pad in the caliper.
11   Reinstall the caliper (see Section 5).
12   Depress the brake pedal a few times to bring the pads in contact with the disc.
13   Using channel lock pliers, bend the ears on the upper edge of the plate assembly until they are flush with the caliper housing, with no radial clearance.

1989 and later models

14   Remove the cover from the brake fluid reservoir and siphon off two-thirds of the fluid into a container and discard it.
15   Loosen the rear wheel lug nuts, raise the rear of the vehicle and place it securely on jackstands. Release the parking brake handle.
16   Remove the wheel, then reinstall one lug nut, flat side against the disc, to hold the disc in place.
17   Remove the spring pins from the caliper with a drift punch and hammer. Make sure the outside diameter of the punch is the same size as the outside diameter of the pins. If you use a punch that's too small in

diameter, it may jam in the end of the hollow pins and flare the ends, making them very difficult to remove from the caliper.
18   Remove the springs from the inner and outer pad flanges. **Warning**: *Wear safety goggles during this procedure - the springs can fly off forcefully when pried loose.*
19   Lift the outer pad through the caliper opening and remove it.
20   Lift the inner pad through the caliper opening and remove it. If necessary, push on the bridge and move the caliper housing toward the center of the vehicle to provide enough clearance for removal.
21   Using a small screwdriver, remove the flexible two-way check valve from the end of the caliper piston. If leakage is noted at the caliper assembly, refer to Section 7 and overhaul the caliper.
22   **Note:** *GM recommends using a piston rotator wrench to bottom out the pistons prior to installing new pads. If you don't have this special tool, you'll have to unbolt the caliper housing and slide it off the disc to bottom out the piston. The piston rotator wrench has pins which engage the holes in the face of the piston assembly. Insert the pins into the holes and rotate the piston assembly until it bottoms in the caliper bore.*
23   If you don't have a rotator wrench, remove the rear caliper assembly (see Section 5), place the tips of a pair of needle-nose pliers into the holes in the face of the piston and rotate the piston until it bottoms in the bore.
24   After you have bottomed the piston in the caliper bore, lubricate a new two-way check valve and install it in the piston face.
25   Install the inner pad with the wear sensor at the rear of the pad. Make sure the pad pins on the back of the inner pad engage the holes on the front of the piston. If you have a piston rotator wrench, you can use it to turn the piston until the holes align with the pins; if you don't have a rotator wrench, turn the piston as described in Step 23 with a pair of needle-nose pliers until the holes are aligned with the pins on the back of the pad.
26   Install the outer pad.
27   Using a small hammer and a brass punch (not a steel one), tap in one spring pin until it is through both pads and slightly into the inner section of the caliper housing.
28   Complete the pin installation by tapping in both pins until the end of each pin just protrudes from the inner face of the caliper housing.
29   Make sure the springs are centered on the pad flanges with each spring end projecting under the pins an equal amount.
30   If you removed the caliper to bottom the piston, install it now (see Section 5).
31   Remove the wheel lug nuts securing the disc to the hub.
32   Install the wheels. Tighten the lug nuts securely.
33   Lower the vehicle and tighten the lug nuts to the torque listed in the Chapter 1 Specifications.
34   Depress the brake pedal a few times to

bring the pads in contact with the disc.
35   Check the brake fluid level and add some, if necessary (see Chapter 1).

---

7   Disc brake caliper (rear) - overhaul

Warning: *The dust created by the brake system may contain asbestos, which is harmful to your health. Never blow it out with compressed air and do not inhale any of it. An approved filtering mask should be worn whenever servicing the brake system. Do not, under any circumstances, use petroleum-based solvents to clean brake parts. Use brake system cleaner only.*
Note: *If an overhaul is indicated, (usually because of fluid leakage) explore all options before beginning the job. New and factory rebuilt calipers are available on an exchange basis, which makes this job quite easy. If you decide to rebuild the calipers, make sure rebuild kits are available before proceeding.*

1988 and earlier models

Refer to illustrations 7.5, 7.7, 7.26 and 7.28

1   Remove the caliper (see Section 5).
2   Remove the brake pads from the caliper (see Section 6).
3   Remove the shoe dampening spring from the end of the caliper piston.
4   Place the caliper in a vise equipped with soft jaws and cushion the interior with a piece of wood or shop towels.
5   Move the parking brake lever back and forth to work the piston out of the caliper bore. If the piston will not come out, remove the lever retaining nut and lever and use a wrench to rotate the actuator screw in the

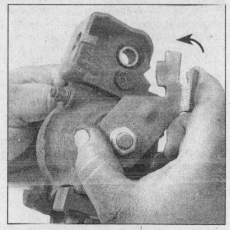

7.5 While pulling out on the piston, ratchet the parking brake lever counterclockwise (towards the parking brake cable bracket); each time the parking brake lever reaches the limit of its travel, rotate it back in a clockwise direction (the piston will retract a little bit each time you rotate the lever clockwise but not as far as it comes out each time you ratchet the lever counterclockwise)

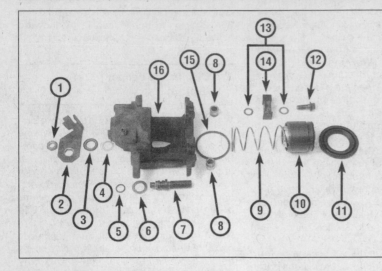

7.7 Rear brake caliper components (1988 and earlier models) - exploded view

1	Parking brake lever nut	9	Piston return spring
2	Parking brake lever	10	Piston
3	Parking brake lever seal	11	Piston dust boot
4	Nylon anti-friction washer	12	Brake hose fitting banjo bolt
5	Actuator screw O-ring	13	Banjo bolt sealing washers
6	Actuator screw thrust washer	14	Brake hose fitting
7	Actuator screw	15	Piston seal
8	Caliper pin bushings	16	Caliper housing

same direction as the parking brake is applied until the piston comes out of the cylinder **(see illustration)**.

6   Remove the balance spring.

7   Remove the retaining nut and parking brake lever, then remove the lever seal and anti-friction washer **(see illustration)**.

8   Press on the threaded end of the actuator screw to remove it from the housing.

9   Carefully pry out the dust boot with a screwdriver **(see illustration 4.5)**.

10   Remove the piston seal with a small wood or plastic tool **(see illustration 4.6)**. Using a metal tool may damage the caliper bore or seal groove.

11   If not previously removed, remove the banjo fitting bolt, banjo fitting and copper washers.

12   If it is damaged, remove the parking brake lever mounting bracket (if it isn't damaged, don't remove it).

13   Inspect the caliper bore and piston seal groove for scoring, nicks, corrosion and wear. Use crocus cloth to polish out light corrosion. Replace the caliper if you can't remove the corrosion in and around the seal groove.

14   Clean all parts not included in the caliper repair kit with brake system cleaner. Never use gasoline, kerosene or other petroleum-based cleaning solvents. Place the caliper on a clean workbench.

15   Use unlubricated compressed air to dry the parts and blow out all passages in the caliper housing and bleeder valve.

16   Install the bleeder valve and tighten it securely.

17   If removed, install the parking brake lever mounting bracket and tighten the bolt securely.

18   Install the banjo fitting, using new copper washers. Tighten the retaining bolt to the torque listed in this Chapter's Specifications.

19   Lubricate the new piston seal with clean brake fluid and install it in the caliper bore groove. Make sure the seal is not twisted.

20   Attach the boot to the piston with the inside lip of the boot in the piston groove and the boot fold toward the end of the piston that contacts the inner brake pad.

21   Install the thrust washer on the actuator screw with the bearing surface toward the caliper housing (copper side facing the piston assembly).

22   Lubricate the shaft seal with brake fluid and install it on the actuator screw.

23   Lubricate the actuator screw with brake fluid and install it in the piston.

24   Install the balance spring in the piston recess, making sure the bottom end of the spring seats in the recess at the bottom of the caliper bore.

25   Lubricate the piston and caliper bore with brake fluid and start the piston assembly into the caliper bore.

26   Using a piston compressor or other suitable tool, push the piston in until it bottoms in the caliper bore **(see illustration)**. Before removing the tool, lubricate the anti-friction washer and lever seal with silicone grease and install them over the end of the actuating screw, making sure that the sealing bead on the lever seal is against the housing. Install the lever over the actuating screw, then rotate the lever slightly away from the stop on the housing and hold it while installing the lever retaining nut. Tighten the nut to the torque listed in this Chapter's Specifications,

then rotate the lever back to the stop.

27   Position the outside of the boot in the caliper recess. Using a seal driver and hammer, seat the boot in the recess.

28   Install the dampening spring in the groove in the piston end. **Note:** *It may be necessary to move the parking brake lever off its stop so the piston may be extended slightly, making the spring groove accessible. If this is necessary, push the piston back into the bottom of the caliper bore before installing the caliper* **(see illustration)**.

29   Install the caliper (see Section 5).

1989 and later models

30   Remove the caliper (see Section 5).

31   Place the rear caliper assembly on a workbench and remove the nut, lever and lever seal.

32   Inspect the bridge and bracket for cracks and other damage

33   Before you remove the piston, place a clean shop towel over the bridge (if you haven't already removed it) and under the caliper housing. Use a wrench to turn the actuator screw in the parking brake "apply" direction. This will work the piston assembly out of the caliper housing.

7.26 Using a piston compressor to bottom the caliper piston in the bore

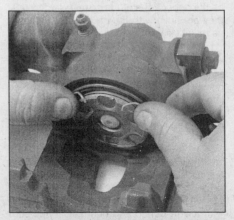

7.28 Install a new pad dampening spring in its groove in the piston; make sure that both ends are positioned as shown

8.5 Checking the disc runout with a dial indicator

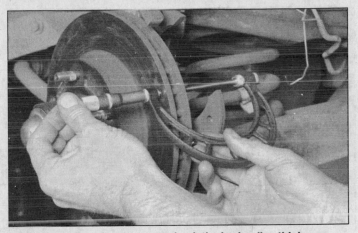

8.6 Using a micrometer to check the brake disc thickness

34   Inspect the piston for score marks, nicks, corrosion and worn or damaged chrome plating. If damage is evident, replace the caliper.

35   Press on the threaded end of the actuator screw to remove it from the housing, then remove the balance spring.

36   Remove the shaft seal and thrust washer from the actuator screw. Discard the seal.

37   Inspect the actuator screw for cracks and thread damage. If any wear or damage is evident, replace the screw.

38   Carefully pry out the dust boot with a screwdriver **(see illustration 4.5)**.

39   Remove the piston seal with a small wood or plastic tool **(see illustration 4.6)**. Using a metal tool may damage the caliper bore or seal groove.

40   Inspect the caliper bore and piston seal groove for scoring, nicks, corrosion and wear. Use crocus cloth to polish out light corrosion. Replace the caliper if you can't remove the corrosion in and around the seal groove.

41   Remove the bleeder valve cap and bleeder valve from the caliper housing.

42   Clean all parts not included in the caliper repair kit with brake system cleaner. Never use gasoline, kerosene or other petroleum-based cleaning solvents. Place the caliper on a clean workbench. Use unlubricated compressed air to dry the parts and blow out all passages in the caliper housing and bleeder valve.

43   Install the bridge and bridge bolts, if you removed them, and tighten the bolts to the torque listed in this Chapter's Specifications.

44   Install the bleeder valve and tighten it securely. Lubricate the new piston seal with clean brake fluid and install it in the caliper bore groove. Make sure the seal is not twisted.

45   Attach the boot to the piston with the inside lip of the boot in the piston groove and the boot fold toward the end of the piston that contacts the inner brake pad.

46   Install the thrust washer on the actuator screw with the bearing surface toward the caliper housing (copper side facing the piston assembly).

47   Lubricate the shaft seal with brake fluid and install it on the actuator screw.

48   Lubricate the actuator screw with brake fluid and install the actuator screw, shaft seal and thrust washer in the caliper housing.

49   Install the balance spring in the piston recess, making sure the bottom end of the spring seats in the recess at the bottom of the caliper bore.

50   Lubricate the outside of the piston with clean brake fluid and push the piston toward the bottom of the caliper bore. When the piston contacts the actuator screw, turn the actuator screw to thread it into the piston and continue turning it until the piston is retracted all the way into the caliper bore.

51   Install the lever seal over the end of the actuator screw. The rubber sealing bead on the lever seal should be against the lever and the copper colored side should be facing the caliper housing.

52   Hold the lever against its stop on the caliper housing and tighten the nut (this prevents accidental application of the parking brake mechanism).

53   Install the lever and nut. The hex hole in the lever must engage the hex on the actuator screw. Tighten the nut to the torque listed in this Chapter's Specifications.

54   Position the outside of the boot in the caliper recess. Using a seal driver and hammer, seat the boot in the recess.

55   Install the brake pads (see Section 6).

56   Install the caliper (see Section 5).

8   Brake disc - inspection, removal and installation

Refer to illustrations 8.5 and 8.6

1   Loosen the wheel lug nuts, raise the vehicle and place it securely on jackstands.

2   Remove the wheel and reinstall the lug nuts, flat side against the disc, to retain the disc to the hub.

3   Remove the brake caliper assembly (see Section 3 or 5). **Note:** *It is not necessary to disconnect the brake hose.* After removing the caliper mounting bolts, hang the caliper out of the way on a piece of wire. Never hang the caliper by the brake hose because damage to the hose will occur.

4   Inspect the disc surfaces. Light scoring or grooving is normal, but deep grooves or severe erosion is not. If pulsating has been noticed during application of the brakes, suspect disc runout.

5   Attach a dial indicator to the caliper mounting bracket, turn the disc and note the amount of runout **(see illustration)**. Check both inboard and outboard surfaces. If the runout is more than the maximum allowable, the disc must be removed from the vehicle and taken to an automotive machine shop for resurfacing.

6   Using a micrometer, measure the thickness of the disc **(see illustration)**. If it is less than the minimum thickness cast into the disc, replace the disc with a new one. Also measure the thickness at several points to determine variations in the surface. Any variation over 0.0005-inch may cause pedal pulsations during brake application. If this condition exists and the thickness is not below the minimum, the disc can be removed and taken to an automotive machine shop for resurfacing.

7   To remove the disc, remove the two lug nuts that were installed in Step 3, then slide the disc off the hub.

8   Installation is the reverse of removal.

9   Drum brake shoes - replacement

Refer to Illustrations 9.5a through 9.5ad and 9.6

Warning: *Drum brake shoes must be replaced on both wheels at the same time - never replace the shoes on only one wheel. Also, the dust created by the brake system may contain asbestos, which is harmful to your health. Never blow it out with compressed air and do not inhale any of it. An approved filtering mask should be worn whenever servicing the brake system. Do not, under any circumstances, use petroleum-based solvents to clean brake parts. Use brake system cleaner only.*

9.5a Drum brake components (1992 and earlier models - left side shown)

1	Return spring	6	Return spring	11	Return spring
2	Secondary shoe	7	Actuator lever	12	Parking brake lever
3	Hold down spring	8	Hold down spring	13	Parking brake strut
4	Adjuster screw spring	9	Primary shoe	14	Wheel cylinder
5	Adjuster screw assembly	10	Actuator link	15	Strut spring

Caution: *Whenever the brake shoes are replaced, the retractor and hold-down springs should also be replaced. Due to the continuous heating/cooling cycle that the springs are subjected to, they lose their tension over a period of time and may allow the* shoes to drag on the drum and wear at a much faster rate than normal.

1   Loosen the wheel lug nuts.

2   Raise the vehicle and support it securely on jackstands.

3   Release the parking brake handle.

4   Remove the wheel and mark the relationship of the brake drum to the wheel flange. **Note:** *All four rear shoes must be replaced at the same time, but to avoid mixing up parts, work on only one brake assembly at a time.*

9.5b Remove the brake drum and clean the brake assembly with brake system cleaner - DO NOT use compressed air to blow the dust from the brake assembly

9.5c Remove the return springs using a brake spring tool

9.5d Remove the hold-down springs and pins by pushing the retainer in and turning it 90-degrees - the tool shown here is available at most auto parts stores

9.5e Lift up on the actuator lever and remove the actuating link from the anchor pin pivot along with the actuator lever and return spring

9.5f Spread the shoes apart and remove the parking brake strut

9.5g With the shoe assembly spread to clear the hub flange, lift it from the backing plate

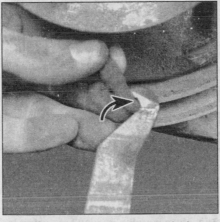

9.5h Disconnect the parking brake lever from the cable in the direction shown (arrow) and remove the shoe assembly

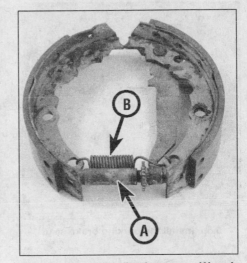

9.5i Remove the adjusting screw (A) and spring (B) from the shoe assembly, making sure to note the direction in which they are installed

5   Refer to the accompanying illustrations and perform the brake shoe replacement procedure. If you're working on a 1992 or earlier model, follow illustrations 9.5a through 9.5x (see illustrations). If you're working on a 1993 or later model, begin with illustration 9.5y. Be sure to stay in order and read the caption under each illustration. **Note:** *If the brake drum cannot be easily pulled off the axle and shoe assembly, make sure that the*

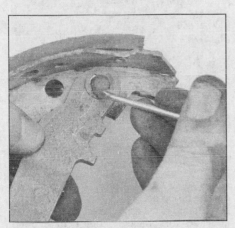

9.5j Remove the parking brake lever by prying the O-clip off

9.5k Install the parking brake lever on the new brake shoe by pressing the C-clip into place with needle-nose pliers

9.5l Lubricate the contact surfaces of the backing plate with high-temperature grease

9.5m Lubricate the adjuster screw with high-temperature grease prior to installation

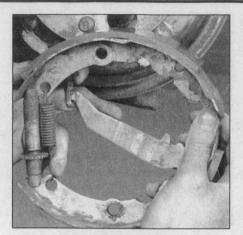

9.5n Connect the parking brake lever to the cable

9.5o Spread the brake assembly apart sufficiently to clear the hub flange and raise it into position

9.5p Install the parking brake strut

9.5q Make sure the parking brake strut is positioned in the shoes properly (arrows)

9.5r Install the hold-down pin and spring on the primary brake shoe

9.5s Install the actuating link

9.5t Install the actuator pivot, lever and return spring

9.5u Install the hold-down spring assembly on the secondary shoe

parking brake is completely released, then squirt some penetrating oil around the center hub area. Allow the oil to soak in and try to pull the drum off. If the drum still cannot be pulled off, the brake shoes will have to be retracted. This is accomplished by first removing the lanced cutout in the brake drum with a hammer and chisel (1992 and earlier models) or removing the rubber plug from the backing plate (1993 and later models). With the cutout removed, disengage the lever from the adjusting screw wheel with one small screwdriver while turning the adjusting wheel with another small screwdriver, moving the shoes away from the drum. The drum may now be pulled off.

6   Before reinstalling the drum it should be checked for cracks, score marks, deep scratches and hard spots, which will appear as small discolored areas. If the hard spots cannot be removed with emery cloth or sand-

9.5v Install the return springs - the special brake spring pliers shown make this step much easier and safer (they're available at most auto parts stores)

9.5w Center the brake shoe assembly so the drum will slide over it

9.5x Adjust the star wheel so the shoes just barely drag on the drum, then back-off the adjustment until the shoes don't drag

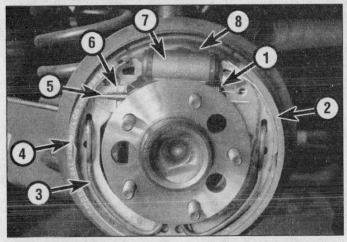

9.5y Drum brake components - 1993 and later models

1	Actuator spring	5	Adjusting screw
2	Trailing shoe	6	Actuator lever
3	Retractor spring	7	Wheel cylinder
4	Leading shoe	8	Backing plate

9.5z Use a pair of needle-nose pliers to remove the actuator spring

9.5aa Wedge a flat-bladed screwdriver under the spring and pry it out of the leading brake shoe, then remove the shoe, adjusting screw and actuator lever

9.5ab Lift the retractor spring from the trailing brake shoe and swing the shoe out from the hub area to gain access to the parking brake cable

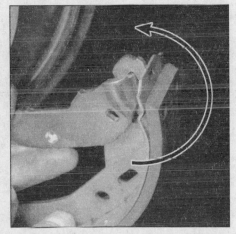

9.5ac Rotate the brake shoe to release the parking brake lever from the shoe

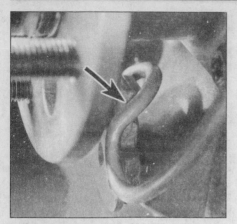

9.5ad Use a screwdriver to pry the retractor spring over the alignment peg (arrow) - to install the new shoes on these models, perform steps 9.5l and 9.5m, then reverse the removal steps and proceed to Steps 9.5w and 9.5x

paper or if any of the other conditions listed above exist, the drum must be taken to an automotive machine shop to have it turned. If the drum will not "clean up" before the maximum drum diameter is reached in the machining operation, the drum will have to be replaced with a new one. **Note**: *The maximum diameter is cast into the brake drum* **(see illustration)**.

7   Install the brake drum. It is not necessary to install a wheel stud lock washer.
8   Mount the wheel, install the wheel lugs, then lower the vehicle.
9   Make a number of forward and reverse stops to adjust the brakes until a satisfactory pedal action is obtained.

---

10 Wheel cylinder - removal, overhaul and installation

Refer to illustrations 10.4, 10.5, 10.7 and 10.13

Removal

1   Raise the rear of the vehicle and support it securely on jackstands.
2   Remove the brake shoe assembly (see Section 9).

9.6 The drum has a maximum permissible diameter cast into it which must not be exceeded when removing scoring or other service imperfections in the friction surface

3   Carefully clean all dirt and foreign material from around the wheel cylinder.
4   Unscrew the brake fluid inlet fitting **(see illustration)**. Don't pull the line away from the wheel cylinder.
5   Remove the wheel cylinder retainer by using a pair of screwdrivers to pry off the clip **(see illustration)**. Immediately plug the brake line to prevent fluid loss and contamination.
6   Remove the wheel cylinder from the brake backing plate and place it on a clean workbench.

Overhaul

7   Remove the bleeder screw, seals, pistons, boots and spring assembly from the cylinder body **(see illustration)**.
8   Clean the wheel cylinder with brake system cleaner. Do not, under any circumstances, use petroleum-based solvents to clean brake parts.
9   Use unlubricated compressed air to remove excess fluid from the wheel cylinder and to blow out the passages.
10   Check the cylinder bore for corrosion and scoring. Crocus cloth may be used to remove light corrosion and stains, but the cylinder must be replaced with a new one if the defects can't be removed easily, or if the bore is scored.

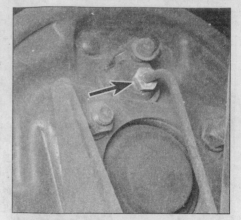

10.4 A flare-nut wrench should be used to disconnect the brake line

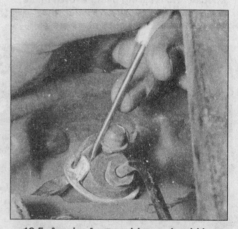

10.5 A pair of screwdrivers should be used to remove the wheel cylinder retainer

11   Lubricate the new seals with brake fluid.
12   Assemble the brake cylinder, making sure the boots are properly seated.

Installation

13   Place the wheel cylinder in position and use a wooden block wedged against the axle flange to hold it in place **(see illustration)**.
14   Install the retainer over the wheel cylinder using a 1-1/8 inch 12 point socket to

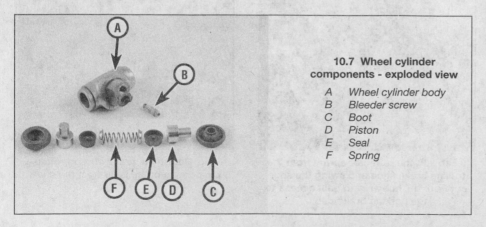

10.7 Wheel cylinder components - exploded view

A   Wheel cylinder body
B   Bleeder screw
C   Boot
D   Piston
E   Seal
F   Spring

10.13 A wood block should be used to hold the wheel cylinder in position

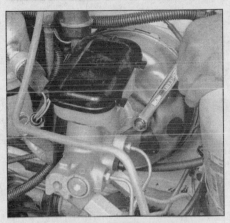

11.4 Remove the master cylinder mounting nuts

11.9 Remove the proportioner valves (1986 and earlier models shown)

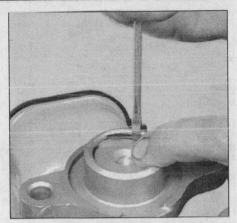

11.12 Press down on the piston and remove the lock ring

11.13 Remove the primary piston assembly

11.15 Pry the plastic reservoir from the cylinder body

11.16 Remove the reservoir grommets

press it into place.

15   Connect the brake line, tightening the fitting securely. Install brake shoe assembly (see Section 9).

11   Master cylinder - removal, overhaul and installation

Refer to illustrations 11.4, 11.9, 11.12, 11.13, 11.15, 11.16, 11.20a, 11.20b, 11.28, 11.30, 11.32, 11.33a, 11.33b, 11.33c, 11.33d, 11.33e, 11.33f, 11.34, 11.35a, 11.35b, 11.35c, 11.35d, 11.35e and 11.36

Note 1: *Before deciding to overhaul the master cylinder, check on the availability and cost of a new or factory rebuilt unit and the availability of a rebuild kit.*

Note 2: *This procedure does not apply to vehicles with ABS.*

1   A master cylinder overhaul kit should be purchased before beginning this procedure. The kit will include all the replacement parts necessary for the overhaul procedure. The rubber replacement parts, particularly the seals, are the key to fluid control within the master cylinder. As such, it is very important that they be installed securely and facing in the proper direction. Be careful during the rebuild procedure that no grease or

petroleum-based solvents come in contact with the rubber parts.

Removal

2   Completely cover the front fender and cowling area of the vehicle, as brake fluid can ruin painted surfaces if it is spilled.

3   Disconnect the brake line connections at the master cylinder, using a flare nut wrench, if available. Rags or newspapers should be placed under the master cylinder to soak up the fluid that will drain out.

4   Remove the two master cylinder mounting nuts **(see illustration)**, move the bracket retaining the combination valve forward slightly (if equipped), taking care not to bend the hydraulic lines running to the combination valve. Remove the master cylinder from the vehicle.

Overhaul

5   Remove the reservoir cover or cap and reservoir diaphragm, then discard any remaining fluid in the reservoir.

6   Clamp the master cylinder flange in a vise. Don't apply pressure to the master cylinder body.

7   If equipped, remove the brake fluid level sensor. Use needle-nose pliers to compress the locking tabs at the inner side of the mas-

ter cylinder.

8   On 1987 and later models, drive out the spring pins with a 1/8-inch punch. Be careful not to damage the reservoir or master cylinder body when driving out the pins.

9   Remove the proportioner valves (1986 and earlier models) or the proportioner valve caps, O-rings and springs (1987 and later models) **(see illustration).** You may have to use needle-nose pliers to remove the proportioner valve pistons - be careful not to scratch or damage the piston stems.

10   Remove the proportioner valve seals.

11   Inspect the proportioner valve pistons for corrosion and deformation and replace them if necessary.

12   Remove the primary piston lock ring by depressing the piston and prying the ring out with a screwdriver **(see illustration).**

13   Remove the primary piston assembly **(see illustration).**

14   Remove the secondary piston assembly. It may be necessary to remove the cylinder from the vise, invert it and tap it against a wood block.

15   Place the master cylinder in a vise and pry the reservoir from the cylinder body with a prybar **(see illustration).** On 1987 and later model master cylinders, remove the reservoir by pulling it straight up.

16   Remove the reservoir grommets or O-

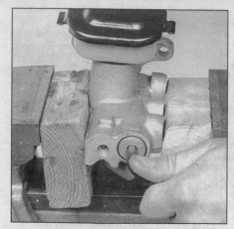

11.20a Remove the switch piston plug (1986 and earlier models)

11.20b Remove the switch piston assembly (1986 and earlier models)

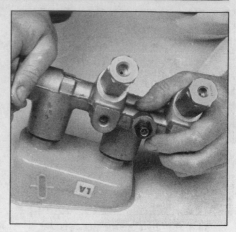

11.28 Use a rocking motion when pressing the reservoir onto the master cylinder

11.30 The secondary piston seals must be installed with the lips facing outwards

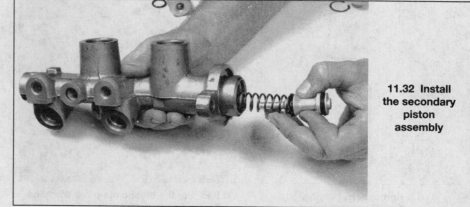

11.32 Install the secondary piston assembly

rings from the master cylinder body **(see illustration)**.

17   Inspect the reservoir for cracks and distortion. Replace it if damage is noted.

18   Be sure to note the installed direction of the old seal lips so the new seals can be installed the same way. The primary piston assembly is serviced as an assembly, while the secondary piston seals can be serviced separately. Clean all parts with brake cleaner. Lubricate all rubber parts with clean brake fluid to ease reassembly.

19   Do not attempt to remove the quick take-up valve from the cylinder body, as this valve is not serviceable.

20   On 1986 and earlier models, remove the switch piston plug and the switch piston assembly **(see illustrations)**. It may be necessary to lightly tap the master cylinder to remove the piston.

21   Inspect the cylinder bore for corrosion and damage. If any corrosion or damage is found, replace the master cylinder body with a new one, as abrasives cannot be used on the bore.

22   Lubricate the new O-rings, proportioner valve seals and proportioner valve pistons with silicone grease supplied in the repair kit.

23   On 1987 and later models, install the new seals on the proportioner valve pistons

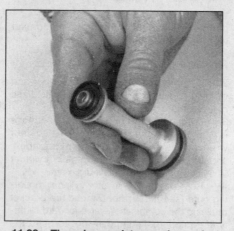

11.33a The primary piston seal must be installed with the lip facing away from the piston

with the seal lips facing up, towards the cap.

24   Install the proportioner valve pistons and seals in the master cylinder body.

25   Install the springs in the master cylinder body.

26   Install new O-rings in the grooves of the proportioner valve caps and install the caps in the master cylinder. Tighten the caps to the torque listed in this Chapter's Specifications.

27   Lubricate the new reservoir grommets

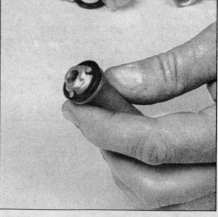

11.33b Install the seal guard over the seal

(or O-rings) with silicone grease and press the grommets into the master cylinder body, making sure they are properly seated.

28   Lay the reservoir on a hard surface and press the master cylinder body onto the reservoir, either by using a rocking motion or by pressing it straight down onto the master cylinder body **(see illustration)**.

29   Drive in the spring pins to retain the reservoir, using care not to damage the reservoir or master cylinder body (1987 and later models).

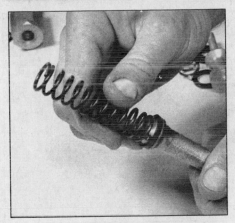

11.33c Place the primary piston spring in position

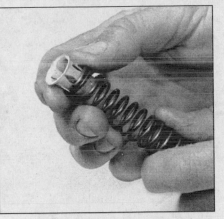

11.33d Insert the spring retainer into the spring

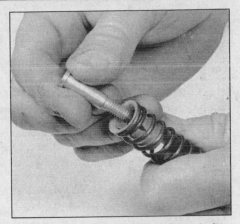

11.33e Insert the spring retaining bolt through the retainer and spring and thread it into the piston

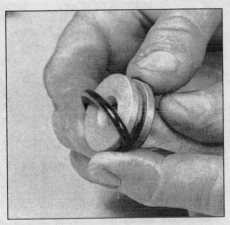

11.33f Install the O-ring on the piston

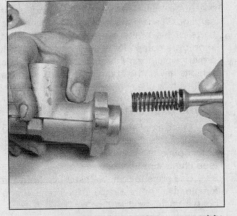

11.34 Install the primary piston assembly in the body

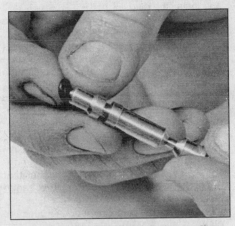

11.35a Install the small O-ring on the switch piston (1986 and earlier models)

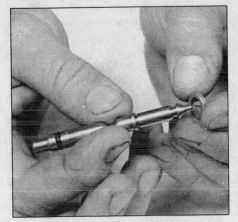

11.35b Install the metal retainer on the switch piston (1986 and earlier models)

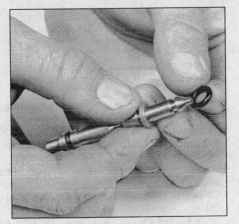

11.35c Install the large O-ring on the switch piston (1986 and earlier models)

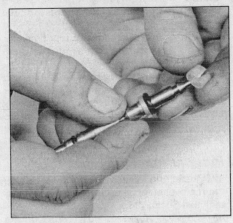

11.35d Install the plastic retainer on the switch piston (1986 and earlier models)

30 Remove the old seals from the secondary piston assembly and install the new seals so the cups face out **(see illustration)**.
31 Attach the spring retainer to the secondary piston assembly.
32 Lubricate the cylinder bore and secondary piston assembly with clean brake fluid

and install the spring and secondary piston assembly into the cylinder **(see illustration)**.
33 Disassemble the primary piston assembly, noting the position of the parts, then lubricate the new seals with clean brake fluid and install them on the piston **(see illustrations)**.
34 Lubricate the primary piston assembly

and install it in the cylinder bore. Depress it and install the lock ring **(see illustration)**.
35 On 1986 and earlier models, install the new O-rings on the switch piston, lubricate the piston with brake fluid and carefully insert it back into the master cylinder **(see illustrations)**. Install a new O-ring on the piston plug

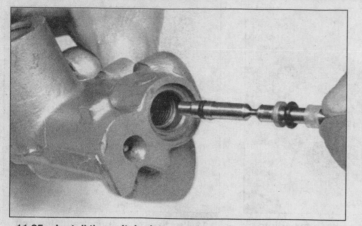

11.35e Install the switch piston assembly into the cylinder body (1986 and earlier models)

11.36 Install the reservoir diaphragm into the cover (1986 and earlier models)

and install the plug.

36   On 1986 and earlier models, attach the diaphragm to the cover **(see illustration)**.

37   **Note**: *Whenever the master cylinder is removed, the complete hydraulic system must be bled*. The time required to bleed the system can be reduced if the master cylinder is filled with fluid and bench bled (refer to Steps 38 through 41) before the master cylinder is installed on the vehicle.

38   Insert threaded plugs of the correct size into the cylinder outlet holes and fill the reservoir with brake fluid. The master cylinder should be supported in such a manner that brake fluid will not spill during the bench bleeding procedure.

39   Loosen one plug at a time and push the piston assembly into the bore to force air from the master cylinder. To prevent air from being drawn back into the cylinder, the appropriate plug must be replaced before allowing the piston to return to its original position.

40   Stroke the piston three or four times for each outlet to ensure that all air has been expelled.

41   Refill the master cylinder reservoirs and install the cap or diaphragm and cover assembly. **Note**: *The reservoirs should only be filled to the top of the reservoir divider to prevent overflowing when the cover is installed.*

Installation

42   Install the master cylinder by reversing the removal steps, then bleed the brake system (see Section 15).

43   Test the brakes carefully before driving the vehicle in traffic.

12 Brake hoses and lines - inspection and replacement

Refer to illustration 12.2

1   Every six months, with the vehicle raised and placed securely on jackstands, the flexible hoses which connect the steel brake lines with the front and rear brake assemblies

should be inspected for cracks, chafing of the outer cover, leaks, blisters and other damage. These are important and vulnerable parts of the brake system and inspection should be complete. A light and mirror will prove helpful for a thorough check. If a hose exhibits any of the above conditions, replace it with a new one.

Front brake hose

2   Using a back-up wrench, disconnect the brake line from the hose fitting, being careful not to bend the frame bracket or brake line **(see illustration)**.

3   Use pliers to remove the U-clip from the female fitting at the bracket, then remove the hose from the bracket.

4   At the caliper end of the hose, remove the bolt from the fitting block, then remove the hose and the copper gaskets on either side of the fitting block.

5   When installing the hose, always use new sealing washers on either side of the fitting block and lubricate all bolt threads with clean brake fluid before installation.

6   With the fitting flange engaged with the caliper locating ledge, attach the hose to the caliper.

7   Without twisting the hose, install the female fitting in the hose bracket. It will fit the bracket in only one position.

8   Install the U-clip retaining the female fitting to the frame bracket.

9   Using a back-up wrench, attach the brake line to the hose fitting.

10   When the brake hose installation is complete, there should be no kinks in the hose. Make sure the hose does not contact any part of the suspension. Check this by turning the wheels to the extreme left and right positions. If the hose makes contact, remove the hose and correct the installation as necessary.

Rear brake hose

11   Using a back-up wrench, disconnect the hose at both ends, being careful not to bend the bracket or steel lines **(see illustration 12.2)**.

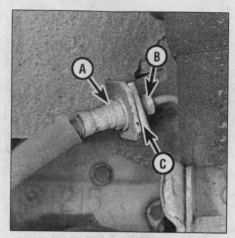

12.2 Using a back-up wrench on the flexible hose side of the fitting (A), loosen the tube nut (B) with a flare nut wrench, then remove the U-clip (C) from the hose fitting

12   Remove the two U-clips with pliers and separate the female fittings from the brackets.

13   Unbolt the hose retaining clip and remove the hose.

14   Without twisting the hose, install the female ends of the hose in the frame brackets. It will fit the bracket in only one position.

15   Install the U-clips retaining the female end to the bracket.

16   Using a back-up wrench, attach the steel line fittings to the female fittings. Again, be careful not to bend the bracket or steel line.

17   Check that the hose installation did not loosen the frame bracket. Tighten the bracket if necessary.

18   Fill the master cylinder reservoir and bleed the system (see Section 15).

Steel brake lines

19   When replacing brake lines be sure to use the correct parts. Never substitute copper tubing because copper is subject to fatigue cracking and corrosion. The outside

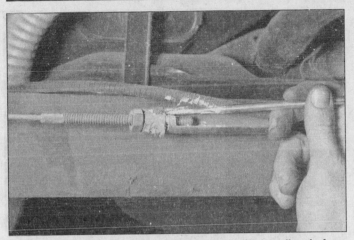

13.3 Lubricate the threads of the parking brake equalizer before adjusting the cable

14.10 Remove the brake booster mounting nuts (arrows)

diameter of the tubing is used for sizing.

20 Prefabricated brake line, with the tube ends already flared and fittings installed, is available at auto parts stores and dealer parts departments.

21 When installing the new brake line, make sure it's securely supported in the brackets and has plenty of clearance from moving or hot components.

22 After installation, check the master cylinder fluid level and add fluid as necessary (see Chapter 1). Bleed the brake system (see Section 15) and test the brakes carefully before driving the vehicle in traffic.

13 Parking brake - adjustment

Refer to illustration 13.3

Drum brake models

1 Apply the parking brake pedal exactly three ratchet clicks.

2 Raise the rear of the vehicle and support it securely on jackstands. Block the front wheels.

3 Before adjusting, make sure the threads of the parking brake equalizer are lubricated liberally with multi-purpose grease **(see illustration)**.

4 Tighten the adjusting nut until the right rear wheel can just be turned rearward with two hands, but locks when forward motion is attempted.

5 Release the parking brake pedal and check to make sure the rear wheels turn freely in both directions with no drag.

6 Lower the vehicle.

Disc brake models

7 Release the parking brake.

8 Raise the rear of the vehicle and support it securely on jackstands. Block the front wheels.

9 Hold the brake cable stud and tighten the equalizer nut until there is no cable slack.

10 Make sure the caliper levers are against

the stops on the caliper housing after tightening the equalizer nut.

11 If the levers are off the stops, loosen the cable until the levers return to the stops.

12 Operate the parking brake several times to check the adjustment. A properly adjusted brake cable will require 14 to 16 notches of movement at the pedal when enough force is applied to lock the rear wheels.

13 Lower the vehicle. The levers must be on the caliper stops after adjustment. Back off the parking brake equalizer if the levers are not against the stops when the vehicle is lowered.

14 Power brake booster - check, removal, and installation

Refer to illustration 14.10

1 The power brake unit requires no special maintenance apart from periodic inspection of the hoses and inspection of the air filter beneath the boot at the pedal pushrod end.

2 Dismantling of the power brake unit requires special tools. If a problem develops, it is recommended that a new or factory-exchange unit be installed rather than trying to overhaul the original booster.

Operating check

3 Depress the brake pedal several times with the engine off and make sure there's no change in the pedal reserve distance.

4 Depress the pedal and start the engine. If the pedal goes down slightly, operation is normal.

Airtightness check

5 Start the engine and turn it off after one or two minutes. Depress the brake pedal slowly several times. If pedal resistance increases each time (gets harder to push down), the booster is airtight.

6 Depress the brake pedal while the engine is running, then stop the engine with

the pedal depressed. If there's no change in the pedal reserve travel after holding the pedal for 30 seconds, the booster is airtight.

Removal and installation

7 Remove the mounting nuts which hold the master cylinder to the power brake unit. Position the master cylinder out of the way, being careful not to strain the lines leading to the master cylinder. If there is any doubt as to the flexibility of the lines, disconnect them at the cylinder and plug the ends.

8 Disconnect the vacuum hose leading to the front of the power brake booster. Cover the end of the hose.

9 Inside the vehicle, disconnect the power brake pushrod from the brake pedal. Do not force the pushrod to the side when disconnecting it.

10 Remove the four booster mounting nuts and carefully lift the unit out of the engine compartment **(see illustration)**.

11 When installing, loosely install the four mounting nuts and connect the pushrod to the brake pedal. Tighten the nuts to the torque listed in this Chapter's Specifications and reconnect the vacuum hose and master cylinder. If the hydraulic brake lines were disconnected, the entire brake system must be bled to eliminate any air which has entered the system (see Section 15).

15 Hydraulic system - bleeding

Refer to illustration 15.19

1 Bleeding the hydraulic system is necessary to remove air whenever it is introduced into the brake system.

2 It may be necessary to bleed the system at all four brakes if air as entered the system due to low fluid level, or if the brake lines have been disconnected at the master cylinder.

3 If a brake line was disconnected only at one wheel, then only that wheel cylinder or caliper must be bled.

4 If a brake line is disconnected at a fitting

15.19 Details of the brake bleeding procedure

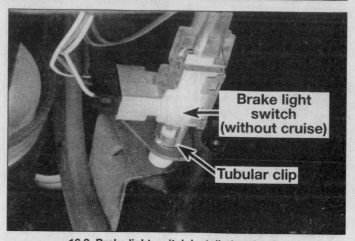

Brake light switch (without cruise)

Tubular clip

16.3 Brake light switch installation details

located between the master cylinder and any of the brakes, that part of the system served by the disconnected line must be bled.

Conventional brake system

5   If the master cylinder has been removed from the vehicle or is suspected of having, air in the bore, the master cylinder must be bled before any wheel cylinder or caliper is bled. Follow Steps 6 through 15 to bleed the master cylinder while it is installed on the vehicle.

6   Remove the vacuum reserve from the brake power booster by applying the brake several times with the engine off.

7   Remove the master cylinder reservoir cover and fill the reservoir with brake fluid. Keep checking the fluid level often during the bleeding operation, adding fluid as necessary to keep the reservoir full. Reinstall the cover.

8   Disconnect the forward brake line connection at the master cylinder.

9   Fill the master cylinder with brake fluid until it begins to flow from the forward line connector port. Have a container and shop rags handy to catch and clean up spilled fluid.

10   Reconnect the forward brake line to the master cylinder.

11   Have an assistant depress the brake pedal very slowly, one time only, and hold it down.

12   Loosen the forward brake line at the master cylinder to purge the air from the bore, retighten the connection, then have the brake pedal released slowly.

13   Wait 15 seconds (this is important).

14   Repeat the sequence, including the 15 second wait, until all air is removed from the bore.

15   After the forward port has been completely purged of air, bleed the rear port in the same manner.

16   To bleed the individual wheel cylinders or calipers, first refer to Steps 6 and 7.

17   Have an assistant on hand, as well as a supply of new brake fluid, an empty clear plastic container, a length of 3/16-inch plastic, rubber or vinyl tubing to fit over the

bleeder valve and a wrench to open and close the bleeder valve. The vehicle may have to be raised and placed on jackstands for clearance.

18   Beginning at the right rear wheel, loosen the bleeder valve slightly, then tighten it to a point where it is snug but can still be loosened quickly and easily.

19   Place one end of the tubing over the bleeder valve and submerge the other end in brake fluid in the container **(see illustration)**.

20   Have the assistant pump the brakes a few times to get pressure in the system, then hold the pedal firmly depressed.

21   While the pedal is held depressed, open the bleeder valve just enough to allow a flow of fluid to leave the valve. Watch for air bubbles to exit the submerged end of the tube. When the fluid flow slows after a couple of seconds, close the valve again and have your assistant release the pedal.

22   Repeat Steps 20 and 21 until no more air is seen leaving the tube, then tighten the bleeder valve and proceed to the left front wheel, the left rear wheel and the right front wheel, in that order, and perform the same procedure. Be sure to check the fluid in the master cylinder reservoir frequently.

23   Never use old brake fluid because it absorbs moisture which will deteriorate the brake system components and could cause the fluid to boil, which could render the brake system inoperative.

24   Refill the master cylinder with fluid at the end of the operation. Check the operation of the brakes. The pedal should feel solid when depressed, with no sponginess. **Warning:** *Do not operate the vehicle if you are in doubt about the effectiveness of the brake system.*

Anti-lock Brake System (ABS)

25   The rear brakes on models equipped with ABS require a slightly different bleeding procedure.

26   Turn the ignition key to the On position, which will activate the hydraulic pump and charge up the accumulator.

27   Connect a length of tubing to the right

rear caliper bleeder valve **(see illustration 15.19)**. Place the other end of the tubing in a container partially filled with clean brake fluid.

28   Have an assistant depress the brake pedal and hold it in the applied position. SLOWLY loosen the bleeder valve and allow the fluid to flow for ten seconds, then close the valve. **Warning:** *When the pedal is depressed, the brake fluid in the rear calipers is under extremely high pressure and careless opening of the bleeder valves may cause the fluid to shoot out with great force.* **Caution:** *Don't let the pump run for more than one minute at a time without letting it cool off for a few minutes.*

29   Repeat the operation until the stream of fluid is free of air bubbles.

30   Check the fluid level in the reservoir, topping it up if necessary.

31   Repeat Steps 26 through 30 on the left rear caliper.

32   The front brakes may be bled using the standard brake bleeding procedure described earlier in this Section.

16   Brake light switch - removal, installation and adjustment

Refer to illustration 16.3

1   The switch is located on a flange or bracket protruding from the brake pedal support.

2   With the brake pedal in the fully released position. the plunger on the body of the switch should be completely pressed in. When the pedal is pushed in, the plunger releases and sends electrical current to the brake lights.

3   If the brake lights are inoperative and it has been determined that the bulbs are not burned out, push the brake light switch into the tubular clip, noting that audible clicks can be heard as the serrated portion of the switch is pushed through the clip toward the brake pedal **(see illustration)**.

4   Pull the brake pedal all the way to the rear against the pedal stop until no further

clicks can be heard. This will seal the switch in the tubular clip and provide the correct adjustment.

5 Release the brake pedal and repeat Step 4 to ensure that no further clicks can be heard.

6 Make sure the brake lights are working.

7 If the lights do not work when the pedal is depressed, check for power to the switch. If power is available on one terminal, depress the pedal and check for power at the other terminal.

a) *If no power is present on either terminal, trace and repair the circuit between the switch and the fuse block.*

b) *If power is present at one terminal of the switch but, when the pedal is depressed is not present at the other terminal, replace the switch.*

c) *If the switch is operating properly but the brake lights don't operate, trace and repair the circuit between the switch and the brake lights.*

8 After installing a new switch, adjust it by performing Steps 3 through 6.

---

17 Anti-lock Brake System (ABS) - general information

Some 1992 and later models are equipped with an anti-lock brake system (ABS) which provides optimal deceleration while maintaining directional stability and vehicle steerability, even under severe braking conditions on less-than-ideal road surfaces. It accomplishes this task by monitoring the rotational speed of the front and rear wheels and controls the brake line hydraulic pressure to all four wheels during braking.

Components

Hydraulic modulators

A hydraulic brake modulator is attached to the side of the brake master cylinder and controls pressure generated by the brake master cylinder. It proportions this pressure to each wheel based on the input from the input control module.

Wheel speed sensors

A speed sensor and a toothed ring are installed at each wheel. The sensor generates electrical signals, indicating wheel rotational speed, and sends these signals to the control module.

Electronic Brake Control Module (EBCM)

The control module is located under the dash panel. The function of the control module is to accept and process information received from the wheel speed sensors and send electrical signals to the modulator on the master cylinder. This controls hydraulic line pressure to all four wheels to prevent wheel lock-up. The control module also constantly monitors the ABS system, even under driving conditions, to find faults within the system.

When the control module finds a fault, a diagnostic code will be stored in the control unit which, when retrieved by a dealer service technician, will indicate the problem area or component.

ABS warning light (amber)

The electronic control unit monitors itself and all other ABS components. If there's a problem in any portion of the system, but it doesn't affect ABS braking ability, the ABS warning light will flash on and off, alerting the driver to the problem and reminding him that repairs should be made as soon as possible. If the ABS light comes on and stays on (i.e. doesn't flash), there's a serious problem in the system and NO anti-lock braking is available (but the system will continue to function in the normal, non-ABS mode). If this condition occurs, repairs should be made immediately.

Diagnosis and repair

If the ABS light comes on and flashes, or stays on, while the vehicle is in operation, the ABS system requires attention. Although troubleshooting the ABS system is beyond the scope of the home mechanic, you can perform a few preliminary checks before taking the vehicle to a dealer service department for diagnosis.

a) *Check the hydraulic brake fluid level in the master cylinder reservoir, adding fluid if necessary (see Chapter 1).*

b) *Verify that the electronic brake control module unit electrical connector is securely connected and is free of corrosion.*

c) *Inspect the electrical connectors at each speed sensor, modulator and all connection locations. Make sure each electrical connector is securely connected and is free of corrosion.*

d) *Check the system fuses, replacing them as necessary. If the above preliminary checks don't rectify the problem, the vehicle should be diagnosed by a dealer service department. Due to the rather complex nature of this system, and the high operating pressures involved, all actual repair work must be done by a dealer service department.*

Notes

Chapter 10
Suspension and steering systems

Contents

Specifications

General

Power steering fluid type	See Chapter 1

Torque Specifications

Ft-lbs (unless otherwise indicated)

Front suspension

Stabilizer bar mounting plate-to-frame bolts	40
Stabilizer bar bushing clamp bolts	32
Control arm pivot bolt nuts	61
Balljoint pinch bolt nut	33
Balljoint-to-control arm bolt/nut	13
Driveaxle/hub nut	See Chapter 8
Hub and bearing retaining bolts	
1985 and earlier	63
1986	70
1987	
Without heavy-duty brakes	63
With heavy-duty brakes	77
1988 on	
Without heavy-duty brakes	63
With heavy-duty brakes	70
Strut damper shaft nut	65
Strut upper mounting nuts	18
Strut-to-steering knuckle nuts	
1994 and earlier	140
1995 and later	122

Torque Specifications

Rear suspension

Ft-lbs (unless otherwise indicated)

Shock absorber upper mounting nut
1992 and earlier..	28
1993 through 1995	16
1996	21

Shock absorber lower mounting bolts/nuts
1992 and earlier..	44
1993 through 1995	50
1996	43

Track bar bolt at axle
1992 and earlier..	44
1993 on	50

Track bar mounting nut at upper bracket
1992 and earlier..	35
1993 on	38

Control arms to bracket nuts................................	84
Control arm brackets-to-underbody	28

Hub and bearing assembly bolts
1992 and earlier..	44
1993 on	60

Steering system

Airbag module screws	24 in-lbs

Steering gear mounting bolt nuts
1992 and earlier..	70
1993 on	66

Intermediate shaft pinch bolts
1984 and earlier..	45
1985 on	35

Steering wheel-to-steering column nut	30
Tie-rod end-to-steering knuckle nut......................	31 to 52

1   Suspension system - general information

Refer to illustrations 1.1 and 1.3

Warning: *Whenever any of the suspension or steering fasteners or removed, they must be inspected and, if necessary, replaced with new ones of the same part number or of original equipment quality and design. Torque specifications must be followed for proper reassembly and component retention. Never attempt to heat or straighten any suspension or steering components. Instead, replace any bent or damaged part with a new one.*

Note: *These vehicles have a combination of standard and metric fasteners on the various suspension and steering components, so it would be a good idea to have both types of tools available when beginning work.*

1   The vehicles covered by this manual feature an independent front suspension of the MacPherson Strut design. This design uses a combination strut and shock absorber assembly which is mounted directly to the steering knuckle. A control arm, which pivots on the engine cradle, is also attached to the steering knuckle by way of a balljoint **(see illustration).**

2   To minimize the transmission of vibration to the body, rubber bushings are used in the control arm pivots in the engine cradle.

The cradle also uses rubber bushings for isolation from the body. The upper end of the strut is isolated by a rubber mount which contains a bearing that allows it to pivot as the wheels are turned.

3   The rear suspension consists of a rear axle assembly, two coil springs, two shock absorbers and a track bar. The rear axle has two control arms welded to it, which are used to mount the axle assembly to the body. These control arms, together with the track bar and shock absorbers, maintain the proper geometric relationship of the axle assembly to the body under the forces created by accelerating, braking and cornering. In addition, a non-serviceable stabilizer bar is welded to the inside of the axle housing **(see illustration).**

4   The two coil springs support the weight of the car in the rear and are retained between seats in the underbody and rear axle housing. A rubber insulator is used to isolate the spring from the underbody seat.

5   The shock absorbers are conventional sealed hydraulic units. They are non-adjustable, non-refillable and cannot be disassembled. They are mounted at the bottom to a bracket on the axle housing and at the top to the body.

6   The track bar attaches to the left side of the axle housing and to the right side of the underbody to control side movement of the

axle assembly. Non-replaceable rubber bushings are used for mounting both ends of the bar.

7   The rear hub and bearing assemblies, mounted to either end of the rear axle, are single, sealed units and the bearing is not replaceable separate from the hub assembly.

8   An option to the conventional rear shock absorbers is GM's Superlift system. This system gives the car greater load carrying capacity by maintaining a level ride under heavy loads. The system consists of normal hydraulic shock absorbers with a pliable neoprene boot and an air cylinder, and is adjusted for different loads by varying the air pressure. Both Superlift shocks are filled by flexible air lines connected to one air valve located inside the fuel fill door. They are mounted in the same location as conventional shocks and are designed so that the shock absorber function is not impaired in the event of accidental air loss.

9   While the air lines used in the Superlift system are flexible, care should be taken not to kink them and to keep them a safe distance from all exhaust system parts.

10   To maintain the best ride characteristics with an empty car, the air pressure within the Superlift system should be kept at a minimum of 10 psi. To adjust for loads, the air pressure may be increased up to a maximum of 90 psi.

Component location

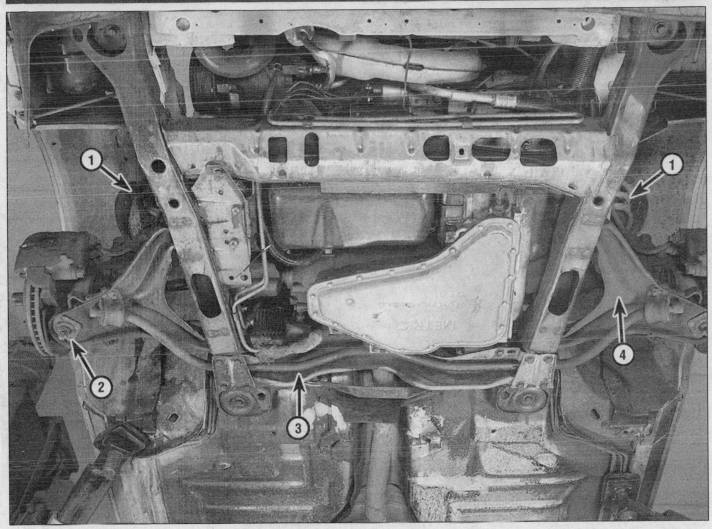

1.1 Typical front suspension components

1	Strut assembly	2	Lower balljoint	3	Stabilizer bar	4 Control arm

2   Suspension system - inspection

1   The suspension components should normally last a long time, except in cases where damage has occurred due to an accident. The suspension parts, however, should be checked from time to time for signs of wear, which will result in a loss of precision handling and riding comfort.

2   Check that the suspension components have not sagged due to wear. Do this by parking the car on a level surface and visually checking that the car sits level. This will normally occur only after many miles and will usually appear more on the driver's side of the vehicle.

3   Put the car in gear and release the hand brake. Grip the steering wheel at the top with both hands and rock it back and forth. Listen for any squeaks or metallic noises. Feel for free play. If any of these conditions is found, have an assistant do the rocking while the source of the trouble is located.

4   Check the shock absorbers, as these are the parts of the suspension system likely to wear out first. If there is any evidence of fluid leakage, they will definitely need replacing. Bounce the car up and down vigorously. It should feel stiff, and well damped by the shock absorbers. As soon as the bouncing is stopped the car should return to its normal position without excessive up and down movement. Do not replace the shock absorbers as single units, but rather in pairs.

5   Check all rubber bushings for signs of deterioration and cracking.

Component location

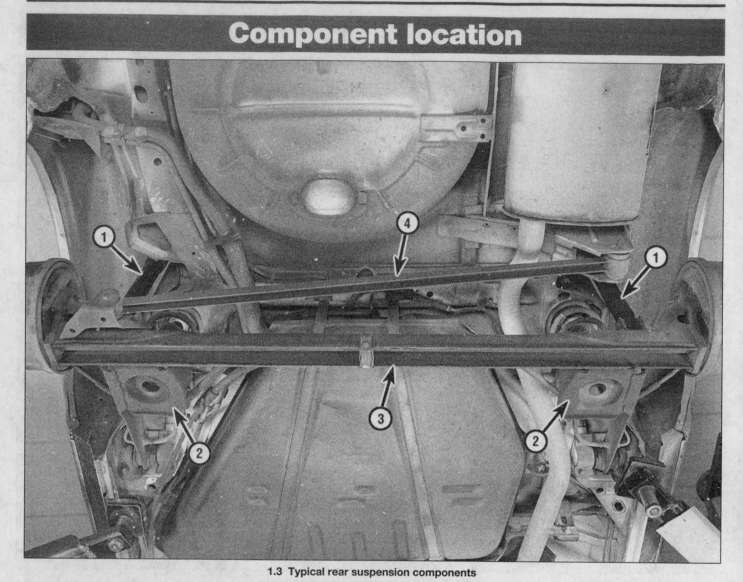

1.3 Typical rear suspension components

1	Shock absorber	2	Coil spring	3	Axle assembly	4	Track bar

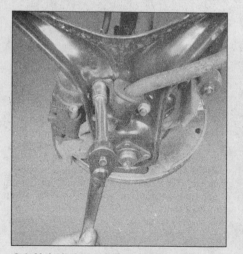

3.4 Unbolt the stabilizer bar bracket from the control arm

3.5 Remove the stabilizer bar mounting plate from the engine cradle

3   Stabilizer bar - removal and installation

Refer to illustrations 3.4, 3.5 and 3.6

1   Raise the front of the car and support it on jackstands.

2   Remove the bolts that connect the front exhaust crossover pipe to the front intermediate pipe.

3   Disconnect the front crossover pipe from the exhaust manifold and remove it.

4   Remove the bolts that secure the stabilizer brackets to the control arm and remove the brackets **(see illustration)**.

5   Remove the bolts that secure the stabilizer mounting plates to the engine cradle and remove both plates **(see illustration)**.

6   Remove the stabilizer bar from its recesses in the engine cradle, complete with bushings and brackets. The bushings need

3.6 Remove the stabilizer bar complete with bushings and brackets

4.4 Remove the pinch bolt that secures the balljoint to the steering knuckle

4.5 Detach the balljoint from the steering knuckle

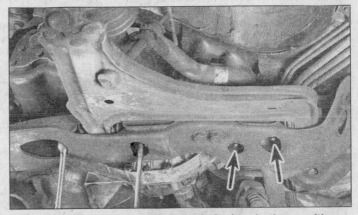

4.6 Remove the control arm pivot bolts (one is shown with a ratchet and wrench on it and the other one is indicated by arrows)

not be removed from the stabilizer bar unless either the bushings or the bar are being replaced **(see illustration)**.

7   Inspect the bushings to be sure they are not hardened, cracked or excessively worn, and replace if necessary.

8   Installation is the reverse of the removal procedure.

4   Control arm - removal and installation

Refer to illustrations 4.4, 4.5, 4.6 and 4.7

1   Loosen the wheel lug nuts. Raise the front of the vehicle and support it securely on jackstands.

2   If only one control arm is being removed, disconnect only that end of the stabilizer bar. If both control arms are being removed, remove the stabilizer bar completely (see Section 3).

3   Remove the wheel.

4   Remove the bolt that retains the balljoint to the steering knuckle **(see illustration)**.

5   Separate the balljoint from the steering knuckle **(see illustration)**.

6   Remove the control arm pivot bolts that

secure the control arm to the engine cradle **(see illustration)**.

7   Remove the control arm. The balljoint does not have to be removed from the control arm unless it needs replacing **(see illustration)**.

8   Inspect the control arm bushings for hardening, cracking or excessive wear and replace if necessary.

9   Installation of the control arm is the reverse of the removal procedure. **Note:** *Do not tighten the pivot bolts to the torque listed in this Chapter's Specifications until the outer end of the control arm has been raised with a floor jack to simulate normal ride height.*

5   Control arm balljoint - replacement

Refer to illustration 5.7

1   Raise the front of the car and support it on jackstands.

2   Remove the wheel.

3   Separate the balljoint from the steering knuckle (see Section 4).

4   Using a 1/8-inch drill bit, drill approximately 1/4-inch deep into the center of the

4.7 Remove the control arm from the engine cradle

rivets that secure the balljoint to the control arm.

5   Using a 1/2-inch drill bit, drill just deep enough to remove the rivet heads.

6   Punch out the remainder of the rivets and remove the balljoint.

7   When reinstalling the balljoint to the

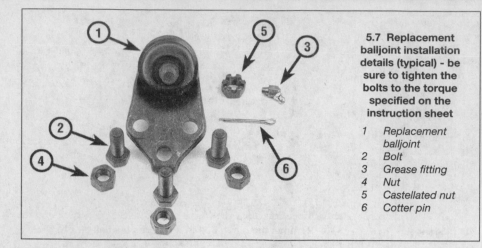

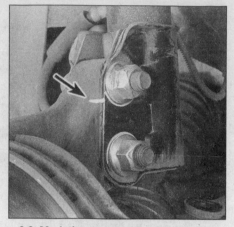

5.7 Replacement balljoint installation details (typical) - be sure to tighten the bolts to the torque specified on the instruction sheet

1   Replacement balljoint
2   Bolt
3   Grease fitting
4   Nut
5   Castellated nut
6   Cotter pin

control arm, use the nuts and bolts supplied with the new balljoint to replace the rivets **(see illustration)**. Tighten the nuts to the torque specified in the instruction sheet that came with the replacement balljoint.

8   Install the balljoint into the steering knuckle, tightening the pinch bolt and nut to the torque specified in the instruction sheet that came with the replacement balljoint.

9   Mount the wheel and lower the car to the ground.

6   Strut service preparation

Refer to illustration 6.2

1   To eliminate the need to readjust the camber setting when servicing the strut mount, jounce bumper, strut shield, spring seat or spring insulator, or when removing the driveaxles, the following marking procedure should be preformed prior to such operations. **Note:** *This procedure is only to return the camber to its approximate setting. The camber setting as well as the toe-in setting should be checked and adjusted after any major service to the front suspension.*

2   Use a sharp tool to scribe a line on the knuckle marking the relationship of the strut to the knuckle **(see illustration)**.

3   After completing the required service, be sure that these marks are properly aligned.

6.2 Mark the strut-to-steering knuckle relationshop and draw a line around the nuts with paint or a scribe

7   Strut assembly - removal and installation

Refer to illustrations 7.4, 7.5 and 7.7

Removal

1   Raise the front of the vehicle and support it securely on jackstands.

2   Remove the wheel.

3   Refer to Section 6 and scribe the strut assembly to retain the same camber adjustment upon reinstallation.

4   Loosen, but do not yet remove, the two strut-to-steering knuckle bolts **(see illustration)**.

5   Loosen, but do not yet remove, the three nuts securing the top of the strut assembly to the strut tower, underneath the hood **(see illustration)**. **Warning:** *Don't loosen the large center nut.*

6   Disconnect the brake line clip from its mounting tab on the strut.

7   Remove all of the loosened bolts and lift out the strut assembly **(see illustration)**. Be

7.4 Break loose the two strut-to-steering knuckle nuts and bolts

7.5 Loosen the three strut upper mounting nuts

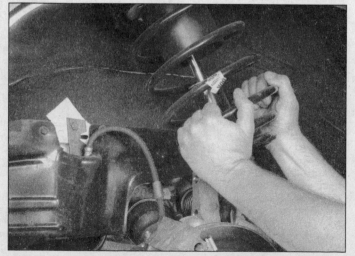

7.7 Carefully remove the strut assembly

8.4 A spring compressor must be used to disassemble the strut

8.6 With the spring compressed, remove the upper retaining nut

8.14 Place the coil spring onto the lower insulator, with the end of the spring butted against the spring stop on the insulator

careful not to damage the driveaxle boot or the brake hose during removal.

8   If the strut assembly needs to be disassembled for spring or strut unit replacement, follow the procedure described in Section 8.

Installation

9   Position the strut assembly in its proper location and install its upper and lower mounting bolts.

10   Place a jack under the control arm to hold it in position, if necessary.

11   Install the brake line clip to its mounting tab on the strut.

12   Tighten all the strut mounting nuts to the torque values listed in this Chapter's Specifications.

13   Install the wheel and lug nuts, then lower the vehicle. Tighten the lug nuts to the torque listed in the Chapter 1 Specifications.

14   Have the front end alignment checked and, if necessary, adjusted.

8   Strut assembly - overhaul

Refer to illustrations 8.4, 8.6 and 8.14
Warning: *Disassembling a strut is a potentially dangerous job. Be very careful and follow the instructions exactly or serious injury may result. Use only a high quality spring compressor and carefully follow the manufacturer's instructions furnished with the tool. After removing the coil spring from the strut assembly, set it aside in a safe, isolated area.*

1   The spring on the strut is under considerable pressure, requiring that a spring compressor be used to compress the spring and disengage its components. Do not attempt to disassemble the strut without a compressor,

as serious injury can occur.

2   A spring compressor can either be rented on a daily basis from an equipment rental agency, or one can be purchased at a tool supply house or some auto parts stores.

3   Hold the strut in a vise, using wood blocks to cushion the jaws, preventing damage to the strut body.

4   Follow the manufacturer's instructions for the particular spring compressor being used. Slightly compress the spring, making sure that the jaws of the compressor are firmly seated around the coils and cannot slip off **(see illustration)**.

5   Tighten the compressor from side to side, a little at a time, until the spring seat is clear of the uppermost coil. This can be confirmed by wiggling the spring.

6   With the spring firmly compressed and clear of its seat, remove the top locknut and washer **(see illustration)**.

7   Pull the mount off the top of the shock absorber assembly.

8   Remove the spring seat, bumper, shield and insulator.

9   Remove the spring from the strut unit. Depending on the type of spring compressor used, you may have to loosen the compressor until the tension on the spring is relieved, then lift the spring from the strut. Although some compressors allow you to lift the spring off the shock absorber in its compressed state, this could prove dangerous should the compressor and spring be jostled and accidentally disengaged from each other. **Warning**: *Always keep your head away from the ends of the spring.*

10   The spring should be checked for cracking or deformation of any kind. If the vehicle was sagging in the front, this is an indication that the springs are in need of replacement.

11   Test the strut damper unit as described in Section 9.

12   If the spring compressor was removed from the spring, reinstall it and compress the spring. With the strut mounted in a vise with protective wood blocks, install the spring.

13   Install the insulator, shield and bumper to the shock body.

14   Install the spring seat, with the flat por-

tion of the seat facing the flange at the bottom of the strut **(see illustration)**.

15   Install the mount assembly.

16   Install the lockwasher and locknut to the top of the piston rod, tightening the nut to the torque listed in this Chapter's Specifications.

17   Carefully relieve tension on the spring by loosening the compressor from side to side, a little at a time. Check to be sure the top of the spring is raised properly into its seat.

9   Strut assembly - general information

1   To test the strut assembly after the coil spring has been removed (as described in Section 8), hold it in an upright position and work the piston rod up and down its full length of travel. If you can feel a strong resistance because of hydraulic pressure, the strut damper is functioning properly. If you feel no substantial resistance, or there is a sudden free movement in travel, the strut should be replaced.

2   If there is fluid leakage evident on the outside of the strut, the strut should be replaced.

3   Although it is possible to disassemble the strut unit and install new oil and parts on some models, the work is very intricate and demands extreme cleanliness. Some special tools will also be necessary. Because of this, it would be wise for the home mechanic to take the strut to a dealer service department or other repair shop to install a replacement cartridge.

10   Front hub and bearing assembly - removal and installation

Refer to illustration 10.6
1   Break loose the driveaxle/hub nut.
2   Raise the front of the vehicle and support it securely on jackstands.
3   Remove the front wheel. Insert a punch

10.6 Remove the front hub and bearing retaining bolts

11.6 Pressing out a wheel stud from the hub and bearing assembly

12.1 Location of the upper shock absorber mounting nut (arrow)

through the caliper and into the disc to allow removal of the hub nut (see Chapter 8, if necessary) It may be necessary to tap the hub and bearing assembly from the knuckle as you do this.

4   Remove the brake caliper as described in Chapter 9. **Note:** *It is not necessary to disconnect the brake line.* Support the caliper out of the way with a piece of wire - don't let it hang by the brake hose.

5   Remove the brake disc.

6   Remove the hub and bearing assembly attaching bolts **(see illustration).**

7   Using a two-jaw puller, remove the hub and bearing assembly from the driveaxle (see Chapter 8, if necessary). It may also be necessary to tap the hub and bearing assembly from the knuckle as you do this.

8   Spin the bearing with your finger and check for any roughness or noise. Check the bearing mating surfaces and steering knuckle bore for dirt or nicks. This assembly is a sealed unit and if the bearing needs replacing, the entire hub and bearing assembly must be replaced.

9   If the hub and bearing assembly is being replaced, a new steering knuckle seal must be installed in the steering knuckle prior to installation of the hub and bearing assembly. This is done by applying grease to the seal and its bore in the steering knuckle and then tapping the seal into place using a hammer and a seal driver or large socket.

10   Install the hub and bearing assembly onto the driveaxle. Install the hub nut onto the driveaxle and tighten it until the hub and bearing assembly is seated.

11   Install the shield and hub assembly attaching bolts.

12   Install the brake disc and caliper (see Chapter 9).

13   Install the wheel and lower the car to the ground.

15   Tighten the hub nut to the torque listed in the Chapter 8 Specifications. Tighten the wheel lug nuts to the torque listed in the Chapter 1 Specifications.

11   Front wheel stud - replacement

Refer to illustration 11.6

1   Raise the front of the car and support it on jackstands.

2   Remove the wheel.

3   Remove the brake caliper as described in Chapter 9.

4   Remove the brake disc as described in Chapter 9.

5   Remove the splash shield.

6   Position the stud to be replaced at either the 5 or 7 o'clock position. Install a lug nut onto the end of the stud and, using a stud remover, balljoint press or equivalent, press the stud from the hub flange **(see illustration).**

7   Remove the lug nut, then the stud.

8   With the stud hole at either the 5 or 7 o'clock position, insert the new stud in the hole, making sure the serrations are aligned with those made by the original bolt.

9   Place four flat washers over the outside end of the stud, then thread a lug nut onto the stud.

10   Tighten the lug nut until the stud head seats against the rear of the hub. Remove the lug nut and washers.

11   Reinstall the splash shield, brake disc and caliper (see Chapter 9).

12   Install the wheel and lower the vehicle to the ground. Tighten the lug nuts to the torque listed in the Chapter 1 Specifications.

12   Rear shock absorbers - removal, inspection and installation

Refer to illustrations 12.1 and 12.5

1   In the rear compartment of the vehicle, open the access panel in the trim cover (wagon models only) and loosen, but do not remove, the upper mounting nut **(see illustration).** The damper rod must be kept from turning while the nut is loosened.

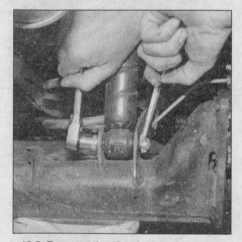

12.5 Remove the shock absorber lower mounting bolt

2   Raise the rear of the vehicle and support it securely on jackstands placed under the frame (not under the rear axle).

3   Support the axle with a floor jack placed under the spring seat. **Warning:** *The jack must remain in this position throughout the entire procedure.*

4   Remove the shock absorber upper mounting nut.

5   Remove the shock absorber lower mounting nut and bolt and remove the shock absorber **(see illustration).** It may be necessary to pry the lower end of the shock absorber out of the mounting bracket.

6   The shock absorber should be compressed and extended its full length several times to check for any free movement of the shaft, noise, or fluid leakage. If any of these conditions are found, the shocks should be replaced with a new set.

7   To install, place a new rubber bushing and washers on the top of the shock absorber, then guide the shock into position.

8   Place the lower end of the shock in its mount and install the bolt and nut, but don't tighten the nut yet.

9   Raise the axle to simulate normal ride

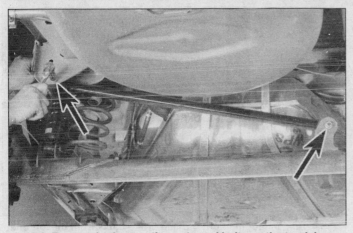

13.2 Remove both mounting nuts and bolts on the track bar

14.9 After lowering the rear axle, remove the coil springs

height, then tighten the lower mounting bolt and nut to the torque listed in this Chapter's Specifications.

10   Install the upper bushing, washers and nut, then tighten the nut to the torque listed in this Chapter's Specifications. If the damper rod turns as the nut is tightened, hold it with a wrench.

11   Lower the floor jack and move it ot the other side, then repeat the procedure to change the other shock absorber.

12   On wagon models, close the access panel in the trim cover.

13   Track bar - removal and installation

Refer to illustration 13.2

1   Raise the rear of the vehicle and support it securely on jackstands. Support the rear axle with a floor jack.

2   Remove the nuts and bolts securing the track bar at both ends **(see illustration)**.

3   Remove the track bar.

4   Inspect the bushings for hardening, cracking or excessive wear. If they exhibit any of these conditions, the track bar must be replaced.

5   To install, place the left end of the track bar in the body mount and loosely install the bolt and nut. The open side of the bar must face to the rear.

6   Place the other end of the bar in the axle mount and loosely install the bolt and nut. Both nuts must face the rear of the car.

7   Raise the rear axle to simulate normal ride height.

8   Tighten both nuts to the torque listed in this Chapter's Specifications, then lower the vehicle to the ground.

14   Rear coil springs and insulators - removal and installation

Refer to illustration 14.9

1   Raise the rear of the vehicle and support it with jackstands placed under the frame.

2   Support the rear axle with a floor jack.

3   Remove the wheels and brake drums.

4   Disconnect the parking brake cable by loosening the adjustment nut and prying forward on the parking brake equalizer lever to disconnect the forward cable from the equalizer lever.

5   Twist the equalizer lever and disengage it from the pivot mount on the body.

6   Remove the bolts attaching the brake line brackets to the chassis on both the left and right sides.

7   Remove the track bar as described in Section 16.

8   Remove the shock absorber lower attaching nuts and bolts from both shock absorbers.

9   Slowly lower the rear axle enough to remove the springs and insulators **(see illustration)**. Do not suspend the rear axle by the brake hoses, as this will damage the hoses.

10   If the insulators are worn, cracked or damaged, they should be replaced.

11   Inspect the springs for cracks or other damage. If they exhibit any of these conditions, or if the car has been sagging in the rear, the springs should be replaced. The rear springs should always be replaced as a pair.

12   Installation is the reverse of the removal procedure. **Note:** *When installing the springs, be sure they are in the proper position with the large coil to the bottom.*

13   Adjust the parking brake as described in Chapter 9.

15   Control arm bushings - replacement

Refer to illustration 15.8

1   Loosen the wheel lug nuts, raise the rear of the vehicle and support it securely on jackstands placed under the frame.

2   Support the rear axle with a floor jack.

3   Remove the wheels and brake drums.

4   If the right control arm bushing is being replaced, loosen the parking brake adjustment nut and disconnect the forward cable from the parking brake equalizer lever by pry-

15.8 Remove the four control arm mounting bolts

ing forward on the equalizer lever. Twist the equalizer lever to disengage it from the pivot mount on the body.

5   Remove the bolts attaching the brake line brackets to the chassis.

6   Remove the shock absorber lower attaching nuts and bolts.

7   Remove the springs.

8   Remove the bolts securing the control arm bracket to the underbody **(see illustration)** and allow the control arm to rotate downward.

9   Remove the control arm bracket from the control arm.

10   Removal of the old bushing and installation of the new one should be done using a special press made for this purpose. Properly sized sockets and a long bolt, nut and washers can also be used. When installing, the cutouts on the rubber portion of the bushing must face toward the front and rear.

11   Remount the control arm bracket to the control arm and check that it is positioned at a 45-degree angle to the lower edge of the control arm. When the proper angle is set, tighten the nut to the torque listed in this Chapter's Specifications.

12   Install the various components by reversing the removal procedure. Do not

16.2 Disconnect the brake line brackets from the rear axle control arms

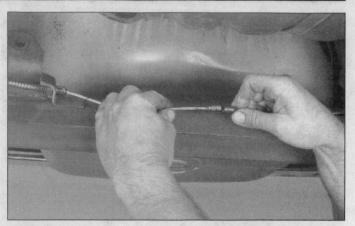

16.4 Disconnect the right parking brake cable from the left one

tighten the shock absorber lower mounting nuts or the track bar fasteners to the torque listed in this Chapter's Specifications until the suspension has been raised to simulate normal ride height.

13   Adjust the parking brake as described in Chapter 9.

16   Rear axle assembly - removal and installation

Refer to illustrations 16.2, 16.4, 16.6, 16.9, 16.12a and 16.12b

Removal

1   Remove the coil springs as described in Section 17.
2   Disconnect the brake lines from the control arms **(see illustration)**.
3   Disconnect and cap the rigid brake lines from both rear brake cylinders.
4   Disconnect the right rear parking brake cable from the left rear parking brake cable **(see illustration)**.
5   Disconnect the right rear and left rear parking brake cables from their brackets on the rear axle.
6   Remove the bolts securing the rear parking brake cable guide to the underbody

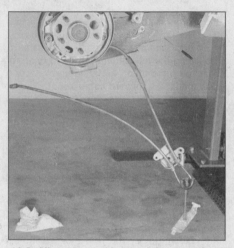

16.6 Allow the parking brake assembly to hang from the right backing plate

and allow the entire parking brake assembly to hang from the right rear backing plate **(see illustration)**.
7   Remove the bolts securing the hub and bearing assembly to the rear axle and remove the assemblies along with the brake backing plates.
8   While an assistant steadies the rear axle on the jack, remove the bolts securing the

16.9 Carefully remove the rear axle

control arm brackets to the body.
9   Lower the rear axle and remove it from under the car **(see illustration)**.
10   If the rear axle is being replaced, remove the control arm brackets from the control arms and install them on the new axle.
11   Inspect the control arm bushings for cracking, hardening or other damage and replace if necessary as described in Section 18.

16.12a Support the rear axle so that the lower edge of the control arm is on a horizontal plane

16.12b The angle of the control arm bracket to lower edge of the control arm should be 45-degrees

Installation

12   Prior to installation, lay the axle on a flat surface and, using an angle measuring instrument, make sure the lower edge of the control arms are on a horizontal plane **(see illustration)**. Measure the control arm brackets. These should be on an angle of 45-degrees to the horizontal plane or the lower edge of the control arm **(see illustration)**. If they are at a different angle, loosen the bracket nuts and adjust them to a 45-degree angle.

13   Installation of the rear axle is the reverse of the removal procedure. Raise the rear axle to simulate normal ride height before tightening the track bar and shock absorber fasteners to the torque listed in this Chapter's Specifications.

14   Bleed the brake system as described in Chapter 9.

15   Adjust the parking brake as described in Chapter 9.

17   Rear hub and bearing assembly - removal and installation

1   Loosen the rear wheel lug nuts, raise the rear of the vehicle and support it securely on jackstands.

2   Remove the wheel and brake drum (or caliper and disc).

3   Remove the brake shoes as described in Chapter 9.

4   Remove the bolts securing the hub and bearing assembly to the rear axle and remove the assembly.

5   Spin the bearing with your fingers and check for any roughness or noise. This assembly is a sealed unit and if the bearing is bad the entire hub and bearing assembly must be replaced.

6   Installation is the reverse of the removal procedure. Be sure to tighten the bolts to the torque listed in this Chapter's Specifications.

18   Rear wheel stud - replacement

1   Loosen the rear wheel lug nuts, raise the rear of the vehicle and support it securely on jackstands.

2   Remove the wheel and brake drum.

3   Install a lug nut on the end of the stud and press the stud from its seat. Alternately, you may be able to knock the stud out with a hammer.

4   Remove the lug nut and remove the stud.

5   Insert the new stud in the hole, making sure the serrations are aligned with those made by the original bolt.

6   Place four flat washers over the stud and thread a lug nut onto the stud.

7   Tighten the lug nut until the stud head seats against the rear of the hub. Remove the lug nut and washers.

8   Install the brake drum (or disc and caliper) and wheel and lower the vehicle to the ground. Tighten the lug nuts to the torque listed in the Chapter 1 Specifications.

19   Steering system - general information

Warning: *Whenever any of the steering fasteners are removed, they must be inspected and, if necessary, replaced with new ones of the same part number or of original equipment quality and design. Torque specifications must be followed for proper reassembly and component retention. Never attempt to heat or straighten any suspension or steering components. Instead, replace any bent or damaged part with a new one.*

1   All models covered by this manual use a rack-and-pinion steering system. The components making up the system are the steering wheel, steering column, intermediate shaft, rack-and-pinion steering gear assembly, tie-rods and steering knuckles. The power steering system uses a belt-driven pump to provide hydraulic pressure.

2   In a manual system, the motion of turning the steering wheel is transferred through the column and intermediate shaft to the pinion shaft in the rack-and-pinion assembly. Teeth on the pinion shaft are meshed with teeth on the rack, so when the shaft is turned, the rack is moved left or right in the housing. Attached to each end of the rack are tie-rods which, in turn, are attached to the steering knuckles on the front wheels. This left and right movement of the rack is the direct force which turns the wheels.

3   The power steering system operates in essentially the same way as the manual system, except that the power rack-and-pinion system uses hydraulic pressure to boost the manual steering force. A rotary control valve in the rack-and-pinion assembly directs hydraulic fluid from the power steering pump to either side of the integral rack piston, which is attached to the rack. Depending on which side of the piston this hydraulic pressure is applied to, the rack will be forced either left or right, which moves the tie-rods, etc.

4   If the power steering system loses its hydraulic pressure it will still function manually, though with increased effort.

5   The steering column is of the collapsible, energy-absorbing type, designed to compress in the event of a front end collision to minimize injury to the driver. The column also houses the ignition switch lock, key warning buzzer, turn signal controls, headlight dimmer control and windshield wiper controls. The ignition and steering wheel can both be locked while the car is parked to inhibit theft.

6   Due to the column's collapsible design, it is important that only original equipment screws, bolts and nuts be used as designated and that they be tightened to the specified torque values. Other precautions particular to this design are noted in appropriate Sections.

7   In addition to the standard steering column, optional tilt and key release versions are also offered. The tilt model can be set in five different positions, while with the key release model the ignition key is locked in the column until a lever is depressed to extract it.

8   Because disassembly of the steering column is more often performed to repair a switch or other electrical part than to correct a problem in the steering functioning, the steering column disassembly and reassembly procedure is included in Chapter 12.

20   Steering wheel - removal and installation

Refer to illustrations 20.3, 20.4a, 20.4b, 20.5a, 20.5b, 20.6, 20.7, 20.8 and 20.9

Warning: *Some models covered by this manual are equipped with airbags. Always turn the steering wheel to the straight ahead position, place the ignition switch in the Lock position and disable the airbag system before working in the vicinity of the impact sensors, steering column or instrument panel to avoid the possibility of accidental deployment of the airbag(s), which could cause personal injury (see Chapter 12 for the airbag disarming procedure). Do not use electrical test equipment on any of the airbag system wiring or connectors or tamper with them in any way.*

Caution: *If the vehicle is equipped with a Delco Loc II audio system, make sure you have the correct activation code before disconnecting the battery.*

1   Park the vehicle with the wheels pointing straight ahead. Disconnect the cable from the negative terminal of the battery. On airbag-equipped models, also disarm the airbag system before proceeding (see Chapter 12).

2   On models without an airbag, the horn pad is attached to the steering wheel with various combinations of clips and/or screws.

3   On airbag models, use a number 30 Torx bit and remove the two screws that secure the airbag module to the steering wheel **(see illustration)**.

20.3 Use a Torx bit to remove the two airbag module screws from behind the steering wheel

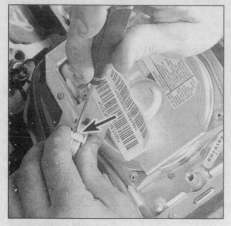

20.4a Use a small screwdriver to release the plastic locking clip (arrow) from the airbag module connector, then . . .

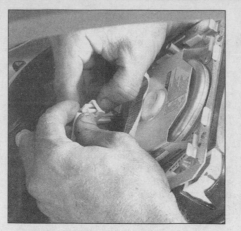

20.4b . . . squeeze the tab and separate the airbag connector

20.5a Remove the steering wheel nut retainer, if equipped

20.5b Remove the steering wheel nut with a deep socket

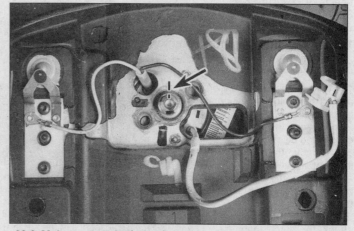

20.6 Make two marks (arrow) to show alignment of the wheel to the shaft before removal

4   Lift the airbag module carefully away from the steering wheel and disconnect the yellow airbag electrical connector. This is a two-part disconnection, as there is a plastic clip that must be removed before the connector can be disconnected **(see illustra-**

tions). Remove the module. **Warning:** *When carrying the airbag module, keep the driver's side of it away from your body, and when you set it down in a safe area, have the driver's side facing up.*

5   Remove the steering wheel nut retainer

(if equipped) and the steering wheel nut **(see illustrations)**.

6   Mark the relationship of the steering wheel to the shaft **(see illustration)**.

7   Install a steering wheel puller (available at most auto parts stores) and turn the center bolt until the wheel is free **(see illustration)**.

8   Remove the puller and disconnect the horn and ground connector **(see illustration)**. Remove the steering wheel. **Warning:** *Don't allow the steering shaft to turn with the steering wheel removed. If the shaft turns, the airbag SIR coil assembly (the mechanism which protects the airbag wiring when the steering wheel is turned) will become uncentered, which may cause the airbag harness to break when the vehicle is returned to service.*

9   Installation is reverse of removal. On airbag models, before the steering wheel is installed, make sure the SIR coil is centered **(see illustration)**. If it isn't, see Chapter 12, Section 26 for the centering procedure. Connect the airbag connector to the back of the airbag module just as it was before steering wheel removal, i.e. with the plastic locking device in place. Be sure to tighten the steering wheel nut and air bag screws to the torque listed in this Chapter's Specifications.

20.7 A steering wheel puller threads into two holes in the steering wheel - tightening the center bolt removes the wheel

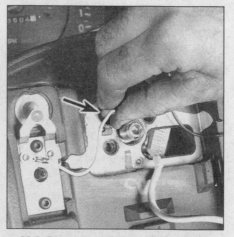

20.8 Disconnect the horn and ground wire connector

20.9 When properly aligned, the airbag coil will be centered with the marks aligned (in circle here) and the tab fitted between the projections on the top of the steering column (arrow)

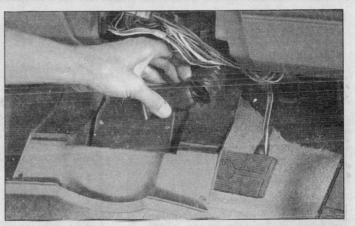

21.4 Remove the steering column trim cover from the dash and disconnect the vent tube if equipped

10   Refer to chapter 12 for the procedure to enable the airbag system.

21   Steering column - removal and installation

Refer to illustrations 21.4 and 21.9

Warning: *Some models covered by this manual are equipped with airbags. Always disable the airbag system before working in the vicinity of the impact sensors, steering column or instrument panel to avoid the possibility of accidental deployment of the airbag(s), which could cause personal injury (see Chapter 12 for the airbag disarming procedure). The yellow wires and connectors routed through the instrument panel are for this system. Do not use electrical test equipment on these yellow wires or tamper with them in any way while working under the instrument panel.*

1   Although it is not mandatory, the steering column removal operation can be made much easier by first removing the front seat.
2   Disconnect the negative cable at the battery terminal. **Caution:** *If the vehicle is equipped with a Delco Loc II audio system, make sure you have the correct activation code before disconnecting the battery. See the information at the front of this manual for the radio re-activation procedure.*
3   If the column is to be disassembled after it is removed from the vehicle, the steering wheel should be removed as described in Section 20. If the column is to be kept as one piece, removal of the steering wheel is not necessary.
4   Remove the screws securing the steering column trim cover to the dash and lift off the cover. On cars with air conditioning, disconnect the vent hose when you remove the cover **(see illustration)**.
5   Disconnect all electrical connections from the steering column, including those from the dimmer switch, windshield wiper switch, ignition switch, back-up light switch and turn signal switch.
6   Disconnect the shift indicator cable by

prying the clip from the shaft bowl.
7   Disconnect the shift cable from the column by removing the clip, pin retainer and washer.
8   Use a screwdriver to pry back the plastic cover over the intermediate shaft so the U-joint is exposed. Remove the locking bolt and nut. **Caution:** *On airbag-equipped models, do not allow the steering column to rotate after the steering shaft has been disconnected, as damage to the SIR coil may result. To prevent rotation, place the ignition key in the LOCK position.*
9   Remove the three bolts and one nut securing the steering column to the support **(see illustration)** and remove the column.
10   Because of its collapsible design, the steering column is very susceptible to damage when removed from the car. Be careful not to lean on or drop the column as this could weaken the column structure and impair its performance.
11   If the car has been in an accident which resulted in frame damage, major body damage or in which the steering column was impacted, the column could be damaged or misaligned and should be checked a qualified shop.
12   The steering column is installed by reversing the sequence of the removal operation. **Note:** *When reattaching the shift indicator cable clip to the shift bowl, place the shift lever in the Neutral position, then position the clip on the edge of the bowl so that the shift indicator pointer is pointing to the N. Push the clip onto the bowl.*

22   Steering knuckle - removal and installation

1   Remove the hub and bearing assembly as described in Section 10.
2   Mark the relationship of the strut to the steering knuckle **(see illustration 6.2)**.
3   Detach the tie-rod end from the steering knuckle (see Section 23).
4   Detach the control arm balljoint from the

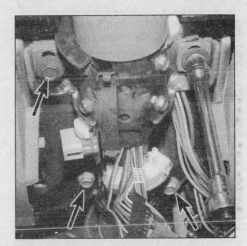

21.9 Remove the steering column mounting nut and bolts

steering knuckle (see Section 4).
5   Remove the strut-to-steering knuckle bolts and remove the steering knuckle.
6   If the steering knuckle is being replaced, install a new steering knuckle seal into the new knuckle. This is done by greasing both the seal and the knuckle bore and then tapping the seal into place using a hammer and socket.
7   Connect the strut to the steering knuckle and install the bolts. Line up the alignment marks and tighten the bolts to the torque listed in this Chapter's Specifications.
8   Insert the balljoint stud into the steering knuckle.
9   Install the balljoint pinch bolt and nut. Tighten the nut to the torque listed in this Chapter's Specifications.
10   Install the hub and bearing assembly, shield, brake disc and caliper (see Chapter 9).
11   Connect the tie-rod end to the steering knuckle (see Section 23).
12   Install the wheel and lower the car to the ground. Tighten the lug nuts to the torque listed in the Chapter 1 Specifications. Tighten the driveaxle/hub nut to the torque listed in the Chapter 8 Specifications.

23.2 Mark the relationship of the tie-rod end to the tie-rod

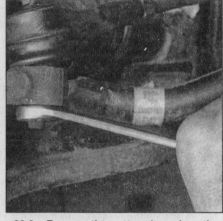

23.3a Remove the cotter pin and castle nut from the tie-rod end stud . . .

23.3b . . . then separate the tie-rod end from the steering knuckle arm with a two-jaw puller - DO NOT pound on the stud!

23 Tie-rod end - removal and installation

Refer to illustrations 23.2, 23.3a and 23.3b

Removal

1   Loosen the wheel lug nuts, raise the front of the vehicle and support it securely on jackstands. Remove the wheel.
2   Loosen the tie-rod end jam nut enough to mark the relationship of the tie-rod end to the threads of the tie-rod **(see illustration)**.
3   Remove the cotter pin and castle nut from the tie-rod end stud, then disconnect the tie-rod end from the steering knuckle arm with a two-jaw puller **(see illustrations)**.
4   Unscrew the tie-rod end from the tie-rod.

Installation

5   Thread the tie-rod end onto the tie-rod up to the marked position, then connect the tie-rod end to the steering knuckle arm. Install the castle nut and tighten it to the torque listed in this Chapter's Specifications. Install a new cotter pin. If the hole in the stud won't line up with one of the castellations, tighten the nut a little more until they do. Never loosen the nut to allow cotter pin installation.
6   Install the wheel and lug nuts. Lower the vehicle and tighten the lug nuts to the torque listed in the Chapter 1 Specifications.
7   Have the front end alignment checked and, if necessary, adjusted.

24 Steering gear boots - replacement

1   Loosen the wheel lug nuts, raise the front of the vehicle and support it securely on jackstands. Remove the wheel.
2   Remove the tie-rod end and jam nut (see Section 23).
3   Remove the steering gear boot clamps and slide the boot off.

4   Before installing the new boot, wrap the threads and serrations on the end of the tie-rod with tape so the small end of the new boot isn't damaged.
5   Slide the new boot onto the tie-rod, making sure the ends of the boot seat correctly in their grooves on the steering gear and the tie-rod. Install new clamps and tighten them securely.
6   Remove the tape and install the tie-rod end (see Section 23).
7   Install the wheel and lug nuts. Tighten the lug nuts to the torque listed in the Chapter 1 Specifications.

25 Steering gear - removal and installation

Refer to illustration 25.10

Warning: *On airbag-equipped models, make sure the steering shaft is not turned while the steering gear is removed or you could damage the airbag system. To prevent the shaft from turning, place the ignition key in the LOCK position or thread the seat belt through the steering wheel and clip it into place.*
Caution: *If the vehicle is equipped with a Delco Loc II audio system, make sure you have the correct activation code before disconnecting the battery.*

Removal

1   Disconnect the cable from the negative terminal of the battery. **Warning:** *On air-bag-equipped models, disarm the airbag system (see Chapter 12).*
2   Move the steering column intermediate shaft seal upwards and remove the pinch bolt attaching the intermediate shaft to the steering gear input shaft.
3   On power steering-equipped models, remove the air cleaner for clearance.
4   Loosen the front wheel lug nuts. Raise the front of the vehicle and support it securely on jackstands placed under the body, not under the cradle. On power steering-equipped models, place newspapers and a drain pan under the steering gear.

5   Remove both front wheels.
6   Detach the tie-rod ends from the steering knuckle arms (see Section 23).
7   If equipped, remove the air management pipe bracket bolt from the crossmember.
8   Place a jack under the cradle rear crossmember to support it and remove the two rear cradle mounting bolts. Loosen the cradle front mounting bolts and lower the rear of the cradle five inches. **Caution:** *Lowering more than this may damage engine components near the cowl.*
9   If equipped, remove the steering gear heat shield. On models equipped with power steering, detach the fluid lines from the steering gear.
10   Remove the two steering gear mounting bolts and remove the assembly through the left wheel opening **(see illustration)**.

Installation

11   Installation is the reverse of the removal procedure.
12   If equipped with power steering, add power steering fluid (see Chapter 1) and bleed the power steering system (see Section 29).
13   Have the front end alignment checked and, if necessary, adjusted.

25.10 Steering rack mounting bolt/nut (arrow) - left-side shown, right-side similar

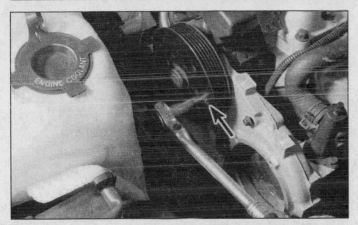

27.6 Using a socket and short extension inserted through one of the holes in the pulley (arrow), remove the three pump mounting bolts - rotate the pulley to access each bolt

28.5 Remove the power steering pump mounting bolts (one is shown with a socket on it and the other one is indicated by an arrow)

26 Power steering pump (four-cylinder engines) - removal and installation

1   Disconnect the negative cable at the battery terminal. **Caution:** *If the vehicle is equipped with a Delco Loc II audio system, make sure you have the correct activation code before disconnecting the battery. See the information at the front of this manual for the radio re-activation procedure.* Raise the front of the vehicle and support it securely on jackstands.
2   Disconnect the pressure hose from its fitting on the rear of the pump
3   Remove the clamp securing the flexible hose to the rigid steel line and disconnect the hose from the line.
4   Loosen the pump attaching bolts and nuts on both sides of the pump, move the pump toward the engine and remove the belt from the pulley.
5   Remove the bolt and spacer from the upper rear mount of the pump.
6   Remove the three bolts holding the left pump bracket to the engine block.
7   Remove the pump and left pump bracket.
8   Remove the pump from the pump bracket.
9   Remove the three bolts securing the right bracket to the pump.
10   Install the pump by reversing the removal procedure. Fill the pump with power steering fluid and adjust the belt tension as described in Chapter 1. Bleed the power steering system (see Section 29).

27 Power steering pump (2.8/3.1L V6 engines) - removal and installation

Refer to illustrations 27.6
1   Disconnect the negative cable at the battery terminal. **Caution:** *If the vehicle is*

equipped with a Delco Loc II audio system, make sure you have the correct activation code before disconnecting the battery. See the information at the front of this manual for the radio re-activation procedure.
2   Disconnect the electrical connector from the blower motor.
3   Remove the blower motor.
4   Drain the coolant (see Chapter 1) and disconnect the heater hose at the water pump.
5   Disconnect the pressure and return hoses at the connection shown.
6   Loosen the pump mounting bolts, move the pump toward the engine and remove the belt from the pulley **(see illustration)**.
7   Remove the mounting bolts and lift the pump from the engine compartment.
8   Special tools are needed to transfer the pulley to the new pump. If the tools are not available, take the pump to a dealer service department or other repair shop.
9   Install the pump by reversing the removal procedure.
10   Fill the pump with power steering fluid and adjust the belt tension as described in Chapter 1. Bleed the power steering system (see Section 29).

28 Power steering pump (3.0, 3.3 and 3.8L engines) - removal and installation

Refer to illustration 28.5
1   Disconnect the negative battery cable. **Caution:** *If the vehicle is equipped with a Delco Loc II audio system, make sure you have the correct activation code before disconnecting the battery. See the information at the front of this manual for the radio re-activation procedure.*
2   Remove the air cleaner for working clearance.
3   Remove the alternator (see Chapter 5).
4   Raise the vehicle and support it securely on jackstands.

5   Remove the rear adjustment nut from the pump **(see illustration)**.
6   Remove the alternator adjustment bracket.
7   Remove the pump belt.
8   Remove the two studs retaining the alternator mounting bracket by using two nuts tightened against each other on the end of the stud to act as a bolt head. After the studs have been removed, lift out the alternator bracket.
9   Remove the two bolts attaching the pump rear adjusting bracket to the engine block.
10   Disconnect the pump pressure hose by using a thin 1-inch wrench to support the flange and a 5/8-inch flare nut wrench to disconnect the line.
11   The pump, along with the brackets, can now be removed from the vehicle.
12   Installation is the reverse of the removal procedure.
13   Fill the pump with power steering fluid and adjust the belt tension as described in Chapter 1. Bleed the power steering system (see Section 29).

29 Power steering system - bleeding

1   Following any operation in which the power steering fluid lines have been disconnected, the power steering system must be bled of air to obtain proper steering performance.
2   With the front wheels turned all the way to the left, check the power steering fluid level and, if low, add fluid until it reaches the Cold mark on the dipstick.
3   Start the engine and allow it to run at fast idle. Recheck the fluid level and add more if necessary to reach the Cold mark on the dipstick.
4   Bleed the system by turning the wheels from side to side, without hitting the stops. This will work the air out of the system. Be careful that the reservoir does not run empty of fluid.

5   When the air is worked out of the system, return the wheels to the straight ahead position and leave the car running for several more minutes before shutting it off.

6   Road test the car to be sure the steering system is functioning normally and is free from noise.

7   Recheck the fluid level to be sure it is up to the Hot mark on the dipstick while the engine is at normal operating temperature. Add fluid if low.

30 Wheels and tires - general information

Refer to illustrations 30.1 and 30.4

1   All models covered by this manual are equipped with metric-sized fiberglass or steel belted radial tires **(see illustration)**. Use of other size or type of tires may affect the ride and handling of the car. Do not mix different types of tires, such as radials and bias belted, on the same car as handling may be seriously affected.

2   It is recommended that tires be replaced in pairs on the same axle, but if only one tire is being replaced, be sure it is of the same size, structure and tread design as the other.

3   Because tire pressure has a substantial effect on handling and wear, the pressure on all tires should be checked at least once a month or before any extended trips and set to the correct pressure. Tire pressure should be checked and adjusted with the tires cold.

4   To achieve the maximum life of your tires they should be rotated at 7500 miles and then again at every 15,000-mile interval **(see illustration)**.

5   The tires should be replaced when the depth of the tread is a minimum of 1/16-in (1.5 mm). Correct tire pressures and driving techniques have an important influence on tire life. Heavy cornering, excessively rapid acceleration and sharp braking increase tire

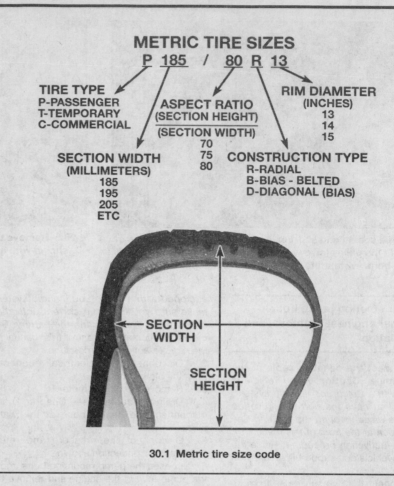

30.1 Metric tire size code

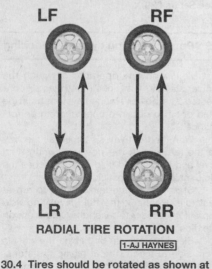

RADIAL TIRE ROTATION

1-AJ HAYNES

30.4 Tires should be rotated as shown at recommended intervals

wear. Extremely worn tires are not only very susceptible to going flat but are especially dangerous in wet weather conditions.

6   The tire tread pattern can give a good indication of problems in the maintenance or adjustment of tires, suspension and front end components (see Section 1).

7   Wheels must be replaced if they are bent, dented, leak air, have elongated bolt holes, are heavily rusted, out of vertical symmetry or if the lug nuts won't stay tight. Wheel repairs that use welding or peening are not recommended, as this can weaken the metal.

8   Tire and wheel balance is important in the overall handling, braking and performance of the car. Unbalanced wheels can adversely affect handling and ride characteristics as well as tire life. Whenever a tire is installed on a wheel, the tire and wheel should be balanced by a shop with the proper equipment.

9   These models are equipped with a compact spare tire, which is designed to save space in the trunk as well as being easier to handle due to its lighter weight. The spare tire pressure should be checked at least once a month, and maintained at 70 psi.

10   The compact spare tire and wheel are designed for use with each other only, and neither the tire nor the wheel should be coupled with other types or size of wheels and tires.

11   Because the compact spare is designed as a temporary replacement for an out-of-service standard wheel and tire, the compact spare should be used on the car only until the standard wheel and tire are repaired or replaced. Continuous use of the compact spare at speeds of over 50 mph is not recommended. In addition, the expected tread life of the compact spare is only 3000 miles.

31 Wheels and tires - removal and installation

1   With the car on a level surface, the parking brake on and the car in gear (manual transaxles should be in Reverse, automatic transaxles should be in Park) remove the hub trim ring and loosen, but do not remove, the wheel lug nuts.

2   Using a jack positioned in the proper location on the car, raise the car just enough so that the tire clears the ground.

3   Remove the lug nuts.

4   Remove the wheel.

5   If a flat tire is being replaced, make sure that there is adequate ground clearance for the new inflated tire, then mount the wheel and tire on the wheel studs.

6   Apply a light coat of spray lubricant or light oil to the wheel stud threads and install the lug nuts snugly with the cone-shaped end

facing the wheel.

7   Lower the car until the tire contacts the ground.

8   Tighten the lug nuts evenly and in a cross pattern to the torque listed in the Chapter 1 Specifications.

9   Lower the car and remove the jack.

10   Replace the hub trim ring.

32   Front end alignment - general information

Refer to illustration 32.4

1   A front end alignment refers to the adjustments made to the front wheels so that they are in proper angular relationship to the suspension and the ground. Front wheels that are out of proper alignment not only affect steering control, but also increase tire wear. The only front end adjustments required on these vehicles are camber and toe-in.

2   Getting the proper front wheel alignment is a very exacting process and one in which complicated and expensive machines are necessary to perform the job properly. Because of this, it is advisable to have a specialist with the proper equipment perform these tasks.

3   We will, however, use this space to give you a basic idea of what is involved with front end alignment so you can better understand the process and deal intelligently with shops which do this work.

4   Toe-in is the turning in of the front wheels **(see illustration)**. The purpose of a toe specification is to ensure parallel rolling of the front wheels. In a car with zero toe-in, the distance between the front edges of the wheels will be the same as the distance between the rear edges of the wheels. The actual amount of toe-in is normally only a fraction of an inch. This is because even when the wheels are set to toe-in slightly when the vehicle is standing still, they tend to roll paral-

lel on the road when the car is moving.

5   Toe-in adjustment is controlled by the tie-rod end's position on the tie-rod. Incorrect toe-in will cause the tires to wear improperly by making them scrub against the road surface.

6   Camber is the tilting of the front wheels from vertical when viewed from the front of the vehicle **(see illustration 32.4)**. When the wheels tilt outward at the top, the camber is said to be positive (+). When the wheels tilt

inward at the top the camber is negative (-). The amount of tilt is measured in degrees from the vertical and this measurement is called the camber angle. This angle affects the amount of tire tread which contacts the road and compensates for changes in the suspension geometry when the car is cornering or traveling over undulating surface.

7   The camber is adjusted by altering the relationship of the steering knuckle to the strut.

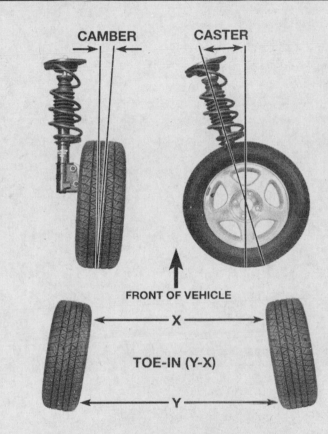

32.4 Camber, caster and toe-in angles

Notes

Chapter 11 Body

Contents

1 General information

Warning: *Some models covered by this manual are equipped with airbags. Always disable the airbag system before working in the vicinity of the impact sensors, steering column or instrument panel to avoid the possibility of accidental deployment of the airbag(s), which could cause personal injury (see Chapter 12). The yellow wires and connectors routed through the instrument panel are for this system. Do not use electrical test equipment on these yellow wires or tamper with them in any way while working under the instrument panel.* **Caution:** *If the vehicle is equipped with a Delco Loc II audio system, make sure you have the correct activation code before disconnecting the battery. See the information at the front of this manual for the radio re-activation procedure.*

The vehicles covered by this manual are available in three models: Two-door coupe, four-door sedan and a four-door wagon. Differences between the various models are noted where appropriate in the service procedures within this Chapter.

These vehicles are of unitized construction, in which the body is designed to provide vehicle rigidity so that a separate frame is not necessary. Front and rear frame side rails, integral with the body, support the front end sheet metal, front and rear suspension systems and other mechanical components. Due to this type of construction, it is very important that, in the event of collision damage, the

underbody be thoroughly checked by a facility with the proper equipment to do so.

Only general body maintenance practices and body panel repair procedures within the scope of the do-it-yourselfer are included in this Chapter.

2 Body - maintenance

1　The condition of your vehicle's body is very important, because the resale value depends a great deal on it. It is much more difficult to repair a neglected or damaged body than it is to repair mechanical components. The hidden areas of the body, such as the wheel wells, the frame and the engine compartment, are equally important, although obviously do not require as frequent attention as the rest of the body.

2　Once a year, or every 12,000 miles, it is a good idea to have the underside of the body and the frame steam cleaned. All traces of dirt and oil will be removed and the underside can then be inspected carefully for rust, damaged brake lines, frayed electrical wiring, damaged cables, and other problems. The front suspension components should be greased after completion of this job.

3　At the same time, clean the engine and the engine compartment using either a steam cleaner or a water soluble degreaser.

4　The wheel wells should be given particular attention, as undercoating can peel away and stones and dirt thrown up by the tires can cause the paint to chip and flake, allowing

rust to set in. If rust is found, clean down to the bare metal and apply an anti-rust paint.

5　The body should be washed once a week (or when dirty). Wet the vehicle thoroughly to soften the dirt, then wash it down with a soft sponge and plenty of clean, soapy water. If the surplus dirt is not washed off very carefully, it will in time wear down the paint.

6　Spots of tar or asphalt coating thrown up from the road should be removed with a cloth soaked in solvent.

7　Once every six months, give the body and chrome trim a thorough waxing. If a chrome cleaner is used to remove rust from any of the vehicle's plated parts, remember that the cleaner also removes part of the chrome, so use it sparingly.

3 Upholstery and carpets - maintenance

1　Every three months remove the carpets or mats and clean the interior of the vehicle (more frequently if necessary). Vacuum the upholstery and carpets to remove loose dirt and dust.

2　If the upholstery is soiled, apply upholstery cleaner with a damp sponge and wipe it off with a clean, dry cloth.

3　Leather upholstery requires special care. Stains should be removed with warm water and a very mild soap solution. Use a clean, damp cloth to remove the soap, then wipe again with a dry cloth. Never use gasoline, nail polish remover or thinner to clean leather upholstery.

4   In areas where the interior of the vehicle is subject to bright sunlight, cover leather seats with a sheet if the vehicle is to be left out for any length of time.

4   Vinyl trim - maintenance

Vinyl trim should not be cleaned with detergents, caustic soaps or petroleum-based cleaners. Plain soap and water or a mild vinyl cleaner is best for stains. Test a small area for color fastness. Bubbles under the vinyl can be corrected by piercing them with a pin and then working the air out.

5   Hinges and locks - maintenance

Every 3000 miles or three months, the door, hood and trunk/liftgate hinges and locks should be lubricated with a few drops of oil. The door, trunk and liftgate striker plates should also be given a thin coat of grease to reduce wear and ensure free movement.

6   Body repair - minor damage

See photo sequence

Repair of minor scratches

1   If the scratch is very superficial and does not penetrate to the metal of the body, repair is very simple. Lightly rub the scratched area with a fine rubbing compound to remove loose paint and built-up wax. Rinse the area with clean water.

2   Apply touch-up paint to the scratch, using a small brush. Continue to apply thin layers of paint until the surface of the paint in the scratch is level with the surrounding paint. Allow the new paint at least two weeks to harden, then blend it into the surrounding paint by rubbing with a very fine rubbing compound. Finally, apply a coat of wax to the scratch area.

3   If the scratch has penetrated the paint and exposed the metal of the body, causing the metal to rust, a different repair technique is required. Remove all loose rust from the bottom of the scratch with a pocket knife, then apply rust inhibiting paint to prevent the formation of rust in the future. Using a rubber or nylon applicator, coat the scratched area with glaze-type filler. If required, the filler can be mixed with thinner to provide a very thin paste, which is ideal for filling narrow scratches. Before the glaze filler in the scratch hardens, wrap a piece of smooth cotton cloth around the tip of a finger. Dip the cloth in thinner and then quickly wipe it along the surface of the scratch. This will ensure that the surface of the filler is slightly hollow. The scratch can now be painted over as described earlier in this section.

Repair of dents

4   When repairing dents, the first job is to pull the dent out until the affected area is as close as possible to its original shape. There is no point in trying to restore the original shape completely as the metal in the damaged area will have stretched on impact and cannot be restored to its original contours. It is better to bring the level of the dent up to a point which is about 1/8-inch below the level of the surrounding metal. In cases where the dent is very shallow, it is not worth trying to pull it out at all.

5   If the back side of the dent is accessible, it can be hammered out gently from behind using a soft-face hammer. While doing this, hold a block of wood firmly against the opposite side of the metal to absorb the hammer blows and prevent the metal from being stretched.

6   If the dent is in a section of the body which has double layers, or some other factor that makes it inaccessible from behind, a different technique is required. Drill several small holes through the metal inside the damaged area, particularly in the deeper sections. Screw long, self-tapping screws into the holes just enough for them to get a good grip in the metal. Now the dent can be pulled out by pulling on the protruding heads of the screws with locking pliers.

7   The next stage of repair is the removal of paint from the damaged area and from an inch or so of the surrounding metal. This is easily done with a wire brush or sanding disk in a drill motor, although it can be done just as effectively by hand with sandpaper. To complete the preparation for filling, score the surface of the bare metal with a screwdriver or the tang of a file (or drill small holes in the affected area). This will provide a good grip for the filler material. To complete the repair, see the Section on *filling and painting*.

Repair of rust holes or gashes

8   Remove all paint from the affected area and from an inch or so of the surrounding metal, using a sanding disk or wire brush mounted in a drill motor. If these are not available, a few sheets of sandpaper will do the job just as effectively.

9   With the paint removed you will be able to determine the severity of the corrosion and decide whether to replace the whole panel, if possible, or repair the affected area. New body panels are not as expensive as most people think and it is often quicker to install a new panel than to repair large areas of rust.

10   Remove all trim pieces from the affected area except those which will act as a guide to the original shape of the damaged body, such as headlight shells, etc. Using metal snips or a hacksaw blade, remove all loose metal and any other metal that is badly affected by rust. Hammer the edges of the hole in to create a slight depression for the filler material.

11   Wire brush the affected area to remove the powdery rust from the surface of the metal. If the back of the rusted area is accessible, treat it with rust inhibiting paint.

12   Before filling is done, block the hole in some way. This can be done with sheet metal riveted or screwed into place, or by stuffing the hole with wire mesh.

13   Once the hole is blocked off, the affected area can be filled and painted.

Filling and painting

14   Many types of body fillers are available, but generally speaking, body repair kits which contain filler paste and a tube of resin hardener are best for this type of repair work. A wide, flexible plastic or nylon applicator will be necessary for imparting a smooth and contoured finish to the surface of the filler material. Mix up a small amount of filler on a clean piece of wood or cardboard (use the hardener sparingly). Follow the manufacturer's instructions on the package, otherwise the filler will set incorrectly.

15   Using the applicator, apply the filler paste to the prepared area. Draw the applicator across the surface of the filler to achieve the desired contour and to level the filler surface. As soon as a contour that approximates the original one is achieved, stop working the paste. If you continue, the paste will begin to stick to the applicator. Continue to add thin layers of paste at 20-minute intervals until the level of the filler is just above the surrounding metal.

16   Once the filler has hardened, the excess can be removed with a body file. From then on, progressively finer grades of sandpaper should be used, starting with a 180-grit paper and finishing with 600-grit wet-or-dry paper. Always wrap the sandpaper around a flat rubber or wooden block, otherwise the surface of the filler will not be completely flat. During the sanding of the filler surface, the wet-or-dry paper should be periodically rinsed in water. This will ensure that a very smooth finish is produced in the final stage.

17   At this point the repair area should be surrounded by a ring of bare metal, which in turn should be encircled by the finely feathered edge of good paint. Rinse the repair area with clean water until all of the dust produced by the sanding operation is gone.

18   Spray the entire area with a light coat of primer. This will reveal any imperfections in the surface of the filler. Repair the imperfections with fresh filler paste or glaze filler and once more smooth the surface with sandpaper. Repeat this spray-and-repair procedure until you are satisfied that the surface of the filler and the feathered edge of the paint are perfect. Rinse the area with clean water and allow it to dry completely.

19   The repair area is now ready for painting. Spray painting must be carried out in a warm, dry, windless and dust free atmosphere. These conditions can be created if you have access to a large indoor work area, but if you are forced to work in the open, you will have to pick the day very carefully. If you are working indoors, dousing the floor in the

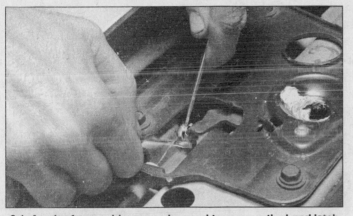

9.1 A pair of screwdrivers can be used to remove the hood latch release cable from the locking mechanism

9.2 Prying the cable out of the retaining bracket

work area with water will help settle the dust which would otherwise be in the air.

20   If the repair area is confined to one body panel, mask off the surrounding panels. This will help minimize the effects of a slight mismatch in paint color. Trim pieces such as chrome strips, door handles, etc., will also need to be masked off or removed. Use masking tape and several thicknesses of newspaper for the masking operations.

21   Before spraying, shake the paint can thoroughly, then spray a test area until the spray painting technique is mastered. Cover the repair area with a thick coat of primer. The thickness should be built up using several thin layers of primer, rather than one thick one. Using 600-grit wet-or-dry sandpaper, rub down the surface of the primer until it is very smooth. While doing this, the work area should be thoroughly rinsed with water and the wet-or-dry sandpaper periodically rinsed as well. Allow the primer to dry before spraying additional coats.

22   Spray on the top coat, again building up the thickness by using several thin layers of paint. Begin spraying in the center of the repair area and then, using a circular motion, work out until the whole repair area and about two inches of the surrounding original paint is covered. Remove all masking material 10 to 15 minutes after spraying on the final coat of paint. Allow the new paint at least two weeks to harden, then use a very fine rubbing compound to blend the edges of the new paint into the existing paint. Finally, apply a coat of wax.

7   Body repair - major damage

1   Major damage must be repaired by an auto body shop specifically equipped to perform unibody repairs. These shops have available the specialized equipment required to do the job properly.

2   If the damage is extensive, the underbody must be checked for proper alignment or the vehicle's handling characteristics may be adversely affected and other components may wear at an accelerated rate.

3   Due to the fact that all of the major body components (hood, fenders, etc.) are separate and replaceable units, any seriously damaged components should be replaced rather than repaired. Sometimes these components can be found in a wrecking yard that specializes in used vehicle components, often at considerable savings over the cost of new parts.

8   Hood - removal and installation

1   Raise the hood.

2   Place protective pads along the edges of the engine compartment to prevent damage to the painted surfaces.

3   Scribe lines around the mounting bracket, so the hood can be installed in the same position.

4   Scribe around the bracket-to-hood bolts so they can be aligned quickly and accurately during installation.

5   With an assistant supporting the weight of the hood, remove the bracket bolts and remove the hood from the vehicle.

6   Installation is the reverse of removal, taking care to align the brackets and bolts with the markings made prior to removal.

9   Hood latch release cable - replacement

Refer to illustrations 9.1, 9.2, 9.3 and 9.4

Warning: *Some models covered by this manual are equipped with airbags. Always disable the airbag system before working in the vicinity of the impact sensors, steering column or instrument panel to avoid the possibility of accidental deployment of the airbag(s), which could cause personal injury (see Chapter 12). The yellow wires and connectors routed through the instrument panel are for this system. Do not use electrical test equipment on these yellow wires or tamper with them in any way.*

Caution: *If the vehicle is equipped with a Delco Loc II or Theftlock audio system, make sure you have the correct activation code before disconnecting the battery.*

1   In the engine compartment, disconnect the release cable from the latch mechanism **(see illustration)**.

2   Pry the cable from the retaining bracket with a screwdriver **(see illustration)**.

3   In the passenger compartment, remove the left kick panel **(see illustration)**.

4   Remove the two bolts holding the T-handle to its bracket **(see illustration)**.

9.3 Remove these two screws to remove the kick panel

9.4 After removing the two retaining bolts the entire cable assembly can be removed from the vehicle

These photos illustrate a method of repairing simple dents. They are intended to supplement *Body repair - minor damage* in this Chapter and should not be used as the sole instructions for body repair on these vehicles.

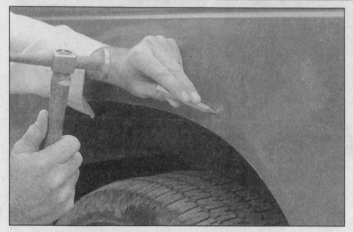

1   If you can't access the backside of the body panel to hammer out the dent, pull it out with a slide-hammer-type dent puller. In the deepest portion of the dent or along the crease line, drill or punch hole(s) at least one inch apart . . .

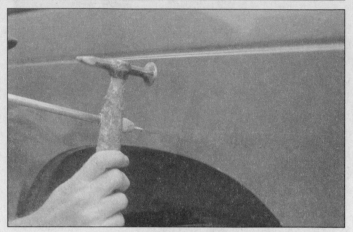

2   . . . then screw the slide-hammer into the hole and operate it. Tap with a hammer near the edge of the dent to help 'pop' the metal back to its original shape. When you're finished, the dent area should be close to its original contour and about 1/8-inch below the surface of the surrounding metal

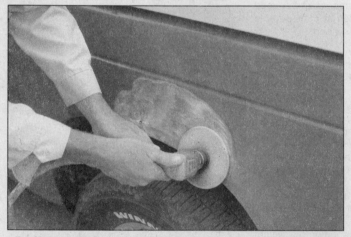

3   Using coarse-grit sandpaper, remove the paint down to the bare metal. Hand sanding works fine, but the disc sander shown here makes the job faster. Use finer (about 320-grit) sandpaper to feather-edge the paint at least one inch around the dent area

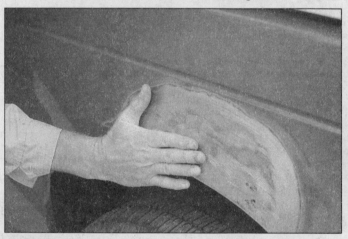

4   When the paint is removed, touch will probably be more helpful than sight for telling if the metal is straight. Hammer down the high spots or raise the low spots as necessary. Clean the repair area with wax/silicone remover

5   Following label instructions, mix up a batch of plastic filler and hardener. The ratio of filler to hardener is critical, and, if you mix it incorrectly, it will either not cure properly or cure too quickly (you won't have time to file and sand it into shape)

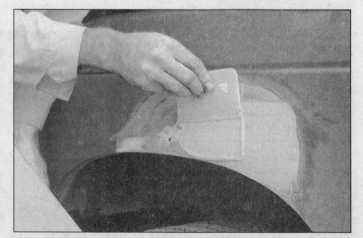

6   Working quickly so the filler doesn't harden, use a plastic applicator to press the body filler firmly into the metal, assuring it bonds completely. Work the filler until it matches the original contour and is slightly above the surrounding metal

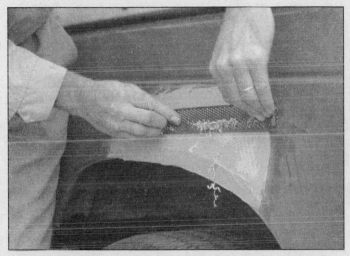

7   Let the filler harden until you can just dent it with your fingernail. Use a body file or Surform tool (shown here) to rough-shape the filler

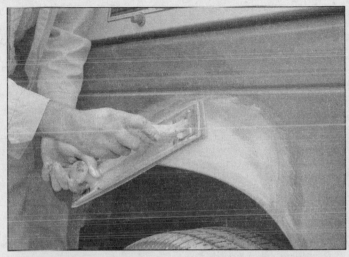

8   Use coarse-grit sandpaper and a sanding board or block to work the filler down until it's smooth and even. Work down to finer grits of sandpaper - always using a board or block - ending up with 360 or 400 grit

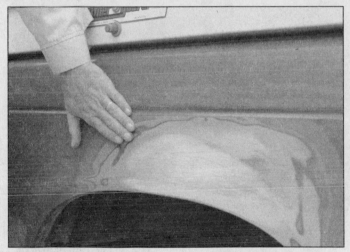

9   You shouldn't be able to feel any ridge at the transition from the filler to the bare metal or from the bare metal to the old paint. As soon as the repair is flat and uniform, remove the dust and mask off the adjacent panels or trim pieces

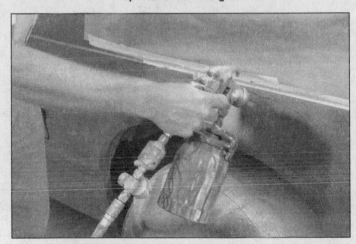

10   Apply several layers of primer to the area. Don't spray the primer on too heavy, so it sags or runs, and make sure each coat is dry before you spray on the next one. A professional-type spray gun is being used here, but aerosol spray primer is available inexpensively from auto parts stores

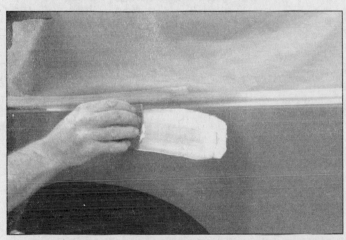

11   The primer will help reveal imperfections or scratches. Fill these with glazing compound. Follow the label instructions and sand it with 000 or 400-grit sandpaper until it's smooth. Repeat the glazing, sanding and respraying until the primer reveals a perfectly smooth surface

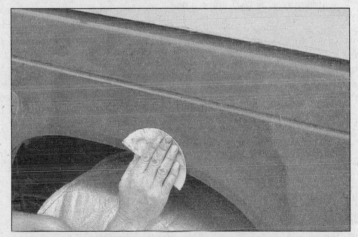

12   Finish sand the primer with very fine sandpaper (400 or 600-grit) to remove the primer overspray. Clean the area with water and allow it to dry. Use a tack rag to remove any dust, then apply the finish coat. Don't attempt to rub out or wax the repair area until the paint has dried completely (at least two weeks)

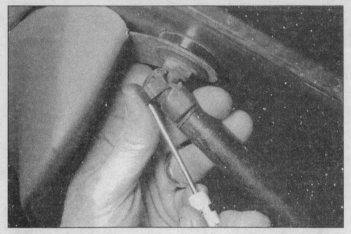

10.2 Use a screwdriver to pry the retaining clip from the support

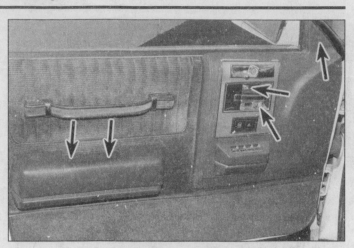

13.1 Remove the door panel retaining screws (arrows)

5   Connect string or thin wire to the end of the cable and remove the cable by pulling it through into the passenger compartment.

6   Installation is the reverse of removal after connecting the string or wire to the new cable and pulling it into position.

10   Liftgate supports - removal and installation

Refer to illustration 10.2

1   Support the liftgate in the fully open position.

2   Use a screwdriver to remove the clips from the ends **(see illustration)** and remove the supports.

3   Installation is the reverse of removal, taking care to replace the supports with ones of the correct length and capacity.

11   Liftgate - removal and installation

Removal

1   Open the rear liftgate and support it with a prop.

2   Place protective pads along the edges of the liftgate opening to prevent damage to the painted surfaces while work is being performed.

3   Remove the trim panel covering the liftgate-to-body pins.

4   Detach the liftgate supports from the liftgate (see Section 10).

5   Place a 5/32-inch metal rod on the pointed end of the hinge pin. Strike the rod sharply with a hammer to shear off the retaining clip tabs and drive the pin out of the hinge. With the help of an assistant, remove the liftgate from the vehicle.

Installation

6   Installation is the reverse of removal, but new retaining clips must be installed with their tabs toward the head of the pins before the pins are driven into place.

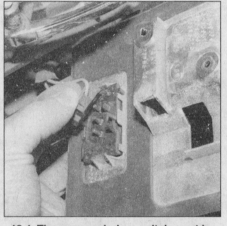

13.4 The power window switch must be disconnected to remove the door trim panel

12   Door lock knob - removal and installation

1   Remove the control handle bezel screws to gain access to the back side of the lock knob.

2   Insert a small screwdriver behind the leading end of the lock knob and pry it away from the locking rod, located behind the knob.

3   After the end of the rod is free from the knob, slide the knob forward and remove it.

4   To install the knob, place the bezel in position with the lock rod through the hole, and insert the small end of the knob rearward into place until the end of the rod engages the depression in the front end of the knob.

13   Door trim panel - removal and installation

Refer to illustrations 13.1, 13.4, and 13.6

1   Remove all of the trim panel retaining screws **(see illustration)**. **Note:** *Some models may have two large screws hidden under the armrest.*

13.6 A trim panel removal tool should be used to pry the door panel off

2   Remove the inside door locking knob (see Section 12).

3   On models with remote control mirrors, remove the escutcheon and disengage the control cable end from the escutcheon.

4   On power window equipped models, disconnect the electrical connector from the switch **(see illustration)**.

5   Remove the window regulator handle, if equipped (see Section 14).

6   Pry the trim panel loose by working around the outer circumference, using a trim panel removal tool or a large screwdriver to disengage the plastic retainers. These retainers fit very tightly and care must be taken not to destroy them during removal **(see illustration)**.

7   On models with courtesy lights in the door panels, unplug the electrical connectors.

8   Remove the panel by pushing up and out to disengage it from the top of the door.

9   Carefully peel back the water deflector for access to the inner door panel.

10   Installation is the reverse of removal, noting the following:

11   Before attaching the trim panel to the door, make sure all the plastic trim retainers are undamaged and installed tightly in the panel.

14.2a The window regulator handle is retained by a spring clip

14.2b A special tool is available to remove the window crank

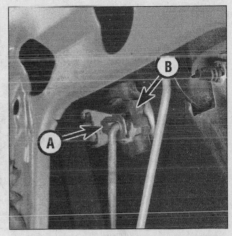

15.2 After removing the metal clip (A) and detaching the lock rod, the retaining clip (B) can be pried off to remove the lock cylinder

12   If the retainer is to be replaced with a new one, start the retainer flange into the cutout attachment hole in the trim panel, then rotate the retainer until the flange is fully engaged.

13   When attaching the door trim panel to the door, locate the top of the panel over the upper flange of the inner door panel and press down on the trim panel to engage the upper retaining clips.

14   Position the trim panel on the inner door panel so that the panel retainers are aligned with the holes in the door panel and tap the retainers into the holes with the palm of your hand or a rubber mallet.

14   Window regulator handle - removal and installation

Refer to illustrations 14.2a and 14.2b

1   Push the trim panel away from the handle to expose the spring clip.

2   Insert two small screwdrivers or a special forked tool (available at auto parts stores) between the handle and the plastic washer and push the spring clip off the shaft **(see illustrations)**.

3   To install, replace the spring clip and press the handle into place.

15   Door lock cylinder - removal and installation

Refer to illustration 15.2

1   Raise the window, remove the trim panel (see Section 13) and peel back the water deflector sufficiently to gain access to the lock cylinder **(see illustration)**.

2   Pry up the end of the metal clip and slide the clip off the lock cylinder lever. Disconnect the lock cylinder actuating rod from the lever **(see illustration)**.

3   Use a screwdriver to slide the lock cylinder retaining clip forward until it is disen-

gaged and the lock cylinder can be removed.

4   Installation is the reverse of removal, making sure the gasket is correctly installed.

16   Door lock assembly - removal and installation

1   Raise the door glass, remove the door trim panel and peel back the water deflector for access to the lock rods.

2   Disconnect the inside lock rod, the inside handle and lock cylinder lock rods.

3   Remove the retaining screws, lower the lock assembly and disengage the outside handle from the lock rod. Remove the assembly from the door.

4   After installing the spring clips to the lock assembly, installation is the reverse of removal. Tighten the retaining screws securely.

17   Door outside handle - removal and installation

1   With the window in the full up position, remove the door trim panel and peel the water deflector back sufficiently to expose the access hole.

2   Disengage the lock rod from the outside handle.

3   Remove the two attaching nuts from the handle studs.

4   Remove the handle by sliding it forward while rotating it up to disengage it from the attaching nut holes.

5   Installation is the reverse of removal.

18   Door window glass - replacement

Due to the requirements for special adhesives and handling techniques, window

19.2 Use a 5/32-inch drill bit to remove the rivet holding the lock cylinder retaining clip

glass should be replaced by a dealer service department or auto glass shop.

19   Rear compartment lid lock cylinder - removal and installation

Refer to illustration 19.2

1   Open the rear compartment and remove the lock cylinder emblem (if equipped).

2   Using a 5/32-inch drill bit, drill out the rivet holding the lock cylinder retainer to the lid **(see illustration)**.

3   Use a screwdriver to slide the lock cylinder retainer forward until it is disengaged and the lock cylinder can be removed.

4   Remove the cylinder from the vehicle.

5   Installation is the reverse of removal, making sure the lock cylinder shaft engages with the lock and the gasket mates with the outer panel to form a watertight seal. Check the lock cylinder with the key for proper operation then install a new rivet or screw.

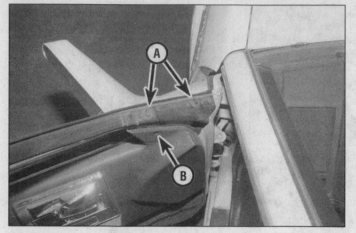

21.2 Remove the two outer retaining screws (A), then remove the door panel to gain access to the final retaining nut (B)

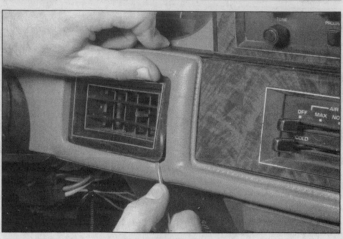

24.1 Be very careful when removing the vents from the trim pad to avoid tearing the pad

20 Luggage compartment lid lock assembly - removal and installation

1   Open the luggage compartment lid.
2   Use a flat blade screwdriver to slide the lock cylinder retainer forward until it is disengaged and the lock cylinder can be removed.
3   Remove the cylinder from the vehicle.
4   Installation is the reverse of removal.

21 Exterior mirror - removal and installation

Refer to illustration 21.2

1   Remove the trim panel or bezel. On some models it may be necessary to remove the door trim panel and peel the water deflector back for access to the retaining nuts.
2   Remove the retaining nuts and lift the mirror from the vehicle **(see illustration)**. On remote control mirrors, detach the cable clip and remove the mirror and cable as an assembly.
3   Installation is the reverse of removal, making sure the mirror gasket is properly aligned.

22 Fixed glass - replacement

Due to the requirements for special adhesives and handling techniques, the fixed glass, such as the windshield, rear and side glass, should be replaced by a dealer service department or auto glass shop.

23 Console - removal and installation

Warning: *Some models covered by this manual are equipped with airbags. Always disable the airbag system before working in the vicinity of the impact sensors, steering column or instrument panel to avoid the possibility of accidental deployment of the airbag(s), which could cause personal injury (see Chapter 12). The yellow wires and connectors routed through the instrument panel are for this system. Do not use electrical test equipment on these yellow wires or tamper with them in any way.*
1   Disconnect the negative cable at the battery. **Caution:** *If the vehicle is equipped with a Delco Loc II audio system, make sure*
you have the correct activation code before disconnecting the battery. See the information at the front of this manual for the radio re-activation procedure.
2   Remove the front compartment by pulling up on it.
3   Remove the shift knob button by inserting a screwdriver in the notch and prying up.
4   Remove the snap-ring in the recess of the knob and remove the shift knob.
5   Remove the four retaining screws holding the cover plate and lift the cover plate up enough to disconnect the indicator bulb. Remove the cover plate.
6   Separate the upper console from the lower console by removing the three attaching screws.
7   Remove the four screws holding the lower console to the floor and disconnect the rear courtesy light.
8   Lift the lower console from the vehicle.

24 Instrument panel trim plates - removal and installation

Refer to illustrations 24.1, 24.2, 24.3, 24.4, 24.5 and 24.6

Warning: *Some models covered by this manual are equipped with airbags. Always disable the airbag system before working in the vicinity of the impact sensors, steering column or instrument panel to avoid the possibility of accidental deployment of the airbag(s), which could cause personal injury (see Chapter 12). The yellow wires and connectors routed through the instrument panel are for this system. Do not use electrical test equipment on these yellow wires or tamper with them in any way.*

1   Insert a screwdriver or putty knife between air vent and the trim pad and gently pry the vent out **(see illustration)**.
2   Remove the remaining vents the same way **(see illustration)**.
3   Remove the three screws retaining the steering column trim collar and remove the

24.2 Once the vents have been detached, remove the screw(s) that secure the trim pad to the dash

24.3 Steering column trim covers

24.4 Location of the trim pad retaining screws

24.5 Remove the cluster trim retaining screws (arrows)

24.6 To install the vent, insert one end
and push

collar **(see illustration)**.

4   With the ashtray open, remove the six screws retaining the trim pad **(see illustration)**

5   To remove the cluster trim cover remove the eight screws holding the cover to the instrument panel **(see illustrations)**.

6   Installation is the reverse of the removal procedure **(see illustration)**.

25 Fender liner and fender (front) - removal and installation

Fender liner

1   Loosen the wheel lug nuts, raise the front of the vehicle and support it securely on jackstands. Remove the wheel.

2   The fender liner is held in place either with screws or special plastic retainers. When removing plastic retainers, use wire cutters or a similar tool to pry the heads of the retainers out of the retainer bodies to release them (just pry the heads out - don't cut them off). Once the heads have been pried up, remove the retainers.

3   Once all the screws or retainers have been removed, detach the fender liner and remove it from the wheel well.

4   Install the fender liner by reversing the removal procedure. If plastic retainers are used, install them in their holes and push the heads in to lock them in place. Tighten the wheel lug nuts to the torque listed in the Chapter 1 Specifications.

Fender

Warning: *Before working in the vicinity of airbag components (on models so equipped), refer to Chapter 12 for the airbag system disabling procedure.*

5   Loosen the wheel lug nuts, raise the front of the vehicle and support it securely on jackstands. Remove the wheel.

6   Remove the fender liner (see Steps 2 and 3).

7   Open the hood and remove the bolts along the top of the fender.

8   Detach the electrical connectors from the parking light and turning light, if equipped.

9   Remove the fasteners connecting the fender to the bumper fascia and any brackets. Also from the fasteners at the rear of the fender securing it to the body.

10   Carefully lift the fender from the vehicle, taking care not to scratch any surrounding paint.

11   Installation is the reverse of removal. Tighten the wheel lug nuts to the torque listed in the Chapter 1 Specifications.

Notes

Chapter 12
Chassis electrical system

Contents

1 General Information

The electrical system is a 12-volt, negative ground type. Power for the lights and all electrical accessories is supplied by a lead/acid-type battery which is charged by the alternator. This chapter covers repair and service procedures for the various electrical components not associated with the engine. Information on the battery, alternator, distributor and starter motor can be found in Chapter 5.

It should be noted that whenever portions of the electrical system are worked on, the negative battery cable should be disconnected to prevent electrical shorts and/or fires. **Caution:** *If the vehicle is equipped with a Delco Loc II audio system, make sure you have the correct activation code before disconnecting the battery. See the information at the front of this manual for the radio re-activation procedure.* **Note 1:** *Information concerning digital instrumentation and dash-related accessories is not included in this manual. Problems involving these components should be referred to a dealer service department or other repair shop.*

2 Electrical troubleshooting - general information

A typical electrical circuit consists of an electrical component, any switches, relays, motors, etc. related to that component and the wiring and connectors that connect the component to both the battery and the chassis. To aid in locating a problem in any electrical circuit, wiring diagrams are included at the end of this book.

Before tackling any troublesome electrical circuit, first study the appropriate diagrams to get a complete understanding of what makes up that individual circuit. Trouble spots, for instance, can often be narrowed down by noting if other components related to that circuit are operating properly or not. If several components or circuits fail at one time, chances are the problem lies in the fuse or ground connection, as several circuits often are routed through the same fuse and ground connections.

Electrical problems often stem from simple causes, such as loose or corroded connections, a blown fuse or melted fusible link. Prior to any electrical troubleshooting, always visually check the condition of the fuse, wires and connections in the problem circuit.

If testing instruments are going to be utilized, use the diagrams to plan ahead of time where you will make the necessary connections in order to accurately pinpoint the trouble spot.

The basic tools needed for electrical troubleshooting include a circuit tester or voltmeter (a 12-volt bulb with a set of test leads can also be used), an ohmmeter or a continuity tester (which includes a bulb, battery and set of test leads), and a jumper wire, preferably with a circuit breaker incorporated, which can be used to bypass electrical components.

Voltage checks should be performed if a circuit is not functioning properly.

Connect one lead of a circuit tester to either the negative battery terminal or a known good ground. Connect the other lead to a connector in the circuit being tested, preferably nearest to the battery or fuse. If the bulb of the tester goes on, voltage is reaching that point, which means the part of the circuit between that connector and the battery is problem free. Continue checking along the entire circuit in the same fashion. When you reach a point where no voltage is present, the problem lies between there and the last good test point. Most of the time the problem is due to a loose connection. **Note:** *Keep in mind that some circuits receive voltage only when the ignition key is in the Accessory or Run position.*

A method of finding shorts in a circuit is to remove the fuse and connect a test light or voltmeter in its place to the fuse terminals. There should be no load in the circuit. Move the wiring harness from side to-side while watching the test light. If the bulb goes on, there is a short to ground somewhere in that area, probably where insulation has rubbed off of a wire. The same test can be performed on other components of the circuit, including the switch.

A ground check should be done to see if a component is grounded properly. Disconnect the battery and connect one lead of a self-powered test light, such as a continuity tester, to a known good ground. Connect the other lead to the wire or ground connection being tested. If the bulb goes on, the ground is good. If the bulb does not go on, the ground is not good.

A continuity check is performed to see if a circuit, section of circuit or individual component is passing electricity properly. Disconnect the battery and connect one lead of a self-powered test light, such as a continuity tester, to one end of the circuit. If the bulb goes on, there is continuity, which means the circuit is passing electricity properly. Switches can be checked in the same way.

Remember that all electrical circuits are composed basically of electricity running from the battery, through the wires, switches, relays, etc. to the electrical component (light bulb, motor, etc.). From there it is run to the body (ground), where it is passed back to the battery. Any electrical problem is basically an interruption in the flow of electricity to and from the battery.

3 Fuses - general information

Refer to illustration 3.3

The electrical circuits of the vehicle are protected by a combination of fuses, circuit breakers and fusible links. The fuse block is located in one of three places; On the underside of the instrument panel on the driver's side, under the radio in the center of the dash or in the glove box. Check your owner's manual for the location of the fuse box in your particular vehicle.

Each of the fuses is designed to protect a specific circuit, as identified on the fuse cover. Spare fuses and a special removal tool are included in the fuse box cover.

Miniaturized fuses are employed in the fuse blocks. These compact fuses, with blade terminal design, allow fingertip removal and replacement. If an electrical component fails, always check the fuse first. The best

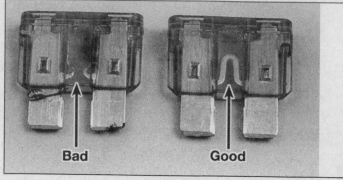

3.3 When a fuse blows, the element between the terminal melts - the fuse on the left is blown, the fuse on the right is good

way to check the fuses is with a test light. Check for power at the exposed terminal tips of each fuse. If power is present at one side of the fuse but not the other, the fuse is blown. A blown fuse can also be identified by visually inspecting it **(see illustration)**.

Fuses are replaced by simply pulling out the old one and pushing in the new one.

Be sure to replace blown fuses with the correct type. Fuses of different ratings are physically interchangeable, but only fuses of the proper rating should be used. Replacing a fuse with one of a higher or lower value than specified is not recommended. Each electrical circuit needs a specific amount of protection. The amperage value of each fuse is molded into the fuse body.

If the replacement fuse immediately fails, don't replace it again until the cause of the problem is isolated and corrected. In most cases, this will be a short circuit in the wiring caused by a broken or deteriorated wire.

4 Fusible links - general information

Refer to illustration 4.1

In addition to fuses, the wiring is protected by fusible links **(see illustration)**. These links are used in circuits which are not ordinarily fused, such as the ignition circuit.

Although the fusible links appear to be a

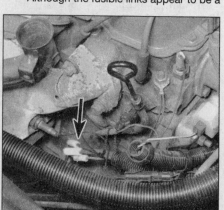

4.1 The fusible links are attached to the starter and can be easily reached

heavier gauge than the wire they are protecting, the appearance is due to the thick insulation. All fusible links are several wire gauges smaller than the wire they are designed to protect. The location of the fusible links on your particular vehicle may be determined by referring to the wiring diagrams at the end of this book.

The fusible links cannot be repaired, but a new link of the same size wire can be put in its place. The procedure is as follows:

a) *Disconnect the negative cable at the battery.*
b) *Disconnect the fusible link from the starter solenoid.*
c) *Cut the damaged fusible link out of the wiring just behind the connector.*
d) *Strip the insulation approximately 1/2-inch.*
e) *Position the connector on the new fusible link and crimp it into place.*
f) *Use rosin core solder at each end of the new link to obtain a good solder joint.*
g) *Use plenty of electrical tape around the soldered joint. No wires should be exposed.*
h) *Connect the fusible link at the starter solenoid. Connect the battery ground cable. Test the circuit for proper operation.*

5 Circuit breakers - general information

A circuit breaker is used to protect the headlight wiring and is located in the light switch. An electrical overload in the system will cause the lights to go on and off, or in some cases to remain off. If this happens, check the entire headlight circuit immediately. Once the overload condition is corrected, the circuit breaker will function normally. Circuit breakers are also used with accessories such as power windows, power door locks and the rear window defogger.

6 Turn signal and hazard flashers - check and replacement

1 Small canister-shaped flasher units are incorporated into the electrical circuits for the directional signals and hazard warning lights.

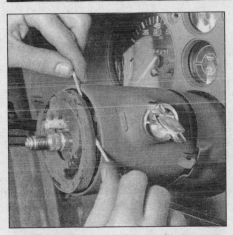

7.3 Screwdrivers can be used to remove the lock plate cover

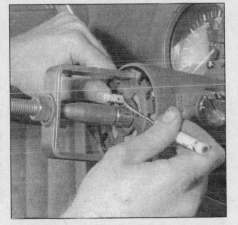

7.4 After relieving the tension on the locking ring, screwdrivers can be used to remove it

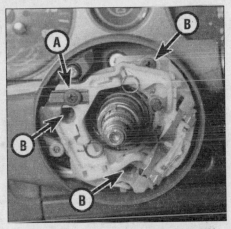

7.7a Removing the retaining screw (A) from the turn signal lever, then the turn signal switch retaining screws (B)

2   When the units are functioning properly, an audible click can be heard with the circuit in operation. If the turn signals fail on one side only and the flasher unit cannot be heard, a faulty bulb is indicated.

3   If the turn signal fails on both sides, the problem many be due to a blown fuse, faulty flasher unit or switch, or a broken or loose connection. If the fuse has blown, check the wiring for a short before installing a new fuse.

4   The hazard warning lights are checked the same way.

5   The hazard warning flasher is located in the convenience center adjacent to the fuse block. The fuse block could be in one of three places: Under the dash in the far left corner, in the glove box, or in a swing panel under the radio. Your owners manual will give you the exact location of the fuse box.

6   The turn signal flasher is mounted behind the ashtray assembly on early models and on right side of the steering column on later models and retained by a spring clip.

7   When replacing either of the flasher units, be sure to buy a replacement of the same capacity. Compare the new flasher to the old one before installing it.

7   Steering column switches and ignition key lock cylinder - removal and installation

Refer to illustrations 7.3, 7.4, 7.7a, 7.7b, 7.9, 7.11, 7.15, 7.17 and 7.21

Warning: *Some models covered by this manual are equipped with an airbag. Always disable the airbag system before working in the vicinity of the impact sensors, steering column or instrument panel to avoid the possibility of accidental deployment of the airbag, which would cause personal injury (see Section 26). The yellow wires and connectors routed through the instrument panel are for this system. Do not use electrical test equipment on these yellow wires or tamper with them in any way.*

1   Park the vehicle with the wheels pointing straight ahead. Disconnect the negative

7.7b Use a small Phillips screwdriver to remove the hazard flasher knob

cable at the battery. **Caution:** *If the vehicle is equipped with a Delco Loc II audio system, make sure you have the correct activation code before disconnecting the battery. See the information at the front of this manual for the radio re-activation procedure.*

Turn signal switch

2   Remove the steering wheel (see Chapter 10). If the vehicle is equipped with an airbag, remove the SIR coil (see Section 26). **Caution:** *Don't push down on the coil's centering spring. If you do, the coil will have to be recentered as described in Section 26.*

3   Pry the lock plate cover off, using two screwdrivers **(see illustration).**

4   Push the lock ring in sufficiently to allow removal of the ring retainer with two screwdrivers **(see illustration).**

5   Remove the lock plate.

6   Remove the retaining screw and remove the turn signal lever.

7   Remove the three retaining screws and the hazard switch button **(see illustrations).**

8   Remove the trim panel from beneath the steering column to gain access to the turn signal switch harness (see Chapter 11).

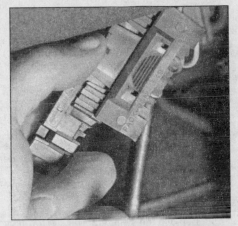

7.9 The turn signal electrical connector can be unplugged after removal of the trim panel

9   Unplug the switch electrical connector **(see illustration).**

10   Remove the steering column retaining bracket bolts and nuts, then lower the bracket (see Chapter 10).

11   Remove the switch assembly and harness, carefully guiding the harness and connector out of the column. For ease of

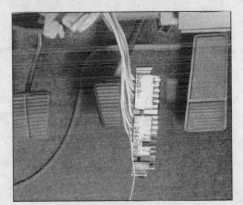

7.11 A thin piece of wire should be fastened to the connector to aid in the installation of the new harness

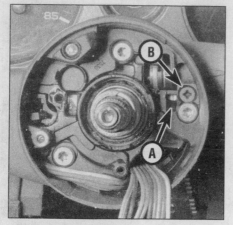

7.15 Needle-nose pliers can be used to remove the warning buzzer switch (A), then remove the ignition switch retaining screw (B)

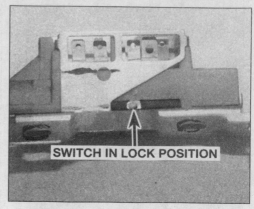

7.17 Warning buzzer switch assembled

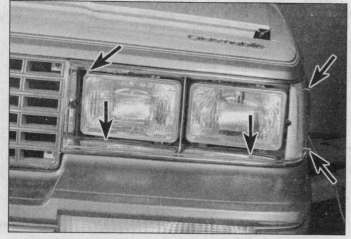

7.21 The ignition switch should be placed in the lock position prior to installation

reassembly, tie a string or fasten a thin wire to the harness connector to use in pulling the connector back into the narrow confines of the steering column **(see illustration)**.

12   Installation is the reverse of removal. If the vehicle is equipped with an airbag, make sure the SIR coil is centered (see Section 26).

Ignition key lock cylinder

13   Perform Steps 1 through 9 and pull the turn signal switch up sufficiently to provide access to the ignition switch.

14   With the key in the On position, remove the ignition warning buzzer switch contacts with needle-nose pliers.

15   Remove the switch retaining screw **(see illustration)**.

16   Withdraw the switch from the steering column.

17   Installation is the reverse of removal, paying attention to the following points:

a) *Assemble the ignition warning buzzer switch and spring before inserting them* **(see illustration)**.

b) *When installing the turn signal actuator arm, make sure it is securely engaged in the lever mechanism before tightening the screw.*

Ignition switch

18   Unbolt the steering column bracket from the dash (see Chapter 10) and lower the column.

19   Unplug the electrical connector from the switch.

20   Turn the ignition key to the LOCK position. Remove the two screws securing the switch to the steering column and remove the switch.

21   To install the switch, reverse the removal procedure, but make sure the new switch is set in the Lock position **(see illustration)**. This can be determined by inserting a small screwdriver in the actuating rod slot and then moving the switch slide all the way to the left, then back one detent. **Caution:** *Use only the original screws or genuine factory replacements. Longer or thicker screws could cause the collapsible design of the steering column to become impaired.*

8   Headlight - removal and installation

Refer to illustrations 8.2 and 8.3

Sealed beam headlights

Removal

1   When replacing the headlight, do not turn the spring-loaded adjusting screws or the headlight aim will be changed.

2   Remove the headlight bezel retaining screws and the decorative bezel **(see illustration)**.

3   Remove the four screws which secure the retaining ring **(see illustration)** and withdraw the ring. Support the light as this is done.

4   Pull the light away, unplug the connector and remove it from the vehicle.

Installation

5   Position the new unit close enough to connect the wires. Make sure the numbers molded into the lens are at the top.

6   Install the retaining ring and mounting screws.

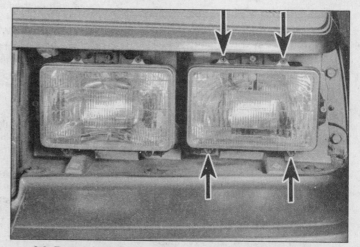

8.2 Location of the retaining screws on the headlight bezel (this vehicle has five screws securing the bezel - other models may have either four or six screws)

8.3 Remove the four retaining screws (arrows) to change the headlight

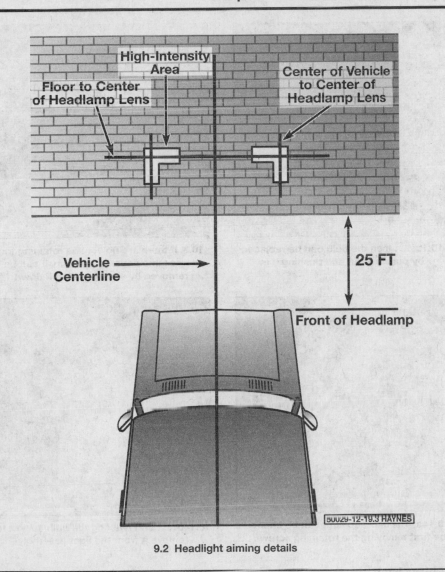

9.2 Headlight aiming details

Headlights have two spring loaded adjusting screws, one on the top controlling up and down movement and one on the side controlling left and right movement.

There are several methods of adjusting the headlights. The simplest method uses a blank wall set at 25 feet in front of the vehicle and a level floor.

Preparation

1   Park the vehicle on a level floor 25 feet from the wall.

2   Position masking tape vertically on the screen in reference to the vehicle centerline and the centerlines of both headlights as shown **(see illustration)**. **Note:** *If the vehicle has a four headlight system, four vertical lines plus the vehicle centerline will be used.*

3   Position a horizontal tape line in reference to the centerline of all the headlights. **Note:** *It may be easier to position the tape on the screen with the vehicle parked only a few inches away.*

Adjustment

4   Adjustment should be made with the vehicle sitting level, the gas tank half-full and no unusually heavy load in the vehicle.

5   Starting with the low beam adjustment, position the high-intensity zone so it is two inches below the horizontal line and two inches to the right of the headlight vertical line. Adjustment is made by turning the top adjusting screw clockwise to raise the beam and counterclockwise to lower the beam. The adjusting screw on the side should be used in the same manner to move the beam left or right.

6   With the high beams on, the high-intensity zone should be vertically centered with the exact center just below the horizontal line. **Note:** *It may not be possible to position the headlight aim exactly for both high and low beams. If a compromise must be made, keep in mind that the low beams are the most used and have the greatest effect on driver safety.*

7   Install the bezel and check for proper operation. If the adjusting screws were not turned, the headlight should not require adjustment.

Composite headlights

Caution: *The composite headlights have halogen bulbs which contain a gas under pressure. Handling a bulb improperly could cause it to shatter into flying glass fragments. To help avoid personal injury, be sure to turn off the headlights and allow the bulb to cool before changing bulbs. Leave the headlights off until the bulb change is complete. Always wear eye protection when changing a halogen bulb. Handle the bulb only by its base. Avoid touching the glass. If you do touch the glass, clean it off with rubbing alcohol. Do not drop or scratch the glass. Keep moisture away. Place the used bulb in the new bulb carton and dispose of it properly. Keep halogen bulbs out of the reach of children.*

8   When replacing composite-type bulbs on some models, it may be necessary to remove the grille and the headlight assembly.

9   Locate the bulb lock ring on the back of the headlight assembly and turn it counterclockwise until it's loose.

10   With a vertical rocking motion, pull the bulb to the rear.

11   With one hand, grip the wire harness end of the bulb. Do not grip the wires. With the other hand, grip the base of the bulb. Do not grip the bulb glass. Pull the bulb and base apart. **Note:** *The bulbs for high and low beams are the same and have two separate filaments. Instead of using a new bulb for a burned out light, low and high beam bulbs can be interchanged.*

12   Installation is the reverse of removal.

9   Headlights - adjustment

Refer to illustration 9.2

Note: *It is important that the headlights are aimed correctly. If adjusted incorrectly they could blind the driver of an oncoming car and cause a serious accident or seriously reduce your ability to see the road.*

10   Bulb replacement

Refer to illustrations 10.1a, 10.1b, 10.3, 10.13, 10.14a and 10.14b

Warning: *On models equipped with an airbag, always disable the airbag system before working in the vicinity of the steering column, instrument panel or airbag system components to prevent accidental deployment of the airbag, which could cause personal injury (see Section 26).*

Front end

Parking and turn signal bulbs

1   The turn signal and side marker light bulb can be replaced from outside the engine compartment after removing the five Torx screws and removing the facia panel. The

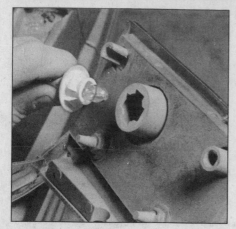

10.1a The side lamp is removed by twisting it . . .

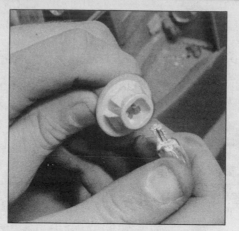

10.1b . . . then the bulb can be replaced by pulling it out and pushing it in

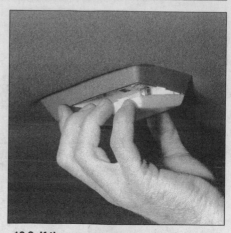

10.3 If there are no screws retaining the dome lamp cover in position, it can be removed by simply pulling it down

10.13 The tail light assembly is held in place by four wing nuts

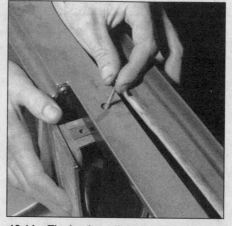

10.14a The back-up light can be changed be first removing the retaining screw . . .

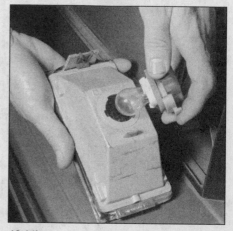

10.14b . . . and twisting the bulb socket to remove it from the light assembly

side marker bulb is located at the end of the facia panel. The front turn signal bulb can be reached through the slot in the front bumper. Turn the bulbs to remove them from the housings **(see illustrations)**.

Interior

Courtesy lights
2   The lower courtesy light bulbs are replaced by pushing up and turning to the left to unlatch the bulb from the socket.

Dome light
3   On some models, screws retain the dome lamp lens. On others, grasp the lens to remove it **(see illustrations)**. Remove the bulb by pulling it straight down.

Instrument panel lights
4   Most instrument panel bulbs can be replaced after removal of the instrument cluster (see Section 15). If a bulb is located in a recess and cannot be grasped with the fingers, push a suitable piece of tubing, such as vacuum hose, over the bulb and pull straight out to remove it.

Ashtray light
5   Remove the ashtray and remove the console cover for access to the bulb.

Glovebox light
6   Open the glove box, remove the striker assembly and remove the bulb.

Heater and air conditioner control light
7   Remove the left side trim pad and instrument panel trim cover. Remove the screws retaining the control to the instrument panel.
8   Pull the control out sufficiently to gain access to the bulb socket and remove it. Remove the bulb from the socket.

Radio bulb
9   Remove the radio.
10   Remove the top cover from the radio, grasp the bulb and pull straight out.

Console
11   Remove the console cover retaining screws and pull the cover up sufficiently to gain access to the bulb socket. Twist the

socket counterclockwise to remove it and then remove the bulb.

Rear end

Courtesy light
12   The rear compartment courtesy light bulb is contained in a plastic housing. Use a screwdriver to pry the housing out of the panel for access to the bulb.

Tail and back-up lights
13   Remove the four plastic wing nuts and remove the tail light assembly. Turn the bulb socket to remove, then push the bulb in and turn it counterclockwise to remove it **(see illustration)**.
14   The back-up light bulb is replaced by removing the retaining screw and carefully prying out the lamp assembly **(see illustrations)**. The bulb is removed in the same manner as the tail lights.

License plate
15   Access to the license plate lamp is gained by removing the two screws and removing the lamp assembly. Turn and pull the bulb to remove it.

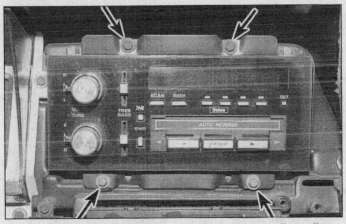

11.6 Remove the four retaining screws to remove the radio

11.13 The front speakers are held in by two retaining bolts

11 Radio and speakers - removal and installation

Refer to illustrations 11.6 and 11.13

Warning: *On models equipped with an airbag, always disable the airbag system before working in the vicinity of the steering column, instrument panel or airbag system components to prevent accidental deployment of the airbag, which could cause personal injury (see Section 26).*

Note: *Detach the cable from the negative terminal of the battery prior to removing the radio or speakers.*

Delco Loc II general information

1 Some audio systems in the models covered by this manual feature the Delco Loc II anti-theft feature. In this system, the owner can program a secret code into the radio which will automatically scramble if the radio is deprived of battery power, rendering it inoperative.
2 Before beginning any procedure which requires the battery to be disconnected or the radio to be removed, make sure you know the secret code stored in the radio. It must be entered after the battery is reconnected.
3 The radio can also be unlocked before battery power is disconnected by entering the secret code, at which time the display on the radio will momentarily indicate "-" then the clock will be displayed.
4 If you don't know your secret code or encounter difficulty in reactivating the radio, consult your dealer service department.

Removal and installation

5 Remove the instrument panel trim plate.
6 Remove the radio retaining screws **(see illustration).**
7 Pull the radio out sufficiently for access to the antenna cable.
8 Unplug the antenna cable from the back of the radio.

9 Unplug the electrical connectors from the radio by depressing the tabs.
10 Lift the radio from the dash.
11 Installation is the reverse of removal.

Speakers

Front

12 Remove the speaker grille by carefully prying up on it, and lift the grille from the instrument panel.
13 Remove the two screws attaching the speaker to the instrument panel **(see illustration)** and lift the speaker sufficiently to disconnect the wiring.
14 Remove the speaker.
15 Installation is the reverse of removal.

Rear

Wagon

16 Remove the two plastic retaining screws and remove the speaker cover trim panel.
17 Pull the carpet back sufficiently for clearance and swing the speaker and cover assembly into the rear compartment.
18 Disconnect the wires and remove the speaker.
19 Installation is the reverse of removal.

Sedan

20 The speakers are accessible after opening the trunk. Remove the nut and speaker cover, then unplug the electrical connector from the speaker.
21 Disengage the speaker retaining clip and remove the speaker.
22 Installation is the reverse of removal.

12 Radio antenna - removal and installation

Standard antenna

1 The antenna mast can be removed by simply unscrewing it from its base.
2 The antenna body and cable assembly can be removed after the mast has been removed by unbolting it from the fender.
3 Installation is the reverse of removal,

taking care to locate the studs securely in the fender.

Power antenna

4 Turn the steering wheel to the far left position.
5 Disconnect the negative cable from the battery. **Caution:** *If the vehicle is equipped with a Delco Loc II audio system, make sure you have the correct activation code before disconnecting the battery. See the information at the front of this manual for the radio re-activation procedure.*
6 Remove the right inner fender splash shield, which is held in place by four plastic studs and three screws.
7 Remove the Phillips head screw retaining the antenna mast escutcheon to the fender.
8 Disconnect the antenna lead and motor wires.
9 Remove the two bolts from the lower bracket.
10 Carefully pull the antenna and wiring assembly down through the wheel opening.
11 Installation is the reverse of removal.

13 Speedometer - removal and installation

Warning: *On models equipped with an airbag, always disable the airbag system before working in the vicinity of the steering column, instrument panel or airbag system components to prevent accidental deployment of the airbag, which could cause personal injury (see Section 26).*

1 Disconnect the negative cable at the battery.
2 Remove the instrument panel cluster housing (see Section 15).
3 Remove the instrument panel trim.
4 Remove the retaining screws and lift the speedometer assembly from the cluster.
5 Installation is the reverse of removal. If the vehicle speed sensor (VSS) has been removed with the speedometer, it must be reinstalled for proper operation of the lock-up torque converter.

14   Speedometer cable - replacement

1   Disconnect the cable from the negative battery terminal. **Caution:** *If the vehicle is equipped with a Delco Loc II audio system, make sure you have the correct activation code before disconnecting the battery. See the information at the front of this manual for the radio re-activation procedure.*
2   Remove the steering column trim plate.
3   Remove the instrument cluster trim plate and pad.
4   After removing the four cluster retaining screws, pull the cluster out carefully so as not to disconnect the cluster wiring until there is sufficient clearance to reach the speedometer cable retaining collar.
5   Press the clip on the cable casing toward the cluster to disconnect it.
6   Disconnect the cable at the transaxle or cruise control transducer.
7   Slide the old cable out from the upper end of the casing, or, if broken, from both ends of the casing.
8   If the speedometer operation has been noisy, but the speedometer cable appears to be in good condition, take a short piece of speedometer cable with a tip to fit the speedometer and insert it in the speedometer socket. Spin the piece of cable between your fingers. If binding is noted, the speedometer is faulty and should be repaired or replaced with a new one.
9   Inspect the speedometer cable casing for sharp bends and breaks, especially at the transaxle end. If breaks are noted, replace the casing with a new one.
10   When installing the cable, perform the following steps to ensure quiet operation.
11   Wipe the cable clean with a lint-free cloth.
12   Flush the bore of the casing with solvent and blow it dry with compressed air.
13   Place some speedometer cable lubricant in the palm of one hand.
14   Feed the cable through the lubricant and into the casing until lubricant has been applied to the lower two-thirds of the cable. Do not over-lubricate.
15   Seat the upper cable tip in the speedometer and snap the retainer onto the housing.
16   The remaining installation steps are the reverse of removal.

15   Instrument cluster - removal and installation

Warning: *On models equipped with an airbag, always disable the airbag system before working in the vicinity of the steering column, instrument panel or airbag system components to prevent accidental deployment of the airbag, which could cause personal injury (see Section 26).*
1   Disconnect the negative cable at the

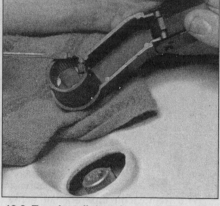

19.1 Carefully pry up on the wiper arm to remove it

battery. **Caution:** *If the vehicle is equipped with a Delco Loc II audio system, make sure you have the correct activation code before disconnecting the battery. See the information at the front of this manual for the radio re-activation procedure.*
2   Remove the left side trim panels.
3   Remove the cluster retaining screws.
4   Pull the cluster out, disconnect the speedometer cable and wiring and remove it from the instrument panel.
5   Installation is the reverse of removal.

16   Cluster panel instruments (except speedometer) - removal and installation

Warning: *On models equipped with an airbag, always disable the airbag system before working in the vicinity of the steering column, instrument panel or airbag system components to prevent accidental deployment of the airbag, which could cause personal injury (see Section 26).*
1   Disconnect the negative cable from battery. **Caution:** *If the vehicle is equipped with a Delco Loc II audio system, make sure you have the correct activation code before disconnecting the battery. See the information at the front of this manual for the radio re-activation procedure.*
2   Remove the instrument panel cluster.
3   Remove the cluster mask.
4   Remove the retaining bolts and lift the instruments from the cluster.
5   Installation is the reverse of removal.

17   Headlight switch - removal and installation

Warning: *On models equipped with an airbag, always disable the airbag system before working in the vicinity of the steering column, instrument panel or airbag system components to prevent accidental deploy-*

19.2 To reinstall the wiper arm, first align the slot with the notch on the shaft and press it on until it seats into position

ment of the airbag, which could cause personal injury (see Section 26).
1   Disconnect the negative cable from the battery. **Caution:** *If the vehicle is equipped with a Delco Loc II audio system, make sure you have the correct activation code before disconnecting the battery. See the information at the front of this manual for the radio re-activation procedure.*
2   Remove the left side instrument panel trim.
3   Remove the retaining screws and lift the switch from the instrument panel.
4   Installation is the reverse of removal.

18   Rear window washer/wiper and rear window defogger switches - removal and installation

1   Disconnect the negative cable at the battery. **Caution:** *If the vehicle is equipped with a Delco Loc II audio system, make sure you have the correct activation code before disconnecting the battery. See the information at the front of this manual for the radio re-activation procedure.*
2   Remove the right side instrument panel trim cover.
3   Remove the retaining screws and lift the appropriate switch from the trim cover.
4   Installation is the reverse of removal.

19   Windshield wiper arm - removal and installation

Refer to illustrations 19.1 and 19.2
1   Using rags to protect the paint and wiper arm, carefully pry up on the arm to release it from the shaft **(see illustration)**.
2   To reinstall the wiper arm, align the slot in the arm with the ridge in the wiper shaft and firmly push it into place **(see illustration)**.

20.3a To gain access to the wiper motor crank arm, first remove the top cowl retaining bolts . . .

20.3b . . . then remove the retaining bolt under the cowl at each end

20 Windshield wiper motor - removal and installation

Refer to illustrations 20.3a, 20.3b, 20.4, and 20.7

1   Disconnect the negative cable at the battery.
2   Remove the wiper arms.
3   Remove the retaining screws holding the cowl panel. A number 15 Torx bit will be needed to remove two of the eleven screws **(see illustrations)**.
4   To avoid problems on reinstallation, use paint or a sharp scribe to mark the position of the motor crank arm to the wiper linkage **(see illustration)**.
5   Disconnect the motor crank arm from the wiper linkage.
6   Disconnect the wiring and washer hoses from the wiper motor.
7   Remove the three motor-to-body attaching screws **(see illustration)** and carefully remove the wiper motor from the vehicle.
8   Installation is the reverse of the removal procedure, noting that the paint marks on the wiper linkage should be aligned for proper operation.

21 Parking brake switch - replacement

1   Remove the console cover.
2   Unplug the electrical connector from the switch.
3   Remove the screw retaining the switch to the parking brake and remove the switch.
4   Installation is the reverse of removal.

22 Cruise control - description and check

The cruise control system maintains vehicle speed with a vacuum actuated servo motor located in the engine compartment, which is connected to the throttle linkage by a cable. The system consists of the servo motor, clutch switch, brake switch, trans-

20.4 Mark the relationship of the motor crank arm to the wiper linkage

ducer (early models) control switches, a relay and associated vacuum hoses.

Because of the complexity of the cruise control system and the special tools and techniques required for diagnosis, repair should be left to a dealer service department or other repair shop. However, it is possible for the home mechanic to make simple checks of the wiring and vacuum connections for minor faults which can be easily repaired. These include:

a) *Inspect the cruise control actuating switches for broken wires and loose connections.*
b) *Check the cruise control fuse.*
c) *The cruise control system is operated by vacuum so it's critical that all vacuum switches, hoses and connections are secure. Check the hoses in the engine compartment and under the dash at the vacuum release switch for tight connections, cracks and obvious vacuum leaks.*

23 Rear defogger (electric grid type) - check and repair

Refer to illustrations 23.4 and 23.11

1   This option consists of a rear window with a number of horizontal elements baked

20.7 Remove the three wiper motor mounting bolts (arrows)

into the glass surface during the glass forming operation.
2   Small breaks in the element can be successfully repaired without removing the rear window.
3   To test the grids for proper operation, turn on the system.
4   Ground one lead of a test light and carefully touch the other lead to each element line **(see illustration)**.

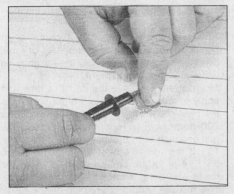

23.4 When measuring the voltage at the rear window defogger grid, wrap a piece of aluminum foil around the positive probe of the voltmeter and press the foil against the wire with your finger

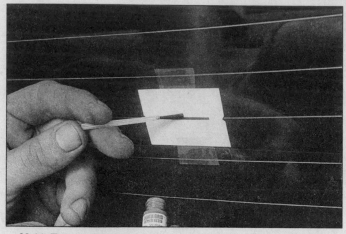

23.11 To use a defogger repair kit, apply masking tape to the inside of the window at the damaged area, then brush on the special conductive coating

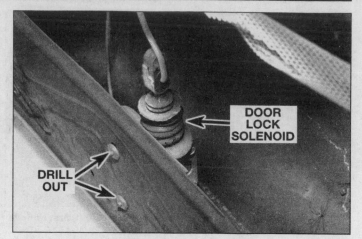

24.2 The door lock actuator is secured by two large rivets. To remove these rivets, knock the center of each rivet out with a narrow punch, then drill the heads off, being careful not to enlarge the holes in the door sheetmetal

5   The brilliance of the test light should increase as the lead is moved across the element from right to left. If the test light glows brightly at both ends of the lines, check for a loose ground wire. All of the lines should be checked in at least two places.

6   To repair a break in a line, it is recommended that a repair kit specifically for this purpose be purchased from a GM dealer parts department or auto parts store. Included in the repair kit will be a decal, a container of silver plastic and hardener, a mixing stick and instructions.

7   To repair a break, first turn off the system and allow it to de-energize for a few minutes.

8   Lightly buff the element area with fine steel wool then clean it thoroughly with rubbing alcohol.

9   Use the decal supplied in the repair kit or apply strips of electrician's tape above and below the area to be repaired. The space between the pieces of tape should be the same width as the existing lines. This can be checked from outside the vehicle. Press the tape tightly against the glass to prevent seepage.

10   Mix the hardener and silver plastic thoroughly.

11   Using the wood spatula, apply the silver plastic mixture between the pieces of tape, overlapping the undamaged area slightly on either end **(see illustration)**.

12   Carefully remove the decal or tape and apply a constant stream of hot air directly to the repaired area. A heat gun set at 500 to 700-degrees F is recommended. Hold the gun one inch from the glass for two minutes.

13   If the new element appears off color, tincture of iodine can be used to clean the repair and bring it back to the proper color. This mixture should not remain on the repair for more than 30 seconds.

14   Although the defogger is now fully operational, the repaired area should not be disturbed for at least 24 hours.

24   Power door lock system - general information

Refer to illustration 24.2

The power door lock system operates the door lock actuators mounted in each door. The system consists of the switches, actuators and associated electrical wiring. Diagnosis can usually be limited to simple checks of the wiring connections and actuators for minor faults which can be easily repaired. These include:

a) *Checking the system fuse and/or circuit breaker.*
b) *Checking the switch wiring for damage or loose connections.*
c) *Checking the switches for continuity.*
d) *Removing the door panel(s) and checking the actuator electrical connections for looseness or damage. Inspect the actuator rods to make sure they are not bent, damaged or binding. The actuator can be checked by applying battery power momentarily. A solid click indicates the solenoid is operating properly.*

2   If you determine that the door lock actuator is faulty, remove the door trim panel (see Chapter 11), detach the lock rod from the actuator and drill out the two large rivets securing the actuator to the inner sheetmetal of the door **(see illustration)**. The new actuator can be secured with new rivets (although a special rivet gun is required due to the large size of the rivets), or with nuts and bolts of the appropriate size.

25   Power window system - general information

The power window system operates the electric motors mounted in the doors which lower and raise the windows. The system consists of the control switches, the motors, glass mechanisms (regulators) and associ-

ated wiring.

Diagnosis can usually be limited to simple checks of the electrical connections and motors for minor faults which can be easily repaired. These include:

a) *Inspecting the power window actuating switches and wiring for broken wires or loose connections.*
b) *Checking the power window fuse and/or circuit breaker.*
c) *Removing the door panel(s) and checking the power window motor electrical connections for looseness and damage, and inspecting the glass mechanisms for damage which could cause binding.*

26   Airbag - general information and precautions

General information

1   Some later models are equipped with a Supplemental Inflatable Restraint (SIR) system, more commonly known as an airbag. This system is designed to protect the driver from serious injury in the event of a head-on or frontal collision. It consists of an airbag module in the center of the steering wheel, two discriminating (crash) sensors mounted at the front and the interior of the vehicle, an arming sensor located behind the glove box, an SIR coil assembly mounted under the steering wheel and a diagnostic module located inside the passenger compartment under the dash.

Airbag module and SIR coil

2   The airbag inflator module contains a housing incorporating the cushion (airbag) and inflator unit, mounted in the center of the steering wheel. The inflator assembly is mounted on the back of the housing over a hole through which gas is expelled, inflating the bag almost instantaneously when an electrical signal is sent from the system. The airbag steering column coil assembly is

mounted on the steering column under the steering wheel and carries this signal to the module. The coil assembly can transmit an electrical signal regardless of steering wheel position.

Sensors

3   The system has three sensors: a forward discriminating sensor mounted on the radiator support and a passenger compartment discriminating sensor mounted under the front of the center console. These sensors are basically pressure sensitive switches that complete an electrical circuit during an impact of sufficient G force. The electrical signal from these sensors is sent to the arming sensor which then completes the circuit and inflates the airbag.

Diagnostic Energy Reserve Module (DERM)

4   The DERM supplies the current to the airbag system in the event of the collision, even if battery power is cut off. It checks this system every time the vehicle is started, causing the "AIR BAG" light to go on then off, if the system is operating properly. If there is a fault in the system, the light will go on and stay on and the DERM will store fault codes indicating the nature of the fault. If the AIR

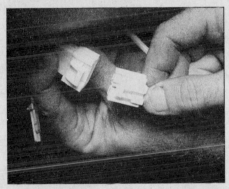

26.10 The airbag Connector Position Assurance (CPA) connector is located at the base of the steering column; always unlock and unplug it before removing the steering wheel or working in the area of the steering wheel

BAG light goes on and stays on, the vehicle should be taken to your dealer immediately for service.

Operation

5   For the airbag(s) to deploy, an impact of sufficient force must occur within 30-degrees of the vehicle centerline. When this condition occurs, the circuit to the airbag inflator is closed and the airbag inflates. If the battery is destroyed by the impact, or is too low to power the inflator, a back-up power supply inside the diagnostic/energy reserve module supplies current to the airbag.

Self-diagnosis system

6   A self-diagnosis circuit in the module displays a light when the ignition switch is turned to the On position. If the system is operating normally, the light should go out after seven flashes. If the light doesn't come on, or doesn't go out after seven flashes, or if it comes on while you're driving the vehicle, there's a malfunction in the SIR system. Have it inspected and repaired as soon as possible. Do not attempt to troubleshoot or service the SIR system yourself. Even a small mistake could cause the SIR system to malfunction when you need it.

Servicing components near the SIR system

7   Nevertheless, there are times when you need to remove the steering wheel, radio or service other components on or near the instrument panel or at the front of the vehicle. At these times, you'll be working around components and wiring harnesses for the SIR system. SIR system wiring is easy to identify; they're all covered by a bright yellow conduit. Do not unplug the connectors for the SIR system wiring, except to disable the system. And do not use electrical test equipment on the SIR system wiring. **Always disable the SIR system before working near the SIR system components or related wiring.**

Disabling the SIR system

Refer to illustration 26.10

8   Turn the steering wheel to the straight

ahead position, place the ignition switch key in the Lock position and remove the key. Remove the airbag fuse from the fuse block (see Section 3). It's also a good idea to disconnect the cable from the negative terminal of the battery, although this is not actually specified by the manufacturer. **Caution:** *If the vehicle is equipped with a Delco Loc II audio system, make sure you have the correct activation code before disconnecting the battery. See the information at the front of this manual for the radio re-activation procedure.*

9   Remove the steering column covers and the left sound insulator panel below the instrument panel (see Chapter 11).

10   Unplug the yellow Connector Position Assurance (CPA) steering column harness connector **(see illustration)**.

Enabling the SIR system

11   After you've disabled the airbag and performed the necessary service, plug in the steering column CPA connectors. Reinstall the steering column lower trim panel, and the sound insulator panel.

12   Install the airbag fuse. Connect the negative battery terminal.

Removing, centering and installing the SIR coil

Refer to illustrations 26.15a, 26.15b, 26.16 and 26.18

13   Anytime some part of the steering system is disassembled for service or replacement, the steering column should be immobilized to ensure that the SIR coil doesn't become uncentered (moved). This can occur, for example, if the steering column is separated from the steering gear, or if the centering spring is pushed down, allowing the hub to rotate while the coil is removed from the steering column. If the coil becomes accidentally uncentered, re-center it as follows before reassembling the steering system:

14   Make sure that the wheels are pointed straight ahead.

15   Remove the coil assembly snap-ring **(see illustration)** and remove the coil assembly **(see illustration)**.

26.15a To release the SIR coil from the steering shaft, remove this snap-ring . . .

26.15b . . . then remove the coil

16   Holding the coil assembly with its bottom side facing up, depress the spring lock **(see illustration)** and rotate the hub in the direction of the arrow until it stops (the arrow is on the back of the coil assembly). The coil ribbon should be wound up snug against the center hub.

17   Rotate the coil hub in the opposite direction two and three-quarters turns, then release the spring lock. The coil is now centered.

18   Install the SIR coil and secure it with the snap-ring. The tab will be at the top and the marks aligned when the coil is properly installed **(see illustration)**.

27   Wiring diagrams - general information

Since it isn't possible to include all wiring diagrams for every year covered by this manual, the following diagrams are those that are typical and most commonly needed.

Prior to troubleshooting any circuits, check the fuse and circuit breakers (if equipped) to make sure they're in good con-

26.16 To center the SIR coil, hold it with its underside facing up, depress the spring lock and rotate the hub in the direction of the arrow on the coil assembly until it stops

26.18 When properly installed, the airbag coil will be centered with the marks aligned (circle) and the tab fitted between the projections on the top of steering column (arrow)

dition. Make sure the battery is properly charged and check the cable connections (see Chapter 1).

When checking a circuit, make sure that all connectors are clean, with no broken or loose terminals. When unplugging a connector, do not pull on the wires. Pull only on the connector housings themselves.

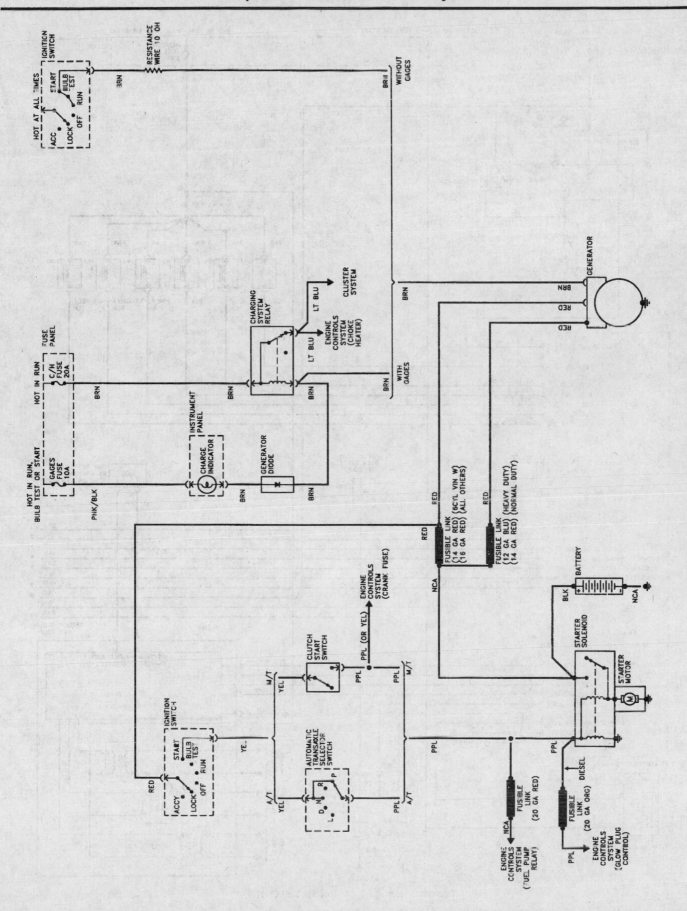

Typical starting and charging system

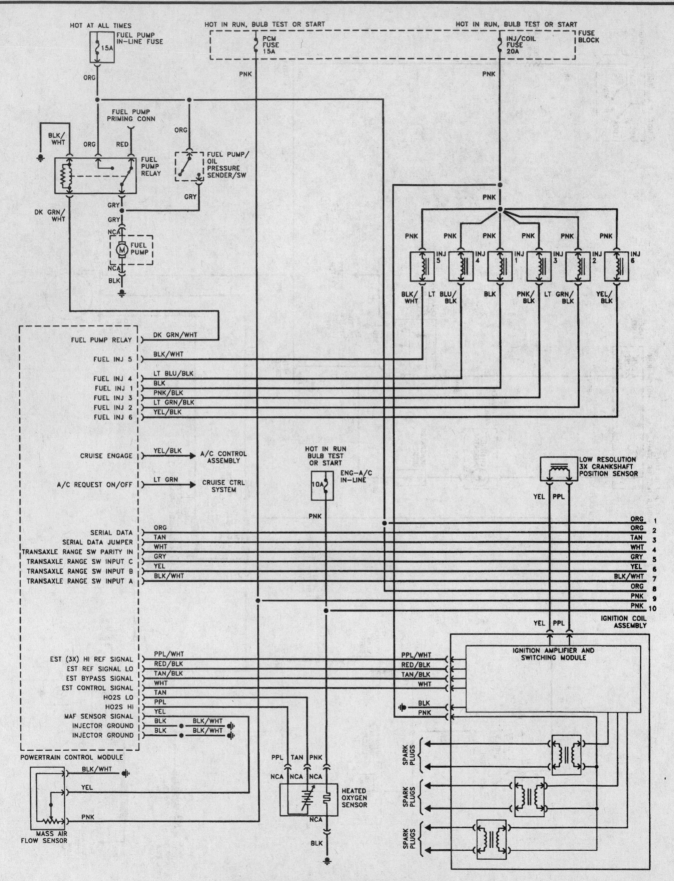

Typical 3.1L engine control system (1 of 3)

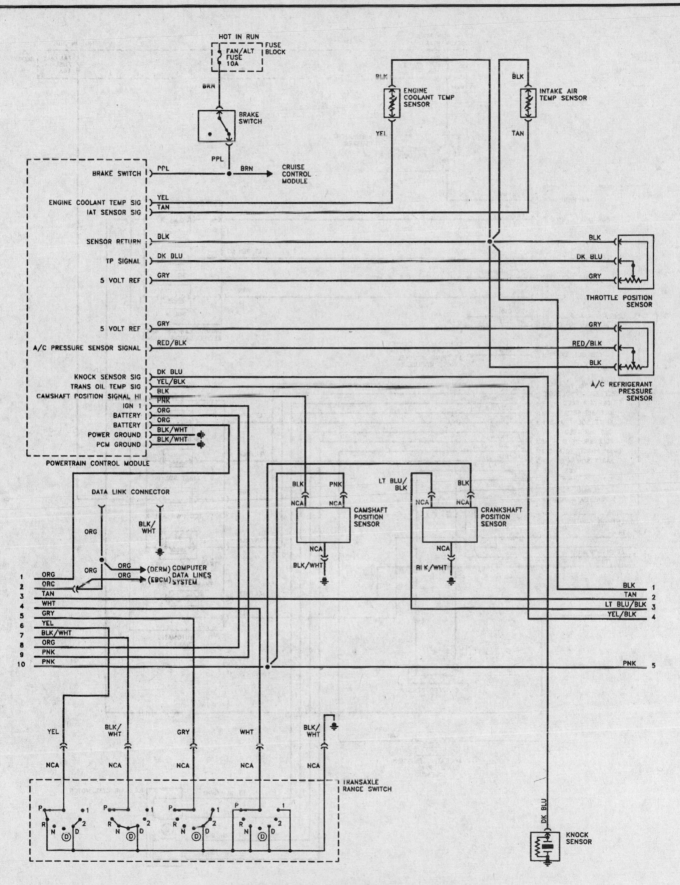

Typical 3.1L engine control system (2 of 3)

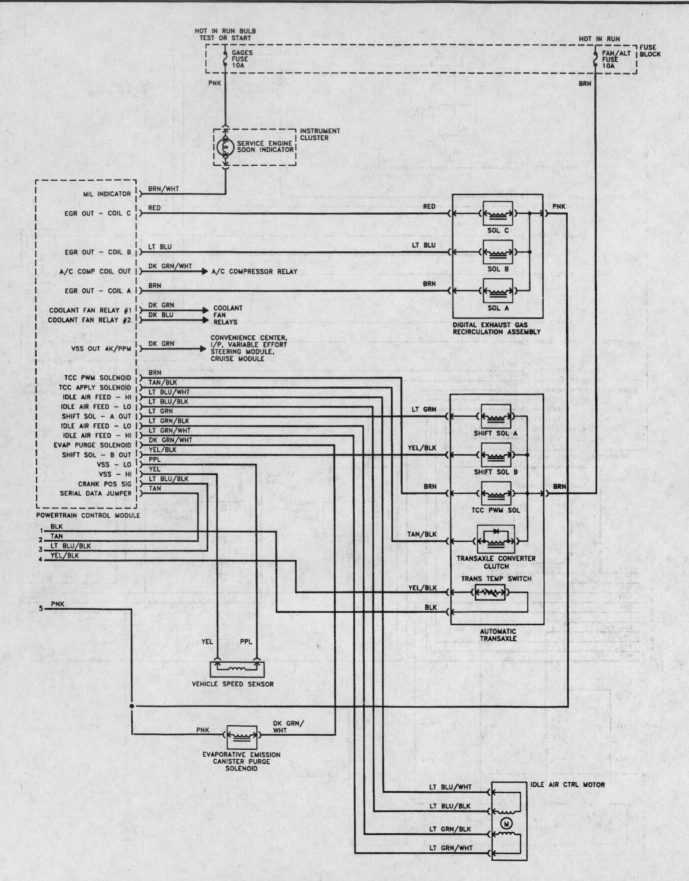

Typical 3.1L engine control system (3 of 3)

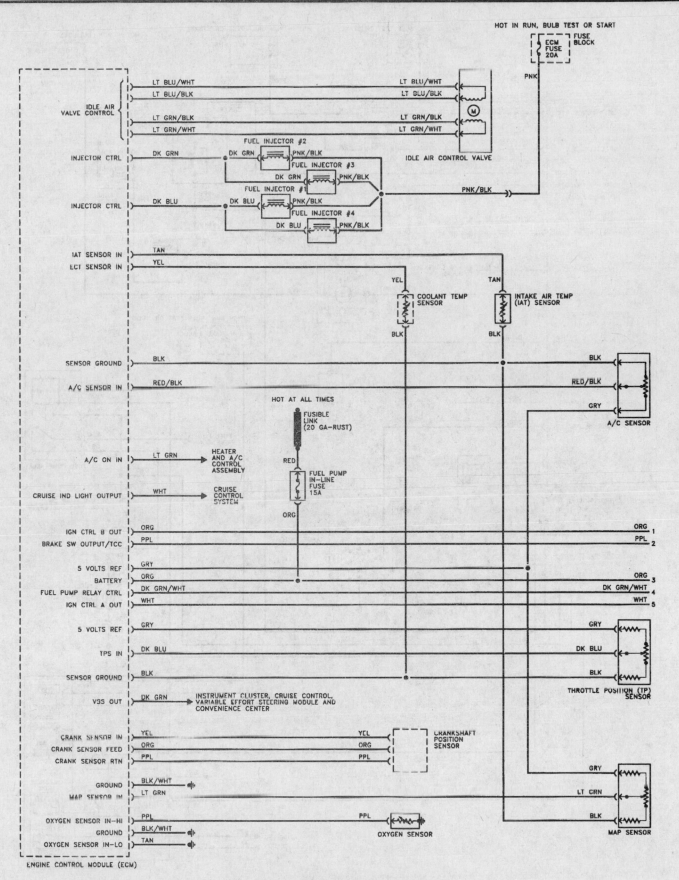

Typical 2.2L engine control system (1 of 2)

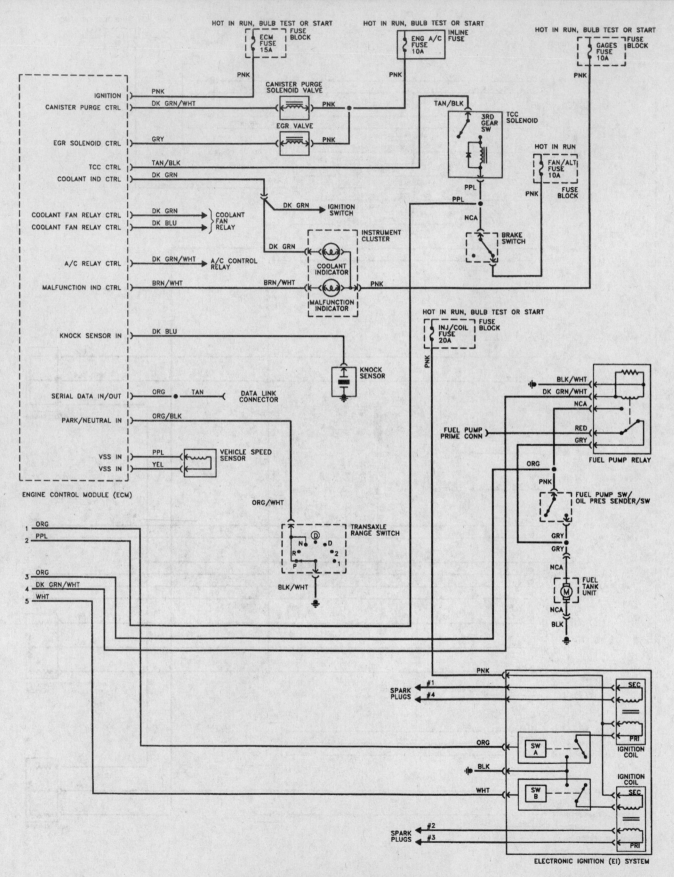

Typical 2.2L engine control system (2 of 2)

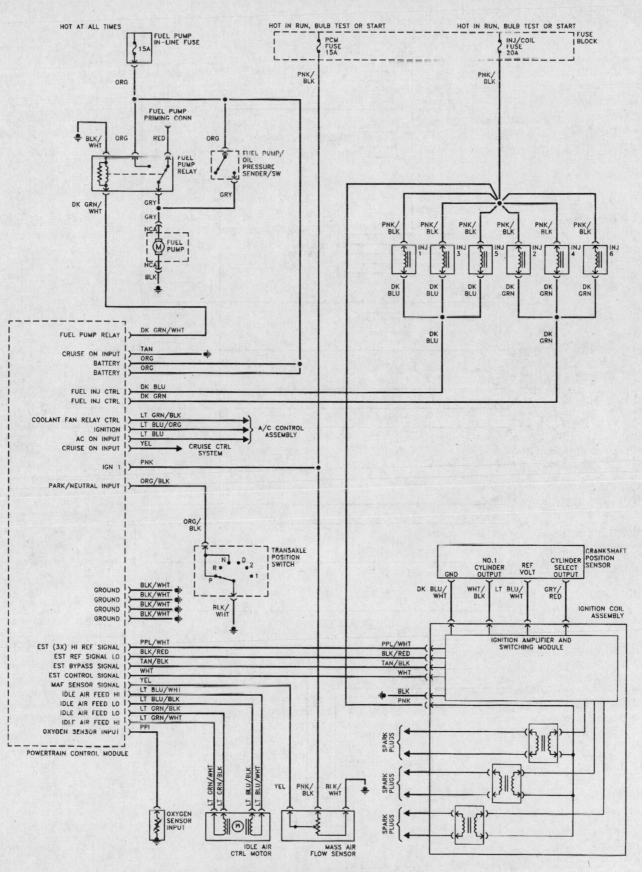

Typical 3.3L engine control system (1 of 2)

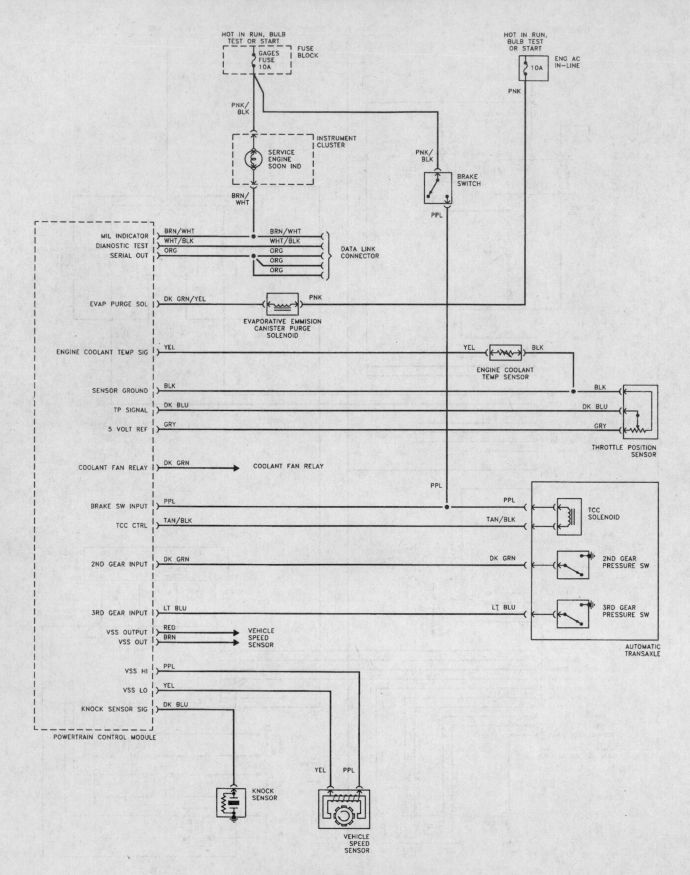

Typical 3.3L engine control system (2 of 2)

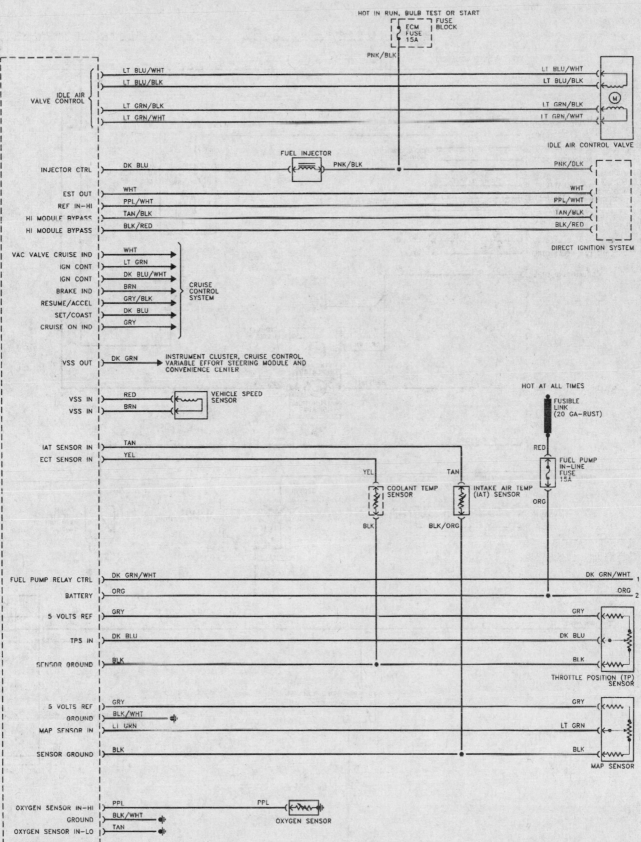

Typical 2.5L engine control system (1 of 2)

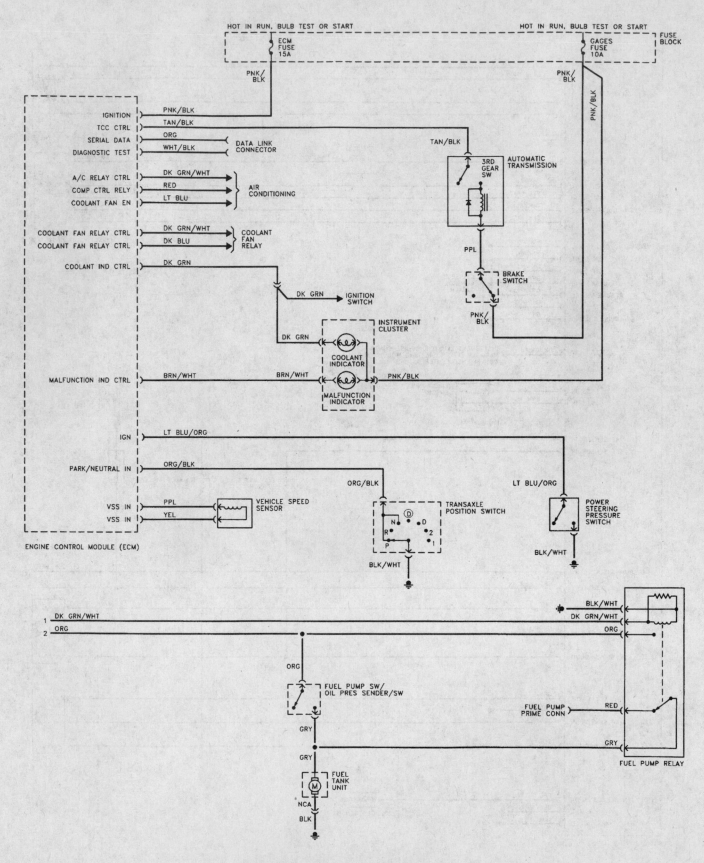

Typical 2.5L engine control system (2 of 2)

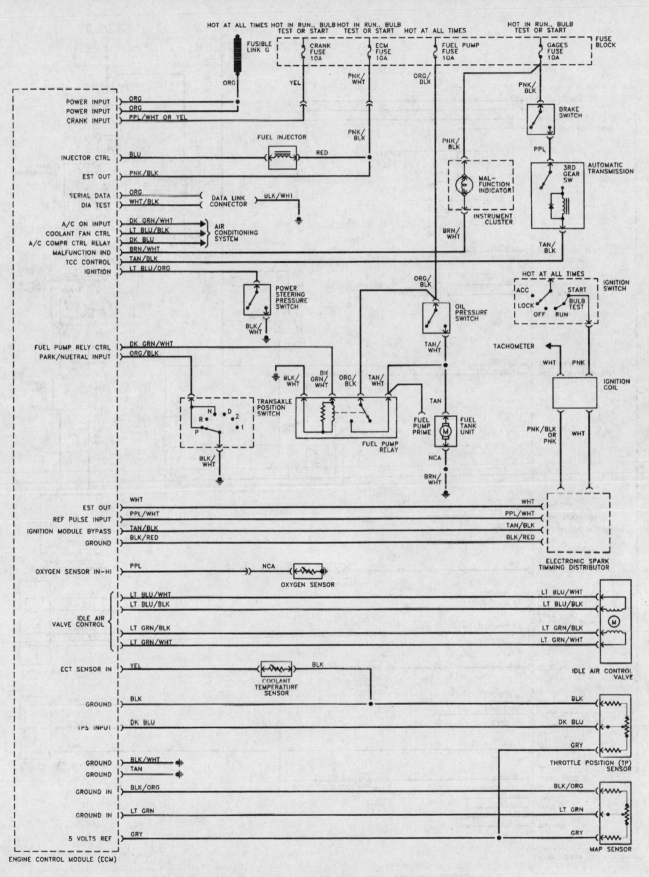

Typical 1986 and earlier model electronic fuel injection system

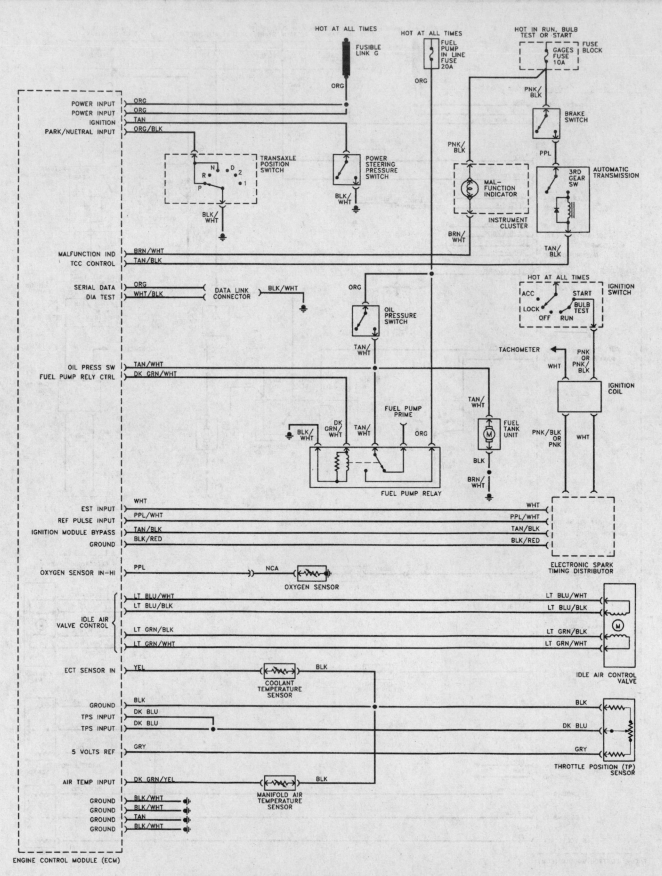

Typical 1986 and earlier model multi-port fuel injection system (1 of 2)

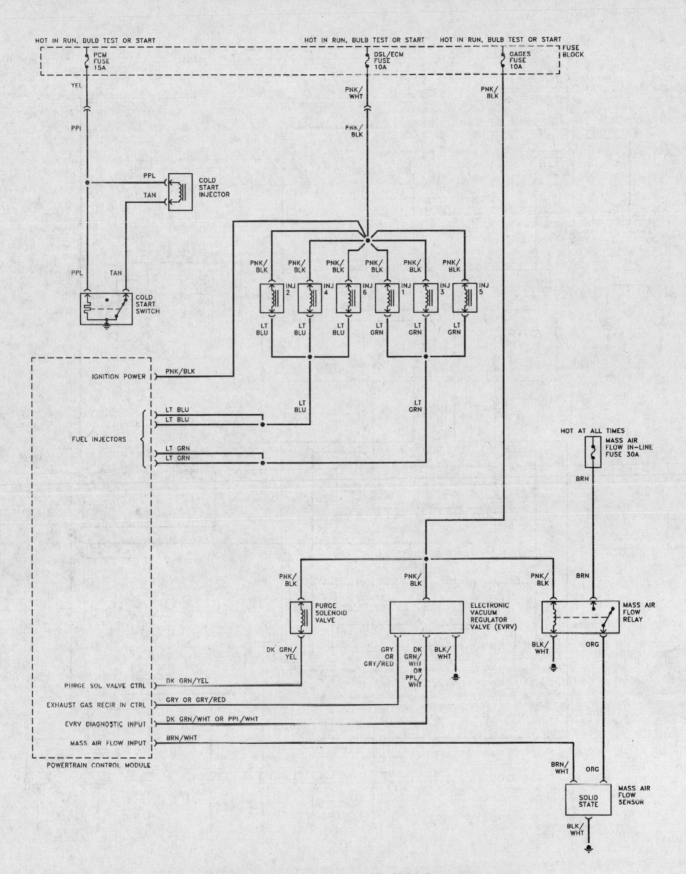

Typical 1986 and earlier model multi-port fuel injection system (2 of 2)

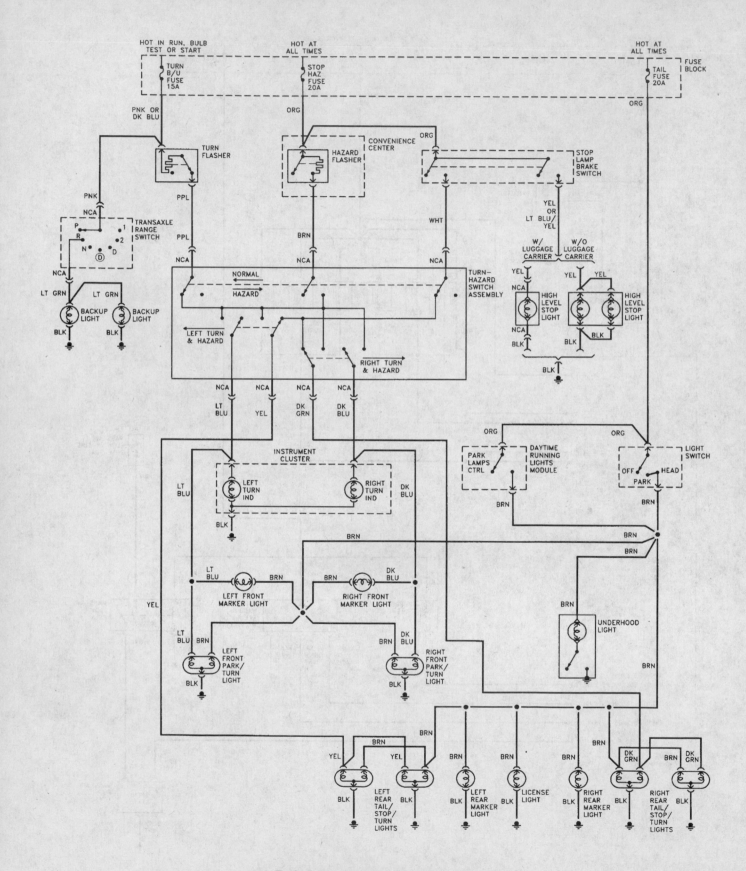

Typical exterior and backup lamp system

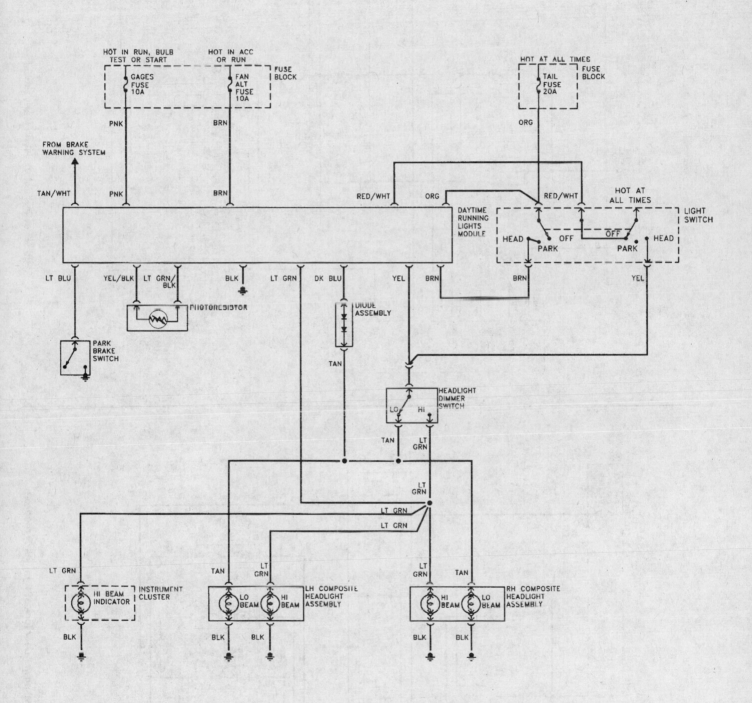

Typical headlight system

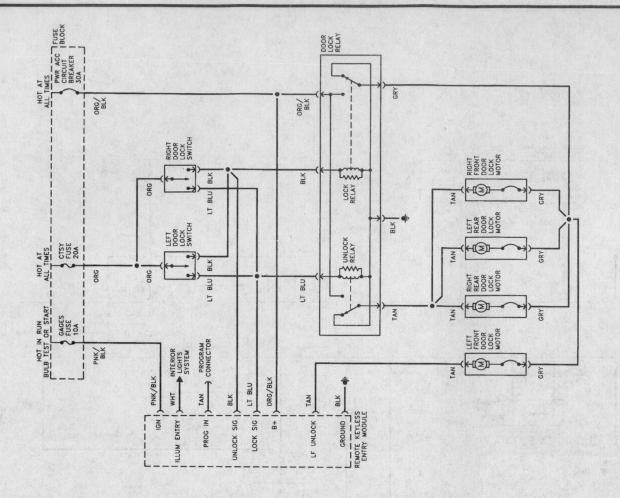

Typical keyless entry system (early models)

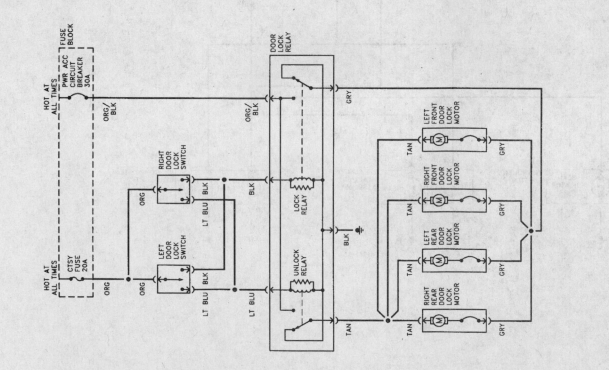

Typical power door lock system (early models)

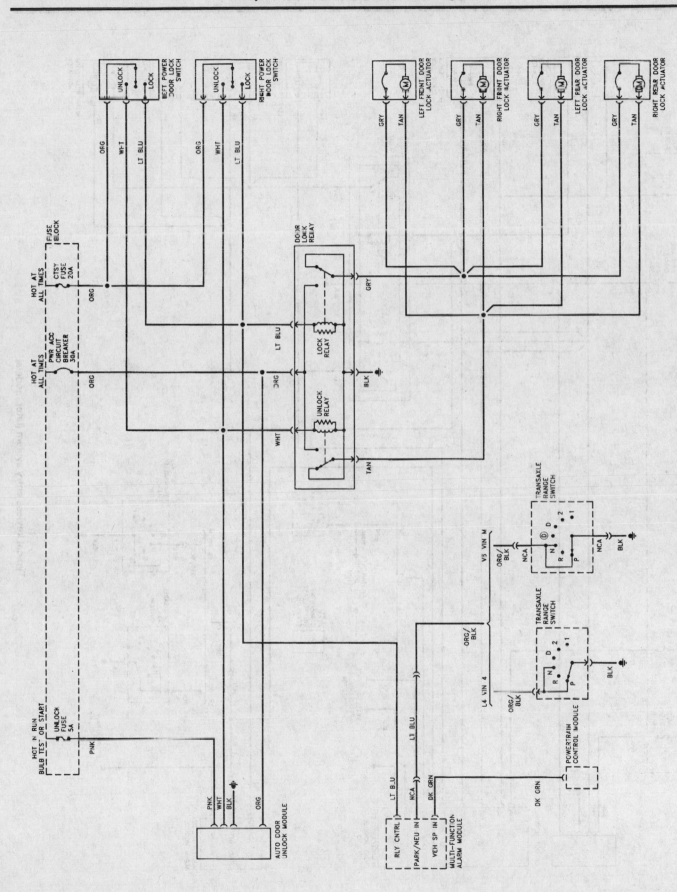

Typical power door lock system (later models)

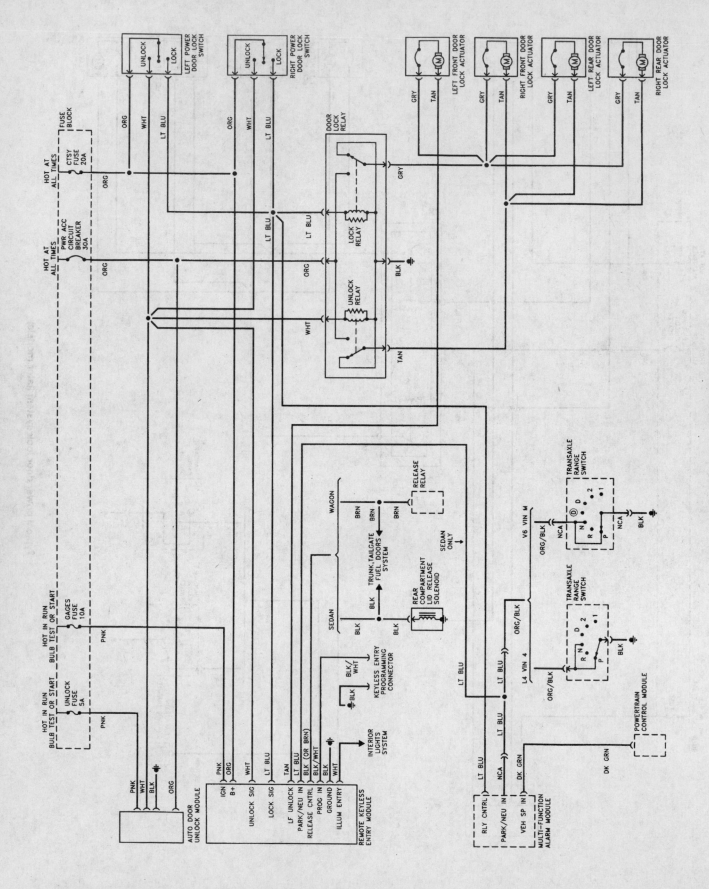

Typical keyless entry system (later models)

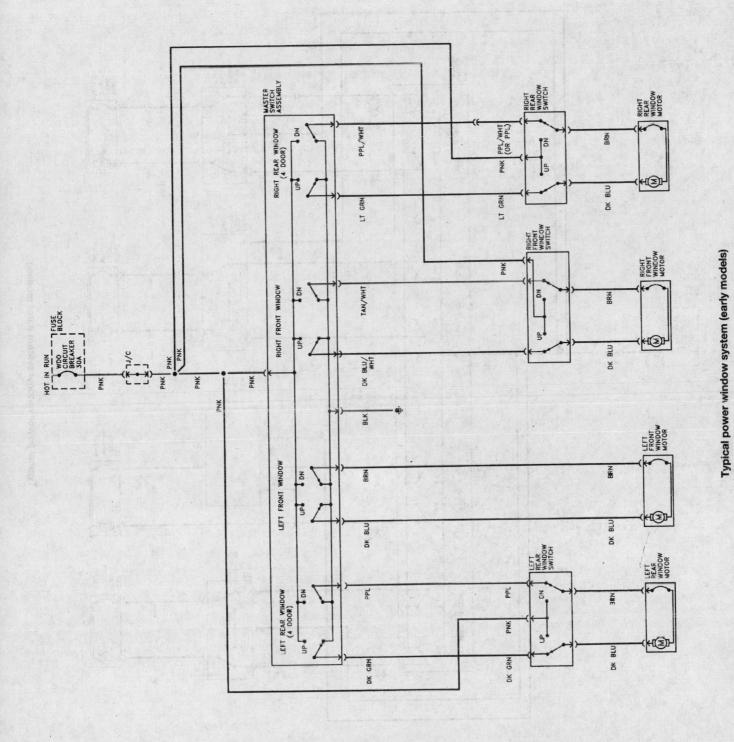

Typical power window system (early models)

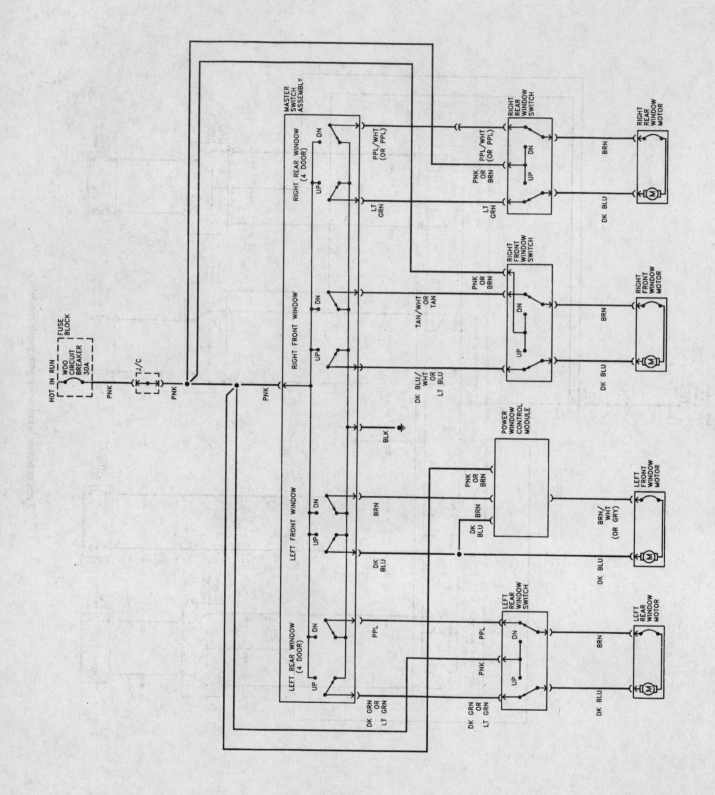

Typical power window system (later models)

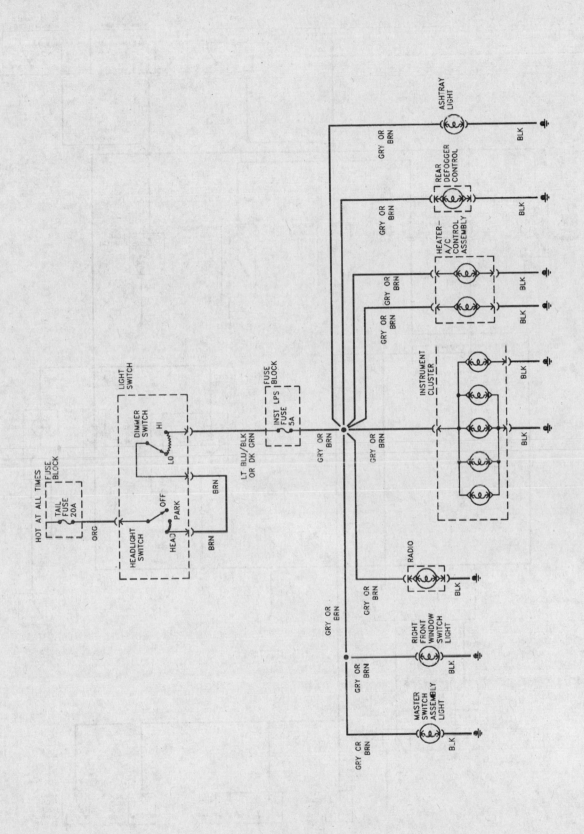

Typical interior illumination system

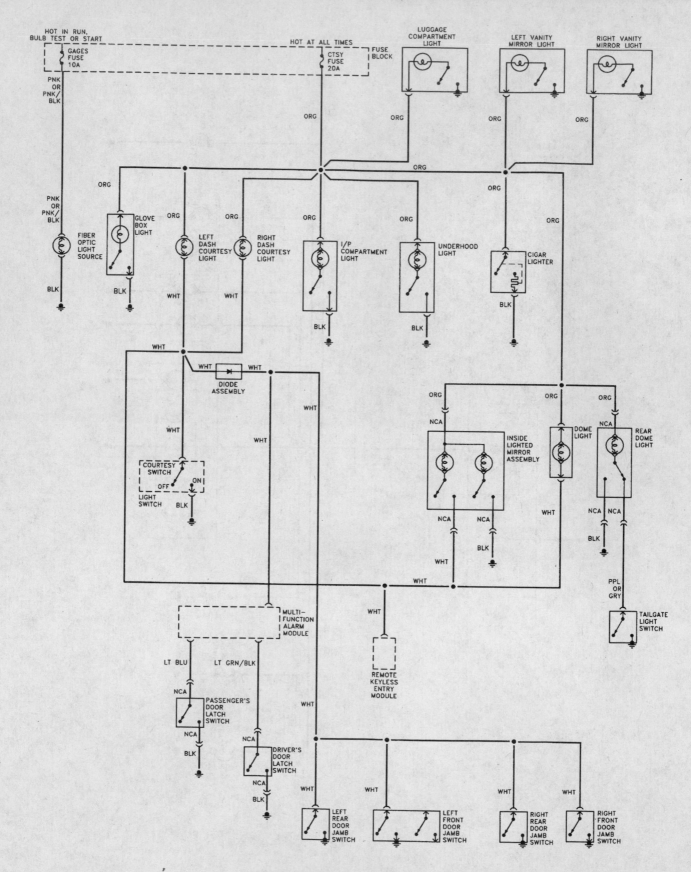

Typical courtesy lamps system

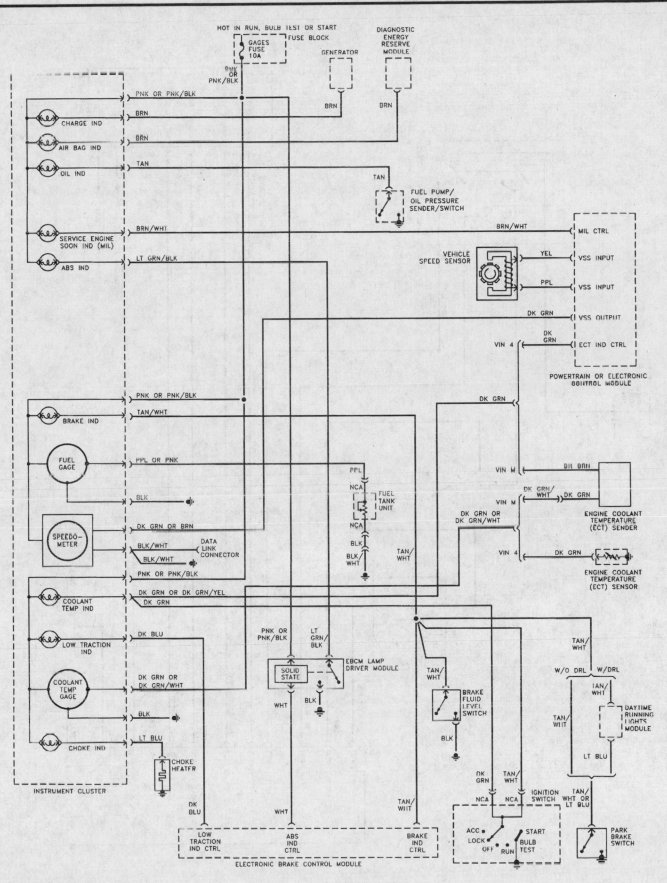

Typical warning lamp system

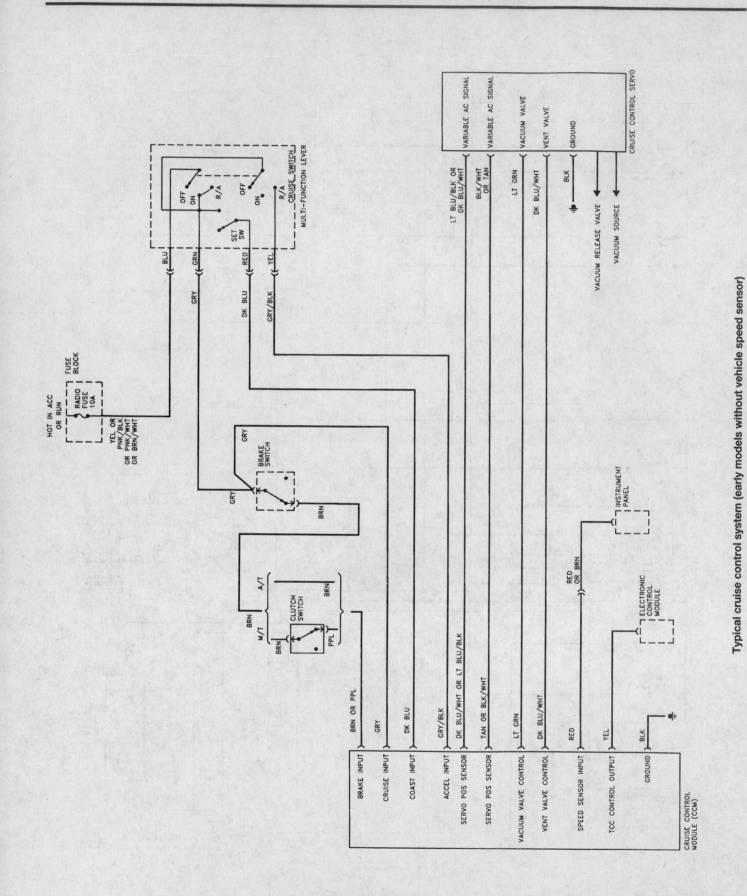

Typical cruise control system (early models without vehicle speed sensor)

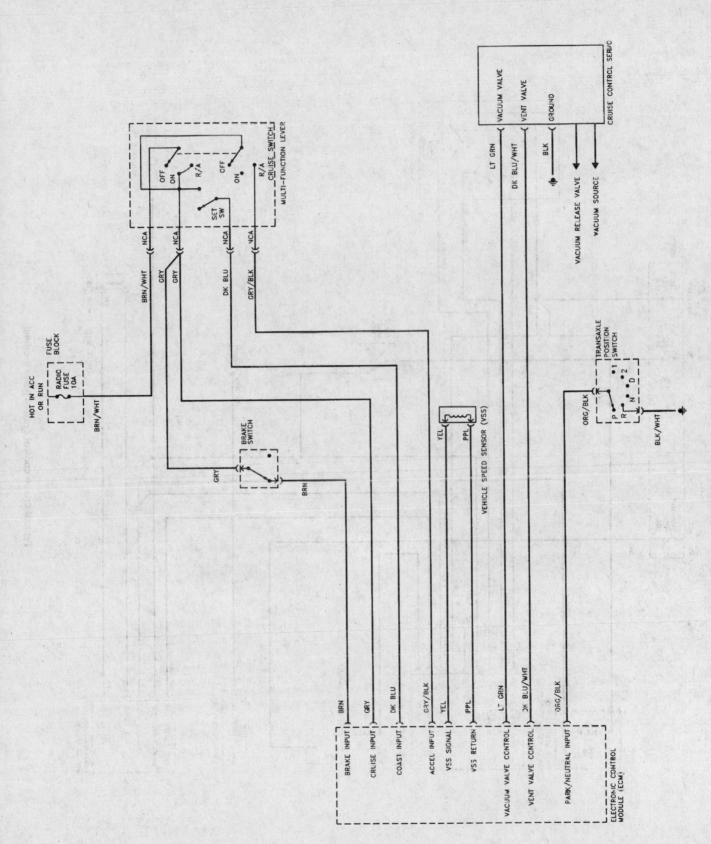

Typical cruise control system (early models with vehicle speed sensor)

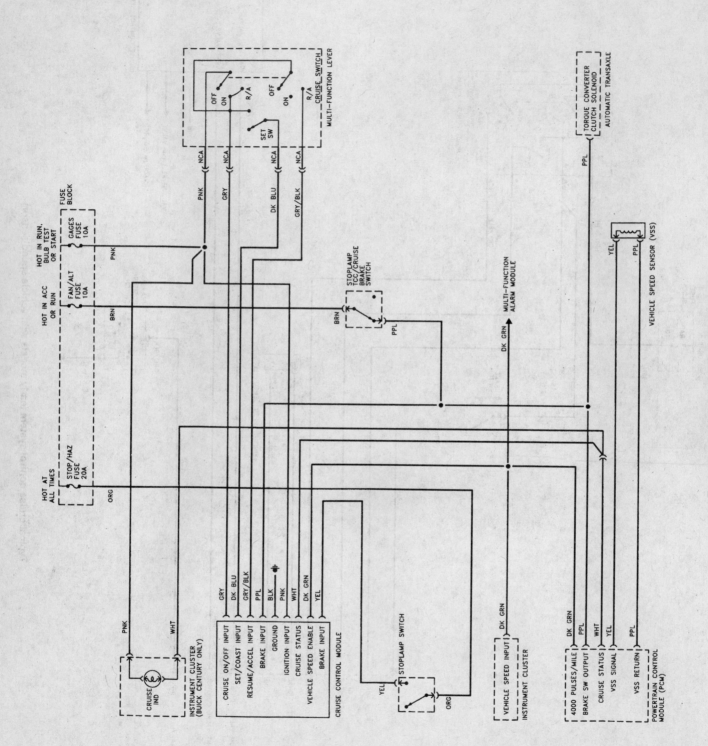

Typical cruise control system (later models)

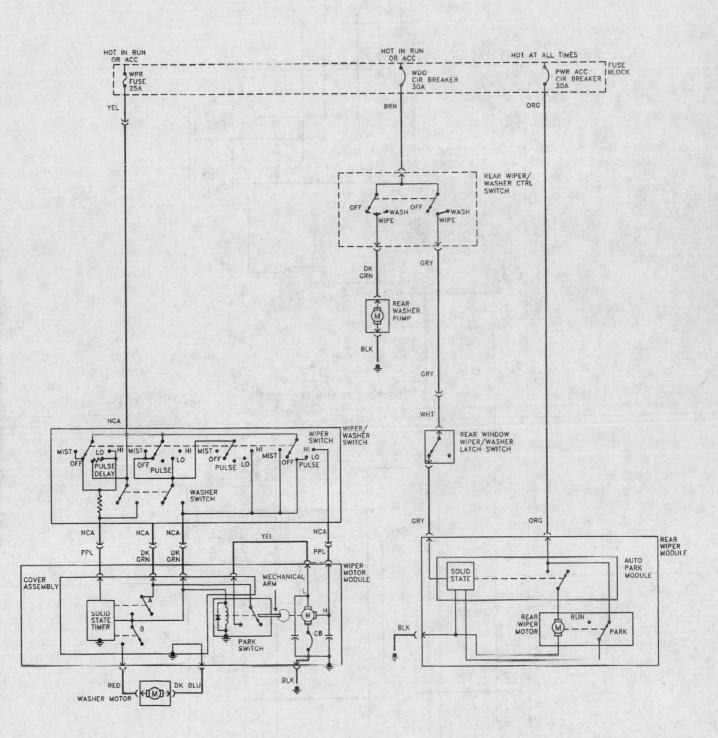

Typical windshield wiper/washer (later models)

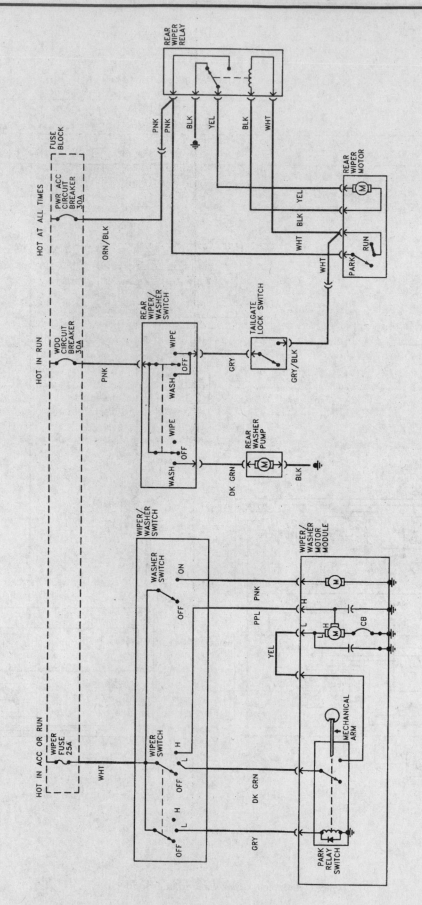

Typical 2-speed windshield wiper/washer system (early models)

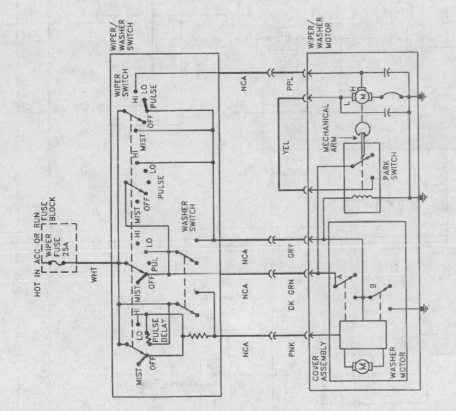

Typical pulse windshield wiper/washer system (early models)

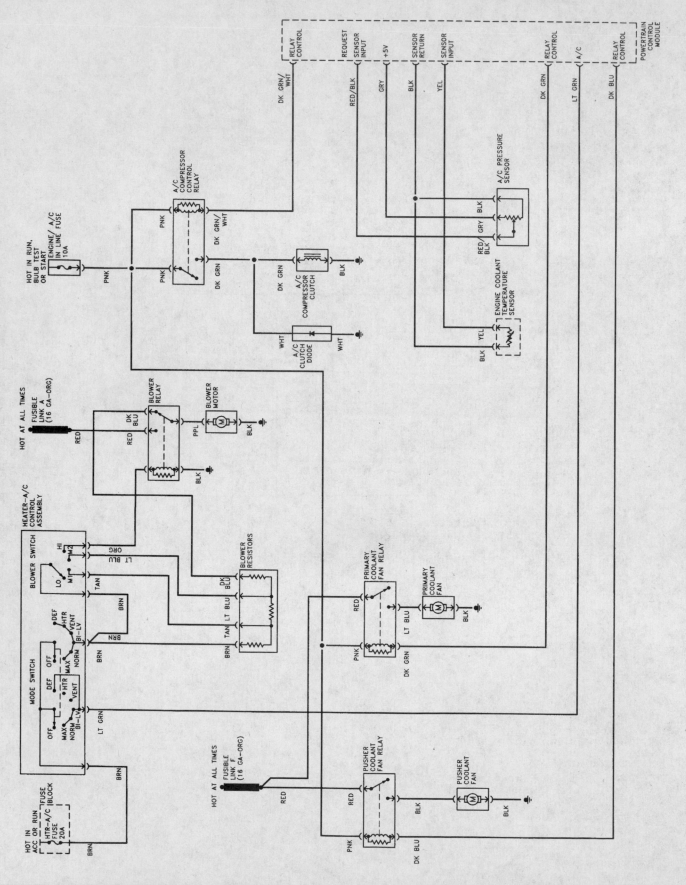

Typical air conditioning system (1994 and later Ciera models)

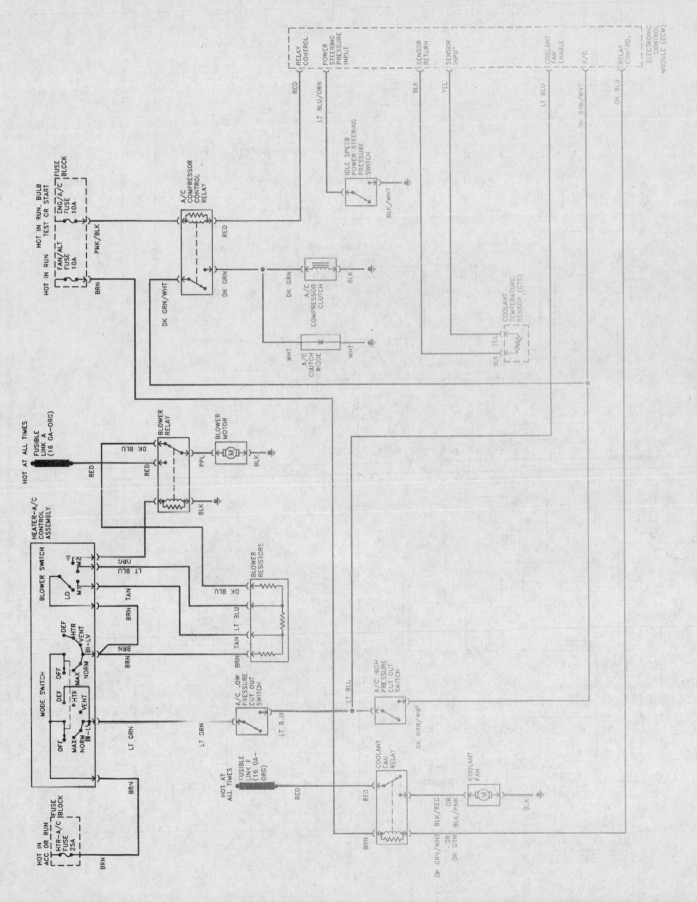

Typical air conditioning system (1990 through 1993 Ciera models)

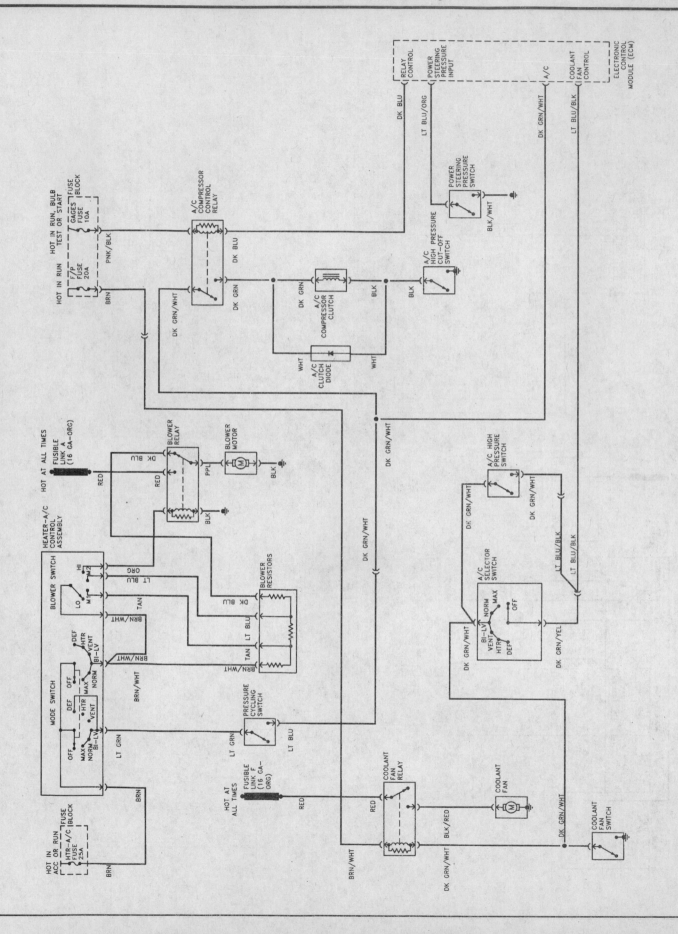

Typical air conditioning system (1988 and earlier Ciera models)

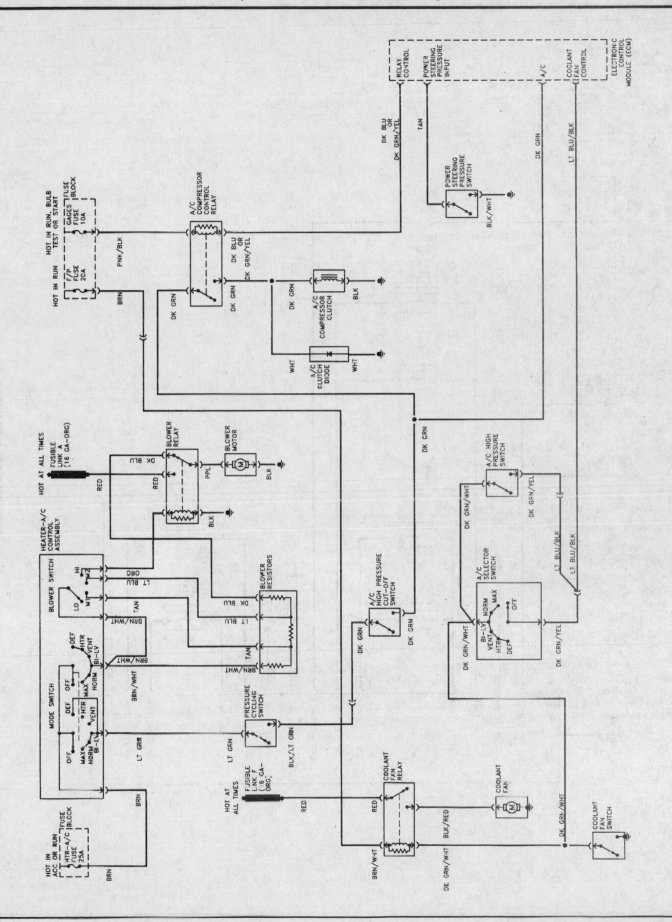

Typical air conditioning system (1986 and earlier Celebrity models)

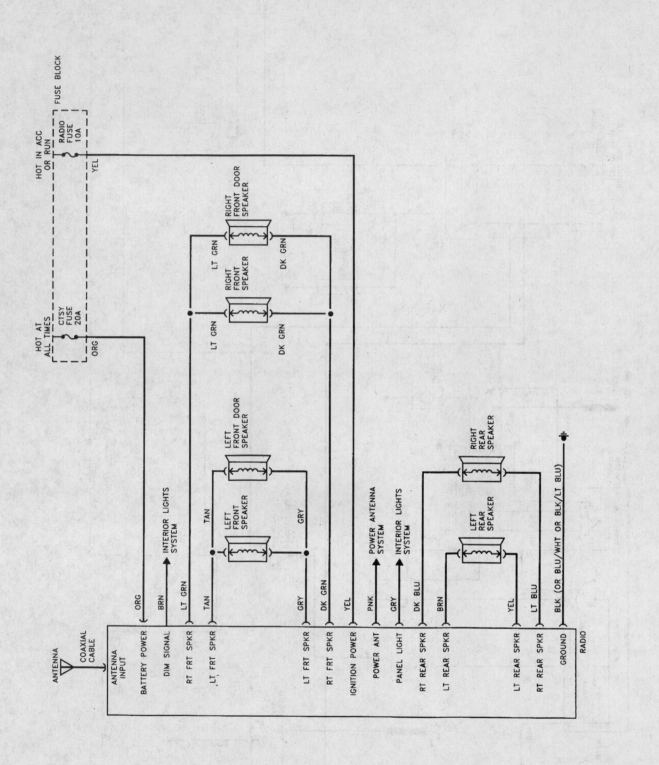

Typical (standard) radio system

Index

Haynes Automotive Manuals

HAYNES XTREME CUSTOMIZING
11101 Sport Compact Customizing
11102 Sport Compact Performance
11110 In-car Entertainment
11150 Sport Utility Vehicle Customizing
11213 Acura
11255 Full-size Pick-ups
11314 Ford Focus
11315 Full-size Ford Pick-ups
11373 Honda Civic

ACURA
12020 Integra '86 thru '89 & Legend '86 thru '90
12021 Integra '90 thru '93 & Legend '91 thru '95

AMC
Jeep CJ - see JEEP (50020)
14020 Concord/Hornet/Gremlin/Spirit '70 thru '83
14025 (Renault) Alliance & Encore '83 thru '87

AUDI
15020 4000 all models '80 thru '87
15025 5000 all models '77 thru '83
15026 5000 all models '84 thru '88

AUSTIN
Healey Sprite - see MG Midget (66015)

BMW
18020 3/5 Series '82 thru '92
18021 3 Series including Z3 '92 thru '98
18022 3-Series, E46 chassis '99 thru '05, Z4 models '03 thru '05
18025 320i all 4 cyl models '75 thru '83
18050 1500 thru 2002 except Turbo '59 thru '77

BUICK
19010 Buick Century '97 thru '05
Century (front-wheel drive) - see GM (38005)
19020 Buick, Oldsmobile & Pontiac Full-size (Front wheel drive) '85 thru '05
19025 Buick Oldsmobile & Pontiac Full-size (Rear wheel drive) '70 thru '90
19030 Mid-size Regal & Century '74 thru '87
Regal - see GENERAL MOTORS (38010)
Skyhawk - see GM (38030)
Skylark - see GM (38020, 38025)
Somerset - see GENERAL MOTORS (38025)

CADILLAC
21030 Cadillac Rear Wheel Drive '70 thru '93
Cimarron, Eldorado & Seville - see GM (38015, 38030, 38031)

CHEVROLET
10305 Chevrolet Engine Overhaul Manual
24010 Astro & GMC Safari Mini-vans '85 thru '03
24015 Camaro V8 all models '70 thru '81
24016 Camaro all models '82 thru '92, Cavalier - see GM (38015), Celebrity - see GM (38005)
24017 Camaro & Firebird '93 thru '02
24020 Chevelle, Malibu, El Camino '69 thru '87
24024 Chevette & Pontiac T1000 '76 thru '87
Citation - see GENERAL MOTORS (38020)
24027 Colorado & GMC Canyon '04 thru '06
24032 Corsica/Beretta all models '87 thru '96
24040 Corvette all V8 models '68 thru '82
24041 Corvette all models '84 thru '96
24045 Full-size Sedans Caprice, Impala, Biscayne, Bel Air & Wagons '69 thru '90
24046 Impala SS & Caprice and Buick Roadmaster '91 thru '96
Lumina '90 thru '94 - see GM (38010)
24048 Lumina & Monte Carlo '95 thru '05
Lumina APV - see GM (38035)
24050 Luv Pick-up all 2WD & 4WD '72 thru '82
Malibu - see GM (38026)
24055 Monte Carlo all models '70 thru '88
Monte Carlo '95 thru '01 - see LUMINA
24059 Nova all V8 models '69 thru '79
24060 Nova/Geo Prizm '85 thru '92
24064 Pick-ups '67 thru '87 - Chevrolet & GMC, all V8 in-line 6 cyl, 2WD & 4WD '67 thru '87; Suburbans, Blazers & Jimmys '67 thru '91
24065 Pick-ups '88 thru '98 - Chevrolet & GMC, all full-size models '88 thru '98; C/K Classic '99 & '00; Blazer & Jimmy '92 thru '94; Suburban '92 thru '99; Tahoe & Yukon '95 thru '99
24066 Pick-ups '99 thru '06 - Chevrolet Silverado & GMC Sierra '99 thru '06; Suburban/Tahoe/Yukon/Yukon XL/Avalanche '00 thru '06
24070 S-10 & GMC S-15 Pick-ups '82 thru '93
24071 S-10, Sonoma & Jimmy '94 thru '04
24072 Chevrolet TrailBlazer & TrailBlazer EXT, GMC Envoy & Envoy XL, Oldsmobile Bravada '02 thru '06
24075 Sprint '85 thru '88, Geo Metro '89 thru '01
24080 Vans - Chevrolet & GMC '68 thru '96
24081 Chevrolet Express & GMC Savana Full-size Vans '96 thru '05

CHRYSLER
10310 Chrysler Engine Overhaul Manual
25015 Chrysler Cirrus, Dodge Stratus, Plymouth Breeze, '95 thru '00
25020 Full-size Front-Wheel Drive '88 thru '93
K-Cars - see DODGE Aries (30008)
Laser - see DODGE Daytona (30030)
25025 Chrysler LHS, Concorde & New Yorker, Dodge Intrepid, Eagle Vision, '93 thru '97
25026 Chrysler LHS, Concorde, 300M, Dodge Intrepid '98 thru '03
25027 Chrysler 300 & Dodge Charger & Magnum '05 thru '07
25030 Chrysler/Plym. Mid-size '82 thru '95
Rear-wheel Drive - see DODGE (30050)
25035 PT Cruiser all models '01 thru '03
25040 Chrysler Sebring/Dodge Avenger '95 thru '05, Dodge Stratus '01 thru '05

DATSUN
28005 200SX all models '80 thru '83
28007 B-210 all models '73 thru '78
28009 210 all models '78 thru '82
28012 240Z, 260Z & 280Z Coupe '70 thru '78
28014 280ZX Coupe & 2+2 '79 thru '83
300ZX - see NISSAN (72010)
28018 510 & PL521 Pick-up '68 thru '73
28020 510 all models '78 thru '81
28022 620 Series Pick-up all models '73 thru '79
720 Series Pick-up - see NISSAN (72030)
28025 810/Maxima all gas models, '77 thru '84

DODGE
400 & 600 - see CHRYSLER (25030)
30008 Aries & Plymouth Reliant '81 thru '89
30010 Caravan & Ply. Voyager '84 thru '95
30011 Caravan & Ply. Voyager '96 thru '02
30012 Challenger/Plymouth Saporro '78 thru '83
Challenger '67-'76 - see DART (30025)
30013 Caravan, Chrysler Voyager, Town & Country '03 thru '06
30016 Colt/Plymouth Champ '78 thru '87
30020 Dakota Pick-ups all models '87 thru '96
30021 Durango '98 & '99, Dakota '97 thru '99
30022 Dodge Durango models '00 thru '03 Dodge Dakota models '00 thru '04
30023 Dodge Durango '04 thru '06, Dakota '05 and '06
30025 Dart, Challenger/Plymouth Barracuda & Valiant 6 cyl models '67 thru '76
30030 Daytona & Chrysler Laser '84 thru '89
Intrepid - see Chrysler (25025, 25026)
30034 Dodge & Plymouth Neon '95 thru '99
30035 Omni & Plymouth Horizon '78 thru '90
30036 Dodge and Plymouth Neon '00 thru '05
30040 Pick-ups all full-size models '74 thru '93
30041 Pick-ups all full-size models '94 thru '01
30042 Dodge Full-size Pick-ups '02 thru '05
30045 Ram 50/D50 Pick-ups & Raider and Plymouth Arrow Pick-ups '79 thru '93
30050 Dodge/Ply./Chrysler RWD '71 thru '89
30055 Shadow/Plymouth Sundance '87 thru '94
30060 Spirit & Plymouth Acclaim '89 thru '95
30065 Vans - Dodge & Plymouth '71 thru '03

EAGLE
Talon - see MITSUBISHI (68030, 68031)
Vision - see CHRYSLER (25025)

FIAT
34010 124 Sport Coupe & Spider '68 thru '78
34025 X1/9 all models '74 thru '80

FORD
10355 Ford Automatic Transmission Overhaul
10320 Ford Engine Overhaul Manual
36004 Aerostar Mini-vans '86 thru '97
Aspire - see FORD Festiva (36030)
36006 Contour/Mercury Mystique '95 thru '00
36008 Courier Pick-up all models '72 thru '82
36012 Crown Victoria & Mercury Grand Marquis '88 thru '06
36016 Escort/Mercury Lynx '81 thru '90
36020 Escort/Mercury Tracer '91 thru '00
Expedition - see FORD Pick-up (36059)
36022 Ford Escape & Mazda Tribute '01 thru '03
36024 Explorer & Mazda Navajo '91 thru '01
36025 Ford Explorer & Mercury Mountaineer '02 thru '06
36028 Fairmont & Mercury Zephyr '78 thru '83
36030 Festiva & Aspire '88 thru '97
36032 Fiesta all models '77 thru '80
36034 Focus all models '00 thru '05
36036 Ford & Mercury Full-size '75 thru '87
36044 Ford & Mercury Mid-size '75 thru '86
36048 Mustang V8 all models '64-1/2 thru '73
36049 Mustang II 4 cyl, V6 & V8 '74 thru '78
36050 Mustang & Mercury Capri '79 thru '86
36051 Mustang all models '94 thru '04
36052 Mustang '05 thru '07
36054 Pick-ups and Bronco '73 thru '79
36058 Pick-ups and Bronco '80 thru '96
36059 F-150 & Expedition '97 thru '03, F-250 '97 thru '99 & Lincoln Navigator '98 thru '02
36060 Super Duty Pick-up, Excursion '99 thru '06
36061 F-150 full-size '04 thru '06
36062 Pinto & Mercury Bobcat '75 thru '80
36066 Probe all models '89 thru '92
36070 Ranger/Bronco II gas models '83 thru '92
36071 Ford Ranger '93 thru '05 & Mazda Pick-ups '94 thru '05
36074 Taurus & Mercury Sable '86 thru '95
36075 Taurus & Mercury Sable '96 thru '01
36078 Tempo & Mercury Topaz '84 thru '94
36082 Thunderbird/Mercury Cougar '83 thru '88
36086 Thunderbird/Mercury Cougar '89 thru '97
36090 Vans all V8 Econoline models '69 thru '91
36094 Vans full size '92 thru '05
36097 Windstar Mini-van '95 thru '03

GENERAL MOTORS
10360 GM Automatic Transmission Overhaul
38005 Buick Century, Chevrolet Celebrity, Olds Cutlass Ciera & Pontiac 6000 '82 thru '96
38010 Buick Regal, Chevrolet Lumina, Oldsmobile Cutlass Supreme & Pontiac Grand Prix front wheel drive '88 thru '05
38015 Buick Skyhawk, Cadillac Cimarron, Chevrolet Cavalier, Oldsmobile Firenza Pontiac J-2000 & Sunbird '82 thru '94
38016 Chevrolet Cavalier/Pontiac Sunfire '95 thru '04
38017 Chevrolet Cobalt & Pontiac G5 '05 thru '07
38020 Buick Skylark, Chevrolet Citation, Olds Omega, Pontiac Phoenix '80 thru '85
38025 Buick Skylark & Somerset, Olds Achieva, Calais & Pontiac Grand Am '85 thru '98
38026 Chevrolet Malibu, Olds Alero & Cutlass, Pontiac Grand Am '97 thru '03
38027 Chevrolet Malibu '04 thru '07
38030 Cadillac Eldorado & Oldsmobile Toronado '71 thru '85, Seville '80 thru '85, Buick Riviera '79 thru '85
38031 Cadillac Eldorado & Seville '86 thru '91, DeVille & Buick Riviera '86 thru '93, Fleetwood & Olds Toronado '86 thru '92
38032 DeVille '94 thru '05, Seville '92 thru '04
38035 Chevrolet Lumina APV, Oldsmobile Silhouette & Pontiac Trans Sport '90 thru '96
38036 Chevrolet Venture, Olds Silhouette, Pontiac Trans Sport & Montana '97 thru '05
General Motors Full-size Rear-wheel Drive - see BUICK (19025)

GEO
Metro - see CHEVROLET Sprint (24075)
Prizm - see CHEVROLET (24060) or TOYOTA (92036)
40030 Storm all models '90 thru '93
Tracker - see SUZUKI Samurai (90010)

GMC
Vans & Pick-ups - see CHEVROLET

HONDA
42010 Accord CVCC all models '76 thru '83
42011 Accord all models '84 thru '89
42012 Accord all models '90 thru '93
42013 Accord all models '94 thru '97
42014 Accord all models '98 thru '02
42015 Honda Accord models '03 thru '05
42020 Civic 1200 all models '73 thru '79
42021 Civic 1300 & 1500 CVCC '80 thru '83
42022 Civic 1500 CVCC all models '75 thru '79
42023 Civic all models '84 thru '91
42024 Civic & del Sol '92 thru '95
42025 Civic '96 thru '00, CR-V '97 thru '01, Acura Integra '94 thru '00
Passport - see ISUZU Rodeo (47017)
42026 Civic '01 thru '04, CR-V '02 thru '04
42035 Honda Odyssey models '99 thru '04
42037 Honda Pilot '03 thru '07, Acura MDX '01 thru '07
42040 Prelude CVCC all models '79 thru '89

HYUNDAI
43010 Elantra all models '96 thru '01
43015 Excel & Accent all models '86 thru '98

ISUZU
Hombre - see CHEVROLET S-10 (24071)
47017 Rodeo '91 thru '02, Amigo '89 thru '02, Honda Passport '95 thru '02
47020 Trooper '84 thru '91, Pick-up '81 thru '93

JAGUAR
49010 XJ6 all 6 cyl models '68 thru '86
49011 XJ6 all models '88 thru '94
49015 XJ12 & XJS all 12 cyl models '72 thru '85

JEEP
50010 Cherokee, Comanche & Wagoneer Limited all models '84 thru '01
50020 CJ all models '49 thru '86
50025 Grand Cherokee all models '93 thru '04
50029 Grand Wagoneer & Pick-up '72 thru '91
50030 Wrangler all models '87 thru '03
50035 Liberty '02 thru '04

KIA
54070 Sephia '94 thru '01, Spectra '00 thru '04

LEXUS
ES 300 - see TOYOTA Camry (92007)

LINCOLN
Navigator - see FORD Pick-up (36059)
59010 Rear Wheel Drive all models '70 thru '05

MAZDA
61010 GLC (rear wheel drive) '77 thru '83
61011 GLC (front wheel drive) '81 thru '85
61015 323 & Protegé '90 thru '00
61016 MX-5 Miata '90 thru '97
61020 MPV all models '89 thru '94
Navajo - see FORD Explorer (36024)
61030 Pick-ups '72 thru '93
Pick-ups '94 on - see Ford (36071)
61035 RX-7 all models '79 thru '85
61036 RX-7 all models '86 thru '91
61040 626 (rear wheel drive) '79 thru '82
61041 626 & MX-6 (front wheel drive) '83 thru '92
61042 626 '93 thru '01, MX-6/Ford Probe '93 thru '01

MERCEDES-BENZ
63012 123 Series Diesel '76 thru '85
63015 190 Series 4-cyl gas models, '84 thru '88
63020 230, 250 & 280 6 cyl sohc '68 thru '72
63025 280 123 Series gas models '77 thru '81
63030 350 & 450 all models '71 thru '80

MERCURY
64200 Villager & Nissan Quest '93 thru '01
All other titles, see FORD listing.

MG
66010 MGB Roadster & GT Coupe '62 thru '80
66015 MG Midget & Austin Healey Sprite Roadster '58 thru '80

MITSUBISHI
68020 Cordia, Tredia, Galant, Precis & Mirage '83 thru '93
68030 Eclipse, Eagle Talon & Plymouth Laser '90 thru '94
68031 Eclipse '95 thru '01, Eagle Talon '95 thru '98
68035 Mitsubishi Galant '94 thru '03
68040 Pick-up '83 thru '96, Montero '83 thru '93

NISSAN
72005 300ZX all models incl. Turbo '84 thru '89
72015 Altima all models '93 thru '04
72020 Maxima all models '85 thru '92
72021 Maxima all models '93 thru '01
72030 Pick-ups '80 thru '97, Pathfinder '87 thru '95
72031 Frontier Pick-up '98 thru '04, Xterra '00 thru '04, Pathfinder '96 thru '04
72040 Pulsar all models '83 thru '86
72050 Sentra all models '82 thru '94
72051 Sentra & 200SX all models '95 thru '04
72060 Stanza all models '82 thru '90

OLDSMOBILE
73015 Cutlass '74 thru '88
For other OLDSMOBILE titles, see BUICK, CHEVROLET or GM listings.

PLYMOUTH
For PLYMOUTH titles, see DODGE.

PONTIAC
79008 Fiero all models '84 thru '88
79018 Firebird V8 models except Turbo '70 thru '81
79019 Firebird all models '82 thru '92
79040 Mid-size Rear-wheel Drive '70 thru '87
For other PONTIAC titles, see BUICK, CHEVROLET or GM listings.

PORSCHE
80020 911 Coupe & Targa models '65 thru '89
80025 914 all 4 cyl models '69 thru '76
80030 924 all models incl. Turbo '76 thru '82
80035 944 all models incl. Turbo '83 thru '89

RENAULT
Alliance, Encore - see AMC (14020)

SAAB
84010 900 including Turbo '79 thru '88

SATURN
87010 Saturn all models '91 thru '02
87011 Saturn Ion '03 thru '07
87020 Saturn all L-series models '00 thu '04

SUBARU
89002 1100, 1300, 1400 & 1600 '71 thru '79
89003 1600 & 1800 2WD & 4WD '80 thru '94
89100 Legacy models '90 thru '99
89101 Legacy & Forester '00 thru '06

SUZUKI
90010 Samurai/Sidekick/Geo Tracker '86 thru '01

TOYOTA
92005 Camry all models '83 thru '91
92006 Camry all models '92 thru '96
92007 Camry/Avalon/Solara/Lexus ES 300 '97 thru '01
92008 Toyota Camry, Avalon and Solara & Lexus ES 300/330 all models '02 thru '05
92015 Celica Rear Wheel Drive '71 thru '85
92020 Celica Front Wheel Drive '86 thru '99
92025 Celica Supra all models '79 thru '92
92030 Corolla all models '75 thru '79
92032 Corolla rear wheel drive models '80 thru '87
92035 Corolla front wheel drive models '84 thru '92
92036 Corolla & Geo Prizm '93 thru '02
92037 Corolla models '03 thru '05
92040 Corolla Tercel all models '80 thru '82
92045 Corona all models '74 thru '82
92050 Cressida all models '78 thru '82
92055 Land Cruiser FJ40/43/45/55 '68 thru '82
92056 Land Cruiser FJ60/62/80/FZJ80 '80 thru '96
92065 MR2 all models '85 thru '87
92070 Pick-up all models '69 thru '78
92075 Pick-up all models '79 thru '95
92076 Tacoma '95 thru '04, 4Runner '96 thru '02, T100 '93 thru '98
92078 Tundra '00 thru '05, Sequoia '01 thru '05
92080 Previa all models '91 thru '95
92081 Prius '01 thru '08
92082 RAV4 all models '96 thru '05
92085 Tercel all models '87 thru '94
92090 Sienna all models '98 thru '02
92095 Highlander & Lexus RX-330 '99 thru '06

TRIUMPH
94007 Spitfire all models '62 thru '81
94010 TR7 all models '75 thru '81

VW
96008 Beetle & Karmann Ghia '54 thru '79
96009 New Beetle '98 thru '05
96016 Rabbit, Jetta, Scirocco, & Pick-up models '75 thru '92 & Convertible '80 thru '92
96017 Golf, GTI & Jetta '93 thru '98, Cabrio '95 thru '98
96018 Golf, GTI, Jetta & Cabrio '98 thru '02
96020 Rabbit, Jetta, Pick-up diesel '77 thru '84
96023 Passat '98 thru '01, Audi A4 '96 thru '01
96030 Transporter 1600 all models '68 thru '79
96035 Transporter 1700, 1800, 2000 '72 thru '79
96040 Type 3 1500 & 1600 '63 thru '73
96045 Vanagon air-cooled models '80 thru '83

VOLVO
97010 120, 130 Series & 1800 Sports '61 thru '73
97015 140 Series all models '66 thru '74
97020 240 Series all models '76 thru '93
97040 740 & 760 Series all models '82 thru '88

TECHBOOK MANUALS
10205 Automotive Computer Codes
10206 OBD-II & Electronic Engine Management Systems
10210 Automotive Emissions Control Manual
10215 Fuel Injection Manual, 1978 thru 1985
10220 Fuel Injection Manual, 1986 thru 1999
10225 Holley Carburetor Manual
10230 Rochester Carburetor Manual
10240 Weber/Zenith/Stromberg/SU Carburetor
10305 Chevrolet Engine Overhaul Manual
10310 Chrysler Engine Overhaul Manual
10320 Ford Engine Overhaul Manual
10330 GM and Ford Diesel Engine Repair
10333 Building Engine Power Manual
10340 Small Engine Repair Manual
10345 Suspension, Steering & Driveline
10355 Ford Automatic Transmission Overhaul
10360 GM Automatic Transmission Overhaul
10405 Automotive Body Repair & Painting
10410 Automotive Brake Manual
10415 Automotive Detailing Manual
10420 Automotive Electrical Manual
10425 Automotive Heating & Air Conditioning
10430 Automotive Reference Dictionary
10435 Automotive Tools Manual
10440 Used Car Buying Guide
10445 Welding Manual
10450 ATV Basics
10452 Scooters, Automatic Transmission 50cc to 250cc

SPANISH MANUALS
98903 Reparación de Carrocería & Pintura
98904 Carburadores para los modelos Holley & Rochester
98905 Códigos Automotrices de la Computadora
98910 Frenos Automotriz
98913 Electricidad Automotriz
98915 Inyección de Combustible 1986 al 1999
99040 Chevrolet & GMC Camionetas '67 al '87
99041 Chevrolet & GMC Camionetas '88 al '98
99042 Chevrolet Camionetas Cerradas '68 al '95
99055 Dodge Caravan & Ply. Voyager '84 al '95
99075 Ford Camionetas y Bronco '80 al '94
99077 Ford Camionetas Cerradas '69 al '91
99088 Ford Modelos de Tamaño Mediano '75 al '86
99091 Ford Taurus & Mercury Sable '86 al '95
99095 GM Modelos de Tamaño Grande '70 al '88
99100 GM Modelos de Tamaño Mediano '70 al '88
99106 Jeep Cherokee, Wagoneer & Comanche '84 al '00
99110 Nissan Camionetas '80 al '96, Pathfinder '87 al '95
99118 Nissan Sentra '82 al '94
99125 Toyota Camionetas y 4-Runner '79 al '95

Over 100 Haynes motorcycle manuals also available

10-07

Haynes North America, Inc., 861 Lawrence Drive, Newbury Park, CA 91320 • (805) 498-6703